FOURTH EDITION

The Norton Field Guide to Writing
with readings

FOURTH EDITION

The Norton
Field Guide
to Writing

with readings

Richard Bullock
WRIGHT STATE UNIVERSITY

Maureen Daly Goggin
ARIZONA STATE UNIVERSITY

W. W. NORTON & COMPANY

New York • London

W. W. Norton & Company has been independent since its founding in 1923, when William Warder Norton and Mary D. Herter Norton first published lectures delivered at the People's Institute, the adult education division of New York City's Cooper Union. The firm soon expanded its program beyond the Institute, publishing books by celebrated academics from America and abroad. By mid-century, the two major pillars of Norton's publishing program — trade books and college texts — were firmly established. In the 1950s, the Norton family transferred control of the company to its employees, and today — with a staff of four hundred and a comparable number of trade, college, and professional titles published each year — W. W. Norton & Company stands as the largest and oldest publishing house owned wholly by its employees.

Copyright © 2016, 2013, 2009, 2007, 2006 by W. W. Norton & Company, Inc.

Editor: Marilyn Moller
Project Editors: Rebecca Homiski and Christine D'Antonio
Developmental Editor: John Elliott
Assistant Editor: Claire Wallace
Manuscript Editor: Jude Grant
Managing Editor, College: Marian Johnson
Managing Editor, College Digital Media: Kim Yi
Production Manager: Andy Ensor
Media Editor: Erica Wnek
Media Project Editor: Cooper Wilhelm

Media Editorial Assistant: Ava Bramson
Marketing Manager, Composition: Megan Zwilling
Design Director: Jillian Burr
Book Designer: Anna Palchik
Photo Editor: Nelson Colón
Photo Research: Dena Digilio Betz
Permissions Manager: Megan Jackson
Permissions Clearing: Bethany Salminen
Composition: Cenveo® Publisher Services
Manufacturing: LSC Communications - Crawfordsville

The Library of Congress has cataloged an earlier edition as follows:
Library of Congress Cataloging-in-Publication Data
Names: Bullock, Richard H. (Richard Harvey) author. | Goggin, Maureen Daly, author.
Title: The Norton Field Guide to writing, with readings / Richard Bullock ; Maureen Daly Goggin.
Description: Fourth Edition | New York : W.W. Norton & Company, [2016] | Includes bibliographical references and index.
Identifiers: LCCN 2015044571 | ISBN 9780393264371 (pbk.)
Subjects: LCSH: English language—Rhetoric—Handbooks, manuals, etc. | English language—Grammar—Handbooks, manuals, etc. | Report writing—Handbooks, manuals, etc. | College readers.
Classification: LCC PE1408 .B8838245 2016 | DDC 808/.042—dc23 LC record available at http://lccn.loc.gov/2015044571

This edition: **ISBN 978-0-393-61737-5**

W. W. Norton & Company, Inc., 500 Fifth Avenue, New York, NY 10110-0017
wwnorton.com

W. W. Norton & Company Ltd., 15 Carlisle Street, London W1D 3BS

6 7 8 9 0

Preface

The Norton Field Guide to Writing began as an attempt to offer the kind of writing guides found in the best rhetorics in a format as user-friendly as the best handbooks, and on top of that, to be as brief as could be. We wanted to create a handy guide to help college students with all their written work. Just as there are field guides for bird watchers, for gardeners, and for accountants, this would be one for writers. In its first three editions, the book has obviously touched a chord with many writing instructors, and it's become the best-selling college rhetoric — a success that leaves us humbled and grateful. Student success is now on everyone's mind. As teachers, we want our students to succeed, and first-year writing courses offer one of the best opportunities to help them develop the skills and habits of mind they need to succeed, whatever their goals may be. To that end, we've added a new part on academic literacies, with chapters on reading and writing in academic contexts, summarizing and responding, and developing academic habits of mind.

The Norton Field Guide still aims to offer both the guidance new teachers and first-year writers need and the flexibility many experienced teachers want. From our own experiences as teachers and WPAs, we've seen how well explicit guides to writing work for students and novice teachers. But too often, writing textbooks provide far more information than students need or instructors can assign and as a result are bigger and more expensive than they should be. So we've tried to provide enough structure without too much detail—to give the information college writers need to know while resisting the temptation to tell them everything there is to know.

Most of all, we've tried to make the book easy to use, with menus, directories, a glossary/index, and color-coded links to help students find what they're looking for. The links are also the way we keep the book brief: chapters are short, but the links send students to pages elsewhere in the book *if* they need more detail.

What's in the Book

The Norton Field Guide covers 14 genres often assigned in college. Much of the book is in the form of guidelines, designed to help students consider the choices they have as writers. The book is organized into eight parts:

1. **ACADEMIC LITERACIES.** Chapters 1–4 focus on writing and reading in academic contexts, summarizing and responding, and developing academic habits of mind.

2. **RHETORICAL SITUATIONS.** Chapters 5–9 focus on purpose, audience, genre, stance, and media and design. In addition, almost every chapter includes tips to help students focus on their rhetorical situations.

3. **GENRES.** Chapters 10–23 cover 14 genres, 4 of them — literacy narrative, textual analysis, report, and argument — treated in greater detail. Chapter 24 helps students choose genres when they need to.

4. **PROCESSES.** Chapters 25–32 offer advice for generating ideas and text, drafting, revising and rewriting, editing, proofreading, compiling a portfolio, collaborating with others, and writing as inquiry.

5. **STRATEGIES.** Chapters 33–44 cover ways of developing and organizing text — writing effective beginnings and endings, titles and thesis statements, comparing, describing, taking essay exams, and so on.

6. **RESEARCH/DOCUMENTATION.** Chapters 45–53 offer advice on how to do academic research; work with sources; quote, paraphrase, and summarize source materials; and document sources using MLA and APA styles. Chapters 51 and 52 present the "official MLA style" introduced in 2016.

7. **MEDIA/DESIGN.** Chapters 54–58 give guidance on choosing the appropriate print, electronic, or spoken medium; designing text; using images and sound; giving spoken presentations; and writing online.

8. **READINGS.** Chapters 59–69 provide readings in ten genres, plus one chapter of readings that mix genres. Discussion questions are color-coded to refer students to relevant details elsewhere in the book.

What's Online

Ebooks. All versions of *The Norton Field Guide* are available as ebooks and include all the readings and images found in the print books. A fraction of the price of the print books, our ebooks allow students to access the entire book, search, highlight, bookmark, and take / share notes with ease, and can be viewed on — and synched between — all computers and mobile devices.

Norton/write. Just a click away with no passcode required, find a library of model student papers; more than 1,000 online exercises and quizzes; research and plagiarism tutorials; documentation guidelines for MLA, APA, *Chicago*, and CSE styles; MLA citation drills—and more. All MLA materials reflect 2016 MLA style. Access the site at wwnorton.com/write.

A companion website includes worksheets and templates, additional chapters, and more. Access the site at wwnorton.com/write/fieldguide.

What's Available for Instructors

A Guide to Teaching with *The Norton Field Guides*. Written by Richard Bullock and several other teachers, this is a comprehensive guide to teaching first-year writing, from developing a syllabus to facilitating group work, teaching multimodal writing to assessing student writing. Free of charge.

Coursepacks are available for free and in a variety of formats, including *Blackbaord*, *Desire2Learn*, *Moodle*, *Canvas*, and *Angel*—and work within your existing learning management system, so there's no new system to learn, and access is free and easy. The *Field Guide* Coursepack includes model student papers; reading comprehension quizzes; reading strategy exercises; quizzes and exercises on grammar and research; documentation guidelines; and author biographies. Coursepacks are ready to use, right from the start — but are also easy to customize, using the system you already know and understand. Access the Coursepack at wwnorton.com/instructors.

PowerPoints. Ready-made PowerPoints feature genre organization flowcharts and documentation maps from the book to help you show examples during class. Download the PowerPoints at wwnorton.com/instructors.

Worksheets available in Word and PDF can be edited, downloaded, and printed with guidance on editing paragraphs, responding to a draft, and more. Download the worksheets at wwnorton.com/instructors.

Highlights

It's easy to use. Menus, directories, and a glossary/index make it easy for students to find what they're looking for. Color-coded templates and documentation maps even make MLA and APA documentation easy.

It has just enough detail, with short chapters that include color-coded links sending students to more detail *if* they need more.

It's uniquely flexible for teachers. Short chapters can be assigned in any order — and color-coded links help draw from other chapters as need be.

What's New

A new part on academic literacies: with chapters on writing and reading in academic contexts, summarizing and responding, and developing academic habits of mind. Chapter 1 lists the WPA outcomes, showing students what's expected of writers in colleges and universities across the nation. (Part 1)

A new chapter on summarizing and responding, two fundamental moves required of college writers across disciplines. The chapter also includes guidance in writing a summary-response essay, a common assignment in many composition classes today. (Chapter 3)

A new chapter on developing academic habits of mind: engagement, persistence, flexibility, creativity, and other such habits, including all the ones identified in the *Framework for Success in College Writing*. (Chapter 4)

New MLA guidelines: Chapters 51 and 52 have been updated to reflect the new "official MLA style" introduced in 2016. All the MLA-style essays in the book have been updated as well.

Chapters on literary analyses: with an album of 5 stories and poems. (Chapters 17, 64)

26 new readings: 4 new essays in the rhetoric, 16 in the anthology; 5 stories and poems.

Ways of Teaching with *The Norton Field Guide to Writing*

The Norton Field Guide is designed to give you both support and flexibility. It has clear assignment sequences if you want them, or you can create your own. If, for example, you assign a position paper, there's a full chapter. If you want students to use sources, add the appropriate research chapters. If you want them to submit a topic proposal, add that chapter.

If you're a new teacher, the genre chapters offer explicit assignment sequences—and the color-coded links will remind you of detail you may want to bring in. The instructor's manual offers advice on creating a syllabus, responding to writing, and more.

If you focus on genres, there are complete chapters on all the genres college students are often assigned. Color-coded links will help you bring in details about research or other writing strategies as you wish.

If you organize your course thematically, a Thematic Guide will lead you to readings on 23 themes. Chapter 27 on generating ideas can help get students thinking about a theme. You can also assign them to do research on the theme, starting with Chapter 46 on finding sources, or perhaps with Chapter 25 on writing as inquiry. If they then write in a particular genre, there will be a chapter to guide them.

If you want students to do research, there are 9 chapters on the research process, including guidelines and sample papers for MLA and APA styles.

If you focus on modes, you'll find chapters on using narration, description, and so on as strategies for many writing purposes, and links that lead students through the process of writing an essay organized around a particular mode.

If you teach a stretch, ALP, IRW, or dual credit course, the academic literacies chapters offer explicit guidelines to help students write and read in academic contexts, summarize and respond to what they read, and develop academic habits of mind that will help them succeed in college.

If you teach online, the book is available as an ebook — and a companion Coursepack includes exercises, quizzes, video tutorials, and more.

Acknowledgments

As we've traveled around the country and met many of the students, teachers, and WPAs who are using *The Norton Field Guide*, we've been gratified to hear that so many find it helpful, to the point that some students tell us that they aren't going to sell it back to the bookstore when the term ends — the highest form of praise. As much as we like the positive response, though, we are especially grateful when we receive suggestions for ways the book might be improved. In this fourth edition, as we did in the third edition, we have tried to respond to the many good suggestions we've gotten from students, colleagues, reviewers, and editors. Thank you all, both for your kind words and for your good suggestions.

Some people need to be singled out for thanks, especially Marilyn Moller, the guiding editorial spirit of the *Field Guide* through all four editions. When we presented Marilyn with the idea for this book, she encouraged us and helped us conceptualize it — and then taught us how to write a textbook. The quality of the *Field Guide* is due in large part to her knowledge of the field of composition, her formidable editing and writing skills, her sometimes uncanny ability to see the future of the teaching of writing — and her equally formidable, if not uncanny, stamina.

Developmental editor John Elliott has shepherded both the third and the fourth editions through their revisions and additions with a careful hand and a clear eye for appropriate content and language. His painstaking editing shows throughout the book, and we're grateful for his ability to make us appear to be better writers than we are.

Many others have contributed, too. Thanks to project editors Christine D'Antonio, Rebecca Homiski, and Katie Callahan for their energy, patience, and great skill in coordinating the tightly scheduled production process for the book. Claire Wallace managed the reviewing process and brought her own astute eye to evaluating all the readings, and more. *The Norton Field Guide* is more than just a print book, and we thank Erica Wnek, Kim Yi, Mateus Teixeira, Patrick Cartelli, Ava Bramson, and Cooper Wilhelm for creating and producing the superb ebook and instructors' site. Anna Palchik designed the award-winning, user-friendly, and attractive interior, Carin Berger created the beautiful new cover design, and Debra Morton Hoyt, Michael Wood, and Tiani Kennedy further enhanced the design and coordinated it all, inside and out. Andy Ensor transformed a scribbled-over manuscript into a finished product with extraordinary speed and precision, while Jude Grant copyedited. Megan Jackson and Bethany Salminen cleared text permissions, coping efficiently with ongoing changes, and Nelson Colón cleared permission for the images found by Dena Digilio Betz. Steve Dunn, Lib Triplett, Megan Zwilling, Maureen Connolly, and Doug Day helped us all keep our eyes on the market. Thanks to all, and to Roby Harrington, Drake McFeely, and Julia Reidhead for supporting this project in the first place.

Rich has many, many people at Wright State University to thank for their support and assistance. Jane Blakelock has taught Rich most of what he knows about electronic text and writing on and for the web and has assembled an impressive list of useful links for the book's website. Adrienne Cassel, now at Sinclair Community College, and Catherine Crowley read and commented on many drafts. Peggy Lindsey (now at Georgia Southern University) shared her students' work and the idea of using charts to show how various genres might be organized. Brady Allen, Debbie Bertsch (now at Columbus State Community College), Vicki Burke, Melissa Carrion, Jimmy Chesire, Carol Cornett, Mary Doyle, Byron Crews, Deborah Crusan, Sally DeThomas, Stephanie Dickey, Scott Geisel, Karen Hayes, Chuck Holmes, Beth Klaisner, Nancy Mack, Marty Maner, Cynthia Marshall, Sarah McGinley, Kristie McKiernan, Michelle Metzner, Kristie Rowe, Bobby Rubin, Cathy Sayer, David Seitz, Caroline Simmons, Tracy Smith, Rick Strader, Mary Van Loveren, and A. J. Williams responded to drafts, submitted good models of student writing, contributed to the instructor's manual, tested the *Field Guide* in their classes, provided support, and shared with Rich some of their best teaching ideas. Henry Limouze and then Carol Loranger, chairs of the English Department, gave him room to work on this project with patience and good humor. Sandy Trimboli, Becky Traxler, and Lynn Morgan, the secretaries to the writing programs, kept him anchored. And he thanks especially the more than 300 graduate teaching assistants and 10,000 first-year students who class-tested various editions of the *Field Guide* and whose experiences helped — and continue to help — to shape it.

At Arizona State, Maureen wants to acknowledge the unwavering support of Neal A. Lester, Vice President of Humanities and Arts and former chair of the English Department, and the assistance of Jason Diller, her former graduate research assistant, and Judy Holiday, her former graduate mentee, for their reading suggestions. She thanks her colleagues, all exemplary teachers and mentors, for creating a supportive intellectual environment, especially Patricia Boyd, Peter Goggin, Mark Hannah, Kathleen Lamp, Elenore Long, Paul Matsuda, Keith Miller, Ersula Ore, Alice Robison, Shirley Rose, and Doris Warriner. Thanks also go to ASU instructors and first-year students who have used the *Field Guide* and have offered good suggestions. Finally, Maureen wants to pay tribute to her students, who are themselves among her best teachers.

Thanks to the teachers across the country who reviewed the third edition of the *Field Guide* and helped shape this fourth edition: Neal Abramson, Richland College; Marian Anders, Alamance Community College; Bonnie Asselin, Abraham Baldwin Agricultural College; Lillie Bailey, Virginia State University; Jacqueline Blackwell, Thomas Nelson Community College; Dean Blumberg, Horry–Georgetown Technical College; Ronald Brooks, Oklahoma State University; Belinda Bruner, Oklahoma State University; Laurie Buchanan, Clark State Community College; Judi Buenaflor, Northampton Community College; Jeaneen Canfield, Oklahoma State University; John Castellarin, Germanna Community College; Sheila Chase, Arkansas State University–Beebe; W. Scott Cheney, Collin College; Robert Ransom Cole, Auburn University at Montgomery; Candace Cooper, Collin College; Amy Decker, Germanna Community College; Regina Dickerson, University of Nevada, Las Vegas; Courtney Doi, Alamance Community College; Summer Doucet, Baton Rouge Community College; Barbara Dumont, Joliet Junior College; Julie Dunlop, Central New Mexico Community College; Lexy Durand, Alamance Community College; Mary Sue Fox, Central New Mexico Community College; Deborah Goodwyn, Virginia State University; Bruce Gospin, Northampton Community College; Michael Hedges, Horry Georgetown Technical College; Kalissa Hendrickson, Arizona State University; Matthew Henry, Richland College; Missy James, Tallahassee Community College; David Jones, Arkansas State University–Beebe; Sheikh Umarr Kamarah, Virginia State University; Erin Kelley, Richland College; Cecilia Kennedy, Clark State Community College; Myleah Kerns, Thomas

Nelson Community College; Guy Krueger, University of Mississippi; Sharon Gavin Levy, Northampton Community College; Jan Look, Joliet Junior College; Terri Mann, El Paso Community College; Margaret Marangione, Blue Ridge Community College; William McGee Jr., Joliet Junior College; Heath Mensher, Northampton Community College; Cathryn Meyer, Tallahassee Community College; Rosemary Mink, Mohawk Valley Community College; David Nackley, Mohawk Valley Community College; Michael Neil, Highland Park High School; Clarence Nero, Baton Rouge Community College; Tanya Nichols, Fresno State University; Nancy Noel, Germanna Community College; Stephen Nowka, Clark State Community College; Joseph Paretta, Northampton Community College; Eden Pearson, Des Moines Area Community College; Robert Pontious, Brunswick Community College; Donna Porche-Frilot, Baton Rouge Community College; Tony Procell, El Paso Community College; Bonnie Proudfoot, Hocking College; Sayanti Ganguly Puckett, Johnson County Community College; Anthony Rapino, Northampton Community College; Brenda Reid, Tallahassee Community College; Marilyn Senter, Johnson County Community College; Maureen Sherbondy, Alamance Community College; Vivian Walters, Arkansas State University–Beebe; Jay Branagan Webb, Richland College; Antoinette Whalen, Richland College; Tammy Wolf, Central New Mexico Community College.

The Norton Field Guide has also benefited from the good advice and conversations we've had with writing teachers across the country, including (among many others) Maureen Mathison, Susan Miller, Tom Huckin, Gae Lyn Henderson, and Sundy Watanabe at the University of Utah; Christa Albrecht-Crane, Doug Downs, and Brian Whaley at Utah Valley State College; Anne Dvorak and Anya Morrissey at Longview Community University; Jeff Andelora at Mesa Community College; Robin Calitri at Merced College; Lori Gallinger, Rose Hawkins, Jennifer Nelson, Georgia Standish, and John Ziebell at the Community College of Southern Nevada; Stuart Blythe at Indiana University–Purdue University Fort Wayne; Janice Kelly at Arizona State University; Jeanne McDonald at Waubonsee Community College; Web Newbold, Mary Clark-Upchurch, Megan Auffart, Matt Balk, Edward James Chambers, Sarah Chavez, Desiree Dighton, Ashley Ellison, Theresa Evans, Keith Heller, Ellie Isenhart, Angela Jackson-Brown, Naoko Kato, Yuanyuan Liao, Claire Lutkewitte, Yeno Matuki, Casey McArdle, Tibor

Munkacsi, Dani Nier-Weber, Karen Neubauer, Craig O'Hara, Martha Payne, Sarah Sandman, and Kellie Weiss at Ball State University; Patrick Tompkins at Tyler Community College; George Kanieski and Pamela Hardman at Cuyahoga Community College; Daniela Regusa, Jeff Partridge, and Lydia Vine at Capital Community College; Elizabeth Woodworth, Auburn University–Montgomery; Stephanie Eason at Enterprise Community College; Kate Geiselman at Sinclair Community College; Ronda Dively at Southern Illinois University; Debra Knutson at Shawnee State University; Guy Shebat and Amy Flick at Youngstown State University; and Martha Tolleson, Toni McMillen, and Patricia Gerecci at Collin College.

We wouldn't have met most of these people without the help of the Norton travelers, the representatives who spend their days visiting faculty, showing and discussing the *Field Guide* and Norton's many other fine textbooks. Thanks especially to Hayley Bartholomew, Kathy Carlsen, Scott Cook, John Darger, Marilyn Rayner, Peter Wentz, Mary Helen Willett, Lauren Winkler, and all the other Norton travelers. And we'd especially like to thank Mike Wright, Lib Triplett, Ashley Cain, and Doug Day for promoting this book so enthusiastically and professionally.

It's customary to conclude by expressing gratitude to one's spouse and family, and for good reason. Writing and revising *The Norton Field Guide* over the past several years, we have enjoyed the loving and unconditional support of our spouses, Barb and Peter, who provide the foundation for all we do. Thank you. We couldn't have done it without you.

How to Use This Book

There's no one way to do anything, and writing is no exception. Some people need to do a lot of planning on paper; others write entire drafts in their heads. Some writers compose quickly and loosely, going back later to revise; others work on one sentence until they're satisfied with it, then move on to the next. And writers' needs vary from task to task, too: sometimes you know what you're going to write about and why, but need to figure out how to do it; other times your first job is to come up with a topic. *The Norton Field Guide* is designed to allow you to chart your own course as a writer, offering guidelines that suit your writing needs. It is organized in nine parts:

1. **ACADEMIC LITERACIES**: The chapters in this part will help you know what's expected in the reading and writing you do for academic purposes, and in summarizing and responding to what you read. One chapter even provides tips for developing habits of mind that will help you succeed in college, whatever your goals.

2. **RHETORICAL SITUATIONS**: No matter what you're writing, it will always have some purpose, audience, genre, stance, and medium and design. This part will help you consider each of these elements, as well as the particular kinds of rhetorical situations created by academic assignments.

3. **GENRES**: Use these chapters for help with specific kinds of writing, from abstracts to lab reports to memoirs and more. You'll find more detailed guidance for four especially common assignments: literacy narratives, textual analyses, reports, and arguments. There's also help with choosing which genre to use when an assignment doesn't specify one.

4. **PROCESSES**: These chapters offer general advice for all writing situations—from generating ideas and text to drafting, revising and rewriting, compiling a portfolio—and more.

5. **STRATEGIES**: Use the advice in this part to develop and organize your writing—to write effective beginnings and endings, to guide readers through your text, and to use comparison, description, dialogue, and other strategies as appropriate.

6. **RESEARCH / DOCUMENTATION**: Use this section for advice on how to do research, work with sources, and compose and document research-based texts using MLA and APA styles.

7. **MEDIA / DESIGN**: This section offers guidance in designing your work and using visuals and sound, and in deciding whether and how to deliver what you write on paper, on screen, or in person.

8. **READINGS**: This section includes readings in 10 genres, and one chapter of texts that mix genres — 42 readings in all that provide good examples of the kinds of writing you yourself may be assigned to do.

Ways into the Book

The Norton Field Guide gives you the writing advice you need, along with the flexibility to write in the way that works best for you. Here are some of the ways you can find what you need in the book.

Brief menus.   Inside the front cover you'll find a list of all the chapters; start here if you are looking for a chapter on a certain kind of writing or a general writing issue. Inside the back cover is a menu of all the readings in the book.

Complete contents.   Pages xix–xxxix contain a detailed table of contents. Look here if you need to find a reading or a specific section in a chapter.

Guides to writing.   If you know the kind of writing you need to do, you'll find guides to writing 14 common genres in Part 2. These guides are designed to help you through all the decisions you have to make — from coming up with a topic to editing and proofreading your final draft.

Color-coding.   The parts of this book are color-coded for easy reference: light blue for **ACADEMIC LITERACIES**, red for **RHETORICAL SITUATIONS**, green for **GENRES**, lavender for **PROCESSES**, orange for **STRATEGIES**, blue for **RESEARCH / DOCUMENTATION**, gold for **MEDIA / DESIGN**, and apple green for the **READINGS**. You'll find a key to the colors on the front cover flap and also at the foot of each left-hand page. When you see a word highlighted in a color, that tells you where you can find additional detail on the topic.

Glossary / index. At the back of the book is a combined glossary and index, where you'll find full definitions of key terms and topics, along with a list of the pages where everything is covered in detail.

Directories to MLA and APA documentation. A brief directory inside the back cover will lead you to guidelines on citing sources and composing a list of references or works cited. The documentation models are color-coded so you can easily see the key details.

The website. You can also start at wwnorton.com/write/fieldguide. There you'll find model essays; worksheets; MLA and APA guidelines; more than 1,000 exercises focused on sentences, language, and punctuation; an online handbook; and more.

Ways of Getting Started

If you know your genre, simply turn to the appropriate genre chapter. There you'll find model readings, a description of the genre's Key Features, and a Guide to Writing that will help you come up with a topic, generate text, organize and write a draft, get response, revise, edit, and proofread. The genre chapters also point out places where you might need to do research, use certain writing strategies, design your text a certain way — and direct you to the exact pages in the book where you can find help doing so.

If you know your topic, you might start with some of the activities in Chapter 27, Generating Ideas and Text. From there, you might turn to Chapter 46, for help Finding Sources on the topic. When it comes time to narrow your topic and come up with a thesis statement, Chapter 34 can help. If you get stuck at any point, you might turn to Chapter 25, Writing as Inquiry; it provides tips that can get you beyond what you already know about your topic. If your assignment or your thesis defines your genre, turn to that chapter; if not, consult Chapter 25 for help determining the appropriate genre, and then turn to that genre chapter. The genre chapters point out places where you might need to do more research, use certain writing strategies, design your text a certain way — and direct you to the exact pages in the book where you can find help doing so.

Contents

Part 2   Rhetorical Situations   53

Part 4   Processes   279

Part 5   Strategies   329

Part 6   Doing Research   433

Part 8   Readings   637

Thematic Guide to the Readings

xxxix

Ethics

Food

Gender

Government and Politics

History

World Cultures and Global Issues

FOURTH EDITION

The Norton Field Guide to Writing
with readings

part 1

Academic Literacies

Whenever we enter a new community — start a new job, move to a new town, join a new club — there are certain things we need to learn. The same is true upon entering the academic world. We need to be able to **READ** and **WRITE** in certain ways. We're routinely called on to **SUMMARIZE** something we've heard or read, and to **RESPOND** in some way. And to succeed, we need to develop certain **HABITS OF MIND** — everyday things such as asking questions and being persistent. The following chapters provide guidelines to help you develop these fundamental academic literacies — and know what's expected of you in academic communities.

Academic Literacies

Writing in Academic Contexts **1**

Write an essay arguing whether genes or environment do more to determine people's intelligence. Research and write a report on the environmental effects of electricity-generating windmills. Work with a team to write a proposal and create a multimedia presentation for a sales campaign. Whatever you're studying, you're surely going to be doing a lot of writing, in classes from various disciplines — the above assignments, for example, are from psychology, environmental science, and marketing. Academic writing can serve a number of different purposes — to **ARGUE** for what you think about a topic and why, to **REPORT** on what's known about an issue, to **PROPOSE A SOLUTION** for some problem, and so on. Whatever your topics or purposes, all academic writing follows certain conventions, ones you'll need to master in order to join the conversations going on across campus. This chapter describes what's expected of academic writing — and of academic writers.

▲ 156–82
129–55
235–42

What's Expected of Academic Writing

Evidence that you've considered the subject thoughtfully. Whether you're composing a report, an argument, or some other kind of writing, you need to demonstrate that you've thought seriously about the topic and done any necessary research. You can use various ways to show that you've considered the subject carefully, from citing authoritative sources to incorporating information you learned in class to pointing out connections among ideas.

academic literacies   rhetorical situations   genres   processes   strategies   research MLA / APA   media / design   readings

An indication of why your topic matters. You need to help your readers understand why your topic is worth exploring and why your writing is worth reading. Even if you are writing in response to an assigned topic, you can better make your point and achieve your purpose by showing your readers why your topic is important and why they should care about it. For example, in "Throwing Like a Girl," James Fallows explains why his topic, the differences between the ways men and women throw a baseball, is worth writing about:

> The phrase "throwing like a girl" has become an embattled and offensive one. Feminists smart at its implication that to do something "like a girl" is to do it the wrong way. Recently, on the heels of the O. J. Simpson case, a book appeared in which the phrase was used to help explain why male athletes, especially football players, were involved in so many assaults against women. Having been trained (like most American boys) to dread the accusation of doing anything "like a girl," athletes were said to grow into the assumption that women were valueless, and natural prey.

By explaining that the topic matters because it reflects attitudes about gender that have potentially serious consequences, he gives readers reason to read on about the mechanics of "throwing like a girl."

A response to what others have said. Whatever your topic, it's unlikely that you'll be the first one to write about it. And if, as this chapter assumes, all academic writing is part of a larger conversation, you are in a way adding your own voice to that conversation. One good way of doing that is to present your ideas as a response to what others have said about your topic — to begin by quoting, paraphrasing, or summarizing what others have said and then to agree, disagree, or both.

For example, in an essay arguing that organ sales will save lives, Joanna MacKay says, "Some agree with Pope John Paul II that the selling of organs is morally wrong and violates 'the dignity of the human person.'" But she then responds — and disagrees, arguing that "the morals we hold are not absolute truths" and that "peasants of third world countries" might not agree with the pope.

A clear, appropriately qualified thesis.   When you write in an academic context, you're expected to state your main point explicitly, often in a **THESIS** statement. MIT student Joanna MacKay states her thesis clearly in her essay "Organ Sales Will Save Lives": "Governments should not ban the sale of human organs; they should regulate it." Often you'll need to **QUALIFY** your thesis statement to acknowledge that the subject is complicated and there may be more than one way of seeing it or exceptions to the generalization you're making about it. Here, for example, is a qualified thesis, from an essay evaluating the movie *Juno* by Ali Heinkamp, a student at Wright State University: "Although the situations *Juno's* characters find themselves in and their dialogue may be criticized as unrealistic, the film, written by Diablo Cody and directed by Jason Reitman, successfully portrays the emotions of a teen being shoved into maturity way too fast." Heinkamp makes a claim that *Juno* achieves its main goal, while acknowledging at the beginning of the sentence that the film may be flawed.

345–47
346–47

Good reasons supported by evidence.   You need to provide good reasons for your thesis and evidence to support those reasons. For example, Joanna MacKay offers several reasons why sales of human kidneys should be legalized: there is a surplus of kidneys, the risk to the donor is not great, and legalization would allow the trade in kidneys to be regulated. Evidence to support your reasons sometimes comes from your own experience but more often from published research and scholarship, research you do yourself or firsthand accounts by others.

Compared with other kinds of writing, academic writing is generally expected to be more objective and less emotional. You may find *Romeo and Juliet* deeply moving or cry when you watch *Titanic* — but when you write about the play or the film for a class, you must do so using evidence from the text to support your thesis. You may find someone's ideas deeply offensive, but you should respond to them with reason rather than with emotional appeals or personal attacks.

Acknowledgment of multiple perspectives.   Debates and arguments in popular media are often framed in "pro/con" terms, as if there were only two sides to any given issue. Once you begin seriously studying a topic, though, you're likely to find that there are several sides and that each of them deserves serious consideration. In your academic writing, you need to represent fairly the range of perspectives on your topic — to explore three, four, or more positions on it as you research and write. In her report, "Does Texting Affect Writing," Marywood University student Michaela Cullington, for example, examines texting from several points of view: teachers' impressions of the influence of texting on student writing, the results of several research studies, and her own survey research.

A confident, authoritative stance.   If one goal of academic writing is to contribute to a larger conversation, your tone should convey confidence and establish your authority to write about your subject. Ways to achieve such a tone include using active verbs ("X claims" rather than "it seems"), avoiding such phrases as "in my opinion" and "I think," and writing in a straightforward, direct style. Your writing should send the message that you've done the research, analysis, and thinking and know what you're talking about. For example, here is the final paragraph of Michaela Cullington's essay on texting and writing:

> On the basis of my own research, expert research, and personal obser-vations, I can confidently state that texting is not interfering with students' use of standard written English and has no effect on their writing abilities in general. It is interesting to look at the dynamics of the arguments over these issues. Teachers and parents who claim that they are seeing a decline in the writing abilities of their students and children mainly support the negative-impact argument. Other teach-ers and researchers suggest that texting provides a way for teens to practice writing in a casual setting and thus helps prepare them to write formally. Experts and students themselves, however, report that they see no effect, positive or negative. Anecdotal experiences should not overshadow the actual evidence.

Cullington's use of simple, declarative sentences ("Other teachers and researchers suggest..."; "Anecdotal experiences should not overshadow...") and her straightforward summary of the arguments surrounding texting,

along with her strong, unequivocal ending ("texting is not interfering with students' use of standard written English"), lend her writing a confident tone. Her stance sends the message that she's done the research and knows what she's talking about.

Carefully documented sources. Clearly acknowledging sources and documenting them carefully and correctly is a basic requirement of academic writing. When you use the words or ideas of others — including visuals, video, or audio — those sources must be documented in the text and in a works cited or references list at the end. (If you're writing something that will appear online, you may also refer readers to your sources by using hyperlinks in the text; ask your instructor if you need to include a list of references or works cited as well.)

Careful attention to correctness. Whether you're writing something formal or informal, in an essay or an email, you should always write in complete sentences, use appropriate capitalization and punctuation, and check that your spelling is correct. In general, academic writing is no place for colloquial language, slang, or texting abbreviations. If you're quoting someone, you can reproduce that person's writing or speech exactly, but in your own writing you try hard to be correct — and always proofread carefully.

What's Expected of College Writers: The WPA Outcomes

Writing is not a multiple-choice test; it doesn't have right and wrong answers that are easily graded. Instead, your readers, whether they're teachers or anyone else, are likely to read your writing with various things in mind: does it make sense, does it meet the demands of the assignment, is the grammar correct, to name just a few of the things readers may look for. Different readers may notice different things, so sometimes it may seem to you that their response — and your grade — is unpredictable. It should be good to know, then, that writing teachers across the nation have come to some agreement on certain "outcomes," what college students should know and be able to do by the time you finish a first-year writing course. These outcomes have been defined by the National Council of Writing Program Administrators (WPA). Here's a brief summary of these outcomes and how *The Norton Field Guide* can help you meet them.

Knowledge of Rhetoric

- *Understand the rhetorical situation of texts that you read and write.* See Chapters 5–9 and the many prompts for Considering the Rhetorical Situation throughout the book.
- *Read and write texts in a number of different genres and understand how your purpose may influence your writing.* See Chapters 10–22 for guidelines on writing in thirteen genres, Chapter 23 on mixing genres, and Chapter 24 for help choosing genres when you need to.
- *Adjust your voice, tone, level of formality, design, and medium as is necessary and appropriate.* See Chapter 8 on stance and tone and Chapter 9 for help thinking about medium and design.
- *Choose the media that will best suit your audience, purpose, and the rest of your rhetorical situation.* See Chapters 9 and 54.

Critical Thinking, Reading, and Composing

- *Read and write to inquire, learn, think critically, and communicate.* See Chapters 1 and 2 on academic writing and reading, and Chapter 25 on writing as inquiry. Chapters 10–13 provide genre-specific prompts to help you think critically about a draft.
- *Read for content, argumentative strategies, and rhetorical effectiveness.* Chapter 7 provides guidance on reading texts with a critical eye, Chapter 11 teaches how to analyze a text, and Chapter 47 shows how to evaluate sources.
- *Find and evaluate popular and scholarly sources.* Chapter 46 teaches how to use databases and other methods to find sources, and Chapter 47 shows how to evaluate the sources you find.

- *Use sources in various ways to support your ideas.* Chapter 36 suggests strategies for supporting your ideas, and Chapter 49 shows how to incorporate ideas from sources into your writing to support your ideas.

Processes

- *Use writing processes to compose texts and explore ideas in various media.* Part 4 covers all stages of the processes writers use, from generating ideas and text to drafting to getting response and revising to editing and proofreading. Each of the thirteen genre chapters (10–22) includes a guide that leads you through the process of writing in that genre.
- *Collaborate with others on your own writing and on group tasks.* Chapter 26 offers guidelines for working with others, Chapter 30 provides general prompts for getting and giving response, and Chapters 10–13 provide genre-specific prompts for reading a draft with a critical eye.
- *Reflect on your own writing processes.* Chapters 10–13 provide genre-specific questions to help you take stock of your work, and Chapter 29 offers guidance in thinking about your own writing process. Chapter 32 provides prompts to help you reflect on a writing portfolio.

Knowledge of Conventions

- *Use correct grammar, punctuation, and spelling.* Chapter 31 provides tips to help you edit and proofread for your writing. Chapters 10–13 offer genre-specific advice for editing and proofreading.
- *Understand and use genre conventions and formats in your writing.* Chapter 7 provides an overview of genres and how to think about them. Part 3 covers thirteen genres, describing the key features and conventions of each one.
- *Understand intellectual property and document sources appropriately.* Chapter 50 offers guidance on the ethical use of sources, Chapter 51 provides an overview of documentation styles, and Chapters 52 and 53 provide templates for documenting in MLA and APA styles.

2 Reading in Academic Contexts

We read newspapers to know about the events of the day. We read textbooks to learn about history, chemistry, and other academic topics — and other academic sources to do research and develop arguments. We read tweets and blogs to follow (and participate in) conversations about issues that interest us. And as writers, we read our own writing to make sure it says what we mean it to say and proofread our final drafts to make sure they say it correctly. In other words, we read many kinds of texts for many different purposes. This chapter offers a number of strategies for various kinds of reading you do in academic contexts.

TAKING STOCK OF YOUR READING

One way to become a better reader is to understand your reading process; if you know what you do when you read, you're in a position to decide what you need to change or improve. Consider the answers to the following questions:

- What do you read for pleasure? for work? for school? Consider all the sorts of reading you do: books, magazines, and newspapers, websites, *Facebook*, texts, blogs, product instructions.

- When you're facing a reading assignment, what do you do? Do you do certain things to get comfortable? Do you play music or seek quiet? Do you plan your reading time or set reading goals for yourself? Do you flip through or skim the text before settling down to read it, or do you start at the beginning and work through it?

- When you begin to read something for an assignment, do you make sure you understand the purpose of the assignment — why you

must read this text? Do you ever ask your instructor (or whoever else assigned the reading) what its purpose is?

- How do you motivate yourself to read material you don't have any interest in? How do you deal with boredom while reading?

- Does your mind wander? If you realize that you haven't been paying attention and don't know what you just read, what do you do?

- Do you ever highlight, underline, or annotate text as you read? Do you take notes? If so, what do you mark or write down? Why?

- When you read text you don't understand, what do you do?

- As you anticipate and read an assigned text, what attitudes or feelings do you typically have? If they differ from reading to reading, why do they?

- What do you do when you've finished reading an assigned text? Write out notes? Think about what you've just read? Move on to the next task? Something else?

- How well do your reading processes work for you, both in school and otherwise? What would you like to change? What can you do to change?

The rest of this chapter offers advice and strategies that you may find helpful as you work to improve your reading skills.

READING STRATEGICALLY

Academic reading is challenging because it makes several demands on you at once. Textbooks present new vocabulary and new concepts, and picking out the main ideas can be difficult. Scholarly articles present content and arguments you need to understand, but they often assume that readers already know key concepts and vocabulary and so don't generally provide background information. As you read more texts in an academic field and begin to participate in its conversations, the reading will become easier, but in the meantime you can develop strategies that will help you to read effectively.

Thinking about What You Want to Learn

To learn anything, we need to place new information into the context of what we already know. For example, to understand photosynthesis, we need to already know something about plants, energy, and air, among other things. To learn a new language, we draw on similarities and differences between it and any other languages we know. A method of bringing to conscious attention our current knowledge on a topic and of helping us articulate our purposes for reading is a list-making process called KWL+. To use it, create a table with three columns:

K: What I _Know_	W: What I _Want_ to Know	L: What I _Learned_

Before you begin reading a text, list in the "K" column what you already know about the topic. Brainstorm ideas, and list terms or phrases that come to mind. Then group them into categories. Also before reading, or after reading the first few paragraphs, list in the "W" column questions you have that you expect, want, or hope to be answered as you read. Number or reorder the questions by their importance to you.

Then, as you read the text or afterward, list in the "L" column what you learned from the text. Compare your "L" list with your "W" list to see what you still want or need to know (the "+") — and what you learned that you didn't expect.

Previewing the Text

It's usually a good idea to start by skimming a text — read the title and subtitle, any headings, the first and last paragraphs, the first sentences of all the other paragraphs. Study any illustrations and other visuals. Your

goal is to get a sense of where the text is heading. At this point, don't stop to look up unfamiliar words; just mark them in some way to look up later.

Adjusting Your Reading Speed to Different Texts

Different texts require different kinds of effort. Some that are simple and straightforward can be skimmed fairly quickly. With academic texts, though, you usually need to read more slowly and carefully, matching the pace of your reading to the difficulty of the text. You'll likely need to skim the text for an overview of the basic ideas and then go back to read it closely. And then you may need to read it yet again. (But do try always to read quickly enough to focus on the meanings of sentences and paragraphs, not just individual words.) With visual texts, too, you'll often need to look at them several times, moving from gaining an overall impression to closely examining the structure, layout, and other visual features — and exploring how those features relate to any accompanying verbal text.

Looking for Organizational Cues

As you read, look for cues that signal the way the text's ideas are organized and how each part relates to the ones around it:

The introductory paragraph and thesis often offer a preview of the topics to be discussed and the order in which they will be addressed. Here, for example, is a typical thesis statement for a report: *Types of prisons in the United States include minimum and medium security, close security, maximum security, and supermax.* The report that follows should explain each type of prison in the order stated in the thesis.

Transitions help **GUIDE READERS** in following the direction of the writer's thinking from idea to idea. For example, "however" indicates an idea that contradicts or limits what has just been said, while "furthermore" indicates one that adds to or supports it.

349

Headings identify a text's major and minor sections, by means of both the headings' content and their design.

Thinking about Your Initial Response

Some readers find it helps to make brief notes about their first response to a text, noting their reaction and thinking a little about why they reacted as they did.

What are your initial reactions? Describe both your intellectual reaction and any emotional reaction, and identify places in the text that caused you to react as you did. An intellectual reaction might consist of an evaluation ("I disagree with this position because . . ."), a connection ("This idea reminds me of . . ."), or an elaboration ("Another example of this point is . . ."). An emotional reaction could include approval or disapproval ("YES! This is exactly right!" "NO! This is so wrong!"), an expression of feeling ("This passage makes me so sad"), or one of appreciation ("This is said so beautifully"). If you had no particular reaction, note that, too.

What accounts for your reactions? Are they rooted in personal experiences? aspects of your personality? positions you hold on an issue? As much as possible, you want to keep your opinions from interfering with your understanding of what you're reading, so it's important to try to identify those opinions up front.

Dealing with Difficult Texts

Let's face it: some texts are difficult. You may have no interest in the subject matter, or lack background knowledge or vocabulary necessary for understanding the text, or simply not have a clear sense of why you have to read the text at all. Whatever the reason, reading such texts can be a challenge. Here are some tips for dealing with them:

Look for something familiar.   Texts often seem difficult or boring because we don't know enough about the topic or about the larger conversation surrounding it to read them effectively. By skimming the headings, the abstract or introduction, and the conclusion, you may find something that relates to something you already know or are at least interested in — and being aware of that prior knowledge can help you see how this new material relates to it.

Look for "landmarks."   Reading a challenging academic text the first time through can be like driving to an unfamiliar destination on roads you've never traveled: you don't know where you're headed, you don't recognize anything along the way, and you're not sure how long getting there will take. As you drive the route again, though, you see landmarks along the way that help you know where you're going. The same goes for reading a difficult text: sometimes you need to get through it once just to get some idea of what it's about. On the second reading, now that you have "driven the route," look for the ways that the parts of the text relate to one another, to other texts or course information, or to other knowledge you have.

Monitor your understanding.   You may have had the experience of reading a text and suddenly realizing that you have no idea what you just read. Being able to monitor your reading — to sense when you aren't understanding the text and need to reread, focus your attention, look up unfamiliar terms, take some notes, or take a break — can make you a more efficient and better reader. Keep these questions in mind as you read: What is my purpose for reading this text? Am I understanding it? Does it make sense? Should I slow down, reread, annotate? skim ahead and then come back? pause to reflect?

Be persistent.   Research shows that many students respond to difficult texts by assuming they're "too dumb to get it" — and quit reading. Successful students, on the other hand, report that if they keep at a text, they will come to understand it. Some of them even see difficult texts as challenges: "I'm going to keep working on this until I make sense of it."

Remember that reading is an active process, and the more you work at it the more successful you will be.

Annotating

Many readers find it helps to annotate as they read: highlighting keywords, phrases, sentences; connecting ideas with lines or symbols; writing comments or questions in the margin or on sticky notes; circling new words so you can look up the definitions later; noting anything that seems noteworthy or questionable. Annotating forces you to read for more than just the surface meaning. Especially when you are going to be writing about or responding to a text, annotating creates a record of things you may want to refer to.

Annotate as if you're having a conversation with the author, someone you take seriously but whose words you do not accept without question. Put your part of the conversation in the margin, asking questions, talking back: "What's this mean?" "So what?" "Says who?" "Where's evidence?" "Yes!" "Whoa!" or even ☺ or ☹ or texting shorthand like LOL or INTRSTN. If you're reading a text online, you may be able to copy it and annotate it electronically. If so, make your annotations a different color from the text itself.

55–56 What you annotate depends upon your **PURPOSE**, or what you're most interested in. If you're analyzing a text that makes an explicit argu- 345–47 ment, you would probably underline the **THESIS STATEMENT**, and then 358–67 the **REASONS AND EVIDENCE** that support that statement. It might help to restate those ideas in your own words in the margins — in order to understand them, you need to put them in your own words! If you are trying to 28–29 **IDENTIFY PATTERNS**, you might highlight each pattern in a different color or mark it with a sticky note and write any questions or notes about it in that color. You might annotate a visual text by circling and identifying important parts of the image.

There are some texts that you cannot annotate, of course — library books, some materials you read on the web, and so on. Then you will need to use sticky notes or make notes elsewhere, and you might find it useful to keep a reading log for this purpose.

A Sample Annotated Text

Here is an excerpt from Justice: What's the Right Thing to Do?, *a book by Harvard professor Michael J. Sandel, annotated by a writer who was doing research for a report on the awarding of military medals:*

What Wounds Deserve the Purple Heart?

On some issues, questions of virtue and honor are too obvious to deny. Consider the recent debate over who should qualify for the Purple Heart. Since 1932, the U.S. military has awarded the medal to soldiers wounded or killed in battle by enemy action. In addition to the honor, the medal entitles recipients to special privileges in veterans' hospitals.

> *Purple Heart given for wounding or death in battle.*

Since the beginning of the current wars in Iraq and Afghanistan, growing numbers of veterans have been diagnosed with post-traumatic stress disorder and treated for the condition. Symptoms include recurring nightmares, severe depression, and suicide. At least three hundred thousand veterans reportedly suffer from traumatic stress or major depression. Advocates for these veterans have proposed that they, too, should qualify for the Purple Heart. Since psychological injuries can be at least as debilitating as physical ones, they argue, soldiers who suffer these wounds should receive the medal.

> *PTSD increasingly common among veterans.*

> *Argument: Vets with PTSD should be eligible for PH because psych. injuries are as serious as physical.*

After a Pentagon advisory group studied the question, the Pentagon announced, in 2009, that the Purple Heart would be reserved for soldiers with physical injuries. Veterans suffering from mental disorders and psychological trauma would not be eligible, even though they qualify for government-supported medical treatment and disability payments. The Pentagon offered two reasons for its decision: traumatic stress disorders are not intentionally caused by enemy action, and they are difficult to diagnose objectively.

> *2009: Military says no: PTSD injuries "not intentionally caused by enemy" and are hard to diagnose.*

Did the Pentagon make the right decision? Taken by themselves, its reasons are unconvincing. In the Iraq War, one of the most common injuries recognized with the Purple Heart has been a punctured eardrum, caused by explosions at close range. But unlike bullets and bombs, such explosions are not a deliberate enemy tactic intended to injure or kill; they are (like traumatic stress) a damaging side effect of battlefield action. And while traumatic disorders may be more difficult

> *PTSD is like punctured eardrums, which do get the PH.*

to diagnose than a broken limb, the injury they inflict can be more severe and long-lasting.

PH "honors sacrifice, not bravery." Injury enough. So what kind of injury?

As the wider debate about the Purple Heart revealed, the real issue is about the meaning of the medal and the virtues it honors. What, then, are the relevant virtues? Unlike other military medals, <u>the Purple Heart honors sacrifice, not bravery</u>. It requires no heroic act, only an injury inflicted by the enemy. The question is what kind of injury should count.

Wow: one vet's group insists that for PH, soldier must <u>bleed</u>!

A veteran's group called the Military Order of the Purple Heart opposed awarding the medal for psychological injuries, claiming that doing so would "debase" the honor. A spokesman for the group stated that "shedding blood" should be an essential qualification. He didn't explain why bloodless injuries shouldn't count. But Tyler E. Boudreau, a former Marine captain who favors including psychological injuries, offers a compelling analysis of the dispute. He attributes the opposition to a deep-seated attitude in the military that views post-traumatic stress as a kind of weakness. "The same culture that demands tough-mindedness also encourages skepticism toward the suggestion that the violence of war can hurt the healthiest of minds . . . Sadly, <u>as long as our military culture bears at least a quiet contempt for the psychological wounds of war, it is unlikely those veterans will ever see a Purple Heart</u>."

Good quote!

Argument based on different ideas about what counts as a military virtue.

So the debate over the Purple Heart is more than a medical or clinical dispute about how to determine the veracity of injury. At the heart of the disagreement are rival conceptions of <u>moral character and military valor</u>. Those who insist that only bleeding wounds should count believe that post-traumatic stress reflects a weakness of character unworthy of honor. Those who believe that psychological wounds should qualify argue that veterans suffering long-term trauma and severe depression have sacrificed for their country as surely, and as honorably, as those who've lost a limb. The dispute over the Purple Heart illustrates the moral logic of Aristotle's theory of justice. We can't determine who deserves a military medal without asking what virtues the medal properly honors. And to answer that question, we have to assess competing conceptions of character and sacrifice.

— Michael J. Sandel, *Justice: What's the Right Thing to Do?*

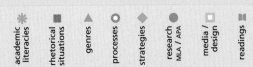

Coding

You may also find it useful to record your thoughts as you read by using a coding system — for example, using "X" to indicate passages that contradict your assumptions, or "?" for ones that puzzle you. You can make up your own coding system, of course, but you could start with this one*:

- ✔ Confirms what you thought
- X Contradicts what you thought
- ? Puzzles you
- ?? Confuses you
- ! Surprises you
- ☆ Strikes you as important
- → Is new or interesting to you

You might also circle new words that you'll want to look up later and highlight or underline key phrases.

Summarizing

Writing a summary, boiling down a text to its main ideas, can help you understand it. To do so, you need to identify which ideas in the text are crucial to its meaning. Then you put those crucial ideas into your own words, creating a brief version that accurately sums up the text. Here, for example, is a summary of Sandel's analysis of the Purple Heart debate:

> In "What Wounds Deserve the Purple Heart?," Harvard professor Michael J. Sandel explores the debate over eligibility for the Purple Heart, the medal given to soldiers who die or are wounded in battle. Some argue that soldiers suffering from post-traumatic stress disorder

---

*Adapted from Harvey Daniels and Steven Zemelman, *Subjects Matter: Every Teacher's Guide to Content-Area Reading.*

should qualify for the medal because psychological injuries are as serious as physical ones. However, the military disagrees, since PTSD injuries are not "intentionally caused by enemy action" and are hard to diagnose. Sandel observes that the dispute centers on how "character" and "sacrifice" are defined. Those who insist that soldiers must have had physical wounds to be eligible for the Purple Heart see psychological wounds as reflecting "weakness of character," while others argue that veterans with PTSD and other psychological traumas have sacrificed honorably for their country.

Thinking about How the Text Works: What It Says, What It Does

Sometimes you'll need to think about how a text works, how its parts fit together. You may be assigned to analyze a text, or you may just need to make sense of a difficult text, to think about how the ideas all relate to one another. Whatever your purpose, a good way to think about a text structure is by **OUTLINING** it, paragraph by paragraph. If you're interested in analyzing its ideas, look at what each paragraph *says*; if, on the other hand, you're concerned with how the ideas are presented, pay attention to what each paragraph *does*.

293–95 ○

What it says.   Write a sentence that identifies what each paragraph says. Once you've done that for the whole text, look for patterns in the topics the writer addresses. Pay attention to the order in which the topics are presented. Also look for gaps, ideas the writer has left unsaid. Such paragraph-by-paragraph outlining of the content can help you see how the writer has arranged ideas and how that arrangement builds an argument or develops a topic. Here, for example, is an outline of Michael Granof's proposal, "Course Requirement: Extortion"; the essay may be found on pages 235–37. The numbers in the left column refer to the essay's paragraphs.

1   College textbooks cost several times more than other books.
2   However, a proposed solution to the cost problem would only make things worse.

3   This proposal, to promote sales of used textbooks, would actually cause textbook costs to rise, because the sale of used books is a main reason new texts cost so much.

4   There is another way to lower costs.

5   Used textbooks are already being marketed and sold very efficiently.

6   Because of this, most new textbook sales take place in the first semester after they're published, forcing publishers to raise prices before used books take over the market.

7   In response, textbooks are revised every few years, whether or not the content is outdated, and the texts are "bundled" with other materials that can't be used again.

8–9 A better solution would be to consider textbooks to be like computer software and issue "site licenses" to universities. Once instructors choose textbooks, the university would pay publishers fees per student for their use.

10   Publishers would earn money for the use of the textbooks, and students' costs would be much lower.

11   Students could use an electronic text or buy a print copy for additional money. The print copies would cost less because the publisher would make most of its profits on the site license fees.

12   This arrangement would have no impact on teaching, unlike other proposals that focus on using electronic materials or using "no frills" textbooks and might negatively affect students' learning.

13   This proposal would reduce the cost of attending college and help students and their families.

What it does. Identify the function of each paragraph. Starting with the first paragraph, ask, What does this paragraph do? Does it introduce a topic? provide background for a topic to come? describe something? define something? entice me to read further? something else? What does the second paragraph do? the third? As you go through the text, you may identify groups of paragraphs that have a single purpose. Here is a functional outline of Granof's essay (again, the numbers on the left refer to the paragraphs):

1	Introduces the topic by defining a problem
2	Introduces a flawed solution
3	Explains the flawed solution and the problem with it
4	Introduces a better solution
5–7	Describes the current situation and the dynamics of the problem
8	Outlines the author's proposed solution
9–10	Explains the proposed solution
11–12	Describes the benefits and effects of the proposed solution
13	Concludes

Reading Visual Texts

Photos, drawings, graphs, diagrams, and charts are frequently used to help convey important information and often make powerful arguments themselves. So learning to read and interpret visual texts is just as necessary as it is for written texts.

Taking visuals seriously. Remember that visuals are texts themselves, not just decoration. When they appear as part of a written text, they may introduce information not discussed elsewhere in the text. Or they might illustrate concepts hard to grasp from words alone. In either case, it's important to pay close attention to any visuals in a written text.

Looking at any title, caption, or other written text that's part of a visual will help you understand its main idea. It might also help to think about its purpose: Why did the writer include it? What information does it add or emphasize? What argument is it making? See, for example, how a psychology textbook uses visuals to help explain two ways that information can be represented:

Analogical and Symbolic Representations

When we think about information, we use two basic types of internal representations: analogical and symbolic.

Analogical representations usually correspond to images. They have some characteristics of actual objects. Therefore, they are analogous to actual objects. For example, maps correspond to geographical layouts. Family trees depict branching relationships between relatives. A clock corresponds directly to the passage of time. **Figure 2.1a** is a drawing of a violin from a particular perspective. This drawing is an analogical representation.

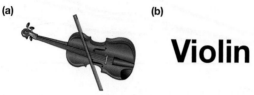

Figure 2.1 Analogical Versus Symbolic Representations

(a)   **(b)**

(a) Analogical representations, such as this picture of a violin, have some characteristics of the objects they represent.
(b) Symbolic representations, such as the word *violin*, are abstract and do not have relationships to the physical qualities of objects.

By contrast, **symbolic representations** are abstract. These representations usually consist of words or ideas. They do not have relationships to physical qualities of objects in the world. The word *hamburger* is a symbolic representation that usually represents a cooked patty of beef served on a bun. The word *violin* stands for a musical instrument (**Figure 2.1b**).
— Sarah Grison, Todd Heatherton, and Michael Gazzaniga, *Psychology in Your Life*

The headings tell you the topic: analogical and symbolic representations. The paragraphs define the two types of representation, and the illustrations present a visual example of each type. The visuals make the information in the written text easier to understand by illustrating the differences between the two.

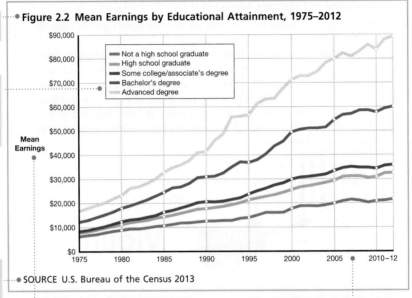

Title: Indicates the topic.

Figure 2.2 Mean Earnings by Educational Attainment, 1975–2012

Legend: Explains the symbols used. Here, colors show the different categories.

Legend:
- Not a high school graduate
- High school graduate
- Some college/associate's degree
- Bachelor's degree
- Advanced degree

Mean Earnings

Source: The origin of the data.

SOURCE U.S. Bureau of the Census 2013

Y-axis: Defines the independent variable (something that doesn't change depending on other factors).

X-axis: Defines the dependent variable (something that changes, depending on other factors).

Reading charts and graphs. To read the information in charts and graphs, you need to look for different things depending on what type of chart or graph you're considering. A line graph, for example, usually contains certain elements: title, legend, x-axis, y-axis, and source information. Figure 2.2 shows one such graph taken from a sociology textbook.

Other types of charts and graphs include some of these same elements. But the specific elements vary according to the different kinds of information being presented, and some charts and graphs can be challenging to read. For example, the chart in Figure 2.3, from the same textbook, includes elements of both bar and line graphs to depict two trends at once: the red line shows the percentage of women in the United States

academic literacies · rhetorical situations · genres · processes · strategies · research MLA / APA · media / design · readings

Figure 2.3 Women's Participation in the Labor Force in the United States, 1948–2012

*Women in the labor force as a percent of all civilian women age sixteen and over.

†Women in the labor force as a percent of the total labor force (both men and women) age sixteen and over.

SOURCE U.S. Bureau of Labor Statistics 2014

who were in the labor force over a sixty-five-year period, and the blue bars show the percentage of U.S. workers who were women during that same period. Both trends are shown in two-year increments. To make sense of this chart, you need to read the title, the y-axis labels, and the labels and their definitions carefully.

Reading Onscreen

Research shows that we tend to read differently onscreen than we do when we read print texts: we skim and sample, often reading a sentence or two and then jumping to another site, another text. If we need to scroll the page to continue, we often don't bother. In general, we don't read as carefully as we do when reading print texts, and we're less likely to reread or take other steps if we find that we don't understand something. Following are some strategies that might help you read effectively onscreen.

Adjust your reading speed and effort to your purpose.   Many students use the web to get an overview of a topic and find potential sources. In that case, skimming and browsing are sensible and appropriate tactics. If you're reading to evaluate a source or find specific information on a topic, though, you probably need to read more slowly and carefully.

Keep your purpose in mind as you read.   Clicking on hyperlinks and jumping from site to site can be tempting. Resist the temptation! Making a list of specific questions you're seeking to answer can help you stay focused and on task.

Print out longer texts.   Some people find reading online to be harder on their eyes than reading pages of print, and many find that they comprehend and remember information in longer texts better if they read them in print. Reading a long text is similar to walking through an unfamiliar neighborhood: we form a mental map of the text as we read and then associate the information with its location in the text, making remembering easier. Since forming such a map is more difficult when reading an electronic text, printing out texts you need to read carefully may be a good strategy.

READING CRITICALLY

113–14 ▲

To read academic texts effectively, you need to read them critically, to look beyond the words on the page or screen to the **RHETORICAL CONTEXT** of the text and the argument it makes. Academic texts — both the ones you read and the ones you write — are parts of ongoing scholarly conversations, in which writers respond to the ideas and assertions of others in order to advance knowledge. To enter those conversations, you must first read carefully and critically to understand the rhetorical situation

and the larger context within which a writer wrote and the argument the text makes.

Considering the Rhetorical Situation

As a reader, you need to think about the message that the writer wants to articulate, including the intended audience and the writer's attitude toward that audience and the topic, as well as about the genre, medium, and design of the text.

PURPOSE　What is the writer's purpose? To entertain? inform? persuade readers to think something or take some action? What is *your* purpose for reading this text?

　55–56

AUDIENCE　Who is the intended audience? Are you a member of that group? If not, should you expect that you'll need to look up unfamiliar terms or concepts or that you'll run into assumptions you don't necessarily share? How is the writer addressing the audience — as an expert addressing those less knowledgeable? an outsider addressing insiders?

　57–60

GENRE　What is the genre? Is it a report? an argument? an analysis? something else? Knowing the genre can help you to anticipate certain key features.

　61–63

STANCE　Who is the writer, and what is his or her stance? Critical? Curious? Opinionated? Objective? Passionate? Indifferent? Something else? Knowing the stance affects the way you understand a text, whether you're inclined to agree or disagree with it, to take it seriously, and so on.

　64–67

MEDIA / DESIGN　What is the medium, and how does it affect the way you read? If it's a print text, what do you know about the publisher? If it's on the web, who sponsors the site, and when was it last updated? Are there any headings, summaries, or other elements that highlight key parts of the text?

　68–70

Identifying Patterns

Look for notable patterns in the text — recurring words and their synonyms, as well as repeated phrases, metaphors and other images, and
types of sentences. Some readers find it helps to highlight patterns in
various colors. Does the author repeatedly rely on any particular writing

419–27
380–87

strategies: **NARRATION**? **COMPARISON**? Something else?

Another kind of pattern it might be important to consider is the kind
of evidence the text provides. Is it more opinion than facts? nothing but
statistics? If many sources are cited, is the information presented in any

478–90

patterns — as **QUOTATIONS**? **PARAPHRASES**? **SUMMARIES**? Are there repeated
references to certain experts or sources?

In visual texts, look for patterns of color, shape, and line. What's in
the foreground, and what's in the background? What's completely visible,
partly visible, or hidden? In both verbal and visual texts, look for omissions
and anomalies: What isn't there that you would expect to find? Is there
anything that doesn't really fit in?

If you discover patterns, then you need to consider what, if anything,
they mean in terms of what the writer is saying. What do they reveal about
the writer's underlying premises and beliefs? What do they tell you about
the writer's strategies for persuading readers to accept the truth of what
he or she is saying?

See how color-coding an essay by *New York Times* columnist William
Safire on the meaning of the Gettysburg Address reveals several patterns
in the language Safire uses. In this excerpt from the essay, which was
published just before the first anniversary of the September 11, 2001, terrorist attacks, Safire develops his analysis through several patterns. Religious references are colored yellow; references to a "national spirit," green;
references to life, death, and rebirth, blue; and places where Safire directly
addresses the reader, gray.

> But the selection of this poetic political sermon as the oratorical cen-
> terpiece of our observance need not be only an exercise. . . . now, as
> then, a national spirit rose from the ashes of destruction.
> Here is how to listen to Lincoln's all-too-familiar speech with new
> ears.

In those 266 words, you will hear the word *dedicate* five times. . . .

Those five pillars of dedication rested on a fundament of religious metaphor. From a president not known for his piety — indeed, often criticized for his supposed lack of faith — came a speech rooted in the theme of national resurrection. The speech is grounded in conception, birth, death, and rebirth.

Consider the barrage of images of birth in the opening sentence. . . .

Finally, the nation's spirit rises from this scene of death: "that this nation, under God, shall have a new birth of freedom." Conception, birth, death, rebirth. The nation, purified in this fiery trial of war, is resurrected. Through the sacrifice of its sons, the sundered nation would be reborn as one. . . .

Do not listen on Sept. 11 only to Lincoln's famous words and comforting cadences. Think about how Lincoln's message encompasses but goes beyond paying "fitting and proper" respect to the dead and the bereaved. His sermon at Gettysburg reminds "us the living" of our "unfinished work" and "the great task remaining before us" — to resolve that this generation's response to the deaths of thousands of our people leads to "a new birth of freedom."

The color coding helps us to see patterns in Safire's language, just as Safire reveals patterns in Lincoln's words. He offers an interpretation of Lincoln's address as a "poetic political sermon," and the words he uses throughout support that interpretation. At the end, he repeats the assertion that Lincoln's address is a sermon, inviting us to consider it differently. Safire's repeated commands ("Consider," "Do not listen," "Think about") offer additional insight into how he wishes to position himself in relation to his readers.

Analyzing the Argument

All texts make some kind of argument, claiming something and then offering reasons and evidence as support for any claim. As a critical reader, you need to look closely at the argument a text makes — to recognize all the claims it makes, consider the support it offers for those claims, and decide how you want to respond. What do you think, and why? Here are some questions to consider when analyzing an argument:

345–47
5
358–59
359–67

- *What claim is the text making?* What is the writer's main point? Is it stated as a **THESIS**, or only implied? Is it limited or **QUALIFIED** somehow? If not, should it have been?

- *How is the claim supported?* What **REASONS** does the writer provide for the claim, and what **EVIDENCE** is given for the reasons? What kind of evidence is it? Facts? Statistics? Examples? Expert opinions? Images? How convincing do you find the reasons and evidence? Is there enough evidence?

370
367
367–69

- *What appeals besides logical ones are used?* Does the writer appeal to readers' **EMOTIONS**? try to establish **COMMON GROUND**? demonstrate his or her **CREDIBILITY** as trustworthy and knowledgeable? How successful are these appeals?

368–69

- *Are any **COUNTERARGUMENTS** acknowledged?* If so, are they presented accurately and respectfully? Does the writer concede any value to them or try to refute them? How successfully does he or she deal with them?

- *What outside sources of information does the writer cite?* What kinds of sources are they, and how credible do they seem? Are they current and authoritative? How well do they support the argument?

370–72

- *Do you detect any **FALLACIES**?* Fallacies are arguments that involve faulty reasoning. Because they often seem plausible, they can be persuasive. It is important, therefore, that you question the legitimacy of such reasoning when you run across it.

Believing and Doubting

One way to develop a response to a text is to play the Believing and Doubting Game, sometimes called reading with and against the grain. Your goal is to **LIST** or **FREEWRITE** notes as you read, writing out as many reasons as you can think of for believing what the writer says (reading with the grain) and then as many as you can for doubting it (reading against the grain).

290–91
289–90

First, try to look at the world through the writer's perspective. Try to understand his or her reasons for arguing as he or she does, even if you strongly disagree. Then reread the text, trying to doubt everything in it: try to find every flaw in the argument, every possible way it can be refuted — even if you totally agree with it. Developed by writing theorist Peter Elbow, the believing and doubting game helps you consider new ideas and question ideas you already have — and at the same time will see where you stand in relation to the ideas in the text you're reading.

Considering the Larger Context

All texts are part of ongoing conversations with other texts that have dealt with the topic of the text. An essay arguing for handgun trigger locks is part of an ongoing conversation on gun control, which is itself part of a conversation on individual rights and responsibilities. Academic texts document their sources in part to show their relationship to the ongoing scholarly conversation on a particular topic. In fact, any time you're reading to learn, you're probably reading for some larger context. Whatever your reading goals, being aware of that larger context can help you better understand what you're reading. Here are some specific aspects of the text to pay attention to:

Who else cares about this topic? Especially when you're reading in order to learn about a topic, the texts you read will often reveal which people or groups are part of the conversation — and might be sources of further reading. For example, an essay describing the formation of Mammoth Cave in Kentucky could be of interest to geologists, spelunkers, travel writers, or tourists. If you're reading such an essay while doing research on the cave, you should consider how the audience to whom the writer is writing determines the nature of the information provided — and its suitability as a source for your research.

What conversations is this text part of? Does the text refer to any concepts or ideas that give you some sense that it's part of a larger conversation? An argument on airport security measures, for example, is part of larger conversations about government response to terrorism, the limits of freedom in a democracy, and the possibilities of using technology to detect weapons and explosives, among others.

What terms does the writer use?   Do any terms or specialized language reflect the writer's allegiance to a particular group or academic discipline? If you run across words like *false consciousness*, *ideology*, and *hegemony*, for example, you might guess that the text was written by a Marxist scholar.

What other writers or sources does the writer cite?   Do the other writers have a particular academic specialty, belong to an identifiable intellectual school, share similar political leanings? If an article on politics cites Paul Krugman and Barbara Ehrenreich in support of its argument, you might assume that the writer holds liberal opinions; if it cites Ross Douthat and Amity Schlaes, the writer is likely a conservative.

IF YOU NEED MORE HELP

See Chapter 47, **EVALUATING SOURCES**, for questions to help you analyze a text's rhetorical situation. See also Chapter 27 on **GENERATING IDEAS AND TEXT**; you can adapt those methods as ways of looking at texts, especially clustering and cubing. And see also Chapter 29 on **ASSESSING YOUR OWN WRITING**, Chapter 30 on **GETTING RESPONSE AND REVISING**, and Chapter 31 on **EDITING AND PROOFREADING** if you need advice for reading your own writing.

469–72
289–97
301–5
306–12
313–17

Summarizing and Responding: *Where Reading Meets Writing*

Summarizing a text helps us to see and understand its main points and to think about what it says. Responding to that text then prompts us to think about — *and say* — what we think. Together, summarizing and responding to texts is one way that we engage with the ideas of others. In a history course, you might summarize and respond to an essay arguing that Civil War photographers did not accurately capture the realities of the battle-field. In a philosophy course, you might summarize Plato's "Allegory of the Cave "and respond to its portrayal of knowledge as shadows on a wall.

And in much of the writing that you do, you'll need to cite the ideas of others, both as context for your own thinking and as evidence to support your arguments. In fact, unless you're Adam, there's probably no topic you'll write about that someone else hasn't already written about — and one way of introducing what you have to say is as a response to something others have said about your topic. A good way of doing that is by summarizing what they've said, using the summary as a launching pad for what you say. This chapter offers advice for summarizing and responding, writing tasks you'll have occasion to do in many of your college classes — and provides a short guide to writing a summary/response essay, a common assignment in composition classes.

SUMMARIZING

In many of your college courses, you'll likely be asked to summarize what someone else has said. Boiling down a text to its basic ideas helps you focus on the text, figure out what the writer has said, and understand (and remember) what you're reading. In fact, summarizing is an essential academic skill, a way to incorporate the ideas of others into your own writing. Following are some guidelines for summarizing effectively:

Read the text carefully.   To write a good summary, you need to read the original text carefully to capture the writer's intended meaning as clearly and evenhandedly as you can. Start by **SKIMMING** the text to get a general sense of what it's saying. If some parts don't make sense, don't worry; at this point, you're reading just to get the gist. Then reread the text more slowly, **ANNOTATING** it paragraph by paragraph. If there's an explicit **THESIS** stating the main point, highlight it in some way. Then try to capture the main idea of each paragraph in a single sentence.

12–13

16–18
345–47

State the main points concisely and accurately.   Summaries of a complete text are generally between 100 and 250 words in length, so you need to choose your words carefully and to focus only on the text's main ideas. Leave out supporting evidence, anecdotes, and counterarguments unless they're crucial to understanding the text. For instance, in summarizing "Throwing Like a Girl," James Fallows's essay explaining the mechanics of throwing baseballs (see p. 137), you would omit his discussion of Bill and Hillary Clinton throwing out the first ball at two Major League games.

Describe the text accurately and fairly — and using neutral language. Present the author's ideas evenhandedly and fairly; a summary isn't the place to share your opinion of what the text says. Use neutral verbs such as *states*, *asserts*, or *concludes*, not verbs that imply praise or criticism like *proves* or *complains*.

487–90

Use SIGNAL PHRASES to distinguish what the author says from what you say.   Introducing a statement with phrases such as "he says" or "the essay concludes" indicates explicitly that you're summarizing what the author said. When first introducing an author, you may need to say something about his or her credentials. For example:

> In "Always Living in Spanish," Spanish professor Marjorie Agosín describes her need to connect with her childhood by writing in Spanish.

James Fallows, a contributing editor at the *Atlantic,* explains the mechanics of throwing baseballs in "Throwing Like a Girl."

Later in the text, you may need to refer to the author again as you summarize specific parts of the text. These signal phrases are typically briefer: *In Agosín's view . . . , Fallows then argues . . .*

Use quotations sparingly, if at all. You may need to **QUOTE** keywords or memorable phrases, but most or all of a summary should be written in your own words, using your own sentence structures.

480

DOCUMENT any text you summarize in a works-cited or references list. A summary of a lengthy work should include **IN-TEXT DOCUMENTATION** noting the pages summarized; they aren't needed with a brief text like the one summarized below (see p. 142).

496–99
MLA 503–9
APA 552–56

An Example Summary

In "The Reason College Costs More than You Think," Jon Marcus, a higher-education editor at the *Hechinger Report*, reports that a major reason why college educations are so expensive is the amount of time students stay in college. Although almost all first-year students and their families assume that earning a bachelor's degree will take four years, the reality is that more than half of all students take longer, with many taking six years or more. This delay happens for many reasons, including students changing majors, having to take developmental courses, taking fewer courses per term than they could have, and being unable to register for required courses. As a result, their expenses are much greater — financial aid seldom covers a fifth or sixth year, so students must borrow money to finish — and the additional time they spend in college is time they aren't working, leading to significant losses in wages.

This summary begins with a signal phrase stating the author's name and credentials and the title of the text being summarized. The summary includes only the main ideas, in the summary writer's own words.

RESPONDING

When you summarize a text, you show that you understand its main ideas; responding to a text pushes you to engage with those ideas — and gives you the opportunity to contribute your ideas to a larger conversation. You can respond in various ways, for instance, by taking a **POSITION** on the text's argument, by **ANALYZING THE TEXT** in some way, or by **REFLECTING** on what it says.

156–82
94–128
245–52

Deciding How to Respond

You may be assigned to write a specific kind of response — an argument or analysis, for instance — but more often than not, the nature of your response is left largely up to you. If so, you'll need to read closely and critically to understand what the text says; to get a sense of how — and how well — it does so; and to think about your own reaction to it. Only then can you decide how to respond. You can respond to what the text says (its ideas), to how it says it (the way it's written), or to where it leads your own thinking (your own personal reaction). Or you might write a response that mixes those ways of responding. You might, for example, combine a personal reaction with an examination of how the writing caused that reaction.

If you're responding to what a text says, you might agree or disagree with the author's argument, supporting your position with good reasons and evidence for your response. You might agree with parts of the argument and disagree with others. You might find that the author has ignored or downplayed some important aspect of the topic that needs to be discussed or at least acknowledged. Here are some questions to consider that can help you think about what a text says:

- What does the writer claim?
358–67
- What **REASONS** and **EVIDENCE** does he or she provide to support that claim?

- What parts of the text do you agree with? Is there anything you disagree with — and if so, why?
- Does the writer represent any views other than his or her own? If not, what other perspectives should be considered?
- Are there any aspects of the topic that the writer overlooks or ignores?
- If you're responding to a visual text, how do the design and any images contribute to your understanding of what the text "says"?

Here is a brief response to Jon Marcus's "The Reason College Costs More than You Think," one that responds to his argument:

> It's true that one reason college costs so much more is that students take longer than four years to finish their degrees, but Jon Marcus's argument in "The Reason College Costs More than You Think" is flawed in several ways. He ignores the fact that over the past years state governments have reduced their subsidies to state-supported colleges and universities, forcing higher tuition; and that federal scholarship aid has declined as well, forcing students to pay a greater share of the costs. He doesn't mention the increased number of administrators or the costs of fancy athletic facilities and dormitories. Ultimately, his argument places most of the blame for higher college costs on students, who, he asserts, make poor choices by changing majors and "taking fewer courses per term than they could." College is supposed to present opportunities to explore many possible career paths, so changing majors should be considered a form of growth and education. Furthermore, many of us are working full-time to pay the high costs of college, leaving us with little extra time to study for four or five courses at once and sometimes forcing us to take fewer classes per term because that's all we can afford. Marcus is partly right — but he gets much of the problem wrong.

If you're focusing on the way a text is written, you'll consider what elements the writer uses to convey his or her message — facts, stories, images, and so on. You'll likely pay attention to the writer's word choices and look for any patterns that lead you to understand the text in a particular way. To think about the way a text is written, you might find some of these questions helpful:

- What is the writer's message? Is there an explicit statement of that message?
- How well has the writer communicated the message?
- How does the writer support what he or she says: by citing facts or statistics? by quoting experts? by noting personal experiences? Are you persuaded?
- Are there any words, phrases, or sentences that you find notable, and that contribute to the text's overall effect?

- How does the text's design affect your response to it? If it's a **VISUAL TEXT** — a photo or ad, for example — how do the various parts of the text contribute to its message?

Here is a brief response to Marcus's essay that analyzes the various ways it makes its argument:

> In "The Reason College Costs More than You Think," *Time* magazine writer Jon Marcus argues that although several factors contribute to high college costs, the main one is how long it takes students to graduate. Marcus introduces this topic by briefly profiling a student who is in his fifth year of school and has run out of financial aid because he "changed majors and took courses he ended up not needing." This profile gives a human face to the topic, which Marcus then develops with statistics about college costs and the numbers of students who take more than four years to finish. Marcus's purpose is twofold: to inform readers that the assumption that most students finish college in four years is wrong, and to persuade them that poor choices like those this student made are the primary reason college takes so long and costs so much. He acknowledges that the extra costs are "hidden" and "not entirely the student's fault" and suggests that poor high school preparation and unavailable required courses play a role, as do limits on financial aid. However, his final paragraph quotes the student as saying of the extra years, "That's time you're wasting that you could be out making money." As the essay's final statement, this assertion that spending more time in school is time wasted and that the implicit goal of college is career preparation reinforces Marcus's argument that college *should* take only four years and that students who take longer are financially irresponsible.

If you're reflecting on your own reaction to a text, you might focus on how your personal experiences or beliefs influenced the way you understood the text, or on how it reinforced or prompted you to reassess some of those beliefs. You could also focus on how it led you to see the topic in new ways — or note questions that it's led you to wonder about. Some questions that may help you reflect on your own reaction to a text include:

- How did the text affect you personally?
- Is there anything in the text that really got your attention? If so, what?
- Do any parts of the text provoke an emotional reaction — make you laugh or cry, make you uneasy? What prompted that response?
- Does the text bring to mind any memories or past experiences? Can you see anything related to you and your life in the text?
- Does the text remind you of any other texts?
- Does the text support (or challenge) any of your beliefs? How?
- Has reading this text given you any new ideas or insight?

Here is a brief response to Jon Marcus's essay that reflects on an important personal issue:

Jon Marcus's "Why College Costs More than You Think" made me think hard about my own educational plans. Because I'm working to pay for as much of my education as I can, I'm taking a full load of courses so I can graduate in four years, but truth be told I'm starting to question the major I've chosen. That's one aspect of going to college that Marcus fails to discuss: how your major affects your future career choices and earnings — and whether or not some majors that don't lead immediately to a career, are another way of "wasting" your time. After taking several courses in English and philosophy, I find myself fascinated by the study of literature and ideas. If I decide to major in one or both of those subjects, am I being impractical? Or am I "following my heart," as Steve Jobs said in his Stanford commencement speech? Jobs did as he told those graduates to do, and it worked out well for him, so maybe majoring in something "practical" is less practical than it seems. If I graduate in four years and am "out making money" but doing something I don't enjoy, I might be worse off than if I take longer in college but find a path that is satisfying and enriching.

WRITING A SUMMARY / RESPONSE ESSAY

You may be assigned to write a full essay that summarizes and responds to something you've read. Following is one such essay. It was written by Jacob MacLeod, a student at Wright State University, and responds to a *New York Times* column by Nicholas Kristof, "Our Blind Spot about Guns" (see p. 161).

JACOB MacLEOD

Guns and Cars Are Different

In "Our Blind Spot about Guns," *The New York Times* columnist Nicholas Kristof compares guns to cars in order to argue for sensible gun regulation. Kristof suggests that gun regulations would dramatically decrease the number of deaths caused by gun use. To demonstrate this point, he shows that the regulations governments have instituted for cars have greatly decreased the number of deaths per million miles driven. Kristof then argues that guns should be regulated in the same way that cars are, that car regulation provides a model for gun regulation. I agree with Kristof that there should be more sensible gun regulation, but I have difficulty accepting that all of the regulations imposed on cars have made them safer, and I also believe that not all of the safety regulations he proposes for guns would necessarily have positive effects.

Kristof is right that background checks for those who want to buy guns should be expanded. According to Daniel Webster, director of the Johns Hopkins Center for Gun Policy and Research, state laws prohibiting firearm ownership by members of high-risk groups, such as perpetrators of domestic violence and the mentally ill, have been shown to reduce violence. Therefore, Webster argues, universal background checks would significantly reduce the availability of guns to high-risk groups, as well as reducing the number of guns diverted to the illegal market by making it easier to prosecute gun traffickers.

Kristof also argues that lowering the speed limit made cars safer. However, in 1987, forty states raised their top speed limit from 55 to 65 miles per hour. An analysis of this change by the University of California Transportation Center shows that after the increase, traffic fatality rates on interstate highways in those forty states decreased between 3.4 percent and 5.1 percent. After the higher limits went into effect, the study suggested, some drivers may have switched to safer interstates from other, more dangerous roads, and highway patrols

may have focused less on enforcing interstate speed limits and more on activities yielding greater benefits in terms of safety (Lave and Elias 58–61). Although common sense might suggest that lowered speed limits would mean safer driving, research showed otherwise, and the same may be true for gun regulation.

Gun control advocates argue that more guns mean more deaths. However, an article by gun rights advocates Don B. Kates and Gary Mauser argues that murder rates in many developed nations have bear no relation to the rate of gun ownership (652). The authors cite data on firearms ownership in the United States and England that suggest that crime rates are lowest where the density of gun ownership is highest and highest where gun density is lowest (653) and that increased gun ownership has often coincided with significant reductions in violence. For example, in the United States in the 1990s, criminal violence decreased, even though gun ownership increased (656). However, the authors acknowledge that "the notion that more guns reduce crime is highly controversial" (659).

All in all, then, Kristof is correct to suggest that sensible gun regulation is a good idea in general, but the available data suggest that some of the particular measures he proposes should not be instituted. I agree that expanding background checks would be a good way to regulate guns and that failure to require them would lead to more guns in the hands of criminals. While background checks are a good form of regulation, however, lower speed limits and trigger locks are not. The problem with this solution is that although it is based on commonsense thinking, the empirical data show that it may not work.

Works Cited

Kates, Don B., and Gary Mauser. "Would Banning Firearms Reduce Murder and Suicide? A Review of International and Some Domestic Evidence." *Harvard Journal of Law and Public Policy*, vol. 30, no. 2, Jan. 2007, pp. 649-94, www.law.harvard.edu/students/orgs/jlpp/ Vol30_No2_KatesMauseronline.pdf. Accessed 4 Oct. 2014.

Kristof, Nicholas. "Our Blind Spot about Guns." *The New York Times*, 31 July 2014, www.nytimes.com/2014/07/31/opinion/nicholas-kristof-our-blind-spot-about-guns.html. Accessed 4 Oct. 2014.

Lave, Charles, and Patrick Elias. "Did the 65 mph Speed Limit Save Lives?" *Accident Analysis & Prevention*, vol. 26, no. 1, Feb. 1994, pp. 49-62, www.sciencedirect.com/science/article/pii/000145759490068X. Accessed 4 Oct. 2014.

Webster, Daniel. "Why Expanding Background Checks Would, in Fact, Reduce Gun Crime." Interview by Greg Sargent. *The Washington Post,* 3 Apr. 2013, www.washingtonpost.com/blogs/plum-line/wp/2013/04/03/why-expanding-background-checks-would-in-fact-reduce-gun-crime/. Accessed 5 Oct. 2014.

In his response, MacLeod both agrees and disagrees with Kristof's argument, using several sources to support his argument that some of Kristof's proposals may not work. MacLeod states his thesis at the end of the first paragraph, after his summary, and ends with a balanced assessment of Kristof's proposals. He cites several sources, both in the text with signal phrases and in-text documentation and at the end in a works-cited section.

Key Features of Summary/Response Essays

A clearly identified author and title.   Usually the author and title of the text being summarized are identified in a signal phrase in the first sentence. The author (or sometimes the title) may then be referred to in an abbreviated form if necessary in the rest of the essay: for example, "Kristof argues . . ." or "according to 'Our Blind Spot about Guns' . . ."

A concise summary of the text.   The summary presents the main and supporting ideas in the text, usually in the order in which they appear. MacLeod, for example, reduces Kristof's argument to four sentences that capture Kristof's main points while leaving out his many examples.

An explicit response.   Your essay should usually provide a concise statement (one sentence if possible) of your overall response to the text.

- *If you're responding to the argument,* you'll likely agree or disagree (or both), and so your response itself will constitute an argument, with an explicit thesis statement. For example, MacLeod first agrees with Kristof that "there should be more sensible gun regulation," but then introduces a two-part thesis: that not all automobile regulations have made cars safer, and that not all gun regulations would make guns safer.
- *If you're analyzing the text,* you'll likely need to explain what you think the author is saying and how the text goes about conveying that

message. An analysis of Kristof's text, for example, might focus on his comparison of automobile regulations with gun regulations.

- *If you're responding with a reflection,* you might explore the ideas, emotions, or memories that the text evokes, the effects of its ideas on your own beliefs, or how your own personal experiences support or contradict the author's position. One response to Kristof's essay might begin by expressing surprise at the comparison of guns to cars and then explore the reasons you find that comparison surprising, leading to a new understanding of the ways regulations can work to save lives.

Support for your response.   Whatever your response, you need to offer reasons and evidence to support what you say.

- *If you're responding to what the text says,* you may offer facts, statistics, anecdotal evidence, and textual evidence, as MacLeod does. You'll also need to consider — and acknowledge — any possible counterarguments, positions other than yours.

- *If you're responding to the way the text is written,* you may identify certain patterns in the text that you think mean something, and you'll need to cite evidence from the text itself. For example, Kristof twice invokes a popular slogan among gun rights advocates, "Guns don't kill people. People kill people," changing "guns" to "cars" to advance his argument that regulating guns may make them safer, just as has happened with cars.

- *If you're reflecting on your own reaction to the text,* you may connect its ideas with your own experiences or beliefs or explore how the text reinforced, challenged, or altered your beliefs. A staunch gun-rights advocate, for example, might find in Kristof's essay a reasonable middle ground too often lacking in polarized debates like the one on gun control.

Ways of Organizing a Summary and Response Essay

You can organize a summary and response essay in various ways. You may want to use a simple, straightforward structure that starts out by

345–47
summarizing the text and then gives the **THESIS** of your response followed by details that develop the thesis.

[Summary, followed by response]

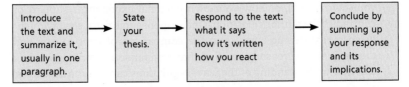

| Introduce the text and summarize it, usually in one paragraph. | State your thesis. | Respond to the text: what it says how it's written how you react | Conclude by summing up your response and its implications. |

Or you may want to start out with the thesis and then, depending on whether your response focuses on the text's argument or its rhetorical choices, provide a paired summary of each main point or each aspect of the writing and a response to it.

[Introduction and thesis, followed by point-by-point summary and response]

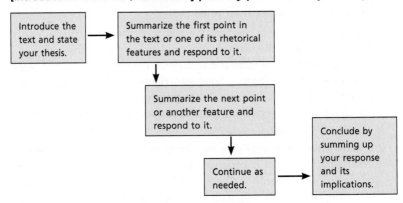

| Introduce the text and state your thesis. | Summarize the first point in the text or one of its rhetorical features and respond to it. |

| Summarize the next point or another feature and respond to it. |

| Continue as needed. | Conclude by summing up your response and its implications. |

IF YOU NEED MORE HELP

298–300
301–5
306–12
313–17
491–95
See Chapter 28 for guidelines on **DRAFTING** and Chapter 34 for help writing a thesis and coming up with a title. See Chapter 29 on **ASSESSING YOUR OWN WRITING**, Chapter 30 on **GETTING RESPONSE AND REVISING**, and Chapter 31 on **EDITING AND PROOFREADING**. See Chapter 50 on **ACKNOWLEDGING SOURCES AND AVOIDING PLAGIARISM**.

Developing Academic Habits of Mind 4

A little advice from Serena Williams: "Stick to it and work hard." She wasn't just talking about tennis, and her words resonate for all of us, for everything we set out to do. And here's Michael Jordan, who tells us "Never quit!" and then goes on to issue a warning: "If you quit once, it becomes a habit." Serena Williams and Michael Jordan may be two of the greatest athletes ever, but neither of them was born a champion. They became great by working hard, hanging in there, never giving up.

They succeeded, in other words, by developing certain habits of mind that can serve us all well — and that are especially valuable when it comes to succeeding in school. This chapter is about developing *academic habits of mind*. Just as Serena Williams wasn't born with her powerful serve, none of us was born knowing how to write academic papers or ace exams. But we too can learn and can develop the habits we need to succeed. This chapter offers advice for developing habits of mind that writing teachers nationwide have identified as essential for college success.

Engage

We all know people who see school as a series of hoops to jump through, who seem uninvolved — and even bored. We also know people who are passionate about something — a video game, a hobby, a profession — and who invest themselves, their time, and their emotions wholeheartedly in those activities. Successful students make that investment in school.

In other words, they engage with what they're studying, what they're doing, and what they're learning.

Think about your purpose for being in college.   What are your goals? To get a degree? To qualify for a particular job or profession? To find intellectual stimulation? To explore life? Try to define why you are in school, both in larger terms ("to get a degree in accounting") and in terms of the specific courses you are taking ("Learning to write better will help me be a better student in general and communicate effectively at work").

Fight off boredom.   Every job, including the job of being a student, includes some tasks that are dull but need to be done. When you encounter such a task, ask yourself how it helps you reach a larger goal. Shooting a hundred free throws for practice may not seem interesting, but it can help you win games. When you're listening to a lecture or reading a textbook, take notes, highlight, and annotate; doing that forces you to pay attention and increases what you remember and learn. Trying to identify the main ideas as you listen to a lecture will help you stay focused. When you're studying, try alternating between different tasks: reading, writing, doing problem sets, drawing, and so on.

If you get distracted, figure out ways to deal with it.   It's hard to engage with what you're reading or studying when you're thinking about something else — paying a tuition bill, the last episode of *The Walking Dead*, whatever. Try taking a few moments to write out what's on your mind, in a journal or somewhere else. Sometimes that simple act frees your mind to think about your work, even if it doesn't solve anything.

Raise your hand.   When you think you know the answer to a teacher's question (or when you yourself have a question), raise your hand. Most teachers appreciate students who take chances and who participate in class. At the same time, be polite: don't monopolize discussion or interrupt others when they're speaking.

Get involved. Get to know other students; study with them; join a campus organization. People who see themselves as part of something larger, even just a study group with three or four others, engage more in what they're doing than those who try to go it alone.

Be Curious

When we're young, we're curious about everything, and we learn by asking questions (why? why *not*?) and by exploring our surroundings (digging holes, cutting up magazines, investigating attics and basements). As we get older, though, we focus on things that interest us — and may as a result start to ignore other things or even to forget how to explore. In college, you'll be asked to research, study, and write about many topics you know nothing about. Seize the opportunity. Be curious! And take a tip from Dr. Seuss: "The more that you read, the more things you will know. / The more that you learn, the more places you'll go."

Ask questions. It's tempting to stay within our comfort zones, thinking about things we know and like, listening to those whose views we tend to agree with — to say what we already think rather than to stop and think. Resist that temptation! Take every opportunity to ask questions, to learn more about things you're already interested in, and especially to learn about things you don't (yet) know anything about. As marine biologist Sylvia Earle says, "The best scientists and explorers have the attributes of kids! They ask questions and have a sense of wonder. They have curiosity. Who, what, where, why, when, and how! They never stop asking questions, and I never stop asking questions, just like a five year old."

Listen! Pay attention to what others say, including those who you don't necessarily agree with. The words and ideas of others can challenge the way we think, prompt us to rethink what we think — and spark our curiosity: Why does X think that? What do *I* think — *and why*? Why do my neighbors oppose the Common Core? What do educators think about it? Paying attention to all sides of an argument, doing research to find out what others have said about a topic, or searching social media to see the latest postings on a trending topic are all ways you can listen in on (and engage in) conversations on important issues of all kinds.

Be Open to New Ideas

No matter where you're in school, you're going to encounter ideas and concepts and even facts that challenge your own beliefs; you're also likely to meet people whose backgrounds and ways of looking at life are very different from your own. Be open-minded, open to new ideas and to what others think and say. Consider the perspectives and arguments of others. Learning involves accepting new ideas, acknowledging the value of different perspectives, and coming to understand our own beliefs in new ways. Listen to what others say, and think before you respond.

- *Treat the ideas of others with respect,* whether you agree with them or not, and encourage others to do the same. We don't open up if we don't feel safe.

- *Try to withhold judgment.* Be willing to listen to the thoughts of others and to consider ideas that may at first seem alien or weird (or wrong). Remember that your weird is likely someone else's normal — and the reverse.

- *Look for common ground between your perspectives and those of others —* places where you can agree, even in the midst of serious disagreement.

Be Flexible

Being flexible means being adaptable. In college, you'll likely face novel situations and need to find new ways to address problems, such as juggling school, work, and family; adjusting to roommates and making new friends; and figuring out how to do unfamiliar new assignments and how to take tests. You'll even have to do new kinds of writing: lab reports, reflections,

academic literacies | rhetorical situations | genres | processes | strategies | research MLA / APA | media / design | readings

literacy narratives, and many, many more; if your school writing up until this point has usually (or always) called for a five-paragraph theme, that's not going to be the case anymore.

Look for new ways to do things.   As the saying goes, "If all you have is a hammer, everything looks like a nail." Look for other tools to add to your toolbox: try solving math problems with words or by drawing, or starting a writing project by sketching out the parts.

Try not to see things as right or wrong, good or bad.   Be willing to consider alternative points of view and to withhold judgment. Often ideas or actions can only be judged in context; they may be true in some cases or in part, and you often need to understand the larger situation or take into account various perspectives. For example, you may believe that lying is wrong, but is it excusable if telling the truth will cause someone pain? You find a required reading assignment boring and useless, but why, then, did your instructor assign it?

Approach academic assignments rhetorically.   Analyze each assignment's purpose, intended audience, and the rest of its **RHETORICAL SITUATION**. Think about what's required in terms of content and format — and also about what's appropriate in terms of language and style. And what's expected in the discipline: informal language, sentence fragments, and photographs without captions might be appropriate for a sociology blog, for example, whereas a research project for a history course might have different requirements for how it's organized, formatted, and documented.

■ 53–70

Be Creative

If you think that creativity is something artists have (and are born with), think again. From the young man selling homemade granola at a local farm market to the woman who puts together an eye-catching outfit from thrift-store bins, many of us are at work expressing ourselves in distinctive ways. Psychologists tell us that acting creatively opens us up to becoming more creative — and it is safe to say that doing so will make your work more productive and very likely more fun.

289–97 ◯

- *Play with ideas.* Freewrite. Make lists. Try looping, clustering, and the other ways of **GENERATING IDEAS** covered in this book. Take some time to think about the ideas you come up with.

- *Don't wait until the last minute.* Some students say they do better under the pressure of a deadline. Don't believe it! It's *always* better to give yourself time to think, to explore ideas, to "sleep on" assignments that first stump you.

- *Take risks!* Explore questions and topics that you haven't thought about before. Try out methods you haven't used previously. Challenge yourself to come up with ten ideas. Or twenty.

- *Ask questions.* And remember that there's no such thing as a dumb question.

Persist

Sometimes the key to success is simply sticking to the task at hand: ignoring distractions, hanging in there, forgetting frustration, getting the work done even in the face of setbacks and failures. Here's some advice from actress and singer Julie Andrews: "Perseverance is failing 19 times and succeeding the 20th."

293–95 ◯
19–20 ❋
16–18

- *Don't quit.* Assume that you can complete the task, and make up your mind to do it. If you're reading a book that seems hopelessly confusing or over your head, for example, keep at it until it starts to make sense. Reread, **OUTLINE CHAPTERS**, **SUMMARIZE**, **ANNOTATE**, and do whatever else you need to do to understand it.

- *Remember that sometimes you'll encounter setbacks* — and that the goal (a passing grade, a degree, a job) is still reachable if you keep trying. Those who play video games know that failing is an inherent part of playing them; the same is true of many other things as well.

academic literacies | rhetorical situations | genres | processes | strategies | research MLA / APA | media / design | readings

- *Make a plan and establish a schedule,* and stick to.
- *Break large projects into smaller goals.* Especially with assignments that call for a huge amount of work, approach it in stages: focus on getting through the next chapter, the next draft, the next whatever. It may be good to "keep your eyes on the prize," but it's usually best to take it one step at a time.
- *When you're working on several assignments, tackle the hardest ones first.* Work on them when you're fresh and your mind is clear.
- *If you don't understand something, ask for clarification.* Better to admit to confusion than to act as if you know something when you don't.
- *Ask for help when you need it.* Teachers are usually happy to help students during office hours or by appointment, before or after class, or over email. Get to know your teachers: they're there to help you.
- *Take advantage of whatever help is available* at your school's writing center or learning center and in class. An important part of being persistent is getting help when you need it.

Reflect

Pay attention to the ways you work and make decisions. Reflect on the ways you think and on how you think about the world. This kind of "meta-cognitive" thinking is one of the most important habits of mind, and it's one that will continue to serve you well throughout your life.

- *Figure out when you are most efficient* and do your best work — and try to schedule your work accordingly.
- *Pay attention to what you're reading and how you're doing it.* Think about why you're reading *x*, and use **READING STRATEGIES** appropriate to your purpose. If you lose the thread of an explanation or argument, figure out where you got lost and why.

  ✳ 10–32

- *After completing an assignment, reflect in writing* on what you did well, what problems you had, and how you solved them (or not). What would you do differently next time — or if you had more time? You'll find prompts for "Taking Stock of Your Work" at the end of Chapters 10–13 that can help.

- *Troubleshoot.* Pay attention to bumps in the road as you encounter them. Try to understand what caused the problem, what you did to solve it, how successful you were and why.

- *Try to focus on your achievements, what you can do*, rather than on what you may not be able to do or to do as well as you'd like.

Take Responsibility

In one way or another, all the habits of mind discussed above involve taking responsibility for your own actions. It may be tempting to blame others or society or bad luck for problems in your academic life, but the more you take ownership of your own learning, the more control you have over the results. Some ways you can enhance your sense of responsibility and demonstrate it include these:

- *Acknowledge that how much you learn and what grades you get depend mostly on you.* Teachers often say that they don't *give* grades, students *earn* grades — an important difference.

- *Treat school as you do a job,* one for which you must show up on time, perform tasks at a certain level of competence, and meet deadlines. In college, where your time is mostly unstructured, you have to become your own boss. So attend class regularly, follow instructions, and turn in assignments on time.

- *Get organized.* Maintain a calendar so you know what's due when. Create a schedule for your day that includes time for class, studying, working, and personal activities. Develop a system for organizing your written work and notes for each course you're taking. Learn where to find the materials you need to do your classwork.

478–95
496–99

- *Use research sources responsibly.* QUOTE , PARAPHRASE , and SUMMARIZE the work of others accurately and DOCUMENT it correctly. Give appropriate credit to those whose ideas and words you are using.

part 2

Rhetorical Situations

Whenever we write, whether it's a text to a friend or a toast for a wedding, an English essay or a résumé, we face some kind of rhetorical situation. We have a PURPOSE, a certain AUDIENCE, a particular STANCE, a GENRE, and a MEDIUM to consider—and often as not a DESIGN. All are important elements that we need to think about carefully. The following chapters offer brief discussions of those elements of the rhetorical situation, along with questions that can help you make the choices you need to as you write. See also the GENRE chapters for guidelines for considering your rhetorical situation in each of these specific kinds of writing.

Rhetorical Situations

Purpose 5

All writing has a purpose. We write to explore our thoughts and emotions, to express ourselves, to entertain; we write to record words and events, to communicate with others, to try to persuade others to believe as we do or to behave in certain ways. In fact, we often have several purposes at the same time. We may write an essay in which we try to explain something to an audience, but at the same time we may be trying to persuade that audience of something. Look, for example, at this passage from a 2012 *New York Times* op-ed essay by economist and editorial columnist Paul Krugman about social and economic trends among "the traditional working-class family" — declining rates of marriage and of male participation in the labor force and increasing numbers of out-of-wedlock births. Krugman asserts that the primary reason for those statistics is a "drastic reduction in the work opportunities available to less-educated men":

> Most of the numbers you see about income trends in America focus on households rather than individuals, which makes sense for some purposes. But when you see a modest rise in incomes for the lower tiers of the income distribution, you have to realize that all — yes, all — of this rise comes from the women, both because more women are in the paid labor force and because women's wages aren't as much below male wages as they used to be.
>
> For lower-education working men, however, it has been all negative. Adjusted for inflation, entry-level wages of male high school graduates have fallen 23 percent since 1973. Meanwhile, employment benefits have collapsed. In 1980, 65 percent of recent high-school graduates working in the private sector had health benefits, but, by 2009, that was down to 29 percent.
>
> So we have become a society in which less-educated men have great difficulty finding jobs with decent wages and good benefits.
>
> —Paul Krugman, "Money and Morals"

academic literacies   rhetorical situations   genres   processes   strategies   research MLA / APA   media / design   readings

Krugman is reporting information here, outlining how the earnings and benefits of less-educated men have dropped over the last forty years. He is also making an argument, that these economic setbacks are the cause of the social ills among working-class Americans and not, as some would have it, the result of them. (Krugman, writing for a newspaper, is also using a style — including dashes, contractions, and other informal elements — that strives to be engaging while it informs and argues.)

Even though our purposes may be many, knowing our primary reason for writing can help us shape that writing and understand how to proceed with it. Our purpose can determine the genre we choose, our audience, even the way we design what we write.

Identify your purpose.   While a piece of writing often has many purposes, a writer usually focuses on one. When you get an assignment or see a need to write, ask yourself what the primary purpose of the writing task is: to entertain? to inform? to persuade? to demonstrate your knowledge or your writing ability? What are your own goals? What are your audience's expectations, and do they affect the way you define your purpose?

Thinking about Purpose

- *What do you want your audience to do, think, or feel?* How will your readers use what you tell them?

- *What does this writing task call on you to do?* Do you need to show that you have mastered certain content or skills? Do you have an assignment that specifies a particular **STRATEGY** or **GENRE** — to compare two things, perhaps, or to argue a position?

- *What are the best ways to achieve your purpose?* What **STANCE** should you take? Should you write in a particular genre? Do you have a choice of **MEDIUM**, and does your text require any special format or **DESIGN** elements?

* academic literacies ■ rhetorical situations ▲ genres ○ processes ◆ strategies ● research MLA / APA ☐ media / design ▮ readings

Audience   **6**

Who will read (or hear) what you are writing? A seemingly obvious but crucially important question. Your audience affects your writing in various ways. Consider a piece of writing as simple as a text from a mother to her son:

> *Pls. take chicken out to thaw and feed Annye. Remember Dr. Wong at 4.*

On the surface, this brief note is a straightforward reminder to do three things. But in fact it is a complex message filled with compressed information for a specific audience. The writer (the mother) counts on the reader (her son) to know a lot that can be left unsaid. She expects that he knows that the chicken is in the freezer and needs to thaw in time to be cooked for dinner; she knows that he knows who Annye is (a pet?), what he or she is fed, and how much; she assumes that he knows who (and where) Dr. Wong is. She doesn't need to spell out any of that because she knows what her son knows and what he needs to know — and in her text she can be brief. She understands her audience. Think how different such a reminder would be were it written to another audience — a babysitter, perhaps, or a friend helping out while Mom is out of town.

What you write, how much you write, how you phrase it, even your choice of **GENRE** (memo, essay, email, note, speech) — all are influenced by the audience you envision. And your audience will interpret your writing according to their own expectations and experiences, not yours.

61–63

When you are a student, your audience is most often your teachers, so you need to be aware of their expectations and know the conventions (rules, often unstated) for writing in specific academic fields. You may make statements that seem obvious to you, not realizing that your instructors may consider them assertions that must be proved with evidence of one sort or another. Or you may write more or less formally than teachers expect. Understanding your audience's expectations — by asking outright, by reading materials in your field of study, by trial and error — is important to your success as a college writer.

This point is worth dwelling on. You are probably reading this textbook for a writing course. As a student, you will be expected to produce essays with few or no errors. If you correspond with family, friends, or coworkers using email and texts, you may question such standards; after all, many of the messages you get in these contexts are not grammatically perfect. But in a writing class, the instructor needs to see your best work. Whatever the rhetorical situation, your writing must meet the expectations of your audience.

Identify your audience.　Audiences may be defined as *known, multiple,* or *unknown. Known audiences* can include people with whom you're familiar as well as people you don't know personally but whose needs and expectations you do know. You yourself are a known, familiar audience, and you write to and for yourself often. Class notes, to-do lists, reminders, and journals are all written primarily for an audience of one: you. For that reason, they are often in shorthand, full of references and code that you alone understand.

Other known, familiar audiences include anyone you actually know — friends, relatives, teachers, classmates — and whose needs and expectations you understand. You can also know what certain readers want and need, even if you've never met them personally, if you write for them within a specific shared context. Such a known audience might include PC gamers who read cheat codes that you have posted on the internet for beating a game; you don't know those people, but you know roughly what they know about the game and what they need to know, and you know how to write about it in ways they will understand.

You often have to write for *multiple audiences.* Business memos or reports may be written initially for a supervisor, but he or she may pass them along to others. Grant proposals may be reviewed by four to six levels of readers — each, of course, with its own expectations and perspectives.

Even writing for a class might involve multiple audiences: your instructor and your classmates.

Unknown audiences can be the most difficult to address since you can't be sure what they know, what they need to know, how they'll react. Such an audience could be your downstairs neighbor, with whom you've chatted occasionally in the laundry room. How will she respond to your letter asking her to sponsor you in an upcoming charity walk? Another unknown audience — perhaps surprisingly — might be many of your instructors, who want — and expect! — you to write in ways that are new to you. While you can benefit from analyzing any audience, you need to think most carefully about those you don't know.

Thinking about Audience

- *Whom do you want to reach?* To whom are you writing (or speaking)?
- *What is your audience's background — their education and life experiences?* It may be important for you to know, for example, whether your readers attended college, fought in a war, or have young children.
- *What are their interests?* What do they like? What motivates them? What do they care about?
- *Is there any demographic information that you should keep in mind?* Consider whether race, gender, sexual orientation, disabilities, occupation, religious beliefs, economic status, and so on should affect what or how you write. For example, writers for *Men's Health*, *InStyle*, and *Out* must consider the particular interests of each magazine's readers.
- *What political circumstances may affect their reading?* What attitudes — opinions, special interests, biases — may affect the way your audience reads your piece? Are your readers conservative, liberal, or middle of the road? Politics may take many other forms as well — retirees on a fixed income may object to increased school taxes, so a letter arguing for such an increase would need to appeal to them differently than would a similar letter sent to parents of young children.

- *What does your audience already know — or believe — about your topic? What do you need to tell them? What is the best way to do so?* Those retirees who oppose school taxes already know that taxes are a burden for them; they may need to know why schools are justified in asking for more money every few years. A good way to explain this may be with a bar graph showing how property values benefit from good schools with adequate funding. Consider which **STRATEGIES** will be effective — narrative, comparison, something else?

329

- *What's your relationship with your audience, and how should it affect your language and tone?* Do you know them, or not? Are they friends? colleagues? mentors? adversaries? strangers? Will they likely share your **STANCE**? In general, you need to write more formally when you're addressing readers you don't know, and you may address friends and colleagues more informally than you would a boss.

64–67

- *What does your audience need and expect from you?* Your history professor, for example, may need to know how well you can discuss the economy of the late Middle Ages in order to assess your learning; he may expect you to write a carefully reasoned argument, drawing conclusions from various sources, with a readily identifiable thesis in the first paragraph. Your boss, on the other hand, may need an informal email that briefly lists your sales contacts for the day; she may expect that you list the contacts in the order in which you saw them, that you clearly identify each one, and that you briefly say how well each contact went. What **GENRE** is most appropriate?

71

- *What kind of response do you want?* Do you want readers to believe or do something? to accept as valid your information on a topic? to understand why an experience you once had matters to you?

591

- *How can you best appeal to your audience?* Is there a particular **MEDIUM** that will best reach them? Are there any **DESIGN** requirements? (Elderly readers may need larger type, for instance.)

Genres are kinds of writing. Letters, profiles, reports, position papers, poems, blog posts, instructions, parodies — even jokes — are genres. For example, here is the beginning of a **PROFILE** of a mechanic who repairs a specific kind of automobile:

224–34

> Her business card reads Shirley Barnes, M.D., and she's a doctor, all right — a Metropolitan Doctor. Her passion is the Nash Metropolitan, the little car produced by Austin of England for American Motors between 1954 and 1962. Barnes is a legend among southern California Met lovers — an icon, a beacon, and a font of useful knowledge and freely offered opinions.

A profile offers a written portrait of someone or something that informs and sometimes entertains, often examining its subject from a particular angle — in this case, as a female mechanic who fixes Nash Metropolitans. While the language in this example is informal and lively ("she's a doctor, all right"), the focus is on the subject, Shirley Barnes, "M.D." If this same excerpt were presented as a poem, however, the new genre would change our reading:

> Her business card reads
> Shirley Barnes, M.D.,
> and she's a doctor, all right
> — a Metropolitan Doctor.
> Her passion is the Nash Metropolitan,
> the little car produced by Austin of England
> for American Motors between 1954 and 1962.
> Barnes is a legend
> among southern California Met lovers
> — an icon,

a beacon,

and a font of useful knowledge and

freely offered opinions.

The content hasn't changed, but the different presentation invites us to read not only to learn about Shirley Barnes but also to explore the significance of the words and phrases on each line, to read for deeper meaning and greater appreciation of language. The genre thus determines how we read and how we interpret what we read.

Genres help us write by establishing features for conveying certain kinds of content. They give readers clues about what sort of information they're likely to find and so help them figure out how to read ("This article begins with an abstract, so it's probably a scholarly source" or "Thank goodness! I found the instructions for editing videos on my phone"). At the same time, genres are flexible; writers often tweak the features or combine elements of different genres to achieve a particular purpose or connect with an audience in a particular way. Genres also change as writers' needs and available technologies change. For example, computers have enabled us to add audio and video content to texts that once could appear only on paper.

Identify your genre. Does your writing situation call for a certain **GENRE**? A memo? A report? A proposal? A letter? Some situations may call for **MIXING GENRES**. Academic assignments generally specify the genre ("take a position," "analyze the text"), but if not, see Chapter 24 for help **CHOOSING GENRES** — or ask your instructor.

71 ▲

265–72

273–78 ▲

Thinking about Genre

- *How does your genre affect what content you can or should include?* Objective information? Researched source material? Your own opinions? Personal experience? A mix?

329 ◆

- *Does your genre call for any specific* **STRATEGIES**? Profiles, for example, usually include some narration; lab reports often explain a process.

academic literacies ❋ rhetorical situations ■ genres ▲ processes ○ strategies ◆ research MLA / APA ● media / design ☐ readings ▨

- *Does your genre require a certain organization?* **PROPOSALS**, for instance, usually need to show a problem exists before offering a solution. Some genres leave room for choice. Business letters delivering good news might be organized differently than those making sales pitches.

▲ 235–44

- *Does your genre affect your tone?* An abstract of a scholarly paper calls for a different **TONE** than a memoir. Should your words sound serious and scholarly? brisk and to the point? objective? opinionated? Sometimes your genre affects the way you communicate your **STANCE**.

■ 65

■ 64–67

- *Does the genre require formal (or informal) language?* A letter to the mother of a friend asking for a summer job in her bookstore calls for more formal language than does an email to the friend thanking him for the lead.

- *Do you have a choice of medium?* Some genres call for print; others for an electronic medium. Sometimes you have a choice: a résumé, for instance, can be printed to bring to an interview, or it may be downloaded or emailed. Some teachers want reports turned in on paper; others prefer that they be emailed or posted in the class course management system. If you're not sure what **MEDIUM** you can use, ask.

☐ 591

- *Does your genre have any design requirements?* Some genres call for paragraphs; others require lists. Some require certain kinds of fonts — you wouldn't use **impact** for a personal narrative, nor would you likely use chiller for an invitation to Grandma's sixty-fifth birthday party. Different genres call for different **DESIGN** elements.

☐ 591

8 Stance

Whenever you write, you have a certain stance, an attitude toward your topic. The way you express that stance affects the way you come across to your audience as a writer and a person. This email from a college student to his father, for example, shows a thoughtful, reasonable stance for a carefully researched argument:

> Hi Dad,
> I'll get right to the point: I'd like to buy a car. I saved over $4,500 from working this summer, and I've found three different cars that I can get for under $3,000. That'll leave me $1,400 to cover the insurance. I can park in Lot J, over behind Monte Hall, for $75 for both semesters. And I can earn gas and repair money by upping my hours at the cafeteria. It won't cost you any more, and if I have a car, you won't have to come and pick me up when I want to come home. May I buy it?
> Love,
> Michael

While such a stance can't guarantee that Dad will give permission, it's more likely to produce results than this version:

> Hi Dad,
> I'm buying a car. A guy in my Western Civ course has a cool Nissan he wants to get rid of. I've got $4,500 saved from working this summer, it's mine, and I'm going to use it to get some wheels. Mom said you'd freak if I did, but I want this car. OK?
> Michael

The writer of the first email respects his reader and offers reasoned arguments and evidence of research to convince him that buying a car is an action that will benefit them both. The writer of the second, by contrast, seems impulsive, ready to buy the first car that comes along, and defiant —

academic literacies | rhetorical situations | genres | processes | strategies | research MLA / APA | media / design | readings

he's picking a fight. Each email reflects a certain stance that shows the writer as a certain kind of person dealing with a topic in a certain way and establishing a certain relationship with his audience.

Identify your stance.   What is your attitude toward your topic? Objective? Critical? Curious? Opinionated? Passionate? Indifferent? Your stance may be affected by your relationship to your **AUDIENCE**. How do you want them to see you? As a colleague sharing information? As a good student showing what you can do? As an advocate for a position? Often your stance is affected by your **GENRE**: for example, lab reports require an objective, unemotional stance that emphasizes the content and minimizes the writer's own attitudes. Memoir, by comparison, allows you to reveal your feelings about your topic. Your stance is also affected by your **PURPOSE**, as the two emails about cars show. Your stance in a piece written to entertain will likely differ from the stance you'd adopt to persuade.

57–60

71

55–56

You communicate (or downplay) your stance through your tone — through the words you use and other ways your text expresses an attitude toward your subject and audience. For example, in an academic essay you would state your position directly — "the *Real Housewives* series reflects the values of American society today" — a confident, authoritative tone. In contrast, using qualifiers like "might" or "I think" can give your writing a wishy-washy, uncertain tone: "I think the *Real Housewives* series might reflect some of the values of American society today." The following paragraph, from an essay analyzing a text, has a sarcastic tone that might be appropriate for a comment on a blog post but that isn't right for an academic essay:

> In "Just Be Nice," Stephen M. Carter complains about a boy who wore his pants too low, showing his underwear. Is that really something people should worry about? We have wars raging and terrorism happening every day, and he wants to talk about how inconsiderate it is for someone to wear his pants too low? If by that boy pulling his pants up, the world would be a better place and peace would break out in the Middle East, I'm sure everyone would buy a belt.

This writer clearly thinks Carter's complaint is trivial in comparison with the larger issues of the day, but her sarcastic tone belittles Carter's argument instead of answering it with a serious counterargument. Like every other element of writing, your tone must be appropriate for your rhetorical situation.

Just as you likely alter what you say depending on whether you're speaking to a boss, an instructor, a parent, or a good friend, so you need to make similar adjustments as a writer. It's a question of appropriateness: we behave in certain ways in various social situations, and writing is a social situation. You might sign an email to a friend with an XO, but in an email to your supervisor you'll likely sign off with a "Many thanks" or "Sincerely." To write well, you need to write with integrity, to say as much as possible what you wish to say; yet you also must understand that in writing, as in speaking, your stance and tone need to suit your purpose, your relationship to your audience, the way in which you wish your audience to perceive you, and your medium.

In writing as in other aspects of life, the Golden Rule applies: "Do unto audiences as you would have them do unto you." Address readers respectfully if you want them to respond to your words with respect.

Thinking about Stance

- *What is your stance, and how does it relate to your purpose for writing?*
  If you feel strongly about your topic and are writing an argument that tries to persuade your audience to feel the same way, your stance and your **PURPOSE** fit naturally together. But suppose you are writing about the same topic with a different purpose — to demonstrate the depth of your knowledge about the topic, for example, or your ability to consider it in a detached, objective way. You will need to adjust your stance to meet the demands of this different purpose.

- *How should your stance be reflected in your tone?* Can your tone grow directly out of your stance, or do you need to "tone down" your attitude toward the topic or take a different tone altogether? Do you want to be seen as reasonable? angry? thoughtful? gentle? funny? ironic? If you're writing about something you want to be seen as taking very

55–56

academic literacies   rhetorical situations   genres   processes   strategies   research MLA / APA   media / design   readings

seriously, be sure that your language and even your font reflect that seriousness. Check your writing for words that reflect the tone you want to convey — and for ones that do not (and revise as necessary).

- *How is your stance likely to be received by your audience?* Your tone and especially the attitude it projects toward your **AUDIENCE** will affect how they react to the content of what you say.

57–60

- *Should you openly discuss your stance?* Do you want or need to announce your own perspective on your topic? Will doing so help you reach your audience, or would it be better not to say directly where you're coming from?

9 Media/Design

In its broadest sense, a medium is a go-between: a way for information to be conveyed from one person to another. We communicate through many media, verbal and nonverbal: our bodies (we catch someone's eye, wave, nod); our voices (we whisper, talk, shout, groan); and various technologies, including handwriting, print, telephone, radio, CD, film, and computer.

Each medium has unique characteristics that influence both what and how we communicate. As an example, consider this message: "I haven't told you this before, but I love you." Most of the time, we communicate such a message in person, using the medium of voice (with, presumably, help from eye contact and touch). A phone call will do, though most of us would think it a poor second choice, and a handwritten letter or note would be acceptable, if necessary. Few of us would break such news on a website, with a tweet, or during a radio call-in program.

By contrast, imagine whispering the following sentence in a darkened room: "By the last decades of the nineteenth century, the territorial expansion of the United States had left almost all Indians confined to reservations." That sentence starts a chapter in a history textbook, and it would be strange indeed to whisper it into someone's ear. It is appropriate, however, in the textbook, in print or in an e-book, or on a *PowerPoint* slide accompanying an oral presentation.

As you can see, we can often choose among various media depending on our purpose and audience. In addition, we can often combine media to create **MULTIMEDIA** texts. And different media allow us to use different ways or modes of expressing meaning, from words to images to sound to hyperlinks, that can be combined into **MULTIMODAL** formats.

No matter the medium or media, a text's design affects the way it is received and understood. A typed letter on official letterhead sends a different message than the same words handwritten on pastel stationery. Classic type

595 □

academic literacies

rhetorical situations

genres

processes

strategies

research MLA / APA

media / design

readings

sends a different message than *flowery italics*. Some genres and media (and audiences) demand **PHOTOS**, **DIAGRAMS**, or color. Some information is easier to explain — and read — in the form of a **PIE CHART** or a **BAR GRAPH** than in the form of a paragraph. Some reports and documents are so long and complex that they need to be divided into sections, which are then best labeled with **HEADINGS**. These are some of the elements to consider when you are thinking about how to design what you write.

☐ 609–11

☐ 604–5

Identify your media and design needs.   Does your writing situation call for a certain medium and design? A printed essay? An oral report with visual aids? A blog? A podcast? Academic assignments often assume a particular medium and design, but if you're unsure about your options or the degree of flexibility you have, check with your instructor.

Thinking about Media

- *What medium are you using* — print? spoken? electronic? a combination? — and how does it affect the way you will create your text? A printed résumé is usually no more than one page long; a scannable résumé sent via email has no length limits. An oral presentation should contain detailed information; accompanying slides should provide only an outline.

- *How does your medium affect your organization and* **STRATEGIES**? Long paragraphs are fine on paper but don't work well on the web. On presentation slides, phrases or keywords work better than sentences. In print, you need to define unfamiliar terms; on the web, you can sometimes just add a link to a definition found elsewhere.

◆ 329

- *How does your medium affect your language?* Some print documents require a more formal voice than spoken media; email and texting often invite greater informality.

- *How does your medium affect what modes of expression you use?* Should your text include photos, graphics, audio or video files, or links? Do you need slides, handouts, or other visuals to accompany an oral presentation?

Thinking about Design

- *What's the appropriate look for your* RHETORICAL SITUATION? Should your text look serious? whimsical? personal? something else? What design elements will suit your audience, purpose, stance, genre, and medium?

- *What elements need to be designed?* Is there any information you would like to highlight by putting it in a box? Are there any key terms that should be boldfaced? Do you need navigation buttons? How should you indicate links?

- *What font(s) are appropriate* to your audience, purpose, stance, genre, and medium?

- *Are you including any* VISUALS? Should you? Will your AUDIENCE expect or need any? Is there any information in your text that would be easier to understand as a chart or graph? If you need to include video or audio clips, how should the links be presented?

- *Should you include headings?* Would they help you organize your materials and help readers follow the text? Does your GENRE or MEDIUM require them?

- *Should you use a specific format?* MLA? APA?

academic literacies ❋
rhetorical situations ◼
genres ▲
processes ○
strategies ◆
research MLA / APA ●
media / design ☐
readings ◗

part 3

Genres

When we make a shopping list, we automatically write each item we need in a single column. When we email a friend, we begin with a salutation: "Hi, Brian." Whether we are writing a letter, a résumé, or a proposal, we know generally what it should contain and what it should look like because we are familiar with each of those genres. Genres are kinds of writing, and texts in any given genre share goals and features—a proposal, for instance, generally starts out by identifying a problem and then suggests a certain solution. The chapters in this part provide guidelines for writing in thirteen common academic genres. First come detailed chapters on four genres often assigned in writing classes—LITERACY NARRATIVES, TEXTUAL ANALYSES, REPORTS, and ARGUMENTS— followed by brief chapters on NINE OTHER GENRES and two on MIXING and CHOOSING GENRES.

Genres

Writing a Literacy Narrative 10

Narratives are stories, and we read and tell them for many different purposes. Parents read their children bedtime stories as an evening ritual. College applicants write about significant moments in their lives. In *psychology* courses, you may write a personal narrative to illustrate how individuals' stories inform the study of behavior. In *education* courses, you may share stories of your teaching experiences. And in *computer science* courses, you may write programming narratives to develop programming skills.

This chapter provides detailed guidelines for writing a specific kind of narrative: a literacy narrative, in which a writer explores his or her experiences with reading, writing, or both. We'll begin with three good examples, the first annotated to point out the key features found in most literacy narratives.

EMILY VALLOWE

Write or Wrong Identity

Emily Vallowe wrote this literacy narrative for a writing class at the University of Mary Washington in Virginia. In it, she explores her lifelong identity as a writer — and her doubts about that identity.

I'm sitting in the woods with a bunch of Catholic people I just met yesterday. Suddenly, they ask me to name one of the talents God has given me. I panic for a split second and then breathe an internal sigh of relief. I tell them I'm a writer. As the group leaders move on to question someone else, I sit trying to mentally catch my breath. It will take a moment before the terror leaves my forearms, chest, and stomach,

Attention-getting opening.

but I tell myself that I have nothing to fear. I am a writer. Yes, I most definitely am a writer. *Now breathe,* I tell myself . . . *and suppress that horrifying suspicion that you are actually not a writer at all.*

The retreat that prepared me for my eighth-grade confirmation was not the first time I found myself pulling out the old "I'm a writer" card and wondering whether I was worthy enough to carry this sacred card in the wallet of my identity. Such things happen to people with identity crises.

Clearly described details.

In kindergarten I wrote about thirty books. They were each about five pages long, with one sentence and a picture on each page. They were held together with three staples on the left side or top and had construction paper covers with the book's title and the phrase "By Emily Vallowe" written out in neat kindergarten-teacher handwriting. My mom still has all of these books in a box at the bottom of her closet.

One day at the very end of the school year, my kindergarten teacher took me to meet my future first-grade teacher, Mrs. Meadows. I got to make a special trip to meet her because I had been absent on the day the rest of the kindergarteners had gone to meet their future teachers. Mrs. Meadows's classroom was big and blue and different from the kindergarten class, complete with bigger, different kids (I think Mrs. Meadows had been teaching third or fourth graders that year, so her students were much older than I was). During this visit, Mrs. Meadows showed me a special writing desk, complete with a small, old-fashioned desk lamp (with a lamp shade and everything). I'm not sure if I understood why she was showing me this writing area. She may have said that she'd heard good things about me.

Vallowe traces her identity as a writer through her life.

This handful of images is all I can remember about the most significant event in my writing life. I'm not sure why I connect the memory of my kindergarten books with the image of me sitting in Mrs. Meadows's old classroom (for by the time I had her she was in a room on the opposite side of the school). I guess I don't even know exactly when this major event happened. Was it kindergarten? First grade? Somewhere in between? All I know is that some event occurred in early elementary school that made me want to be a writer. I don't even clearly remember what this event was, but it is something that has actively affected me for the fourteen years since then.

5

academic literacies ✳ | rhetorical situations ■ | genres ▲ | processes ○ | strategies ◆ | research MLA / APA ● | media / design ▢ | readings Ⅲ

I have wanted to be a writer my entire life — or at least that's what I tell people. Looking back, I don't know if I ever *wanted* to be a writer. The idea might never have even occurred to me. Yet somehow I was marked as a writer. My teachers must have seen something in my writing that impressed them and clued me in on it. Teachers like to recognize kids for their strengths, and at the age of five, I probably started to notice that different kids were good at different things: Bobby was good at t-ball; Sally was good at drawing; Jenny could run really fast. I was probably starting to panic at the thought that I might not be good at anything — and then a teacher came along and told me I was good at writing. Someone gave me a compliment, and I ran with it. I declared myself to be a writer and have clung to this writer identity ever since.

There are certain drawbacks to clinging to one unchanging identity since the age of five. Constant panic is one of these drawbacks. It is a strange feeling to grow up defining yourself as something when you don't know if that something is actually true. By the time I got to middle school, I could no longer remember having become a writer; I had just always been one — and had been one without any proof that I deserved to be called one. By the age of ten, I was facing a seasoned writer's terror of "am I any good?!" and this terror has followed me throughout my entire life since then. Every writing assignment I ever had was a test — a test to see if I was a real writer, to prove myself to teachers, to classmates, to myself. I approached every writing assignment thinking, "I am supposed to be good at this," not "I am going to try to make this good," and such an attitude is not a healthy way to approach anything.

Ongoing discussion of the central issue: is she a writer or not?

It doesn't help that if I am a writer, I am a very slow one. I can't sit down and instantly write something beautiful like some people I know can. I have been fortunate to go to school with some very smart classmates, some of whom can whip out a great piece of writing in minutes. I still find these people threatening. If they are faster than I am, does that make them better writers than I am? *I thought I was supposed to be "the writer"!*

My obsession with being "the" writer stems from my understanding of what it means to be "the" anything. My childhood was marked by a belief in many abstract absolutes that I am only now allowing to crumble. I was born in Chicago (and was thus the fourth generation of my family to live there), but I grew up in northern Virginia. I came to look down on my Virginia surroundings because I had been taught to view Chicago as this great Mecca — the world's most amazing city to which I must someday return, and to which all other places on earth pale in comparison. Throughout my childhood, I gathered that Chicago is a real city in which average people live and which has an economy historically based in shipping and manufacturing; Washington, D.C., on the other hand, where my dad works, has a population that includes a bizarre mix of impoverished people and the most influential leaders and diplomats in the world — and so manufactures nothing but political power. People in Chicago know how to deal with snow; Virginians panic at the *possibility* of snow. Chicago rests on soil that is so fertile it's *black*; Virginia does not even have soil — it has reddish clay suitable for growing nothing except tobacco. Even Chicago's tap water tastes amazing; D.C.'s tap water is poisoned with lead. I grew up thinking that every aspect of Chicago was perfect — so perfect that Chicago became glorious to the point of abstraction. No other city could compare, and after a while I forgot *why* no other city could compare. I just knew that Chicago was "the" city . . . and that if "the" city exists, there must also be an abstract "the" everything.

I grew up with this and many other abstract ideals that I would 10 defend against my friends' attacks . . . until I learned that they were just abstractions — and so was I. My writing identity was just another ideal, an absolute that I clung to without any basis in fact. I used to use writing as an easy way to define myself on those over-simplistic surveys teachers always asked us to fill out in elementary and middle school — the surveys that assumed that someone could know all about me simply by finding out my favorite color, my favorite TV show, or my hobbies. I used to casually throw out the "I'm a writer" card just to get these silly surveys over with. "I'm a writer" was just an easy answer to the complicated question, "Who are you?" I always thought the surveys avoided asking this question, but maybe I was the one avoid-ing it. For years, I had been defining myself as "the writer" without really pondering what this writer identity meant. Is a writer simply someone who writes all the time? Well, I often went through long stretches in which I did not write anything, so this definition did not seem to suit me. Is a writer someone who is good at writing? Well, I've already mentioned that I've been having "am I any good?!" thoughts

Vallowe examines the roots of her identity as a writer — and why she questions that identity.

since elementary school, so this definition didn't seem to fit me, either. I was identifying myself as "the writer" as an abstraction, without any just cause to do so.

The funny thing is that I recognized my writing identity as an abstract ideal before I recognized any of the other ideals I was clinging to, but that didn't make the situation any better. It is one thing to learn that dead people have been voting in Chicago elections for decades, and so perhaps Chicago isn't the perfect city, but what happens when the absolute ideal is you? More important, what would happen if *this* absolute were to crumble? It was terrifying to think that I might discover that I was not a writer because to not be a writer was to suddenly be nothing. If a writer was the only thing that I had ever been, what would happen if writing was a lie? I would vanish. Looking back, the logical part of my brain tells me that, if I am not a writer, I am still plenty of other things: I am a Catholic; I am a Vallowe; people tell me that I have other good qualities. But when facing these horrifying spells of writer's doubt, my brain doesn't see these other things. I am driven only by the fear of nothingness and the thought that I have to be a writer because I'm not good at anything else.

Am I really not good at anything else? I used to blame this entire writer's complex on whoever it was that told me I was a writer. If that person hadn't channeled this burdensome identity into me, I might never have expected great literary things from myself, and life would have been easier. I had these thoughts until one day in high school I mentioned something to my mom about the fact that I'd been writing since I was five years old. My mom corrected me by saying that I'd been writing since I was three years old. At the age of three I couldn't even physically form letters, but apparently I would dictate stories to my mom on a regular basis. My mom explained to me how I would run to her and say, "Mommy, Mommy, write my story for me!"

She continues to explore her identity as a writer.

This new information was both comforting and unsettling. On one hand, it was a great relief to know that I had been a writer all along — that I would have been a writer even if no one had told me that I was one. On the other hand, the knowledge that I had been a writer all along drove me into an entirely new realm of panic.

I've been a writer my entire life?

WHAT?!

15

I've been a writer since I was three? Three? *Three* years old: How is that even possible? I didn't know it was possible to be anything at age three, let alone the thing that might define me for my entire life.

I have been taught that each person has a vocation — a calling that he or she must use to spread God's love to others. Yet I've also assumed that one must go on some sort of journey to figure out what this vocation is. If I found my vocation at the age of three, have I skipped this journey? And if I've skipped the journey, does that mean that the vocation isn't real? Or am I just really lucky for having found my vocation so early? Was I really born a writer? Was I born to do one thing and will I do that one thing for my entire life? Can anything be that consistent? That simple? And if I am living out some divine vocation, is that any comfort at all? If I am channeling some divine being in my writing, and everything I write comes from some outside source, where does that leave me? Am I nothing even if I am a writer?

This questioning has not led me to any comforting conclusions. I still wonder if my writer identity has been thrust upon me, and what it means to have someone else determine who I am. If I am a writer, then I am someone who passionately seeks originality — someone who gets pleasure from inventing entire fictional worlds. Yet if someone — either a teacher or a divine being — is channeling an identity into me, then I am no more original than the characters that I create in my fiction. If my identity is not original, then this identity is not real, and if I am not real . . . I can't even finish this sentence.

I don't know if I really wrote thirty books in kindergarten. It might have been twenty — or fifteen — or ten — or five. I might have made up that part about the special writing desk in Mrs. Meadows's old classroom. I don't know if God predestined me to write masterpieces or if a teacher just casually mentioned that I wrote well and I completely overreacted to the compliment. Questioning my identity as "the writer" has led me to new levels of fear and uncertainty, but this questioning is not going to stop. Even if I one day sit, withered and gray, with a Nobel Prize for Literature proudly displayed on my desk as I try to crank out one last novel at the age of ninety-two, my thoughts will probably drift back to Mrs. Meadows and those books I wrote in kindergarten. In my old age, I still might not understand my writer identity,

Ending refers back to the opening anecdote.

Conclusion is tentative (since the end of the story is decades in the future).

but maybe by that point, I will have written a novel about a character with an identity crisis — and maybe the character will have come through all right.

In this literacy narrative, Vallowe reflects on the origins of her identity as a writer: her early teachers, her parents, God, herself. The significance of her story lies in her inability to settle on any one of these possibilities.

MARJORIE AGOSÍN

Always Living in Spanish: Recovering the Familiar, through Language

Marjorie Agosín, a Spanish professor at Wellesley College, wrote this literacy narrative for Poets & Writers *magazine in 1999. Originally written in Spanish, it tells of Agosín's Chilean childhood and her continuing connection to the Spanish language.*

In the evenings in the northern hemisphere, I repeat the ancient ritual that I observed as a child in the southern hemisphere: going out while the night is still warm and trying to recognize the stars as it begins to grow dark silently. In the sky of my country, Chile, that long and wide stretch of land that the poets blessed and dictators abused, I could easily name the stars: the three Marias, the Southern Cross, and the three Lilies, names of beloved and courageous women.

But here in the United States, where I have lived since I was a young girl, the solitude of exile makes me feel that so little is mine, that not even the sky has the same constellations, the trees and the fauna the same names or sounds, or the rubbish the same smell. How does one recover the familiar? How does one name the unfamiliar? How can one be another or live in a foreign language? These are the dilemmas of one who writes in Spanish and lives in translation.

Since my earliest childhood in Chile I lived with the tempos and the melodies of a multiplicity of tongues: German, Yiddish, Russian, Turkish, and many Latin songs. Because everyone was from somewhere else, my relatives laughed, sang, and fought in a Babylon of languages. Spanish was reserved for matters of extreme seriousness, for commercial transactions, or for illnesses, but everyone's mother tongue was always associated with the memory of spaces inhabited in the past: the shtetl, the flowering and vast Vienna avenues, the minarets of Turkey, and the Ladino whispers of Toledo. When my paternal grandmother sang old songs in Turkish, her voice and body assumed the passion of one who was there in the city of Istanbul, gazing by turns toward the west and the east.

Destiny and the always ambiguous nature of history continued my family's enforced migration, and because of it I, too, became one who had to live and speak in translation. The disappearances, torture, and clandestine deaths in my country in the early seventies drove us to the United States, that other America that looked with suspicion at those who did not speak English and especially those who came from the supposedly uncivilized regions of Latin America. I had left a dangerous place that was my home, only to arrive in a dangerous place that was not: a high school in the small town of Athens, Georgia, where my poor English and my accent were the cause of ridicule and insult. The only way I could recover my usurped country and my Chilean childhood was by continuing to write in Spanish, the same way my grandparents had sung in their own tongues in diasporic sites.

The new and learned English language did not fit with the visceral 5 emotions and themes that my poetry contained, but by writing in Spanish I could recover fragrances, spoken rhythms, and the passion of my own identity. Daily I felt the need to translate myself for the strangers living all around me, to tell them why we were in Georgia, why we are different, why we had fled, why my accent was so thick, and why I did not look Hispanic. Only at night, writing poems in Spanish, could I return to my senses, and soothe my own sorrow over what I had left behind.

This is how I became a Chilean poet who wrote in Spanish and lived in the southern United States. And then, one day, a poem of mine was translated and published in the English language. Finally, for the first time since I had left Chile, I felt I didn't have to explain myself. My poem, expressed in another language, spoke for itself . . . and for me.

Sometimes the austere sounds of English help me bear the solitude of knowing that I am foreign and so far away from those about whom

I write. I must admit I would like more opportunities to read in Spanish to people whose language and culture is also mine, to join in our common heritage and in the feast of our sounds. I would also like readers of English to understand the beauty of the spoken word in Spanish, that constant flow of oxytonic and paraoxytonic syllables (*Vérde qué té quiéro vérde*),* the joy of writing — of dancing — in another language. I believe that many exiles share the unresolvable torment of not being able to live in the language of their childhood.

I miss that undulating and sensuous language of mine, those baroque descriptions, the sense of being and feeling that Spanish gives me. It is perhaps for this reason that I have chosen and will always choose to write in Spanish. Nothing else from my childhood world remains. My country seems to be frozen in gestures of silence and oblivion. My relatives have died, and I have grown up not knowing a young generation of cousins and nieces and nephews. Many of my friends disappeared, others were tortured, and the most fortunate, like me, became guardians of memory. For us, to write in Spanish is to always be in active pursuit of memory. I seek to recapture a world lost to me on that sorrowful afternoon when the blue electric sky and the Andean cordillera bade me farewell. On that, my last Chilean day, I carried under my arm my innocence recorded in a little blue notebook I kept even then. Gradually that diary filled with memoranda, poems written in free verse, descriptions of dreams and of the thresholds of my house surrounded by cherry trees and gardenias. To write in Spanish is for me a gesture of survival. And because of translation, my memory has now become a part of the memory of many others.

Translators are not traitors, as the proverb says, but rather splendid friends in this great human community of language.

Agosín's narrative uses vivid detail to bring her childhood in Chile to life for her readers. Her love for her homeland and its people is clear, as is the significance of her narrative — with her childhood home gone, to write in Spanish is a "gesture of survival."

---

*"*Vérde qué té quiéro vérde*" ("Green, how I want you, green"): the opening line of a famous Spanish poem that demonstrates the interplay of words with the main stress on the final syllable (oxytonic) and those with the main stress on the next-to-last syllable (paroxytonic) in Spanish. [Editor's note]

SHANNON NICHOLS

"Proficiency"

In the following literacy narrative, Shannon Nichols, a student at Wright State University, describes her experience taking the standardized writing proficiency test that high school students in Ohio must pass to graduate. She wrote this essay for a college writing course, where her audience included her classmates and instructor.

The first time I took the ninth-grade proficiency test was in March of eighth grade. The test ultimately determines whether students may receive a high school diploma. After months of preparation and anxiety, the pressure was on. Throughout my elementary and middle school years, I was a strong student, always on the honor roll. I never had a GPA below 3.0. I was smart, and I knew it. That is, until I got the results of the proficiency test.

Although the test was challenging, covering reading, writing, math, and citizenship, I was sure I had passed every part. To my surprise, I did pass every part—except writing. "Writing! Yeah right! How did I manage to fail writing, and by half a point, no less?" I thought to myself in disbelief. Seeing my test results brought tears to my eyes. I honestly could not believe it. To make matters worse, most of my classmates, including some who were barely passing eighth-grade English, passed that part.

Until that time, I loved writing just as much as I loved math. It was one of my strengths. I was good at it, and I enjoyed it. If anything, I thought I might fail citizenship. How could I have screwed up writing? I surely spelled every word correctly, used good grammar, and even used big words in the proper context. How could I have failed?

Finally I got over it and decided it was no big deal. Surely I would pass the next time. In my honors English class I worked diligently, passing with an A. By October I'd be ready to conquer that writing test. Well, guess what? I failed the test again, again with only 4.5 of the 5 points needed to pass. That time I did cry, and even went to my English teacher, Mrs. Brown, and asked, "How can I get A's in all my English classes but fail the writing part of the proficiency test twice?" She couldn't answer my question. Even my friends and classmates were confused. I felt like a failure. I had disappointed my family and seriously let myself down. Worst of all, I still couldn't figure out what I was doing wrong.

academic literacies · rhetorical situations · genres · processes · strategies · research MLA / APA · media / design · readings

I decided to quit trying so hard. Apparently — I told myself — the people grading the tests didn't have the slightest clue about what constituted good writing. I continued to excel in class and passed the test on the third try. But I never again felt the same love of reading and writing.

This experience showed me just how differently my writing could be judged by various readers. Obviously all my English teachers and many others enjoyed or at least appreciated my writing. A poem I wrote was put on television once. I must have been a pretty good writer. Unfortunately the graders of the ninth-grade proficiency test didn't feel the same, and when students fail the test, the state of Ohio doesn't offer any explanation.

After I failed the test the first time, I began to hate writing, and I started to doubt myself. I doubted my ability and the ideas I wrote about. Failing the second time made things worse, so perhaps to protect myself from my doubts, I stopped taking English seriously. Perhaps because of that lack of seriousness, I earned a 2 on the Advanced Placement English Exam, barely passed the twelfth-grade proficiency test, and was placed in developmental writing in college. I wish I knew why I failed that test because then I might have written what was expected on the second try, maintained my enthusiasm for writing, and continued to do well.

Nichols's narrative focuses on her emotional reaction to failing a test that she should have passed easily. The contrast between her demonstrated writing ability and her repeated failures creates a tension that captures readers' attention. We want to know what will happen to her.

For four more literacy narratives, see CHAPTER 59.

Key Features / Literacy Narratives

A well-told story. As with most narratives, those about literacy often set up some sort of situation that needs to be resolved. That need for resolution makes readers want to keep reading. We want to know whether Nichols ultimately will pass the proficiency test. Some literacy narratives simply explore the role that reading or writing played at some time in someone's life — assuming, perhaps, that learning to read or write is a challenge to be met.

Vivid detail.   Details can bring a narrative to life for readers by giving them vivid mental sensations of the sights, sounds, smells, tastes, and textures of the world in which your story takes place. The details you use when describing something can help readers picture places, people, and events; dialogue can help them hear what is being said. We get a picture of Agosín's Chilean childhood when she writes of the "blue electric sky" and her "little blue notebook" in which she described her "house surrounded by cherry trees and gardenias." Similarly, we can picture and hear Vallowe as a little girl running to her mother and saying, "Mommy, Mommy, write my story for me!"

Some indication of the narrative's significance.   By definition, a literacy narrative tells something the writer remembers about learning to read or write. In addition, the writer needs to make clear why the incident matters to him or her. You may reveal its significance in various ways. Nichols does it when she says she no longer loves to read or write. Agosín points out that she writes in Spanish because "nothing else from my childhood world remains. . . . To write in Spanish is for me a gesture of survival." The trick is to avoid tacking a brief statement about your narrative's significance onto the end as if it were a kind of moral of the story. Vallowe's narrative would be less effective if, instead of questioning her identity as a writer from several perspectives, she had simply said, "I became a writer at the age of three."

A GUIDE TO WRITING LITERACY NARRATIVES

Choosing a Topic

In general, it's a good idea to focus on a single event that took place during a relatively brief period of time. For example:

- any early memory about writing or reading that you recall vividly
- someone who taught you to read or write

- a book or other text that has been significant for you in some way
- an event at school that was related to reading or writing and that you found interesting, humorous, or embarrassing
- a writing or reading task that you found (or still find) especially difficult or challenging
- a memento that represents an important moment in your literacy development (perhaps the start of a **LITERACY PORTFOLIO**)

326–27

- the origins of your current attitudes about writing or reading
- learning to text, learning to write email appropriately, creating and maintaining a *Facebook* page or blog

Make a list of possible topics, and then choose one that you think will be interesting to you and to others — and that you're willing to share with others. If several seem promising, try them out on a friend or classmate. Or just choose one and see where it leads; you can switch to another if need be. If you have trouble coming up with a topic, try **FREEWRITING**, **LISTING**, **CLUSTERING**, or **LOOPING**.

289–92

Considering the Rhetorical Situation

PURPOSE Why do you want to tell this story? To share a memory with others? To fulfill an assignment? To teach a lesson? To explore your past learning? Think about the reasons for your choice and how they will shape what you write.

55–56

AUDIENCE Are your readers likely to have had similar experiences? Would they tell similar stories? How much explaining will you have to do to help them understand your narrative? Can you assume that they will share your attitudes toward your story, or will you have to work at making them see your perspective? How much about your life are you willing to share with this audience?

57–60

64–67

STANCE What attitude do you want to project? Affectionate? Neutral? Critical? Do you wish to be sincere? serious? humorously detached? self-critical? self-effacing? something else? How do you want your readers to see you?

68–70

MEDIA / DESIGN Will your narrative be in print? presented orally? online? Should you use photos, tables, graphs, or video or audio clips? Is there a font that conveys the right tone? Do you need headings?

Generating Ideas and Text

Good literacy narratives share certain elements that make them interesting and compelling for readers. Remember that your goals are to tell the story as clearly and vividly as you can and to convey the meaning the incident has for you today. Start by thinking about what you already know about writing a literacy narrative. Then write out what you remember about the setting of your narrative and those involved, perhaps trying out some of the methods in the chapter on **GENERATING IDEAS AND TEXT**. You may also want to **INTERVIEW** a teacher or parent who figures in your narrative.

289–92
463–64

Explore what you already know about writing a literacy narrative. Think about recent occasions when you've had to narrate a story, either orally or in writing, in school or out. Take a few moments to think about a couple of those occasions, especially ones involving your reading, writing, or learning to do something. Why and to whom were you telling these stories? How successful do you think your narratives were? What aspects of telling the story did you feel most confident about or do especially well? What could you have done better? What do you still need to learn about writing a literacy narrative?

Describe the setting. Where does your narrative take place? List the places where your story unfolds. For each place, write informally for a few minutes, **DESCRIBING** what you remember:

399–407

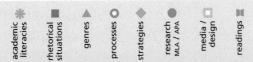

- *What do you see?* If you're inside, what color are the walls? What's hanging on them? What can you see out any windows? What else do you see? Books? Lined paper? Red ink? Are there people? places to sit? a desk or a table?

- *What do you hear?* A radiator hissing? Leaves rustling? The wind howling? Rain? Someone reading aloud? Shouts? Cheers? Children playing? Music? The chime of a text arriving on your phone?

- *What do you smell?* Sweat? Perfume? Incense? Food cooking?

- *How and what do you feel?* Nervous? Happy? Cold? Hot? A scratchy wool sweater? Tight shoes? Rough wood on a bench?

- *What do you taste?* Gum? Mints? Graham crackers? Juice? Coffee?

Think about the key people. Narratives include people whose actions play an important role in the story. In your literacy narrative, you are probably one of those people. A good way to develop your understanding of the people in your narrative is to write about them:

- *Describe each person in a paragraph or so.* What do the people look like? How do they dress? How do they speak? Quickly? Slowly? With an accent? Do they speak clearly, or do they mumble? Do they use any distinctive words or phrases? You might begin by describing their movements, their posture, their bearing, their facial expressions. Do they have a distinctive scent?

- *Recall (or imagine) some characteristic dialogue.* A good way to bring people to life and move a story along is with **DIALOGUE**, to let readers hear them rather than just hearing about them. Try writing six to ten lines of dialogue between two people in your narrative. If you can't remember an actual conversation, make up one that could have happened. (After all, you are telling the story, and you get to decide how it is to be told.) Try to remember (and write down) some of the characteristic words or phrases that the people in your narrative used. 408–13

Write about "what happened." At the heart of every good **NARRATIVE** is the answer to the question "What happened?" The action in a literacy 419–27 narrative may be as dramatic as winning a spelling bee or as subtle as a conversation between two friends; both contain action, movement, or change that the narrative tries to capture for readers. A good story dramatizes the action. Try **SUMMARIZING** the action in your narrative in a paragraph—try to capture what happened. Use active and specific verbs (*pondered, shouted, laughed*) to describe the action as vividly as possible.

486–87 ◆

Consider the significance of the narrative.　You need to make clear the ways in which any event you are writing about is significant for you now. Write a page or so about the meaning it has for you. How did it change or otherwise affect you? What aspects of your life now can you trace to that event? How might your life have been different if this event had not happened or had turned out differently? Why does this story matter to you?

Ways of Organizing a Literacy Narrative

293–94 ○

Start by **OUTLINING** the main events in your narrative. Then think about how you want to tell the story. Don't assume that the only way to tell your story is just as it happened. That's one way—starting at the beginning of the action and continuing to the end. But you could also start in the middle—or even at the end. Shannon Nichols, for example, could have begun her narrative by telling how she finally passed the proficiency test and then gone back to tell about the times she tried to pass it, even as she was an A student in an honors English class. Several ways of organizing a narrative follow.

[Chronologically, from beginning to end]

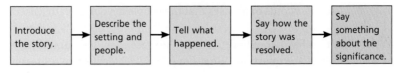

academic literacies | rhetorical situations | genres | processes | strategies | research MLA / APA | media / design | readings

[Beginning in the middle]

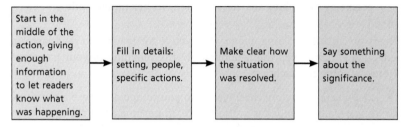

Start in the middle of the action, giving enough information to let readers know what was happening. → Fill in details: setting, people, specific actions. → Make clear how the situation was resolved. → Say something about the significance.

[Beginning at the end]

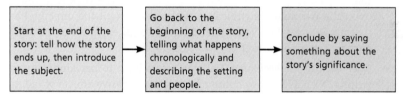

Start at the end of the story: tell how the story ends up, then introduce the subject. → Go back to the beginning of the story, telling what happens chronologically and describing the setting and people. → Conclude by saying something about the story's significance.

Writing Out a Draft

Once you have generated ideas and thought about how you want to organize your narrative, it's time to begin **DRAFTING**. Do this quickly—try to write a complete draft in one sitting, concentrating on getting the story on paper or screen and on putting in as much detail as you can. Some writers find it helpful to work on the beginning or ending first. Others write out the main event first and then draft the beginning and ending. 298–300

Draft a **BEGINNING**.   A good narrative grabs readers' attention right from the start. Here are some ways of beginning: 331–39

- *Jump right in.* Sometimes you may want to get to the main action as quickly as possible. Nichols, for example, begins as she takes the ninth-grade proficiency test for the first time.

- *Describe the context.* You may want to provide background information at the start of your narrative, as Vallowe does with an anecdote exposing her fears that she may not be who she thinks she is.

- *Describe the setting, especially if it's important to the narrative.* Agosín begins by describing the constellations in her native Chile.

339–42 **Draft an ENDING.** Think about what you want readers to read last. An effective ending helps them understand the meaning of your narrative. Here are some possibilities:

- *End where your story ends.* It's up to you to decide where a narrative ends. Vallowe ends far in the future, in her imagined old age.

- *Say something about the significance of your narrative.* Nichols observes that she no longer loves to write, for example. The trick is to touch upon the narrative's significance without stating it too directly, like the moral of a fable. Vallowe and Agosín both explore the meaning of their experiences over several paragraphs.

- *Refer back to the beginning.* Vallowe refers back to her kindergarten writing; Nichols ends by contemplating the negative effects of failing the proficiency test.

- *End on a surprising note.* Agosín catches our attention when she tells us of the deaths and disappearances of her friends and relatives.

344–45 **Come up with a title.** A good **TITLE** indicates something about the subject of your narrative—and makes readers want to take a look. Nichols's title, "'Proficiency,'" is also her subject; her use of quote marks around this word calls its meaning into question in a way that might make readers wonder — and read on. Vallowe focuses on the significance of her narrative: "Write or Wrong Identity." Agosín makes her title an expression of her sense of identity: "Always Living in Spanish."

Considering Matters of Design

You'll probably write your narrative in paragraph form, but think about the information you're presenting and how you can design it to enhance your story and appeal to your audience.

- What would be an appropriate **FONT**? Something serious, like Times Roman? Something whimsical, like *Comic Sans*? Something else?

601–2

- Would it help your readers if you added **HEADINGS** in order to divide your narrative into shorter sections?

604–5

- Would photographs or other **VISUALS** show details better than you can describe them with words alone? If you're writing about learning to read, for example, you might scan in an image of one of the first books you read. Or if your topic is learning to write, you could include something you wrote. You could even include a video or audio recording. Would your narrative best be conveyed as a multimodal composition that combines written text, images, and video or audio?

607–15

Getting Response and Revising

The following questions can help you study your draft with a critical eye. **GETTING RESPONSE** from others is always good, and these questions can guide their reading, too. Make sure they know your purpose and audience.

306–7

- Do the title and first few sentences make readers want to read on? If not, how else might you begin?

- Is the sequence of events in the narrative clear? Does it flow, and are there effective transitions? Does the narrative get sidetracked at any point?

- Is anything confusing?

- Is there enough detail, and is it interesting? Will readers be able to imagine the setting? Can they picture the characters and sense what they're like? Would it help to add some dialogue so that readers can "hear" them?

- Are visuals used effectively and integrated smoothly with the written text? If there are no visuals, would using some strengthen the narrative?

- Have you made the narrative meaningful enough for readers so that they wonder and care about what will happen?

- Do you narrate any actions clearly? vividly? Does the action keep readers engaged?
- Is the significance of the narrative clear?
- Is the ending satisfying? What are readers left thinking?

307–10 ○

The preceding questions should identify aspects of your narrative you need to work on. When it's time to **REVISE**, make sure your text appeals to your audience and achieves your purpose as successfully as possible.

Editing and Proofreading

313–16 ○

Readers equate correctness with competence. Once you've revised your draft, follow these guidelines for **EDITING** a narrative:

419–27 ◆
349

- Make sure events are **NARRATED** in a clear order and include appropriate time markers, **TRANSITIONS**, and summary phrases to link the parts and show the passing of time.
- Be careful that verb tenses are consistent throughout. If you start your narrative in the past tense ("he *taught* me how to use a computer"), be careful not to switch to the present ("So I *look* at him and *say* . . . ") along the way.
- Check to see that verb tenses correctly indicate when an action took place. If one action took place before another action in the past, for example, you should use the past perfect tense: "I forgot to dot my i's, a mistake I *had made* many times before."

408–13 ◆

- Punctuate **DIALOGUE** correctly. Whenever someone speaks, surround the speech with quotation marks ("No way," I said). Periods and commas go inside quotation marks; exclamation points and question marks go inside if they're part of the quotation, outside if they're part of the whole sentence:

  INSIDE   Opening the door, Ms. Cordell announced, "Pop quiz!"
  OUTSIDE   It wasn't my intention to announce "I hate to read"!

316–17 ○

- **PROOFREAD** your finished narrative carefully before turning it in.

Taking Stock of Your Work

- How well do you think you told the story?
- What did you do especially well?
- What could still be improved?
- How did you go about coming up with ideas and generating text?
- How did you go about drafting your narrative?
- Did you use photographs or any other visual or audio elements? What did they add? Can you think of such elements you might have used?
- How did others' responses influence your writing?
- What would you do differently next time?

IF YOU NEED MORE HELP

See also **MEMOIRS** (Chapter 18), a kind of narrative that focuses more generally on a significant event from your past, and **REFLECTIONS** (Chapter 21), a kind of essay for thinking about a topic in writing. See Chapter 32 if you are required to submit your literacy narrative as part of a writing **PORTFOLIO**.

▲ 216–23
245–52

⬤ 318–28

11 Analyzing Texts

Both the *Huffington Post* and *National Review Online* cover the same events, but each one interprets them differently. All toothpaste ads claim to make teeth "the whitest." The Environmental Protection Agency is a guardian of America's air, water, and soil — or an unconstitutional impediment to economic growth, depending on which politician is speaking. Those are but three examples that demonstrate why we need to be careful, analytical readers of magazines, newspapers, blogs, websites, ads, political documents, even textbooks.

Text is commonly thought of as words, as a piece of writing. In the academic world, however, text can include not only writing but images — photographs, illustrations, videos, films — and even sculptures, buildings, and music and other sounds. And many texts combine words, images, and sounds. We are constantly bombarded with texts: on the web, in print, on signs and billboards, even on our clothing. Not only does text convey information, but it also influences how and what we think. We need to read, then, to understand not only what texts say but also how they say it and how they try to persuade or influence what we think.

Because understanding how texts say what they say and achieve their effects is so crucial, assignments in many disciplines ask you to analyze texts. You may be asked to analyze candidates' speeches in a *political science* course or to analyze the imagery in a poem for a *literature* class. In a *statistics* course, you might analyze a set of data — a numerical text — to find the standard deviation from the mean.

This chapter offers detailed guidelines for writing an essay that closely examines a text both for what it says and for how it does so, with the goal of demonstrating for readers how — and how well — the text achieves its effects. We'll begin with three good examples, the first annotated to point out the key features found in most textual analyses.

academic literacies · rhetorical situations · genres · processes · strategies · research MLA / APA · media / design · readings

HANNAH BERRY

The Fashion Industry: Free to Be an Individual

Hannah Berry wrote this analysis of two visual texts, shoe ads, for a first-year writing course at Wright State University.

As young women, we have always been told through the medium of advertisement that we must use certain products to make ourselves beautiful. For decades, ads for things like soap, makeup, and mouthwash have established a sort of misplaced control over our lives, telling us what will make us attractive and what will not. Recently, however, a new generation of advertisement has emerged in the fashion industry, one that cleverly equates the products shown in the ads with the quest for confident individuality. Ads such as the two for Clarks and Sorel discussed below encourage us to break free from the standard beauty mold and be ourselves; using mostly imagery, they remind us that being unique is the true origin of beauty.

The first ad promotes Clarks fashion as band geek chic, quite literally raising a unique personality onto a pedestal, with the subject poised on a decorative stone platform as shown in fig. 1. Photographed in standing profile, this quirky-looking young woman is doing what she loves — playing some kind of trumpet — and looks great doing it. She is wearing her hair in a French twist with a strand tucked behind her ear, as if she recently moved it out of her face to play the music she loves without distraction. The downturn of her nose points to the short gray-black dress that stops several inches above her knees but covers her chest and shoulders modestly, with a collar situated at the base of her neck and sleeves that reach for her elbows. The dress is plain, but it is a perfect fit for the personality implied in the photo. Set against the background of a light-tan wall, the model leans back slightly as if supporting the weight of her instrument. Her right knee is bent while her left knee remains straight. The positioning of her legs not only accentuates her unbalanced posture but also points out the pair of simple brown pumps that complete the look. She wears the shoes with a pair of socks in a much darker shade of brown pulled up around her shins. Around her ankles are sandy-colored rings of shaggy fabric that are most likely attached to the socks, giving the whole outfit a sense of nerdy flair. Her expression is a simple mix of calm and concentration. It's as if the photographer happened to take the picture while she was practicing for a school recital.

Attention to the context of the ads Berry will analyze.

Clear thesis.

Detailed description of the first text.

Illustrations are labeled in MLA format.

Fig. 1. Clarks ad shows a band geek doing what she loves (Clarks).

academic literacies · rhetorical situations · genres · processes · strategies · research MLA / APA · media / design · readings

Clarks has taken what looks like your average high school student and dressed her in an outfit that speaks to her own distinctive character and talents. The image sparks the idea that her beauty comes from an internal base of secure self-confidence and moves outward to infuse her physical appearance and sense of style. This ad urges us to celebrate individuality with the right look. Using an image alone, Clarks advertises its products with the simple promise that they will support you in doing what you love and keep you original.

Analysis of the first text.

Taking a narrower perspective on originality, the ad for Sorel boots shown in fig. 2 dramatizes the idea that spontaneity is key to a distinctive personal identity. This abstract idea is depicted in a vividly concrete way, using the featured fur-topped boots as a base for encouraging a bold sense of self. The ad dares us to break free from the mold of society and do something "fearless" (Sorel). It shows us a dark-haired, red-lipped woman sitting in a formal French upholstered chair in a dark-blue, elaborately paneled parlor. An expression of triumph and mischief adorns her sultry visage. She's wearing a revealing short white dress that overlaps slightly around her chest and falls strategically over her hips so that large portions of her upper thighs are visible. Feathers in autumn colors cover her shoulders, and a gold belt accentuates her waist. Next to her is a polished wood table supporting a lighted candle, a small glass vase of pink and white flowers, and a black-and-white-patterned orb. There is a dormant, ornate fireplace to her left. But what makes this scene extraordinary is what seems to have taken place moments before the picture was taken. One of the young woman's feet, clad in the devil-red black-laced boots being advertised, rests defiantly on top of the shattered remains of a crystal chandelier. In her right hand, the woman holds an old-looking shotgun with her forefinger still resting on the trigger.

Description of the second text.

Speculation about the story behind the image.

In Sorel's explosive ad, it is apparent that the woman not only shot down the ceiling fixture but also has no regrets about doing so. Her white dress represents a sort of purity and innocence that is completely contradicted by the way she wears it — and by the boots. They gave her the power to shoot down the chandelier, the push she needed to give in to a long-held desire that perhaps she couldn't have indulged in without the extra help. They symbolize her liberty to decide to be herself and do what she wants. Along with the white dress, the formal decor represents the bounds that society tells her she must fit into — but that she decides

Analysis of the second text.

Fig. 2. Sorel ad flaunts devil-red boots worn by a fearless woman with a shotgun (Sorel).

to take a potshot at instead. Focusing on the beauty of inner power, not just the power of outer beauty, this Sorel ad punctuates its bold visual statement with a single verbal phrase: "Après anything" (Sorel). In the French language, the word *après* means "after." So, the ad suggests, no matter what outrageous or outlandish deed you do, the Sorel boots will be there for you, suitable for slipping into afterward like a negligee.

With these pioneering fashion ads that celebrate blowing your own horn or shooting up fancy French lighting fixtures for fun, young women are told to accessorize their inner beauty with articles of clothing geared toward their distinctive individual desires. "You don't have to just try to be beautiful in the ways other women do," they say; "you can strike out on your own, and our products will help you do it." The extent to which women will respond to these messages remains to be seen, but certainly the ads themselves achieve a strikingly different look. Whether celebrating individual talents or random acts of defiance in our everyday lives, they dare us to accessorize our personalities.

Conclusion ties together the strands of the analysis.

Works Cited

Clarks. Advertisement. *Lucky*, Sept. 2011, p. 55.
Sorel. Advertisement. *Lucky*, Sept. 2011, p. 65.

Berry summarizes each ad clearly and focuses her analysis on a theme running through both ads: that clothing is an expression of one's individuality. She describes patterns of images in both ads as evidence.

DANIELLE ALLEN

Our Declaration

Danielle Allen is a political philosopher who teaches at the Institute for Advanced Study in Princeton, New Jersey. This analysis is a chapter from her book Our Declaration: A Reading of the Declaration of Independence in Defense of Equality.

There's something quite startling about the phrase "We hold these truths to be self-evident." Perhaps it can be made visible most easily with a comparison.

The Catholic Church, too, is committed to a set of truths. At every mass priest and parishioners together recite a list of their beliefs called the *Credo*. One version, called the Apostles' Creed, starts like this: "I believe in God, the Father almighty, creator of heaven and earth. I believe in Jesus Christ, his only son and Lord." Each section begins with the words "I believe," and that's why this recitation is called the *Credo*. Latin, "credo" simply means "I believe."

The Declaration launches its list of truths altogether differently. Jefferson and his colleagues do not say, "I believe," or even "we believe," that all men are created equal. Instead, they say, "We hold these truths to be self-evident," and then they give us a set of either three or five truths, depending on how you count.

What's the difference between "We believe" and "We hold these truths to be self-evident"? In the Catholic *Credo*, when one says, "I believe," the basis for that belief is God's revealed word. In contrast, when Jefferson and his colleagues say, "We hold these truths to be self-evident," they are claiming to know the truths thanks to their own powers of perception and reasoning. These truths are self-evident, and so humans can grasp and hold them without any external or divine assistance.

In order to understand what "We hold these truths to be self-evident" really means, then, it is important to know what "self-evident" means.   5

Sometimes people take it to mean that we can instantly understand an idea, but that's not really right. It's true that sometimes the idea of self-evidence is used for things that we simply perceive. For instance, when I look out my window I immediately perceive that the world includes things like trees and flowers. If outside my window there are many different kinds of tree — hickory and maple and oak, for instance — when I look at them, I nonetheless rapidly perceive that they are all the same kind of thing. That many different kinds of a particular sort of growing thing are all trees is self-evident. We can call this self-evidence from sense perception.

The immediacy of perception, though, is not the same as instantly understanding an idea. And, in fact, to call a proposition self-evident is not at all to say that you will instantly get it. It means instead that if you look into the proposition, if you entertain it, if you reflect upon it, you will inevitably come to affirm it. All the evidence that you

academic literacies

rhetorical situations

genres

processes

strategies

research MLA / APA

media / design

readings

need in order to believe the proposition exists within the proposition itself.

This second kind of self-evidence comes not from perception but from logic and how language works.

For instance, we define a chair as an object with a seat and some structure of legs to hold that seat up; and the artifact serves the purpose of having someone sit on it. Then, if I say that a chair is for sitting on, I am expressing a self-evident truth based only on the definition of a chair. Of course a chair is for sitting on! That is how I've defined the word, after all. That's a pretty trivial example of self-evidence. If that were all there were to the idea of self-evidence, it wouldn't be very interesting.

So here is where matters get more interesting: one can string together more than one kind of self-evident proposition — let's call them "premises" — in order to lead to a new piece of knowledge, a conclusion, which will also count as self-evident, since it has been deduced from a few basic self-evident premises.

Aristotle called this method of stringing together valid premises to yield a self-evident conclusion, a syllogism. Above, I said that "syllogism" is a technical word. Here is a basic example:

FIRST PREMISE: *Bill Gates is a human being.*
SECOND PREMISE: *All human beings are mortal.*
CONCLUSION: *Bill Gates is mortal.*

This is a bit like math. We can use a Venn diagram to show how the syllogism works. Venn diagrams represent sets of things and how they overlap, and the argument of a syllogism can be thought of as expressing facts about sets and their members. Bill Gates is in the set of human beings. And the set of human beings is entirely contained within the set of mortals. It follows that Bill Gates is in the set of mortals. The validity of this syllogism becomes self-evident when those facts are represented as in this Venn diagram:

Now, in this syllogism, our two premises are both self-evident truths based on sense perception. We know Bill Gates is a human being by looking at and listening to him. As to the idea that human beings are mortal, we know that human beings die by seeing it happen all around us and never seeing a counterexample. Then we take these two

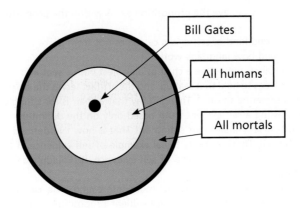

premises, each self-evident through sense perception, and generate a third self-evident proposition, in this case a conclusion, through deduction. From the two premises, we can deduce the certain conclusion that Bill Gates will die.

The Declaration introduces a similar kind of argument when it says, "We hold these truths to be self-evident." At first glance, it looks as if we just have three separate self-evident truths. But if we look closer, we notice that our truths also represent an argument with two premises, which are true from sense perception, and a conclusion that is deduced from them.

Here's how it works.

After the Declaration says, "We hold these truths to be self-evident," the text proceeds to identify three truths: one about human beings, one about government, and one about revolution. The truth about human beings, though, is a three-part truth.

It is self-evidently true:

> *that all men are created equal, that they are endowed by their Creator with certain unalienable Rights, that among these are Life, Liberty and the pursuit of Happiness.*

15

How do these three claims make a single truth? Human beings are equal in all acquiring the same rights at the moment of their creation. From the moment of their emergence as living beings, human beings seek to survive, to be free from domination, and to be happy. This is something we simply observe about human beings. For that matter, we observe it about other animals, too. For instance, I've never seen a cat that didn't want to survive, to be free, and to be happy.

Then, with the next truth, we come to the difference between human beings and animals. The Declaration says, it is self-evidently true

—*That to secure these rights, Governments are instituted among Men, deriving their just powers from the consent of the governed.*

This is a truly salient point. The signers are saying that, in contrast to the animal kingdom, the world of human beings is indeed full of kingdoms and other kinds of governments. The so-called animal kingdom is a kingdom only metaphorically. There are no governments among animals. Animals have social hierarchies, and they have their own methods for seeking their survival, freedom, and happiness, but human beings use politics. Human beings display self-conscious thought about social organization, and politics is the activity that flows from that self-consciousness about power. Again, this is simply a matter of observation. From the beginning of time to the present day, human beings have formed governments. Human beings have done this just as regularly as birds build nests.

Then the Declaration puts these first two truths together. Since 20 human beings seek their own survival, freedom, and happiness, and since they have a special tool for doing so — namely, the ability to form governments — it makes sense for them to stick with any particular version of that tool, any particular government, only if it's doing the work it's been built to do.

Compare it to a bird with a nest. What's the point of a bird's staying in a nest if it turns out that the nest has been built out of material inimical or poisonous to the bird? What's the use, in other words, of having a government, if it doesn't serve the purposes of protecting life, liberty, and the pursuit of happiness for which governments are set up in the first place?

The Declaration puts it this way: It is self-evidently true

— That whenever any Form of Government becomes destructive of these ends, it is the Right of the People to alter or to abolish it, and to institute new Government, laying its foundation on such principles and organizing its powers in such form, as to them shall seem most likely to effect their Safety and Happiness.

From the facts, first, that people are simply wired, as are all animals, to seek their survival, freedom, and happiness, and, second, that human beings use governments as their central instrument for protecting their life, liberty, and pursuit of happiness, we can deduce that people have a right to change governments that aren't working for them.

This makes an argument that goes like this:

PREMISE 1: All people have rights to life, liberty, and the pursuit of happiness.

PREMISE 2: Properly constituted government is necessary to their securing their rights

CONCLUSION: All people have a right to a properly constituted government.

In fact, a philosopher would say that a premise is missing from that argument and that the full formally valid syllogism would look like this: 25

PREMISE 1: All people have rights to life, liberty, and the pursuit of happiness.

PREMISE 2: Properly constituted government is necessary to their securing these rights.

PREMISE 3: [All people have a right to whatever is necessary to secure what they have a right to].

CONCLUSION: All people have a right to a properly constituted government.

Politicians often craft maxims simply by dropping out pieces of their argument. With the missing premise inserted, the Declaration's truths fit together almost like the pieces of a mathematical equation; we intuitively feel the puzzle pieces snap together. That is how self-evidence should feel.

academic literacies · rhetorical situations · genres · processes · strategies · research MLA / APA · media / design · readings

Allen's analysis focuses on the Declaration's second sentence, unpacking its logic through a careful examination of its key term, "self-evident," and explaining how the rest of the sentence forms a syllogism that "snaps together." She looks carefully at every word, restricting her analysis here to a very brief part of the text — but provides insights that illuminate the whole document.

SAM ANDERSON

Just One More Game . . . : Angry Birds, Farmville, and Other Hyperaddictive Stupid Games

Journalist and critic Sam Anderson analyzes the lure of video games in this essay, which appeared in print in the New York Times Sunday Magazine *and simultaneously online at* <u>nytimes.com</u>. *In addition to the text reproduced here, the online version, available via* <u>wwnorton.com/write/fieldguidelinks</u>, *includes illustrations, a simulation of the online game Kick Ass, and personal narratives of Anderson's video gaming experiences.*

In 1989, as communism was beginning to crumble across Eastern Europe, just a few months before protesters started pecking away at the Berlin Wall, the Japanese game-making giant Nintendo reached across the world to unleash upon America its own version of freedom. The new product was the Game Boy — a hand-held, battery-powered plastic slab that promised to set gamers loose, after all those decades of sweaty bondage, from the tyranny of rec rooms and pizza parlors and arcades.

The unit came bundled with a single cartridge: *Tetris*, a simple but addictive puzzle game whose goal was to rotate falling blocks — over and over and over and over and over and over and over — in order to build the most efficient possible walls. (Well, it was complicated. You were both building walls and not building walls; if you built them right, the walls disappeared, thereby ceasing to be walls.) This turned out to be a perfect symbiosis of game and platform. *Tetris*'s graphics were simple enough to work on the Game Boy's small gray-scale screen; its motion was slow enough not to blur; its action was a repetitive, storyless puzzle that could be picked up, with no loss of potency, at any moment, in any situation. The pairing went on to sell more than 70 million copies, spreading the freedom of compulsive wall-building into every breakfast nook and bank line in the country.

And so a tradition was born: a tradition I am going to call (half descriptively, half out of revenge for all the hours I've lost to them) "stupid games." In the nearly 30 years since *Tetris*'s invention — and especially over the last five, with the rise of smartphones — *Tetris* and its offspring (*Angry Birds*, *Bejeweled*, *Fruit Ninja*, etc.) have colonized our pockets and our brains and shifted the entire economic model of the video-game industry. Today we are living, for better and worse, in a world of stupid games.

Game-studies scholars (there are such things) like to point out that games tend to reflect the societies in which they are created and played. Monopoly, for instance, makes perfect sense as a product of the 1930s — it allowed anyone, in the middle of the Depression, to play at being a tycoon. Risk, released in the 1950s, is a stunningly literal expression of cold-war realpolitik. Twister is the translation, onto a game board, of the mid-1960s sexual revolution. One critic called it "sex in a box."

Tetris was invented exactly when and where you would expect — 5 in a Soviet computer lab in 1984 — and its game play reflects this origin. The enemy in *Tetris* is not some identifiable villain (Donkey Kong, Mike Tyson, Carmen Sandiego) but a faceless, ceaseless, reasonless force that threatens constantly to overwhelm you, a churning production of blocks against which your only defense is a repetitive, meaningless sorting. It is bureaucracy in pure form, busywork with no aim or end, impossible to avoid or escape. And the game's final insult is that it annihilates free will. Despite its obvious futility, somehow we can't make ourselves stop rotating blocks. *Tetris*, like all the stupid games it spawned, forces us to choose to punish ourselves.

In 2009, 25 years after the invention of *Tetris*, a nearly bankrupt Finnish company called Rovio hit upon a similarly perfect fusion of game and device: *Angry Birds*. The game involves launching peevish birds at green pigs hiding inside flimsy structures. Its basic mechanism — using your index finger to pull back a slingshot, over and over and over and over and over and over and over — was the perfect use of the new technology of the touch screen: simple enough to lure a suddenly immense new market of casual gamers, satisfying enough to hook them.

Within months, *Angry Birds* became the most popular game on the iPhone, then spread across every other available platform. Today it has been downloaded, in its various forms, more than 700 million times. It has also inspired a disturbingly robust merchandising empire: films, T-shirts, novelty slippers, even plans for *Angry Birds* "activity parks" featuring play equipment for kids. For months, a sign outside my local auto-repair shop promised, "Free *Angry Birds* pen with service." The game's latest iteration, *Angry Birds Space*, appeared a couple weeks ago with a promotional push from Wal-Mart, T-Mobile, National Geographic Books, MTV and NASA. (There was an announcement on the International Space Station.) *Angry Birds*, it seems, is our *Tetris*: the string of digital prayer beads that our entire culture can twiddle in moments of rapture or anxiety — economic, political or existential. . . .

Humans have always played stupid games. Dice are older than recorded history. Ancient Egyptians played a board game called Senet, which archaeologists believe was something like sacred backgammon. We have rock-paper-scissors, tick-tack-toe, checkers, dominoes and solitaire — small, abstract games in which sets of simple rules play out in increasingly complex scenarios. (Chess, you might say, is the king of stupid games: the tide line where stupid games meet genius.)

But pre-*Tetris* games were different in a primal way. They required human opponents or at least equipment — the manipulation of three-dimensional objects in space. When you sat down to play them, chances were you meant to sit down and play them.

Stupid games, on the other hand, are rarely occasions in themselves. They are designed to push their way through the cracks of other occasions. We play them incidentally, ambivalently, compulsively, almost accidentally. They're less an activity in our day than a blank space in our day; less a pursuit than a distraction from other pursuits. You glance down to check your calendar and suddenly it's 40 minutes later and there's only one level left before you jump to the next stage, so you might as well just launch another bird. . . . 10

Then, in 2007, the iPhone appeared. Games were much easier to develop and easier to distribute through Apple's app store. Instead of just passing their work around to one another on blogs, independent game designers suddenly had a way to reach everyone — not just hardcore gamers, but their mothers, their mailmen and their college professors. Consumers who never would have put a quarter into an arcade or even set eyes on an Xbox 360 were now carrying a sophisticated game console with them, all the time, in their pockets or their purses.

This had a profound impact on game design. In the era of consoles, most games were designed to come to life on a stationary piece of furniture — a television or a desktop computer. The games were built accordingly, around long narratives (quests, wars, the rise and fall of civilizations) that could be explored comfortably while sitting cross-legged on a living-room carpet.

Smartphone games are built on a very different model. The iPhone's screen is roughly the size of a playing card; it responds not to the fast-twitch button combos of a controller but to more intuitive and intimate motions: poking, pinching, tapping, tickling. This has encouraged a very different kind of game: Tetris-like little puzzles, broken into discrete bits, designed to be played anywhere, in any context, without a manual, by any level of player. (Charles Pratt, a researcher in New York University's Game Center, refers to such games as "knitting games.") You could argue that these are *pure* games: perfectly designed minisystems engineered to take us directly to the core of gaming pleasure without the distraction of narrative. The *Angry Birds* creators like to compare their game with *Super Mario Brothers*. But the first and simplest level of *Super Mario Brothers* takes about a minute and a half to finish. The first level of *Angry Birds* takes around 10 seconds. . . .

There are people who see the proliferation of stupid games as a good thing. In fact, they believe that games may be the answer to all of humanity's problems. In her book *Reality Is Broken*, Jane McGonigal argues that play is possibly the best, healthiest, most productive activity a human can undertake — a gateway to our ideal psychological state. Games aren't an escape from reality, McGonigal contends, they are an optimal form of engaging it. In fact, if we could just find a way to impose game mechanics on top of everyday life, humans would be infinitely better off. We might even use these approaches to help solve real-world problems like obesity, education and government abuse. Some proponents point to successful examples of games applied to everyday life: Weight Watchers and frequent-flier miles, for example.

Corporations, of course, have been using similar strategies for decades, hooking consumers on products by giving them constant small victories for spending money (think of the old Monopoly game

15

promotion at McDonald's). The buzzword for this is "gamification" and the ubiquity of computers and smartphones has only supercharged these tendencies. Gartner, a technology research firm, predicted last year that, in the near future, "a gamified service for consumer-goods marketing and customer retention will become as important as Facebook, eBay or Amazon." Companies have already used online games to sneakily advertise sugary cereals directly to children.

Although there is a certain utopian appeal to McGonigal's "games for change" model, I worry about the dystopic potential of gamification. Instead of just bombarding us with jingles, corporations will be able to inject their messages directly into our minds with ads disguised as games. Gamification seeks to turn the world into one giant chore chart covered with achievement stickers — the kind of thing parents design for their children — though it raises the potentially terrifying question of who the parents are. This, I fear, is the dystopian future of stupid games: amoral corporations hiring teams of behavioral psychologists to laser-target our addiction cycles for profit. . . .

[Game designer Frank] Lantz seemed undisturbed by the dark side of stupid games, like addiction or cynical corporate hijacking. He said that real games are far too fragile and complex to be engineered by corporations and that their appeal goes much deeper than reward schedules. "It's as hard to make a really good game as it is to make a really good movie or opera or hat," he told me. "Sure, there's mathematics to it, but it's also a piece of culture. The type of game you play is also a part of how you think about yourself as a person. There's no formula that's going to solve that equation. It's impossible, because it's infinitely deep and wonderful."

As for my nightmare vision of a world splintered by addiction to stupid games, Lantz had a different perspective. He said that he liked to think *Drop7* [a game Lantz designed that combines elements of *Tetris* and Sudoku] was not only addictive but also, on some level, about addiction. Games, he told me, are like "homebrew neuroscience" — "a little digital drug you can use to run experiments on your own brain." Part of the point of letting them seduce you, as Lantz sees it, is to come out the other side a more interesting and self-aware person; more conscious of your habits, weaknesses, desires and strengths. "It's like heroin that is abstracted or compressed or stylized," he said. "It gives you a window into your brain that doesn't crush your brain."

I tried to think about what — if anything — I had learned from this window into my brain. Like their spiritual forefather, *Tetris*, most stupid games are about walls: building them, scaling them, knocking them down. Walls made of numbers, walls made of digital bricks, walls with green pigs hiding behind them. They're like miniature boot camps of containment. Ultimately, I realized, these games are also about a more subtle and mysterious form of wall-building: the internal walls we build to compartmentalize our time, our attention, our lives. The legendary game designer Sid Meier once defined a game as, simply, "a series of interesting choices." Maybe that's the secret genius of stupid games: they force us to make a series of interesting choices about what matters, moment to moment, in our lives. . . .

■■ For four more textual analyses, see CHAPTER 60.

Anderson describes Tetris and other games clearly and outlines their relationship to older "stupid games." He interprets the "gamification" of American culture positively and provides evidence from experts as well as the games themselves, including the playable online Kick Ass game, to support his interpretation.

Key Features / Textual Analysis

A summary or description of the text. Your readers may not know the text you are analyzing, so you need to include it or tell them about it before you analyze it. Allen's text, the Declaration of Independence, is well known, so she assumes that her readers already know its first sentences. Texts that are not so well known require a more detailed summary or description. For example, Berry includes the ads she analyzes and also describes them in detail.

Attention to the context. Texts don't exist in isolation: they are influenced by and contribute to ongoing conversations, controversies, debates, and cultural trends. To understand a particular text, you need to understand its larger context. Anderson begins by offering a brief history of handheld video games, and Berry places shoe ads into the context of fashion advertising.

A clear interpretation or judgment.   Your goal in analyzing a text is to lead readers through careful examination of the text to some kind of interpretation or reasoned judgment, sometimes announced clearly in a thesis statement. When you interpret something, you explain what you think it means, as Berry does when she argues that the two ads suggest that our clothing choices enhance our individuality. She might instead have chosen to judge the effectiveness of the ads, perhaps noting that they promise the impossible: uniqueness through mass-produced clothing. Anderson judges "stupid games" to be positive, as "they force us to make a series of interesting choices about what matters, moment to moment, in our lives."

Reasonable support for your conclusions.   Written analysis of a text is generally supported by evidence from the text itself and sometimes from other sources as well. The writer might support his or her interpretation by quoting words or passages from a verbal text or referring to images in a visual text. Allen, for example, interprets the term "self-evident" by referring to formal logic, Venn diagrams, and the Catholic *Credo*. Berry examines patterns of both language and images in her analysis of two ads. Anderson quotes expert game designers to support his thesis. Note that the support you offer for your interpretation need only be "reasonable" — there is never only one way to interpret something.

A GUIDE TO WRITING TEXTUAL ANALYSES

Choosing a Text to Analyze

Most of the time, you will be assigned a text or a type of text to analyze: a poem in a literature class, the work of a political philosopher in a political science class, a speech in a history or communications course, a painting or sculpture in an art class, a piece of music in a music theory course. If you must choose a text to analyze, look for one that suits the demands of the assignment—one that is neither too large or complex to analyze thoroughly (a Dickens novel or a Beethoven symphony is probably too big) nor too brief or limited to generate sufficient material (a ten-second TV news brief or a paragraph from *Moneyball* would probably be too small). You might also choose to analyze three or four texts by examining elements common to all. Be sure you understand what the assignment asks you to do, and ask your instructor for clarification if you're not sure.

Considering the Rhetorical Situation

55–56 **PURPOSE** Why are you analyzing this text? To demonstrate that you understand it? To show how its argument works — or doesn't? Or are you using the text as a way to make some other point?

57–60 **AUDIENCE** Are your readers likely to know your text? How much detail will you need to supply?

64–67 **STANCE** What interests you (or not) about your text? Why? What do you know or believe about it, and how will your own beliefs affect your analysis?

68–70 **MEDIA / DESIGN** Will your analysis appear in print? on the web? How will your medium affect your analysis? If you are analyzing a visual text, you will probably need to include an image of it.

Generating Ideas and Text

In analyzing a written text, your goal is to understand what it says, how it works, and what it means. To do so, you may find it helpful to follow a certain sequence: read, respond, summarize, analyze, and draw conclusions from your analysis.

Read to see what the text says. Start by reading carefully, to get a sense of what it says. This means first skimming to **PREVIEW THE TEXT**, rereading 12–13 16–18 for the main ideas, then questioning and **ANNOTATING**.

14 Consider your **INITIAL RESPONSE**. Once you have a sense of what the text says, what do you think? What's your reaction to the argument, the

academic literacies · rhetorical situations · genres · processes · strategies · research MLA / APA · media / design · readings

tone, the language, the images? Do you find the text difficult? puzzling? Do you agree with what the writer says? disagree? agree *and* disagree? Your reaction to a text can color your analysis, so start by thinking about how you react — and why. Consider both your intellectual and any emotional reactions. Identify places in the text that trigger or account for those reactions. If you think that you have no particular reaction or response, try to articulate why. Whatever your response, think about what accounts for it.

Next, consolidate your understanding of the text by **SUMMARIZING** what it says in your own words. You may find it helpful to **OUTLINE** its main ideas. For instance, Allen carefully maps out the parts of the syllogism at the heart of her analysis.

● 486–87
◎ 293–95

Decide what you want to analyze. Having read the text carefully, think about what you find most interesting or intriguing and why. Does the argument interest you? its logic? its attempt to create an emotional response? its reliance on the writer's credibility or reputation? its use of design to achieve its aims? its context? Does the text's language, imagery, or structure intrigue you? something else? You might begin your analysis by exploring what attracted your notice.

Think about the larger context. All texts are part of larger conversations with other texts that have dealt with the same topic. An essay arguing for handgun trigger locks is part of an ongoing conversation about gun control, which is itself part of a conversation on individual rights and responsibilities. Academic texts include documentation in part to weave in voices from the conversation. And, in fact, any time you're reading to learn, you're probably reading for some larger context. Whatever your reading goals, being aware of that larger context can help you better understand what you're reading. Here are some specific aspects of the text to pay attention to:

- *Who else cares about this topic?* Especially when you're reading in order to learn about a topic, the texts you read will often reveal which people or groups are part of the conversation — and might be sources of further reading. For example, an essay describing the formation of Mammoth Cave could be of interest to geologists, spelunkers, travel writers, or tourists. If you're reading such an essay while doing research on the cave, you should consider how the audience addressed determines the nature of the information provided — and its suitability as a source for your research.

- **Ideas.** Does the text refer to any concepts or ideas that give you some sense that it's part of a larger conversation? An argument on airport security measures, for example, is part of larger conversations about government response to terrorism, the limits of freedom in a democracy, and the possibilities of using technology to detect weapons and explosives, among others.

- **Terms.** Is there any terminology or specialized language that reflects the writer's allegiance to a particular group or academic discipline? If you run across words like *false consciousness*, *ideology*, and *hegemony*, for example, you might guess the text was written by a Marxist scholar.

- **Citations.** Whom does the writer cite? Do the other writers have a particular academic specialty, belong to an identifiable intellectual school, share similar political leanings? If an article on politics cites Michael Moore and Barbara Ehrenreich in support of its argument, you might assume the writer holds liberal opinions; if it cites Rush Limbaugh and Sean Hannity, the writer is likely a conservative.

Write a brief paragraph describing the larger context surrounding the text and how that context affects your understanding of the text.

Consider what you know about the writer. What you know about the person who created a text can influence your understanding of it. His or her **CREDENTIALS**, other work, reputation, stance, and beliefs are all useful windows into understanding a text. You may need to conduct an online search to find information on the writer. Then write a sentence or two summarizing what you know about the writer and how that information affects your understanding of the text.

470 ●

Study how the text works. Written texts are made up of various components, including words, sentences, paragraphs, headings, lists,

punctuation — and sometimes images as well. Look for patterns in the way these components are used and try to decide what those patterns reveal about the text. How do they affect its message? See the sections on **THINKING ABOUT HOW THE TEXT WORKS** and **IDENTIFYING PATTERNS** for specific guidelines on examining patterns this way. Then write a sentence or two describing the patterns you've discovered and how they contribute to what the text says.

20–22
28–29

Analyze the argument. Every text makes an argument and provides some kind of support for it. An important part of understanding any text is to recognize its argument — what the writer wants the audience to believe, feel, or do. Here are some questions you'll want to consider when you analyze an argument:

- *What is the claim?* What is the main point the writer is trying to make? Is there a clearly stated **THESIS**, or is the thesis merely implied? Is it appropriately qualified?

345–47

- *What support does the writer offer for the claim?* What **REASONS** are given to support the claim? What **EVIDENCE** backs up those reasons? Facts? Statistics? Examples? Testimonials by authorities? Anecdotes or stories? Are the reasons and evidence appropriate, plausible, and sufficient? Are you convinced by them? If not, why not?

358–59

- *How does the writer appeal to readers?* Does he or she appeal to your **EMOTIONS**? rely on **LOGIC**? try to establish **COMMON GROUND**? demonstrate **CREDIBILITY**?

370
356–67
367

- *How evenhandedly does the writer present the argument?* Is there any mention of **COUNTERARGUMENTS**? If so, how does the writer deal with them? By refuting them? By acknowledging them and responding to them reasonably? Does the writer treat other arguments respectfully? dismissively?

367–69
369

- *Does the writer use any logical **FALLACIES**?* Are the arguments or beliefs of others distorted or exaggerated? Is the logic faulty?

370–72

- *What authorities or other sources of outside information does the writer use?* How are they used? How credible are they? Are they in any way biased or otherwise unreliable? Are they current?

- *How does the writer address you as the reader?*   Does the writer assume that readers know something about what is being discussed? Does his or her language include you or exclude you? (Hint: If you see the word *we*, do you feel included?) Do you sense that you and the writer share any beliefs or attitudes? If the writer is not writing to you, what audience is the target? How do you know?

Then write a brief paragraph summarizing the argument the text makes and the main way the writer argues it, along with your reactions to or questions about that argument.

In analyzing a visual text, your goal is to understand its intended effect on viewers as well as its actual effect, the ways it creates that effect, and its relationship to other texts. If the visual text accompanies a written one, you need to understand how the texts work together to convey a message or make an argument.

Describe the text.   Your first job is to examine the image carefully. Focus on specific details; given the increasing use of *Photoshop* and other digital image manipulation tools, you can usually assume that every detail in the image is intentional. Ask yourself these questions:

- What kind of image is it? Does it stand alone, or is it part of a group? Are there typical features of this kind of image that it includes — or lacks?

- What does the image show? What stands out? What is in the background? Are some parts of the image grouped together or connected? Or set apart from one another?

- As you look at the image, does the content seem far away, close up, or in between? Are you level with it, looking down from above, or looking up from below? What is the effect of your viewing position?

- Does the image tell or suggest a story, about what has happened (as in Berry's ad for Sorel shoes) or is about to happen?

- Does the image allude to or refer to anything else? For example, the Starbucks logo features the image of a Siren, the mythical beings who lured sailors to their doom.

Explore your response. Images, particularly those in advertisements, are often trying to persuade us to buy something or to feel, think, or behave a certain way. News photographs and online videos also try to evoke **EMOTIONAL** responses, from horror over murdered innocents to amusement at cute kittens. Think about your response:

◆ 370

- How does the image make you feel? What emotional response, if any, does the image make you feel? Sympathy? Concern? Anger? Happiness? Contentment? Something else?

- What does the image lead you to think about? What connections does it have to things in your life, in the news, in your knowledge of the world?

- Do the image and any words accompanying seem to be trying to persuade you to think or do something? Do they do so directly, such as by pointing out the virtues of a product (Buick Encore: "Sized to Fit Your Life")? Or indirectly, by setting a tone or establishing a mood (the Clarks shoe ad that Berry analyzes)?

- Does the **GENRE** affect your response? For example, do you expect to laugh at a comic? feel empathy with victims of a tragedy in a photo accompanying a news story? find a satirical editorial cartoon offensive?

▲ 71

Consider the context. Like written texts, visual texts are part of larger conversations with other texts that have dealt with the same topic or used similar imagery. This editorial cartoon on global warming, for example, is part of an ongoing conversation about climate change and the role our lifestyles play in it:

Consider what you know about the artist or sponsor. Editorial cartoons, like the one above, are usually signed, and information about the artist and his or her other work is usually readily available on the Web. Many commercials and advertisements, however, are created by ad agencies, so the organization or company that sponsored or posted the image should be identified and researched. How does that information affect your understanding of the text?

Decide on a focus for your analysis. What do you find most interesting about the text, and why? Its details and the way they work together

(or not)? The argument it makes? The way it uses images to appeal to its audience? The emotional response it evokes? The way any words and images work together to deliver a message? These are just some ways of thinking about a visual text, ones that can help you find a focus.

However you choose to focus your analysis, it should be limited in scope so that you can zero in on the details of the visual you're analyzing. Here, for example, is an excerpt from an essay by an art historian responding to a statement made by President Barack Obama that manufacturing skills may be worth more than a degree in art history.

> *"I promise you, folks can make a lot more potentially with skilled manufacturing or the trades than they might with an art history degree."* President Barack Obama

> Charged with interrogating this quote from the president, I Google "Obama art history." I click on the first result, a video from CNN, in which the quote is introduced by a gray-haired man in a dark and serious suit, standing in front of a bank of monitors in a digitally created nonspace. The camera cuts from this man to President Obama, who stands in shirtsleeves, his tie slightly loosened. His undershirt is visible through his buttondown under the intense light from what I assume is the work-day sun.

> Behind him is a crowd of men and women in more casual clothing, some wearing sweatshirts that have the name of a union printed across them. Their presence creates a spectrum of skin tones. Each person was clearly vetted for visual effect, as were the president's and the newscaster's costumes, the size of their flag lapel pins, the shape of the microphones they speak into, and the angle of the light on their faces. The president makes the comment in question, immediately declares his love for art history, and says that he doesn't want to get a bunch of angry emails from art historians. The crowd behind him laughs and the clip cuts off abruptly.

> A click away, I find a digitized copy of a handwritten note from President Obama, apologizing to an angry art history professor who emailed him to complain about his comments. The card on which the note is written is plain, undecorated save for two lines of text printed in a conservative, serif font in a shade of blue that is just on the vibrant side of navy — THE WHITE HOUSE — and under it in smaller letters,

WASHINGTON. Its tasteful, minimal aesthetic pulls double duty, meant to convey both populist efficiency (note the absence of gold gilding) and stern superiority (you know where Washington is, right?). It sets up a productive contrast with the friendliness of the president's own handwriting, particularly his looping signature, soft on the outside with a strong slash through the middle.

Like the video of the president's speech, it is a screen-scale tour de force of political imagecraft, certainly produced with the full knowledge that it would be digitized and go viral, at least among a particular demographic.

—Joel Parsons, "Richness in the Eye of the Beholder"

Parsons begins by describing the images — Obama's clothing, the people standing behind him, the letterhead on his note card, his "looping

President Obama speaking at a General Electric plant in Waukesha, Wisconsin, 2014.

THE WHITE HOUSE
WASHINGTON

Ann —

Let me apologize for my off-the-cuff remarks. I was making a point about the job market, not the value of art history. As it so happens, art history was one of my favorite subjects in high school, and it has helped me take in a great deal of joy in my life that

I might otherwise have missed.

So please pass on my apology for the glib remark to the entire department, and understand that I was trying to encourage young people who may not be predisposed to a four year college experience to be open to technical training that can lead them to an honorable career.

Sincerely,

Obama's apology note to Ann Johns, art history professor at the University of Texas at Austin.

signature" — followed by an analysis of how every aspect of the video and the note card was "certainly produced with the full knowledge that it would be digitized and go viral." Notice as well that Parsons's analysis focuses more on the visual aspects of the video and note card than on what was said or written. And in a part of his essay not shown here, he notes that his analysis is grounded in "tools . . . he learned in a first-year art history course" — a not-so-subtle response to what President Obama said.

Coming Up with a Thesis

355–73 ◆

When you analyze a text, you are basically **ARGUING** that the text should be read or seen in a certain way. Once you've studied the text thoroughly, you need to identify your analytical goal: do you want to show that the text has a certain meaning? uses certain techniques to achieve its purposes? tries to influence its audience in particular ways? relates to some larger context in some significant manner? should be taken seriously — or not?

345–47 ◆

something else? Come up with a tentative **THESIS** to guide your thinking and analyzing — but be aware that your thesis may change as you continue to work.

Ways of Organizing a Textual Analysis

Examine the information you have to see how it supports or complicates your thesis. Look for clusters of related information that you can use to

293–95 ○

structure an **OUTLINE**. Your analysis might be structured in at least two ways. You might, as Anderson does, discuss patterns, elements, or themes that run through the text. Alternatively, you might analyze each text or section of text separately, as Berry does. Following are graphic representations of some ways of organizing a textual analysis.

[Thematically]

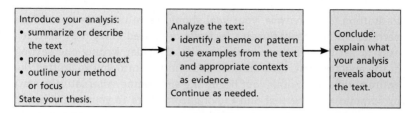

[Part by part, or text by text]

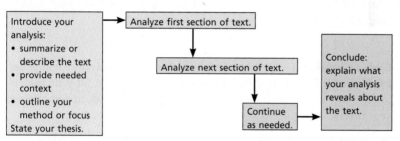

[Spatially, as the text is likely to be experienced by viewers]

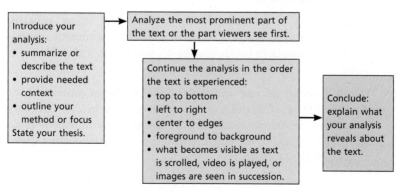

Writing Out a Draft

In drafting your analysis, your goal should be to integrate the various parts into a smoothly flowing, logically organized essay. However, it's easy to get bogged down in the details. Consider writing one section of the analysis first, then another and another until you've drafted the entire middle; then draft your beginning and ending. Alternatively, start by summarizing the text and moving from there to your analysis and then to your ending. However you do it, you need to support your analysis with evidence: from the text itself (as Berry's analysis of advertisements does), or from **RESEARCH** on the larger context of the text (as Allen does), or by incorporating various experts' views of your subject (as Anderson does).

433

331–38

Draft a BEGINNING. The beginning of an essay that analyzes a text generally has several tasks: to introduce or summarize the text for your readers, to offer any necessary information on the larger context, and to present your thesis.

486–87

- *Summarize or describe the text.* If the text is one your readers don't know, you need to **SUMMARIZE** or **DESCRIBE** it early on to show that you understand it fully. For example, Berry begins each analysis of a shoe advertisement with a description of its content.

- *Show the text.* If you're analyzing a visual text online, consider starting off with an image, a video, or a link to it or something similar, as Anderson does by illustrating his essay with a playable video game.

- *Provide a context for your analysis.* If there is a larger context that is significant for your analysis, you might mention it in your introduction. Allen does this by comparing the Declaration's statement about self-evident truths to the statements of belief in the Apostles' Creed of the Catholic Church.

- *State your* **THESIS**. Berry ends her first paragraph by stating her thesis explicitly: These ads "for Clarks and Sorel. . . encourage us to break free from the standard beauty mold and be ourselves; using mostly imagery, they remind us that being unique is the true origin of beauty."

345–47

Draft an ENDING. Think about what you want your readers to take away from your analysis, and end by getting them to focus on those thoughts.

338–42

- *Restate your thesis — and say why it matters.* Berry, for example, ends by asserting that the ads she examines invite women to "be ourselves" by "accessoriz[ing] our personalities."
- *Explain what your analysis reveals.* Your analysis should tell your readers something about the way the text works or about what it means or says. Allen, for example, concludes by noting that "the Declaration's truths fit together almost like the pieces of a mathematical equation; we intuitively feel the puzzle pieces snap together. That is how self-evidence should feel."

Come up with a TITLE. A good title indicates something about the subject of your analysis — and makes readers want to see what you have to say about it. Berry's title provides a preview of her thesis that the ads she is analyzing are selling a vision of clothing as a vehicle for being unique, while Anderson's title tells us that his topic is video games while enticing us to read on with provocative language like "hyperaddictive" and "stupid."

344–45

Considering Matters of Design

- If you cite written text as evidence, be sure to set long quotations and **DOCUMENTATION** according to the style you're using.

496–99

604–5

- If your essay is lengthy, consider whether **HEADINGS** would make your analysis easier for readers to follow.

- If you're analyzing a visual text, include a copy of the image and a caption identifying it.

- If you're submitting your essay electronically, provide links to whatever text you are analyzing.

- If you're analyzing an image or a screen shot, consider annotating elements of it right on the image.

Getting Response and Revising

306–7

The following questions can help you and others study your draft with a critical eye. Make sure that anyone you ask to read and **RESPOND** to your text knows your purpose and audience.

- Is the beginning effective? Does it make a reader want to continue?

- Does the introduction provide an overview of your analysis? Is your thesis clear?

- Is the text described or summarized clearly and sufficiently?

- Is the analysis well organized and easy to follow? Do the parts fit together coherently? Does it read like an essay rather than a collection of separate bits of analysis?

- Does each part of the analysis relate to and support the thesis?

- Is anything confusing or in need of more explanation?

- Are all quotations accurate and correctly documented?

- Is it clear how the analysis leads to the interpretation? Is there adequate evidence to support the interpretation?

- Does the ending make clear what your analysis shows?

Then it's time to **REVISE**. Make sure your text appeals to your audience and think hard about whether it will achieve your purpose.

307–10

Editing and Proofreading

Readers equate correctness with competence. Once you've revised your draft, edit carefully:

- Is your **THESIS** clearly stated?
- Check all **QUOTATIONS**, **PARAPHRASES**, and **SUMMARIES** for accuracy and form. Be sure that each has the required **DOCUMENTATION**.
- Make sure that your analysis flows clearly from one point to the next and that you use **TRANSITIONS** to help readers move through your text.
- **PROOFREAD** your finished analysis carefully before turning it in.

345–47

478–90
496–99

349

316–17

Taking Stock of Your Work

Take stock of what you've written and learned by writing out answers to these questions:

- How did you go about analyzing the text? What methods did you use — and which ones were most helpful?
- How did you go about drafting your essay?
- How well did you organize your written analysis? What, if anything, could you do to make it easier to read?
- Did you provide sufficient evidence to support your analysis?
- What did you do especially well?
- What could still be improved?
- Did you include any visuals, and if so, what did they add? Could you have shown the same thing with words?

- How did other readers' responses influence your writing?
- What would you do differently next time?
- Are you pleased with your analysis? What did it teach you about the text you analyzed? Did it make you want to study more works by the same writer or artist?

IF YOU NEED MORE HELP

See Chapter 28 for guidelines on **DRAFTING**, Chapter 29 on **ASSESSING YOUR OWN WRITING**, Chapter 30 on **GETTING RESPONSE AND REVISING**, and Chapter 31 on **EDITING AND PROOFREADING**. See Chapter 32 if you are required to submit your analysis in a writing **PORTFOLIO**. See Chapter 56 for help **USING VISUALS**.

298–300 ○
301–5
306–12
313–17
318–28
607–15 ▫

✳ academic literacies
■ rhetorical situations
▲ genres
○ processes
◆ strategies
● research MLA / APA
▫ media / design
▌ readings

Reporting Information 12

Many kinds of writing report information. Newspapers report on local and world events; textbooks give information about biology, history, writing; websites provide information about products (*jcrew.com*), people (*pharrellwilliams.com*), institutions (*smithsonian.org*). We write out a lot of information ourselves, from a note we post on our door saying we've gone to choir practice to a text we send to tell a friend where to meet us for dinner and how to get there.

College assignments often call for reporting information as well. In a *history* class, you may be assigned to report what you've learned about the state of U.S. relations with Japan just before the bombing of Pearl Harbor. A *biology* course may require you to report the effects of an experiment in which plants are deprived of sunlight for different periods of time. In a *nursing* class, you may have to report the changes in a patient's symptoms after the administration of a particular drug.

This chapter focuses on reports that are written to inform readers about a particular topic. Very often this kind of writing calls for some kind of research: you need to know your subject in order to report on it! When you write to report information, you are the expert. We'll begin with three good examples, the first annotated to show the key features found in most reports.

MICHAELA CULLINGTON

Does Texting Affect Writing?

This essay by a student at Marywood University was published in Young Scholars in Writing, *a journal of undergraduate writing published by the University of Missouri–Kansas City.*

It's taking over our lives. We can do it almost anywhere — walking to class, waiting in line at the grocery store, or hanging out at home. It's quick, easy, and convenient. It has become a concern of doctors, parents, and teachers alike. What is it? It's texting!

Text messaging — or texting, as it's more commonly called — is the process of sending and receiving typed messages via a cellular phone. It is a common means of communication among teenagers and is even becoming popular in the business world because it allows quick messages to be sent without people having to commit to a telephone conversation. A person is able to say what is needed, and the other person will receive the information and respond when it's convenient to do so.

Definitions of key terms.

In order to more quickly type what they are trying to say, many people use abbreviations instead of words. The language created by these abbreviations is called textspeak. Some people believe that using these abbreviations is hindering the writing abilities of students, and others argue that texting is actually having a positive effect on writing. In fact, it seems likely that texting has no significant effect on student writing.

Here's the thesis.

Concerns about Textspeak

A September 2008 article in *USA Today* entitled "Texting, Testing Destroys Kids' Writing Style" summarizes many of the most common complaints about the effect of texting. It states that according to the National Center for Education Statistics, only 25% of high school seniors are "proficient" writers. The article quotes Jacquie Ream, a former teacher and author of *K.I.S.S.— Keep It Short and Simple*, a guide for writing more effectively. Ream states, "[W]e have a whole generation being raised without communication skills." She blames the use of acronyms and shorthand in text messages for students' inability to spell and ultimately to write well. Ream also points out that students struggle to convey emotion in their writing because, as she states, in text messages "emotions are always sideways smiley faces."

Analysis of causes and effects.

This debate became prominent after some teachers began to believe   5 they were seeing a decline in the writing abilities of their students. Many attributed this perceived decline to the increasing popularity of text messaging and its use of abbreviations. Naomi Baron, a linguistics professor at American University, blames texting for what she sees as the fact that "so much of American society has become sloppy and laissez faire about

academic literacies | rhetorical situations | genres | processes | strategies | research MLA / APA | media / design | readings

the mechanics of writing" ("Should"). Teachers report finding "2" for "to," "gr8" for "great," "dat" for "that," and "wut" for "what," among other examples of textspeak, in their students' writing. A Minnesota teacher of the seventh and ninth grades says that she has to spend extra time in class editing papers and must "explicitly" remind her students that it is not acceptable to use text slang and abbreviations in writing (Walsh). Another English teacher believes that text language has become "second nature" to her students (Carey); they are so used to it that they do not even catch themselves doing it.

Many also complain that because texting does not stress the importance of punctuation, students are neglecting it in their formal writing. Teachers say that their students are forgetting commas, apostrophes, and even capital letters to begin sentences. Another complaint is that text messages lack emotion. Many argue that texts lack feeling because of their tendency to be short, brief, and to the point. Because students are not able to communicate emotion effectively through texts, some teachers worry, they may lose the ability to do so in writing.

To get a more personal perspective on the question of how teachers perceive texting to be influencing student writing, I interviewed two of my former high school teachers — my junior-year English teacher and my senior-year theology teacher. Both teachers stress the importance of writing in their courses. They maintain that they notice text abbreviations in their students' writing often. To correct this problem, they point it out when it occurs and take points off for its use. They also remind their students to use proper sentence structure and complete sentences. The English teacher says that she believes texting inhibits good writing — it reinforces simplistic writing that may be acceptable for conversation but is "not so good for critical thinking or analysis." She suggests that texting tends to generate topic sentences without emphasizing the following explanation. According to these teachers, then, texting is inhibiting good writing. However, their evidence is limited, based on just a few personal experiences rather than on a significant amount of research.

Responses to Concerns about Textspeak

In response to these complaints that texting is having a negative impact on student writing, others insist that texting should be viewed as beneficial because it provides students with motivation to write, practice in specific writing skills, and an opportunity to gain confidence in their writing. For example, Betty Sternberg and her coauthors argue that texting is a good way to motivate students: teens enjoy texting, and if they frequently write through texts, they will be more motivated to write formally. Texting also helps to spark students' creativity, these authors argue, because they are always coming up with new ways to express their ideas (417).

In addition, because they are engaging in written communication rather than oral speech, texting teens learn how to convey their message to a reader in as few words as possible. In his book *Txtng: The Gr8 Db8*, David Crystal discusses a study that concludes that texting actually helps foster "the ability to summarize and express oneself concisely" in writing (168). Furthermore, Crystal explains that texting actually helps people to "sharpen their diplomatic skills . . . [because] it allows more time to formulate their thoughts and express them carefully" (168). One language arts teacher from Minnesota believes that texting helps students develop their own "individual voice" (qtd. in Walsh). Perfecting such a voice allows the writer to offer personal insights and express feelings that will interest and engage readers.

Synthesis of various sources of information. Quotations are introduced with signal phrases.

Supporters of texting also argue that it not only teaches elements 10 of writing but provides extra practice to those who struggle with the conventions of writing. As Crystal points out, children who struggle with literacy will not choose to use a technology that requires them to do something that is difficult for them. However, if they do choose to text, the experience will help them "overcome their awkwardness and develop their social and communication skills" (*Txtng* 171). Shirley Holm, a junior high school teacher, describes texting as a "comfortable form of communication" (qtd. in Walsh). Teenagers are used to texting, enjoy doing so, and as a result are always writing. Through this experience of writing in ways they enjoy, they can learn to take pleasure in writing formally. If students are continually writing in some form, they will eventually develop better skills.

Furthermore, those who favor texting explain that with practice comes the confidence and courage to try new things, which some observers believe they are seeing happen with writing as a result of texting. Teenagers have, for example, created an entirely new language — one that uses abbreviations and symbols instead of words, does not require punctuation, and uses short, incomplete phrases throughout the entire

academic literacies   rhetorical situations   genres   processes   strategies   research MLA / APA   media / design   readings

conversation. It's a way of speaking that is a language in and of itself. Crystal, among others, sees this "language evolution" as a positive effect of texting; he seems, in fact, fascinated that teenagers are capable of creating such a phenomenon, which he describes as the "latest manifestation of the human ability" (*Txtng* 175). David Warlick, a teacher and author of books about technology in the classroom, would agree with Crystal. He believes students should be given credit for "inventing a new language ideal for communicating in a high-tech world" (qtd. in Carey).

Methods

I decided to conduct my own research into this controversy. I wanted to get different, more personal, perspectives on the issue. First, I surveyed seven students on their opinions about the impact of texting on writing. Second, I questioned two high school teachers, as noted above. Finally, in an effort to compare what students are actually doing to people's perceptions of what they are doing, I analyzed student writing samples for instances of textspeak.[1]

To let students speak for themselves, I created a list of questions for seven high school and college students, some of my closest and most reliable friends. Although the number of respondents was small, I could trust my knowledge of them to help me interpret their responses. In addition, these students are very different from one another, and I believed their differences would allow for a wide array of thoughts and opinions on the issue. I was thus confident in the reliability and diversity of their answers but was cautious not to make too many assumptions because of the small sample size.

Firsthand research: interviews and survey.

I asked the students how long they had been texting; how often they texted; what types of abbreviations they used most and how often they used them; and whether they noticed themselves using any type of textspeak in their formal writing. In analyzing their responses, I looked for commonalities to help me draw conclusions about the students' texting habits and if/how they believed their writing was affected.

I created a list of questions for teachers similar to the one for the students and asked two of my high school teachers to provide their input. I asked if they had noticed their students using textspeak in their writing assignments and, if so, how they dealt with it. I also asked if they believed texting had a positive or negative effect on writing. Next, I asked if they were texters themselves. And, finally, I solicited their

15

opinions on what they believed should be done to prevent teens from using text abbreviations and other textspeak in their writing.

I was surprised at how different the students' replies and opinions were from the teachers'. I decided to find out for myself whose impressions were more accurate by comparing some students' actual writing with students' and teachers' perceptions of that writing. To do this I looked at twenty samples of student writing — end-of-semester research arguments written in two first-year college writing courses with different instructors. The topics varied from increased airport security after September 11 to the weapons of the Vietnam War to autism, and lengths ranged from eight to ten pages. To analyze the papers for the presence of textspeak, I looked closely for use of abbreviations and other common slang terms, especially those usages which the students had stated in their surveys were most common. These included "hbu" ("How about you?"); "gtg" ("Got to go"); and "cuz" ("because"). I also looked for the numbers 2 and 4 used instead of the words "to" and "for."

Comparison and contrast.

Discussion of Findings

My research suggests that texting actually has a minimal effect on student writing. It showed that students do not believe textspeak is appropriate in formal writing assignments. They recognize the difference between texting friends and writing formally and know what is appropriate in each situation. This was proven true in the student samples, in which no examples of textspeak were used. Many experts would agree that there is no harm in textspeak, as long as students continue to be taught and reminded that occasions where formal language is expected are not the place for it. As Crystal explains, the purpose of the abbreviations used in text messages is not to replace language but rather to make quick communications shorter and easier, since in a standard text message, the texter is allowed only 160 characters for a communication ("Texting" 81).

Dennis Baron, an English and linguistics professor at the University of Illinois, has done much research on the effect of technology on writing, and his findings are aligned with those of my own study. In his book *A Better Pencil: Readers, Writers, and the Digital Revolution,* he concludes that students do not use textspeak in their writing. In fact, he suggests students do not even use abbreviations in their text messages very often. Baron says that college students have "put away such

Summary and quotations of sources.

academic literacies | rhetorical situations | genres | processes | strategies | research MLA / APA | media / design | readings

childish things, and many of them had already abandoned such signs of middle-school immaturity in high school" (qtd. in Golden).

In surveying the high school and college students, I found that most have been texting for a few years, usually starting around ninth grade. The students said they generally text between thirty and a hundred messages every day but use abbreviations only occasionally, with the most common being "lol" ("Laugh out loud"), "gtg" ("Got to go"), "hbu" ("How about you?"), "cuz" ("because"), and "jk" ("Just kidding"). None of them believed texting abbreviations were acceptable in formal writing. In fact, research has found that most students report that they do not use textspeak in formal writing. As one Minnesota high school student says, "[T]here is a time and a place for everything," and formal writing is not the place for communicating the way she would if she were texting her friends (qtd. in Walsh). Another student admits that in writing for school she sometimes finds herself using these abbreviations. However, she notices and corrects them before handing in her final paper (Carey). One teacher reports that, despite texting, her students' "formal writing remains solid." She occasionally sees an abbreviation; however, it is in informal, "warm-up" writing. She believes that what students do in everyday writing is up to them as long as they use standard English in formal writing (qtd. in Walsh).

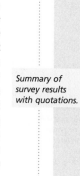

Summary of survey results with quotations.

Also supporting my own research findings are those from a study which took place at a midwestern research university. This study involved eighty-six students who were taking an Introduction to Education course at the university. The participants were asked to complete a questionnaire that included questions about their texting habits, the spelling instruction they had received, and their proficiency at spelling. They also took a standardized spelling test. Before starting the study, the researchers had hypothesized that texting and the use of abbreviations would have a negative impact on the spelling abilities of the students. However, they found that the results did not support their hypothesis. The researchers did note that text messaging is continuing to increase in popularity; therefore, this issue should continue to be examined (Shaw et al.).

Summary of research that supports her own.

20

I myself am a frequent texter. I chat with my friends from home every day through texting. I also use texting to communicate with my school friends, perhaps to discuss what time we are going to meet for dinner or to ask quick questions about homework. According to my cell phone bill, I send and receive around 6,400 texts a month. In the messages I send, I

Pertinent personal experience.

rarely notice myself using abbreviations. The only time I use them is if I do not have time to write out the complete phrase. However, sometimes I find it more time-consuming to try to figure out how to abbreviate something so that my message will still be comprehensible.

Since I rarely use abbreviations in my texting, I never use them in my formal writing. I know that they are unacceptable and that it would make me look unintelligent if I included acronyms and symbols instead of proper and formal language. I also have not noticed an effect on my spelling as a result of texting. I am confident in my spelling abilities, and even when I use an abbreviation, I know how to spell the word(s) it stands for.

Conclusion: summary of research and restatement of claim.

On the basis of my own research, expert research, and personal observations, I can confidently state that texting is not interfering with students' use of standard written English and has no effect on their writing abilities in general. It is interesting to look at the dynamics of the arguments over these issues. Teachers and parents who claim that they are seeing a decline in the writing abilities of their students and children mainly support the negative-impact argument. Other teachers and researchers suggest that texting provides a way for teens to practice writing in a casual setting and thus helps prepare them to write formally. Experts and students themselves, however, report that they see no effect, positive or negative. Anecdotal experiences should not overshadow the actual evidence.

Note

1. All participants in the study have given permission for their responses to be published.

Works Cited

Baron, Dennis. *A Better Pencil: Readers, Writers, and the Digital Revolution.* Oxford UP, 2009.

Carey, Bridget. "The Rise of Text, Instant Messaging Vernacular Slips into Schoolwork." *Miami Herald,* 6 Mar. 2007, *Academic OneFile,* search.ebscohost.com/login.aspx?.direct=true&db=edsgao&AN=edsgcl.160190230&site=eds-live. Accessed 27 Oct. 2009.

Crystal, David. "Texting." *ELT Journal,* vol. 62, no. 1, Jan. 2008, pp. 77-83. *Academic OneFile,* search.ebscohost.com/login.aspx?direct=true&db=edsgao&AN=edsgcl.177163353&site=eds-live. Accessed 8 Nov. 2009.

———. *Txtng: The Gr8 Db8.* Oxford UP, 2008.

Golden, Serena. Rev. of *A Better Pencil*. *Inside Higher Ed*, 18 Sept. 2009, insidehighered.com/news/2009/09/18/barron. Accessed 9 Nov. 2009.

Shaw, Donita M., et al. "An Exploratory Investigation into the Relationship between Text Messaging and Spelling." *New England Reading Association Journal*, vol. 43, no. 1, pp. 57-62. *EBSCO Discovery Service for Marywood University*, search.ebscohost.com/login.aspx?direct=true&db=edb&AN=25648081&site=eds-live. Accessed 8 Nov. 2009.

"Should We Worry or LOL?" *NEA Today*, Mar. 2004, p. 12. *ProQuest*, search.proquest.com/docview/198894194?accountid=42654. Accessed 27 Oct. 2009.

Sternberg, Betty, et al. "Enhancing Adolescent Literacy Achievement through Integration of Technology in the Classroom." *Reading Research Quarterly*, vol. 42, no. 3, July-Sept. 2007, pp. 416-20. *ProQuest*, search.proquest.com/docview/212128056?accountid=42654. Accessed 8 Nov. 2009.

"Texting, Testing Destroys Kids' Writing Style." *USA Today Magazine*, vol. 137, no. 2760, Sept. 2008, p. 8. *ProQuest*, search.proquest.com/docview/214595644?accountid=42654. Accessed 9 Nov. 2009.

Walsh, James. "Txt Msgs Creep in2 class; Some Say That's gr8." *McClatchy-Tribune News Service*, 23 Oct. 2007. *ProQuest*, search.proquest.com/docview/456879133?accountid=42654. Accessed 27 Oct. 2009.

Cullington's essay examines whether or not texting affects students' writing. Her information is based on both published scholarship and a small survey of students and teachers.

JAMES FALLOWS

Throwing Like a Girl

In the following report for the Atlantic, national correspondent James Fallows explores the art of throwing a baseball and the misconceptions that lead to the phrase "throwing like a girl."

Most people remember the 1994 baseball season for the way it ended — with a strike rather than a World Series. I keep thinking about the way it began. On opening day, April 4, Bill Clinton went to Cleveland and, like many Presidents before him, threw out a ceremonial first pitch. That same day Hillary Rodham Clinton went to Chicago and, like no First Lady before her, also threw out a first ball, at a Cubs game in Wrigley Field.

The next day photos of the Clintons in action appeared in newspapers around the country. Many papers, including *The New York Times* and *The Washington Post*, chose the same two photos to run. The one of Bill Clinton showed him wearing an Indians cap and warm-up jacket. The President, throwing lefty, had turned his shoulders sideways to the plate in preparation for delivery. He was bringing the ball forward from behind his head in a clean-looking throwing action as the photo was snapped. Hillary Clinton was pictured wearing a dark jacket, a scarf, and an oversized Cubs hat. In preparation for her throw she was standing directly facing the plate. A right-hander, she had the elbow of her throwing arm pointed out in front of her. Her forearm was tilted back, toward her shoulder. The ball rested on her upturned palm. As the picture was taken, she was in the middle of an action that can only be described as throwing like a girl.

The phrase "throwing like a girl" has become an embattled and offensive one. Feminists smart at its implication that to do something "like a girl" is to do it the wrong way. Recently, on the heels of the O. J. Simpson case, a book appeared in which the phrase was used to help explain why male athletes, especially football players, were involved in so many assaults against women. Having been trained (like most American boys) to dread the accusation of doing anything "like a girl," athletes were said to grow into the assumption that women were valueless, and natural prey.

Hillary and Bill Clinton throw the first ball at two games in 1994.

I grant the justice of such complaints. I am attuned to the hurt caused by similar broad-brush stereotypes when they apply to groups I belong to—"dancing like a white man," for instance, or "speaking foreign languages like an American," or "thinking like a Washingtonian."

Still, whatever we want to call it, the difference between the two Clintons in what they were doing that day is real, and it is instantly recognizable. And since seeing those photos I have been wondering, Why, exactly, do so many women throw "like a girl"? If the motion were easy to change, presumably a woman as motivated and self-possessed as Hillary Clinton would have changed it. (According to her press secretary, Lisa Caputo, Mrs. Clinton spent the weekend before opening day tossing a ball in the Rose Garden with her husband, for practice.) Presumably, too, the answer to the question cannot be anything quite as simple as, Because they *are* girls.

A surprising number of people think that there is a structural difference between male and female arms or shoulders—in the famous "rotator cuff," perhaps—that dictates different throwing motions. "It's in the shoulder joint," a well-educated woman told me recently. "They're hinged differently." Someday researchers may find evidence to support a biological theory of throwing actions. For now, what you'll hear if you ask an orthopedist, an anatomist, or (especially) the coach of a women's softball team is that there is no structural reason why men and women should throw in different ways. This point will be obvious to any male who grew up around girls who liked to play baseball and became good at it. It should be obvious on a larger scale this summer, in broadcasts of the Olympic Games. This year [1996], for the first time, women's fast-pitch softball teams will compete in the Olympics. Although the pitchers in these games will deliver the ball underhand, viewers will see female shortstops, center fielders, catchers, and so on pegging the ball to one another at speeds few male viewers could match.

Even women's tennis is a constant if indirect reminder that men's and women's shoulders are "hinged" the same way. The serving motion in tennis is like a throw—but more difficult, because it must be coordinated with the toss of the tennis ball. The men in professional tennis serve harder than the women, because they are bigger and stronger. But women pros serve harder than most male amateurs have ever done, and the service motion for good players is the same for men and women alike. There is no expectation in college or pro tennis that because of their anatomy female players must "serve like a girl." "I know many women who can throw a lot harder and better than the normal male," says Linda Wells, the coach of the highly successful women's softball team at Arizona State University. "It's not gender that makes the difference in how they throw."

At a superficial level it's easy to tick off the traits of an awkward-looking throw. The fundamental mistake is the one Mrs. Clinton appeared to be making in the photo: trying to throw a ball with your body facing the target, rather than rotating your shoulders and hips ninety degrees away from the target and then swinging them around in order to accelerate the ball. A throw looks bad if your elbow is lower than your shoulder as your arm comes forward (unless you're throwing sidearm). A throw looks really bad if, as the ball leaves your hand, your wrist is "inside your elbow"—that is, your elbow joint is bent in such a way that your forearm angles back toward your body and your wrist is closer to your head than your elbow is. Slow-motion film of big-league pitchers shows that when they release the ball, the throwing arm is fully extended and straight from shoulder to wrist. The combination of these three elements—head-on stance, dropped elbow, and wrist inside the elbow—mechanically dictates a pushing rather than a hurling motion, creating the familiar pattern of "throwing like a girl."

It is surprisingly hard to find in the literature of baseball a deeper explanation of the mechanics of good and bad throws. Tom Seaver's pitching for the Mets and the White Sox got him into the Hall of Fame, but his book *The Art of Pitching* is full of bromides that hardly clarify the process of throwing, even if they might mean something to accomplished pitchers. His chapter "The Absolutes of Pitching Mechanics," for instance, lays out these four unhelpful principles: "Keep the Front Leg Flexible!" "Rub Up the Baseball!" "Hide the Baseball!" "Get It Out, Get It Up!" (The fourth refers to the need to get the ball out of the glove and into the throwing hand in a quick motion.)

A variety of other instructional documents, from *Little League's* 10 *Official How-to-Play Baseball Book* to *Softball for Girls & Women*, mainly reveal the difficulty of finding words to describe a simple motor activity that everyone can recognize. The challenge, I suppose, is like that of writing a manual on how to ride a bike, or how to kiss. Indeed, the most useful description I've found of the mechanics of throwing comes from a man whose specialty is another sport: Vic Braden made his name as a tennis coach, but he has attempted to analyze the physics of a wide variety of sports so that they all will be easier to teach.

Braden says that an effective throw involves connecting a series of links in a "kinetic chain." The kinetic chain, which is Braden's tool for analyzing most sporting activity, operates on a principle like that of crack-the-whip. Momentum builds up in one part of the body. When that part is suddenly stopped, as the end of the "whip" is stopped in crack-the-whip, the momentum is transferred to and concentrated in the next link in the chain. A good throw uses six links of chain, Braden says. The first two links involve the lower body, from feet to waist. The first motion of a throw (after the body has been rotated away from the target) is to rotate the legs and hips back in the direction of the throw, building up momentum as large muscles move body mass. Then those links stop—a pitcher stops turning his hips once they face the plate—and the momentum is transferred to the next link. This is the torso, from waist to shoulders, and since its mass is less than that of the legs, momentum makes it rotate faster than the hips and legs did. The torso stops when it is facing the plate, and the momentum is transferred to the next link—the upper arm. As the upper arm comes past the head, it stops moving forward, and the momentum goes into the final links—the forearm and wrist, which snap forward at tremendous speed.

This may sound arcane and jerkily mechanical, but it makes perfect sense when one sees Braden's slow-mo movies of pitchers in action. And it explains why people do, or don't, learn how to throw. The implication of Braden's analysis is that throwing is a perfectly natural action (millions and millions of people can do it), but not at all innate. A successful throw involves an intricate series of actions coordinated among muscle groups, as each link of the chain is timed to interact with the next. Like bike riding or skating, it can be learned by anyone—male or female. No one starts out knowing how to ride a bike or throw a ball. Everyone has to learn.

Fallows describes in detail what distinguishes a successful baseball throw from an awkward-looking one, concluding with the point that throwing a baseball effectively is a learned activity. He draws on various sources—including a women's softball coach, a tennis coach, and his own observations—to support his claim. Notice how he establishes the context for his essay by focusing on the differences between the stances of the Clintons when photographed throwing a baseball.

JON MARCUS

The Reason College Costs More than You Think

Writing online for Time *in 2014, Hechinger Report editor Jon Marcus examines the length of time students take to graduate and how that affects the cost of getting a degree.*

When Alex Nichols started as a freshman at the University of Mississippi, he felt sure he'd earn his bachelor's degree in four years. Five years later, and Nichols is back on the Oxford, Mississippi, campus for what he hopes is truly his final semester.

"There are a lot more students staying another semester or another year than I thought there would be when I got here," Nichols says. "I meet people once a week who say, 'Yes, I'm a second-year senior,' or, 'I've been here for five years.'"

They're likely as surprised as Nichols still to be toiling away in school.

The Lyceum, the oldest building at the University of Mississippi.

Nearly nine out of 10 freshmen think they'll earn their bachelor's degrees within the traditional four years, according to a nationwide survey conducted by the Higher Education Research Institute at UCLA. But the U.S. Department of Education reports that fewer than half that many actually will. And about 45 percent won't have finished even after six years.

That means the annual cost of college, a source of so much anxiety   5 for families and students, often overlooks the enormous additional expense of the extra time it will actually take to graduate.

"It's a huge inconvenience," says Nichols, whose college career has been prolonged for the common reason that he changed majors and took courses he ended up not needing. His athletic scholarship — Nichols was a middle-distance runner on the cross-country team — ran out after four years. "I had to get some financial help from my parents."

The average added cost of just one extra year at a four-year public university is $63,718 in tuition, fees, books, and living expenses, plus lost wages each of those many students could have been earning had they finished on time, according to the advocacy group Complete College America.

A separate report by the Los Angeles-based Campaign for College Opportunity finds that the average student at a California State University campus who takes six years instead of four to earn a bachelor's degree will spend an additional $58,000 and earn $52,900 less over their lifetimes than a student who graduates on time, for a total loss of $110,900.

"The cost of college isn't just what students and their families pay in tuition or fees," says Michele Siqueiros, the organization's executive director. "It's also about time. That's the hidden cost of a college education."

So hidden that most families still unknowingly plan on four years   10 for a bachelor's degree, says Sylvia Hurtado, director of the Higher Education Research Institute at UCLA.

Although the institute does not poll parents in its annual survey, "that high percentage of freshmen [who are confident they'll finish in four years] is probably reflecting their parents' expectation — 'This is costing me a lot, so you're going to be out in four years.' So the students think, 'Sure, why not?' I don't think the parents even initially entertain or plan for six years or some possible outcome like that."

Yet many students almost immediately doom themselves to taking longer, since they register for fewer courses than they need to stay on track. Surveys of incoming freshmen in California and Indiana who said they expected to graduate in four years found that half signed up for fewer courses than they'd needed to meet that goal, according to a new report by the higher-education consulting firm HCM Strategists.

It's not entirely the students' fault.

More than half of community-college students are slowed down by having to retake subjects such as math and reading that they should have learned in high school, says Complete College America. And at some schools, budget cuts have made it difficult to register for the courses students do need to take. Two-thirds of students at one California State University campus weren't able to get into their required courses, according to a 2010 study by the University of California's Civil Rights Project.

Most state financial-aid programs, meanwhile, cover only four years.   15 "They do not fund a fifth or sixth year," says Stan Jones, president of Complete College America and a former Indiana commissioner of higher education. "And by that time the parents' resources and the students' resources have run out. So that fifth year is where you borrow."

Students at the most elite colleges and universities tend not to have this problem, which means that schools with some of the highest annual tuition can turn out to be relative bargains. These schools "would have a revolt if their students had to go a fifth year," Jones says. "But that recognition has really not hit the public sector yet, about the hidden cost of that extra year."

Policymakers urge speeding students through remedial classes more quickly, adding more sections of required courses so students can get in when they need them, and encouraging students to take 15 credits per semester instead of the typical 12.

Change won't come soon enough for Nichols, who is determined that it won't take more than one extra semester to finish his degree in integrated marketing communications.

"That's time you're wasting," he says, "that you could be out making money."

Marcus combines information from various research institutes, advocacy groups, surveys, and academic sources to support his argument. His statistics are given

a human face by quotations from a student who is taking longer to graduate than he expected.

For four more reports, see CHAPTER 61.

Key Features / Reports

A tightly focused topic.   The goal of this kind of writing is to inform readers about something without digressing—and without, in general, bringing in the writer's own opinions. All three examples focus on a particular topic—texting, throwing a baseball, and the cost of college — and present information about the topics evenhandedly.

Accurate, well-researched information.   Reports usually require some research. The kind of research depends on the topic. Library research to locate scholarly sources may be necessary for some topics—Cullington, for example, uses various sources available through her library's database. Other topics may require field research—interviews, observations, and so on. Fallows interviewed two coaches in addition to reading several books on pitching baseballs.

Synthesis of ideas.   Reports do more than present lists of unconnected facts; they **SYNTHESIZE IDEAS** by showing patterns in and relationships among the information presented. Marcus compares undergraduate students' expectations of finishing college in four years with statistics showing that more than half will take longer. Fallows combines observations of women pitching baseballs and serving tennis balls to refute claims that their arms are structured differently from men's.

473–77

Various writing strategies.   Presenting information usually requires various organizing patterns—defining, comparing, classifying, explaining processes, analyzing causes and effects, and so on. Fallows explains the process governing throwing a baseball and classifies different ways of throwing. Marcus analyzes the financial effects of delaying graduation, and Cullington analyzes the effects (or lack of effects) of texting on students' writing ability.

Clear definitions. Reports need to provide clear definitions of any key terms that their audience may not know. Cullington defines both *texting* and *textspeak*. Fallows defines several pitching terms, such as *inside your elbow*.

Appropriate design. Reports often combine paragraphs with information presented in lists, tables, diagrams, and other illustrations. When you're presenting information, you need to think carefully about how to design it—numerical data, for instance, can be easier to understand and remember in a table than in a paragraph. Often a photograph can bring a subject to life, as do the photos on page 138, which accompany "Throwing Like a Girl." The caption provides important information that is explained more fully in the essay itself. Online reports offer the possibility of video and audio clips as well as links to source materials and more detailed information.

A GUIDE TO WRITING REPORTS

Choosing a Topic

Whether you get to choose your topic or are working with an assigned one, see if you can approach the topic from an angle that interests you.

If you get to choose. What interests you? What do you wish you knew more about? The possible topics for informational reports are limitless, but the topics that you're most likely to write well on are those that engage you. They may be academic in nature or reflect your personal interests or both. If you're not sure where to begin, here are some places to start:

- an intriguing technology: hybrid cars, touchscreens, tooth whiteners
- sports: soccer, snowboarding, ultimate Frisbee, basketball
- an important world event: the Arab Spring, the fall of Rome, the Black Death

- a historical period: the African diaspora, the Middle Ages, the Ming dynasty, the Great Depression
- a common object: hoodies, gel pens, mascara, Post-it notes
- a significant environmental issue: melting Arctic ice, deer overpopulation, mercury and the fish supply
- the arts: hip-hop, outsider art, the Crystal Bridges Museum of American Art, Savion Glover, Mary Cassatt

LIST a few possibilities, and then choose one that you'd like to know more about—and that your audience might find interesting, too. You might start out by phrasing your topic as a question that your research will attempt to answer. For example:

290–91

How is *Google* different from *Yahoo!*?

How was the Great Pyramid constructed?

What kind of training do football referees receive?

If your topic is assigned. If your assignment is broad—"Explain some aspect of the U.S. government"—try focusing on a more limited topic within the larger topic: federalism, majority rule, political parties, states' rights. Even if an assignment seems to offer little flexibility — "Explain the physics of roller coasters" — your task is to decide how to research the topic—and sometimes even narrow topics can be shaped to fit your own interests and those of your audience.

Considering the Rhetorical Situation

PURPOSE   Why are you presenting this information? To teach readers about the subject? To demonstrate your research and writing skills? For some other reason?

55–56

AUDIENCE   Who will read this report? What do they already know about the topic? What background information do they

57–60

need in order to understand it? Will you need to define any terms? What do they want or need to know about the topic? Why should they care about it? How can you attract their interest?

64–67 ▨ **STANCE**   What is your own attitude toward your subject? What interests you most about it? What about it seems important?

68–70 ▨ **MEDIA / DESIGN**   What medium are you using? What is the best way to present the information? Will it all be in paragraph form, or is there information that is best presented as a chart, table, or infographic? Do you need headings? Would diagrams, photographs, or other illustrations help you explain the information?

Generating Ideas and Text

Good reports share certain features that make them useful and interesting to readers. Remember that your goal is to present information clearly and accurately. Start by exploring your topic.

Explore what you already know about your topic.   Write out whatever you know or want to know about your topic, perhaps by **FREEWRITING**, 289–92 ○ **LISTING**, or **CLUSTERING**. Why are you interested in this topic? What questions do you have about it? Such questions can help you decide what you'd like to focus on and how you need to direct your research efforts.

Narrow your topic.   To write a good report, you need to narrow your focus—and to narrow your focus, you need to know a fair amount about your subject. If you are assigned to write on a subject like biodiversity, for example, you need to know what it is, what the key issues are, and so on. If you do, you can simply list or brainstorm possibilities, choose one, and start your research. If you don't know much about the subject,

academic literacies | rhetorical situations | genres | processes | strategies | research MLA / APA | media / design | readings

though, you need to do some research to discover focused, workable topics. This research may shape your thinking and change your focus. Start with **SOURCES** that can give you a general sense of the subject, such as a *Wikipedia* entry, a magazine article, a website, perhaps an interview with an expert. Your goal at this point is simply to find out what issues your topic might include and then to focus your efforts on an aspect of the topic you will be able to cover.

445–68

Come up with a tentative thesis.   Once you narrow your topic, write out a statement that explains what you plan to report or explain. A good **THESIS** is potentially interesting (to you and your readers) and limits your topic enough to make it manageable. Fallows phrases his thesis as a question: "Why, exactly, do so many women throw 'like a girl'?" Cullington frames her thesis in relation to the context surrounding her topic: "Some people believe that using these abbreviations is hindering the writing abilities of students, and others argue that texting is actually having a positive effect on writing. In fact, it seems likely that texting has no significant effect on student writing." At this point, however, you need only a tentative thesis that will help focus any research you do.

345–47

Do any necessary research, and revise your thesis.   To focus your research efforts, **OUTLINE** the aspects of your topic that you expect to discuss. Identify any aspects that require additional research and **DEVELOP A RESEARCH PLAN**. Expect to revise your outline as you do your research, since more information will be available for some aspects of your topic than others, some may prove irrelevant to your topic, and some may turn out to be more than you need. You'll need to revisit your tentative thesis once you've done any research, to finalize your statement.

293–94
435–44

Ways of Organizing a Report

Reports can be organized in various ways. Here are three common organizational structures.

[Reports on topics that are unfamiliar to readers]

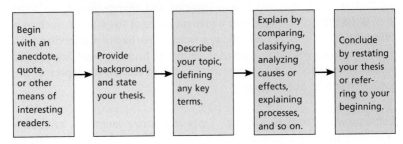

Begin with an anecdote, quote, or other means of interesting readers. → Provide background, and state your thesis. → Describe your topic, defining any key terms. → Explain by comparing, classifying, analyzing causes or effects, explaining processes, and so on. → Conclude by restating your thesis or referring to your beginning.

[Reports on events]

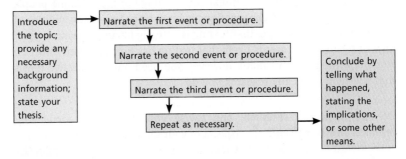

Introduce the topic; provide any necessary background information; state your thesis. → Narrate the first event or procedure. → Narrate the second event or procedure. → Narrate the third event or procedure. → Repeat as necessary. → Conclude by telling what happened, stating the implications, or some other means.

[Reports that compare and contrast]

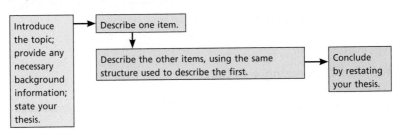

Introduce the topic; provide any necessary background information; state your thesis. → Describe one item. → Describe the other items, using the same structure used to describe the first. → Conclude by restating your thesis.

Many reports use a combination of organizational structures; don't be afraid to use whatever method of organization best suits your material and your purpose.

Writing Out a Draft

Once you have generated ideas and thought about how you want to organize your report, it's time to start **DRAFTING**. Do this quickly — try to write a complete draft in one sitting, concentrating on getting the report on paper or screen and on putting in as much detail as you can.

298–300

Writing that reports information often calls for certain writing strategies. The report on throwing a baseball, for example, **EXPLAINS THE PROCESS** of throwing, whereas the report on college costs **ANALYZES THE EFFECTS** of delaying college graduation. When you're reporting on a topic your readers aren't familiar with, you may wish to **COMPARE** it with something more familiar; you can find useful advice on these and other writing strategies in Part 5 of this book.

414–18
350–54
380–87

Draft a BEGINNING. Essays that report information often need to begin in a way that will get your audience interested in the topic. Here are a few ways of beginning:

331–38

- *Simply state your thesis.* Cullington states her thesis about texting after only a brief introduction. Opening with a thesis works well when you can assume your readers have enough familiarity with your topic that you don't need to give much detailed background information.

- *Start with something that will provoke readers' interest.* Marcus's report begins with an anecdote about a college student.

- *Begin with an illustrative example.* Fallows uses the contrasting photographs of the Clintons throwing baseballs as a way of defining "throwing like a girl."

Draft an ENDING. Think about what you want your readers to read last. An effective ending leaves them thinking about your topic.

338–42

- *Summarize your main points.* This is a good way to end when you've presented several key points you want readers to remember. Cullington ends this way, summarizing the debate about texting's effects and the results of her research.

- *Point out the implications of your report.* Cullington ends by affirming the importance of researched evidence when drawing conclusions not only about texting but in general.

- *Frame your report by referring to its introduction.* Marcus begins and ends his report by quoting the same student.

- *Tell what happened.* If you are reporting on an event, you could conclude by telling how it turns out.

Come up with a title.   You'll want a title that tells readers something about your subject—and makes them want to know more. Cullington's title, "Does Texting Affect Writing?," is a straightforward description of what's to come. Marcus suggests that his essay will disclose the reason college costs more than you think—but doesn't tell us in the title. See the chapter on **GUIDING YOUR READER** for tips on coming up with titles that are informative and enticing enough to make readers wish to read on.

344–49

Considering Matters of Design

You'll probably write the main text of your report in paragraph form, but think about what kind of information you're presenting and how you can design and format it to make it as easy as possible for your readers to understand. You might ask yourself these questions:

- What is an appropriate **FONT**? Something serious like Times Roman, something traditional like Courier, something else?

601–2

- Would it help your readers if you divided your report into shorter sections and added **HEADINGS**?

604–5

- Is there any information that would be easier to follow in a **LIST**?

603

academic literacies   rhetorical situations   genres   processes   strategies   research MLA / APA   media / design   readings

- Could any of your information be summarized in a **TABLE** or **FIGURE**?

609–11

- Do you have any data that readers would more easily understand in the form of a bar **GRAPH**, line graph, or pie chart?

609–11
607–15

- Would **ILLUSTRATIONS** (diagrams, photos, drawings, and so on), video or audio clips, or links help you explain anything in your report?

Getting Response and Revising

The following questions can help you study your draft with a critical eye. **GETTING RESPONSE** from others is always good, and these questions can guide their reading, too. Make sure they know your purpose and audience.

306–7

- Do the title and opening sentences get readers' interest? If not, how might they do so?

- What information does this text provide, and for what purpose?

- Does the introduction explain why this information is being presented? Does it place the topic in a larger context?

- Are all key terms defined that need to be?

- Do you have any questions? Where might more explanation or an example help you understand something better?

- Is any information presented visually, with a chart, graph, table, drawing, or photograph? If so, is it clear how the illustration relates to the written text? Is there any text that would be more easily understood if it were presented visually?

- Is any information presented through digital media, such as hyperlinks, video clips, or audio files? If so, is the relation of these elements to the written text made clear? Would any aspect of the report be clearer if presented using such elements?

- Does the organization help make sense of the information? Does the text include description, comparison, or any other writing strategies? Does the topic or rhetorical situation call for any particular strategies that should be added?

- If the report cites any sources, are they quoted, paraphrased, or summarized effectively (and with appropriate documentation)? Is information from sources introduced with **SIGNAL PHRASES**?

487–90 ●

- Does the report end in a satisfying way? What are readers left thinking?

These questions should identify aspects of your report you need to work on. When it's time to **REVISE**, make sure your report appeals to your audience and achieves your purpose as successfully as possible.

307–10 ◐

Editing and Proofreading

Readers equate correctness with the writer's competence. Once you've revised your draft, follow these guidelines for **EDITING** a report:

313–16 ◐

- Check your use of key terms. Repeating key words is acceptable in reports; using synonyms for unfamiliar words may confuse readers, while the repetition of key words or the use of clearly identified pronouns for them can be genuinely helpful.

349 ◆

- Check to be sure you have **TRANSITIONS** where you need them.

604–5 ▢

- If you have included **HEADINGS**, make sure they're parallel in structure and consistent in design.

607–15 ▢

- Make sure that any photos or other **ILLUSTRATIONS** have captions, that charts and graphs have headings—and that all are referred to in the main text. Use white space as necessary to separate sections of your report and to highlight graphic elements.

496–99 ●

- Check any **DOCUMENTATION** to see that it follows the appropriate style without mistakes.

316–17 ◐

- **PROOFREAD** and spell-check your report carefully.

Taking Stock of Your Work

- How well did you convey the information? Is it complete enough for your audience's needs?

academic literacies ✳ rhetorical situations ■ genres ▲ processes ◐ strategies ◆ research MLA / APA ● media / design ▢ readings ▮

- What strategies did you rely on, and how did they help you achieve your purpose?
- How well did you organize the report?
- How did you go about researching the information for this piece?
- How did you go about drafting this piece?
- Did you use any tables, graphs, diagrams, photographs, illustrations, or other graphics effectively?
- How did others' responses influence your writing?
- What did you do especially well?
- What could still be improved?
- What would you do differently next time?

IF YOU NEED MORE HELP

See Chapter 32 if you are required to submit your report in a writing **PORTFOLIO**.
See also Chapter 14 on **ABSTRACTS** if your report requires one; and Chapter 19 on **PROFILES**, a report based on firsthand research.

● 318–28
▲ 183–87
224–34

13 Arguing a Position

Everything we say or do presents some kind of argument, takes some kind of position. Often we take overt positions: "Everyone in the United States is entitled to affordable health care." "The university needs to offer more language courses." "Photoshopped images should carry disclosure notices." But arguments can be less direct and specific as well, from yellow ribbons that honor U.S. troops to a yellow smiley face, which might be said to argue for a good day.

In college course work, you are constantly called on to argue positions: in an *English* class, you may argue for a certain interpretation of a poem; in a *business* course, you may argue for the merits of a flat tax; in a *linguistics* class, you may argue that English is now a global language. All of those positions are arguable—people of goodwill can agree or disagree with them and present reasons and evidence to support their positions.

This chapter provides guidelines for writing an essay that argues a position. We'll begin with three good examples, the first one annotated to point out key features of this kind of writing.

JOANNA MACKAY

Organ Sales Will Save Lives

In this essay, written for a class on ethics and politics in science, MIT student Joanna MacKay argues that the sale of human organs should be legal.

Clear and
arguable position.

There are thousands of people dying to buy a kidney and thousands of people dying to sell a kidney. It seems a match made in heaven. So why are we standing in the way? Governments should not ban the sale of human organs; they should regulate it. Lives should not be wasted; they should be saved.

156

academic
literacies

rhetorical
situations

genres

processes

strategies

research
MLA / APA

media /
design

readings

About 350,000 Americans suffer from end-stage renal disease, a
state of kidney disorder so advanced that the organ stops functioning
altogether. There are no miracle drugs that can revive a failed kidney,
leaving dialysis and kidney transplantation as the only possible treat-
ments (McDonnell and Mallon, pars. 2 and 3).

Dialysis is harsh, expensive, and, worst of all, only temporary. Acting as an artificial kidney, dialysis mechanically filters the blood of a
patient. It works, but not well. With treatment sessions lasting three
hours, several times a week, those dependent on dialysis are, in a sense,
shackled to a machine for the rest of their lives. Adding excessive stress
to the body, dialysis causes patients to feel increasingly faint and tired,
usually keeping them from work and other normal activities.

Kidney transplantation, on the other hand, is the closest thing to
a cure that anyone could hope for. Today the procedure is both safe
and reliable, causing few complications. With better technology for
confirming tissue matches and new anti-rejection drugs, the surgery is
relatively simple.

But those hoping for a new kidney have high hopes indeed. In the
year 2000 alone, 2,583 Americans died while waiting for a kidney transplant; worldwide the number of deaths is around 50,000 (Finkel 27).
With the sale of organs outlawed in almost every country, the number
of living donors willing to part with a kidney for free is small. When
no family member is a suitable candidate for donation, the patient is
placed on a deceased donors list, relying on the organs from people
dying of old age or accidents. The list is long. With over 60,000 people
in line in the United States alone, the average wait for a cadaverous
kidney is ten long years.

Daunted by the low odds, some have turned to an alternative solution: purchasing kidneys on the black market. For about
$150,000, they can buy a fresh kidney from a healthy, living donor.
There are no lines, no waits. Arranged through a broker, the entire
procedure is carefully planned out. The buyer, seller, surgeons, and
nurses are flown to a predetermined hospital in a foreign country. The operations are performed, and then all are flown back to
their respective homes. There is no follow-up, no paperwork to sign
(Finkel 27).

The illegal kidney trade is attractive not only because of the
promptness but also because of the chance at a living donor. An
organ from a cadaver will most likely be old or damaged, estimated

5

*Necessary back-
ground information.*

to function for about ten years at most. A kidney from a living donor can last over twice as long. Once a person's transplanted cadaverous kidney stops functioning, he or she must get back on the donor list, this time probably at the end of the line. A transplanted living kidney, however, could last a person a lifetime.

While there may seem to be a shortage of kidneys, in reality there is a surplus. In third-world countries, there are people willing to do anything for money. In such extreme poverty these people barely have enough to eat, living in shacks and sleeping on dirt floors. Eager to pay off debts, they line up at hospitals, willing to sell a kidney for about $1,000. The money will go toward food and clothing, or perhaps to pay for a family member's medical operation (Goyal et al. 1590–91). Whatever the case, these people need the money.

Reason (donors need the money) supported by evidence.

There is certainly a risk in donating a kidney, but this risk is not great enough to be outlawed. Millions of people take risks to their health every day for money, or simply for enjoyment. As explained in *The Lancet*, "If the rich are free to engage in dangerous sports for pleasure, or dangerous jobs for high pay, it is difficult to see why the poor who take the lesser risk of kidney selling for greater rewards . . . should be thought so misguided as to need saving from themselves" (Radcliffe-Richards et al. 1951). Studies have shown that a person can live a healthy life with only one kidney. While these studies might not apply to the poor living under strenuous conditions in unsanitary environments, the risk is still theirs to take. These people have decided that their best hope for money is to sell a kidney. How can we deny them the best opportunity they have?

Counterargument (donating a kidney is risky) acknowledged.

Some agree with Pope John Paul II that the selling of organs is morally wrong and violates "the dignity of the human person" (qtd. in Finkel 26), but this is a belief professed by healthy and affluent individuals. Are we sure that the peasants of third-world countries agree? The morals we hold are not absolute truths. We have the responsibility to protect and help those less fortunate, but we cannot let our own ideals cloud the issues at hand.

Counterargument (selling organs is wrong) acknowledged.

10

In a legal kidney transplant, everybody gains except the donor. The doctors and nurses are paid for the operation, the patient receives a new kidney, but the donor receives nothing. Sure, the donor will have the warm, uplifting feeling associated with helping a fellow human being, but this is not enough reward for most people to part with a

Reason (altruism is not enough) supported by evidence.

academic literacies · rhetorical situations · genres · processes · strategies · research MLA / APA · media / design · readings

piece of themselves. In an ideal world, the average person would be altruistic enough to donate a kidney with nothing expected in return. The real world, however, is run by money. We pay men for donating sperm, and we pay women for donating ova, yet we expect others to give away an entire organ for no compensation. If the sale of organs were allowed, people would have a greater incentive to help save the life of a stranger.

While many argue that legalizing the sale of organs will exploit the poorer people of third-world countries, the truth of the matter is that this is already the case. Even with the threat of a $50,000 fine and five years in prison (Finkel 26), the current ban has not been successful in preventing illegal kidney transplants. The kidneys of the poor are still benefiting only the rich. While the sellers do receive most of the money promised, the sum is too small to have any real impact on their financial situation. A study in India discovered that in the long run, organ sellers suffer. In the illegal kidney trade, nobody has the interests of the seller at heart. After selling a kidney, their state of living actually worsens. While the $1,000 pays off one debt, it is not enough to relieve the donor of the extreme poverty that placed him in debt in the first place (Goyal et al. 1591).

Counterargument (poor people are exploited) acknowledged.

These impoverished people do not need stricter and harsher penalties against organ selling to protect them, but quite the opposite. If the sale of organs were made legal, it could be regulated and closely monitored by the government and other responsible organizations. Under a regulated system, education would be incorporated into the application process. Before deciding to donate a kidney, the seller should know the details of the operation and any hazards involved. Only with an understanding of the long-term physical health risks can a person make an informed decision (Radcliffe-Richards et al. 1951).

Reason (regulating organ sales would lead to better decisions).

Regulation would ensure that the seller is fairly compensated. In the illegal kidney trade, surgeons collect most of the buyer's money in return for putting their careers on the line. The brokers arranging the procedure also receive a modest cut, typically around ten percent. If the entire practice were legalized, more of the money could be directed toward the person who needs it most, the seller. By eliminating the middleman and allowing the doctors to settle for lower prices, a regulated system would benefit all those in need of a kidney, both rich

Reason (fairness to sellers) followed by evidence.

and poor. According to Finkel, the money that would otherwise be spent on dialysis treatment could not only cover the charge of a kidney transplant at no cost to the recipient, but also reward the donor with as much as $25,000 (32). This money could go a long way for people living in the poverty of third-world countries.

Critics fear that controlling the lawful sale of organs would be too difficult, but could it be any more difficult than controlling the unlawful sale of organs? Governments have tried to eradicate the kidney market for decades to no avail. Maybe it is time to try something else. When "desperately wanted goods" are made illegal, history has shown that there is more opportunity for corruption and exploitation than if those goods were allowed (Radcliffe-Richards et al. 1951). (Just look at the effects of the prohibition of alcohol, for example.) Legalization of organ sales would give governments the authority and the opportunity to closely monitor these live kidney operations.

Counterargument (controlling organ sales would be difficult) acknowledged.

Regulation would also protect the buyers. Because of the need for secrecy, the current illegal method of obtaining a kidney has no contracts and, therefore, no guarantees. Since what they are doing is illegal, the buyers have nobody to turn to if something goes wrong. There is nobody to point the finger at, nobody to sue. While those participating in the kidney market are breaking the law, they have no other choice. Without a new kidney, end-stage renal disease will soon kill them. Desperate to survive, they are forced to take the only offer available. It seems immoral to first deny them the opportunity of a new kidney and then to leave them stranded at the mercy of the black market. Without laws regulating live kidney transplants, these people are subject to possibly hazardous procedures. Instead of turning our backs, we have the power to ensure that these operations are done safely and efficiently for both the recipient and the donor.

Reason (fairness to buyers) supported by examples.

Those suffering from end-stage renal disease would do anything for the chance at a new kidney, take any risk or pay any price. There are other people so poor that the sale of a kidney is worth the profit. Try to tell someone that he has to die from kidney failure because selling a kidney is morally wrong. Then turn around and try to tell another person that he has to remain in poverty for that same reason. In matters of life and death, our stances on moral issues must be reevaluated. If legalized and regulated, the sale of human organs would save lives. Is it moral to sentence thousands to unnecessary deaths?

Concludes by asking a question for readers to consider.

Works Cited

Finkel, Michael. "This Little Kidney Went to Market." *The New York Times Magazine,* 27 May 2001, pp. 26+.

Goyal, Madhav, et al. "Economic and Health Consequences of Selling a Kidney in India." *Journal of the American Medical Association,* vol. 288, 2002, pp. 1589–92.

McDonnell, Michael B., and William K. Mallon. "Kidney Transplant." *eMedicine Health,* 18 Aug. 2008, www.emedicinehealth.com/articles/24500-1.asp. Accessed 30 Nov. 2008.

Radcliffe-Richards, J., et al. "The Case for Allowing Kidney Sales." *The Lancet,* vol. 351, no. 9120, 27 June 1998, pp. 1950-52.

MacKay clearly states her position at the beginning of her text: "Governments should not ban the sale of human organs; they should regulate it." Her argument appeals to her readers' sense of fairness; when kidney sales are legalized and regulated, both sellers and buyers will benefit from the transaction. She uses MLA style to document her sources.

NICHOLAS KRISTOF

Our Blind Spot about Guns

In this essay, which first appeared in the New York Times in 2014, columnist Nicholas Kristof argues that if guns and their owners were regulated in the same way that cars and their drivers are, thousands of lives could be saved each year.

If we had the same auto fatality rate today that we had in 1921, by my calculations we would have 715,000 Americans dying annually in vehicle accidents.

Instead, we've reduced the fatality rate by more than 95 percent — not by confiscating cars, but by regulating them and their drivers sensibly.

We could have said, "Cars don't kill people. People kill people," and there would have been an element of truth to that. Many accidents are a result of alcohol consumption, speeding, road rage or driver distraction. Or we could have said, "It's pointless because even if you regulate cars, then people will just run each other down with bicycles," and that, too, would have been partly true.

Yet, instead, we built a system that protects us from ourselves. This saves hundreds of thousands of lives a year and is a model of what we should do with guns in America.

Whenever I write about the need for sensible regulation of guns, some readers jeer: *Cars kill people, too, so why not ban cars? Why are you so hypocritical as to try to take away guns from law-abiding people when you don't seize cars?*

That question is a reflection of our national blind spot about guns. The truth is that we regulate cars quite intelligently, instituting evidence-based measures to reduce fatalities. Yet the gun lobby is too strong, or our politicians too craven, to do the same for guns. So guns and cars now each kill more than 30,000 in America every year.

One constraint, the argument goes, is the Second Amendment. Yet the paradox is that a bit more than a century ago, there was no universally recognized individual right to bear arms in the United States, but there was widely believed to be a "right to travel" that allowed people to drive cars without regulation.

A court struck down an early attempt to require driver's licenses, and initial attempts to set speed limits or register vehicles were met with resistance and ridicule. When authorities in New York City sought in 1899 to ban horseless carriages in the parks, the idea was lambasted in the *New York Times* as "devoid of merit" and "impossible to maintain."

Yet, over time, it became increasingly obvious that cars were killing and maiming people, as well as scaring horses and causing accidents. As a distinguished former congressman, Robert Cousins, put it in 1910: "Pedestrians are menaced every minute of the days and nights by a wanton recklessness of speed, crippling and killing people at a rate that is appalling."

Courts and editorial writers alike saw the carnage and agreed that something must be done. By the 1920s, courts routinely accepted driver's license requirements, car registration and other safety measures.

That continued in recent decades with requirements of seatbelts and air bags, padded dashboards and better bumpers. We cracked down on drunken drivers and instituted graduated licensing for young people, while also improving road engineering to reduce accidents. The upshot is that there is now just over 1 car fatality per 100 million miles driven.

Yet as we've learned to treat cars intelligently, we've gone in the opposite direction with guns. In his terrific new book, *The Second Amendment: A Biography,* Michael Waldman, the president of the Brennan Center for Justice at the New York University School of Law, notes that "gun control laws were ubiquitous" in the nineteenth century. Visitors to Wichita, Kansas, for example, were required to check their revolvers at police headquarters.

And Dodge City, symbol of the Wild West? A photo shows a sign on the main street in 1879 warning: "The Carrying of Fire Arms Strictly Prohibited."

Dodge City, Kansas, 1878. The sign reads, "The Carrying of Fire Arms strictly prohibited."

The National Rifle Association supported reasonable gun control for most of its history and didn't even oppose the landmark Gun Control Act of 1968. But, since then, most attempts at safety regulation have stalled or gone backward, and that makes the example of cars instructive.

"We didn't ban cars, or send black helicopters to confiscate them," 15 notes Waldman. "We made cars safer: air bags, seatbelts, increasing the drinking age, lowering the speed limit. There are similar technological and behavioral fixes that can ease the toll of gun violence, from expanded background checks to trigger locks to smart guns that recognize a thumbprint, just like my iPhone does."

Some of these should be doable. A Quinnipiac poll this month found 92 percent support for background checks for all gun buyers.

These steps won't eliminate gun deaths any more than seatbelts eliminate auto deaths. But if a combination of measures could reduce the toll by one-third, that would be 10,000 lives saved every year.

A century ago, we reacted to deaths and injuries from unregulated vehicles by imposing sensible safety measures that have saved hundreds of thousands of lives a year. Why can't we ask politicians to be just as rational about guns?

Kristof argues that because regulating cars has made them much safer, guns should be regulated similarly. He supports his argument with data on fatality rates and the history of automobile and gun regulation in the United States.

ANDREW LEONARD

Black Friday: Consumerism Minus Civilization

This essay arguing that advertising for day-after-Thanksgiving sales has gone too far first appeared on Salon, where it includes several videos and links to other websites, which are underlined in this text. The online version may be accessed via wwnorton.com/write/fieldguidelinks.

Here's a Thanksgiving recipe guaranteed to deliver a nervous breakdown impervious to even the most bleeding-edge psychopharmaceutical wonder drug. Go to *YouTube*, search for "Black Friday

Grown men scream at Justin Bieber in the Macy's Black Friday ad.

commercials," start watching, and then, once you've sated yourself on grown men screaming at Justin Bieber, remakes of Rebecca Black's "Friday," and, most distressingly, the continuing adventures of the Crazy Target Lady, ask yourself this question:

What does it all mean?

I stared into this heart of retail panic darkness, and the more I clicked and pondered, the more confused — (mind-boggled? fascinated? flabbergasted?) — I became. The Crazy Target Lady, so proud of her OCD — obsessive Christmas disorder — is not funny. She's scary. She's why people trample each other to death. She is wrong.

There is a point in our culture beyond which camp and kitsch no longer make the least ironic sense, where consumerism loses its last mooring to civilization, where even seemingly legitimate protest devolves into farce. That point is Black Friday.

Let me be clear. I am not opposed to vigorous sprees of retail 5 spending. For the sake of the U.S. economy, I would love to see a robust Christmas shopping season and I plan to do my part. I find the notion that we should "occupy Black Friday" and withhold our consumer dollars as a way of hitting back at the 1 percent just nutty. Voluntarily subtracting demand from the economy hurts *us*. A general consumer strike would result in more layoffs and pay cuts and bankruptcies and foreclosures. Sure, Wal-Mart would take a hit, but so would Wal-Mart employees.

But there's also a point where healthy consumerism becomes out-of-control marketing-driven commodity fetishism, and when we find ourselves checking our smartphones for last minute online deals while standing in line for a chain store opening at midnight on Thanksgiving, we are clearly too far gone. That's insanity.

And corporate America knows this. The retail moguls are counting on it. They are outright encouraging it — and role-modeling the appropriate behavior for us. The Crazy Target Lady is not a joke. Watch her cannibalize her gingerbread man, or strategize her reverse psychology shopping techniques, or show off her shopping utility belt: You cannot avoid the dual conclusion that a) she is not a healthy woman, and b) she is *America*. She might be a lunatic, but it's a culturally approved lunacy — the kind that keeps the American engine of capitalism all stoked up. The message that keeps getting blasted across my TV is that we should all be more like her — doing our patriotic duty to boost

The Crazy Target Lady models her shopping utility belt.

academic literacies | rhetorical situations | genres | processes | strategies | research MLA / APA | media / design | readings

fourth-quarter retail sales. Sure, you can laugh at her. But then get in line and keep your credit card handy.

But, of course, the big story of this year's Black Friday has been the welcome news that at least some subsection of the population of the United States has come to the realization that it's time to step back from the brink. The budding protests against the decision by some of the country's biggest retailers — Target, Macy's, Best Buy, Kohl's — to move the start of their Black Friday sales to midnight Thanksgiving, or even earlier, is laudable.

The nearly 200,000 signatures on part-time Target employee Anthony Hardwick's petition to "Save Thanksgiving" is proof that both employees and customers of Target are beginning to see this endless race by retailers to one-up each other as dehumanizing and ridiculous. What does a Target employee forced to go to work at 11 p.m. on Thanksgiving have to give thanks for?

(Although, even here, in the protest arena, it's hard to know what 10 to make of the "Respect the Bird" campaign hosted at AllRecipes.com

The "Friday" parody used in the Kohl's campaign.

that mixes pledges to "take back Thanksgiving" with KitchenAid mixer promotions and ads for pop-up turkey timers. Even the protests are inseparable from consumerist mania.)

The chains are lamely defending their move as a response to forces beyond their control:

"As that is the busiest shopping day of the year, it is imperative that we be competitive," said Anahita Cameron, a Target human resources director, in a statement quoted by the *L.A. Times*. "Our guests have expressed that they would prefer to kick off their holiday shopping by heading out after their holiday celebrations rather than getting up in the middle of the night."

Guests? Pre-programmed automatons would be more accurate. I am undoubtedly reading too much into the "Black Friday" parody of Rebecca Black's "Friday" currently touting the midnight Thanksgiving sale at Kohl's, but there is an awfully revealing moment at the very end of the ad.

After the perky Stepford-wife shopper sings joyfully about how she's "been in line since yesterday" and how everybody's going to Kohl's at "midnight, midnight" the ad ends with her observing, with a mild air of perturbance, that she "can't get this darn song out of my head."

Ladies and gentlemen, there's your winner of the 2011 award for honesty in advertising. A commercial attempting to brainwash consumers into lining up for a midnight sale manages also to explicitly reference the difficulty of shaking free from mindless jingles.   15

That's kind of brilliant. But also very wrong. Which makes it the perfect commercial for summing up the culture-wide psychotic spasm that is Black Friday. Stay home Thanksgiving night. Go shopping after getting a full night's rest. Sure, you might miss a sale or two. But you'll be a better human being.

For four more arguments, see CHAPTER 62.

Leonard's claim, that Black Friday represents "out-of-control marketing-driven commodity fetishism" or, more concisely, "insanity," is vividly illustrated by several videos of commercials that provide both background information and evidence for his argument. He acknowledges the need for "vigorous sprees of retail spending" while decrying the "psychotic spasm that is Black Friday."

Key Features / Arguments

A clear and arguable position. At the heart of every argument is a claim with which people may reasonably disagree. Some claims are not arguable because they're completely subjective, matters of taste or opinion ("I hate sauerkraut"), because they are a matter of fact ("The first *Star Wars* movie came out in 1977"), or because they are based on belief or faith ("There is life after death"). To be arguable, a position must reflect one of at least two points of view, making reasoned argument necessary: Guns should (or should not) be regulated; selling human organs should be legal (or illegal). In college writing, you will often argue not that a position is correct but that it is plausible— that it is reasonable, supportable, and worthy of being taken seriously.

Necessary background information. Sometimes we need to provide some background on a topic we are arguing so that readers can understand what is being argued. MacKay establishes the need for kidney donors before launching her argument for legalizing the selling of organs; Kristof describes the history of automobile regulation.

Good reasons. By itself, a position does not make an argument; the argument comes when a writer offers reasons to back up the position. There are many kinds of good reasons. Kristof makes his argument by comparing cars to guns. MacKay bases her argument in favor of legalizing the sale of human organs on the grounds that doing so would save more lives, that impoverished people should be able to make risky choices, and that regulation would protect such people who currently sell their organs on the black market as well as desperate buyers.

Convincing evidence. Once you've given reasons for your position, you then need to offer evidence for your reasons: facts, statistics, expert testimony, anecdotal evidence, case studies, textual evidence. All three arguments use a mix of these types of evidence. MacKay cites statistics about Americans who die from renal failure to support her argument for legalizing organ sales; Kristof shows how regulating cars led to dramatic decreases in driving deaths and injuries. Leonard presents several videos to demonstrate how excessive Black Friday advertising has become.

Appeals to readers' values. Effective arguers try to appeal to readers' values and emotions. MacKay appeals to basic values of compassion and fairness. These are deeply held values that we may not think about very much and as a result may see as common ground we share with the writers. And some of MacKay's evidence appeals to emotion—her descriptions of people dying from kidney disease and of poor people selling their organs are likely to evoke an emotional response in many readers.

A trustworthy tone. Arguments can stand or fall on the way readers perceive the writer. Very simply, readers need to trust the person who's making the argument. One way of winning this trust is by demonstrating that you know what you're talking about. Kristof offers plenty of facts to show his knowledge of the history of automotive regulation — and he does so in a self-assured tone. There are many other ways of establishing yourself (and your argument) as trustworthy — by showing that you have some experience with your subject, that you're fair, and of course that you're honest. Occasionally, an outraged tone such as Leonard's is appropriate, especially when it is tempered by good reasons and qualified as he does in noting that he is "undoubtedly reading too much into the Kohl's . . . parody."

Careful consideration of other positions. No matter how reasonable and careful we are in arguing our positions, others may disagree or offer counterarguments. We need to consider those other views and to acknowledge and, if possible, refute them in our written arguments. MacKay, for example, acknowledges that some believe that selling organs is unethical, but she counters that it's usually healthy, affluent people who say this — not people who need either an organ or the money they could get by selling one.

academic literacies | rhetorical situations | genres | processes | strategies | research MLA / APA | media / design | readings

A GUIDE TO WRITING ARGUMENTS

Choosing a Topic

A fully developed argument requires significant work and time, so choosing a topic in which you're interested is very important. Students often find that widely debated topics such as "animal rights" or "abortion" can be difficult to write on because they don't feel any personal connection to them. Better topics include those that

- interest you right now
- are focused but not too narrowly
- have some personal connection to your life

One good way to **GENERATE IDEAS** for a topic that meets those three criteria is to explore your own roles in life.

289–97

Start with your roles in life. Make four columns with the headings "Personal," "Family," "Public," and "School." Then **LIST** the roles you play that relate to it. Here is a list one student wrote:

290–91

Personal	Family	Public	School
gamer	son	voter	college student
dog owner	younger	homeless-shelter	work-study
old-car owner	brother	volunteer	employee
male	grandson	American	dorm resident
white		resident	primary-education
middle class		of Texas	major

Identify issues that interest you. Think, then, about issues or controversies that may concern you as a member of one or more of those groups. For instance, as a primary-education major, this student cares about the controversy over whether teachers' jobs should be focused on preparing kids for high-stakes standardized tests. As a college student, he cares about the costs of a college education. Issues that stem from these subjects could include the following: Should student progress be measured by standardized tests? Should college cost less than it does?

Pick four or five of the roles you list. In five or ten minutes, identify issues that concern or affect you as a member of each of those roles. It might help to word each issue as a question starting with *Should*.

Frame your topic as a problem.   Most position papers address issues that are subjects of ongoing debate—their solutions aren't easy, and people disagree on which ones are best. Posing your topic as a problem can help you think about the topic, find an issue that's suitable to write about, and find a clear focus for your essay.

For example, if you wanted to write an argument on the lack of student parking at your school, you could frame your topic as one of several problems: What causes the parking shortage? Why are the university's parking garages and lots limited in their capacity? What might alleviate the shortage?

Choose one issue to write about.   Remember that the issue should be interesting to you and have some connection to your life. It is a tentative choice; if you find later that you have trouble writing about it, simply go back to your list of roles or issues and choose another.

Considering the Rhetorical Situation

55–56 ▮	**PURPOSE**	Do you want to persuade your audience to do something? Change their minds? Consider alternative views? Accept your position as plausible — see that you have thought carefully about an issue and researched it appropriately?
57–60 ▮	**AUDIENCE**	Who is your intended audience? What do they likely know and believe about this issue? How personal is it for them? To what extent are they likely to agree or disagree with you — and with one another? Why? What common ground can you find with them?

STANCE
What's your attitude toward your topic, and why? How do you want your audience to perceive your attitude? How do you want your audience to perceive you? As an authority on your topic? As someone much like them? As calm? reasonable? impassioned or angry? something else?

64–67

MEDIA/DESIGN
What media will you use, and how do your media affect your argument? Does your print or online argument call for photos or charts? If you're giving an oral presentation, should you put your reasons and support on slides? If you're writing electronically, should you include audio or video evidence or links to counterarguments or your sources?

68–70

Generating Ideas and Text

Most essays that successfully argue a position share certain features that make them interesting and persuasive. Remember that your goal is to stake out a position and convince your readers that it is plausible.

Explore what you already know about the issue. Write out whatever you know about the issue by **FREEWRITING** or as a **LIST** or **OUTLINE**. Why are you interested in this topic? What is your position on it at this point, and why? What aspect do you think you'd like to focus on? Where do you need to focus your research efforts? This activity can help you discover what more you need to learn. Chances are you'll need to learn a lot more about the issue before you even decide what position to take.

289–291
293–94

Do some research. At this point, try to get an overview. Start with one **GENERAL SOURCE** of information that will give you a sense of the ins and outs of your issue, one that isn't overtly biased. *The atlantic.com, Time.com, Slate,* and other online newspapers and magazines can be good starting points on current issues. For some issues, you may need to **INTERVIEW** an expert. For example, one student who wanted to write about chemical

455–56

463–64

abuse of animals at 4-H competitions interviewed an experienced show competitor. Use your overview source to find out the main questions raised about your issue and to get some idea about the various ways in which you might argue it.

Explore the issue strategically.   Most issues may be argued from many different perspectives. You'll probably have some sense of the different views that exist on your issue, but you should explore multiple perspectives before deciding on your position. The following methods are good ways of exploring issues:

388–98

- As a matter of **DEFINITION**. What is it? How should it be defined? How can *organic* or *genetically modified food* be defined? How do proponents of *organic food* define it—and how do they define *genetically modified food*? How do advocates of *genetically modified food* define it—and how do they define *organic food*? Considering such definitions is one way to identify different perspectives on the topic.

374–79

- As a matter of **CLASSIFICATION**. Can the issue be divided into categories? Are there different kinds of, or different ways of, producing organic foods and genetically modified foods? Do different categories suggest particular positions or perhaps a way of supporting a certain position? Are there other ways of categorizing foods?

380–87

- As a matter of **COMPARISON**. Is one subject being considered better than another? Is organic food healthier or safer than genetically modified food? Is genetically modified food healthier or safer than organic? Is the answer somewhere in the middle?

414–18

- As a matter of **PROCESS**. Should somebody do something? What? Should people buy and eat more organic food? More genetically modified food? Should they buy and eat some of each?

Reconsider whether the issue can be argued.   Is this issue worth discussing? Why is it important to you and to others? What difference will it make if one position or another prevails? Is it **ARGUABLE**? At this point, you want to be sure that your topic is worth arguing about.

353–73

Draft a thesis. Having explored the possibilities, decide your position, and write it out as a complete sentence. For example:

> Parents should be required to have their children vaccinated.
>
> Pod-based coffeemakers should be banned.
>
> Genetically modified foods should be permitted in the United States.

Qualify your thesis. Rather than taking a strict pro or con position, in most cases you'll want to **QUALIFY YOUR POSITION** — in certain circumstances, with certain conditions, with these limitations, and so on. This is not to say that we should settle, give in, sell out; rather, it is to say that our position may not be the only "correct" one and that other positions may be valid as well. **QUALIFYING YOUR THESIS** also makes your topic manageable by limiting it. For example:

357

345–47

> Parents should be required to have their children vaccinated, with only medical exemptions allowed.
>
> Pod-based coffeemakers should be banned unless the pods are recyclable.
>
> Genetically modified foods should be permitted in the United States if they are clearly labeled as such.

Come up with good reasons. Once you have a thesis, you need to come up with good **REASONS** to convince your readers that it's plausible. Write out your position, and then list several reasons. For instance, if your thesis is that pod-based coffeemakers should be banned, two of your reasons might be:

358–59

> The pods cannot be recycled.
>
> Other methods of making coffee are more environmentally sound.

Think about which reasons are best for your purposes. Which seem the most persuasive? Which are most likely to be accepted by your audience? Which seem to matter the most now? If your list of reasons is short or you think you'll have trouble developing them enough to write an appropriate essay, this is a good time to rethink your topic — before you've invested too much time in it.

359–67

Develop support for your reasons. Next you have to come up with **EVIDENCE** to support your reasons: facts, statistics, examples, testimony by authorities and experts, anecdotal evidence, scenarios, case studies and observation, and textual evidence. For some topics, you may want or need to use evidence in visual form like photos, graphs, and charts; online, you could also use video or audio evidence and links to evidence in other websites.

What counts as evidence varies across audiences. Statistical evidence may be required in certain disciplines but not in others; anecdotes may be accepted as evidence in some courses but not in engineering. Some audiences will be persuaded by emotional appeals while others will not. For example, if you argue that foods produced from genetically modified organisms (GMOs) should be allowed to be sold because they're safe, you could support that reason with *facts*: GMOs are tested thoroughly by three separate U.S. government agencies. Or you could support it with *statistics*: A study of 29 years of data on livestock fed GMO feed found that GMO-fed cattle had no adverse health effects. *Expert testimony* might include R. E. Goodman of the Department of Food Science and Technology at the University of Nebraska–Lincoln, who writes that "there is an absence of proof of harm to consumers from commercially available GMOs."

Identify other positions. Now think about positions other than yours and the reasons people are likely to give for those positions. Be careful to represent their points of view as accurately and fairly as you can. Then decide whether you need to acknowledge or to refute each position.

368–69

Acknowledging other positions. Some positions can't be refuted but are too important to ignore, so you need to **ACKNOWLEDGE** concerns and objections they raise to show that you've considered other perspectives. For example, in an essay arguing that vacations are necessary to maintain good health, medical writer Alina Tugend acknowledges that "in some cases, these trips — particularly with entire families in tow — can be stressful in their own way. The joys of a holiday can also include lugging around a ridiculous amount of paraphernalia, jet-lagged children sobbing on airplanes, hotels that looked wonderful on the Web but are in reality

next to a construction site." Tugend's acknowledgment moderates her position and makes her argument appear more reasonable.

Refuting other positions. State the position as clearly and as fairly as you can, and then **REFUTE** it by showing why you believe it is wrong. 369 Perhaps the reasoning is faulty or the supporting evidence inadequate. Acknowledge the merits of the position, if any, but emphasize its short-comings. Avoid the **FALLACY** of attacking the person holding the position 370–72 or bringing up a competing position that no one seriously entertains.

Ways of Organizing an Argument

Readers need to be able to follow the reasoning of your argument from beginning to end; your task is to lead them from point to point as you build your case. Sometimes you'll want to give all the reasons for your argument first, followed by discussion of any other positions. Alternatively, you might discuss each reason and any opposing arguments together.

[Reasons to support your argument, followed by opposing arguments]

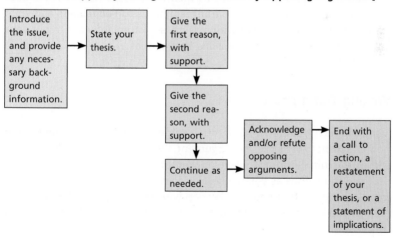

[Reason/opposing argument, reason/opposing argument]

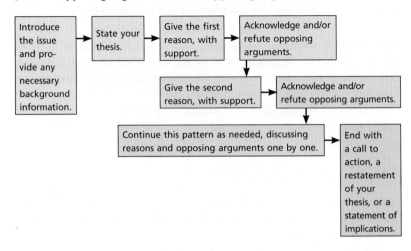

Consider carefully the order in which you discuss your reasons. Usually what comes last makes the strongest impression on readers and what comes in the middle the least impression, so you might want to put your most important or strongest reasons first and last.

Writing Out a Draft

298–300 ○

Once you have generated ideas, done some research, and thought about how you want to organize your argument, it's time to start **DRAFTING**. Your goal in the initial draft is to develop your argument — you can fill in support and transitions as you revise. You may want to write your first draft in one sitting, so that you can develop your reasoning from beginning to end. Or you may write the main argument first and the introduction and

conclusion after you've drafted the body of the essay; many writers find that beginning and ending an essay are the hardest tasks they face. Here is some advice on how you might **BEGIN AND END** your argument:

◆ 331–43

Draft a beginning.   There are various ways to begin an argument essay, depending on your audience and purpose. Here are a few suggestions:

- *Offer background information.* You may need to give your readers information to help them understand your position. MacKay outlines the extent of kidney failure in the United States and the limits of dialysis as treatment.

- *Define a key term.* You may need to show how you're using certain keywords. MacKay, for example, defines *end-stage renal disease* as "a state of kidney disorder so advanced that the organ stops functioning altogether," a **DEFINITION** that is central to her argument.

◆ 388–98

- *Begin with something that will get readers' attention.* MacKay begins emphatically: "There are thousands of people dying to buy a kidney and thousands of people dying to sell a kidney . . . So why are we standing in the way?" Leonard offers still photos from two commercials and links to two more available online.

- *Explain the context for your position.* All arguments are part of a larger, ongoing conversation, so you might begin by showing how your position fits into the arguments others have made. Kristof places his argument about guns in the **CONTEXT** of government regulation of other dangerous technologies.

▲ 110

Draft an ending.   Your conclusion is the chance to wrap up your argument in such a way that readers will remember what you've said. Here are a few ways of concluding an argument essay:

- *Summarize your main points.* Especially when you've presented a complex argument, it can help readers to **SUMMARIZE** your main point. MacKay sums up her argument with the sentence "If legalized and regulated, the sale of human organs would save lives."

● 486–87

- *Call for action*. Kristof does this by asking politicians to consider "sensible safety measures." Leonard presents an alternative to Black Friday's excesses: "Stay home Thanksgiving night. Go shopping after getting a full night's rest."
- *Frame your argument by referring to the introduction.* MacKay does this when she ends by reiterating that selling organs benefits both seller and buyer.

Come up with a title.   Most often you'll want your title to tell readers something about your topic—and to make them want to read on. MacKay's "Organ Sales Will Save Lives" tells us both her topic and position. Kristof's title, "Our Blind Spot about Guns," entices us to find out what that blind spot is. See the

344–49 chapter on **GUIDING YOUR READER** for more advice on composing a good title.

Considering Matters of Design

You'll probably write the main text of your argument in paragraph form, but think about what kind of information you're presenting and how you can design it to make your argument as easy as possible for your readers to understand. Think also about whether any visual or audio elements would be more persuasive than written words.

601–2
- What would be an appropriate **FONT**? Something serious like Times Roman? Something traditional like Courier? Something else?

604–5
- Would it help your readers if you divided your argument into shorter sections and added **HEADINGS**?

603
- If you're making several points, would they be easier to follow if you set them off in a **LIST**?

609–11
- Do you have any supporting evidence that would be easier to understand in the form of a bar **GRAPH**, line graph, or pie chart?

607–15
- Would **ILLUSTRATIONS**—photos, diagrams, or drawings—add support for your argument? Online, would video, audio, or links help?

academic literacies · rhetorical situations · genres · processes · strategies · research MLA / APA · media / design · readings

Getting Response and Revising

At this point you need to look at your draft closely, and if possible **GET RESPONSE** from others as well. Following are some questions for look- ing at an argument with a critical eye.

○ 306–7

- Is there sufficient background or context?
- Have you defined terms to avoid misunderstandings?
- Is the thesis clear and appropriately qualified?
- Are the reasons plausible?
- Is there enough evidence to support these reasons? Will readers accept the evidence as valid and sufficient?
- Can readers follow the steps in your reasoning?
- Have you considered potential objections or other positions? Are there any others that should be addressed?
- Have you cited enough sources, and are these sources credible?
- Are source materials documented carefully and completely, with in-text citations and a works cited or references section?
- Are any visuals or links that are included used effectively and inte- grated smoothly with the rest of the text? If there are no visuals or links, would using some strengthen the argument?

Next it's time to **REVISE**, to make sure your argument offers convincing evidence, appeals to readers' values, and achieves your purpose.

○ 307–10

Editing and Proofreading

Readers equate correctness with competence. Once you've revised your draft, follow these guidelines for **EDITING** an argument:

○ 313–16

- Check to see that your tone is appropriate and consistent throughout, reflects your **STANCE** accurately, and enhances the argument you're making.

▨ 64–67

349
- Be sure readers will be able to follow the argument; check to see you've provided **TRANSITIONS** and summary statements where necessary.

478–90
496–99
- Make sure you've smoothly integrated **QUOTATIONS**, **PARAPHRASES**, and **SUMMARIES** from source material into your writing and **DOCUMENTED** them accurately.

- Look for phrases such as "I think" or "I feel" and delete them; your essay itself expresses your opinion.

607–15
- Make sure that **ILLUSTRATIONS** have captions and that charts and graphs have headings—and that all are referred to in the main text.

- If you're writing online, make sure all your links work.

316–17
- **PROOFREAD** and spell-check your essay carefully.

Taking Stock of Your Work

Take stock of what you've written by writing out answers to these questions:

- What did you do well in this piece?
- What could still be improved?
- How did you go about researching your topic?
- How did others' responses influence your writing?
- How did you go about drafting this piece?
- Did you use visual elements (tables, graphs, diagrams, photographs), audio elements, or links effectively? If not, would they have helped?
- What would you do differently next time?
- What have you learned about your writing ability from writing this piece? What do you need to work on in the future?

318–28
94–128
197–205
235–44

IF YOU NEED MORE HELP

See Chapter 32 if you are required to submit your argument as part of a writing **PORTFOLIO**. See also Chapter 11 on **ANALYZING A TEXT**, Chapter 16 on **EVALUATIONS**, and Chapter 20 on **PROPOSALS** for advice on writing those specific types of arguments.

Abstracts **14**

Abstracts are summaries written to give readers the gist of a **REPORT** or presentation. Sometimes they are published in conference proceedings or databases. In courses in the *sciences, social sciences,* and *engineering,* you may be asked to create abstracts of your proposed projects and completed reports and essays. Abstracts are brief, typically 100–200 words, sometimes even shorter. Three common kinds are *informative abstracts, descriptive abstracts,* and *proposal abstracts.*

▲ 129–55

INFORMATIVE ABSTRACTS

Informative abstracts state in one paragraph the essence of a whole paper about a study or a research project. That one paragraph must mention all the main points or parts of the paper: a description of the study or project, its methods, the results, and the conclusions. Here is an example of the abstract accompanying a seven-page essay that appeared in the *Journal of Clinical Psychology:*

> The relationship between boredom proneness and health-symptom reporting was examined. Undergraduate students ($N = 200$) completed the Boredom Proneness Scale and the Hopkins Symptom Checklist. A multiple analysis of covariance indicated that individuals with high boredom-proneness total scores reported significantly higher ratings on all five subscales of the Hopkins Symptom Checklist (Obsessive–Compulsive, Somatization, Anxiety, Interpersonal Sensitivity, and Depression). The results suggest that boredom proneness may be an important element to consider when assessing symptom reporting. Implications for determining the effects of boredom proneness on

psychological- and physical-health symptoms, as well as the application in clinical settings, are discussed.

— Jennifer Sommers and Stephen J. Vodanovich,
"Boredom Proneness"

The first sentence states the nature of the study being reported. The next summarizes the method used to investigate the problem, and the following one gives the results: students who, according to specific tests, are more likely to be bored are also more likely to have certain medical or psychological symptoms. The last two sentences indicate that the paper discusses those results and examines the conclusion and its implications.

DESCRIPTIVE ABSTRACTS

Descriptive abstracts are usually much briefer than informative abstracts and provide much less information. Rather than summarizing the entire paper, a descriptive abstract functions more as a teaser, providing a quick overview that invites the reader to read the whole. Descriptive abstracts usually do not give or discuss results or set out the conclusion or its implications. A descriptive abstract of the boredom-proneness essay might simply include the first sentence from the informative abstract plus a final sentence of its own:

The relationship between boredom proneness and health-symptom reporting was examined. The findings and their application in clinical settings are discussed.

PROPOSAL ABSTRACTS

Proposal abstracts contain the same basic information as informative abstracts, but their purpose is very different. You prepare proposal abstracts to persuade someone to let you write on a topic, pursue a project, conduct an experiment, or present a paper at a scholarly conference. This kind of abstract is not written to introduce a longer piece but rather to stand alone, and often the abstract is written before the paper itself. Titles and other

academic literacies · rhetorical situations · genres · processes · strategies · research MLA / APA · media / design · readings

aspects of the proposal deliberately reflect the theme of the proposed work, and you may use the future tense, rather than the past, to describe work not yet completed. Here is a possible proposal for doing research on boredom:

> Undergraduate students will complete the Boredom Proneness Scale and the Hopkins Symptom Checklist. A multiple analysis of covariance will be performed to determine the relationship between boredom-proneness total scores and ratings on the five subscales of the Hopkins Symptom Checklist (Obsessive–Compulsive, Somatization, Anxiety, Interpersonal Sensitivity, and Depression).

Key Features / Abstracts

A summary of basic information. An informative abstract includes enough information to substitute for the report itself, a descriptive abstract offers only enough information to let the audience decide whether to read further, and a proposal abstract gives an overview of the planned work.

Objective description. Abstracts present information on the contents of a report or a proposed study; they do not present arguments about or personal perspectives on those contents. The informative abstract on boredom proneness, for example, offers only a tentative conclusion: "The results *suggest* that boredom proneness *may* be an important element to consider."

Brevity. Although the length of abstracts may vary, journals and organizations often restrict them to 120–200 words — meaning you must carefully select and edit your words.

A BRIEF GUIDE TO WRITING ABSTRACTS

Considering the Rhetorical Situation

PURPOSE   Are you giving a brief but thorough overview of a completed study? only enough information to create interest? a proposal for a planned study or presentation?

55–56

55–56 **AUDIENCE** For whom are you writing this abstract? What information about your project will your readers need?

64–67 **STANCE** Whatever your stance in the longer work, your abstract must be objective.

68–70 **MEDIA / DESIGN** How will you set your abstract off from the rest of the text? If you are publishing it online, should it be on a separate page? What format do your readers expect?

Generating Ideas and Text

Write the paper first, the abstract last. You can then use the finished work as the guide for the abstract, which should follow the same basic structure. *Exception:* You may need to write a proposal abstract months before the work it describes will be complete.

345–47 **Copy and paste key statements.** If you've already written the work, highlight your **THESIS**, objective, or purpose; basic information on your methods; your results; and your conclusion. Copy and paste those sentences into a new document to create a rough version of your abstract.

486–87 **Pare down the rough abstract.** **SUMMARIZE** the key ideas in the document, editing out any nonessential words and details. In your first sentence, introduce the overall scope of your study. Also include any other information that seems crucial to understanding your paper. Avoid phrases that add unnecessary words, such as "It is concluded that." In general, you probably won't want to use "I"; an abstract should cover ideas, not say what you think or will do.

Conform to any requirements. In general, an informative abstract should be at most 10 percent as long as the original and no longer than the maximum length allowed. Descriptive abstracts should be shorter still, and proposal abstracts should conform to the requirements of the organization calling for the proposal.

Ways of Organizing an Abstract

[An informative abstract]

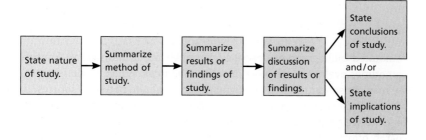

State nature of study. → Summarize method of study. → Summarize results or findings of study. → Summarize discussion of results or findings. → State conclusions of study.

and/or

State implications of study.

[A descriptive abstract]

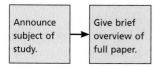

Announce subject of study. → Give brief overview of full paper.

[A proposal abstract]

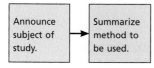

Announce subject of study. → Summarize method to be used.

IF YOU NEED MORE HELP

See Chapter 28 for guidelines on **DRAFTING**, Chapter 29 on **ASSESSING YOUR OWN WRITING**, Chapter 30 on **GETTING RESPONSE AND REVISING**, and Chapter 31 on **EDITING AND PROOFREADING**.

298–300
301–5
313–17

15 Annotated Bibliographies

Annotated bibliographies describe, give publication information for, and sometimes evaluate each work on a list of sources. When we do research, we may consult annotated bibliographies to evaluate potential sources. In some college courses, you may be assigned to create annotated bibliographies to weigh the potential usefulness of sources and to document your search efforts so that teachers can assess your ability to find, describe, and evaluate sources. There are two kinds of annotations, *descriptive* and *evaluative*; both may be brief, consisting only of phrases, or more formal, consisting of sentences and paragraphs. Sometimes an annotated bibliography is introduced by a short statement explaining its scope.

Descriptive annotations simply summarize the contents of each work, without comment or evaluation. They may be very short, just long enough to capture the flavor of the work, like the examples in the following excerpt from a bibliography of books and articles on teen films, published in the *Journal of Popular Film and Television.*

MICHAEL BENTON, MARK DOLAN, AND REBECCA ZISCH

Teen Film$

In the introduction to his book *The Road to Romance and Ruin*, Jon Lewis points out that over half of the world's population is currently under the age of twenty. This rather startling fact should be enough to make most Hollywood producers drool when they think of the potential profits from a target movie audience. Attracting the largest demographic group is, after all, the quickest way to box-office success. In fact, almost from its beginning, the film industry has recognized the importance of the teenaged audience, with characters such as Andy Hardy and locales such as Ridgemont High and the 'hood.

Beyond the assumption that teen films are geared exclusively toward teenagers, however, film researchers should keep in mind that people of all ages have attended and still attend teen films. Popular films about adolescents are also expressions of larger cultural currents. Studying the films is important for understanding an era's common beliefs about its teenaged population within a broader pattern of general cultural preoccupations.

This selected bibliography is intended both to serve and to stimulate interest in the teen film genre. It provides a research tool for those who are studying teen films and their cultural implications. Unfortunately, however, in the process of compiling this list we quickly realized that it was impossible to be genuinely comprehensive or to satisfy every interest.

Doherty, Thomas. *Teenagers and Teenpics: The Juvenilization of American Movies in the 1950s*. Unwin Hyman, 1988. Historical discussion of the identification of teenagers as a targeted film market.

Foster, Harold M. "Film in the Classroom: Coping with 'Teenpics.'" *English Journal*, vol. 76, no. 3, Mar. 1987, pp. 86-88. Evaluation of the potential of using teen films such as *Sixteen Candles*, *The Karate Kid*, *Risky Business*, *The Flamingo Kid*, and *The Breakfast Club* to instruct adolescents on the difference between film as communication and film as exploitation.

Washington, Michael, and Marvin J. Berlowitz."Blaxploitation Films and High School Youth: Swat Superfly." *Jump Cut*, vol. 9, Oct.-Dec. 1975, pp. 23-24. Marxist reaction to the trend of youth-oriented black action films. Article seeks to illuminate the negative influences the films have on high school students by pointing out the false ideas about education, morality, and the black family espoused by the heroes in the films.

These annotations are purely descriptive; the authors express none of their own opinions. They describe works as "historical" or "Marxist" but do not indicate whether they're "good." The bibliography entries are documented in MLA style.

Evaluative annotations offer opinions on a source as well as describe it. They are often helpful in assessing how useful a source will be for your own writing. The following evaluative annotations are from a bibliography by Jessica Ann Olson, a student at Wright State University.

JESSICA ANN OLSON

Global Warming

Gore, Al. *An Inconvenient Truth: The Planetary Emergency of Global Warming and What We Can Do about It.* Rodale, 2006.
This publication, which is based on Gore's slide show on global warming, stresses the urgency of the global warming crisis. It centers on how the atmosphere is very thin and how greenhouse gases such as carbon dioxide are making it thicker. The thicker atmosphere traps more infrared radiation, causing warming of the Earth. Gore argues that carbon dioxide, which is created by burning fossil fuels, cutting down forests, and producing cement, accounts for eighty percent of greenhouse gas emissions. He includes several examples of problems caused by global warming. Penguins and polar bears are at risk because the glaciers they call home are quickly melting. Coral reefs are being bleached and destroyed when their inhabitants overheat and leave. Global warming is now affecting people's lives as well. For example, the highways in Alaska are only frozen enough to be driven on fewer than eighty days of the year. In China and elsewhere, record-setting floods and droughts are taking place. Hurricanes are on the rise. This source's goal is to inform its audience about the ongoing global warming crisis and to inspire change across the world. It is useful because it relies on scientific data that can be referred to easily and it provides a solid foundation for me to build on. For example, it explains how carbon dioxide is produced and how it is currently affecting plants and animals. This evidence could potentially help my research on how humans are biologically affected by global warming. It will also help me structure my essay, using its general information to lead into the specifics of my topic. For example, I could introduce the issue by explaining the thinness of the atmosphere and the effect of greenhouse gases, then focus on carbon dioxide and its effects on organisms.

Parmesan, Camille, and Hector Galbraith. "Executive Summary." *Observed Impacts of Global Climate Change in the U.S.,* Pew Center on Global

Climate Change, Nov. 2004, c2es.org/docUploads/final_ObsImpact.pdf. Accessed 17 Jan. 2007.

This report summarizes recent scientific findings that document the impact changes in the climate have had on the distribution of plants and animals in the United States and on how they interact within their communities. For example, it explains how a shift has taken place in the blooming period for plants and the breeding period for animals caused by global warming. Because of changes in their geographic range, species may interact differently, possibly resulting in population declines. For example, the red fox is now found in areas dominated by the arctic fox and is threatening its survival. The report stresses that such shifts can harm the world's biodiversity. Plants and animals that are rare now face extinction. The annual cycle of carbon dioxide levels in the atmosphere has also changed, largely due to the lengthening of the growing season, affecting basic ecosystem processes. I did not find this report as helpful as other sources because its information is based only on observations made in the United States. The information appears reliable, though, because it is based on scientific evidence. This essay will be helpful to my essay because it focuses on how plants and animals are currently affected, such as their shifting communities and how they are clashing. I could use this to explain human changes by providing evidence of what is happening to other species. This source will not be as helpful in explaining the climate's effects on human biological function in particular, but it will provide some framework. For example, I could explain how the plants that help convert carbon dioxide into oxygen are being harmed and relate that to how the humans will suffer the consequences.

These annotations not only describe the sources in detail, but also evaluate their usefulness for the writer's own project. They show that the writer understands the content of the sources and can relate it to her own anticipated needs as a researcher and writer.

Key Features / Annotated Bibliographies

A statement of scope.   Sometimes you need or are asked to provide a brief introductory statement to explain what you're covering. The authors of the bibliography on teen films introduce their bibliography with three paragraphs establishing a context for the bibliography and announcing their purpose for compiling it.

Complete bibliographic information.   Provide all the information about each source using one documentation system (MLA, APA, or another one) so that you, your readers, or other researchers will be able to find the source easily. It's a good idea to include sources' URLs or **PERMALINKS** to make accessing online sources easier.

443

A concise description of the work.   A good annotation describes each item as carefully and objectively as possible, giving accurate information and showing that you understand the source. These qualities will help to build authority—for you as a writer and for your annotations.

Relevant commentary.   If you write an evaluative bibliography, your comments should be relevant to your purpose and audience. The best way to achieve relevance is to consider what questions a potential reader might have about each source: What are the main points of the source? What is its argument? How current and reliable is it? Will the source be helpful for your project?

Consistent presentation.   All annotations should follow a consistent pattern: if one is written in complete sentences, they should all be. Each annotation in the teen films bibliography, for example, begins with a phrase (not a complete sentence) characterizing the work.

A BRIEF GUIDE TO WRITING ANNOTATED BIBLIOGRAPHIES

Considering the Rhetorical Situation

55–56

PURPOSE   Will your bibliography need to demonstrate the depth or breadth of your research? Will your readers actually track down and use your sources? Do you need or want to convince readers that your sources are good?

academic literacies   rhetorical situations   genres   processes   strategies   research MLA / APA   media / design   readings

AUDIENCE   For whom are you compiling this bibliography? What does your audience need to know about each source?

57–60

STANCE   Are you presenting yourself as an objective describer or evaluator? Or are you expressing a particular point of view toward the sources you evaluate?

64–67

MEDIA / DESIGN   If you are publishing the bibliography electronically, will you provide links from each annotation to the source itself? Online or off, should you distinguish the bibliographic information from the annotation by using a different font?

68–70

Generating Ideas and Text

Decide what sources to include.   You may be tempted to include in a bibliography every source you find or look at. A better strategy is to include only those sources that you or your readers may find potentially useful in researching your topic. For an academic bibliography, you need to consider the qualities in the list below. Some of these qualities should not rule a source in or out; they simply raise issues you need to think about.

- *Appropriateness.* Is this source relevant to your topic? Is it a primary source or a secondary source? Is it aimed at an appropriate audience? General or specialized? Elementary, advanced, or somewhere in between?

- *Credibility.* Is the author reputable? Is the publication, publishing company, or sponsor of the site reputable? Do the ideas more or less agree with those in other sources you've read?

- *Balance.* Does the source present enough evidence for its assertions? Does it show any particular bias? Does it present countering arguments fairly?

- *Timeliness.* Is the source recent enough? Does it reflect current thinking or research about the subject?

If you need help **FINDING SOURCES**, see Chapter 46.

445–68

MLA 500–548 ●
APA 549–89

Compile a list of works to annotate. Give the sources themselves in whatever documentation style is required; see the guidelines for **MLA** and **APA** styles in Chapters 52 and 53.

Determine what kind of bibliography you need to write. Descriptive or evaluative? Will your annotations be in the form of phrases? complete sentences? paragraphs? The form will shape your reading and note taking. If you're writing a descriptive bibliography, your reading goal will be just to understand and capture the writer's message as clearly as possible. If you're writing an evaluative bibliography, you will also need to assess the source as you read in order to include your own opinions of it.

235–44 ▲

Read carefully. To write an annotation, you must understand the source's argument, but when you are writing an annotated bibliography as part of a **PROPOSAL**, you may have neither the time nor the need to read the whole text. Here's a way of quickly determining whether a source is likely to serve your needs:

- Check the publisher or sponsor (university press? scholarly journal? popular magazine? website sponsored by a reputable organization?).
- Read the preface (of a book), abstract (of a scholarly article), introduction (of an article in a nonscholarly magazine or a website).
- Skim the table of contents or the headings.
- Read the parts that relate specifically to your topic.

Research the writer, if necessary. If you are required to indicate the writer's credentials, you may need to do additional research. You may find information by typing the writer's name into a search engine or looking up the writer in *Contemporary Authors*. In any case, information about the writer should take up no more than one sentence in your annotation.

399–407 ◆

Summarize the work in a sentence or two. **DESCRIBE** it as objectively as possible: even if you are writing an evaluative annotation, you can evaluate the central point of a work better by stating it clearly first. *If you're writing a descriptive annotation, you're done.*

Establish criteria for evaluating sources. If you're **EVALUATING** sources for a project, you'll need to evaluate them in terms of their usefulness for your project, their **STANCE**, and their overall credibility.

469–72

64–67

Write a brief evaluation of the source. If you can generalize about the worth of the entire work, fine. You may find, however, that some parts are useful while others are not, and what you write should reflect that mix.

Be consistent—in content, sentence structure, and format.

- **Content.** Try to provide about the same amount of information for each entry. If you're evaluating, don't evaluate some sources and just describe others.

- **Sentence structure.** Use the same style throughout—complete sentences, brief phrases, or a mix.

- **Format.** Use one documentation style throughout; use a consistent **FONT** for each element in each entry—for example, italicize or underline all book titles.

601–2

Ways of Organizing an Annotated Bibliography

Depending on their purpose, annotated bibliographies may or may not include an introduction. Most annotated bibliographies cover a single topic and so are organized alphabetically by author's or editor's last name. When a work lacks a named author, alphabetize it by the first important word in its title. Consult the documentation system you're using for additional details about alphabetizing works appropriately.

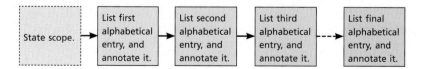

State scope. → List first alphabetical entry, and annotate it. → List second alphabetical entry, and annotate it. → List third alphabetical entry, and annotate it. ⇢ List final alphabetical entry, and annotate it.

Sometimes an annotated bibliography needs to be organized into several subject areas (or genres, periods, or some other category); if so, the entries are listed alphabetically within each category. For example, a bibliography about terrorism breaks down into subjects such as "Global Terrorism" and "Weapons of Mass Destruction."

[Multicategory bibliography]

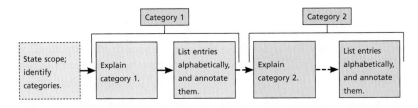

298–300
301–5
306–12
313–17
318–28

IF YOU NEED MORE HELP

See Chapter 28 for guidelines on **DRAFTING**, Chapter 29 on **ASSESSING YOUR OWN WRITING**, Chapter 30 on **GETTING RESPONSE AND REVISING**, and Chapter 31 on **EDITING AND PROOFREADING**. See Chapter 32 if you are required to submit your bibliography in a writing **PORTFOLIO**.

Evaluations 16

ConsumerReports.org evaluates cars and laundry detergents. The *Princeton Review* and *U.S. News & World Report* evaluate colleges and universities. You probably consult such sources to make decisions, and you probably evaluate things all the time—when you recommend a film (or not) or a teacher (ditto). An evaluation is at bottom a judgment; you judge something according to certain criteria, supporting your judgment with reasons and evidence. You need to give your reasons for evaluating it as you do because often your evaluation will affect your audience's actions: they must see this movie, needn't bother with this book, should be sure to have the Caesar salad at this restaurant, and so on.

In college courses, students in *literature, film, drama,* and *art* classes may be assigned to evaluate poems, fiction, movies, plays, and art works,

ConsumerReports.org *uses lab testing to support the evaluations it publishes.*

and those in *business* and *political science* classes may be asked to evaluate advertising or political campaigns or plans for business or public-policy initiatives. In a review that follows, written for a first-year writing class at Wright State University, Ali Heinekamp offers her evaluation of the film *Juno*.

ALI HEINEKAMP

Juno: *Not Just Another Teen Movie*

It all starts with a chair, where Juno (Ellen Page) has unprotected sex with her best friend Bleeker (Michael Cera). Several weeks later, she's at a convenience store, buying a pregnancy test. Only sixteen, Juno faces the terrifying task of telling her parents that she is pregnant. With their support, Juno moves forward in her decision to give birth and give the child to Mark (Jason Bateman) and Vanessa (Jennifer Garner), a wealthy and seemingly perfect married couple looking to adopt. Although the situations *Juno*'s characters find themselves in and their dialogue may be criticized as unrealistic, the film, written by Diablo Cody and directed by Jason Reitman, successfully portrays the emotions of a teen being shoved into maturity way too fast.

Much of the time, *Juno* seems unrealistic because it seems to treat the impact of teen pregnancy so lightly. The consequences of Juno's pregnancy are sugar-coated to such an extent that in many cases, they are barely apparent. The film downplays the emotional struggle that a pregnant woman would feel in deciding to give birth and then put that child up for adoption, and it ignores the discomforts of pregnancy, such as mood swings and nausea.

Likewise, *Juno*'s dialogue is too good to be true—funny and clever, but unrealistic. For example, Juno tells Mark and Vanessa "If I could just have the thing and give it to you now, I totally would. But I'm guessing it looks probably like a sea monkey right now, and we should let it get a little cuter." At another point, talking about her absent mother, Juno says, "Oh, and she inexplicably mails me a cactus every Valentine's Day. And I'm like, 'Thanks a heap, coyote ugly. This cactus-gram stings even worse than your abandonment.'" As funny as they are, the creatively quirky one-liners often go a bit too far, detracting from both the gravity of Juno's situation and the film's believability.

academic literacies | rhetorical situations | genres | processes | strategies | research MLA / APA | media / design | readings

Ellen Page as Juno.

But although the situations and dialogue are unrealistic, the emotional heart of the movie is believable—and moving. Despite the movie's lack of realism in portraying her pregnancy, Juno's vulnerability transforms her character and situation into something much more believable. Juno mentions at various times that her classmates stare at her stomach and talk about her behind her back, but initially she seems unconcerned with the negative attention. This façade falls apart, however, when Juno accuses Bleeker, the baby's father, of being ashamed of the fact that he and Juno have had sex. The strong front she is putting up drops when she bursts out, "At least you don't have to have the evidence under your sweater." This break in Juno's strength reveals her vulnerability and makes her character relatable and believable.

The juxtaposition of Juno's teenage quirks and the adult situation she's in also reminds us of her youth and vulnerability. As a result of the adult situation Juno finds herself in and her generally stoic demeanor, it's easy to see her as a young adult. But the film fills each scene with visual reminders that Juno is just a kid being forced into situations beyond her maturity level. At a convenience store, Juno buys a pregnancy test along with a licorice rope. She calls Women Now, an abortion clinic, on a phone that looks like a hamburger. And while she is giving birth, she wears long, brightly striped socks. These subtle visual cues help us remember the reality of Juno's position as both physically an adult and emotionally an adolescent.

While the dialogue is too clever to be realistic, in the end it's carried by the movie's heart. Scott Tobias from the entertainment website *The A.V. Club* says it best when he writes that the colorful dialogue is often "too ostentatious for its own good, but the film's sincerity is what ultimately carries it across." In fact, intensely emotional scenes are marked by their *lack* of witty dialogue. For example, when Juno runs into Vanessa at the mall, Vanessa, reluctantly at first, kneels down to talk to the baby through Juno's stomach. Vanessa's diction while talking to the baby is so simple, so expected. She simply starts with, "Hi baby, it's me. It's Vanessa," and then continues, "I can't wait to meet you." This simple, everyday statement stands out in comparison to the rest of the well-crafted, humorous script. For her part, Juno simply stares admiringly at Vanessa. She doesn't have to say anything to transform the scene into a powerful one. Another scene in which the dialogue stops being clever is the one in which Juno and Bleeker lie side by side in a hospital bed after Juno has given birth, Juno in tears and Bleeker lost in thought. They don't need to say anything for us to feel their pain at the realization that although the pregnancy is over, it will never truly be in the past. The absence of dialogue in scenes such as these actually contributes to their power. We finally see more than stoicism and sarcasm from Juno: we see caring and fear, which are feelings most would expect of a pregnant teen.

There has been much concern among critics that as a pregnant teenager, Juno doesn't present a good role model for teen girls. Worrying that teens may look up to Juno so much that being pregnant becomes "cool," Dana Stevens writes in *Slate*, "Let's hope that the teenage girls of America don't cast their condoms to the wind in hopes of becoming as cool as 16-year-old Juno MacGuff." But it is not Juno's pregnancy that makes her cool: it is her ability to overcome the difficult obstacles thrown at her, and that strength does make her a good role model. Another critic, Lisa Schwarzbaum from *Entertainment Weekly*, feels that the movie might have been more realistic had Juno chosen to go through with an abortion. It's true that Juno may have chosen the more difficult answer to a teen pregnancy, but she is far from alone in her decision. Perhaps Schwarzbaum underestimates teens in thinking that they would not be able to cope with the emotionally difficult situation Juno chooses. Again, in her strength, Juno is a role model for young women.

academic literacies

rhetorical situations

genres

processes

strategies

research MLA / APA

media / design

readings

Although *Juno* is a comedy filled with improbable situations, exaggerations, and wit, its genuine emotion allows us to connect with and relate to the film. The reality of the characters' emotions in controversial and serious situations allows *Juno* to transcend its own genre. It reaches depths of emotion that are unusual for teenage comedies, proving that *Juno* is not just another teen movie.

Works Cited

Juno. Written by Diablo Cody, directed by Jason Reitman, performance by Ellen Page, Michael Cera, Jennifer Garner, and Jason Bateman. Fox Searchlight, 2007.

Schwarzbaum, Lisa. Review of *Juno. Entertainment Weekly*, 9 Jan. 2008, www.ew.com/article/2008/01/09/juno. Accessed 14 Apr. 2008.

Stevens, Dana. "Superpregnant: How *Juno* Is *Knocked Up* from the Girl's Point of View." Review of *Juno. Slate*, 5 Dec. 2007, www.slate.com/articles/arts/movies/2007/12/superpregnant.html. Accessed 12 Apr. 2008.

Tobias, Scott. Review of *Juno. The A.V. Club*, 6 Dec. 2007, www.avclub.com/review/juno-3171. Accessed 13 Apr. 2008.

Heinekamp quickly summarizes Juno's plot and then evaluates the film according to clearly stated criteria. She responds to several reviewers' comments, joining the critical conversation about the film, and documents her sources in MLA style.

For four more evaluations, see CHAPTER 63.

Key Features / Evaluations

A concise description of the subject.   You should include just enough information to let readers who may not be familiar with your subject understand what it is; the goal is to evaluate, not summarize. Depending on your topic and medium, some of this information may be in visual or audio form. Heinekamp briefly describes *Juno*'s main plot points in her first paragraph, only providing what readers need to understand the context of her evaluation.

Clearly defined criteria.   You need to determine clear criteria as the basis for your judgment. In reviews or other evaluations written for a broad audience, you can integrate the criteria into the discussion as reasons for your assessment, as Heinekamp does in her evaluation of *Juno*. In more formal evaluations, you may need to announce your criteria explicitly. Heinekamp evaluates the film based on the power of its emotion and the realism of its situations, characters, and dialogue.

A knowledgeable discussion of the subject.   To evaluate something credibly, you need to show that you know it yourself and that you've researched what other authoritative sources say. Heinekamp cites many examples from *Juno*, showing her knowledge of the film. She also cites reviews from three internet sources, showing that she's researched others' views as well.

A balanced and fair assessment.   An evaluation is centered on a judgment. Heinekamp concedes that *Juno*'s situations and dialogue are unrealistic, but she says it nevertheless "reaches depths of emotion that are unusual for teenage comedies." It is important that any judgment be balanced and fair. Seldom is something all good or all bad. A fair evaluation need not be all positive or all negative; it may acknowledge both strengths and weaknesses. For example, a movie's soundtrack may be wonderful while the plot is not. Heinekamp criticizes *Juno*'s too-witty dialogue and unrealistic situations, even as she appreciates its heart.

Well-supported reasons.   You need to argue for your judgment, providing reasons and evidence that might include visual and audio as well as verbal material. Heinekamp gives several reasons for her positive assessment of *Juno*—the believability of its characters, the intensely emotional scenes, the strength of the main character as a role model—and she supports these reasons with many quotations and examples from the film.

A BRIEF GUIDE TO WRITING EVALUATIONS

Choosing Something to Evaluate

You can more effectively evaluate a limited subject than a broad one: review certain dishes at a local restaurant rather than the entire menu; review one film or episode rather than all the films by Alfred Hitchcock

academic literacies   rhetorical situations   genres   processes   strategies   research MLA / APA   media / design   readings

or all sixty-two *Breaking Bad* episodes. The more specific and focused your subject, the better you can write about it.

Considering the Rhetorical Situation

PURPOSE Are you writing to affect your audience's opinion of a subject? to help others decide what to see, do, or buy? to demonstrate your expertise in a field?

■ 55–56

AUDIENCE To whom are you writing? What will your audience already know about the subject? What will they expect to learn from your evaluation of it? Are they likely to agree with you or not?

■ 57–60

STANCE What is your attitude toward the subject, and how will you show that you have evaluated it fairly and appropriately? Think about the tone you want to use: should it be reasonable? passionate? critical?

■ 64–67

MEDIA / DESIGN How will you deliver your evaluation? In print? Electronically? As a speech? Can you show images or audio or video clips? If you're submitting your text for publication, are there any format requirements?

■ 68–70

Generating Ideas and Text

Explore what you already know. **FREEWRITE** to answer the following questions: What do you know about this subject or subjects like it? What are your initial or gut feelings, and why do you feel as you do? How does this subject reflect or affect your basic values or beliefs? How have others evaluated subjects like this?

○ 289–90

Identify criteria. Make a list of criteria you think should be used to evaluate your subject. Think about which criteria will likely be important to your **AUDIENCE**. You might find **CUBING** and **QUESTIONING** to be useful processes for thinking about your criteria.

■ 57–60
○ 292–93

Evaluate your subject. Study your subject closely to determine to what extent it meets each of your criteria. You may want to list your criteria and take notes related to each one, or you may develop a rating scale for each criterion to help stay focused on it. Come up with a tentative judgment.

380–87
Compare your subject with others. Often, evaluating something involves **COMPARING AND CONTRASTING** it with similar things. We judge movies in comparison with the other movies we've seen and french fries with the other fries we've tasted. Sometimes those comparisons can be made informally. For other evaluations, you may have to do research—to try on several pairs of jeans before buying any, for example—to see how your subject compares.

345–47
State your judgment as a tentative thesis statement. Your **THESIS STATEMENT** should be one that addresses both pros and cons. "*Hawaii Five-O* is fun to watch despite its stilted dialogue." "Of the five sport-utility vehicles tested, the Toyota 4Runner emerged as the best in comfort, power, and durability, though not in styling or cargo capacity." Both of these examples offer a judgment but qualify it according to the writer's criteria.

Anticipate other opinions. I think Will Ferrell is a comic genius whose movies are first-rate. You think Will Ferrell is a terrible actor who makes awful movies. How can I write a review of his latest film that you will at least consider? One way is by **ACKNOWLEDGING** other opinions—and
368
369
REFUTING those opinions as best I can. I may not persuade you to see Ferrell's next film, but I can at least demonstrate that by certain criteria
433
he should be appreciated. You may need to **RESEARCH** how others have evaluated your subject.

358–59
Identify and support your reasons. Write out all the **REASONS** you can think of that will convince your audience to accept your judgment. Review your list to identify the most convincing or important reasons. Then review
359–67
how well your subject meets your criteria and decide how best to **SUPPORT** your reasons: through examples, authoritative opinions, statistics, visual or audio evidence, or something else.

academic literacies · rhetorical situations · genres · processes · strategies · research MLA / APA · media / design · readings

Ways of Organizing an Evaluation

Evaluations are usually organized in one of two ways. One way is to introduce what's being evaluated, followed by your judgment, discussing your criteria along the way. This is a useful strategy if your audience may not be familiar with your subject.

[Start with your subject]

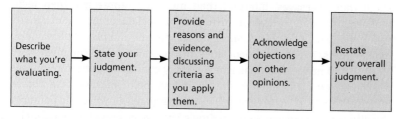

Describe what you're evaluating. → State your judgment. → Provide reasons and evidence, discussing criteria as you apply them. → Acknowledge objections or other opinions. → Restate your overall judgment.

You might also start by identifying your criteria and then follow with a discussion of how well your subject meets those criteria. This strategy foregrounds the process by which you reached your conclusions.

[Start with your criteria]

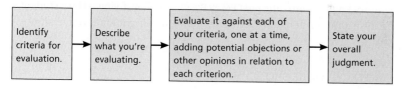

Identify criteria for evaluation. → Describe what you're evaluating. → Evaluate it against each of your criteria, one at a time, adding potential objections or other opinions in relation to each criterion. → State your overall judgment.

IF YOU NEED MORE HELP

See Chapter 28 for guidelines on **DRAFTING**, Chapter 29 on **ASSESSING YOUR OWN WRITING**, Chapter 30 on **GETTING RESPONSE AND REVISING**, and Chapter 31 on **EDITING AND PROOFREADING**. See Chapter 32 if you are required to submit your report in a writing **PORTFOLIO**.

298–300
301–5
306–12
313–17
318–28

17 Literary Analyses

Literary analyses are essays that examine literary texts closely to understand their messages, interpret their meanings, appreciate their techniques, or understand their historical or social contexts. Such texts traditionally include novels, short stories, poems, and plays but may also include films, TV shows, videogames, music, and comics. You might read *Macbeth* and notice that Shakespeare's play contains a pattern of images of blood. You could explore the distinctive point of view in Ambrose Bierce's story "An Occurrence at Owl Creek Bridge." Or you could point out the differences between Stephen King's *The Shining* and Stanley Kubrick's screenplay based on that novel. In all these cases, you use specific analytical techniques to go below the surface of the work to deepen your understanding of how it works and what it means.

You may be assigned to analyze works of literature in courses in *English*, *film*, *drama*, and many other subjects. Here is a sonnet by the nineteenth-century English Romantic poet Percy Bysshe Shelley, followed by a student's analysis of it written for a literature course at Wright State University.

PERCY BYSSHE SHELLEY

Sonnet: "Lift not the painted veil which those who live"

Lift not the painted veil which those who live
Call Life: though unreal shapes be pictured there,
And it but mimic all we would believe
With colours idly spread, —behind, lurk Fear
And Hope, twin Destinies; who ever weave   5

Their shadows, o'er the chasm, sightless and drear.
I knew one who had lifted it — he sought,
For his lost heart was tender, things to love,
But found them not, alas! nor was there aught
The world contains, the which he could approve. 10
Through the unheeding many he did move,
A splendour among shadows, a bright blot
Upon this gloomy scene, a Spirit that strove
For truth, and like the Preacher found it not.

STEPHANIE HUFF

Metaphor and Society in Shelley's "Sonnet"

In his sonnet "Lift not the painted veil which those who live," Percy
Bysshe Shelley introduces us to a bleak world that exists behind veils
and shadows. We see that although fear and hope both exist, truth is
dishearteningly absent. This absence of truth is exactly what Shelley
chooses to address as he uses metaphors of grim distortion and radiant
incandescence to expose the counterfeit nature of our world.

The speaker of Shelley's poem presents bold assertions about the
nature of our society. In the opening lines of the poem, he warns the
reader, "Lift not the painted veil which those who live / Call Life"
(lines 1–2). Here, the "painted veil" serves as a grim metaphor for life.
More specifically, the speaker equates the veil with what people like
to *call* life. In this sense, the speaker asserts that what we believe to
be pure reality is actually nothing more than a covering that masks
what really lies beneath. Truth is covered by a veil of falsehood and is
made opaque with the paint of people's lies.

This painted veil does not completely obstruct our view but rather
distorts what we can see. All that can be viewed through it are "unreal
shapes" (2) that metaphorically represent the people that make up this
counterfeit society. These shapes are not to be taken for truth. They are
unreal, twisted, deformed figures of humanity, people full of falsities
and misrepresentations.

Most people, however, do not realize that the shapes and images
seen through the veil are distorted because all they know of life is the

veil —this life we see as reality only "mimic[s] all we would believe" (3), using "colours idly spread" (4) to create pictures that bear little resemblance to that which they claim to portray. All pure truths are covered up and painted over until they are mere mockeries. The lies that cloak the truth are not even carefully constructed, but are created idly, with little attention to detail. The paint is not applied carefully but merely spread across the top. This idea of spreading brings to mind images of paint slopped on so heavily that the truth beneath becomes nearly impossible to find. Even the metaphor of color suggests only superficial beauty —"idly spread" (4) —rather than any sort of pure beauty that could penetrate the surface of appearances.

What really lies behind this facade are fear and hope, both of which "weave / Their shadows, o'er the chasm, sightless and drear" (5–6). These two realities are never truly seen or experienced, though. They exist only as shadows. Just as shadows appear only at certain times of day, cast only sham images of what they reflect, and are paid little attention, so too do these emotions of hope and fear appear only as brief, ignored imitations of themselves when they enter the artificiality of this chasmlike world. Peering into a chasm, one cannot hope to make out what lies at the bottom. At best one could perhaps make out shadows and even that cannot be done with any certainty as to true appearance. The world is so large, so caught up in itself and its counterfeit ways, that it can no longer see even the simple truths of hope and fear. Individuals and civilizations have become sightless, dreary, and as enormously empty as a chasm.

This chasm does not include *all* people, however, as we are introduced to one individual, in line 7, who is trying to bring to light whatever truth may yet remain. This one person, who defies the rest of the world, is portrayed with metaphors of light, clearly standing out among the dark representations of the rest of mankind. He is first presented to us as possessing a "lost heart" (8) and seeking things to love. It is important that the first metaphor applied to him be a heart because this is the organ with which we associate love, passion, and purity. We associate it with brightness of the soul, making it the most radiant spot of the body. He is then described as a "splendour among shadows" (12), his purity and truth brilliantly shining through the darkness of the majority's falsehood. Finally, he is equated with "a bright blot / Upon this gloomy scene" (12–13), his own bright blaze of authenticity burning in stark contrast to the murky phoniness of the rest of the world.

These metaphors of light are few, however, in comparison to those of grim distortion. So, too, are this one individual's radiance and zeal too little to alter the warped darkness they temporarily pierce. This one person, though bright, is not bright enough to light up the rest of civilization and create real change. The light simply confirms the dark falsity that comprises the rest of the world. Shelley gives us one flame of hope, only to reveal to us what little chance it has under the suffocating veil. Both the metaphors of grim distortion and those of radiant incandescence work together in this poem to highlight the world's counterfeit nature.

Huff focuses her analysis on patterns in Shelley's imagery. In addition, she pays careful attention to individual words and to how, as the poem unfolds, they create a certain meaning. That meaning is her interpretation.

For two more literary analyses, see CHAPTER 64.

Key Features / Literary Analyses

An arguable thesis. A literary analysis is a form of argument; you are arguing that your analysis of a literary work is valid. Your thesis, then, should be arguable, as Huff's is: "[Shelley] uses metaphors of grim distortion and radiant incandescence to expose the counterfeit nature of our world." A mere summary — "Shelley writes about a person who sees reality and seeks love but never finds it" — would not be arguable and therefore is not a good thesis.

Careful attention to the language of the text. The key to analyzing a text is looking carefully at the language, which is the foundation of its meaning. Specific words, images, metaphors—these are where analysis begins. You may also bring in contextual information, such as cultural, historical, or biographical facts, or you may refer to similar texts. But the words, phrases, and sentences that make up the text you are analyzing are your primary source when dealing with texts. That's what literature teachers mean by "close reading": reading with the assumption that every word of a text is meaningful.

Attention to patterns or themes. Literary analyses are usually built on evidence of meaningful patterns or themes within a text or among several texts. These patterns and themes reveal meaning. In Shelley's poem, images of light and shadow and artifice and reality create patterns of meaning, while the poem's many half rhymes (*live / believe*, *love / approve*) create patterns of sound that may contribute to the overall meaning.

A clear interpretation. A literary analysis demonstrates the plausibility of its thesis by using evidence from the text and, sometimes, relevant contextual evidence to explain how the language and patterns found there support a particular interpretation. When you write a literary analysis, you show readers one way the text may be read and understood; that is your interpretation.

MLA style. Literary analyses usually follow MLA style. Even though Huff's essay has no works-cited list, it refers to line numbers using MLA style.

A BRIEF GUIDE TO WRITING LITERARY ANALYSES

Considering the Rhetorical Situation

55–56	**PURPOSE**	What do you need to do? Show that you have examined the text carefully? Offer your own interpretation? Demonstrate a particular analytical technique? Or some combination? If you're responding to an assignment, does it specify what you need to do?
57–60	**AUDIENCE**	What do you need to do to convince your readers that your interpretation is plausible and based on sound analysis? Can you assume that readers are already familiar with the text you are analyzing, or do you need to tell them about it?
64–67	**STANCE**	How can you see your subject through interested, curious eyes—and then step back in order to see what your observations might *mean*?

MEDIA/DESIGN Will your analysis focus on an essentially verbal text or one that has significant visual content, such as a graphic novel? Will you need to show visual elements in your analysis? Will it be delivered in a print, spoken, or electronic medium? Are you required to follow MLA or some other style?

■ 68–70

Generating Ideas and Text

Look at your assignment. Does it specify a particular kind of analysis? Does it ask you to consider a particular theme? To use any specific critical approaches? Look for any terms that tell you what to do, words like *analyze, compare, interpret,* and so on.

Study the text with a critical eye. When we read a literary work, we often come away with a reaction to it: we like it, we hate it, it made us cry or laugh, it perplexed us. That may be a good starting point for a literary analysis, but to write about literature you need to go beyond initial reactions, to think about **HOW THE TEXT WORKS**: What does it *say*, and what does it *do*? What elements make up this text? How do those elements work together or fail to work together? Does this text lead you to think or feel a certain way? How does it fit into a particular context (of history, culture, technology, genre, and so on)?

✳ 20–22

Choose a method for analyzing the text. There are various ways to analyze your subject. Three common focuses are on the text itself, on your own experience reading it, and on other cultural, historical, or literary contexts.

- *The text itself.* Trace the development and expression of themes, characters, and language through the work. How do they help to create the overall meaning, tone, or effect for which you're arguing? To do this, you might look at the text as a whole, something you can understand from all angles at once. You could also pick out parts from the beginning, middle, and end as needed to make your case, **DEFINING**

◆ 388–98

399–407

419–27

key terms, **DESCRIBING** characters and settings, and **NARRATING** key scenes. Huff's essay about the Shelley sonnet offers a text-based analysis that looks at patterns of images in the poem. You might also examine the same theme in several different works.

- *Your own response as a reader.* Explore the way the text affects you or develops meanings as you read through it from beginning to end. By doing such a close reading, you're slowing down the process to notice how one element of the text leads you to expect something, confirming earlier suspicions or surprises. You build your analysis on your experience of reading the text—as if you were pretending to drive somewhere for the first time, though in reality you know the way intimately. By closely examining the language of the text as you experience it, you explore how it leads you to a set of responses, both intellectual and emotional. If you were responding in this way to the Shelley poem, you might discuss how its first lines suggest that while life is an illusion, a veil, one might pull it aside and glimpse reality, however "drear."

427

- *Context.* Analyze the text as part of some **LARGER CONTEXT**—as part of a certain time or place in history or as an expression of a certain culture (how does this text relate to the time and place of its creation?), as one of many other texts like it, a representative of a genre (how is this text like or unlike others of its kind? how does it use, play with, or flout the conventions of the genre?). A context-based approach to the Shelley poem might look at Shelley's own philosophical and religious views and how they may have influenced the poem's characterization of the world we experience as illusory, a "veil."

Read the work more than once.   Reading literature, watching films, or listening to speeches is like driving to a new destination: the first time you go, you need to concentrate on getting there; on subsequent trips, you can see other aspects—the scenery, the curve of the road, other possible routes—that you couldn't pay attention to earlier. When you experience a piece of literature for the first time, you usually focus on the story, the plot, the overall meaning. By experiencing it repeatedly, you can see how its effects are achieved, what the pieces are and how they fit together, where different patterns emerge, how the author crafted the work.

academic literacies   rhetorical situations   genres   processes   strategies   research MLA / APA   media / design   readings

To analyze a literary work, then, plan to read it more than once, with the assumption that every part of the text is there for a reason. Focus on details, even on a single detail that shows up more than once: Why is it there? What can it mean? How does it affect our experience of reading or studying the text? Also, look for anomalies, details that *don't* fit the patterns: Why are they part of the text? What can they mean? How do they affect the experience of the text? See the **READING IN ACADEMIC CONTEXTS** chapter for several different methods for reading a text.

✳ 10–32

Compose a strong thesis. The **THESIS** of a literary analysis should be specific, limited, and open to potential disagreement. In addition, it should be analytical, not evaluative: avoid thesis statements that make overall judgments, such as a reviewer might do: "Virginia Woolf's *The Waves* is a failed experiment in narrative" or "No one has equaled the achievement of *The Lego Movie*." Rather, offer a way of seeing the text: "The choice presented in Robert Frost's 'The Road Not Taken' ultimately makes no difference"; "The plot of *The Lego Movie* reflects contemporary American media culture."

◆ 345–47

Read the text carefully. When you analyze a text, you need to find specific, brief passages that support your interpretation. Then you should interpret those passages in terms of their language, their context, or your reaction to them as a reader. To find such passages, you must read the text closely, questioning it as you go, asking, for example:

- What language provides evidence to support your thesis?
- What does each word (phrase, passage) mean exactly?
- Why does the writer choose *this* language, *these* words? What are the implications or connotations of the language? If the language is dense or difficult, why might the writer have written it that way?
- What images or metaphors are used? What is their effect on the meaning?
- What patterns of language, imagery, or plot do you see? If something is repeated, what significance does the repetition have?
- How does each word, phrase, or passage relate to what precedes and follows it?

- How does the experience of reading the text affect its meaning?
- What words, phrases, or passages connect to a larger **CONTEXT**? What language demonstrates that this work reflects or is affected by that context?
- How do these various elements of language, image, and pattern support your interpretation?

10–32

Your analysis should focus on analyzing and interpreting your subject, not simply summarizing or paraphrasing it. Many literary analyses also use the strategy of **COMPARING** two or more works.

380–87

Find evidence to support your interpretation. The parts of the text you examine in your close reading become the evidence you use to support your interpretation. Some think that we're all entitled to our own opinions about literature. And indeed we are. But when writing a literary analysis, we're entitled only to our own *well-supported* and *well-argued* opinions. When you analyze a text, you must treat it like any other **ARGUMENT**: you need to discuss how the text creates an effect or expresses a theme, and then you have to show **EVIDENCE** from the text—significant plot or structural elements; important characters; patterns of language, imagery, or action—to back up your argument.

355–73
359–67

Pay attention to matters of style. Literary analyses have certain conventions for using pronouns and verbs.

- In informal papers, it's okay to use the first person: "I believe Frost's narrator has little basis for claiming that one road is 'less traveled.'" In more formal essays, make assertions directly; claim authority to make statements about the text: "Frost's narrator has no basis for claiming that one road is 'less traveled.'"
- Discuss textual features in the present tense even if quotations from the text are in another tense: "When Nick finds Gatsby's body floating in the pool, he says very little about it: 'the laden mattress moved irregularly down the pool.'" Describe the historical context of the setting in the past tense: "In the 1920s, such estates as Gatsby's were rare."

Cite and document sources appropriately. Use **MLA** citation and documentation style unless told otherwise. Format **QUOTATIONS** properly, and use **SIGNAL PHRASES** to introduce quoted material.

● MLA 500–548
480–83
487–90

Think about format and design. Brief essays do not require **HEADINGS**; text divisions are usually marked by **TRANSITIONS** between paragraphs. In longer papers, though, headings can be helpful.

◻ 604–5
◆ 349

Organizing a Literary Analysis

[Of a single text]

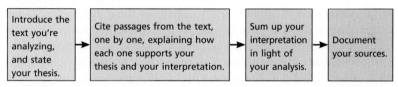

[Comparing two texts]

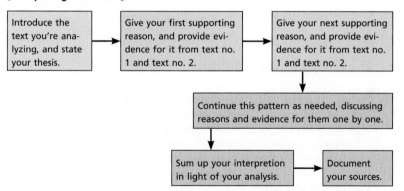

IF YOU NEED MORE HELP

See Chapter 28 for guidelines on **DRAFTING**, Chapter 29 on **ASSESSING YOUR OWN WRITING**, Chapter 30 on **GETTING RESPONSE AND REVISING**, and Chapter 31 on **EDITING AND PROOFREADING**. See Chapter 32 if you are required to submit your analysis in a writing **PORTFOLIO**.

○ 298–300
301–5
306–12
313–17
318–28

18 Memoirs

We write memoirs to explore our past—about shopping for a party dress with Grandma, or driving a car for the first time, or breaking up with our first love. Memoirs focus on events and people and places that are important to us. We usually have two goals when we write a memoir: to capture an important moment and to convey something about its significance for us. You may be asked to write memoirs or personal reflections that include memoirs in *psychology*, *education*, and *English* courses. The following example is from Pulitzer Prize–winning journalist Rick Bragg's autobiography, *All Over but the Shoutin'*. Bragg grew up in Alabama, and in this memoir he recalls when, as a teenager, he paid a final visit to his dying father.

RICK BRAGG

All Over but the Shoutin'

He was living in a little house in Jacksonville, Alabama, a college and mill town that was the closest urban center—with its stoplights and a high school and two supermarkets—to the country roads we roamed in our raggedy cars. He lived in the mill village, in one of those houses the mills subsidized for their workers, back when companies still did things like that. It was not much of a place, but better than anything we had ever lived in as a family. I knocked and a voice like an old woman's, punctuated with a cough that sounded like it came from deep in the guts, told me to come on in, it ain't locked.

It was dark inside, but light enough to see what looked like a bundle of quilts on the corner of a sofa. Deep inside them was a ghost of a man, his hair and beard long and going dirty gray, his face pale and cut with deep grooves. I knew I was in the right house because my daddy's only real possessions, a velvet-covered board pinned with medals, sat inside a glass cabinet on a table. But this couldn't be him.

He coughed again, spit into a can and struggled to his feet, but stopped somewhere short of standing straight up, as if a stoop was all he could manage. "Hey, Cotton Top," he said, and then I knew. My daddy, who was supposed to be a still-young man, looked like the walking dead, not just old but damaged, poisoned, used up, crumpled up and thrown in a corner to die. I thought that the man I would see would be the trim, swaggering, high-toned little rooster of a man who stared back at me from the pages of my mother's photo album, the young soldier clowning around in Korea, the arrow-straight, good-looking boy who posed beside my mother back before the fields and mop handle and the rest of it took her looks. The man I remembered had always dressed nice even when there was no cornmeal left, whose black hair always shone with oil, whose chin, even when it wobbled from the beer, was always angled up, high.

I thought he would greet me with that strong voice that sounded so fine when he laughed and so evil when, slurred by a quart of corn likker, he whirled through the house and cried and shrieked, tormented by things we could not see or even imagine. I thought he would be the man and monster of my childhood. But that man was as dead as a man could be, and this was what remained, like when a snake sheds its skin and leaves a dry and brittle husk of itself hanging in the Johnson grass.

"It's all over but the shoutin' now, ain't it, boy," he said, and when 5 he let the quilt slide from his shoulders I saw how he had wasted away, how the bones seemed to poke out of his clothes, and I could see how it killed his pride to look this way, unclean, and he looked away from me for a moment, ashamed.

He made a halfhearted try to shake my hand but had a coughing fit again that lasted a minute, coughing up his life, his lungs, and after that I did not want to touch him. I stared at the tops of my sneakers, ashamed to look at his face. He had a dark streak in his beard below his lip, and I wondered why, because he had never liked snuff. Now I know it was blood.

I remember much of what he had to say that day. When you don't see someone for eight, nine years, when you see that person's life red on their lips and know that you will never see them beyond this day, you listen close, even if what you want most of all is to run away.

"Your momma, she alright?" he said.

I said I reckon so.

"The other boys? They alright?" 10

I said I reckon so.

Then he was quiet for a minute, as if trying to find the words to a question to which he did not really want an answer.

"They ain't never come to see me. How come?"

I remember thinking, fool, why do you think? But I just choked down my words, and in doing so I gave up the only real chance I would ever have to accuse him, to attack him with the facts of his own sorry nature and the price it had cost us all. The opportunity hung perfectly still in the air in front of my face and fists, and I held my temper and let it float on by. I could have no more challenged him, berated him, hurt him, than I could have kicked some three-legged dog. Life had kicked his ass pretty good.

"How come?" 15

I just shrugged.

For the next few hours—unless I was mistaken, having never had one before—he tried to be my father. Between coughing and long pauses when he fought for air to generate his words, he asked me if I liked school, if I had ever gotten any better at math, the one thing that just flat evaded me. He asked me if I ever got even with the boy who blacked my eye ten years ago, and nodded his head, approvingly, as I described how I followed him into the boys' bathroom and knocked his dick string up to his watch pocket, and would have dunked his head in the urinal if the aging principal, Mr. Hand, had not had to pee and caught me dragging him across the concrete floor.

He asked me about basketball and baseball, said he had heard I had a good game against Cedar Springs, and I said pretty good, but it was two years ago, anyway. He asked if I had a girlfriend and I said, "One," and he said, "Just one?" For the slimmest of seconds he almost grinned and the young, swaggering man peeked through, but disappeared again in the disease that cloaked him. He talked and talked and never said a word, at least not the words I wanted.

He never said he was sorry.

He never said he wished things had turned out different. 20

He never acted like he did anything wrong.

Part of it, I know, was culture. Men did not talk about their

feelings in his hard world. I did not expect, even for a second, that he would bare his soul. All I wanted was a simple acknowledgment that he was wrong, or at least too drunk to notice that he left his pretty wife and sons alone again and again, with no food, no money, no way to get any, short of begging, because when she tried to find work he yelled, screamed, refused. No, I didn't expect much.

After a while he motioned for me to follow him into a back room where he had my present, and I planned to take it and run. He handed me a long, thin box, and inside was a brand-new, well-oiled Remington .22 rifle. He said he had bought it some time back, just kept forgetting to give it to me. It was a fine gun, and for a moment we were just like anybody else in the culture of that place, where a father's gift of a gun to his son is a rite. He said, with absolute seriousness, not to shoot my brothers.

I thanked him and made to leave, but he stopped me with a hand on my arm and said wait, that ain't all, that he had some other things for me. He motioned to three big cardboard egg cartons stacked against one wall.

Inside was the only treasure I truly have ever known.   25

I had grown up in a house in which there were only two books, the King James Bible and the spring seed catalog. But here, in these boxes, were dozens of hardback copies of everything from Mark Twain to Sir Arthur Conan Doyle. There was a water-damaged Faulkner, and the nearly complete set of Edgar Rice Burroughs's *Tarzan*. There was poetry and trash, Zane Grey's *Riders of the Purple Sage,* and a paperback with two naked women on the cover. There was a tiny, old copy of *Arabian Nights,* threadbare Hardy Boys, and one Hemingway. He had bought most of them at a yard sale, by the box or pound, and some at a flea market. He did not even know what he was giving me, did not recognize most of the writers. "Your momma said you still liked to read," he said.

There was Shakespeare. My father did not know who he was, exactly, but he had heard the name. He wanted them because they were pretty, because they were wrapped in fake leather, because they looked like rich folks' books. I do not love Shakespeare, but I still have those books. I would not trade them for a gold monkey.

"They's maybe some dirty books in there, by mistake, but I know you ain't interested in them, so just throw 'em away," he said. "Or at least, throw 'em away before your momma sees 'em." And then I swear to God he winked.

I guess my heart should have broken then, and maybe it did, a little. I guess I should have done something, anything, besides mumble "Thank you, Daddy." I guess that would have been fine, would not have betrayed in some way my mother, my brothers, myself. But I just stood there, trapped somewhere between my long-standing, comfortable hatred, and what might have been forgiveness. I am trapped there still.

For four more memoirs, see CHAPTER 65.

Bragg's memoir illustrates all the features that make a memoir good: how the son and father react to each other creates the kind of suspense that keeps us reading; vivid details and rich dialogue bring the scene to life. His later reflections make the significance of that final meeting very clear.

Key Features / Memoirs

A good story.   Your memoir should be interesting, to yourself and others. It need not be about a world-shaking event, but your topic—and how you write about it—should interest your readers. At the center of most good stories stands a conflict or question to be resolved. The most compelling memoirs feature some sort of situation or problem that needs resolution. That need for resolution is another name for suspense. It's what makes us want to keep reading.

Vivid details.   Details bring a memoir to life by giving readers mental images of the sights, sounds, smells, tastes, and textures of the world in which your story takes place. The goal is to show as well as tell, to take readers there. When Bragg describes a "voice like an old woman's, punctuated with a cough that sounded like it came from deep in the guts," we can hear his dying father ourselves. A memoir is more than simply a report of what happened; it uses vivid details and dialogue to bring the events of the past to life, much as good fiction brings to life events that the writer makes up or embellishes. Depending on your topic and medium, you may want to provide some of the details in audio or visual form.

academic literacies　rhetorical situations　genres　processes　strategies　research MLA / APA　media / design　readings

Clear significance.   Memories of the past are filtered through our view from the present: we pick out some moments in our lives as significant, some as more important or vivid than others. Over time, our interpretations change, and our memories themselves change.

A good memoir conveys something about the significance of its subject. As a writer, you need to reveal something about what the incident means to you. You don't, however, want to simply announce the significance as if you're tacking on the moral of the story. Bragg tells us that he's "trapped between [his] long-standing, comfortable hatred, and what might have been forgiveness," but he doesn't come right out and say that's why the incident is so important to him.

A BRIEF GUIDE TO WRITING MEMOIRS

Choosing an Event to Write About

LIST several events or incidents from your past that you consider significant in some way. They do not have to be earthshaking; indeed, they may involve a quiet moment that only you see as important—a brief encounter with a remarkable person, a visit to a special place, a memorable achievement (or failure), something that makes you laugh whenever you think about it. Writing about events that happened at least a few years ago is often easier than writing about recent events because you can more easily step back and see those events with a clear perspective. To choose the event that you will write about, consider how well you can recall what happened, how interesting it will be to readers, and whether you want to share it with an audience.

290–91

Considering the Rhetorical Situation

PURPOSE   What is the importance of the memory you are trying to convey? How will this story help you understand yourself and your readers understand you, as you were then and as you are now?

55–56

57–60 **AUDIENCE** Who are your readers? Why will they care about your memoir? What do you want them to think of you after reading it? How can you help them understand your experience?

64–67 **STANCE** What impression do you want to give, and how can your words contribute to that impression? What tone do you want to project? Sincere? Serious? Humorous? Detached? Self-critical?

68–70 **MEDIA / DESIGN** Will your memoir be a print document? A speech? Will it be posted on a website? Can you include photographs, audio or video clips, or other visual texts?

Generating Ideas and Text

Think about what happened. Take a few minutes to write out an account 292–93 of the incident: **WHAT** happened, **WHERE** it took place, **WHO** else was involved, what was said, how you feel about it, and so on. Can you identify any tension or conflict that will make for a compelling story? If not, you might want to rethink your topic.

Consider its significance. Why do you still remember this event? What effect has it had on your life? What makes you want to tell someone else about it? Does it say anything about you? What about it might interest someone else? If you have trouble answering these questions, you should probably find another topic. But in general, once you have defined the significance of the incident, you can be sure you have a story to tell—and a reason for telling it.

Think about the details. The best memoirs connect with readers by giving them a sense of what it was like to be there, leading them to experience in words and images what the writer experienced in life. Spend some time 399–407 **DESCRIBING** the incident, writing what you see, hear, smell, touch, and taste when you envision it. Do you have any photos or memorabilia or

other **VISUAL** materials you might include in your memoir? Try writing out **DIALOGUE**, things that were said (or, if you can't recall exactly, things that might have been said). Look at what you come up with—is there detail enough to bring the scene to life? Anything that might be called vivid? If you don't have enough detail, you might reconsider whether you recall enough about the incident to write about it. If you have trouble coming up with plenty of detail, try **FREEWRITING**, **LISTING**, or **LOOPING**.

607–15

408–13

289–91

Ways of Organizing Memoirs

[Tell about the event from beginning to end]

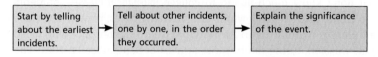

| Start by telling about the earliest incidents. | → | Tell about other incidents, one by one, in the order they occurred. | → | Explain the significance of the event. |

[Start at the end and tell how the event came about]

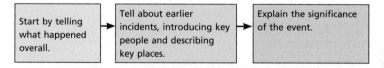

| Start by telling what happened overall. | → | Tell about earlier incidents, introducing key people and describing key places. | → | Explain the significance of the event. |

IF YOU NEED MORE HELP

See Chapter 28 for guidelines on **DRAFTING**, Chapter 29 on **ASSESSING YOUR OWN WRITING**, Chapter 30 on **GETTING RESPONSE AND REVISING**, and Chapter 31 on **EDITING AND PROOFREADING**. See Chapter 32 if you are required to submit your memoir in a writing **PORTFOLIO**.

298–300
301–5
306–12
313–17
318–28

19 Profiles

Profiles are written portraits—of people, places, events, or other things. We find profiles of celebrities, travel destinations, and offbeat festivals in magazines and newspapers, on radio and TV. A profile presents a subject in an entertaining way that conveys its significance, showing us something or someone that we may not have known existed or that we see every day but don't know much about. In college *journalism* classes, students learn to create profiles using words and, in many cases, photos and video as well. Here is a profile of an Air National Guard fighter pilot who faced a suicide mission during the terrorist attacks of September 11, 2001. The writer, Steve Hendrix, writes for the *Washington Post*, where this essay originally appeared.

STEVE HENDRIX

F-16 Pilot Was Ready to Give Her Life on Sept. 11

Late in the morning of the Tuesday that changed everything, Lt. Heather "Lucky" Penney was on a runway at Andrews Air Force Base and ready to fly. She had her hand on the throttle of an F-16 and she had her orders: Bring down United Airlines Flight 93. The day's fourth hijacked airliner seemed to be hurtling toward Washington. Penney, one of the first two combat pilots in the air that morning, was told to stop it.

The one thing she didn't have as she roared into the crystalline sky was live ammunition. Or missiles. Or anything at all to throw at a hostile aircraft.

Except her own plane. So that was the plan.

academic literacies · rhetorical situations · genres · processes · strategies · research MLA / APA · media / design · readings

Penney was to stop Flight 93 — by crashing her own plane into it.

Because the surprise attacks were unfolding, in that innocent age, faster than they could arm war planes, Penney and her commanding officer went up to fly their jets straight into a Boeing 757.

"We wouldn't be shooting it down. We'd be ramming the aircraft," Penney recalls of her charge that day. "I would essentially be a kamikaze pilot."

5

For years, Penney, one of the first generation of female combat pilots in the country, gave no interviews about her experiences on September 11 (which included, eventually, escorting Air Force One back into Washington's suddenly highly restricted airspace).

But 10 years later, she is reflecting on one of the lesser-told tales of that endlessly examined morning: how the first counterpunch the U.S. military prepared to throw at the attackers was effectively a suicide mission.

"We had to protect the airspace any way we could," she said last week in her office at Lockheed Martin, where she is a director in the F-35 program.

Penney, now a major but still a petite blonde with a Colgate grin, is no longer a combat flier. She flew two tours in Iraq and she serves as a part-time National Guard pilot, mostly hauling VIPs around in a military Gulfstream. She takes the stick of her own vintage 1941 Taylorcraft tail-dragger whenever she can.

But none of her thousands of hours in the air quite compare with 10 the urgent rush of launching on what was supposed to be a one-way flight to a midair collision.

First of her kind

She was a rookie in the autumn of 2001, the first female F-16 pilot they'd ever had at the 121st Fighter Squadron of the D.C. Air National Guard. She had grown up smelling jet fuel. Her father flew jets in Vietnam and still races them. Penney got her pilot's license when she was a literature major at Purdue. She planned to be a teacher. But during a graduate program in American studies, Congress opened up combat aviation to women and Penney was nearly first in line.

"I signed up immediately," she says. "I wanted to be a fighter pilot like my dad."

On that Tuesday, they had just finished two weeks of air combat training in Nevada. They were sitting around a briefing table when someone looked in to say a plane had hit the World Trade Center in New York. When it happened once, they assumed it was some yahoo in a Cessna. When it happened again, they knew it was war.

But the surprise was complete. In the monumental confusion of those first hours, it was impossible to get clear orders. Nothing was ready. The jets were still equipped with dummy bullets from the training mission.

As remarkable as it seems now, there were no armed aircraft stand- 15 ing by and no system in place to scramble them over Washington. Before that morning, all eyes were looking outward, still scanning the old Cold War threat paths for planes and missiles coming over the polar ice cap.

"There was no perceived threat at the time, especially one coming from the homeland like that," says Col. George Degnon, vice commander of the 113th Wing at Andrews. "It was a little bit of a helpless feeling, but we did everything humanly possible to get the aircraft armed and in the air. It was amazing to see people react."

Things are different today, Degnon says. At least two "hot-cocked" planes are ready at all times, their pilots never more than yards from the cockpit.

A third plane hit the Pentagon, and almost at once came word that a fourth plane could be on the way, maybe more. The jets would be armed within an hour, but somebody had to fly now, weapons or no weapons.

"Lucky, you're coming with me," barked Col. Marc Sasseville.

They were gearing up in the pre-flight life-support area when Sasseville, struggling into his flight suit, met her eye.   20

"I'm going to go for the cockpit," Sasseville said.

She replied without hesitating.

"I'll take the tail."

It was a plan. And a pact.

"Let's go!"

Penney had never scrambled a jet before. Normally the pre-flight is a   25
half-hour or so of methodical checks. She automatically started going down the list.

"Lucky, what are you doing? Get your butt up there and let's go!" Sasseville shouted.

She climbed in, rushed to power up the engines, screamed for her ground crew to pull the chocks. The crew chief still had his headphones plugged into the fuselage as she nudged the throttle forward. He ran along pulling safety pins from the jet as it moved forward.

She muttered a fighter pilot's prayer — "God, don't let me [expletive] up" — and followed Sasseville into the sky.

They screamed over the smoldering Pentagon, heading north-west at more than 400 mph, flying low and scanning the clear horizon. Her commander had time to think about the best place to hit the enemy.

"We don't train to bring down airliners," said Sasseville, now sta-   30
tioned at the Pentagon. "If you just hit the engine, it could still glide and you could guide it to a target. My thought was the cockpit or the wing."

He also thought about his ejection seat. Would there be an instant just before impact?

"I was hoping to do both at the same time," he says. "It probably wasn't going to work, but that's what I was hoping."

Penney worried about missing the target if she tried to bail out.

"If you eject and your jet soars through without impact ..." she trails off, the thought of failing more dreadful than the thought of dying.

But she didn't have to die. She didn't have to knock down an air- 35 liner full of kids and salesmen and girlfriends. They did that themselves.

It would be hours before Penney and Sasseville learned that United 93 had already gone down in Pennsylvania, an insurrection by hostages willing to do just what the two Guard pilots had been willing to do: Anything. And everything.

"The real heroes are the passengers on Flight 93 who were willing to sacrifice themselves," Penney says. "I was just an accidental witness to history."

She and Sasseville flew the rest of the day, clearing the airspace, escorting the president, looking down onto a city that would soon be sending them to war.

She's a single mom of two girls now. She still loves to fly. And she still thinks often of that extraordinary ride down the runway a decade ago.

"I genuinely believed that was going to be the last time I took 40 off," she says. "If we did it right, this would be it."

 For four more profiles, see CHAPTER 66.

This profile focuses on Lt. Heather "Lucky" Penney's role in responding to the attempted attack on Washington, D.C. The writer engages our interest first by recounting Penney's orders to stop Flight 93 — and then by revealing that Penney would have to do so by flying her fighter plane into the airliner. The rest of the profile shows how she and her commander came to be in that situation and how it played out.

Key Features / Profiles

An interesting subject. The subject may be something unusual, or it may be something ordinary shown in an intriguing way. You might profile an interesting person (like Heather "Lucky" Penney), a place (like the cockpit of an F-16), or an event (like scrambling a fighter plane on a suicide mission).

Any necessary background. A profile usually includes just enough information to let readers know something about the subject's larger context. Hendrix tells us how Penney became a fighter pilot and that she is still involved in aviation but leaves out other details about her life that don't matter for this profile.

An interesting angle. A good profile captures its subject from a particular angle. Sometimes finding an angle will be fairly easy because your topic — like preparing to fly a plane into a terrorist-controlled airliner — is offbeat enough to be interesting in and of itself. Other topics, though, may require you to find a particular aspect that you can focus on. For example, a profile of a person might focus on the important work the person does or a challenging hobby he or she pursues; it would likely ignore aspects of the person's life that don't relate to that angle.

A firsthand account. Whether you are writing about a person, place, or event, you need to spend time observing and interacting with your subject. With a person, interacting means watching and conversing. Journalists tell us that "following the guy around," getting your subject to do something and talk about it at the same time, yields excellent material for a profile. When one writer met Theodor Geisel (Dr. Seuss) before profiling him, she asked him not only to talk about his characters but also to draw one—resulting in an illustration for her profile. With a place or event, interacting may mean visiting and participating, although sometimes you may gather even more information by playing the role of the silent observer.

Engaging details. You need to include details that bring your subject to life. These may include *specific information* ("The crew chief still had his headphones plugged into the fuselage as she nudged the throttle forward."); *sensory images* ("she roared into the crystalline sky"); *figurative language* ("She had grown up smelling jet fuel."); *dialogue* ("'I'm going to go for the cockpit,' Sasseville said. . . . 'I'll take the tail.'"); and *anecdotes* ("They were sitting around a briefing table when someone looked in to say a plane had hit the World Trade Center in New York"). Choose details that show rather than tell — that let your audience see and hear your subject rather than merely read an abstract description of it. Sometimes you may let them see and hear it literally, by including *photographs* or *video and audio clips*. And be sure all the details create some *dominant impression* of your subject: the impression that we get out of this profile, for example, is of a modest but heroic woman willing to sacrifice her life to protect her country.

A BRIEF GUIDE TO WRITING PROFILES

Choosing a Suitable Subject

290–91 ○

A person, a place, an event—whatever you choose, make sure it's something that arouses your curiosity and that you're not too familiar with. Knowing your subject too well can blind you to interesting details. **LIST** five to ten interesting subjects that you can experience firsthand. Obviously, you can't profile a person who won't be interviewed or a place or activity that can't be observed. So before you commit to a topic, make sure you'll be able to carry out firsthand research and not find out too late that the people you need to interview aren't willing or that places you need to visit are off-limits.

Considering the Rhetorical Situation

55–56 ■

PURPOSE   Why are you writing the profile? What angle will best achieve your purpose? How can you inform *and engage* your audience?

57–60 ■

AUDIENCE   Who is your audience? How familiar are they with your subject? What expectations of your profile might they have? What background information or definitions do you need to provide? How interested will they be—and how can you get their interest?

STANCE   What view of your subject do you expect to present? Sympathetic? Critical? Sarcastic? Will you strive for a carefully balanced perspective?

64–67

MEDIA / DESIGN   Will your profile be a print document? electronic? an oral presentation? Can (and should) you include images or any other visuals? Will it be recorded as an audio file or multimodal text?

68–70

Generating Ideas and Text

Explore what you already know about your subject.   Why do you find this subject interesting? What do you know about it now? What do you expect to find out about it from your research? What preconceived ideas about or emotional reactions to this subject do you have? Why do you have them? It may be helpful to try some of the activities in the chapter on **GENERATING IDEAS AND TEXT**.

289–97

Visit your subject.   If you're writing about an amusement park, go there; if you're profiling the man who runs the carousel, make an appointment to meet and interview him. Get to know your subject—if you profile Ben and Jerry, sample the ice cream! Take photos or videos if there's anything you might want to show visually in your profile. Find helpful hints for **OBSERVING** and **INTERVIEWING** in the chapter on finding sources.

463–66

If you're planning to interview someone, prepare questions.   Hendrix likely asked Heather Penney questions like "What led you to become a fighter pilot?" "How long does a pre-flight check normally take?"

Do additional research.   You may be able to write a profile based entirely on your field research. You may, though, need to do some library or web **RESEARCH** as well, to deepen your understanding, get a different perspective, or fill in gaps. Often the people you interview can help you find sources

433

Research can lead you to more than just text sources. These photos of Heather Penney and Marc Sasseville were found with a Google search.

of additional information; so can the sponsors of events and those in charge of places. To learn more about a city park, for instance, contact the government office that maintains it. Download any good photos of your subject that you find online (such as the photos of Heather Penney and Marc Sasseville), both to refer to as you write and to illustrate your profile.

Analyze your findings. Look for patterns, images, recurring ideas or phrases, and engaging details. Look for contrasts or discrepancies: between a subject's words and actions, between the appearance of a place and what goes on there, between your expectations and your research findings. Hendrix probably expected Penney to be an enthusiastic pilot but may not have expected that she had gotten her pilot's license while still an undergraduate literature major. You may find the advice in the **READING IN ACADEMIC CONTEXTS** chapter helpful here.

10–32 ✳

Come up with an angle. What's most memorable about your subject? What most interests you? What will interest your audience? Hendrix focuses on a woman who was one of the first female F-16 pilots and one of two pilots ready to undertake a suicide mission. Sometimes you'll know your angle from the start; other times you'll need to look further into your topic. You might try **CLUSTERING**, **CUBING**, **FREEWRITING**, and **LOOPING**, activities that will help you look at your topic from many different angles.

289–92

Note details that support your angle. Use your angle to focus your research and generate text. Try **DESCRIBING** your subject as clearly as you can, **COMPARING** your subject with other subjects of its sort, writing **DIALOGUE** that captures your subject. Hendrix, for instance, describes Heather Penney as "a petite blonde with a Colgate grin," providing details that help us see his subject, and he quotes Penney to give a sense of her attitude toward her experience: "We had to protect the airspace any way we could." Engaging details will bring your subject to life for your audience. Together, these details should create a dominant impression of your subject.

399–407
380–87
408–13

Ways of Organizing a Profile

[As a narrative]

One common way to organize a profile is by **NARRATING**. For example, if you are profiling a chess championship, you may write about it chronologically, creating suspense as you move from start to finish. The profile of Heather Penney's flight is organized this way.

419–27

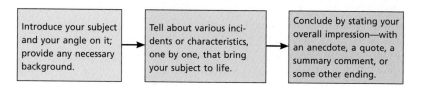

Introduce your subject and your angle on it; provide any necessary background. → Tell about various incidents or characteristics, one by one, that bring your subject to life. → Conclude by stating your overall impression—with an anecdote, a quote, a summary comment, or some other ending.

[As a description]

Sometimes you may organize a profile by **DESCRIBING** — a person or a place, for instance.

399–407

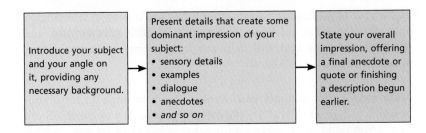

Introduce your subject and your angle on it, providing any necessary background.

Present details that create some dominant impression of your subject:
- sensory details
- examples
- dialogue
- anecdotes
- *and so on*

State your overall impression, offering a final anecdote or quote or finishing a description begun earlier.

IF YOU NEED MORE HELP

See Chapter 28 for guidelines on **DRAFTING**, Chapter 29 on **ASSESSING YOUR OWN WRITING**, Chapter 30 on **GETTING RESPONSE AND REVISING**, and Chapter 31 on **EDITING AND PROOFREADING**. See Chapter 32 if you are required to submit your analysis in a writing **PORTFOLIO**.

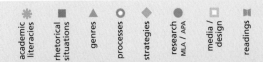

academic literacies　rhetorical situations　genres　processes　strategies　research MLA / APA　media / design　readings

Proposals 20

Proposals are part of our personal lives: lovers propose marriage, friends propose sharing dinner and a movie, you offer to pay half the cost of a car and insurance if your parents will pay the other half. They are also part of our academic and professional lives: student leaders lobby for lights on bike paths. *Musicians, artists, writers,* and *educators* apply for grants. Researchers in all fields of the *humanities, social sciences, sciences,* and *technology* seek funding for their projects. In business, contractors bid on building projects and companies and freelancers solicit work from potential clients. These are all examples of proposals, ideas put forward for consideration that say, "Here is a solution to a problem" or "This is what ought to be done." For example, here is a proposal for reducing the costs of college textbooks, written by an accounting professor at the University of Texas who is chairman of the university's Co-op Bookstore and himself a textbook author.

MICHAEL GRANOF

Course Requirement: Extortion

By now, entering college students and their parents have been warned: textbooks are outrageously expensive. Few textbooks for semester-long courses retail for less than $120, and those for science and math courses typically approach $180. Contrast this with the $20 to $30 cost of most hardcover best sellers and other trade books.

Perhaps these students and their parents can take comfort in knowing that the federal government empathizes with them, and in an attempt to ease their pain Congress asked its Advisory Committee

on Student Financial Assistance to suggest a cure for the problem. Unfortunately, though, the committee has proposed a remedy that would only worsen the problem.

The committee's report, released in May, mainly proposes strengthening the market for used textbooks—by encouraging college bookstores to guarantee that they will buy back textbooks, establishing online book swaps among students, and urging faculty to avoid switching textbooks from one semester to the next. The fatal flaw in that proposal (and similar ones made by many state legislatures) is that used books are the cause of, not the cure for, high textbook prices.

Yet there is a way to lighten the load for students in their budgets, if not their backpacks. With small modifications to the institutional arrangements between universities, publishers, and students, textbook costs could be reduced—and these changes could be made without government intervention.

Today the used-book market is exceedingly well organized and efficient. Campus bookstores buy back not only the books that will be used at their university the next semester but also those that will not. Those that are no longer on their lists of required books they resell to national wholesalers, which in turn sell them to college bookstores on campuses where they will be required. This means that even if a text is being adopted for the first time at a particular college, there is almost certain to be an ample supply of used copies.

As a result, publishers have the chance to sell a book to only one of the multiple students who eventually use it. Hence, publishers must cover their costs and make their profit in the first semester their books are sold—before used copies swamp the market. That's why the prices are so high.

As might be expected, publishers do what they can to undermine the used-book market, principally by coming out with new editions every three or four years. To be sure, in rapidly changing fields like biology and physics, the new editions may be academically defensible. But in areas like algebra and calculus, they are nothing more than a transparent attempt to ensure premature textbook obsolescence. Publishers also try to discourage students from buying used books by bundling the text with extra materials like workbooks and CDs that are not reusable and therefore cannot be passed from one student to another.

The system could be much improved if, first of all, colleges and publishers would acknowledge that textbooks are more akin to

5

academic literacies   rhetorical situations   genres   processes   strategies   research MLA / APA   media / design   readings

computer software than to trade books. A textbook's value, like that of a software program, is not in its physical form, but rather in its intellectual content. Therefore, just as software companies typically "site license" to colleges, so should textbook publishers.

Here's how it would work: A teacher would pick a textbook, and the college would pay a negotiated fee to the publisher based on the number of students enrolled in the class. If there were 50 students in the class, for example, the fee might be $15 per student, or $750 for the semester. If the text were used for ten semesters, the publisher would ultimately receive a total of $150 ($15 × 10) for each student enrolled in the course, or as much as $7,500.

In other words, the publisher would have a stream of revenue for as long as the text was in use. Presumably, the university would pass on this fee to the students, just as it does the cost of laboratory supplies and computer software. But the students would pay much less than the $900 a semester they now typically pay for textbooks. 10

Once the university had paid the license fee, each student would have the option of using the text in electronic format or paying more to purchase a hard copy through the usual channels. The publisher could set the price of hard copies low enough to cover only its production and distribution costs plus a small profit, because it would be covering most of its costs and making most of its profit by way of the license fees. The hard copies could then be resold to other students or back to the bookstore, but that would be of little concern to the publisher.

A further benefit of this approach is that it would not affect the way courses are taught. The same cannot be said for other recommendations from the Congressional committee and from state legislatures, like placing teaching materials on electronic reserve, urging faculty to adopt cheaper "no frills" textbooks, and assigning mainly electronic textbooks. While each of these suggestions may have merit, they force faculty to weigh students' academic interests against their fiscal concerns and encourage them to rely less on new textbooks.

Neither colleges nor publishers are known for their cutting-edge innovations. But if they could slightly change the way they do business, they would make a substantial dent in the cost of higher education and provide a real benefit to students and their parents.

■■ For four more proposals, see CHAPTER 67.

This proposal clearly defines the problem—some textbooks cost a lot—and explains why. It proposes a solution to the problem of high textbook prices and offers reasons why this solution will work better than others. Its tone is reasonable and measured, yet decisive.

Key Features / Proposals

A well-defined problem. Some problems are self-evident and relatively simple, and you would not need much persuasive power to make people act—as with the problem "This university discards too much paper." While some people might see nothing wrong with throwing paper away, most are likely to agree that recycling is a good thing. Other issues are controversial: some people see them as problems while others do not, such as this one: "Motorcycle riders who do not wear helmets risk serious injury and raise health-care costs for everyone." Some motorcyclists believe that wearing or not wearing a helmet should be a personal choice; you would have to present arguments to convince your readers that not wearing a helmet is indeed a problem needing a solution. Any written proposal must establish at the outset that there is a problem—and that it's serious enough to require a solution. For some topics, visual or audio evidence of the problem may be helpful.

A recommended solution. Once you have defined the problem, you need to describe the solution you are suggesting and to explain it in enough detail for readers to understand what you are proposing. Again, photographs, diagrams, or other visuals may help. Sometimes you might suggest several solutions, weigh their merits, and choose the best one.

A convincing argument for your proposed solution. You need to convince readers that your solution is feasible—and that it is the best way to solve the problem. Sometimes you'll want to explain in detail how your proposed solution would work. See, for example, how the textbook proposal details the way a licensing system would operate. Visuals may strengthen this part of your argument as well.

Granof's proposal for reducing textbook prices via licensing fees might benefit from a photograph like this one, which provides a comparison of other approaches to the problem.

A response to anticipated questions. You may need to consider any questions readers may have about your proposal—and to show how its advantages outweigh any disadvantages. Had the textbook proposal been written for college budget officers, it would have needed to anticipate and answer questions about the costs of implementing the proposed solution.

A call to action. The goal of a proposal is to persuade readers to accept your proposed solution. This solution may include asking readers to take action.

An appropriate tone. Since you're trying to persuade readers to act, your tone is important—readers will always react better to a reasonable, respectful presentation than to anger or self-righteousness.

A BRIEF GUIDE TO WRITING PROPOSALS

Deciding on a Topic

Choose a problem that can be solved. Complex, large problems, such as poverty, hunger, or terrorism, usually require complex, large solutions. Most of the time, focusing on a smaller problem or a limited aspect of a large problem will yield a more manageable proposal. Rather than tackling the problem of world poverty, for example, think about the problem faced by people in your community who have lost jobs and need help until they find employment.

Considering the Rhetorical Situation

55–56 ■ **PURPOSE**   Do you have a stake in a particular solution, or do you simply want to eliminate the problem by whatever solution might be adopted?

57–60 ■ **AUDIENCE**   Do your readers share your view of the problem as a serious one needing a solution? Are they likely to be open to possible solutions or resistant? Do they have the authority to carry out a proposed solution?

64–67 ■ **STANCE**   How can you show your audience that your proposal is reasonable and should be taken seriously? How can you demonstrate your own authority and credibility?

68–70 ■ **MEDIA / DESIGN**   How will you deliver your proposal? In print? Electronically? As a speech? Would visuals, or video or audio clips help support your proposal?

Generating Ideas and Text

Explore potential solutions to the problem. Many problems can be solved in more than one way, and you need to show your readers that

you've examined several potential solutions. You may develop solutions on your own; more often, though, you'll need to do **RESEARCH** to see how others have solved—or tried to solve—similar problems. Don't settle on a single solution too quickly—you'll need to **COMPARE** the advantages and disadvantages of several solutions in order to argue convincingly for one.

● 433

◆ 380–87

Decide on the most desirable solution(s).   One solution may be head and shoulders above others—but be open to rejecting all the possible solutions on your list and starting over if you need to, or to combining two or more potential solutions in order to come up with an acceptable fix.

Think about why your solution is the best one.   Why did you choose your solution? Why will it work better than others? What has to be done to enact it? What will it cost? What makes you think it can be done? Writing out answers to these questions will help you argue for your solution: to show that you have carefully and objectively outlined a problem, analyzed the potential solutions, weighed their merits, and determined the reasons the solution you propose is the best.

Ways of Organizing a Proposal

You can organize a proposal in various ways, but always you will begin by establishing that there is a problem. You may then identify several possible solutions before recommending one of them or a combination of several. Sometimes, however, you might discuss only a single solution.

[Several possible solutions]

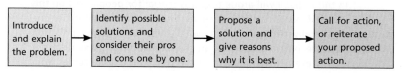

| Introduce and explain the problem. | → | Identify possible solutions and consider their pros and cons one by one. | → | Propose a solution and give reasons why it is best. | → | Call for action, or reiterate your proposed action. |

[A single solution]

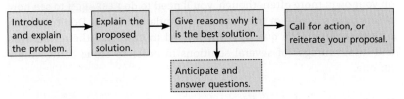

TOPIC PROPOSALS

Instructors often ask students to write topic proposals to ensure that their topics are appropriate or manageable. Some instructors may also ask for an 188–96 ▲ **ANNOTATED BIBLIOGRAPHY** showing that appropriate sources of information are available—more evidence that the project can be carried out. Here a first-year student proposes a topic for an assignment in a writing course in which she has been asked to take a position on a global issue.

JENNIFER CHURCH

Biodiversity Loss and Its Effect on Medicine

The loss of biodiversity—the variety of organisms found in the world—is affecting the world every day. Some scientists estimate that we are losing approximately one hundred species per day and that more than a quarter of all species may vanish within fifty years. I recently had the issue of biodiversity loss brought to my attention in a biological sciences course that I am taking this quarter. I have found myself interested in and intrigued by the subject and have found an abundance of information both in books and on the Internet.

In this paper, I will argue that it is crucial for people to stop this rapid loss of our world's biodiversity. Humans are the number-one cause of biodiversity loss in the world. Whether through pollution or toxins, we play a crucial role in the extinction of many different species. For example, 80 percent of the world's medicine comes from

biological species and their habitats. One medicine vanishing due to biodiversity loss is TAXOL. Found in the Wollemi pine tree, TAXOL is one of the most promising drugs for the treatment of ovarian and breast cancer. If the Wollemi pine tree becomes extinct, we will lose this potential cure.

I will concentrate primarily on biodiversity and its effects on the medical field. If we keep destroying the earth's biodiversity at the current rate, we may lose many opportunities to develop medicines we need to survive. The majority of my information will be found on the Internet, because there are many reliable Web sites from all around the world that address the issue of biodiversity loss and medicine.

Church defines and narrows her topic (from biodiversity loss to the impact of that loss on medicine), discusses her interest, outlines her argument, and discusses her research strategy. Her goal is to convince her instructor that she has a realistic writing project and a clear plan.

Key Features / Topic Proposals

You'll need to explain what you want to write about, why you want to explore it, and what you'll do with your topic. Unless your instructor has additional requirements, here are the features to include:

A concise discussion of the subject.   Topic proposals generally open with a brief discussion of the subject, outlining any important areas of controversy or debate associated with it and clarifying the extent of the writer's current knowledge of it. In its first two paragraphs, Church's proposal includes a concise statement of the topic she wishes to address.

A clear statement of your intended focus.   State what aspect of the topic you intend to write on as clearly as you can, narrowing your focus appropriately. Church does so by stating her intended topic—loss of biodiversity—and then showing how she will focus on the importance of biodiversity to the medical field.

A rationale for choosing the topic.   Tell your instructor why this topic interests you and why you want to write about it. Church both states what made her interested in her topic and hints at a practical reason for choosing it: plenty of information is available.

Mention of resources.   To show your instructor that you can achieve your goal, you need to identify the available research materials.

298–300
301–5
306–12
313–17
318–28

IF YOU NEED MORE HELP

See Chapter 28 for guidelines on **DRAFTING**, Chapter 29 on **ASSESSING YOUR OWN WRITING**, Chapter 30 on **GETTING RESPONSE AND REVISING**, and Chapter 31 on **EDITING AND PROOFREADING**. See Chapter 32 if you are required to submit your proposal in a writing **PORTFOLIO**.

academic literacies   rhetorical situations   genres   processes   strategies   research MLA / APA   media / design   readings

Reflections **21**

Sometimes we write essays just to think about something—to speculate, ponder, probe; to play with an idea, develop a thought; or simply to share something. Reflective essays are our attempt to think something through by writing about it and to share our thinking with others. If such essays make an argument, it is about things we care or think about more than about what we believe to be "true." In college, you might be asked in courses across the curriculum to write formal or informal reflections in the form of essays, journals, design reports, or learning logs. Have a look at one example of a reflection by Jonathan Safran Foer, a novelist who lives in Brooklyn. This essay originally appeared on the Op-Ed page of the *New York Times*.

JONATHAN SAFRAN FOER

My Life as a Dog

For the last twenty years, New York City parks without designated dog runs have permitted dogs to be off-leash from 9 p.m. to 9 a.m. Because of recent complaints from the Juniper Park Civic Association in Queens, the issue has been revisited. On December 5, the Board of Health will vote on the future of off-leash hours.

Retrievers in elevators, Pomeranians on No. 6 trains, bull mastiffs crossing the Brooklyn Bridge . . . it is easy to forget just how strange it is that dogs live in New York in the first place. It is about as unlikely a place for dogs as one could imagine, and yet 1.4 million of them are among us. Why do we keep them in our apartments and houses, always at some expense and inconvenience? Is it even possible, in a city, to provide a good life for a dog, and what is a "good life"? Does the health board's vote matter in ways other than the most obvious?

I adopted George (a Great Dane/Lab/pit/greyhound/ridgeback/whatever mix—a.k.a. Brooklyn shorthair) because I thought it would be fun. As it turns out, she is a major pain an awful lot of the time.

She mounts guests, eats my son's toys (and occasionally tries to eat my son), is obsessed with squirrels, lunges at skateboarders and Hasids,* has the savant-like ability to find her way between the camera lens and subject of every photo taken in her vicinity, backs her tush into the least interested person in the room, digs up the freshly planted, scratches the newly bought, licks the about-to-be-served, and occasionally relieves herself on the wrong side of the front door. Her head is resting on my foot as I type this. I love her.

Our various struggles—to communicate, to recognize and accommodate each other's desires, simply to coexist—force me to interact with something, or rather someone, entirely "other." George can respond to a handful of words, but our relationship takes place almost entirely outside of language. She seems to have thoughts and emotions, desires and fears. Sometimes I think I understand them; often I don't. She is a mystery to me. And I must be one to her.

Of course our relationship is not always a struggle. My morning walk with George is very often the highlight of my day—when I have my best thoughts, when I most appreciate both nature and the city, and in a deeper sense, life itself. Our hour together is a bit of compensation for the burdens of civilization: business attire, email, money, etiquette, walls, and artificial lighting. It is even a kind of compensation for language. Why does watching a dog be a dog fill one with happiness? And why does it make one feel, in the best sense of the word, human?

It is children, very often, who want dogs. In a recent study, when asked to name the ten most important "individuals" in their lives, 7- and 10-year-olds included two pets on average. In another study, 42 percent of 5-year-olds spontaneously mentioned their pets when asked, "Whom do you turn to when you are feeling, sad, angry, happy, or wanting to share a secret?" Just about every children's book in my local bookstore has an animal for its hero. But then, only a few feet away in the cookbook section, just about every cookbook includes

5

---

*Hasids: a Jewish sect whose members dress distinctively. [Editor's note]

recipes for cooking animals. Is there a more illuminating illustration of our paradoxical relationship with the nonhuman world?

In the course of our lives, we move from a warm and benevolent relationship with animals (learning responsibility through caring for our pets, stroking and confiding in them) to a cruel one (virtually all animals raised for meat in this country are factory farmed—they spend their lives in confinement, dosed with antibiotics and other drugs).

How do you explain this? Is our kindness replaced with cruelty? I don't think so. I think in part it's because the older we get, the less exposure we have to animals. And nothing facilitates indifference or forgetfulness so much as distance. In this sense, dogs and cats have been very lucky: they are the only animals we are intimately exposed to daily.

Folk parental wisdom and behavioral studies alike generally view   10
the relationships children have with companion animals as beneficial. But one does not have to be a child to learn from a pet. It is precisely my frustrations with George, and the inconveniences she creates, that reinforce in me how much compromise is necessary to share space with other beings.

The practical arguments against off-leash hours are easily refuted. One doesn't have to be an animal scientist to know that the more a dog is able to exercise its "dogness"—to run and play, to socialize with other dogs—the happier it will be. Happy dogs, like happy people, tend not to be aggressive. In the years that dogs have been allowed to run free in city parks, dog bites have decreased 90 percent. But there is another argument that is not so easy to respond to: some people just don't want to be inconvenienced by dogs. Giving dogs space necessarily takes away space from humans.

We have been having this latter debate, in different forms, for ages. Again and again we are confronted with the reality—some might say the problem—of sharing our space with other living things, be they dogs, trees, fish, or penguins. Dogs in the park are a present example of something that is often too abstracted or far away to gain our consideration.

The very existence of parks is a response to this debate: earlier New Yorkers had the foresight to recognize that if we did not carve out places for nature in our cities, there would be no nature. It was recently estimated that Central Park's real estate would be worth more than

$500 billion. Which is to say we are half a trillion dollars inconvenienced by trees and grass. But we do not think of it as an inconvenience. We think of it as balance.

Living on a planet of fixed size requires compromise, and while we are the only party capable of negotiating, we are not the only party at the table. We've never claimed more, and we've never had less. There has never been less clean air or water, fewer fish or mature trees. If we are not simply ignoring the situation, we keep hoping for (and expecting) a technological solution that will erase our destruction, while allowing us to continue to live without compromise. Maybe zoos will be an adequate replacement for wild animals in natural habitats. Maybe we will be able to recreate the Amazon somewhere else. Maybe one day we will be able to genetically engineer dogs that do not wish to run free. Maybe. But will those futures make us feel, in the best sense of the word, human?

I have been taking George to Prospect Park twice a day for more than three years, but her running is still a revelation to me. Effort-lessly, joyfully, she runs quite a bit faster than the fastest human on the planet. And faster, I've come to realize, than the other dogs in the park. George might well be the fastest land animal in Brooklyn. Once or twice every morning, for no obvious reason, she'll tear into a full sprint. Other dog owners can't help but watch her. Every now and then someone will cheer her on. It is something to behold.

A vote regarding off-leash hours for dogs sparks Foer's reflection on the relation-ship between dogs and humans. He begins by thinking about his relationship with his own dog, then goes on to consider the paradoxical nature of our treat-ment of animals in general. From there, he moves into a larger discussion of the compromises we make to "share space with other beings." Finally, he brings his reflection back to the personal, describing the joy of watching his dog be herself, off-leash.

▌▌ For four more reflections, see CHAPTER 68.

Key Features / Reflections

A topic that intrigues you.   A reflective essay has a dual purpose: to pon-der something you find interesting or puzzling and to share your thoughts

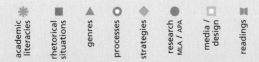

academic literacies   rhetorical situations   genres   processes   strategies   research MLA / APA   media / design   readings

with an audience. Your topic may be anything that interests you. You might write about someone you have never met and are curious about, an object or occurrence that makes you think, a place where you feel comfortable or safe. Your goal is to explore the meaning that the person, object, event, or place has for you in a way that will interest others. One way to do that is by making connections between your personal experience and more general ones that readers may share. Foer writes about his experience with his dog, but in so doing he raises questions and offers insights about the way everyone relates to others, human and nonhuman alike.

Some kind of structure.   A reflective essay can be structured in many ways, but it needs to *be* structured. It may seem to wander, but all its paths and ideas should relate, one way or another. The challenge is to keep your readers' interest as you explore your topic and to leave readers satisfied that the journey was pleasurable, interesting, and profitable. Foer brings his essay full circle, introducing the vote on the off-leash law in his opening, then considering our complex relationship with dogs, and, after suggesting some of the compromises we make to share our world with other nonhuman living things, closing with an indelible image of the joy that freedom from a leash brings.

Specific details.   You'll need to provide specific details to help readers understand and connect with your subject, especially if it's an abstract or unfamiliar one. Foer offers a wealth of details about his dog: "She mounts guests, eats my son's toys (and occasionally tries to eat my son), is obsessed by squirrels, lunges at skateboarders and Hasids." Anecdotes can bring your subject to life: "Once or twice every morning, for no obvious reason, she'll tear into a full sprint. Other dog owners can't help but watch her. Every now and then someone will cheer her on." Reflections may be about causes, such as why dogs make us feel more human; comparisons, such as when Foer compares animals as pets and as food; and examples: "virtually all animals raised for meat in this country are factory farmed." Photographs or other visuals may help provide details as well as set a certain tone for a reflection, as discussed below.

A questioning, speculative tone. In a reflective essay, you are working toward answers, not providing them neatly organized and ready for consumption. So your tone is usually tentative and open, demonstrating a willingness to entertain, accept, and reject various ideas as your essay progresses from beginning to end. Foer achieves this tone by looking at people's relationships with dogs from several different perspectives as well as by asking questions for which he provides no direct answers.

A BRIEF GUIDE TO WRITING REFLECTIONS

Deciding on a Topic

Choose a subject you want to explore. Write a list of things that you think about, wonder about, find puzzling or annoying. They may be big things—life, relationships—or little things—quirks of certain people's behavior, curious objects, everyday events. Try **CLUSTERING** one or more of those things, or begin by **FREEWRITING** to see what comes to mind as you write.

291–92
289–90

Considering the Rhetorical Situation

55–56

PURPOSE   What's your goal in writing this essay? To introduce a topic that interests you? Entertain? Provoke readers to think about something? What aspects of your subject do you want to ponder and reflect on?

57–60

AUDIENCE   Who is the audience? How familiar are they with your subject? How will you introduce it in a way that will interest them?

64–67

STANCE   What is your attitude toward the topic you plan to explore? Questioning? Playful? Critical? Curious? Something else?

academic literacies / rhetorical situations / genres / processes / strategies / research MLA / APA / media / design / readings

68–70

MEDIA / DESIGN   Will your essay be a print document? an oral presentation? Will it be posted on a website or blog? Would it help to include any visuals or video or audio files?

Generating Ideas and Text

Explore your subject in detail.   Reflections often include descriptive details. Foer, for example, **DESCRIBES** the many ways he encounters dogs in New York: "Retrievers in elevators, Pomeranians on No. 6 trains, bull mastiffs crossing the Brooklyn Bridge." Those details provide a base for the speculations to come. You may also make your point by **DEFINING**, **COMPARING**, even **CLASSIFYING**. Virtually any organizing pattern will help you explore your subject.

399–407

388–98
380–87
374–79

Back away.   Ask yourself why your subject matters: why is it important or intriguing or significant? You may try **LISTING** or **OUTLINING** possibilities, or you may want to start **DRAFTING** to see where the writing takes your thinking. Your goal is to think on screen (or paper) about your subject, to play with its possibilities.

290–91
293–95
296–97

Think about how to keep readers with you.   Reflections may seem loose or unstructured, but they must be carefully crafted so that readers can follow your train of thought. It's a good idea to sketch out a rough **THESIS** to help focus your thoughts. You may not include the thesis in the essay itself, but every part of the essay should in some way relate to it.

345–47

Ways of Organizing a Reflective Essay

Reflective essays may be organized in many ways because they mimic the way we think, associating one idea with another in ways that make sense but do not necessarily form a "logical" progression. In general, you might consider organizing a reflection using this overall strategy:

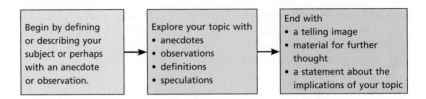

Another way to organize this type of essay is as a series of brief reflections that together create an overall impression:

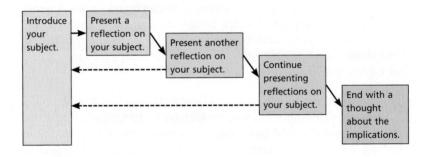

298–300 ⊙
301–5
306–12
313–17
318–28

IF YOU NEED MORE HELP

See Chapter 28 for guidelines on **DRAFTING**, Chapter 29 on ASSESSING YOUR OWN WRITING, Chapter 30 on GETTING RESPONSE AND REVISING, and Chapter 31 on EDITING AND PROOFREADING. See Chapter 32 if you are required to submit your reflection in a writing **PORTFOLIO**.

Résumés and Job Letters 22

Résumés summarize our education, work experience, and other accomplishments for prospective employers. Application letters introduce us to those employers. When you send a letter and résumé applying for a job, you are making an argument for why that employer should want to meet you and perhaps hire you. In a way, the two texts together serve as an advertisement selling your talents and abilities to someone who likely has to sift through many applications to decide whom to invite for an interview. That's why résumés and application letters require a level of care that few other documents do. In the same way, sending a thank-you letter following an interview completes your presentation of yourself to potential employers. Résumés, application letters, and thank-you letters are obviously very different genres—yet they share one common purpose and are done for the same audience. Thus, they are presented together in this chapter.

Social Media and Job Hunting

Social media have become important aspects of finding a job, for both good and ill. In fact, over half of all employers always search for job applicants' online profiles — and in many cases, those profiles lower the applicants' chances of being hired. So it's important to create or revise your profiles on *Facebook, LinkedIn,* and *Twitter,* the three most-searched social media sites, as well as other sites. Emphasize any volunteer or charity work you do, and highlight potential qualifications for and interest in the kind of work you want. Make sure your profiles contain no profanity or references to your sexual activity, or use of alcohol, guns, or illegal drugs—and proofread your posts for grammar and spelling. Your photos of yourself should project a professional image, too. Also, Google yourself to see what a search reveals about you.

You can also use social media to improve your job search. Read the descriptions of positions you would like to have, looking for keywords that describe what employers want in such employees; then use those keywords in your profiles. Also, join *LinkedIn* groups related to your desired job or industry to stay current with the conversations in those fields; then follow the companies where you'd like to work, as new job opportunities are sometimes posted there before they appear in other places.

RÉSUMÉS

A résumé is one of a job seeker's most important tools. If done well, a résumé not only tells potential employers about your education and work history, it says a lot about your attention to detail, writing skills, and professionalism. Taking the time to craft an excellent résumé, then, is time well spent. Here's an example, a résumé written by a college student applying for an internship before his senior year.

Samuel Praeger

28 Murphy Lane
Springfield, OH 45399
937-555-2640
spraeger22@webmail.com

name in boldface

OBJECTIVE To obtain an internship with a public relations firm

objective tailored to specific job sought

EDUCATION
Fall 2012–present

Wittenberg University, Springfield, OH
- BA in Psychology expected in May 2016
- Minor in East Asian Studies

EXPERIENCE
2014–present

Department of Psychology, Wittenberg University
Research Assistant
- Collect and analyze data
- Interview research participants

work experience in reverse chronological order

Summer
2014

Landis and Landis Public Relations, Springfield, OH
Events Coordinator
- Organized local charity events
- Coordinated database of potential donors
- Produced two radio spots for event promotion

Summers
2012, 2013

Springfield Aquatic Club, Springfield, OH
Assistant Swim Coach
- Instructed children ages 5–18 in competitive swimming

HONORS
2015

Psi Chi National Honor Society in Psychology

2013–2015

Community Service Scholarship, Wittenberg University

ACTIVITIES Varsity Swim Team; Ronald McDonald House Fund-raiser

SKILLS Microsoft Office; SPSS for Windows; Prezi; fluent in Japanese

REFERENCES Available upon request

format to fill entire page

Samuel Praeger's résumé is arranged chronologically, and because he was looking for work in a certain field, the résumé is targeted, focusing on his related work and skills and leaving out any references to high school (that he is in college allows readers to assume graduation from high school) or his past job as a house painter, which is not relevant. He describes his work responsibilities using action verbs to highlight what he actually did—produced, instructed, and so on.

Key Features / Résumés

A structure that suits your goals and experience. There are conventional ways of organizing a résumé but no one right way. You can organize a résumé chronologically or functionally, and it can be targeted or not. A *chronological résumé* is the most general, listing pretty much all your academic and work experience from the most recent to the earliest. A *targeted résumé* will generally announce the specific goal up top, just beneath your name, and will offer information selectively, showing only the experience and skills relevant to your goal. A *functional résumé* is organized around various kinds of experience and is not chronological. You might write a functional résumé if you wish to demonstrate a lot of experience in more than one area and perhaps if you wish to downplay dates.

Succinct. A résumé should almost always be short—one page if at all possible. Entries should be parallel but do not need to be written in complete sentences—"Produced two radio spots," for instance, rather than "I produced two radio spots." Use action verbs ("instructed," "produced") to emphasize what you accomplished.

A design that highlights key information. It's important for a résumé to look good and to be easy to skim; typography, white space, and alignment matter. Your name should be bold at the top. Major sections should be labeled with headings, all of which should be in one slightly larger or bolder font. And you need to surround each section and the text as a whole with adequate white space to make the parts easy to read—and to make the entire document look professional.

academic literacies · rhetorical situations · genres · processes · strategies · research MLA / APA · media / design · readings

A BRIEF GUIDE TO WRITING RÉSUMÉS

Considering the Rhetorical Situation

PURPOSE
Are you seeking a job? an internship? some other position? How will the position for which you're applying affect what you include on your résumé?

55–56

AUDIENCE
What sort of employee is the company or organization seeking? What experience and qualities will the person doing the hiring be looking for?

57–60

STANCE
What personal and professional qualities do you want to convey? Think about how you want to come across— as eager? polite? serious? ambitious?— and choose your words accordingly.

64–67

MEDIA / DESIGN
Are you planning to send your résumé and letter as PDFs? on paper? as an email attachment? Whatever your medium, be sure both documents are formatted appropriately and proofread carefully.

68–70

Generating Ideas and Text for a Résumé

Define your objective. Are you looking for a particular job for which you should create a targeted résumé? Are you preparing a generic chronological résumé to use in a search for work of any kind? Defining your objective as specifically as possible helps you decide on the form the résumé will take and the information it will include.

Consider how you want to present yourself. Begin by gathering the information you will need to include. As you work through the steps of putting your résumé together, think about the method of organization that works best for your purpose—chronological, targeted, or functional.

- *Contact information.* At the top of your résumé, list your full name, a permanent address (rather than your school address), a permanent telephone number with area code, and your email address (which should sound professional; addresses like hotbabe334@gmail.com do not make a good first impression on potential employers).

- *Your education.* Start with the most recent: degree, major, college attended, and minor (if any). You may want to list your GPA (if it's over 3.0) and any academic honors you've received. If you don't have much work experience, list education first.

- *Your work experience.* As with education, list your most recent job first and work backward. Include job title, organization name, city and state, start and end dates, and responsibilities. Describe them in terms of your duties and accomplishments. If you have extensive work experience in the area in which you're applying, list that first.

- *Community service, volunteer, and charitable activities.* Many high school students are required to perform community service, and many students participate in various volunteer activities that benefit others. List what you've done, and think about the skills and aptitudes that participation helped you develop or demonstrate.

- *Other activities, interests, and abilities.* What do you do for fun? What skills do your leisure activities require? (For example, if you play a sport, you probably have a good grasp of the value of teamwork. You should describe your skills in a way that an employer might find useful.)

Choose references.   Whether you list references on your résumé or offer to provide them on request, ask people to serve as references for you before you send out a résumé. It's a good idea to provide each reference with a one-page summary of relevant information about you (for example, give professors a list of courses you took with them, including the grades you earned and the titles of papers you wrote).

Choose your words carefully.   Remember, your résumé is a sales document—you're trying to present yourself as someone worth a second look. Focus on your achievements, using action verbs that say what you've done. Be honest—employers expect truthfulness, and embellishing the truth can cause you to lose a job later.

academic literacies   rhetorical situations   genres   processes   strategies   research MLA / APA   media / design   readings

Consider key design elements. Make sure your résumé is centered on the page and that it looks clean and clear. It's usually best to use a single, simple **FONT** (Times New Roman is a good one) throughout and to print on white paper. Use bold type and bullets to make the résumé easy to read, and limit it to no more—and no less—than one full page.

601–2

Edit and proofread carefully. Your résumé must be perfect. Show it to others, and proofread again. You don't want even one typo or other error.

Send the résumé as a PDF. PDFs look the same on all devices, whereas *Word* or other formats may not. Make sure potential employers see your résumé as you intended.

Ways of Organizing a Résumé

If you don't have much work experience or if you've just gone back to school to train for a new career, put education before work experience; if you have extensive work experience in the area in which you're applying, list work before education.

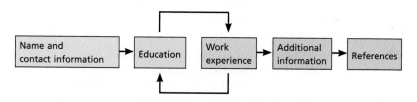

APPLICATION AND THANK-YOU LETTERS

The application letter argues that the writer should be taken seriously as a candidate for a job or some other opportunity. Generally, it is sent together with a résumé, so it doesn't need to give that much information. It does, however, have to make a favorable impression: the way it's written and presented can get you in for an interview—or not. On pages 260 and 261

Application Letter

street address
city, state ZIP
date

28 Murphy Lane
Springfield, OH 45399
May 19, 2015

equal space at top and bottom of page, all text aligning at left margin

line space

recipient's name and title, organization, address

Barbara Jeremiah, President
Jeremiah Enterprises
44322 Commerce Way
Worthington, OH 45322

line space

salutation, with a colon

Dear Ms. Jeremiah:

position identified

I am writing to apply for the public relations internship advertised in the Sunday, May 15, *Columbus Dispatch*. The success of your company makes me eager to work with you and learn from you.

line space between paragraphs

match between experience and job description

My grasp of public relations goes beyond the theories I have learned in the classroom. I worked last summer at Landis and Landis, the Springfield public relations firm, where I was responsible for organizing two charity events that drew over two hundred potential donors each. Since your internship focuses on public relations, my experience in the field will allow me to make a contribution to your company's public relations team.

availability

I will be available to begin any time after May 23, when the spring term at Wittenberg ends. I enclose my résumé, which provides detailed information about my background. I will phone this week to see if I might arrange an interview.

line space

closing

Sincerely,

4 lines space for signature

Samuel Praeger

sender's name, typed

Samuel Praeger

academic literacies · rhetorical situations · genres · processes · strategies · research MLA / APA · media / design · readings

Thank-You Email

	Dear Ms. Jeremiah:	salutation, with a colon
line space		
	Thank you for the opportunity to meet with you yesterday. I enjoyed talking with you and meeting the people who work with you, and I continue to be very interested in becoming an intern with Jeremiah Enterprises.	thanks and confirmation of interest
line space between paragraphs		
	As we discussed, I worked with a public relations firm last summer, and since then I have completed three courses in marketing and public relations that relate directly to the work I would be doing as an intern.	brief review of qualifications
invitation for further contact	I have attached a list of references, as you requested. If you need any more information, please do not hesitate to contact me by email at spraeger22@webmail.com or by phone at 937-555-2640. Thanks again;	attachments
repeat thanks	I hope to hear from you soon.	
line space	Sincerely,	closing
	Samuel Praeger	

is an application letter that Samuel Praeger wrote seeking a position at the end of his junior year. Praeger tailored his letter to one specific reader at a specific organization. The letter cites details, showing that it is not a generic application letter being sent to many possible employers. Rather, it identifies a particular position—the public relations internship—and stresses the fit between Praeger's credentials and the position. Praeger also states his availability. Send a thank-you email to each person who interviewed you within twenty-four hours of the interview; follow up by mailing a printed note that follows the same format as the application letter. Doing so is a way of showing appreciation for the interview and restating your interest in the position. It also shows that you have good manners and understand proper business etiquette. On the previous page is an email Samuel Praeger sent to the person who interviewed him for an internship, thanking the interviewer for her time and the opportunity to meet her, indicating his interest in the position, and reiterating his qualifications.

Key Features / Application and Thank-You Letters

A succinct indication of your qualifications. In an application letter, you need to make clear why you're interested in the position or the organization—and at the same time give some sense of why the person you're writing to should at least want to meet you. In a thank-you letter, you should remind the interviewer of your qualifications.

A reasonable and pleasing tone. When writing application and thank-you letters, you need to go beyond simply stating your accomplishments or saying thank you. Through your words, you need to demonstrate that you will be the kind of employee the organization wants. Presentation is also important—your letter should be neat and error-free.

A conventional, businesslike format. Application and thank-you letters typically follow a prescribed format. The most common is the block format shown in the examples. It includes the writer's address, the date, the recipient's name and address, a salutation, the message, a closing, and a signature.

A BRIEF GUIDE TO WRITING JOB LETTERS

Generating Ideas and Text for Application and Thank-You Letters

Focus. Application and thank-you letters are not personal and should not be chatty. Keep them focused: when you're applying for a position, include only information relevant to the position. Don't make your audience wade through irrelevant side issues. Stay on topic.

academic literacies · rhetorical situations · genres · processes · strategies · research MLA / APA · media / design · readings

State the reason for the letter. Unlike essays, which develop a thesis over several paragraphs, or emails, which announce their topic in a subject line, letters need to explicitly introduce their reason for being written, usually in the first paragraph. When you're applying for something or thanking someone, say so in the first sentence: "I am writing to apply for the Margaret Branscomb Peabody Scholarship for students majoring in veterinary science." "Thank you for meeting with me."

Think of your letter as an argument. When you're asking for a job, you're making an **ARGUMENT**. You're making a claim—that you're qualified for a certain position—and you need to support your claim with reasons and evidence. Praeger, for example, cites his education and his work experience—and he offers to supply references who will support his application.

355–73

Choose an appropriate salutation. If you know the person's name and title, use it: "Dear Professor Turnigan." If you don't know the person's title, one good solution is to address him or her by first and last name: "Dear Julia Turnigan." If, as sometimes happens, you must write to an unknown reader, your options include "To Whom It May Concern" and the more old fashioned "Dear Sir or Madam." Another option in such situations might be to omit the salutation completely and instead use a subject line, for example: "Subject: Public Relations Internship Application." Whenever possible, though, write to a specific person; research or contact the organization and find out whom to write to. Once you've had an interview, write to your interviewer.

Proofread. Few writing situations demand greater perfection than professional letters—especially job letters. Employers receive dozens, sometimes hundreds, of applications, and often can't look at them all. Typos, grammar errors, and other forms of sloppiness prejudice readers against applicants: they're likely to think that if this applicant can't take the time and care to **PROOFREAD**, how badly does he or she want this position? To compete, strive for perfection.

316–17

Ways of Organizing an Application or Thank-You Letter

Application and thank-you letters should both follow a conventional organization, though you might vary the details somewhat. Here are two standard organizations:

[Application letter]

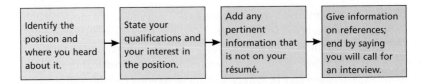

| Identify the position and where you heard about it. | → | State your qualifications and your interest in the position. | → | Add any pertinent information that is not on your résumé. | → | Give information on references; end by saying you will call for an interview. |

[Thank-you letter]

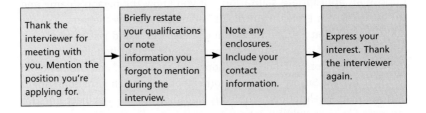

| Thank the interviewer for meeting with you. Mention the position you're applying for. | → | Briefly restate your qualifications or note information you forgot to mention during the interview. | → | Note any enclosures. Include your contact information. | → | Express your interest. Thank the interviewer again. |

IF YOU NEED MORE HELP

See Chapter 28 for guidelines on **DRAFTING**, Chapter 29 on **ASSESSING YOUR OWN WRITING**, Chapter 30 on **GETTING RESPONSE AND REVISING**, and Chapter 31 on **EDITING AND PROOFREADING**.

298–300
301–5
306–12
313–17

academic literacies · rhetorical situations · genres · processes · strategies · research MLA / APA · media / design · readings

Musicians regularly mix genres, blending, for instance, reggae, hip-hop, and jazz to create a unique sound. Like musicians, writers often combine different genres in a single text. An **EVALUATION** of mining practices might include a **PROFILE** of a coal company CEO. A **PROPOSAL** to start a neighborhood watch might begin with a **REPORT** on crime in the area. Here's a column that mixes genres, written by Anna Quindlen for *Newsweek* magazine in 2007.

▲ 197–205
224–34
235–44
129–55

ANNA QUINDLEN

Write for Your Life

The new movie *Freedom Writers* isn't entirely about the themes the trailers suggest. It isn't only about gang warfare and racial tensions and tolerance. It isn't only about the difference one good teacher can make in the life of one messed-up kid. *Freedom Writers* is about the power of writing in the lives of ordinary people. That's a lesson everyone needs. The movie, and the book from which it was taken, track the education of a young teacher named Erin Gruwell, who shows up shiny-new to face a class of what are called, in pedagogical jargon, "at risk" students. It's a mixed bag of Latino, Asian, and black teenagers with one feckless white kid thrown in. They ignore, belittle, and dismiss her as she proffers lesson plans and reading materials seriously out of step with the homelessness, drug use, and violence that are the stuff of their precarious existences.

And then one day, she gives them all marbled composition books and the assignment to write their lives, ungraded, unjudged, and the world breaks open.

Textual analysis

265

"My probation officer thinks he's slick; he swears he's an expert on gangs."

"Sorry, diary, I was going to try not to do it tonight, but the little baggy of white powder is calling my name."

"If you pull up my shirtsleeves and look at my arms, you will see black and blue marks."

"The words 'Eviction Notice' stopped me dead in my tracks."

"When I was younger, they would lock me up in the closet because they wanted to get high and beat up on each other."

Ms. G, as the kids called her, embraced a concept that has been lost in modern life: writing can make pain tolerable, confusion clearer and the self stronger.

Report

How is it, at a time when clarity and strength go begging, that we have moved so far from everyday prose? Social critics might trace this back to the demise of letter writing. The details of housekeeping and child rearing, the rigors of war and work, advice to friends and family: none was slated for publication. They were communications that gave shape to life by describing it for others.

But as the letter fell out of favor and education became professionalized, with its goal less the expansion of the mind than the acquisition of a job, writing began to be seen largely as the purview of writers. Writing at work also became so stylistically removed from the story of our lives that the two seemed to have nothing in common. Corporate prose conformed to an equation: information × polysyllabic words + tortured syntax = aren't you impressed?

Reflection

And in the age of the telephone most communication became evanescent, gone into thin air no matter how important or heartfelt. Think of all those people inside the World Trade Center saying goodbye by phone. If only, in the blizzard of paper that followed the collapse of the buildings, a letter had fallen from the sky for every family member and friend, something to hold on to, something to read and reread. Something real. Words on paper confer a kind of immortality. Wouldn't all of us love to have a journal, a memoir, a letter, from those we have loved and lost? Shouldn't all of us leave a bit of that behind?

The age of technology has both revived the use of writing and provided ever more reasons for its spiritual solace. Emails are letters, after all, more lasting than phone calls, even if many of them r 2 cursory 4 u.

And the physical isolation they and other arms-length cyber-advances create makes talking to yourself more important than ever. That's also what writing is: not just a legacy, but therapy. As the novelist Don DeLillo once said, "Writing is a form of personal freedom. It frees us from the mass identity we see in the making all around us. In the end, writers will write not to be outlaw heroes of some underculture but mainly to save themselves, to survive as individuals."

That's exactly what Gruwell was after when she got the kids in her class writing, in a program that's since been duplicated at other schools. Salvation and survival for teenagers whose chances of either seemed negligible. "Growing up, I always assumed I would either drop out of school or get pregnant," one student wrote. "So when Ms. G started talking about college, it was like a foreign language to me." Maybe that's the moment when that Latina girl began to speak that foreign language, when she wrote those words down. Today she has a college degree.

Argument

One of the texts Erin Gruwell assigned was *The Diary of a Young Girl* by Anne Frank. A student who balked at reading a book about someone so different, so remote, went on to write: "At the end of the book, I was so mad that Anne died, because as she was dying, a part of me was dying with her." Of course Anne never dreamed her diary would be published, much less read by millions of people after her death at the hands of the Nazis. She wrote it for the same reason the kids who called themselves Freedom Writers wrote in those composition books: to make sense of themselves. That's not just for writers. That's for people.

Quindlen argues that writing helps us understand ourselves and our world. She uses several genres to help advance her argument—textual analysis of the film Freedom Writers, *a brief report on the decline of letter writing, and a reflection on the technologies we use to write. Together, these genres help her develop her argument that writing helps us "make sense of [our]selves."*

For four more multigenre texts, see CHAPTER 69.

Key Features / Texts That Mix Genres

One primary genre. Your writing situation will often call for a certain genre that is appropriate for your purpose—an argument, a proposal, a report, a textual analysis, and so forth. Additional genres then play supporting roles. Quindlen's essay, for example, primarily argues a position and mixes in other genres, including report and reflection, to elaborate her argument and bring it to life.

A clear focus. A text that mixes genres approaches the topic several different ways, but each genre must contribute to your main point. One genre may serve as the introduction, and others may be woven throughout the text in other ways, but all must address some aspect of the topic and support the central claim. Quindlen's analysis of the film *Freedom Writers*, for example, supports her claim that writing is one way we learn about ourselves.

Careful organization. A text that combines several genres requires careful organization — the various genres must fit together neatly and clearly. Quindlen opens by analyzing the theme of *Freedom Writers*, noting that it's about "the power of writing in the lives of ordinary people." She then switches genres, reporting on how "we have moved so far from everyday prose" and then reflecting on the consequences of that move.

Clear transitions. When a text includes several genres, those genres need to be connected in some way. Transitions do that, and in so doing, they help readers make their way through the text. Transitions may include words such as "in addition" and "however," and they may also consist of phrases that sum up an idea and move it forward. See, for example, how Quindlen ends one paragraph by quoting Don DeLillo as saying that writers write "to save themselves, to survive as individuals" and then begins the next paragraph by referring to DeLillo's words, saying "That's exactly what Gruwell was after."

Some Typical Ways of Mixing Genres

It's possible to mix almost any genres together. Following are some of the most commonly mixed genres and how they combine with other genres.

academic literacies　rhetorical situations　genres　processes　strategies　research MLA / APA　media / design　readings

Memoirs. Sometimes a personal anecdote can help support an **ARGUMENT** or enhance a **REPORT**. Stories from your personal experience can help readers understand your motivations for arguing a certain position and can enhance your credibility as a writer.

▲ 156–82
129–55

Profiles. One way to bring a **REPORT** on an abstract topic to life is to include a profile of a person, place, or event. For example, if you were writing a report for your boss on the need to hire more sales representatives, including a profile of one salesperson's typical day might drive home the point that your sales force is stretched too thin.

▲ 129–55

Textual analyses. You might need to analyze a speech or other document as part of an **ARGUMENT**, especially on a historical or political topic. For instance, you might analyze speeches by Abraham Lincoln and Jefferson Davis if you're writing about the causes of the Civil War, or an advertisement for e-cigarettes if you're making an argument about teen smoking.

▲ 156–82

Evaluations. You might include an evaluation of something when you write a **PROPOSAL** about it. For example, if you were writing a proposal for additional student parking on your campus, you would need to evaluate the current parking facilities to discuss their inadequacy.

▲ 235–44

A BRIEF GUIDE TO WRITING TEXTS THAT MIX GENRES

Considering the Rhetorical Situation

PURPOSE   Why are you writing this text? To inform? persuade? entertain? explore an idea? something else? What genres will help you achieve your purpose?

■ 55–56

AUDIENCE   Who are your readers? Which genres will help these readers understand your point? Will starting with a memoir or profile draw them in? Will some analysis help them

■ 57–60

understand the topic? Will a profile make the topic less abstract or make them more sympathetic to your claim?

61–63 **GENRE** What is your primary genre? What other genres might support that primary genre?

64–67 **STANCE** What is your stance on your topic—objective? opinionated? something else? Will including a textual analysis or report help you establish an objective or analytical tone? Will some reflection or a brief memoir show your personal connection to your topic?

68–70 **MEDIA / DESIGN** Will your text be an electronic or a print document? an oral presentation? Will it be published on a blog or other website? Should you include illustrations? audio or video clips? Do you need to present any information that would be best shown in a chart or graph?

Generating Ideas and Text

Identify your primary genre. If you're writing in response to an assignment, does it specify a particular genre? Look for key verbs that name specific genres — for example, *analyze*, *argue*, *evaluate*, and so on. Be aware that other verbs imply certain genres: *explain*, *summarize*, *review*, and *describe* ask for a report; *argue*, *prove*, and *justify* signal that you need to argue a position; and *evaluate* and *propose* specify evaluations and proposals.

55–56
57–60 If the choice of genre is up to you, consider your **PURPOSE** and **AUDIENCE** carefully to determine what genre is most appropriate. Consult the appropriate genre chapter to identify the key features of your primary genre and to generate ideas and text.

Determine if other genres would be helpful. As you write a draft, you may identify a need — for a beginning that grabs readers' attention, for a satisfying ending, for ways to make an abstract concept more concrete or to help in analyzing something. At this point, you may want to try mixing

academic literacies
rhetorical situations
genres
processes
strategies
research MLA / APA
media / design
readings

one or more genres within your draft. Determine what genre will help you achieve your purpose and consult the appropriate genre chapter for advice on writing in that genre. Remember, however, that you're mixing genres into your draft to support and enhance it—so your supporting genres may not be as developed as complete texts in that genre would be and may not include all the key features. For example, if you include a brief memoir as part of an argument, it should include a good story and vivid details—but its significance may well be stated as part of the argument rather than revealed through the storytelling itself.

Integrate the genres.   Your goal is to create a focused, unified, coherent text. So you need to make sure that your genres work together to achieve that goal. Make sure that each genre fulfills a purpose within the text—for example, that a textual analysis within an argument provides evidence to support your claim, or that the profile you include in a report provides a clear illustration of the larger subject. Also, use **TRANSITIONS** to help readers move from section to section in your text.

◆ 349

Multigenre Projects

Sometimes a collection of texts can together represent an experience or advance an argument. For example, you might document a trip to the Grand Canyon in an album that contains journal entries written during the trip, photographs, a map of northern Arizona showing the canyon, postcards, an essay on the geology of the canyon, and a souvenir coin stamped with an image of the canyon. Each represents a different way of experiencing the Grand Canyon, and together they offer a multifaceted way to understand your trip.

You might also write in several different genres on the same topic. If you begin by **ARGUING** that the government should provide universal health care, for example, writing a **MEMOIR** about a time you were ill could help you explore a personal connection to the topic. Composing a **PROFILE** of a doctor might give you new insights into the issue, and writing a **PROPOSAL** for how universal health care could work might direct

◆ 355–73
▲ 216–23
224–34
235–44

you to potential solutions. You could assemble all these texts in a folder, with a title page and table of contents so that readers can see how it all fits together — or you could create an online multimodal text, combining text, images, video, sound, and links to other sites.

298–300
301–5
331–43
344–49

IF YOU NEED MORE HELP

See Chapter 28 for guidelines on **DRAFTING**, Chapter 29 on **ASSESSING YOUR OWN WRITING**, Chapter 33 on **BEGINNING AND ENDING**, and Chapter 34 on **GUIDING YOUR READER**.

Choosing Genres **24**

Write an essay responding to one of the course readings. Show how James Joyce uses financial and economic imagery in "Araby." Explore the various policies adopted toward the use of marijuana. Much of the time, your college writing assignments will specify a particular genre, but sometimes — as these examples suggest — they won't. Vague verbs like *discuss* or *explore* may leave you wondering exactly what your instructor expects. This chapter will help you decide what genre(s) to use when an assignment doesn't tell you what to do.

Recognizing Which Genres Are Required

LITERACY NARRATIVE   A personal account of how you learned to read or write or to make meaning through words, pictures, music, or other means. If you're assigned to explore your development as a writer or reader or to describe how you came to be interested in a particular subject or career, you'll likely need to write a literacy narrative or a variation on one. Some terms that might signal a literacy narrative: *describe a learning experience, tell how you learned, trace your development, write a story.*

▲ 73–93

TEXTUAL ANALYSIS or **LITERARY ANALYSIS**   A careful examination of a text both for what it says and for how it says it, with the goal of demonstrating the ways the text achieves certain effects. If your assignment calls on you to look at a nonfiction text to see not only what it says but how it works, you likely need to write a textual analysis. If the text is a short story, novel, poem, or play, you probably need to write a literary analysis. If you are analyzing a text or texts in multiple media, you might choose either genre

▲ 94–128
206–15

or mix the two. Some terms that might signal that a textual or literary analysis is being asked for: *analyze, examine, explicate, read closely, interpret.*

129–55 ▲ **REPORT**   A presentation of information as objectively as possible to inform readers about a subject. If your task is to research a topic and then tell your audience in a balanced, neutral way what you know about it, your goal is probably to write a report. Some terms that might signal that a report is being asked for: *define, describe, explain, inform, observe, record, report, show.*

156–82 ▲ **POSITION PAPER** or **ARGUMENT**   Writing that asserts a belief or claim about an issue — usually stated as a thesis — and supports it with reasons and various kinds of evidence. Some terms that might signal that your instructor wants you to take a position or argue for or against something: *agree or disagree, argue, claim, criticize, defend, justify, position paper, prove.*

183–87 ▲
486–87 ● **ABSTRACT** or **SUMMARY**   A condensation of a text into a briefer version that conveys the main points of the original. If your assignment is to reduce a text, either someone else's or your own, into a single paragraph or so, one of these genres is called for. A summary usually either stands on its own or is inserted within a larger text you're writing; an abstract is a condensation of a text you've written yourself, and you write it either to submit the text for publication or to serve as an introduction to the text. Some terms that might signal that an abstract or summary is expected: *abridge, boil down, compress, condense, recap, summarize.*

188–96 ▲ **ANNOTATED BIBLIOGRAPHY**   A genre that includes an overview of published research and scholarship on a topic. Assignments asking you to list potential sources on a topic with complete publication information for and descriptions or evaluations of each one are likely asking for annotated bibliographies. Some terms that might signal that an annotated bibliography is expected: *an annotated list, list and comment on, list and describe, list and evaluate, list sources.*

197–205 ▲ **EVALUATION**   Writing that makes a judgment about something — a source, poem, film, restaurant, whatever — based on certain criteria. If your instructor asks you to say whether or not you like something or whether it's a good or bad example of a category or better or worse than something else, an evaluation is likely being called for. Some terms that might signal that an evaluation is expected: *assess, critique, evaluate, judge, recommend, review.*

MEMOIR   A genre of writing that focuses on something significant in your past. If you're asked to explore an important moment or event in your life, you're probably being asked to write a memoir. Some terms that likely signal that a memoir is desired: *autobiography, chronicle, narrate, a significant personal memory, a story drawn from your experience.*

▲ 216–23

PROFILE   A type of writing that presents a person, place, or event from an interesting angle in an engaging way and is based on firsthand field research. If your instructor assigns you the task of portraying a subject in a way that is both informative and entertaining, you're likely being asked to write a profile. Some terms that might indicate that a profile is being asked for: *angle, describe, dominant impression, interview, observe, report on.*

▲ 224–34

PROPOSAL   Writing that argues for a particular solution to a problem or suggests some action — or that makes a case for pursuing a certain project. Some terms that might indicate a proposal: *argue for [a solution or action], propose, put forward, recommend.*

▲ 235–44

REFLECTION   A genre of writing that presents a writer's thoughtful, personal exploration of a subject. If your assignment calls on you to think in writing about something or to play with ideas, you are likely being asked to write a reflection. Some terms that may mean that a reflection is called for: *consider, explore, ponder, probe, reflect, speculate.*

▲ 245–52

Dealing with Ambiguous Assignments

Sometimes even the key term in an assignment doesn't indicate clearly which genre is wanted, so you need to read such an assignment especially carefully. A first step might be to consider whether it's asking for a report or an argument. For example, here are two sample assignments:

> Discuss ways in which the invention of gas and incandescent lighting significantly changed people's daily lives in the nineteenth century.
>
> Discuss why Willy Loman in *Death of a Salesman* is, or is not, a tragic hero.

Both assignments use the word *discuss*, but in very different ways. The first may be simply be requesting an informative, researched report: the thesis — new forms of lighting significantly changed people's daily lives in various ways — is already given, and you may be simply expected to research and explain what some of these changes were. It's also possible, though, that this assignment is asking you to make an argument about which of these changes were the most significant ones.

In contrast, *discuss* in the second assignment is much more open-ended. It does not lead to a particular thesis but is more clearly asking you to present an argument: to choose a position (Willy Loman *is* a tragic hero; Willy Loman is *not* a tragic hero; even, possibly, Willy Loman both *is and is not* a tragic hero) and to marshal reasons and evidence from the play to support your position. A clue that an argument is being asked for lies in the way the assignment offers a choice of paths.

Other potentially ambiguous words in assignments are *show* and *explore*, both of which could lead in many directions. If after a careful reading of the entire assignment you still aren't sure what it's asking for, ask your instructor to clarify the appropriate genre or genres.

Mixing Genres

Genres are seldom "pure" — a pure argument, a pure memoir, a pure literary analysis. Most of the writing we read and produce mixes genres to meet the needs of the writer's purpose and audience. For example, writing that **TAKES A POSITION** rarely jumps into the argument immediately. Instead, it may include several paragraphs in which the context for the disputed position is explained or information crucial to the audience's understanding is reported. Sometimes that **REPORT** will be introduced by

156–82 ▲

129–55 ▲

a brief **MEMOIR** that makes the topic personal to the writer and so less abstract. And the argument itself may well do much more than simply take a position — it may **EVALUATE** alternatives and end with a **PROPOSAL**, and even include genres in other media, such as a video clip **PROFILING** the subject of the argument.

▲ 216–23
197–205
235–44
224–34

A decision about whether to mix genres or not should depend primarily on your purpose and audience. If doing so would help you achieve your goal, and you are not restricted to a particular genre, then combining genres is appropriate. Be creative — but not to the extent that you confuse or annoy readers who expect, say, a straightforward academic report. And if you are required to write using a single genre, then you must find ways of making it suit your purpose.

Considering the Rhetorical Situation

If you're still unsure which genre or combination of genres you should use, try exploring your rhetorical situation by answering some or all of the following questions:

PURPOSE   Why are you writing? What do you hope to achieve? What genre(s) do writers typically use to achieve this purpose? Where might you find examples of these genres? What alternatives to these genres are available?

■ 55–56

AUDIENCE   To whom are you writing? How do members of this audience typically communicate with one another? What information do they typically include, and what do they omit? How much information or explanation will they need? Will they expect you to cite the work of others?

■ 57–60

GENRE   What will your audience expect? Which ones do they use themselves in similar situations?

■ 61–63

STANCE   What stance do you wish to project — and what stances are acceptable for your audience and purpose? What is

■ 64–67

your relationship with your audience? Are you writing as an equal, a student, an interested or concerned outsider, something else? What tone is appropriate — objective, impassioned, respectful, informal, something else? What genre(s) will allow you to express that tone?

68–70 ◼

MEDIA / DESIGN What media are typically used to communicate in this situation, and do these media suggest or encourage a particular genre? If so, does the genre require a particular design or format? Are charts, graphs, photos, or other visual elements typically included?

✳ academic literacies

◼ rhetorical situations

▲ genres

○ processes

◆ strategies

● research MLA / APA

▢ media / design

◖ readings

part 4

Processes

To create anything, we generally break the work down into a series of steps. We follow a recipe (or the directions on a box) to bake a cake; we break a song down into different parts and the music into various chords to arrange a piece of music. So it is when we write. We rely on various processes to get from a blank screen or page to a finished product. The chapters that follow offer advice on some of these processes—from WRITING AS INQUIRY and GENERATING IDEAS to DRAFTING to GETTING RESPONSE to EDITING to COMPILING A PORTFOLIO, and more.

Processes

Writing as Inquiry 25

Sometimes we write to say what we think. Other times, however, we write in order to figure out what we think. Much of the writing you do in college will be the latter. Even as you learn to write, you will be writing to learn. This chapter is about writing with a spirit of inquiry — approaching writing projects with curiosity, moving beyond the familiar, keeping your eyes open, tackling issues that don't have easy answers. It's about starting with questions and going from there — and taking risks. As Mark Twain once said, "Sail away from the safe harbor. . . . Explore. Dream. Discover." This chapter offers strategies for doing just that with your writing.

Starting with Questions

The most important thing is to start with questions — with what you don't know rather than with what you do know. Your goal is to learn about your subject and then to learn more. If you're writing about a topic you know well, you want to expand on what you already know. In academic writing, good topics arise from important questions, issues, and problems that are already being discussed. As a writer, you need to find out what's being said about your topic and then see your writing as a way of entering that larger conversation.

So start with questions, and don't expect to find easy answers. If there were easy answers, there would be no reason for discussion — or for you to write. For purposes of inquiry, the best questions can't be answered by looking in a reference book. Instead, they are ones that help you explore what you think — and why. As it happens, many of the strategies in this book can help you ask questions of this kind. Following are some questions to get you started.

* academic literacies
■ rhetorical situations
▲ genres
○ processes
◆ strategies
● research MLA / APA
□ media / design
Ⅲ readings

388–98
How can it be DEFINED?   What is it, and what does it do? Look it up in a dictionary; check *Wikipedia*. Remember, though, that these are only starting points. How *else* can it be defined? What more is there to know about it? If your topic is being debated, chances are that its very definition is subject to debate. If, for instance, you're writing about gay marriage, how you define marriage will affect how you approach the topic.

399–407
How can it be DESCRIBED?   What details should you include? From what vantage point should you describe your topic? If, for example, your topic were the physiological effects of running a marathon, what would those effects be — on the lungs, heart muscles, nerves, brain, and so on? How would you describe the physical experience of running over twenty-six miles from the runner's point of view?

414–18
How can it be EXPLAINED?   What does it do? How does it work? If you were investigating the use of performance-enhancing drugs by athletes, for example, what exactly is the effect of these drugs? What makes them dangerous — and are they always dangerous or only in certain conditions? Why are they illegal — and should they be illegal?

380–87
What can it be COMPARED with?   Again using performance-enhancing drugs by athletes as an example, how does taking such supplements compare with wearing high-tech footwear or uniforms? Does such a comparison make you see taking steroids or other performance-enhancing drugs in a new light?

350–54
What may have CAUSED it? What might be its EFFECTS?   Who or what does it affect? What causes cerebral palsy in children, for example? What are its symptoms? If children with cerebral palsy are not treated, what might be the consequences?

375–79
How can it be CLASSIFIED?   Is it a topic or issue that can be placed into categories of similar topics or issues? What categories can it be placed into? Are there legal and illegal performance-enhancing supplements (human growth hormone and steroids, for instance), and what's the difference? Are some safe and others less safe? Classifying your topic in this way can help you consider its complexities.

How can it be ANALYZED?   What parts can the topic be divided into? For example, if you were exploring the health effects of cell phone use, you might ask what evidence suggests that cell phone radiation causes cancer? What cancers are associated with cell phone use? What do medical experts and phone manufacturers say? How can cell phone users reduce their risk?

▲ 94–128

How can it be interpreted?   What does it really mean? How do you interpret it, and how does your interpretation differ from others? What evidence supports your interpretation, and what argues against it? Imagine you were exploring the topic of sports injuries among young women. Do these injuries reflect a larger cultural preoccupation with competition? a desire to win college scholarships? something else?

What expectations does it raise?   What will happen next? What makes you think so? If this happens, how will it affect those involved? For instance, will the governing bodies of professional sports require more testing of athletes' blood, urine, and hair than they do now? Will such tests be unfair to athletes taking drugs for legitimate medical needs?

What are the different POSITIONS on it?   What controversies or disagreements exist, and what evidence is offered for the various positions? What else might be said? Are there any groups or individuals who seem especially authoritative? If so, you might want to explore what they have said.

▲ 156–82

What are your own feelings about it?   What interests you about the topic? How much do you already know about it? For example, if you're an athlete, how do you feel about competing against others who may have taken supplements? If a friend has problems with drugs, do those problems affect your thinking about drugs in sports? How do you react to what others say about the topic? What else do you want to find out?

Are there other ways to think about it?   Is what seems true in this case also true in others? How can you apply this subject in another situation? Will what works in another situation also work here? What do you have to do to adapt it? Imagine you were writing about traffic fatalities. If replacing stop signs with roundabouts or traffic circles reduced traffic fatalities in England, could doing so also reduce accidents in the United States?

292–93 ◉

You can also start with the journalist's **QUESTIONS**: *Who? What? When? Where? Why? How?* Asking questions from these various perspectives can help you deepen your understanding of your topic by leading you to see it from many angles.

Keeping a Journal

295–96 ◉

One way to get into the habit of using writing as a tool for inquiry is to keep a **JOURNAL**. You can use a journal to record your observations, reactions, whatever you wish. Some writers find journals especially useful places to articulate questions or speculations. You may be assigned by teachers to do certain work in a journal, but in general, you can use a journal to write for yourself. Note your ideas, speculate, digress — go wherever your thoughts lead you.

Keeping a Blog

618–19 ▢

You may also wish to explore issues or other ideas online in the form of a **BLOG**. Most blogs have a comments section that allows others to read and respond to what you write, leading to potentially fruitful discussions. You can also include links to other websites, helping you connect various strands of thought and research. The blogs of others, along with online discussion forums and groups, may also be useful sources of opinion on your topic, but keep in mind that they probably aren't authoritative research sources. There are a number of search engines that can help you find blog posts related to specific topics, including *Google Blog Search*, *Ask*, and *IceRocket*. You can create your own blog on sites such as *Blogger*, *Tumblr*, *Svbtle*, or *WordPress*.

academic literacies · rhetorical situations · genres · processes · strategies · research MLA / APA · media / design · readings

Collaborating 26

Whether you're working in a face-to-face group, posting on an online discussion board or class *Facebook* page, or exchanging drafts with a classmate for peer review, you likely spend a lot of time collaborating with others on writing tasks. Even if you do much of your writing sitting alone at a computer, you probably get help from others at various stages in the writing process — and provide help as well. The fact is that two heads can be better than one — and learning to work well with a team is as important as anything else you'll learn in college. This chapter offers some guidelines for collaborating successfully with other writers.

Some Ground Rules for Face-to-Face Group Work

- Make sure everyone is facing everyone else and is physically part of the group. Doing that makes a real difference in the quality of the interactions — think how much better conversation works when you're sitting around a table than it does when you're sitting in a row.

- Thoughtfulness, respect, and tact are key, since most writers (as you know) are sensitive and need to be able to trust those commenting on their work. Respond to the contributions of others as you would like others to respond to yours.

- Each meeting needs an agenda — and careful attention paid to time. Appoint one person as timekeeper to make sure all necessary work gets done in the available time.

- Appoint another person to be group leader or facilitator. That person needs to make sure everyone gets a chance to speak, no one dominates the discussion, and the group stays on task.

486–87

- Appoint a member of the group to keep a record of the group's discussion, jotting down the major points as they come up and afterward writing a **SUMMARY** of the discussion that the group members then approve.

Online Collaboration

Sometimes you'll need or want to work with one or more people online. Working together online offers many advantages, including the ability to collaborate without being in the same place at the same time. Nonetheless, it also presents some challenges that differ from those of face-to-face group work. When sharing writing or collaborating with others online in other ways, consider the following suggestions:

- As with all online communication, remember that you need to choose your words carefully to avoid inadvertently hurting someone's feelings. Without facial expressions, gestures, and other forms of body language and without tone of voice, your words carry all the weight.

57–60

- Remember that the **AUDIENCE** for what you write may well extend beyond your group — your work might be forwarded to others, so there is no telling who else might read it.
- Decide as a group how best to deal with the logistics of exchanging drafts and comments. You can cut and paste text directly into email, send it as an attachment to a message, or post it to your class course management system site or a file-sharing site like *Dropbox* or *Google Docs*. You may need to use a combination of methods, depending on each group member's access to equipment and software. In any case, name your files carefully so that everyone knows which version to use.

Group Writing Projects

Creating a document with a team is common in business and professional work and in some academic fields as well. Here are some tips for making collaboration of this kind work well:

- *Define the task as clearly as possible.* Make sure everyone understands and agrees with the stated goals.
- *Divide the task into parts.* Decide which parts can be done by individuals, which can be done by a subgroup, and which need to be done by everyone together.
- *Assign each group member certain tasks.* Try to match tasks to each person's skills and interests and to divide the work equally.
- *Establish a deadline for each task.* Allow time for unforeseen problems before the project deadline.
- *Try to accommodate everyone's style of working.* Some people value discussion; others want to get right down to the writing. There's no best way to get work done; everyone needs to be conscious that his or her way is not the only way.
- *Work for consensus — not necessarily total agreement.* Everyone needs to agree that the plan to get the writing accomplished is doable and appropriate — if not exactly the way you would do the project if you were working alone.
- *Make sure everyone performs.* In some situations, your instructor may help, but in others the group itself may have to develop a way to make sure that the work gets done well and fairly. During the course of the project, it's sometimes helpful for each group member to write an assessment both of the group's work and of individual members' contributions.

Writing Conferences

Conferences with instructors or writing tutors can be an especially helpful kind of collaboration. These one-on-one sessions often offer the most strongly focused assistance you can get — and truly valuable instruction. Here are some tips for making the most of conference time:

- *Come prepared.* Bring all necessary materials, including the draft you'll be discussing, your notes, any outlines — and, of course, any questions.

- *Be prompt.* Your instructor or tutor has set aside a block of time for you, and once that time is up, there's likely to be another student writer waiting.

- *Listen carefully, discuss your work seriously, and try not to be defensive.* Your instructor or tutor is only trying to help you produce the best piece possible. If you sense that your work is being misunderstood, explain what you're trying to say. Don't get angry! If a sympathetic reader who's trying to help can't understand what you mean, maybe you haven't conveyed your meaning well enough.

- *Take notes.* During the conference, jot down keywords and suggestions. Immediately afterward, flesh out your notes so you'll have a complete record of what was said.

- *Reflect on the conference.* Afterward, think about what you learned. What do you have to do now? Create a plan for revising or doing further work, and write out questions you will ask at your next conference.

academic literacies

rhetorical situations

genres

processes

strategies

research MLA / APA

media / design

readings

Generating Ideas and Text

All good writing revolves around ideas. Whether you're writing a job-application letter, a sonnet, or an essay, you'll always spend time and effort generating ideas. Some writers can come up with a topic, put their thoughts in order, and flesh out their arguments in their heads; but most of us need to write out our ideas, play with them, tease them out, and examine them from some distance and from multiple perspectives. This chapter offers activities that can help you do just that. *Freewriting, looping, listing,* and *clustering* can help you explore what you know about a subject; *cubing* and *questioning* nudge you to consider a subject in new ways; and *outlining, letter writing, journal keeping,* and *discovery drafting* offer ways to generate a text.

Freewriting

An informal method of exploring a subject by writing about it, freewriting ("writing freely") can help you generate ideas and come up with materials for your draft. Here's how to do it:

1. Write as quickly as you can without stopping for 5 to 10 minutes (or until you fill a screen or page).

2. If you have a subject to explore, write it at the top and then start writing about it, but if you stray, don't worry — just keep writing. If you don't have a subject yet, just start writing and don't stop until the time is up. If you can't think of anything to say, write that ("I can't think of anything to say") again and again until you do — and you will!

3. Once the time is up, read over what you've written, and underline or highlight passages that interest you.

4. Write some more, starting with one of those underlined or highlighted passages as your new topic. Repeat the process until you've come up with a usable topic.

Looping

Looping is a more focused version of freewriting; it can help you explore what you know about a subject. You stop, reflect on what you've written, and then write again, developing your understanding in the process. It's good for clarifying your knowledge and understanding of a subject and finding a focus. Here's what you do:

1. Write for 5 to 10 minutes on whatever you know about your subject. This is your first loop.

2. Read over what you wrote, and then write a single sentence summarizing the most important or interesting idea. You might try completing one of these sentences: "I guess what I was trying to say was . . . " or "What surprises me most in reading what I wrote is . . ." This will be the start of another loop.

3. Write again for 5 to 10 minutes, using your summary sentence as your beginning and your focus. Again, read what you've written, and then write a sentence capturing the most important idea — in a third loop.

Keep going until you have enough understanding of your topic to be able to decide on a tentative focus — something you can write about.

Listing

Some writers find it useful to keep lists of ideas that occur to them while they are thinking about a topic. Follow these steps:

1. Write a list of potential ideas about a topic. Don't try to limit your list — include anything that interests you.

2. Look for relationships among the items on your list: what patterns do you see? If other ideas occur to you, add them to the list.

3. Arrange the items in an order that makes sense for your purpose and can serve as the beginning of an outline for your writing.

Clustering or Mapping Ideas

Clustering (also called idea mapping) is a way of generating and connecting ideas visually. It's useful for seeing how various ideas relate to one another and for developing subtopics. The technique is simple:

1. Write your topic in the middle of a sheet of paper and circle it.

2. Write ideas relating to that topic around it, circle them, and connect them to the central circle.

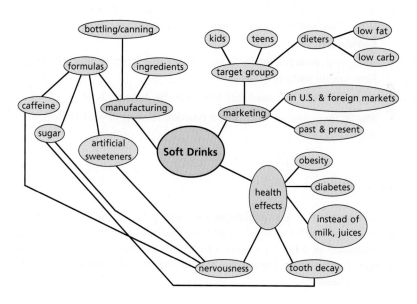

3. Write down examples, facts, or other details relating to each idea, and join them to the appropriate circles.

4. Keep going until you can't think of anything else relating to your topic.

You should end up with various ideas about your topic, and the clusters will allow you to see how they relate to one another. In the example cluster on the topic of "soft drinks" from page 291, note how some ideas link not only to the main topic or related topics but also to other ideas.

Cubing

A cube has six sides. You can examine a topic as you might a cube, looking at it in these six ways:

399–407
- **DESCRIBE** it. What's its color? shape? age? size? What's it made of?

380–87
- **COMPARE** it to something else. What is it similar to or different from?

- Associate it with other things. What does it remind you of? What connections does it have to other things? How would you 374–79 **CLASSIFY** it?

- Analyze it. How is it made? Where did it come from? Where is it going? How are its parts related?

- Apply it. What is it used for? What can be done with it?

156–82
- **ARGUE** for or against it. Choose a position relating to your subject, and defend it.

Questioning

281–84
It's always useful to ask **QUESTIONS**. One way is to start with *What? Who? When? Where? How?* and *Why?* A particular method of exploring a topic is to ask questions as if the topic were a play. This method is especially useful for exploring literature, history, the arts, and the social sciences. Start with these questions:

- *What?* What happens? How is it similar to or different from other actions?
- *Who?* Who are the actors? Who are the participants, and who are the spectators? How do the actors affect the action, and how are they affected by it?
- *When?* When does the action take place? How often does it happen? What happens before, after, or at the same time? Would it be different at another time? Does the time have historical significance?
- *Where?* What is the setting? What is the situation, and what makes it significant?
- *How?* How does the action occur? What are the steps in the process? What techniques are required? What equipment is needed?
- *Why?* Why did this happen? What are the actors' motives? What end does the action serve?

Using Genre Features

Genres typically include particular kinds of information and organize it in particular ways. One way to generate ideas and text, then, is to identify the key features of the genre in which you're writing and use them to guide you as you write. Of course, you may alter the genre's features or combine two or more genres in order to achieve your purpose, but the overall shape and content of the genre can give you a way to develop and organize your ideas and research.

Outlining

You may create an *informal outline* by simply listing your ideas and numbering them in the order in which you want to write about them. You might prefer to make a *working outline*, to show the hierarchy of relationships among your ideas. While still informal, a working outline distinguishes your main ideas and your support, often through simple indentation:

> First main idea
>> Supporting evidence or detail
>> Supporting evidence or detail
>
> Second main idea
>> Supporting evidence or detail
>> Supporting evidence or detail

A *formal outline* shows the hierarchy of your ideas through a system of indenting, numbering, and lettering. Remember that when you divide a point into more specific subpoints, you should have at least two of them — you can't divide something into only one part. Also, try to keep items at each level parallel in structure. Formal outlines work this way:

> Thesis statement
>
> I. First reason
>> A. Supporting evidence
>>> 1. Detail of evidence
>>> 2. Detail of evidence
>> B. Supporting evidence
>
> II. Another reason

Here is a formal outline of the research report by Carolyn Stonehill on pages 579–89, "It's in Our Genes," that shows how she organized it:

> I. Introduction: Reasons for choosing mates
> II. Women
>> A. Experience long pregnancy, childbirth risks, and infant dependence
>> B. Are attracted to signs of resources and protective ability
> III. Men
>> A. Need mates with reproductive fitness
>> B. Are attracted to signs of health and youth

IV. Possible objections to biological theory of selection
    A. Role of culture
        1. Media influence on selection standards
        2. Unclear relation between cause and effect
    B. Role of species-specific development
        1. Symbolic thought as unique human quality
        2. Impossibility of inherited preferences
V. Conclusion: Dominant influence of ancestral strategies

Writing out a formal outline can be helpful when you're dealing with a complex subject; as you revise your drafts, though, be flexible and ready to change your outline as your understanding of your topic develops.

Letter Writing

Sometimes the prospect of writing a report or essay can be intimidating. You may find that simply explaining your topic to someone will help you get started. In that case, write a letter or email to someone you know — your best friend, a parent or grandparent, a sibling — in which you discuss your subject. Explain it in terms that your reader can understand. Use the unsent letter to rehearse your topic; make it a kind of rough draft that you can then revise and develop to suit your actual audience.

Keeping a Journal

Some writers find that writing in a journal helps them generate ideas. Making note of your ideas, thoughts, feelings, or the events of your day can provide a wealth of topics, and a journal can also be a good place to explore what you think and why you think as you do.

Journals are private — you are the only audience — so you can feel free to write whatever comes to mind. And you can do more than write.

If you choose a paper journal, doodle or draw in it, and keep clippings or scraps of paper between the pages; if you keep your journal on a computer, copy and paste interesting images or text you find online. Whatever form your journal takes, feel free to play with its contents, and don't worry about errors or grammar. The goal is to generate ideas; let yourself wander without censoring yourself or fretting that your writing is incorrect or incomplete or incoherent. That's okay.

289–90 ◉
290–91
292

One measure of the success of journaling and other personal writing is length: journal entries, **FREEWRITING**, **LISTING**, **CUBING**, and other types of informal writing are like warm-up exercises to limber you up and get you thinking. If you don't give them enough time and space, they may not do what you want them to. Often, students' best insights appear at the end of their journal entries. Had they stopped before that point, they would never have had those good ideas.

After you've written several journal entries, one way to study the ideas in them is to highlight useful patterns in different colors. For example, journal entries usually include some questioning and speculating, as well as summarizing and paraphrasing. Try color-coding each of these, sentence by sentence, phrase by phrase: yellow for summaries or paraphrases, green for questions, blue for speculations. Do any colors dominate? If, for example, your entries are mostly yellow, you may be restating the course content or quoting from the textbook too much and perhaps need to ask more questions. If you're generating ideas for an essay, you might assign colors to ideas or themes to see which ones are the most promising.

Discovery Drafting

Some writers do best by jumping in and writing. Here are the steps to take if you're ready to write a preliminary **DRAFT**:

298–300 ◉

1. Write your draft quickly, in one sitting if possible.

academic literacies · rhetorical situations · genres · processes · strategies · research MLA / APA · media / design · readings

2. Assume that you are writing to discover what you want to say and how you need to say it — and that you will make substantial revisions in a later part of the process.

3. Don't worry about grammatical or factual correctness — if you can't think of a word, leave a blank space to fill in later. If you're unsure of a date or spelling, put a question mark in parentheses as a reminder to check it later. Just write.

IF YOU NEED MORE HELP

See each of the **GENRE** chapters for specific strategies for generating text in each genre.

▲ 71

28 Drafting

At some point, you need to write out a draft. By the time you begin drafting, you've probably written quite a bit — in the form of notes, lists, outlines, and other kinds of informal writing. This chapter offers some hints on how to write a draft — and reminds you that as you draft, you may well need to get more information, rethink some aspect of your work, or follow new ideas that occur to you as you write.

Establishing a Schedule with Deadlines

435–36

Don't wait until the last minute to write. Computers crash, printers jam. Life intervenes in unpredictable ways. You increase your chances of success immensely by setting and meeting **DEADLINES**: Research done by ___; rough draft done by ___; revisions done by ___; final draft edited, proofread, and submitted by ___. How much time you need varies with each writing task — but trying to compress everything into twenty-four or forty-eight hours before the deadline is asking for trouble.

Getting Comfortable

When are you at your best? When do you have your best ideas? For major writing projects, consider establishing a schedule that lets you write when you stand the best chance of doing good work. Schedule breaks for exercise and snacks. Find a good place to write, a place where you've got a good surface on which to spread out your materials, good lighting, a comfortable chair, and the right tools (computer, pen, paper) for the job. Often, however, we must make do: you may have to do your drafting in a busy computer lab or classroom. The trick is to make yourself as comfortable as you can manage. Sort out what you *need* from what you *prefer*.

Starting to Write

All of the above advice notwithstanding, don't worry so much about the trappings of your writing situation that you don't get around to writing. Write. Start by **FREEWRITING**, start with a first sentence, start with awful writing that you know you'll discard later — but write. That's what gets you warmed up and going.

◉ 289–90

Write quickly in spurts.   Write quickly with the goal of writing a complete draft, or a complete section of a longer draft, in one sitting. If you need to stop in the middle, make some notes about where you were headed when you stopped so that you can easily pick up your train of thought when you begin again.

Break down your writing task into small segments.   Big projects can be intimidating. But you can always write one section or, if need be, one paragraph or even a single sentence — and then another and another. It's a little like dieting. If I think I need to lose twenty pounds, I get discouraged and head for the doughnuts; but if I decide that I'll lose one pound and I lose it, well, I'll lose another — *that* I can do.

Expect surprises.   Writing is a form of thinking; the words you write lead you down certain roads and away from others. You may end up somewhere you didn't anticipate. Sometimes that can be a good thing — but sometimes you can write yourself into a dead end or out onto a tangent. Just know that this is natural, part of every writer's experience, and it's okay to double back or follow a new path that opens up before you.

Expect to write more than one draft.   A first sentence, first page, or first draft represents your attempt to organize into words your thoughts, ideas, feelings, research findings, and more. It's likely that some of that first try will not achieve your goals. That's okay — having writing on screen or on paper that you can change, add to, and cut means you're part of the way there. As you revise, you can fill in gaps and improve your writing and thinking.

Dealing with Writer's Block

You may sit down to write but find that you can't — nothing occurs to you; your mind is blank. Don't panic; here are some ways to get started writing again:

- Think of the assignment as a problem to be solved. Try to capture that problem in a single sentence: "How do I explain the context for my topic?" "What is the best way to organize my argument?" "What am I trying to do in the conclusion?"

- Start early and break the writing task into small segments drafted over several days. Waiting until the night before an assignment is due can create panic — and writer's block

- Stop trying: take a walk, take a shower, do something else. Come back in a half hour, refreshed.

- Open a new document on your computer or get a fresh piece of paper and **FREEWRITE**, or try **LOOPING** or **LISTING**. What are you trying to say? Just let whatever comes come — you may write yourself out of your box.

- If you usually write on your computer, turn it off, get out paper and pencil, and write by hand.

- Try a graphic approach: try **CLUSTERING**, or draw a chart of what you want to say; draw a picture; doodle.

- Do some **RESEARCH** on your topic to see what others have said about it.

- Talk to someone about what you are trying to do. If there's a writing center at your school, talk to a tutor: **GET RESPONSE**. If there's no one to talk to, talk to yourself. It's the act of talking — using your mouth instead of your hands — that can free you up.

289–91 ◉

291–92 ◉

433 ●

306–7 ◉

> **IF YOU NEED MORE HELP**
>
> See the chapter on **GENERATING IDEAS AND TEXT** if you find you need more material. And once you have a draft, see the chapters on **ASSESSING YOUR OWN WRITING** and **GETTING RESPONSE AND REVISING** for help evaluating your draft.

289–97 ◉
301–5
306–12

Assessing Your Own Writing 29

In school and out, our work is continually assessed by others. Teachers determine whether our writing is strong or weak; supervisors decide whether we merit raises or promotions; even friends and relatives size up in various ways the things we do. As writers, we need to assess our own work — to step back and see it with a critical eye. By developing standards of our own and being conscious of the standards others use, we can assess — and shape — our writing, making sure it does what we want it to do. This chapter will help you assess your own written work.

What we write for others must stand on its own because we usually aren't present when it is read — we rarely get to explain to readers why we did what we did and what it means. So we need to make our writing as clear as we can before we submit, post, display, or publish it. It's a good idea to assess your writing in two stages, first considering how well it meets the needs of your particular rhetorical situation, then studying the text itself to check its focus, argument, organization, and clarity. Sometimes some simple questions can get you started:

What works?
What still needs work?
Where do I need to say more (or less)?

Considering the Rhetorical Situation

PURPOSE   What is your purpose for writing? If you have multiple   ■ 55–56
                purposes, list them, and then note which ones are the
                most important. How well does your draft achieve your
                purpose(s)? If you're writing for an assignment, what are

the requirements of the assignment, and does your draft meet those requirements?

57–60 **AUDIENCE** To whom are you writing? What do those readers need and expect, as far as you can tell? Does your draft answer their needs? Do you define any terms and explain any concepts they won't know?

61–63 **GENRE** What is the genre, and what are the key features of that genre? Does your draft include each of those features? If not, is there a good reason?

64–67 **STANCE** Is your attitude toward your topic and your audience clear? Does your language project the personality and tone that you want?

68–70 **MEDIA / DESIGN** What medium (print? spoken? electronic?) or combination of media is your text intended for, and how well does your writing suit it? How well does the design of the text suit your purpose and audience? Does it meet any requirements of the genre or of the assignment, if you're writing for one?

Examining the Text Itself

Look carefully at your text to see how well it says what you want it to say. Start with its focus, and then examine its reasons and evidence, organization, and clarity, in that order. If your writing lacks focus, the revising you'll do to sharpen the focus is likely to change everything else; if it needs more reasons and evidence, the organization may well change.

Consider your focus. Your writing should have a clear point, and every part of the writing should support that point. Here are some questions that can help you see if your draft is adequately focused:

345–47 • What is your **THESIS**? Even if it is not stated directly, you should be able to summarize it for yourself in a single sentence.

- Is your thesis narrow or broad enough to suit the needs and expectations of your audience?
- How does the **BEGINNING** focus attention on your thesis or main point? ◈ 331–38
- Does each paragraph support or develop that point? Do any paragraphs or sentences stray from your focus?
- Does the **ENDING** leave readers thinking about your main point? Is there another way of concluding the essay that would sharpen your focus? ◈ 338–42

Consider the support you provide for your argument. Your writing needs to give readers enough information to understand your points, follow your argument, and see the logic of your thinking. How much information is enough will vary according to your audience. If they already know a lot about your subject or are likely to agree with your point of view, you may need to give less detail. If, however, they are unfamiliar with your topic or are skeptical about your views, you will probably need to provide much more.

- What **REASONS** and **EVIDENCE** do you give to support your thesis? Where might more information be helpful? If you're writing online, could you provide links to it? ◈ 358–67
- What key terms and concepts do you **DEFINE**? Are there any other terms your readers might need to have explained? Could you do so by providing links? ◈ 388–98
- Where might you include more **DESCRIPTION** or other detail? ◈ 399–407
- Do you make any **COMPARISONS**? Especially if your readers will not be familiar with your topic, it can help to compare it with something more familiar. ◈ 380–87
- If you include **NARRATIVE**, how is it relevant to your point? ◈ 419–27
- See Part 5 for other useful **STRATEGIES**. ◈ 329

Consider the organization. As a writer, you need to lead readers through your text, carefully structuring your material so that they will be able to follow your argument.

293–95 ○

- Analyze the structure by **OUTLINING** it. An informal outline will do since you mainly need to see the parts, not the details.

578 ●
510–37 ●

- Is your text complete? Does your genre require an **ABSTRACT**, a **WORKS-CITED LIST**, or any other elements?

349 ◆

- What **TRANSITIONS** help readers move from idea to idea and paragraph to paragraph? Do you need more?

604–5 ☐

- If there are no **HEADINGS**, would adding them help orient readers?

Check for clarity. Nothing else matters if readers can't understand what you write. Following are some questions that can help you see whether your meaning is clear and your text is easy to read:

344–45 ◆

- Does your **TITLE** announce the subject of your text and give some sense of what you have to say? If not, would a more direct title strengthen your argument?

345–47 ◆

- Do you state your **THESIS** directly? If not, will readers easily understand what your main point is? Try stating your thesis outright, and see if it makes your argument easier to follow.

331–38 ◆
338–42 ◆

- Does your **BEGINNING** tell readers what they need to understand your text, and does your **ENDING** help them make sense of what they've just read?

349 ◆

- How does each paragraph relate to the ones before and after? Are those relationships clear — or do you need to add **TRANSITIONS**?

- Do you vary your sentences? If all the sentences are roughly the same length or follow the same subject-verb-object pattern, your text probably lacks any clear emphasis and might even be difficult to read.

607–15 ☐

- Are **VISUALS** clearly labeled, positioned near the text they relate to, and referred to clearly in the text?

478–90 ●

- If you introduce materials from other sources, have you clearly distinguished **QUOTED**, **PARAPHRASED**, or **SUMMARIZED** ideas from your own?

388–98 ◆

- Do you **DEFINE** all the words that your readers may not know?

academic literacies | rhetorical situations | genres | processes | strategies | research MLA / APA | media / design | readings

- Does your punctuation make your writing more clear or less? Incorrect punctuation can make writing difficult to follow or, worse, change the meaning from what you intended. As a best-selling punctuation manual reminds us, there's a considerable difference between "eats, shoots, and leaves" and "eats shoots and leaves."

Thinking about Your Process

Your growth as a writer depends on how well you understand what you do when you write so that you can build on good habits. After you finish a writing project, considering the following questions can help you see the process that led to its creation — and find ways to improve the process next time.

- How would you tell the story of your thinking? Try writing these sentences: "When I first began with my topic, I thought _____. But as I did some thinking, writing, and research about the topic, my ideas changed and I thought _____."

- At some point in your writing, did you have to choose between two or more alternatives? What were they, and how did you choose?

- What was the most difficult problem you faced while writing? How did you go about trying to solve it?

- Whose advice did you seek while researching, organizing, drafting, revising, and editing? What advice did you take, and what did you ignore? Why?

Assessing a Body of Your Work

If you are required to submit a portfolio of your writing as part of a class, you will likely need to write a letter or essay that introduces the portfolio's contents and describes the processes that you used to create them and that ASSESSES THE WRITING IN YOUR PORTFOLIO. See Chapter 32 for detailed advice and a good example of a portfolio self-assessment.

⬤ 322–25

30 Getting Response and Revising

If we want to learn to play a song on the guitar, we play it over and over again until we get it right. If we play basketball or baseball, we likely spend hours shooting foul shots or practicing a swing. Writing works the same way. Making meaning clear can be tricky, and you should plan on revising and, if need be, rewriting in order to get it right. When we speak with someone face-to-face or on the phone or text a friend, we can get immediate response and restate or adjust our message if we've been misunderstood. In most other situations when we write, that immediate response is missing, so we need to seek out responses from readers to help us revise. This chapter includes a list of things for those readers to consider, along with various strategies for subsequent revising and rewriting.

Getting Response

Sometimes the most helpful eyes belong to others: readers you trust, including trained writing-center tutors. They can often point out problems (and strengths) that you simply cannot see in your own work. Ask your readers to consider the specific elements in the list below, but don't restrict them to those elements. Caution: if a reader says nothing about any of these elements, don't be too quick to assume that you needn't think about them yourself.

344–45 • What did you think when you first saw the **TITLE**? Is it interesting? informative? appropriate? Will it attract other readers' attention?

331–38 • Does the **BEGINNING** grab your attention? If so, how does it do so? Does it give enough information about the topic? offer necessary background information? How else might the piece begin?

345–47 • Is there a clear **THESIS**? What is it?

academic literacies

rhetorical situations

genres

processes

strategies

research MLA / APA

media / design

readings

- Is there sufficient **SUPPORT** for the thesis? Is there anywhere you'd like to have more detail? Is the supporting material sufficiently **DOCUMENTED**?

356–67
496–99

- Does the text have a clear pattern of organization? Does each part relate to the thesis? Does each part follow from the one preceding it? Was the text easy to follow? How might the organization be improved?

- Is the **ENDING** satisfying? What did it leave you thinking? How else might the piece end?

338–42

- Can you tell the writer's **STANCE** or attitude toward the subject and audience? What words convey that attitude? Is it consistent throughout?

64–67

- How well does the text meet the needs and expectations of its **AUDIENCE**? Where might readers need more information, guidance, or clarification? How well does it achieve its **PURPOSE**? Does every part of the text help achieve the purpose? Could anything be cut? Should anything be added? Does the text meet the requirements of its **GENRE**? Should anything be added, deleted, or changed to meet those requirements?

57–60
55–56
61–63

Revising

Once you have studied your draft with a critical eye and, if possible, gotten responses from other readers, it's time to revise. Major changes may be necessary, and you may need to generate new material or do some rewriting. But assume that your draft is good raw material that you can revise to achieve your purposes. Revision should take place on several levels, from global (whole-text issues) to particular (the details). Work on your draft in that order, starting with the elements that are global in nature and gradually moving to smaller, more particular aspects. This allows you to use your time most efficiently and take care of bigger issues first. In fact, as you deal with the larger aspects of your writing, many of the smaller ones will be taken care of along the way.

Give yourself time to revise. When you have a due date, set deadlines for yourself that will give you time — preferably several days but as much as your schedule permits — to work on the text before it has to be delivered.

Also, get some distance. Often when you're immersed in a project, you can't see the big picture because you're so busy creating it. If you can, get away from your writing for a while and think about something else. When you return to it, you're more likely to see it freshly. If there's not time to put a draft away for several days or more, even letting it sit overnight or for a few hours can help.

As you revise, assume that nothing is sacred. Bring a critical eye to all parts of a draft, not only to those parts pointed out by your reviewers. Content, organization, sentence patterns, individual words—all are subject to improvement. Be aware that a change in one part of the text may require changes in other parts.

At the same time, don't waste energy struggling with writing that simply doesn't work; you can always discard it. Look for the parts of your draft that do work — the parts that match your purpose and say what you want to say. Focus your efforts on those bright spots, expanding and developing them.

345–47 ◆
55–56 ◼
293–95 ◉

Revise to sharpen your focus. Examine your **THESIS** to make sure it matches your **PURPOSE** as you now understand it. Read each paragraph to ensure that it contributes to your main point; you may find it helpful to **OUTLINE** your draft to help you see all the parts. One way to do this is to highlight one sentence in each paragraph that expresses the paragraph's main idea. Then copy and paste the highlighted sentences into a new document. Does one state the thesis of the entire essay? Do the rest relate to the thesis? Are they in the best order? If not, you need to either modify the parts of the draft that don't advance your thesis or revise your thesis to reflect your draft's focus and to rearrange your points so they advance your discussion more effectively.

331–42 ◆

Read your **BEGINNING AND ENDING** carefully; make sure that the first paragraphs introduce your topic and provide any needed contextual information and that the final paragraphs provide a satisfying conclusion.

Revise to strengthen the argument. If readers find some of your claims unconvincing, you need to provide more information or more support. You may need to define terms you've assumed they will understand, offer additional examples, or provide more detail by describing, explaining

✳ academic literacies ◼ rhetorical situations ▲ genres ◯ processes ◆ strategies ● research MLA / APA ☐ media / design ▌▌ readings

processes, adding dialogue, or using some other **STRATEGIES**. Make sure you show as well as tell — and don't forget that you might need to do so literally, with visuals like photos, graphs, or charts. You might try freewriting, clustering, or other ways of **GENERATING IDEAS AND TEXT**. If you need to provide additional evidence, you might need to do additional **RESEARCH**.

329

289–97
433

Revise to improve the organization.   If you've outlined your draft, number each paragraph, and make sure each one follows from the one before. If anything seems out of place, move it, or if necessary, cut it completely. Check to see if you've included appropriate **TRANSITIONS** or **HEADINGS** to help readers move through the text, and add them as needed. Check to make sure your text meets readers' expectations of the **GENRE** you're writing in.

349

604–5

61–63

Revise for clarity.   Be sure readers will be able to understand what you're saying. Look closely at your **TITLE** to be sure it gives a sense of what the text is about and at your **THESIS**: will readers recognize your main point? If you don't state a thesis directly, consider whether you should. Provide any necessary background information and **DEFINE** any key terms. Make sure you've integrated any **QUOTATIONS**, **PARAPHRASES**, or **SUMMARIES** into your text smoothly. Are all paragraphs focused around one main point? Do the sentences in each paragraph contribute to that point? Finally, consider whether there are any data that would be more clearly presented in a **CHART**, **TABLE**, or **GRAPH**.

344–45
345–47

388–98
478–90

609–11

One way to test whether your text is clear is to switch audiences: write what you're trying to express as if you were talking to an eight-year-old. Your final draft probably won't be written that way, but the act of explaining your ideas to a young audience or readers who know nothing about your topic can help you discover any points that may be unclear.

Read and reread — and reread.   Take some advice from writing theorist Donald Murray:

> Nonwriters confront a writing problem and look away from the text to rules and principles and textbooks and handbooks and models. Writers look at the text, knowing that the text itself will reveal what needs to be done and what should not yet be done or may never be done.

The writer reads and rereads and rereads, standing far back and reading quickly from a distance, moving in close and reading slowly line by line, reading again and again, knowing that the answers to all writing problems lie within the evolving text.

— Donald Murray, *A Writer Teaches Writing*

Rewriting

Some writers find it useful to try rewriting a draft in various ways or from various perspectives just to explore possibilities. Try it! If you find that your original plan works best for your purpose, fine. But you may find that another way will work better. Especially if you're not completely satisfied with your draft, consider the following ways of rewriting. Experiment with your rhetorical situation:

- Rewrite your draft from different points of view, through the eyes of different people perhaps or through the eyes of an animal or even from the perspective of an object. See how the text changes (in the information it presents, its perspective, its voice).

57–60
- Rewrite for a different **AUDIENCE**. How might an email detailing a recent car accident be written to a friend, an insurance agent, a parent?

64–67
- Rewrite in a different **TONE**. If the first draft was temperate and judicious, be extreme; if it was polite, be more direct. If the first draft was in standard English, rewrite it more informally.

61–63
68–70
- Rewrite the draft in a different **GENRE** or **MEDIUM**. Rewrite an essay as a letter, story, poem, speech, comic strip, *PowerPoint* presentation. Which genre and medium work best to reach your intended audience and achieve your purpose?

Ways of rewriting a narrative

408–13
- Rewrite one scene completely in **DIALOGUE**.
- Start at the end of the story and work back to the beginning, or start in the middle and fill in the beginning as you work toward the end.

academic literacies · rhetorical situations · genres · processes · strategies · research MLA / APA · media / design · readings

Ways of rewriting a textual analysis

- **COMPARE** the text you're analyzing with another text (which may be in a completely different genre — film, TV, song lyrics, computer games, poetry, fiction, whatever).

  380–87

- Write a parody of the text you're analyzing. Be as silly and as funny as you can while maintaining the structure of the original text. Alternatively, write a parody of your analysis, using evidence from the text to support an outrageous analysis.

Ways of rewriting a report

- Rewrite for a different **AUDIENCE**. For example, explain a concept to your grandparents; describe the subject of a profile to a visitor from another planet.

  57–60

- Be silly. Rewrite the draft as if for *The Daily Show* or the *Onion*, or rewrite it as if it were written by Bart Simpson.

Ways of rewriting an argument

- Rewrite taking another **POSITION**. Argue as forcefully for that position as you did for your actual one, acknowledging and refuting your original position. Alternatively, write a rebuttal to your first draft from the perspective of someone with different beliefs.

  156–82

- Rewrite your draft as a **STORY**—make it real in the lives of specific individuals. (For example, if you were writing about abortion rights, you could write a story about a young pregnant woman trying to decide what she believes and what to do.) Or rewrite the argument as a fable or parable.

  419–27

- Rewrite the draft as a letter responding to a hostile reader, trying at least to make him or her understand what you have to say.

- Rewrite the draft as an angry letter to someone or as a table-thumping dinner-with-the-relatives discussion. Write from the most extreme position possible.

115–16 ▲

- Write an **ANALYSIS** of the topic of your argument in which you identify, as carefully and as neutrally as you can, the various positions people hold on the issue.

Once you've rewritten a draft in any of these ways, see whether there's anything you can use. Read each draft, considering how it might help you achieve your purpose, reach your audience, convey your stance. Revise your actual draft to incorporate anything you think will make your text more effective, whether it's other genres or a different perspective.

academic literacies

rhetorical situations

genres

processes

strategies

research MLA / APA

media / design

readings

Editing and Proofreading **31**

Your ability to produce clear, error-free writing shows something about your ability as a writer and also leads readers to make assumptions about your intellect, your work habits, even your character. Readers of job-application letters and résumés, for example, may reject applications if they contain a single error, for no other reason than it's an easy way to narrow the field of potential candidates. In addition, they may well assume that applicants who present themselves sloppily in an application will do sloppy work on the job. This is all to say that you should edit and proofread your work carefully.

Editing

Editing is the stage when you work on the details of your paragraphs, sentences, words, and punctuation to make your writing as clear, precise, correct — and effective — as possible. Your goal is not to achieve "perfection" (whatever that may be) so much as to make your writing as effective as possible for your particular purpose and audience. Check a good writing handbook for detailed advice, but the following guidelines can help you check your drafts systematically for some common errors with paragraphs, sentences, and words.

Editing paragraphs

- Does each paragraph focus on one point? Does it have a **TOPIC SENTENCE** ◆ 347–48
  that announces that point, and if so, where is it located? If it's not the first sentence, should it be? If there's no clear topic sentence, should there be one?

313

- Does every sentence relate to the main point of the paragraph? If any sentences do not, should they be deleted, moved, or revised?

329
- Is there enough detail to develop the paragraph's main point? How is the point developed — with narrative? definition? some other **STRATEGY**?

- Where have you placed the most important information — at the beginning? the end? in the middle? The most emphatic spot is at the end, so in general that's where to put information you want readers to remember. The second most emphatic spot is at the beginning.

- Are any paragraphs especially long or short? Consider breaking long paragraphs if there's a logical place to do so — maybe an extended example should be in its own paragraph, for instance. If you have paragraphs of only a sentence or two, see if you can add to them or combine them with another paragraph, unless you're using a brief paragraph to provide emphasis.

349
- Check the way your paragraphs fit together. Does each one follow smoothly from the one before? Do you need to add any **TRANSITIONS**?

331–38
- Does the **BEGINNING** paragraph catch readers' attention? In what other ways might you begin your text?

338–42
- Does the final paragraph provide a satisfactory **ENDING**? How else might you conclude your text?

Editing sentences

- Is each sentence complete? Does it have someone or something (the subject) performing some sort of action or expressing a state of being (the verb)? Does each sentence begin with a capital letter and end with a period, question mark, or exclamation point?

- Check your use of the passive voice. Although there are some rhetorical situations in which the passive voice ("The emperor was assassinated by an anarchist") is more appropriate than the active voice ("An anarchist assassinated the emperor") because you want to emphasize an action rather than who performed it, you'll do well to edit it out unless you have a good reason for using it.

- Check for parallelism. Items in a list or series should be parallel in form—all nouns (lions, tigers, bears), all verbs (hopped, skipped, jumped), all clauses (he came, he saw, he conquered), and so on.

- Do many of your sentences begin with *it* or *there*? Too often these words make your writing wordy and vague or even conceal needed information. Why write "There are reasons we voted for him" when you can say "We had reasons to vote for him"?

- Are your sentences varied? If they all start with the subject or are the same length, your writing might be dull and maybe even hard to read. Try varying your sentence openings by adding **TRANSITIONS**, introductory phrases or clauses. Vary sentence lengths by adding detail to some or combining some sentences.

  349

- Make sure you've used commas correctly. Is there a comma after each introductory element? ("After the lead singer quit, the group nearly disbanded. However, they then produced a string of hits.") Do commas set off nonrestrictive elements—parts that aren't needed to understand the sentence? ("The books I read in middle school, like the Harry Potter series, became longer and more challenging.") Are compound sentences connected with a comma? ("I'll eat broccoli steamed, but I prefer it roasted.")

Editing words

- Are you sure of the meaning of every word? Use a dictionary; be sure to look up words whose meanings you're not sure about. And remember your audience — do you use any terms they'll need to have defined?

- Is any of your language too general or vague? Why write that you competed in a race, for example, if you could say you ran the 4 × 200 relay?

- What about the **TONE**? If your stance is serious (or humorous or critical or something else), make sure that your words all convey that attitude.

  65

- Do any pronouns have vague or unclear antecedents? If you use "he" or "they" or "it" or "these," will readers know whom or what the words refer to?

- Have you used any clichés—expressions that are used so frequently that they are no longer fresh? "Live and let live," avoiding something "like the plague," and similar expressions are so predictable that your writing will almost always be better off without them.

- Be careful with language that refers to others. Make sure that your words do not stereotype any individual or group. Mention age, gender, race, religion, sexual orientation, and so on only if they are relevant to your subject. When referring to an ethnic group, make every effort to use the terms members of the group prefer.

- Edit out language that might be considered sexist. Do you say "he" when you mean "he and she"? Have you used words like *manpower* or *policeman* to refer to people who may be female? If so, substitute less gendered words such as *personnel* or *police officer*. Do your words reflect any gender stereotypes — for example, that all engineers are male, or all nurses female? If you mention someone's gender, is it even necessary? If not, eliminate the unneeded words.

- How many of your verbs are forms of *be* and *do*? If you rely too much on these words, try replacing them with more specific verbs. Why write "She did a proposal for" when you could say "She proposed"?

- Do you ever confuse *its* and *it's*? Use *it's* when you mean *it is* or *it has*. Use *its* when you mean *belonging to it*.

Proofreading

Proofreading is the final stage of the writing process, the point where you clean up your work to present it to your readers. Proofreading is like checking your appearance in a mirror before going into a job interview: being neat and well groomed looms large in creating a good first impression, and the same principle applies to writing. Misspelled words, missing pages, mixed-up fonts, and other lapses send a negative message about your work — and about you. Most readers excuse an occasional error, but by and large readers are an intolerant bunch: too many errors will lead them to declare your writing — and maybe your thinking — flawed. There goes your credibility. So proofread your final draft with care to ensure that your message is taken as seriously as you want it to be.

Up to this point, you've been told *not* to read individual words on the page and instead to read for meaning. Proofreading demands the opposite: you must slow down your reading so that you can see every word, every punctuation mark.

- Use your computer's grammar checker and spelling checker, but only as a first step, and know that they're not very reliable. Computer programs don't read writing; instead, they rely on formulas and banks of words, so what they flag (or don't flag) as mistakes may or may not be accurate. If you were to write, "my brother was diagnosed with a leaning disorder," *leaning* would not be flagged as misspelled because it is a word, even though it's the wrong word in that sentence.

- To keep your eyes from jumping ahead, place a ruler or piece of paper under each line as you read. Use your finger or a pencil as a pointer.

- Some writers find it helpful to read the text one sentence at a time, beginning with the last sentence and working backward.

- Read your text out loud to yourself—or better, to others, who may *hear* problems you can't see. Alternatively, have someone else read your text aloud to you while you follow along on the screen or page.

- Ask someone else to read your text. The more important the writing is, the more important this step is.

- If you find a mistake after you've printed out your text and are unable to print out a corrected version, make the change as neatly as possible in pencil or pen.

32 Compiling a Portfolio

Artists maintain portfolios of their work to show gallery owners, collectors, and other potential buyers. Money managers work with investment portfolios of stocks, bonds, and various mutual funds. And often as part of a writing class, student writers compile portfolios of their work. As with a portfolio of paintings or drawings, a portfolio of writing includes a writer's best work and, sometimes, preliminary and revised drafts of that work, along with a statement by the writer articulating why he or she considers it good. The *why* is as important as the work, for it provides you with an occasion for assessing your overall strengths and weaknesses as a writer. This chapter offers guidelines to help you compile both a *writing portfolio* and a *literacy portfolio*, a project that writing students are sometimes asked to complete as part of a literacy narrative.

Considering the Rhetorical Situation

As with the writing you put in a portfolio, the portfolio itself is generally intended for a particular audience but could serve a number of different purposes. It's a good idea, then, to consider these and the other elements of your rhetorical situation when you begin to compile a portfolio.

<table>
<tr><td>55–56</td><td>PURPOSE</td><td>Why are you creating this portfolio? To show your learning? To create a record of your writing? As the basis for a grade in a course? To organize your research? To explore your literacy? For something else?</td></tr>
<tr><td>57–60</td><td>AUDIENCE</td><td>Who will read your portfolio? What will your readers expect it to contain? How can you help them understand the context or occasion for each piece of writing you include?</td></tr>
</table>

GENRE   What genres of writing should the portfolio contain? Do you want to demonstrate your ability to write one particular type of writing or in a variety of genres? Will your introduction to or assessment of the portfolio be in the form of a letter or an essay? 61–63

STANCE   How do you want to portray yourself in this portfolio? What items should you include to create this impression? What stance do you want to take in your written assessment of its contents? Thoughtful? Enthusiastic? Something else? 64–67

MEDIA / DESIGN   Will your portfolio be in print? Or will it be electronic? Will it include multiple media? Whichever medium you use, how can you help readers navigate its contents? What design elements will be most appropriate to your purpose and medium? 68–70

A WRITING PORTFOLIO

What to Include

A portfolio developed for a writing course typically contains examples of your best work in that course, including any notes, outlines, preliminary drafts, and so on, along with your own assessment of your performance in the course. You might include any of the following items:

- freewriting, outlines, and other work you did to generate ideas
- drafts, rough and revised
- in-class writing assignments
- source material—copies of articles and online sources, observation notes, interview transcripts, and other evidence of your research
- tests and quizzes

- responses to your drafts
- conference notes, error logs, lecture notes, other course materials
- electronic material including visuals, blogs, and multimedia texts
- reflections on your work

What you include will vary depending on what your instructor asks for. You may be asked to include three or four of your best papers or everything you've written. You may also be asked to show work in several different genres. In any case, you will usually need to choose, and to do that you will need to have criteria for making your choices. Don't base your decision solely on grades (unless grades are one criterion); your portfolio should reflect *your* assessment of your work, not your instructor's. What do you think is your best work? your most interesting work? your most ambitious work? Whatever criteria you use, you are the judge.

Organizing a Portfolio

Your instructor may provide explicit guidelines for organizing your portfolio. If not, here are some guidelines. If you set up a way to organize your writing at the start of the course, you'll be able to keep track of it throughout the course, making your job at term's end much easier. Remember that your portfolio presents you as a writer, presumably at your best. It should be neat, well organized, and easy to navigate.

Paper portfolios.   Choose something in which to gather your work. You might use a two-pocket folder, a three-ring binder, or a file folder, or you may need a box, basket, or some other container to accommodate bulky or odd-shaped items.

Label everything. Label each piece at the top of the first page, specifying the assignment, the draft, and the date: "Proposal, Draft 1, 9/12/12"; "Text Analysis, Final Draft, 10/10/12"; "Portfolio Self-Assessment, Final Draft, 12/11/12"; and so on. Write this information neatly on the page,

academic literacies · rhetorical situations · genres · processes · strategies · research MLA / APA · media / design · readings

or put it on a Post-it note. For each assignment, arrange your materials chronologically, with your earliest material (freewriting, for example) on the bottom, and each successive item (source materials, say, then your outline, then your first draft, and so on) on top of the last, ending with your final draft on top. That way readers can see how your writing changed from draft to draft.

Electronic portfolios.   You might also create an electronic portfolio, or e-portfolio, that includes a homepage with links to your portfolio's contents. There are several tools that can help you create an e-portfolio:

- *Online tools.* Several websites, including *Weebly* and *Wix*, offer free tools to help you create a preformatted e-portfolio. For example, *GoogleSites* provides templates you can use to build an e-portfolio, uploading documents, images, and videos from your computer.

- *Blogging tools.* You can create an e-portfolio using a blogging platform, like *Tumblr* or *WordPress*, which allows you to upload files and create a network of linked pages. Readers can then comment on your e-portfolio, just as they might on your blog entries.

- *Wikis.* Wiki-based e-portfolios differ from blog-based ones in the level of interactivity they allow. In addition to commenting, readers may — if you allow them — make changes and add information. *PBworks* is one free provider, as is *WikiSpaces*.

- *Courseware.* Your school may use a learning platform, such as *Blackboard, Desire2Learn,* or *Moodle*, that allows you to create an e-portfolio of your work.

It's also possible to create an electronic portfolio using word processing, spreadsheet, or presentation software. The programs available for your use and the requirements for publishing your portfolio vary from school to school and instructor to instructor; ask your instructor or your school's help desk for assistance (and see Chapter 57 on **WRITING ONLINE** for general guidance).

616–24

Assessing Your Portfolio

An important part of your portfolio is your written self-assessment of your work. This is an opportunity to assess your work with a critical eye and to think about what you're most proud of, what you most enjoyed doing, what you want to improve. It's your chance to think about and say what you've learned during the class. Some instructors may ask you to write out your assessment in essay form, as an additional sample of your writing; others will want you to put it in letter form, which usually allows for a more relaxed and personal tone. Whatever form it takes, your statement should cover the following ground:

- *An evaluation of each piece of writing in the portfolio.* Consider both strengths and weaknesses, and give examples from your writing to support what you say. What would you change if you had more time? Which is your favorite piece, and why? your least favorite?

- *An assessment of your overall writing performance.* What do you do well? What still needs improvement? What do you *want* your work to say about you? What *does* your work say about you?

- *A discussion of how the writing you did in this course has affected your development as a writer.* How does the writing in your portfolio compare with writing you did in the past? What do you know now that you didn't know before? What can you do that you couldn't do before?

- *A description of your writing habits and process.* What do you usually do? How well does it work? What techniques seem to help you most, and why? Which seem less helpful? Cite passages from your drafts that support your conclusions.

- *An analysis of your performance in the course.* How did you spend your time? Did you collaborate with others? Did you have any conferences with your instructor? Did you visit the writing center? Consider how these or any other activities contributed to your success.

academic literacies rhetorical situations genres processes strategies research MLA / APA media / design readings

A Sample Self-Assessment

Here is a self-assessment written by Nathaniel Cooney as part of his portfolio for his first-year writing class at Wright State University.

2 June 2016

Dear Reader,

It is my hope that in reading this letter you will gain an understanding of the projects contained in this portfolio. I enclose three works that I have submitted for an introductory writing class at Wright State University, English 102, Writing in Academic Discourse: an informative report, an argument paper, and a genre project based largely on the content of the argument paper. I selected the topics of these works for two reasons: First, they address issues that I believe to be relevant in terms of both the intended audience (peers and instructors of the course) and the times when they were published. Second, they speak to issues that are important to me personally. Below I present general descriptions of the works, along with my review of their strengths and weaknesses.

My purpose in writing the informative report "Higher Standards in Education Are Taking Their Toll on Students" was to present a subject in a factual manner and to support it with well-documented research. My intent was not to argue a point. However, because I chose a narrowly focused topic and chose information to support a thesis, the report tends to favor one side of the issue over the other. Because as a student I have a personal stake in the changing standards in the formal education system, I chose to research recent changes in higher education and their effects on students. Specifically, I examine students' struggles to reach a standard that seems to be moving further and further beyond their grasp.

I believe that this paper could be improved in two areas. The first is a bias that I think exists because I am a student presenting information from the point of view of a student. It is my hope, however, that my inclusion of unbiased sources lessens this problem somewhat and, furthermore, that it presents the reader with a fair and accurate collection of facts and examples that supports the thesis. My second area of concern is the over-all balance in the paper between outside sources supporting my own thoughts and outside sources supporting opposing points of view. Rereading the paper, I notice many places where I may have worked too hard to include sources that support my ideas.

The second paper, "Protecting Animals That Serve," is an argument intended not only to take a clear position on an issue but also to argue for that position and convince the reader that it is a valid one. That issue is the need for legislation guaranteeing that certain rights of service animals be protected. I am blind and use a guide dog. Thus, this issue is especially important to me. During the few months that I have had him, my guide dog has already encountered a number of situations where intentional or negligent treatment by others has put him in danger. At the time I was writing the paper, a bill was being written in the Ohio House of Representatives that, if passed, would protect service animals and establish consequences for those who violated the law. The purpose of the paper, therefore, was to present the reader with information about service animals, establish the need for the legislation in Ohio and nationwide, and argue for passage of such legislation.

I think that the best parts of my argument are the introduction and the conclusion. In particular, I think that the conclusion does a good job of not only bringing together the various points but also conveying the significance of the issue for me and for others. In contrast, I think that the area most in need of further attention is the body of the paper. While I think the content is strong, I believe the overall organization could be improved. The connections between ideas are unclear in places, particularly in the section that acknowledges opposing viewpoints. This may be due in part to the fact that I had difficulty understanding the reasoning behind the opposing argument.

The argument paper served as a starting point for the genre project, for which the assignment was to revise one paper written for this class in a different genre. My genre project consists of a poster and a brochure. As it was for the argument paper, my

primary goal was to convince my audience of the importance of a particular issue and viewpoint—specifically, to convince my audience to support House Bill 369, the bill being introduced in the Ohio legislature that would create laws to protect the rights of service animals in the state.

Perhaps both the greatest strength and the greatest weakness of the genre project is my use of graphics. Because of my blindness, I was limited in my use of some graphics. Nevertheless, the pictures were carefully selected to capture the attention of readers and, in part, to appeal to their emotions as they viewed and reflected on the material.

I put a great deal of time, effort, and personal reflection into each project. While I am hesitant to say that they are finished and while I am dissatisfied with some of the finer points, I am satisfied with the overall outcome of this collection of works. Viewing it as a collection, I am also reminded that writing is an evolving process and that even if these works never become exactly what I envisioned them to be, they stand as reflections of my thoughts at a particular time in my life. In that respect, they need not be anything but what they already are, because what they are is a product of who I was when I wrote them. I hope that you find the papers interesting and informative and that as you read them, you, too, may realize their significance.

Respectfully,

Nathaniel J. Cooney

Nathaniel J. Cooney

Enclosures (3)

Cooney describes each of the works he includes and considers their strengths and weaknesses, citing examples from his texts to support his assessment.

A LITERACY PORTFOLIO

As a writing student, you may be asked to think back to the time when you first learned to read and write or to remember significant books or other texts you've read, and perhaps to put together a portfolio that chronicles your development as a reader and writer. You may also be asked to put together a literacy portfolio to accompany a **LITERACY NARRATIVE**.

71–93

What you include in such a portfolio will vary depending on what you've kept over the years and what your family has kept. You may have all of your favorite books, stories you dictated to a preschool teacher, notebooks in which you practiced writing the alphabet. Or you may have almost nothing. What you have or don't have is unimportant in the end: what's important is that you gather what you can and arrange it in a way that shows how you think about your development and growth as a literate person. What have been your experiences with reading and writing? What's your earliest memory of learning to write? If you love to read, what led you to love it? Who was most responsible for shaping your writing ability? Those are some of the questions you'll ask if you write a literacy narrative. You might also compile a literacy portfolio as a good way to generate ideas and text for that assignment.

What to Include in a Literacy Portfolio

- school papers
- drawings and doodles from preschool
- favorite books
- photographs you've taken
- drawings
- poems
- letters
- journals and diaries
- lists
- reading records or logs

- electronic texts you've created
- marriage vows
- speeches you've given
- awards you've received

Organizing a Literacy Portfolio

You may wish to organize your material chronologically, but there are other methods of organization to consider as well. For example, you might group items according to where they were written (at home, at school, at work), by genre (stories, poems, essays, letters, notes), or even by purpose (pleasure, school, work, church, and so on). Arrange your portfolio in the way that best conveys who you are as a literate person. Label each item you include, perhaps with a Post-it note, to identify what it is, when it was written or read, and why you've included it in your portfolio. Or you might create an e-portfolio, scanning print items to include in it with electronic items.

Reflecting on Your Literacy Portfolio

- Why did you choose each item?
- Is anything missing? Are there any other important materials that should be here?
- Why is the portfolio organized as it is?
- What does the portfolio show about your development as a reader and writer?
- What patterns do you see? Are there any common themes you've read or written about? Any techniques you rely on? Any notable changes over time?
- What are the most significant items, and why?

part 5

Strategies

Whenever we write, we draw on many different strategies to articulate what we have to say. We may DEFINE key terms, DESCRIBE people or places, and EXPLAIN how something is done. We may COMPARE one thing to another. Sometimes we may choose a pertinent story to NARRATE, and we may even want to include some DIALOGUE. The chapters that follow offer advice on how to use these and OTHER BASIC STRATEGIES for developing and organizing the texts you write.

Strategies

Beginning and Ending **33**

Whenever we pick up something to read, we generally start by looking at the first few words or sentences to see if they grab our attention, and based on them we decide whether to keep reading. Beginnings, then, are important, both attracting readers and giving them some information about what's to come. When we get to the end of a text, we expect to be left with a sense of closure, of satisfaction — that the story is complete, our questions have been answered, the argument has been made. So endings are important, too. This chapter offers advice on how to write beginnings and endings.

Beginning

How you begin depends on your **RHETORICAL SITUATION**, especially your purpose and audience. Academic audiences generally expect your introduction to establish context, explaining how the text fits into some larger conversation, addresses certain questions, or explores an aspect of the subject. Most introductions also offer a brief description of the text's content, often in the form of a thesis statement. The following opening of an essay on the effect of texting on student writing does all of this:

53

> It's taking over our lives. We can do it almost anywhere — walking to class, waiting in line at the grocery store, or hanging out at home. It's quick, easy, and convenient. It has become a concern of doctors, parents, and teachers alike. What is it? It's texting!
>
> Text messaging — or texting, as it's more commonly called — is the process of sending and receiving typed messages via a cellular phone. It is a common means of communication among teenagers and is even becoming popular in the business world because it allows quick messages

331

to be sent without people having to commit to a telephone conversation. A person is able to say what is needed, and the other person will receive the information and respond when it's convenient to do so.

   In order to more quickly type what they are trying to say, many people use abbreviations instead of words. The language created by these abbreviations is called textspeak. Some people believe that using these abbreviations is hindering the writing abilities of students, and others argue that texting is actually having a positive effect on writing. In fact, it seems likely that texting has no significant effect on student writing.   —Michaela Cullington, "Does Texting Affect Writing?"

If you're writing for a nonacademic audience or genre — for a newspaper or a website, for example — your introduction may need to entice your readers to read on by connecting your text to their interests through shared experiences, anecdotes, or some other attention-getting device. Cynthia Bass, writing a newspaper article about the Gettysburg Address on its 135th anniversary, connects that date — the day her audience would read it — to Lincoln's address. She then develops the rationale for thinking about the speech and introduces her specific topic: debates about the writing and delivery of the Gettysburg Address:

November 19 is the 135th anniversary of the Gettysburg Address. On that day in 1863, with the Civil War only half over and the worst yet to come, Abraham Lincoln delivered a speech now universally regarded as both the most important oration in U.S. history and the best explanation — "government of the people, by the people, for the people" — of why this nation exists.

   We would expect the history of an event so monumental as the Gettysburg Address to be well established. The truth is just the opposite. The only thing scholars agree on is that the speech is short — only ten sentences — and that it took Lincoln under five minutes to stand up, deliver it, and sit back down.

   Everything else — when Lincoln wrote it, where he wrote it, how quickly he wrote it, how he was invited, how the audience reacted — has been open to debate since the moment the words left his mouth.

—Cynthia Bass, "Gettysburg Address: Two Versions"

academic literacies | rhetorical situations | genres | processes | strategies | research MLA / APA | media / design | readings

Ways of Beginning

Explain the larger context of your topic. Most essays are part of an ongoing conversation, so you might begin by outlining the context of the subject to which your writing responds. An essay exploring the "emotional climate" of the United States after Barack Obama became president begins by describing the national moods during some of his predecessors' administrations:

> Every president plays a symbolic, almost mythological role that's hard to talk about, much less quantify—it's like trying to grab a ball of mercury. I'm not referring to using the bully pulpit to shape the national agenda but to the way that the president, as America's most inescapably powerful figure, colors the emotional climate of the country. John Kennedy and Ronald Reagan did this affirmatively, expressing ideals that shaped the whole culture. Setting a buoyant tone, they didn't just change movies, music, and television; they changed attitudes. Other presidents did the same, only unpleasantly. Richard Nixon created a mood of angry paranoia, Jimmy Carter one of dreary defeatism, and George W. Bush, especially in that seemingly endless second term, managed to do both at once.
>
> —John Powers, "Dreams from My President"

State your thesis. Sometimes the best beginning is a clear **THESIS** stating your position, like the following statement in an essay arguing that fairy tales and nursery rhymes introduce us to "the rudiments and the humanness of engineering":

◆ 345–47

> We are all engineers of sorts, for we all have the principles of machines and structures in our bones. We have learned to hold our bodies against the forces of nature as surely as we have learned to walk. We calculate the paths of our arms and legs with the computer of our brain, and we catch baseballs and footballs with more dependability than the most advanced weapons systems intercept missiles. We may wonder if human evolution may not have been the greatest engineering feat of all time. And though many of us forget how much we once knew about the principles and practices of engineering, the nursery rhymes and fairy tales of our youth preserve the evidence that we did know quite a bit.
>
> —Henry Petroski, "Falling Down Is Part of Growing Up"

Forecast your organization. You might begin by briefly outlining the way in which you will organize your text. The following example from a scholarly paper on the role of immigrants in the U.S. labor market offers background on the subject and describes the points that the writer's analysis will discuss:

> Debates about illegal immigration, border security, skill levels of workers, unemployment, job growth and competition, and entrepreneurship all rely, to some extent, on perceptions of immigrants' role in the U.S. labor market. These views are often shaped as much by politics and emotion as by facts.
>
> To better frame these debates, this short analysis provides data on immigrants in the labor force at the current time of slowed immigration, high unemployment, and low job growth and highlights eight industries where immigrants are especially vital. How large a share of the labor force are they and how does that vary by particular industry? How do immigrants compare to native-born workers in their educational attainment and occupational profiles?
>
> The answers matter because our economy is dependent on immigrant labor now and for the future. The U.S. population is aging rapidly as the baby boom cohort enters old age and retirement. As a result, the labor force will increasingly depend upon immigrants and their children to replace current workers and fill new jobs. This analysis puts a spotlight on immigrant workers to examine their basic trends in the labor force and how these workers fit into specific industries and occupations of interest.
>
> —Audrey Singer, "Immigrant Workers in the U.S. Labor Force"

Offer background information. If your readers may not know as much as you do about your topic, giving them information to help them understand your position can be important, as David Guterson does in an essay on the Mall of America:

> Last April, on a visit to the new Mall of America near Minneapolis, I carried with me the public-relations press kit provided for the benefit of reporters. It included an assortment of "fun facts" about the mall: 140,000 hot dogs sold each week, 10,000 permanent jobs, 44 escalators and 17 elevators, 12,750 parking places, 13,300 short tons of steel, $1 million in cash disbursed weekly from 8 automatic-teller machines.

The rotunda of the Mall of America.

> Opened in the summer of 1992, the mall was built on the 78-acre site of the former Metropolitan Stadium, a five-minute drive from the Minneapolis–St. Paul International Airport. With 4.2 million square feet of floor space—including twenty-two times the retail footage of the average American shopping center—the Mall of America was "the largest fully enclosed combination retail and family entertainment complex in the United States."
>
> —David Guterson, "Enclosed. Encyclopedic. Endured. One Week at the Mall of America"

Visuals can also help provide context. For example, this essay on the Mall of America might have included a photo like the one on the preceding page to convey the size of the structure.

Define key terms or concepts.   The success of an argument often hinges

388–98

on how key terms are **DEFINED**. You may wish to provide definitions up front, as an advocacy website, *Health Care without Harm*, does in a report on the hazards of fragrances in health-care facilities:

> To many people, the word "fragrance" means something that smells nice, such as perfume. We don't often stop to think that scents are chemicals. Fragrance chemicals are organic compounds that volatilize, or vaporize into the air—that's why we can smell them. They are added to products to give them a scent or to mask the odor of other ingredients. The volatile organic chemicals (VOCs) emitted by fragrance products can contribute to poor indoor air quality (IAQ) and are associated with a variety of adverse health effects.
>
> —"Fragrances," *Health Care without Harm*

Connect your subject to your readers' interests or values.   You'll always want to establish common ground with your readers, and sometimes you may wish to do so immediately, in your introduction, as in this example:

> We all want to feel safe. Most Americans lock their doors at night, lock their cars in parking lots, try to park near buildings or under lights, and wear seat belts. Many invest in expensive security systems, carry pepper spray or a stun gun, keep guns in their homes, or take self-defense classes. Obviously, safety and security are important issues in American life.
>
> —Andy McDonie, "Airport Security: What Price Safety?"

Start with something that will provoke readers' interest.   Anna Quindlen opens an essay on feminism with the following eye-opening assertion:

> Let's use the F word here. People say it's inappropriate, offensive, that it puts people off. But it seems to me it's the best way to begin, when it's simultaneously devalued and invaluable.
> Feminist. Feminist, feminist, feminist.
>
> —Anna Quindlen, "Still Needing the F Word"

Start with an anecdote.   Sometimes a brief **NARRATIVE** helps bring a topic to life for readers. See, for example, how an essay on the dozens, a type of verbal contest played by some African Americans, begins:

419–27

> Alfred Wright, a nineteen-year-old whose manhood was at stake on Longwood Avenue in the South Bronx, looked fairly calm as another teenager called him Chicken Head and compared his mother to Shamu the whale.
> He fingered the gold chain around his thin neck while listening to a detailed complaint about his sister's sexual abilities. Then he slowly took the toothpick out of his mouth; the jeering crowd of young men quieted as he pointed at his accuser.
> "He was so ugly when he was born," Wright said, "the doctor smacked his mom instead of him."
>
> —John Tierney, "Playing the Dozens"

Ask a question.   Instead of a thesis statement, you might open with a question about the topic your text will explore, as this study of the status of women in science does:

> Are women's minds different from men's minds? In spite of the women's movement, the age-old debate centering around this question continues. We are surrounded by evidence of de facto differences between men's and women's intellects—in the problems that interest them, in the ways they try to solve those problems, and in the professions they choose. Even though it has become fashionable to view such differences as environmental in origin, the temptation to seek an explanation in terms of innate differences remains a powerful one.
>
> —Evelyn Fox Keller, "Women in Science: A Social Analysis"

Jump right in.   Occasionally you may wish to start as close to the key action as possible. See how one writer jumps right into his profile of a blues concert:

> Long Tongue, the Blues Merchant, strolls onstage. His guitar rides side-saddle against his hip. The drummer slides onto the tripod seat behind the drums, adjusts the high-hat cymbal, and runs a quick, off-beat tattoo on the tom-tom, then relaxes. The bass player plugs into the amplifier, checks the settings on the control panel, and nods his okay. Three horn players stand off to one side, clustered, lurking like brilliant sorcerer-wizards waiting to do magic with their musical instruments.
>
> —Jerome Washington, "The Blues Merchant"

Ending

53

Endings are important because they're the last words readers read. How you end a text will depend in part on your **RHETORICAL SITUATION**. You may end by wrapping up loose ends, or you may wish to give readers something to think about. Some endings do both, as Cynthia Bass does in a report on the debate over the Gettysburg Address. In her two final paragraphs, she first summarizes the debate and then shows its implications:

> What's most interesting about the Lincoln-as-loser and Lincoln-as-winner versions is how they marshal the same facts to prove different points. The invitation asks Lincoln to deliver "a few appropriate remarks." Whether this is a putdown or a reflection of the protocol of the time depends on the "spin" — an expression the highly politicized Lincoln would have readily understood — which the scholar places on it.
>
>   These diverse histories should not in any way diminish the power or beauty of Lincoln's words. However, they should remind us that history, even the history of something as deeply respected as the Gettysburg Address, is seldom simple or clear. This reminder is especially useful today as we watch expert witnesses, in an effort to divine what the founders meant by "high crimes and misdemeanors," club one another with conflicting interpretations of the same events, the same words, the same precedents, and the same laws.
>
> —Cynthia Bass, "Gettysburg Address: Two Versions"

Bass summarizes the dispute about Lincoln's address and then moves on to discuss the role of scholars in interpreting historical events. Writing during the Clinton impeachment hearings, she concludes by pointing out the way in which expert government witnesses often offer conflicting interpretations of events to suit their own needs. The ending combines several strategies to bring various strands of her essay together, leaving readers to interpret her final words themselves.

Ways of Ending

Restate your main point.   Sometimes you'll simply **SUMMARIZE** your central idea, as in this example from an essay arguing that we have no "inner" self and that we should be judged by our actions alone:

486–87

> The inner man is a fantasy. If it helps you to identify with one, by all means, do so; preserve it, cherish it, embrace it, but do not present it to others for evaluation or consideration, for excuse or exculpation, or, for that matter, for punishment or disapproval.
>   Like any fantasy, it serves your purposes alone. It has no standing in the real world which we share with each other. Those character traits, those attitudes, that behavior—that strange and alien stuff sticking out all over you—*that's the real you!*
>
> —Willard Gaylin, "What You See Is the Real You"

Discuss the implications of your argument.   The following conclusion of an essay on the development of Post-it notes leads readers to consider how failure sometimes leads to innovation:

> Post-it notes provide but one example of a technological artifact that has evolved from a perceived failure of existing artifacts to function without frustrating. Again, it is not that form follows function but, rather, that the form of one thing follows from the failure of another thing to function as we would like. Whether it be bookmarks that fail to stay in place or taped-on notes that fail to leave a once-nice surface clean and intact, their failure and perceived failure is what leads to the true evolution of artifacts. That the perception of failure may take

centuries to develop, as in the case of loose bookmarks, does not reduce the importance of the principle in shaping our world.

—Henry Petroski, "Little Things Can Mean a Lot"

419–27

End with an anecdote, maybe finishing a **NARRATIVE** that was begun earlier in your text or adding one that illustrates the point you are making. See how Sarah Vowell uses a story to end an essay on students' need to examine news reporting critically:

> I looked at Joanne McGlynn's syllabus for her media studies course, the one she handed out at the beginning of the year, stating the goals of the class. By the end of the year, she hoped her students would be better able to challenge everything from novels to newscasts, that they would come to identify just who is telling a story and how that person's point of view affects the story being told. I'm going to go out on a limb here and say that this lesson has been learned. In fact, just recently, a student came up to McGlynn and told her something all teachers dream of hearing. The girl told the teacher that she was listening to the radio, singing along with her favorite song, and halfway through the sing-along she stopped and asked herself, "What am I singing? What do these words mean? What are they trying to tell me?" And then, this young citizen of the republic jokingly complained, "I can't even turn on the radio without thinking anymore."

—Sarah Vowell, "Democracy and Things Like That"

Refer to the beginning.   One way to bring closure to a text is to bring up something discussed in the beginning; often the reference adds to or even changes the original meaning. For example, Amy Tan opens an essay on her Chinese mother's English by establishing herself as a writer and lover of language who uses many versions of English in her writing:

> I am not a scholar of English or literature. I cannot give you much more than personal opinions on the English language and its variations in this country or others.
>
> I am a writer. And by that definition, I am someone who has always loved language. I am fascinated by language in daily life. I spend a

great deal of my time thinking about the power of language — the way it can evoke an emotion, a visual image, a complex idea, or a simple truth. Language is the tool of my trade. And I use them all — all the Englishes I grew up with.

At the end of her essay, Tan repeats this phrase, but now she describes language not in terms of its power to evoke emotions, images, and ideas but in its power to evoke "the essence" of her mother. When she began to write fiction, she says,

> [I] decided I should envision a reader for the stories I would write. And the reader I decided upon was my mother, because these were stories about mothers. So with this reader in mind — and in fact she did read my early drafts — I began to write stories using all the Englishes I grew up with: the English I spoke to my mother, which for lack of a better term might be described as "simple"; the English she used with me, which for lack of a better term might be described as "broken"; my translation of her Chinese, which could certainly be described as "watered down"; and what I imagined to be her translation of her Chinese if she could speak in perfect English, her internal language, and for that I sought to preserve the essence, but neither an English nor a Chinese structure. I wanted to capture what language ability tests can never reveal: her intent, her passion, her imagery, the rhythms of her speech and the nature of her thoughts.
>
> — Amy Tan, "Mother Tongue"

Note how Tan not only repeats "all the Englishes I grew up with" but also provides parallel lists of what those Englishes can do for her: "evoke an emotion, a visual image, a complex idea, or a simple truth," on the one hand, and, on the other, capture her mother's "intent, her passion, her imagery, the rhythms of her speech and the nature of her thoughts."

Propose some action, as in the following conclusion of a report on the consequences of binge drinking among college students:

> The scope of the problem makes immediate results of any interventions highly unlikely. Colleges need to be committed to large-scale and long-term behavior-change strategies, including referral of alcohol abusers

to appropriate treatment. Frequent binge drinkers on college campuses are similar to other alcohol abusers elsewhere in their tendency to deny that they have a problem. Indeed, their youth, the visibility of others who drink the same way, and the shelter of the college community may make them less likely to recognize the problem. In addition to addressing the health problems of alcohol abusers, a major effort should address the large group of students who are not binge drinkers on campus who are adversely affected by the alcohol-related behavior of binge drinkers.

—Henry Wechsler et al., "Health and Behavioral Consequences of Binge Drinking in College: A National Survey of Students at 140 Campuses"

Considering the Rhetorical Situation

As a writer or speaker, think about the message that you want to articulate, the audience you want to reach, and the larger context you are writing in.

| 55–56 | **PURPOSE** | Your purpose will affect the way you begin and end. If you're trying to persuade readers to do something, you may want to open by clearly stating your thesis and end by calling for a specific action. |

| 57–60 | **AUDIENCE** | Who do you want to reach, and how does that affect the way you begin and end? You may want to open with an intriguing fact or anecdote to entice your audience to read a profile, for instance, whereas readers of a report may expect it to conclude with a summary of your findings. |

| 61–63 | **GENRE** | Does your genre require a certain type of beginning or ending? Arguments, for example, often provide a statement of the thesis near the beginning; proposals typically end with a call for some solution. |

| 64–67 | **STANCE** | What is your stance, and can your beginning and ending help you convey that stance? For example, beginning an argument on the distribution of AIDS medications to underdeveloped countries with an anecdote may |

academic literacies · rhetorical situations · genres · processes · strategies · research MLA / APA · media / design · readings

demonstrate concern for the human costs of the disease, whereas starting with a statistical analysis may suggest the stance of a careful researcher. Ending a proposal by weighing the advantages and disadvantages of the solution you propose may make you seem reasonable.

MEDIA/DESIGN Your medium may affect the way you begin and end. A web text, for instance, may open with a homepage listing a menu of the site—and giving readers a choice of where they will begin. With a print text, you get to decide how it will begin and end.

68–70

IF YOU NEED MORE HELP

See also the guides to writing in Chapters 10–13 for ways of beginning and ending a LITERACY NARRATIVE, an essay ANALYZING TEXT, a REPORT, or an ARGUMENT.

89–90
124–25
151–52
179–80

34 Guiding Your Reader

Traffic lights, street signs, and lines on the road help drivers find their way. Readers need similar guidance—to know, for example, whether they're reading a report or an argument, an evaluation or a proposal. They also need to know what to expect: What will the report be about? What perspective will it offer? What will this paragraph cover? What about the next one? How do the two paragraphs relate to each other?

When you write, then, you need to provide cues to help your readers navigate your text and understand the points you're trying to make. This chapter offers advice on guiding your reader and, specifically, on using titles, *thesis statements, topic sentences,* and *transitions.*

Titles

A title serves various purposes, naming a text and providing clues to the content. It also helps readers decide whether they want to read further, so it's worth your while to come up with a title that attracts interest. Some titles include subtitles. You generally have considerable freedom in choosing a title, but always you'll want to consider the **RHETORICAL SITUATION** to be sure your title serves your purpose and appeals to the audience you want to reach.

Some titles simply announce the subject of the text:

"Black Men and Public Space"
The Pencil
"Why Colleges Shower Their Students with A's"
"Does Texting Affect Writing?"

53

Some titles provoke readers or otherwise entice them to read:

> "Kill 'Em! Crush 'Em! Eat 'Em Raw!"
> "Thank God for the Atom Bomb"
> "What Are Homosexuals For?"

Sometimes writers add a subtitle to explain or illuminate the title:

> *Aria: Memoir of a Bilingual Childhood*
> "It's in Our Genes: The Biological Basis of Human Mating Behavior"
> "From Realism to Virtual Reality: Images of America's Wars"

Sometimes when you're starting to write, you'll think of a title that helps you generate ideas and write. More often, though, a title is one of the last things you'll write, when you know what you've written and can craft a suitable name for your text.

Thesis Statements

A thesis identifies the topic of your text along with the claim you are making about it. A good thesis helps readers understand an essay. Working to create a sharp thesis can help you focus both your thinking and your writing. Here are three steps for moving from a topic to a thesis statement:

1. **State your topic as a question.** You may have an idea for a topic, such as "gasoline prices," "analysis of 'real women' ad campaigns," or "famine." Those may be good topics, but they're not thesis statements, primarily because none of them actually makes a statement. A good way to begin moving from topic to thesis statement is to turn your topic into a question:

> What causes fluctuations in gasoline prices?
>
> Are ads picturing "real women" who aren't models effective?
>
> What can be done to prevent famine in Africa?

2. Then turn your question into a position. A thesis statement is an assertion—it takes a stand or makes a claim. Whether you're writing a report or an argument, you are saying, "This is the way I see . . . ," "My research shows . . . ," or "This is what I believe about . . ." Your thesis statement announces your position on the question you are raising about your topic, so a relatively easy way of establishing a thesis is to answer your own question:

> Gasoline prices fluctuate for several reasons.
>
> Ads picturing "real women" instead of models are effective because women can easily identify with them.
>
> The most recent famine in Somalia could have been avoided if certain measures had been taken.

3. Narrow your thesis. A good thesis is specific, guiding you as you write and showing your audience exactly what your essay will cover. The preceding thesis statements need to be qualified and focused—they need to be made more specific. For example:

> Gasoline prices fluctuate because of production procedures, consumer demand, international politics, and oil companies' policies.
>
> Dove's "Campaign for Self-Esteem" and Cover Girl's ads featuring Queen Latifah work because consumers can identify with the women's bodies and admire their confidence in displaying them.
>
> The 2012 famine in Somalia could have been avoided if farmers had received training in more effective methods and had had access to certain technology and if other nations had provided more aid more quickly.

281–84 A good way to narrow a thesis is to ask **QUESTIONS** about it: *Why* do gasoline prices fluctuate? *How* could the Somalia famine have been avoided? The answers will help you craft a narrow, focused thesis.

4. Qualify your thesis. Sometimes you want to make a strong argument and to state your thesis bluntly. Often, however, you need to acknowledge that your assertions may be challenged or may not be unconditionally true. In those cases, consider limiting the scope of your thesis by adding to it such terms as *may*, *probably*, *apparently*, *very likely*, *sometimes*, and *often*.

academic literacies · rhetorical situations · genres · processes · strategies · research MLA / APA · media / design · readings

Gasoline prices *very likely* fluctuate because of production procedures, consumer demand, international politics, and oil companies' policies.

Dove's and Cover Girl's ad campaigns featuring "real women" *may* work because consumers can identify with the women's bodies and admire their confidence in displaying them.

The 2012 famine in Somalia could *probably* have been avoided if farmers had received training in more effective methods and had had access to certain technology and if other nations had provided more aid more quickly.

Thesis statements are typically positioned at or near the end of a text's introduction, to let readers know at the outset what is being claimed and what the text will be aiming to prove. A thesis doesn't necessarily forecast your organization, which may be more complex than the thesis itself. For example, Carolyn Stonehill's research paper, "It's in Our Genes: The Biological Basis of Human Mating Behavior," contains this thesis statement:

While cultural values and messages clearly play a part in the process of mate selection, the genetic and psychological predispositions developed by our ancestors play the biggest role in determining to whom we are attracted.

However, the paper that follows includes sections on "Women's Need to Find a Capable Mate" and "Men's Need to Find a Healthy Mate," in which the "genetic and psychological predispositions" are discussed, followed by sections titled "The Influence of the Media on Mate Selection" and "If Not Media, Then What?" discussing "cultural values and messages." The paper delivers what the thesis includes without following the order in which the thesis presents the topics.

Topic Sentences

Just as a thesis statement announces the topic and position of an essay, a topic sentence states the subject and focus of a paragraph. Good paragraphs focus on a single point, which is summarized in a topic sentence. Usually, but not always, the topic sentence begins the paragraph:

Graduating from high school or college is an exciting, occasionally even traumatic event. Your identity changes as you move from being a high school teenager to a university student or a worker; your connection to home loosens as you attend school elsewhere, move to a place of your own, or simply exercise your right to stay out later. You suddenly find yourself doing different things, thinking different thoughts, fretting about different matters. As recent high school graduate T. J. Devoe puts it, "I wasn't really scared, but having this vast range of opportunity made me uneasy. I didn't know *what* was gonna happen." Jenny Petrow, in describing her first year out of college, observes, "It's a tough year. It was for all my friends."

—Sydney Lewis, *Help Wanted: Tales from the First Job Front*

Sometimes the topic sentence may come at the end of the paragraph or even at the end of the preceding paragraph, depending on the way the paragraphs relate to one another. Other times a topic sentence will summarize or restate a point made in the previous paragraph, helping readers understand what they've just read as they move on to the next point. See how the linguist Deborah Tannen does this in the first paragraphs of an article on differences in men's and women's conversational styles:

I was addressing a small gathering in a suburban Virginia living room— a women's group that had invited men to join them. Throughout the evening, one man had been particularly talkative, frequently offering ideas and anecdotes, while his wife sat silently beside him on the couch. Toward the end of the evening, I commented that women frequently complain that their husbands don't talk to them. This man quickly concurred. He gestured toward his wife and said, "She's the talker in our family." The room burst into laughter; the man looked puzzled and hurt. "It's true," he explained. "When I come home from work I have nothing to say. If she didn't keep the conversation going, we'd spend the whole evening in silence."

This episode crystallizes the irony that although American men tend to talk more than women in public situations, they often talk less at home. And this pattern is wreaking havoc with marriage.

—Deborah Tannen, "Sex, Lies, and Conversation: Why Is It So Hard for Men and Women to Talk to Each Other?"

Transitions

Transitions help readers move from thought to thought—from sentence to sentence, paragraph to paragraph. You are likely to use a number of transitions as you draft; when you're **EDITING**, you should make a point of checking transitions. Here are some common ones:

313–16

- *To signal causes and effects:* accordingly, as a result, because, consequently, hence, so, then, therefore, thus
- *To signal comparisons:* also, in the same way, like, likewise, similarly
- *To signal changes in direction or expections:* although, but, even though, however, in contrast, instead, nevertheless, nonetheless, on the contrary, on the one hand . . . on the other hand, still, yet
- *To signal examples:* for example, for instance, indeed, in fact, such as
- *To signal sequences or similarities:* again; also; and; and then; besides; finally; furthermore; last; moreover; next; too; first, second, third, etc.
- *To signal time relations:* after, as soon as, at first, at the same time, before, eventually, finally, immediately, later, meanwhile, next, simultaneously, so far, soon, then, thereafter
- *To signal a summary or conclusion:* as a result, as we have seen, finally, in a word, in any event, in brief, in conclusion, in other words, in short, in the end, in the final analysis, on the whole, therefore, thus, to summarize

---

IF YOU NEED MORE HELP

See also Chapter 56 on **USING VISUALS, INCORPORATING SOUND** for ways of creating visual signals for your readers.

607–15

35 Analyzing Causes and Effects

Analyzing causes helps us think about why something happened, whereas thinking about effects helps us consider what might happen. When we hear a noise in the night, we want to know what caused it. Children poke sticks into holes to see what will happen. Researchers try to understand the causes of diseases. Writers often have occasion to consider causes or effects as part of a larger topic or sometimes as a main focus: in a **PROPOSAL**, we might consider the effects of reducing tuition or the causes of recent tuition increases; in a **MEMOIR**, we might explore why the person we had a date with failed to show up.

Usually we can only speculate about *probable* causes or *likely* effects. In writing about causes and effects, then, we are generally **ARGUING** for those we consider plausible, not proven. This chapter will help you analyze causes and effects in writing—and to do so in a way that suits your rhetorical situation.

235–44
216–23

355–73

Determining Plausible Causes and Effects

What causes ozone depletion? Sleeplessness? Obesity? And what are their effects? Those are of course large, complex topics, but whenever you have reason to ask why something happened or what could happen, there will likely be several possible causes and just as many predictable effects. There may be obvious causes, though often they will be less important than others that are harder to recognize. (Eating too much may be an obvious cause of being overweight, but *why* people eat too much has several less obvious causes: portion size, advertising, lifestyle, and physiological disorders are only a few possibilities.) Similarly, short-term effects are often less important than long-term ones. (A stomachache may be an

academic literacies · rhetorical situations · genres · processes · strategies · research MLA / APA · media / design · readings

effect of eating too much candy, but the chemical imbalance that can result from consuming too much sugar is a much more serious effect.)

LISTING, **CLUSTERING**, and **OUTLINING** are useful processes for analyzing causes. And at times you might need to do some **RESEARCH** to identify possible causes or effects and to find evidence to support your analysis. When you've identified potential causes and effects, you need to analyze them. Which causes and effects are primary? Which seem to be secondary? Which are most relevant to your **PURPOSE** and are likely to convince your **AUDIENCE**? You will probably have to choose from several possible causes and effects for your analysis because you won't want or need to include all of them.

290–95
433

55–56
57–60

Arguing for Causes or Effects

Once you've identified several possible causes or predictable effects, you need to **ARGUE** that some are more plausible than others. You must provide convincing support for your argument because you usually cannot *prove* that x causes y or that y will be caused by z; you can only show, with good reasons and appropriate evidence, that x is *likely* to cause y or that y will *likely* follow from z. See, for example, how an essay on the psychological basis for risk taking speculates about two potential causes for the popularity of extreme sports:

355–73

> Studies now indicate that the inclination to take high risks may be hardwired into the brain, intimately linked to arousal and pleasure mechanisms, and may offer such a thrill that it functions like an addiction. The tendency probably affects one in five people, mostly young males, and declines with age. It may ensure our survival, even spur our evolution as individuals and as a species. Risk taking probably bestowed a crucial evolutionary advantage, inciting the fighting and foraging of the hunter-gatherer. . . .
>
> As psychologist Salvadore Maddi, PhD, of the University of California at Davis warns, "High-risk takers may have a hard time deriving meaning and purpose from everyday life." Indeed, this peculiar form of dissatisfaction could help explain the explosion of high-risk sports in America and other postindustrial Western nations. In unstable cultures, such as those at war or suffering poverty, people rarely seek

out additional thrills. But in a rich and safety-obsessed country like America, land of guardrails, seat belts, and personal-injury lawsuits, everyday life may have become too safe, predictable, and boring for those programmed for risk taking.   —Paul Roberts, "Risk"

Roberts suggests that genetics is one likely cause of extreme sports and that an American obsession with safety is perhaps a cause of their growing popularity. Notice, however, that he presents these as likely or possible, not certain, by choosing his words carefully: "studies now *indicate*"; "the inclination to take high risks *may* be hardwired"; "[r]isk taking *probably* bestowed a crucial evolutionary advantage"; "this . . . dissatisfaction *could help* explain." Like Roberts, you will almost always need to qualify what you say about causes and effects—to say that something *could explain* (rather than saying it "explains") or that it *suggests* (rather than "shows"). Causes and effects can seldom be proved definitively, so you need to acknowledge that your argument is not the last word on the subject.

Ways of Organizing an Analysis of Causes and Effects

Your analysis of causes and effects may be part of a proposal or some other genre of writing, or you may write a text whose central purpose is to analyze causes or speculate about effects. While there are many ways to organize an analysis of causes and effects, three common ways are to state a cause and then discuss its effects, to state an effect and then discuss its causes, and to identify a chain of causes and effects.

Identify a cause and then discuss its effects.   If you were writing about climate change, you might first show that many scientists fear it will have several effects, including more violent storms, the extinction of various kinds of plants, and elevated sea levels.

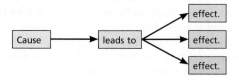

Identify an effect and then trace its causes.   If you were writing about school violence, for example, you might argue that it is a result of sloppy dress, informal teacher-student relationships, low academic standards, and disregard for rules.

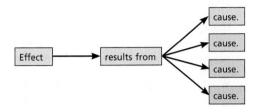

Identify a chain of causes and effects.   You may sometimes discuss a chain of causes and effects. If you were writing about the right to privacy, for example, you might consider the case of Megan's law. A convicted child molester raped and murdered a girl named Megan; the crime caused New Jersey legislators to pass the so-called Megan's law (an effect), which requires that convicted sex offenders be publicly identified. As more states enacted versions of Megan's law, concern for the rights of those who are identified developed—the effect became a cause of further effects.

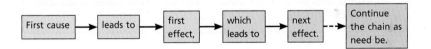

Considering the Rhetorical Situation

As a writer or speaker, you need to think about the message that you want to articulate, the audience you want to reach, and the larger context you are writing in.

PURPOSE   Your main purpose may be to analyze the causes and effects of something. But sometimes you'll have another goal that calls for such analysis — a business report, for

55–56

example, might need to explain what caused a decline in sales.

57–60 **AUDIENCE**   Who is your intended audience, and how will analyzing causes help you reach them? Do you need to tell them why some event happened or what effects resulted?

61–63 **GENRE**   Does your genre require you to analyze causes? Proposals, for example, often need to consider the effects of a proposed solution.

64–67 **STANCE**   What is your stance, and could analyzing causes or effects show that stance? Could it help demonstrate your seriousness or show that your conclusions are reasonable?

68–70 **MEDIA/DESIGN**   You can rely on words to analyze causes, but sometimes a drawing will help readers *see* how causes lead to effects.

---

279 ○

IF YOU NEED MORE HELP

See also the **PROCESSES** chapters for help generating ideas, drafting, and so on if you need to write an entire text whose purpose is to analyze causes or speculate about effects.

Arguing 36

Football fans argue about who's better, Eli or Peyton Manning. Political candidates argue that they have the most experience or best judgment. A toilet paper ad argues that "you deserve a little luxury in your life, and so does your bottom." As you likely realize, we are surrounded by arguments, and much of the work you do as a college student requires you to read and write arguments. When you write a **LITERARY ANALYSIS**, for instance, you argue for a particular interpretation. In a **PROPOSAL**, you argue for a particular solution to a problem. Even a **PROFILE** argues that a subject should be seen in a certain way. This chapter offers advice on some of the key elements of making an argument, from developing an arguable thesis and identifying good reasons and evidence that supports those reasons to building common ground and dealing with viewpoints other than your own.

▲ 206–15

235–44

224–34

Reasons for Arguing

We argue for many reasons, and they often overlap: to convince others that our position on a subject is reasonable, to influence the way they think about a subject, to persuade them to change their point of view or to take some sort of action. In fact, many composition scholars and teachers believe that all writing makes an argument.

As a student, you'll be called upon to make arguments continually: when you participate in class discussions, when you take an essay exam, when you post a comment to an online discussion or a blog. In all these instances, you are adding your opinions to some larger conversation, arguing for what you believe—and why.

Arguing Logically: Claims, Reasons, and Evidence

The basic building blocks of argument are claims, reasons, and evidence that supports those reasons. Using these building blocks, we can construct a strong logical argument.

Claims.   Good arguments are based on arguable claims — statements that reasonable people may disagree about. Certain kinds of statements cannot be argued:

- *Verifiable statements of fact.* Most of the time, there's no point in arguing about facts like "The earth is round" or "George H. W. Bush was America's forty-first president." Such statements contain no controversy, no potential opposition — and so no interest for an audience. However, you might argue about the basis of a fact. For example, until recently it was a fact that our solar system had nine planets, but when further discoveries led to a change in the definition of *planet*, Pluto no longer qualified.

- *Issues of faith or belief.* By definition, matters of faith cannot be proven or refuted. If you believe in reincarnation or don't believe there is an afterlife, there's no way I can convince you otherwise. However, in a philosophy or religion course you may be asked to argue, for example, whether or not the universe must have a cause.

- *Matters of simple opinion or personal taste.* If you think cargo pants are ugly, no amount of arguing will convince you to think otherwise. If you own every Taylor Swift CD and think she's the greatest singer ever, you won't convince your Nirvana-loving parents to like her, too. If matters of taste are based on identifiable criteria, though, they may be argued in an **EVALUATION**, where "Tom Cruise is a terrible actor" is more than just your opinion — it's an assertion you can support with evidence.

197–205

You may begin with an opinion: "I think wearing a helmet makes riding a bike more dangerous, not less." As it stands, that statement can't be considered a claim — it needs to be made more reasonable and informed. To do that, you might reframe it as a question — "Do bike riders who wear helmets get injured more often than those who don't?" — that may be answered as you do research and start to write. Your opinion or question should lead

you to an arguable claim, however, one that could be challenged by another thoughtful person. In this case, for example, your research might lead you to a focused, qualified claim: *Contrary to common sense, wearing a helmet while riding a bicycle increases the chances of injury, at least to adult riders.*

Qualifying a claim.   According to an old saying, there are two sides to every story. Much of the time, though, arguments don't sort themselves neatly into two sides, pro and con. No matter what your topic, your argument will rarely be a simple matter of being for or against; in most cases, you'll want to qualify your claim—that it is true in certain circumstances, with certain conditions, with these limitations, and so on. Qualifying your claim shows that you're reasonable and also makes your topic more manageable by limiting it. The following questions can help you qualify your claim.

- *Can it be true in some circumstances or at some times but not others?* For example, freedom of speech should generally be unrestricted, but individuals can sue for slander or libel.

- *Can it be true only with certain conditions?* For instance, cell phones and computer monitors should be recycled, but only by licensed, domestic recyclers.

- *Can it be true for some groups or individuals but not others?* For example, nearly everyone should follow a low-carb diet, but some people, such as diabetics, should avoid it.

SOME WORDS FOR QUALIFYING A CLAIM

sometimes	nearly	it seems/seemingly
rarely	usually	some
in some cases	more or less	perhaps
often	for the most part	possibly
routinely	in many cases	in most cases

Drafting a thesis statement.   Once your claim is focused and appropriately qualified, it can form the core of your essay's **THESIS STATEMENT**, which announces your position and forecasts the path your argument will follow. For example, here is the opening paragraph of an essay by the

345–47

executive director of the National Congress of American Indians arguing that the remains of Native Americans should be treated with the same respect given to others. The author outlines the context of her argument and then presents her thesis (here, in italics):

> What if museums, universities and government agencies could put your dead relatives on display or keep them in boxes to be cut up and otherwise studied? What if you believed that the spirits of the dead could not rest until their human remains were placed in a sacred area? The ordinary American would say there ought to be a law—and there is, for ordinary Americans. *The problem for American Indians is that there are too many laws of the kind that make us the archeological property of the United States and too few of the kind that protect us from such insults.*   —Susan Shown Harjo, "Last Rites for Indian Dead: Treating Remains Like Artifacts Is Intolerable"

Reasons.   Your claim must be supported by reasons that your audience will accept. A reason can usually be linked to a claim with the word *because*:

CLAIM	+	*BECAUSE*	+	REASON
College students should strive to graduate		*because*		they will earn far more over their lifetimes than those who do not.

Keep in mind that you likely have a further reason, a rule or principle that underlies the reason you link directly to your claim. In this argument, the underlying reason is that isolation from other people is bad. If your audience doesn't accept that principle, you may have to back it up with further reasons or evidence.

To come up with good reasons, start by stating your position and then answering the question *why?*

CLAIM: College students should strive to graduate. *Why?*

REASON: (Because) They will earn far more over their lifetimes than those who do not. *Why?*

UNDERLYING REASON: The economy values college graduates and pays them more.

academic literacies · rhetorical situations · genres · processes · strategies · research MLA / APA · media / design · readings

As you can see, this exercise can continue indefinitely as the underlying reasons grow more and more general and abstract. You can do the same with other positions:

CLAIM: Smoking should be banned. *Why?*

REASON: (Because) It is harmful to smokers and also to nonsmokers.

UNDERLYING REASON: People should be protected from harmful substances.

Evidence. Evidence to support your reasons can come from various sources. In fact, you may need to use several kinds of evidence to persuade your audience that your claim is true. Some of the most common types of evidence include facts, statistics, examples, authorities, anecdotes, scenarios, case studies, textual evidence, and visuals.

Facts are ideas that are proven to be true. Facts can include observations or scholarly research (your own or someone else's), but they need to be accepted as true. If your audience accepts the facts you present, they can be powerful means of persuasion. For example, an essay on junk email offers these facts to demonstrate the seasonal nature of spam:

The flow of spam is often seasonal. It slows in the spring, and then, in the month that technology specialists call "black September"—when hundreds of thousands of students return to college, many armed with new computers and access to fast Internet connections—the levels rise sharply.

—Michael Specter, "Damn Spam"

Specter offers this fact with only a general reference to its origin ("technology specialists"), but given what most people know—or think they know—about college students, it rings true. A citation from a study published by a "technology specialist" would offer even greater credibility.

Statistics are numerical data, usually produced through research, surveys, or polls. Statistics should be relevant to your argument, as current as possible, accurate, and from a reliable source. An argument advocating that Americans should eat less meat presents these data to support the writer's contention that we eat far too much of it:

> Americans are downing close to 200 pounds of meat, poultry, and fish per capita per year (dairy and eggs are separate, and hardly insignificant), an increase of 50 pounds per person from 50 years ago. We each consume something like 110 grams of protein a day, about twice the federal government's recommended allowance; of that, about 75 grams come from animal protein. (The recommended level is itself considered by many dietary experts to be higher than it needs to be.) It's likely that most of us would do just fine on around 30 grams of protein a day, virtually all of it from plant sources.
>
> —Mark Bittman, "Rethinking the Meat-Guzzler"

Bittman's statistics demonstrate the extent to which Americans have increased their meat consumption over the last half century, the proportion of our diets that comes from meat, and, by comparison, how much protein our bodies require—and summarize the heart of his argument in stark numeric terms.

Examples are specific instances that illustrate general statements. In a book on life after dark in Europe, a historian offers several examples to demonstrate his point that three hundred years ago, night—without artificial lighting—was treacherous:

> Even sure-footed natives on a dark night could misjudge the lay of the land, stumbling into a ditch or off a precipice. In Aberdeenshire, a fifteen-year-old girl died in 1739 after straying from her customary path through a churchyard and tumbling into a newly dug grave. The Yorkshireman Arthur Jessop, returning from a neighbor's home on a cold December evening, fell into a stone pit after losing his bearings.
>
> —A. Roger Ekirch, *At Day's Close: Night in Times Past*

Ekirch illustrates his point and makes it come alive for readers by citing two specific individuals' fates.

Authorities are experts on your subject. To be useful, authorities must be reputable, trustworthy, and qualified to address the subject. You should **EVALUATE** any authorities you consult carefully to be sure they have the credentials necessary for readers to take them seriously. When you cite

469–72

academic literacies   rhetorical situations   genres   processes   strategies   research MLA / APA   media / design   readings

experts, you should clearly identify them and the origins of their authority in a **SIGNAL PHRASE**, as does the author of an argument that deforested land can be reclaimed:

487–90

> Reed Funk, professor of plant biology at Rutgers University, believes that the vast areas of deforested land can be used to grow millions of genetically improved trees for food, mostly nuts, and for fuel. Funk sees nuts used to supplement meat as a source of high-quality protein in developing-country diets.
>
> —Lester R. Brown, *Plan B 2.0: Rescuing a Planet under Stress and a Civilization in Trouble*

Brown cites Funk, an expert on plant biology, to support his argument that humans need to rethink the global economy in order to create a sustainable world. Without the information on Funk's credentials, though, readers would have no reason to take his proposal seriously.

Anecdotes are brief **NARRATIVES** that your audience will find believable and that contribute directly to your argument. Anecdotes may come from your personal experience or the experiences of others. In an essay arguing that it's understandable when athletes give in to the temptation to use performance-enhancing drugs, sports blogger William Moller uses an anecdote to show that the need to perform can outweigh the potential negative consequences of using drugs:

419–27

> I spent my high school years at a boarding school hidden among the apple orchards of Massachusetts. Known for a spartan philosophy regarding the adolescent need for sleep, the school worked us to the bone, regularly slamming us with six hours of homework. I pulled a lot more all-nighters (of the scholastic sort) in my years there than I ever did in college. When we weren't in class, the library, study hall, or formal sit-down meals, we were likely found on a sports field. We also had school on Saturday, beginning at 8 a.m. just like every other non-Sunday morning.
>
> Adding kindling to the fire, the students were not your laid-back types; everyone wanted that spot at the top of the class, and social life was rife with competition. The type A's that fill the investment banking,

legal, and political worlds — those are the kids I spent my high school years with.

And so it was that midway through my sophomore year, I found myself on my third all-nighter in a row, attempting to memorize historically significant pieces of art out of E. H. Gombrich's *The Story of Art*. I had finished a calculus exam the day before, and the day before that had been devoted to world history. And on that one cold night in February, I had had enough. I had hit that point where you've had so little sleep over such a long time that you start seeing spots, as if you'd been staring at a bright light for too long. The grade I would compete for the next day suddenly slipped in importance, and I began daydreaming about how easy the real world would be compared to the hell I was going through.

But there was hope. A friend who I was taking occasional study breaks with read the story in the bags beneath my eyes, in the slump of my shoulders, the nervous drumming of my fingers on the chair as we sipped flat, warm Coke in the common room. My personal *deus ex machina*,* he handed me a small white pill.

I was very innocent. I matured way after most of my peers, and was probably best known for being the kid who took all the soprano solos away from the girls in the choir as a first-year student. I don't think I had ever been buzzed, much less drunk. I'd certainly never smoked a cigarette. And knowing full well that what I was doing could be nothing better than against the rules (and less importantly, illegal) I did what I felt I needed to do, to accomplish what was demanded of me. And it worked. I woke up and regained focus like nothing I'd ever experienced. Unfortunately, it also came with serious side effects: I was a hypersensitized, stuffed-up, sweaty, wide-eyed mess, but I studied until the birds started chirping. And I aced my test.

Later I found out the pill was Ritalin, and it was classified as a class 3 drug.† I did it again, too — only a handful of times, as the side effects were so awful. But every time it was still illegal, still against

---

*Deus ex machina: In ancient Greek and Roman drama, a god introduced into the plot to resolve complications.

†Class 3 drug: Drug that is illegal to possess without a prescription.

academic literacies · rhetorical situations · genres · processes · strategies · research MLA / APA · media / design · readings

the rules. And as emphasized above, I was much more worried about the scholastic consequences if I were discovered abusing a prescription drug than the fact that I was breaking the law. Though I was using it in a far different manner than the baseball players who would later get caught with it in their systems, it was still very clearly a "performance-enhancing drug."

Just like every other person on this planet, I was giving in to the incentive scheme that was presented to me. The negative of doing poorly on the test was far greater than the negative of getting caught, discounted by the anesthetic of low probability.

—William Moller, "We, the Public, Place the Best Athletes on Pedestals"

Moller uses this anecdote to demonstrate the truth of his argument, that given the choice between "breaking the rules and breaking my grades" or "getting an edge" in professional sports, just about everyone will choose to break the rules.

Scenarios are hypothetical situations. Like anecdotes, "what if" scenarios can help you describe the possible effects of particular actions or offer new ways of looking at a particular state of affairs. For example, a mathematician presents this lighthearted scenario about Santa Claus in a tongue-in-cheek argument that Christmas is (almost) pure magic:

Let's assume that Santa only visits those who are children in the eyes of the law, that is, those under the age of 18. There are roughly 2 billion such individuals in the world. However, Santa started his annual activities long before diversity and equal opportunity became issues, and as a result he doesn't handle Muslim, Hindu, Jewish and Buddhist children. That reduces his workload significantly to a mere 15% of the total, namely 378 million. However, the crucial figure is not the number of children but the number of homes Santa has to visit. According to the most recent census data, the average size of a family in the world is 3.5 children per household. Thus, Santa has to visit 108,000,000 individual homes. (Of course, as everyone knows, Santa only visits good children, but we can surely assume that, on

an average, at least one child of the 3.5 in each home meets that criterion.)

—Keith Devlin, "The Mathematics of Christmas"

Devlin uses this scenario, as part of his mathematical analysis of Santa's yearly task, to help demonstrate that Christmas is indeed magical—because if you do the math, it's clear that Santa's task is physically impossible.

Case studies and observations feature detailed reporting about a subject. Case studies are in-depth, systematic examinations of an occasion, a person, or a group. For example, in arguing that class differences exist in the United States, sociologist Gregory Mantsios presents studies of three "typical" Americans to show "enormous class differences" in their lifestyles.

Observations offer detailed descriptions of a subject. Here's an observation of the emergence of a desert stream that flows only at night:

> At about 5:30 water came out of the ground. It did not spew up, but slowly escaped into the surrounding sand and small rocks. The wet circle grew until water became visible. Then it bubbled out like a small fountain and the creek began.
>
> —Craig Childs, *The Secret Knowledge of Water*

Childs presents this and other observations in a book that argues (among other things) that even in harsh, arid deserts, water exists, and knowing where to find it can mean the difference between life and death.

478–90 **Textual evidence** includes **QUOTATIONS**, **PARAPHRASES**, and **SUMMARIES**. Usually, the relevance of textual evidence must be stated directly, as excerpts from a text may carry several potential meanings. For example, here is an excerpt from a student essay analyzing the function of the raft in *Huckleberry Finn* as "a platform on which the resolution of conflicts is made possible":

> [T]he scenes where Jim and Huck are in consensus on the raft contain the moments in which they are most relaxed. For instance, in chapter twelve of the novel, Huck, after escaping capture from Jackson's Island, calls the rafting life "solemn" and articulates their experience

as living "pretty high" (Twain 75–76). Likewise, subsequent to escaping the unresolved feud between the Grangerfords and Shepherdsons in chapter eighteen, Huck is unquestionably at ease on the raft: "I was powerful glad to get away from the feuds. . . . We said there warn't no home like a raft, after all. Other places do seem so cramped up and smothery, but a raft don't. You feel mighty free and easy and comfortable on a raft" (Twain 134).

—Dave Nichols, "'Less All Be Friends': Rafts as Negotiating Platforms in Twain's *Huckleberry Finn*"

Huck's own words support Nichols's claim that he can relax on a raft. Nichols strengthens his claim by quoting evidence from two separate pages, suggesting that Huck's opinion of rafts pervades the novel.

Visuals can be a useful way of presenting evidence. Remember, though, that charts, graphs, photos, drawings, and other **VISUAL TEXTS** seldom speak for themselves and thus must be explained in your text. Below, for example, is a photograph of a poster carried by demonstrators at the 2008 Beijing Summer Olympics, protesting China's treatment of Tibetans.

607–15

If you were to use this photo in an essay, you would need to explain that the poster combines the image of a protester standing before a tank during the 1989 Tiananmen Square uprising with the Olympic logo, making clear to your readers that the protesters are likening China's treatment of Tibetans to its brutal actions in the past. Similarly, the poster for a recycling campaign below uses an American flag made from household waste to argue that recycling is patriotic.

 academic literacies

 rhetorical situations

 genres

 processes

 strategies

 research MLA / APA

 media / design

readings

Choosing appropriate evidence. The kinds of evidence you provide to support your argument depends on your RHETORICAL SITUATION. If your purpose is, for example, to convince readers to accept the need for a proposed solution, you'd be likely to include facts, statistics, and anecdotes. If you're writing for an academic audience, you'd be less likely to rely on anecdotes, preferring authorities, textual evidence, statistics, and case studies instead. And even within academic communities different disciplines and genres may focus primarily on different kinds of evidence. If you're not sure what counts as appropriate evidence, ask your instructor for guidance.

53

Convincing Readers You're Trustworthy

For your argument to be convincing, you need to establish your own credibility with readers—to demonstrate your knowledge about your topic, to show that you and your readers share some common ground, and to show yourself to be evenhanded in the way you present your argument.

Building common ground.   One important element of gaining readers' trust is to identify some common ground, some values you and your audience share. For example, to introduce a book arguing for the compatibility of science and religion, author Chet Raymo offers some common memories:

> Like most children, I was raised on miracles. Cows that jump over the moon; a jolly fat man that visits every house in the world in a single night; mice and ducks that talk; little engines that huff and puff and say, "I think I can"; geese that lay golden eggs. This lively exercise of credulity on the part of children is good practice for what follows—for believing in the miracle stories of traditional religion, yes, but also for the practice of poetry or science.
>
> —Chet Raymo, *Skeptics and True Believers: The Exhilarating Connection between Science and Religion*

Raymo presents childhood stories and myths that are part of many people's shared experiences to help readers find a connection between two realms that are often seen as opposed.

Incorporating other viewpoints. To show that you have carefully considered the viewpoints of others, including those who may agree or disagree with you, you should incorporate those viewpoints into your argument by acknowledging, accommodating, or refuting them.

Acknowledging other viewpoints. One essential part of establishing your credibility is to acknowledge that there are viewpoints different from yours and to represent them fairly and accurately. Rather than weakening your argument, acknowledging possible objections to your position shows that you've thought about and researched your topic thoroughly. For example, in an essay about his experience growing up homosexual, writer Andrew Sullivan admits that not every young gay man or woman has the same experience:

> I should add that many young lesbians and homosexuals seem to have had a much easier time of it. For many, the question of sexual identity was not a critical factor in their life choices or vocation, or even a factor at all. —Andrew Sullivan, "What Is a Homosexual?"

In response to a reasonable objection, Sullivan qualifies his assertions, making his own stance appear to be reasonable.

Accommodating other viewpoints. You may be tempted to ignore views you don't agree with, but in fact it's important to demonstrate that you are aware of them and have considered them carefully. You may find yourself conceding that opposing views have some merit and qualifying your claim or even making them part of your own argument. See, for example, how a philosopher arguing that torture is sometimes "not merely permissible but morally mandatory" addresses a major objection to his position:

> The most powerful argument against using torture as a punishment or to secure confessions is that such practices disregard the rights of the individual. Well, if the individual is all that important—and he is— it is correspondingly important to protect the rights of individuals threatened by terrorists. If life is so valuable that it must never be

taken, the lives of the innocents must be saved even at the price of hurting the one who endangers them.

—Michael Levin, "The Case for Torture"

Levin acknowledges his critics' argument that the individual is indeed important but then asserts that if the life of one person is important, the lives of many people must be even more important. In effect, he uses an opposing argument to advance his own.

Refuting other viewpoints. Often you may need to refute other arguments and make a case for why you believe they are wrong. Are the values underlying the argument questionable? Is the reasoning flawed? Is the evidence inadequate or faulty? For example, an essay arguing for the elimination of college athletics scholarships includes this refutation:

> Some argue that eliminating athletics scholarships would deny opportunity and limit access for many students, most notably black athletes. The question is, access to what? The fields of competition or an opportunity to earn a meaningful degree? With the six-year graduation rates of black basketball players hovering in the high 30-percent range, and black football players in the high 40-percent range, despite years of "academic reform," earning an athletics scholarship under the current system is little more than a chance to play sports. —John R. Gerdy, "For True Reform, Athletics Scholarships Must Go"

Gerdy bases his refutation on statistics showing that for more than half of African American college athletes, the opportunity to earn a degree by playing a sport is an illusion.

When you incorporate differing viewpoints, be careful to avoid the **FALLACIES** of attacking the person making the argument or refuting a competing position that no one seriously entertains. It is also important that you not distort or exaggerate opposing viewpoints. If *your* argument is to be persuasive, other arguments should be represented fairly.

◆ 370–72

Appealing to Readers' Emotions

Logic and facts, even when presented by someone who seems reasonable and trustworthy, may not be enough to persuade readers. Many successful arguments include an emotional component that appeals to readers' hearts as well as to their minds. Advertising often works by appealing to its audience's emotions, as in this paragraph from a Volvo ad:

> Choosing a car is about the comfort and safety of your passengers, most especially your children. That's why we ensure Volvo's safety research examines how we can make our cars safer for everyone who travels in them—from adults to teenagers, children to babies. Even those who aren't even born yet. —*Volvo.com*

This ad plays on the fear that children—or a pregnant mother—may be injured or killed in an automobile accident.

Keep in mind that emotional appeals can make readers feel as though they are being manipulated and, consequently, less likely to accept an argument. For most kinds of academic writing, use emotional appeals sparingly.

Checking for Fallacies

Fallacies are arguments that involve faulty reasoning. It's important to avoid fallacies in your writing because they often seem plausible but are usually unfair or inaccurate and make reasonable discussion difficult. Here are some of the most common fallacies:

- **Ad hominem** arguments attack someone's character rather than address the issues. (*Ad hominem* is Latin for "to the man.") It is an especially common fallacy in political discourse and elsewhere: "Jack Turner has no business talking about the way we run things in this city. He's just another flaky liberal." Whether or not Turner is a "flaky liberal" has no bearing on the worth of his argument about "the way we run things in this city"; insulting one's opponents isn't an argument against their positions.

- **Bandwagon appeals** argue that because others think or do something, we should, too. For example, an advertisement for a rifle association suggests that "67 percent of voters support laws permitting concealed weapons. You should, too." It assumes that readers want to be part of the group and implies that an opinion that is popular must be correct.

- **Begging the question** is a circular argument. It assumes as a given what is trying to be proved, essentially supporting an assertion with the assertion itself. Consider this statement: "Affirmative action can never be fair or just because you cannot remedy one injustice by committing another." This statement begs the question because to prove that affirmative action is unjust, it assumes that it is an injustice.

- **Either-or** arguments, also called *false dilemmas*, are oversimplifications that assert there can be only two possible positions on a complex issue. For example, "Those who oppose our actions in this war are enemies of freedom" inaccurately assumes that if someone opposes the war in question, he or she opposes freedom. In fact, people might have many other reasons for opposing the war.

- **False analogies** compare things that resemble each other in some ways but not in the most important respects — for example, "Trees pollute the air just as much as cars and trucks do." Although it's true that plants emit hydrocarbons, and hydrocarbons are a component of smog, they also produce oxygen, whereas motor vehicles emit gases that combine with hydrocarbons to form smog. Vehicles pollute the air; trees provide the air that vehicles' emissions pollute.

- **Faulty causality,** also known as *post hoc, ergo propter hoc* (Latin for "after this, therefore because of this"), assumes that because one event followed another, the first event caused the second—for example, "Legalizing same-sex marriage in Sweden led to a decline in the marriage rate of opposite-sex couples." The statement contains no evidence to show that the first event caused the second.

- **Straw man** arguments misrepresent an opposing position to make it ridiculous or extreme and thus easy to refute, rather than dealing with the actual position. For example, if someone argues that funding for food stamps should be cut, a straw man response would be, "You want the poor to starve," transforming a proposal to cut a specific program into an exaggerated argument that the proposer hasn't made.

- *Hasty generalizations* are conclusions based on insufficient or inappropriately qualified evidence. This summary of a research study is a good example: "Twenty randomly chosen residents of Brooklyn, New York, were asked whether they found graffiti tags offensive; fourteen said yes, five said no, and one had no opinion. Therefore, 70 percent of Brooklyn residents find tagging offensive." In Brooklyn, a part of New York City with a population of over two million, twenty residents is far too small a group from which to draw meaningful conclusions. To be able to generalize, the researcher would have had to survey a much greater percentage of Brooklyn's population.

- *Slippery slope* arguments assert that one event will inevitably lead to another, often cataclysmic event without presenting evidence that such a chain of causes and effects will in fact take place. Here's an example: "If the state legislature passes this 2 percent tax increase, it won't be long before all the corporations in the state move to other states and leave thousands unemployed." According to this argument, if taxes are raised, the state's economy will be ruined—not a likely scenario, given the size of the proposed increase.

Considering the Rhetorical Situation

To argue effectively, you need to think about the message that you want to articulate, the audience you want to persuade, the effect of your stance, and the larger context you are writing in.

55–56 ▮

PURPOSE   What do you want your audience to do? To think a certain way? To take a certain action? To change their minds? To consider alternative views to their current ones? To accept your position as plausible? To see that you have thought carefully about an issue and researched it appropriately?

academic literacies   rhetorical situations   genres   processes   strategies   research MLA / APA   media / design   readings

AUDIENCE Who is your intended audience? What do they likely know and believe about your topic? How personal is it for them? To what extent are they likely to agree or disagree with you? Why? What common ground can you find with them? How should you incorporate other viewpoints they have? What kind of evidence are they likely to accept? 57–60

GENRE What genre will help you achieve your purpose? A position paper? An evaluation? A review? A proposal? An analysis? 61–63

STANCE What's your attitude toward your topic, and why? What strategies will help you to convey that stance? How do you want your audience to perceive you? As an authority on your topic? As someone much like them? As calm? reasonable? impassioned or angry? something else? 64–67

MEDIA / DESIGN What media will you use, and how do your media affect your argument? If you're writing on paper, does your argument call for photos or charts? If you're giving an oral presentation, should you put your reasons and support on slides? If you're writing online, should you add links to sites representing other positions or containing evidence that supports your position? 68–70

37 Classifying and Dividing

Classification and division are ways of organizing information: various items may be classified according to their similarities, or a single topic may be divided into parts. We might classify different kinds of flowers as annuals or perennials, for example, and classify the perennials further as dahlias, daisies, roses, and peonies. We might also divide a flower garden into distinct areas: for herbs, flowers, and vegetables.

Writers often use classification and division as ways of developing and organizing material. This book, for instance, classifies comparison, definition, description, and several other common ways of thinking and writing as strategies. It divides the information it provides about writing into seven parts: "Rhetorical Situations," "Genres," "Processes," and so on. Each part further divides its material into various chapters. Even if you never write a book, you will have occasion to classify and divide material in **ANNOTATED BIBLIOGRAPHIES**, essays **ANALYZING TEXTS**, and other kinds of writing. This chapter offers advice for classifying and dividing information for various writing purposes—and in a way that suits your own rhetorical situation.

188–96 ▲
94–128

Classifying

When we classify something, we group it with similar things. A linguist would classify French and Spanish and Italian as Romance languages, for example—and Russian, Polish, and Bulgarian as Slavic languages. In a hilarious (if totally phony) news story from the *Onion* about a church bake sale, the writer classifies the activities observed there as examples of the seven deadly sins:

academic literacies · rhetorical situations · genres · processes · strategies · research MLA / APA · media / design · readings

> GADSDEN, AL—The seven deadly sins—avarice, sloth, envy, lust, gluttony, pride, and wrath—were all committed Sunday during the twice-annual bake sale at St. Mary's of the Immaculate Conception Church.
>
> —"All Seven Deadly Sins Committed at Church Bake Sale," *The Onion*

The article goes on to categorize the participants' behavior in terms of the sins, describing one parishioner who commits the sin of pride by bragging about her cookies and others who commit the sin of envy by envying the popularity of the prideful parishioner's baked goods (the consumption of which leads to the sin of gluttony). In all, the article notes, "347 individual acts of sin were committed at the bake sale," and every one of them can be classified as one of the seven deadly sins.

Dividing

As a writing strategy, division is a way of breaking something into parts—and a way of making the information easy for readers to follow and understand. See how this example about children's ways of nagging divides their tactics into seven categories:

> James U. McNeal, a professor of marketing at Texas A&M University, is considered America's leading authority on marketing to children. In his book *Kids as Customers* (1992), McNeal provides marketers with a thorough analysis of "children's requesting styles and appeals." He [divides] juvenile nagging tactics into seven major categories. A *pleading* nag is one accompanied by repetitions of words like "please" or "mom, mom, mom." A *persistent* nag involves constant requests for the coveted product and may include the phrase "I'm gonna ask just one more time." *Forceful* nags are extremely pushy and may include subtle threats, like "Well, then, I'll go and ask Dad." *Demonstrative* nags are the most high risk, often characterized by full-blown tantrums in public places, breath holding, tears, a refusal to leave the store. *Sugar-coated* nags promise affection in return for a purchase and may rely on seemingly heartfelt declarations, like "You're

the best dad in the world." *Threatening* nags are youthful forms of blackmail, vows of eternal hatred and of running away if something isn't bought. *Pity* nags claim the child will be heartbroken, teased, or socially stunted if the parent refuses to buy a certain item. "All of these appeals and styles may be used in combination," McNeal's research has discovered, "but kids tend to stick to one or two of each that prove most effective . . . for their own parents."

—Eric Schlosser, *Fast Food Nation:*
The Dark Side of the All-American Meal

Here the writer announces the division scheme of "seven major categories." Then he names each tactic and describes how it works. And notice the italics: each nagging tactic is italicized, making it easy to recognize and follow. Take away the italics, and the divisions would be less visible.

Creating Clear and Distinct Categories

When you classify or divide, you need to create clear and distinct categories. If you're writing about music, you might divide it on the basis of the genre (hip-hop, rock, classical, gospel), artist (male or female, group or solo), or instruments (violins, trumpets, bongos, guitars). These categories must be distinct, so that no information overlaps or fits into more than one category, and they must include every member of the group you're discussing. The simpler the criteria for selecting the categories, the better. The nagging categories in the example from *Fast Food Nation* are based on only one criterion: a child's verbal behavior.

Sometimes you may want to highlight your categories visually to make them easier to follow. Eric Schlosser does that by italicizing each category: the *pleading* nag, the *persistent* nag, the *forceful* nag, and so on. Other **DESIGN** elements—bulleted lists, pie charts, tables, images—might also prove useful.

597–606 ◻

See, for instance, how *The World of Caffeine* authors Bennett Alan Weinberg and Bonnie K. Bealer use a two-column list to show what they say are the differing cultural connotations of coffee and tea:

academic literacies   rhetorical situations   genres   processes   strategies   research MLA / APA   media / design   readings

Coffee Aspect	Tea Aspect
Male	Female
Boisterous	Decorous
Indulgence	Temperance
Hardheaded	Romantic
Topology	Geometry
Heidegger	Carnap
Beethoven	Mozart
Libertarian	Statist
Promiscuous	Pure

—Bennett Alan Weinberg and Bonnie K. Bealer,
The World of Caffeine

Sometimes you might show categories visually, as in this website promoting Michigan apples. Each of the sixteen varieties grown in Michigan is pictured, and its taste, uses, and texture are described.

The photographs allow us to see the differences among the varieties at a glance. The varieties are arranged alphabetically but could have been arranged by color, flavor (sweet or tart), or whether they are best for baking or eating raw.

Considering the Rhetorical Situation

As a writer or speaker, you need to think about the message that you want to articulate, the audience you want to reach, and the larger context you are writing in.

<table>
<tr>
<td>55–56</td>
<td>**PURPOSE**</td>
<td>Your purpose for writing will affect how you classify or divide information. Weinberg and Bealer classify coffee as "boisterous" and tea as "decorous" to help readers understand the cultural styles the two beverages represent, whereas J. Crew might divide sweaters into cashmere, wool, and cotton to help shoppers find and buy things from their website.</td>
</tr>
<tr>
<td>57–60</td>
<td>**AUDIENCE**</td>
<td>What audience do you want to reach, and will classifying or dividing your material help them follow your discussion?</td>
</tr>
<tr>
<td>61–63</td>
<td>**GENRE**</td>
<td>Does your genre call for you to categorize or divide information? A long report might need to be divided into sections, for instance.</td>
</tr>
<tr>
<td>64–67</td>
<td>**STANCE**</td>
<td>Your stance may affect the way you classify information. Weinberg and Bealer's classification of coffee as "Beethoven" and tea as "Mozart" reflects a stance that focuses on cultural analysis (and assumes an audience familiar with the difference between the two composers). If the authors were botanists, they might categorize the two beverages in terms of their biological origins ("seed based" and "leaf based").</td>
</tr>
</table>

MEDIA / DESIGN You can classify or divide in paragraph form, but sometimes a pie chart or list will show the categories better.

68–70

IF YOU NEED MORE HELP

See also **CLUSTERING**, **CUBING**, and **LOOPING**, three methods of generating ideas
discussed in Chapter 30 that can be especially helpful for classifying material. And
see all the **PROCESSES** chapters for guidelines on drafting, revising, and so on if
you need to write a classification essay.

290–92
279

38 Comparing and Contrasting

Comparing things looks at their similarities; contrasting them focuses on their differences. It's a kind of thinking that comes naturally and that we do constantly—for example, comparing Houston with Dallas, iPhones with Androids, or three paintings by Renoir. And once we start comparing, we generally find ourselves contrasting—Houston and Dallas have differences as well as similarities.

As a student, you'll often be asked to compare and contrast paintings or poems or other things. As a writer, you'll have cause to compare and contrast in most kinds of writing. In a **PROPOSAL**, for instance, you will need to compare your solution with other possible solutions; or in an **EVALUATION**, such as a movie review, you might contrast the film you're reviewing with some other film. This chapter offers advice on ways of comparing and contrasting things for various writing purposes and for your own rhetorical situations.

Most of the time, we compare obviously similar things: cars we might purchase, three competing political candidates, two versions of a film. Occasionally, however, we might compare things that are less obviously similar. See how John McMurtry, an ex–football player, compares football with war in an essay arguing that the attraction football holds for spectators is based in part on its potential for violence and injury:

> The family resemblance between football and war is, indeed, striking. Their languages are similar: "field general," "long bomb," "blitz," "take a shot," "front line," "pursuit," "good hit," "the draft," and so on. Their principles and practices are alike: mass hysteria, the art of intimidation, absolute command and total obedience, territorial aggression, censorship, inflated insignia and propaganda, blackboard maneuvers and strategies, drills, uniforms, marching bands, and training

235–44
197–205

academic literacies / rhetorical situations / genres / processes / strategies / research MLA / APA / media / design / readings

camps. And the virtues they celebrate are almost identical: hyper-aggressiveness, coolness under fire, and suicidal bravery.

—John McMurtry, "Kill 'Em! Crush 'Em! Eat 'Em Raw!"

McMurtry's comparison helps focus readers' attention on what he's arguing about football in part because it's somewhat unexpected. But the more unlikely the comparison, the more you might be accused of comparing apples and oranges. It's important, therefore, that the things we compare be legitimately compared—as is the case in the following comparison of the health of the world's richest and poorest people:

> World Health Organization (WHO) data indicate that roughly 1.2 billion people are undernourished, underweight, and often hungry. At the same time, roughly 1.2 billion people are overnourished and overweight, most of them suffering from excessive caloric intake and exercise deprivation. So while 1 billion people worry whether they will eat, another billion should worry about eating too much.
>
> Disease patterns also reflect the widening gap. The billion poorest suffer mostly from infectious diseases—malaria, tuberculosis, dysentery, and AIDS. Malnutrition leaves infants and small children even more vulnerable to such infectious diseases. Unsafe drinking water takes a heavier toll on those with hunger-weakened immune systems, resulting in millions of fatalities each year. In contrast, among the billion at the top of the global economic scale, it is diseases related to aging and lifestyle excesses, including obesity, smoking, diets rich in fat and sugar, and exercise deprivation, that cause most deaths.

—Lester R. Brown, *Plan B 2.0: Rescuing a Planet under Stress and a Civilization in Trouble*

While the two groups of roughly a billion people each undoubtedly have similarities, this selection from a book arguing for global action on the environment focuses on the stark contrasts.

Two Ways of Comparing and Contrasting

Comparisons and contrasts may be organized in two basic ways: block and point by point.

The block method.   One way is to discuss separately each item you're comparing, giving all the information about one item and then all the information about the next item. A report on Seattle and Vancouver, for example, compares the firearm regulations in each city using a paragraph about Seattle and then a paragraph about Vancouver:

> Although similar in many ways, Seattle and Vancouver differ markedly in their approaches to the regulation of firearms. In Seattle, handguns may be purchased legally for self-defense in the street or at home. After a thirty-day waiting period, a permit can be obtained to carry a handgun as a concealed weapon. The recreational use of handguns is minimally restricted.
>
> In Vancouver, self-defense is not considered a valid or legal reason to purchase a handgun. Concealed weapons are not permitted. Recreational uses of handguns (such as target shooting and collecting) are regulated by the province, and the purchase of a handgun requires a restricted-weapons permit. A permit to carry a weapon must also be obtained in order to transport a handgun, and these weapons can be discharged only at a licensed shooting club. Handguns can be transported by car, but only if they are stored in the trunk in a locked box.
>
> —John Henry Sloan et al., "Handgun Regulations, Crime, Assaults, and Homicide: A Tale of Two Cities"

The point-by-point method.   The other way to compare things is to focus on specific points of comparison. In this paragraph, humorist David Sedaris compares his childhood with his partner's, discussing corresponding aspects of the childhoods one at a time:

> Certain events are parallel, but compared with Hugh's, my childhood was unspeakably dull. When I was seven years old, my family moved to North Carolina. When he was seven years old, Hugh's family moved to the Congo. We had a collie and a house cat. They had a monkey and two horses named Charlie Brown and Satan. I threw stones at stop signs. Hugh threw stones at crocodiles. The verbs are the same, but he definitely wins the prize when it comes to nouns and objects. An eventful day for my mother might have involved a trip to the dry cleaner or a conversation with the potato-chip deliveryman. Asked

one ordinary Congo afternoon what she'd done with her day, Hugh's mother answered that she and a fellow member of the Ladies' Club had visited a leper colony on the outskirts of Kinshasa.

—David Sedaris, "Remembering My Childhood on the Continent of Africa"

Using Graphs and Images to Present Comparisons

Some comparisons can be easier to understand if they're presented visually, as a **CHART**, **GRAPH**, or **ILLUSTRATION**. For example, this excerpt from a chart from the *Huffington Post* shows the results of various opinion polls about Americans' identification with a political party in April and May 2012; it allows readers to compare not only percentages of Republicans, Democrats, and Independents but also differences in results among the polls. (In the third column, pop-up links explain that "Pop." means "Population," "A" means "adults," "RV" means "registered voters," and "LV" means "likely voters.")

607–15

Pollster	Dates	Pop.	Democrat	Independent	Republican	Undecided
AP-GfK	5/3–5/7	1,004 A	31	46	22	1
DailyKos/SEIU/ PPP (D)	5/3–5/6	1,000 RV	38	26	35	—
NBC/WSJ	4/13–4/17	800 A	30	42	24	4
CBS/Times	4/13–4/17	957 A	34	36	30	—
Ipsos/Reuters	4/12–4/15	1,044 A	29	49	22	—

—*Huffington Post*

The following bar graph, from an economics textbook, compares the incomes of various professions in the United States, both with one another and with the average U.S. income (defined as 100 percent). Again, it would be possible to write out this information in a paragraph—but it is much easier to understand it this way:

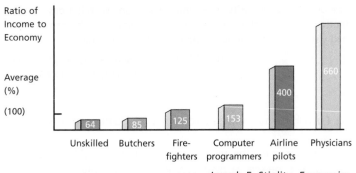

Ratio of Income to Economy

Average (%)

(100)

Unskilled	Butchers	Fire-fighters	Computer programmers	Airline pilots	Physicians
64	85	125	153	400	660

—Joseph E. Stiglitz, *Economics*

Sometimes photographs can make a comparison. The two photos below show an area of Japan before and after the 2011 tsunami.

Ishinomaki Prefecture before the 2011 tsunami (top) and after the storm (bottom).

Using Figurative Language to Make Comparisons

Another way we make comparisons is with figurative language: words and phrases used in a nonliteral way to help readers see a point. Three kinds of figurative language that make comparisons are similes, metaphors, and analogies. When Robert Burns wrote that his love was "like a red, red rose," he was comparing his love with a rose and evoking an image—in this case, a simile—that helps us understand his feelings for her. A simile makes a comparison using *like* or *as*. In the following example, from an article in the food section of the *New York Times*, a restaurant critic uses several similes (underlined) to help us visualize an unusual food dish:

> Once upon a time, possibly at a lodge in Wyoming, possibly at a butcher shop in Maurice, Louisiana, or maybe even at a plantation in South Carolina, an enterprising cook decided to take a boned chicken, a boned duck, and a boned turkey, stuff them one inside the other <u>like Russian dolls</u>, and roast them. He called his masterpiece turducken. . . .
>
> A well-prepared turducken is a marvelous treat, a free-form poultry terrine layered with flavorful stuffing and moistened with duck fat. When it's assembled, it looks <u>like a turkey</u> and it roasts <u>like a turkey</u>, but when you go to carve it, you can slice through it <u>like a loaf of bread</u>. In each slice you get a little bit of everything: white meat from the breast; dark meat from the legs, duck, carrots, bits of sausage, bread, herbs, juices, and chicken, too.
>
> —Amanda Hesser, "Turkey Finds Its Inner Duck (and Chicken)"

Metaphors make comparisons without such connecting words as *like* or *as*. See how desert ecologist Craig Childs uses a metaphor to help us understand the nature of water during a flood in the Grand Canyon:

> Water splashed off the desert and ran all over the surface, looking for the quickest way down. It was too swift for the ground to absorb. When water flows like this, it will not be clean tap water. It will be <u>a gravy of debris</u>, snatching everything it finds.
>
> —Craig Childs, *The Secret Knowledge of Water*

Calling the water "a gravy of debris" allows us to see the murky liquid as it streams through the canyon.

Analogies are extended similes or metaphors that compare something unfamiliar with something more familiar. Arguing that corporations should not patent parts of DNA whose function isn't yet clear, a genetics professor uses the familiar image of a library to explain an unfamiliar concept:

> It's like having a library of books and randomly tearing pages out. You may know which books the pages came from but that doesn't tell you much about them.　　—Peter Goodfellow, quoted in John Vidal and
> John Carvel, "Lambs to the Gene Market"

Sometimes analogies are used for humorous effect as well as to make a point, as in this passage from a critique of history textbooks:

> Another history text—this one for fifth grade—begins with the story of how Henry B. Gonzalez, who is a member of Congress from Texas, learned about his own nationality. When he was ten years old, his teacher told him he was an American because he was born in the United States. His grandmother, however, said, "The cat was born in the oven. Does that make him bread?"
>
> —Frances FitzGerald, *America Revised:*
> *History Schoolbooks in the Twentieth Century*

The grandmother's question shows how an intentionally ridiculous analogy can be a source of humor—and can make a point memorably.

Considering the Rhetorical Situation

As a writer or speaker, you need to think about the message that you want to articulate, the audience you want to reach, and the larger context you are writing in.

55–56 **PURPOSE**　　Sometimes your main purpose for writing will be to compare two or more things. Other times, you may want to compare several things for some other purpose—to compare your views with those of others in an argument essay or to compare one text with another as you analyze them.

AUDIENCE   Who is your audience, and will comparing your topic with   57–60
a more familiar one help them to follow your discussion?

GENRE   Does your genre require you to compare something?   61–63
Evaluations often include comparisons—one book to
another in a review, or ten different cell phones in *Consumer Reports*.

STANCE   Your stance may affect any comparisons you make.   64–67
How you compare two things—evenhandedly, or clearly
favoring one over the other, for example—will reflect
your stance.

MEDIA / DESIGN   Some things you will want to compare with words alone   68–70
(lines from two poems, for instance), but sometimes you
may wish to make comparisons visually (two images juxtaposed on a page, or several numbers plotted on a line
graph).

IF YOU NEED MORE HELP

See **LOOPING** and **CUBING**, two methods of generating ideas discussed in Chapter 27   290–92
that can be especially helpful for comparing and contrasting. If you're writing an   279
essay whose purpose is to compare two or more things, see also the **PROCESSES**
chapters for help drafting, revising, and so on.

39 Defining

Defining something says what it is—and what it is not. A terrier, for example, is a kind of dog. A fox terrier is a small dog now generally kept as a pet but once used by hunters to dig for foxes. Happiness is a jelly donut, at least according to Homer Simpson. All of those are definitions. As writers, we need to define any terms our readers may not know. And sometimes you'll want to stipulate your own definition of a word in order to set the terms of an **ARGUMENT**—as Homer Simpson does with a definition that's not found in any dictionary. This chapter details strategies for using definitions in your writing to suit your own rhetorical situations.

355–73

Formal Definitions

Sometimes to make sure readers understand you, you will need to provide a formal definition. If you are using a technical term that readers are unlikely to know or if you are using a term in a specific way, you need to say then and there what the word means. The word *mutual*, for example, has several dictionary meanings:

> mu•tu•al . . .
>
> **1a:** directed by each toward the other or the others <*mutual* affection> **b:** having the same feelings one for the other <they had long been *mutual* enemies> **c:** shared in common <enjoying their *mutual* hobby> **d:** joint
> **2:** characterized by intimacy
> **3:** of or relating to a plan whereby the members of an organization share in the profits and expenses; *specifically*: of, relating to, or taking the form of an insurance method in which the policyholders constitute the members of the insuring company   —*Merriam-Webster.com*

academic literacies rhetorical situations genres processes strategies research MLA / APA media / design readings

The first two meanings are commonly understood and probably require no definition. But if you were to use *mutual* in the third sense, it might—depending on your audience. A general audience would probably need the definition; an audience from the insurance industry would not. A website that gives basic financial advice to an audience of non-specialists, for instance, offers a specific definition of the term *mutual fund*:

> *Mutual funds* are financial intermediaries. They are companies set up to receive your money and then, having received it, to make investments with the money.
>
> —Bill Barker, "A Grand, Comprehensive Overview to Mutual Funds Investing"

But even writers in specialized fields routinely provide formal definitions to make sure their readers understand the way they are using certain words. See how two writers define the word *stock* as it pertains to their respective (and very different) fields:

> Stocks are the basis for sauces and soups and important flavoring agents for braises. Admittedly, stock making is time consuming, but the extra effort yields great dividends.
>
> —Tom Colicchio, *Think Like a Chef*

> Want to own part of a business without having to show up at its office every day? Or ever? Stock is the vehicle of choice for those who do. Dating back to the Dutch mutual stock corporations of the sixteenth century, the modern stock market exists as a way for entrepreneurs to finance businesses using money collected from investors. In return for ponying up the dough to finance the company, the investor becomes a part owner of the company. That ownership is represented by stock—specialized financial "securities," or financial instruments, that are "secured" by a claim on the assets and profits of a company.
>
> —"Investing Basics: Stocks," *The Motley Fool*

To write a formal definition

- Use words that readers are likely to be familiar with.
- Don't use the word being defined in the definition.

- Begin with the word being defined; include the general category to which the term belongs and the attributes that make it different from the others in that category.

For example:

Term	General Category	Distinguishing Attributes
Stock is	a specialized financial "security"	that is "secured" by a claim.
Photosynthesis is	a process	by which plants use sunlight to create energy.
Astronomers are	scientists	who study celestial objects and phenomena.
Zach Galifianakis,	a comedian,	has acted in several films, including *The Hangover* and *The Campaign.*

Note that the category and distinguishing attributes cannot be stated too broadly; if they were, the definition would be too vague to be useful. It wouldn't be helpful in most circumstances, for example, to say, "Zach Galifianakis is a man who has acted" or "Photosynthesis is something having to do with plants."

Extended Definitions

Sometimes you need to provide a more detailed definition. Extended definitions may be several sentences long or several paragraphs long and may include pictures or diagrams. Sometimes an entire essay is devoted to defining a difficult or important concept. Here is one writer's extended definition of *meme*:

> Richard Dawkins first came up with the idea of a meme in his 1976 book *The Selfish Gene*. Essentially, memes are ideas that evolve according to the same principles that govern biological evolution. Think about all the ideas that you have in your head right now. They are all memes,

and they all came from somewhere. Some of them will have come from friends and some will have come from the internet or television. Examples of memes are musical tunes, jokes, trends, fashions, catch phrases, and car designs. Now, the memes that inhabit your mind are in competition with all the other memes in the *memepool* (the collection of all existing memes). This means that they are all competing to get themselves copied into other people's minds. Some of these memes do quite well. Every time you whistle your favorite tune or utter a useful catch phrase, you are facilitating the spread of those memes. Every time you wear something that is "in fashion" you are helping the idea of that fashion enter other people's minds. Consider the first four notes of Beethoven's 5th symphony, or the "Happy Birthday" song. These are ideas that inhabit our minds and have been very successful at replicating. Not only have these memes found their way into literally millions of minds, they have also managed to leave copies of themselves on paper, in books, on audiotape, on compact disks, and in computer hard-drives.

There is a limited amount of memetic storage space on this planet, so only the best memes manage to implant themselves. Memes that are good at replicating tend to leave more copies of themselves in minds and in other mediums such as books. Memes that are not so good at replicating tend to die out. We can imagine what sorts of memes have become extinct. Ancient songs that were once sung and never written down are one example. Another example is the many stories that were once told but have since slipped into oblivion.

—Brent Silby, "What Is a Meme?"

That definition includes a description of the basic features and behavior of memes, examples of them, and the origin of the term. We can assume that it's written for a general audience, one that doesn't know anything about memes.

Abstract concepts often require extended definitions because by nature they are more complicated to define. There are many ways of writing an extended definition, depending in part on the term being defined and on your audience and purpose. The following examples show some of the methods that can be used for composing extended definitions of *democracy*.

Explore the word's origins. Where did the word come from? When did it first come into use? In the following example, from an essay considering what democracy means in the twenty-first century, the writer started by looking at the word's first known use in English. Though it's from an essay written for a first-year writing course and thus for a fairly general audience, it's a definition that might pique any audience's interest:

> According to the *Oxford English Dictionary*, the term *democracy* first appeared in English in a thirteenth-century translation of Aristotle's works—specifically, in his *Politics*, where he stated that the "underlying principle of democracy is freedom" and that "it is customary to say that only in democracies do men have a share in freedom, for that is what every democracy makes its aim." By the sixteenth century, the word was used much as it is now. One writer in 1586, for instance, defined it in this way: "where free and poore men being the greater number, are lords of the estate."
>
> —Susanna Mejía, "What Does Democracy Mean Now?"

Here's another example, this one written for a scholarly audience, from an essay about women, participation, democracy, and the information age:

> The very word *citizenship* carries with it a connotation of place, a "citizen" being, literally, the inhabitant of a city. Over the years the word has, of course, accumulated a number of associated meanings . . . and the word has come to stand in for such concepts as participation, equality, and democracy. The fact that the concept of locality is deeply embedded in the word *citizen* suggests that it is also fundamental to our current understanding of these other, more apparently abstract words.
>
> In Western thought, the concepts of citizenship, equality, and democracy are closely interlinked and can be traced back to a common source, in Athens in the fifth century B.C. Perhaps it is no accident that it was the same culture which also gave us, in its theater, the concept of the unity of time and space. The Greek city-state has been represented for centuries as the ideal model of democracy, with free and equal access for all citizens to decision making. Leaving aside, for the moment, the question of who was included, and who excluded from this notion of citizenship, we can see that the sense of place is fundamental to this model. Entitlement to participate in the democratic process is circumscribed by geography; it is the inhabitants of the

Norman Rockwell's 1943 painting Freedom of Speech *presents a visual definition of democracy: a citizen stands to speak at a public meeting while his fellow citizens listen attentively.*

geographical entity of the city-state, precisely defined and bounded, who have the rights to citizenship. Those who are not defined as inhabitants of that specific city-state are explicitly excluded, although, of course, they may have the right to citizenship elsewhere.

—Ursula Huws, "Women, Participation, and
Democracy in the Information Society"

Provide details. What are its characteristics? What is it made of? See how a historian explores the basic characteristics of democracy in a book written for an audience of historians:

As a historian I am naturally disposed to be satisfied with the meaning which, in the history of politics, men have commonly attributed to the word—a meaning, needless to say, which derives partly from the experience and partly from the aspirations of mankind. So regarded, the term *democracy* refers primarily to a form of government, and it has always meant government by the many as opposed to government by the one—government by the people as opposed to government by a tyrant, a dictator, or an absolute monarch. . . . Since the Greeks first used the term, the essential test of democratic government has always been this: the source of political authority must be and remain in the people and not in the ruler. A democratic government has always meant one in which the citizens, or a sufficient number of them to represent more or less effectively the common will, freely act from time to time, and according to established forms, to appoint or recall the magistrates and to enact or revoke the laws by which the community is governed. —Carl Becker, *Modern Democracy*

Compare it with other words. How is this concept like other similar things? How does it differ? What is it *not* like? **COMPARE AND CONTRAST** it. See how a political science textbook defines a *majoritarian democracy* by comparing its characteristics with those of a *consensual democracy*:

380–87

A majoritarian democracy is one

1. having only two major political parties, not many
2. having an electoral system that requires a bare majority to elect one clear winner in an election, as opposed to a proportional

academic
literacies

rhetorical
situations

genres

processes

strategies

research
MLA / APA

media /
design

readings

electoral system that distributes seats to political parties according to the rough share of votes received in the election

3. a strong executive (president or prime minister) and cabinet that together are largely independent of the legislature when it comes to exercising the executive's constitutional duties, in contrast to an executive and cabinet that are politically controlled by the parties in the legislature and therefore unable to exercise much influence when proposing policy initiatives.

> —Benjamin Ginsberg, Theodore J. Lowi, and Margaret Weir,
> *We the People: An Introduction to American Politics*

And here's an example in which democracy is contrasted with various other forms of governments of the past:

> Caesar's power derived from a popular mandate, conveyed through established republican forms, but that did not make his government any the less a dictatorship. Napoleon called his government a democratic republic, but no one, least of all Napoleon himself, doubted that he had destroyed the last vestiges of the democratic republic.
>
> —Carl Becker, *Modern Democracy*

Give examples. See how the essayist E. B. White defines democracy by giving some everyday examples of considerate behavior, humility, and civic participation—all things he suggests constitute democracy:

> It is the line that forms on the right. It is the don't in "don't shove." It is the hole in the stuffed shirt through which the sawdust slowly trickles; it is the dent in the high hat. Democracy is the recurrent suspicion that more than half of the people are right more than half of the time. . . . Democracy is a letter to the editor.   —E. B. White, "Democracy"

White's definition is elegant because he uses examples that his readers will know. His characteristics—metaphors, really—define democracy not as a conceptual way of governing but as an everyday part of American life.

374–79

Classify it.   Often it is useful to divide or **CLASSIFY** a term. The ways in which democracy unfolds are complex enough to warrant entire text-books, of course, but the following definition, from a political science textbook, divides democracy into two kinds, representative and direct:

> A system of government that gives citizens a regular opportunity to elect the top government officials is usually called a representative democracy or republic. A system that permits citizens to vote directly on laws and policies is often called a direct democracy. At the national level, America is a representative democracy in which citizens select government officials but do not vote on legislation. Some states, however, have provisions for direct legislation through popular refer-endum. For example, California voters in 1995 decided to bar undocu-mented immigrants from receiving some state services.
>
> —Benjamin Ginsberg, Theodore J. Lowi, and Margaret Weir,
> *We the People: An Introduction to American Politics*

Stipulative Definitions

Sometimes a writer will stipulate a certain definition, essentially saying, "This is how I'm defining x." Such definitions are not usually found in a dictionary—and at the same time are central to the argument the writer is making. Here is one example, from an essay by Toni Morrison. Describing a scene from a film in which a newly arrived Greek immigrant, working as a shoe shiner in Grand Central Terminal, chases away an African American competitor, Morrison calls the scene an example of "race talk," a concept she then goes on to define:

> This is race talk, the explicit insertion into everyday life of racial signs and symbols that have no meaning other than pressing African Americans to the lowest level of the racial hierarchy. Popular culture, shaped by film, theater, advertising, the press, television, and litera-ture, is heavily engaged in race talk. It participates freely in this most enduring and efficient rite of passage into American culture: negative appraisals of the native-born black population. Only when the lesson

academic literacies　rhetorical situations　genres　processes　strategies　research MLA / APA　media / design　readings

of racial estrangement is learned is assimilation complete. Whatever the lived experience of immigrants with African Americans—pleasant, beneficial, or bruising—the rhetorical experience renders blacks as noncitizens, already discredited outlaws.

All immigrants fight for jobs and space, and who is there to fight but those who have both? As in the fishing ground struggle between Texas and Vietnamese shrimpers, they displace what and whom they can. Although U.S. history is awash in labor battles, political fights and property wars among all religious and ethnic groups, their struggles are persistently framed as struggles between recent arrivals and blacks. In race talk the move into mainstream America always means buying into the notion of American blacks as the real aliens. Whatever the ethnicity or nationality of the immigrant, his nemesis is understood to be African American.　　—Toni Morrison, "On the Backs of Blacks"

The following example is from a book review of Nancy L. Rosenblum's *Membership and Morals: The Personal Uses of Pluralism in America*, published in the *American Prospect*, a magazine for readers interested in political analysis. In it a Stanford law professor outlines a definition of "the democracy of everyday life":

Democracy, in this understanding of it, means simply treating people as equals, disregarding social standing, avoiding attitudes of either deference or superiority, making allowances for others' weaknesses, and resisting the temptation to respond to perceived slights. It also means protesting everyday instances of arbitrariness and unfairness—from the rudeness of the bakery clerk to the sexism of the car dealer or the racism of those who vandalize the home of the first black neighbors on the block.　　—Kathleen M. Sullivan, "Defining Democracy Down"

Considering the Rhetorical Situation

As a writer or speaker, you need to think about the message that you want to articulate, the audience you want to reach, and the larger context you are writing in.

PURPOSE Your purpose for writing will affect any definitions you include. Would writing an extended definition help you explain something? Would stipulating definitions of key terms help you shape an argument? Could an offbeat definition help you entertain your readers?

AUDIENCE What audience do you want to reach, and are there any terms your readers are unlikely to know (and therefore need to be defined)? Are there terms they might understand differently from the way you're defining them?

GENRE Does your genre require you to define terms? Chances are that if you're reporting information you'll need to define some terms, and some arguments rest on the way you define key terms.

STANCE What is your stance, and do you need to define key terms to show that stance clearly? How you define *fetus*, for example, is likely to reveal your stance on abortion.

MEDIA / DESIGN Your medium will affect the form your definitions take. In a print text, you will need to define terms in your text; if you're giving a speech or presentation, you might also provide images of important terms and their definitions. In an electronic text, you may be able to define terms by linking to an online dictionary definition.

IF YOU NEED MORE HELP

See also the **PROCESSES** chapters for help generating ideas, drafting, revising, and so on if you are writing a whole essay dedicated to defining a term or concept.

academic literacies   rhetorical situations   genres   processes   strategies   research MLA / APA   media / design   readings

Describing 40

When we describe something, we indicate what it looks like—and sometimes how it sounds, feels, smells, and tastes. Descriptive details are a way of showing rather than telling, of helping readers see (or hear, smell, and so on) what we're writing about—that the sky is blue, that Miss Havisham is wearing an old yellowed wedding gown, that the chemicals in the beaker have reacted and smell like rotten eggs. You'll have occasion to describe things in most of the writing you do—from describing a favorite hat in a MEMOIR to detailing a chemical reaction in a lab report. This chapter will help you work with description—and, in particular, help you think about the use of *detail*, about *objectivity and subjectivity*, about *vantage point*, about creating a clear *dominant impression*, and about using description to fit your rhetorical situation.

▲ 216–23

Detail

The goal of using details is to be as specific as possible, providing information that will help your audience imagine the subject or make sense of it. See, for example, how Nancy Mairs, an author with multiple sclerosis, describes the disease in clear, specific terms:

> During its course, which is unpredictable and uncontrollable, one may lose vision, hearing, speech, the ability to walk, control of bladder and/ or bowels, strength in any or all extremities, sensitivity to touch, vibration, and/or pain, potency, coordination of movements—the list of possibilities is lengthy and, yes, horrifying. One may also lose one's sense of humor. That's the easiest to lose and the hardest to survive without.
>
> In the past ten years, I have sustained some of these losses. Characteristic of MS are sudden attacks, called exacerbations, followed by

remissions, and these I have not had. Instead, my disease has been slowly progressive. My left leg is now so weak that I walk with the aid of a brace and a cane, and for distances I use an Amigo, a variation on the electric wheelchair that looks rather like an electrified kiddie car. I no longer have much use of my left hand. Now my right side is weakening as well. I still have the blurred spot in my right eye. Overall, though, I've been lucky so far.   —Nancy Mairs, "On Being a Cripple"

Mairs's gruesome list demonstrates, through *specific details*, how the disease affects sufferers generally and her in particular. We know far more after reading this text than we do from the following more general description, from a National Multiple Sclerosis Society brochure:

> Multiple sclerosis is a chronic, unpredictable disease of the central nervous system (the brain, optic nerves, and spinal cord). It is thought to be an autoimmune disorder. This means the immune system incorrectly attacks the person's healthy tissue.
>
> MS can cause blurred vision, loss of balance, poor coordination, slurred speech, tremors, numbness, extreme fatigue, problems with memory and concentration, paralysis, and blindness. These problems may be permanent, or they may come and go.
>
> —National Multiple Sclerosis Society, *Just the Facts*

Specific details are also more effective than labels, which give little meaningful information. Instead of saying that someone is a "moron" or "really smart," it's better to give details so that readers can understand the reasons behind the label: what does this person *do* or *say* that makes him or her deserve this label? See, for example, how the writer of a news story about shopping on the day after Thanksgiving opens with a description of a happy shopper:

> Last Friday afternoon, the day ritualized consumerism is traditionally at its most frenetic, Alexx Balcuns twirled in front of a full-length mirror at the Ritz Thrift Shop on West Fifty-seventh Street as if inhabited by the soul of Eva Gabor in *Green Acres*. Ms. Balcuns was languishing in a $795 dyed-mink parka her grandmother had just bought her. Ms. Balcuns is six.
>
> —Ginia Bellafante, "Staying Warm and Fuzzy during Uncertain Times"

The writer might simply have said, "A spoiled child admired herself in the mirror." Instead, she shows her subject twirling and "languishing" in a "$795 dyed-mink parka" and seemingly possessed by the soul of the actress Eva Gabor—all details that create a far more vivid description.

Sensory details help readers imagine sounds, odors, tastes, and physical sensations in addition to sights. In the following example, writer Scott Russell Sanders recalls sawing wood as a child. Note how visual details, odors, and even the physical sense of being picked up by his father mingle to form a vivid scene:

> As the saw teeth bit down, the wood released its smell, each kind with its own fragrance, oak or walnut or cherry or pine—usually pine because it was the softest, easiest for a child to work. No matter how weathered and gray the board, no matter how warped and cracked, inside there was this smell waiting, as of something freshly baked. I gathered every smidgen of sawdust and stored it away in coffee cans, which I kept in a drawer of the workbench. When I did not feel like hammering nails I would dump my sawdust on the concrete floor of the garage and landscape it into highways and farms and towns, running miniature cars and trucks along miniature roads. Looming as huge as a colossus, my father worked over and around me, now and again bending down to inspect my work, careful not to trample my creations. It was a landscape that smelled dizzyingly of wood. Even after a bath my skin would carry the smell, and so would my father's hair, when he lifted me for a bedtime hug.
>
> —Scott Russell Sanders, *The Paradise of Bombs*

Whenever you describe something, you'll select from many possible details you might use. Simply put, to exhaust all the details available to describe something is impossible—and would exhaust your readers as well. To focus your description, you'll need to determine the kinds of details appropriate for your subject. They will vary, depending on your **PURPOSE**.   ▌55–56
See, for example, how the details might differ in three different genres:

- For a **MEMOIR** *about an event,* you might choose details that are significant for you, that evoke the sights, sounds, and other sensations that give meaning to your event.   ▲ 216–23

224–34

- For a **PROFILE**, you're likely to select details that will reinforce the dominant impression you want to give, that portray the event from the perspective you want readers to see.

- *For a lab report,* you need to give certain specifics — what equipment was used, what procedures were followed, what exactly were the results.

Deciding on a focus for your description can help you see it better, as you'll look for details that contribute to that focus.

Objectivity and Subjectivity

Descriptions can be written with objectivity, with subjectivity, or with a mixture of both. Objective descriptions attempt to be uncolored by personal opinion or emotion. Police reports and much news writing aim to describe events objectively; scientific writing strives for objectivity in describing laboratory procedures and results. See, for example, the following objective account of what happened at the World Trade Center on September 11, 2001:

> **World Trade Center Disaster — Tuesday, September 11, 2001**
>
> On Tuesday, September 11, 2001, at 8:45 a.m. New York local time, One World Trade Center, the north tower, was hit by a hijacked 767 commercial jet airplane loaded with fuel for a transcontinental flight. Two World Trade Center, the south tower, was hit by a similar hijacked jet eighteen minutes later, at 9:03 a.m. (In separate but related attacks, the Pentagon building near Washington, D.C., was hit by a hijacked 757 at 9:43 a.m., and at 10:10 a.m. a fourth hijacked jetliner crashed in Pennsylvania.) The south tower, WTC 2, which had been hit second, was the first to suffer a complete structural collapse, at 10:05 a.m., 62 minutes after being hit itself, 80 minutes after the first impact. The north tower, WTC 1, then also collapsed, at 10:29 a.m., 104 minutes after being hit. WTC 7, a substantial forty-seven-story office building in its own right, built in 1987, was damaged by the collapsing towers, caught fire, and later in the afternoon also totally collapsed.
>
> — "World Trade Center," *GreatBuildings.com*

academic literacies · rhetorical situations · genres · processes · strategies · research MLA / APA · media / design · readings

Subjective descriptions, on the other hand, allow the writer's opinions and emotions to come through. A house can be described as comfortable, with a lived-in look, or as rundown and in need of a paint job and a new roof. Here's a subjective description of the planes striking the World Trade Center, as told by a woman watching from a nearby building:

> Incredulously, while looking out [the] window at the damage and carnage the first plane had inflicted, I saw the second plane abruptly come into my right field of vision and deliberately, with shimmering intention, thunder full-force into the south tower. It was so close, so low, so huge and fast, so intent on its target that I swear to you, I swear to you, I felt the vengeance and rage emanating from the plane.
>
> —Debra Fontaine, "Witnessing"

Vantage Point

Sometimes you'll want or need to describe something from a certain vantage point. Where you locate yourself in relation to what you're describing will determine what you can perceive (and so describe) and what you can't. You may describe your subject from a *stationary vantage point*, from which you (and your readers) see your subject from one angle only, as if you were a camera. This description of one of three photographs that captured a woman's death records only what the camera saw from one angle at one particular moment:

> The first showed some people on a fire escape—a fireman, a woman and a child. The fireman had a nice strong jaw and looked very brave. The woman was holding the child. Smoke was pouring from the building behind them. A rescue ladder was approaching, just a few feet away, and the fireman had one arm around the woman and one arm reaching out toward the ladder.
>
> —Nora Ephron, "The Boston Photographs"

By contrast, this description of a drive to an Italian villa uses a *moving vantage point*; the writer recounts what he saw as he passed through a gate in a city wall, moving from city to country:

> La Pietra—"the stone"—is situated one mile from the Porta San Gallo, an entry to the Old City of Florence. You drive there along the Via Bolognese, twisting past modern apartment blocks, until you come to a gate, which swings open—and there you are, at the upper end of a long lane of cypresses facing a great ocher palazzo; with olive groves spreading out on both sides over an expanse of fifty-seven acres. There's something almost comically wonderful about the effect: here, the city, with its winding avenue; there, on the other side of a wall, the country, fertile and gray green.   —James Traub, "Italian Hours"

The description of quarries in the following section uses *multiple vantage points* to capture the quarries from many perspectives.

This ad for Adidas sports apparel combines photos of two basketball games, one in New York City and one in Ho Chi Minh City, to show the universality of the game. Both photos use a stationary vantage point, looking down on the court from above the backboard.

SOMEWHERE ON AN AIRPLANE A MAN IS TRYING TO RIP OPEN A SMALL BAG OF PEANUTS.

The visual image of vast sky and desert in this Harley-Davidson motorcycle ad creates a dominant impression of spaciousness and freedom that contrasts with the written text to argue that riding on a Harley is far better than sitting on a cramped airplane.

Dominant Impression

With any description, your aim is to create some dominant impression—the overall feeling that the individual details add up to. The dominant impression may be implied, growing out of the details themselves. For example, Scott Russell Sanders's memory of the smell of sawdust creates a dominant impression of warmth and comfort: the "fragrance . . . as of something freshly baked," sawdust "stored . . . away in coffee cans," a young boy "lifted . . . for a bedtime hug." Sometimes, though, a writer will state the dominant impression directly, in addition to creating it with details. In an essay about Indiana limestone quarries, Sanders makes the dominant impression clear from the start: "they are battlefields."

> The quarries will not be domesticated. They are not backyard pools; they are battlefields. Each quarry is an arena where violent struggles have taken place between machines and planet, between human ingenuity and brute

resisting stone, between mind and matter. Waste rock litters the floor and brim like rubble in a bombed city. The ragged pits might have been the basements of vanished skyscrapers. Stones weighing tens of tons lean against one another at precarious angles, as if they have been thrown there by some gigantic strength and have not yet finished falling. Wrecked machinery hulks in the weeds, grimly rusting, the cogs and wheels, twisted rails, battered engine housings, trackless bulldozers and burst boilers like junk from an armored regiment. Everywhere the ledges are scarred from drills, as if from an artillery barrage or machine-gun strafing. Stumbling onto one of these abandoned quarries and gazing at the ruins, you might be left wondering who had won the battle, men or stone.

—Scott Russell Sanders, *The Paradise of Bombs*

The rest of his description, full of more figurative language ("like rubble in a bombed city," "like junk from an armored regiment," "as if from an artillery barrage or machine-gun strafing") reinforces the direct "they are battlefields" statement.

Organizing Descriptions

You can organize descriptions in many ways. When your description is primarily visual, you will probably organize it spatially: from left to right, top to bottom, outside to inside. One variation on this approach is to begin with the most significant or noteworthy feature and move outward from that center, as Ephron does. Or you may create a chronological description of objects as you move past or through them in space, as Traub does in his description of his drive. You might even pile up details to create a dominant impression, as Sanders and Mairs do, especially if your description draws on senses besides vision.

Considering the Rhetorical Situation

As a writer or speaker, you need to think about the message that you want to articulate, the audience you want to reach, and the larger context you are writing in.

academic literacies · rhetorical situations · genres · processes · strategies · research MLA / APA · media / design · readings

PURPOSE

Your purpose may affect the way you use description. If you're arguing that a government should intervene in another country's civil war, for example, describing the anguish of refugees from that war could make your argument more persuasive. If you're analyzing a painting, you will likely need to describe it.

55–56

AUDIENCE

Who is your audience, and will they need detailed description to understand the points you wish to make?

57–60

GENRE

Does your genre require description? A lab report generally calls for you to describe materials and results; a memoir about grandma should probably describe her— her smile, her dress, her apple pie.

61–63

STANCE

The way you describe things can help you convey your stance. For example, the details you choose can show you to be objective (or not), careful or casual.

64–67

MEDIA / DESIGN

Your medium will affect the form your description can take. In a print or spoken text, you will likely rely on words, though you may also include visuals. In an electronic text, you can easily provide links to visuals as well as audio clips and so may need fewer words of your own.

68–70

IF YOU NEED MORE HELP

See also **FREEWRITING**, **CUBING**, and **LISTING**, three methods of generating ideas that can be especially helpful for developing detailed descriptions. Sometimes you may be assigned to write a whole essay describing something: see the **PROCESSES** chapters for help drafting, revising, and so on.

289–97
279

41 Dialogue

216–23
224–34
206–15
156–82

Dialogue is a way of including people's own words in a text, letting readers hear those people's voices—not just what you say about them. **MEMOIRS** and **PROFILES** often include dialogue, and many other genres do as well: **LITERARY ANALYSES** often quote dialogue from the texts they analyze, and essays **ARGUING A POSITION** might quote an authoritative source as support for a claim. This chapter provides brief guidelines for the conventions of paragraphing and punctuating dialogue and offers some good examples of how you can use dialogue most effectively to suit your own rhetorical situations.

Why Add Dialogue?

Dialogue is a way of bringing in voices other than your own, of showing people and scenes rather than just telling about them. It can add color and texture to your writing, making it memorable. Most important, however, dialogue should be more than just colorful or interesting. It needs to contribute to your rhetorical purpose, to support the point you're making. See how dialogue is used in the following excerpt from a magazine profile of the Mall of America, how it gives us a sense of the place that the journalist's own words could not provide:

> Two pubescent girls in retainers and braces sat beside me sipping coffees topped with whipped cream and chocolate sprinkles, their shopping bags gathered tightly around their legs, their eyes fixed on the passing crowds. They came, they said, from Shakopee—"It's no-where," one of them explained. The megamall, she added, was "a buzz at first, but now it seems pretty normal. 'Cept my parents are like Twenty Questions every time I want to come here. 'Specially since the shooting."

> On a Sunday night, she elaborated, three people had been wounded when shots were fired in a dispute over a San Jose Sharks jacket. "In the *mall*," her friend reminded me. "Right here at megamall. A shooting."
> "It's like nowhere's safe," the first added.
>
> —David Guterson, "Enclosed. Encyclopedic. Endured. One Week at the Mall of America"

Of course it was the writer who decided whom and what to quote, and Guterson deliberately chose words that capture the young shoppers' speech patterns, quoting fragments ("In the *mall*. . . . Right here at megamall. A shooting"), slang ("a buzz at first," "my parents are like Twenty Questions"), even contractions ("'cept," "'specially").

Integrating Dialogue into Your Writing

There are certain conventions for punctuating and paragraphing dialogue:

- *Punctuating.* Enclose each speaker's words in quotation marks, and put any end punctuation—periods, question marks, and exclamation marks—inside the closing quotation mark. Whether you're transcribing words you heard or making them up, you will sometimes need to add punctuation to reflect the rhythm and sound of the speech. In the last sentence of the example below, see how Chang-Rae Lee adds a comma after *well* and italicizes *practice* to show intonation—and attitude.

- *Paragraphing.* When you're writing dialogue that includes more than one speaker, start a new paragraph each time the speaker changes.

- *Signal phrases.* Sometimes you'll need to introduce dialogue with SIGNAL PHRASES—"I said," "she asked," and so on—to make clear who is speaking. At times, however, the speaker will be clear enough, and you won't need any signal phrases.

487–90

Here is a conversation between a mother and her son that illustrates each of the conventions for punctuating and paragraphing dialogue:

> "Whom do I talk to?" she said. She would mostly speak to me in Korean, and I would answer back in English.

"The bank manager, who else?"

"What do I say?"

"Whatever you want to say."

"Don't speak to me like that!" she cried.

"It's just that you should be able to do it yourself," I said.

"You know how I feel about this!"

"Well, maybe then you should consider it *practice*," I answered lightly, using the Korean word to make sure she understood.

—Chang-Rae Lee, "Coming Home Again"

Interviews

Interviews are a kind of dialogue, with different conventions for punctuation. When you're transcribing an interview, give each speaker's name each time he or she speaks, starting a new line but not indenting, and do not use quotation marks. Here is an excerpt from a National Public Radio interview that Audie Cornish conducted with writer Susan Cain:

> **Audie Cornish:** In the 1940s and '50s, the message to most Americans was, don't be shy. And in the era of reality television, Twitter and relentless self-promotion, it seems that cultural mandate is in overdrive.
>
> A new book tells the story of how things came to be this way, and it's called *Quiet: The Power of Introverts in a World that Can't Stop Talking*. The author is Susan Cain, and she joins us from the NPR studios in New York to talk more about it. Welcome, Susan.
>
> **Susan Cain:** Thank you. It's such a pleasure to be here, Audie.
>
> **Cornish:** Well, we're happy to have you. And to start out — I think we should get this on the record — do you consider yourself an introvert or an extrovert?
>
> **Cain:** Oh, I definitely consider myself an introvert, and that was part of the fuel for me to write the book.
>
> **Cornish:** And what's the difference between being an introvert versus being shy? I mean, what's your definition?
>
> **Cain:** So introversion is really about having a preference for lower-stimulation environments — so just a preference for quiet, for less noise, for less action — whereas extroverts really crave more stimulation

academic literacies / rhetorical situations / genres / processes / strategies / research MLA / APA / media / design / readings

in order to feel at their best. And what's important to understand about this is that many people believe that introversion is about being antisocial. And that's really a misperception because actually, it's just that introverts are differently social. So they would prefer to have, you know, a glass of wine with a close friend as opposed to going to a loud party full of strangers.

Now shyness, on the other hand, is about a fear of negative social judgment. So you can be introverted without having that particular fear at all, and you can be shy but also be an extrovert.

Cornish: And in the book, you say that there's a spectrum. So if some people are listening and they think, well, I, too, like a glass of wine and a party. It's like we all have these tendencies.

Cain: Yeah, yeah. That's an important thing. And, in fact, Carl Jung, the psychologist who first popularized these terms all the way back in the 1920s — even he said there's no such thing as a pure introvert or a pure extrovert, and he said such a man would be in a lunatic asylum.

Cornish: That makes me worry because I took your test in the book and I'm like, 90 percent extroverted, basically.

[*soundbite of laughter*]

Cornish: Now, you mentioned going back into the history. And I want to talk more about that because I was really fascinated by how you showed how this extrovert ideal — you call it — came to be. When did being introverted move from being a character trait to being looked at as a problem?

Cain: Yeah. What I found is, to some extent, we've always had an admiration for extroversion in our culture. But the extrovert ideal really came to play at the turn of the 20th century, when we had the rise of big business. And so suddenly, people were flocking to the cities, and they were needing to prove themselves in big corporations — at job interviews and on sales calls.

And so at that moment in time, we moved from what cultural historians call a culture of character to a culture of personality. So during the culture of character, what was important was the good deeds that you performed when nobody was looking. You know, Abraham Lincoln is the embodiment of the culture of character, and people celebrated him back then for being a man who did not offend by superiority.

But at the turn of the century, when we moved into this culture of personality, suddenly, what was admired was to be magnetic and charismatic. And then at the same time, we suddenly had the rise of movies and movie stars. And movie stars, of course, were the embodiment of what it meant to be a charismatic figure. And so part of people's fascination with these movie stars was for what they could learn from them, and bring with them to their own jobs.

—"Quiet, Please: Unleashing 'The Power of Introverts'"

In preparing the interview transcript for publication, NPR had to add punctuation, which of course was not part of the oral conversation, and probably deleted pauses and verbal expressions such as *um* and *uh*. At the same time, the editor kept informal constructions, such as incomplete sentences, which are typical answers to questions ("Yeah.") to maintain the oral flavor of the interview and to reflect Cain's voice.

Considering the Rhetorical Situation

As a writer or speaker, you need to think about the message that you want to articulate, the audience you want to reach, and the larger context of your writing.

55–56 **PURPOSE**   Your purpose will affect any use of dialogue. Dialogue can help bring a profile to life and make it memorable. Interviews with experts or firsthand witnesses can add credibility to a report or argument.

57–60 **AUDIENCE**   Whom do you want to reach, and will dialogue help? Sometimes actual dialogue can help readers hear human voices behind facts or reason.

61–63 **GENRE**   Does your genre require dialogue? If you're evaluating or analyzing a literary work, for instance, you may wish to include dialogue from that work. If you're writing a profile of a person or event, dialogue can help you bring your subject to life. Similarly, an interview with an expert can add credibility to a report or argument.

STANCE What is your stance, and can dialogue help you communicate that stance? For example, excerpts of an interview may allow you to challenge someone's views and make your own views clear.

64–67

MEDIA / DESIGN Your medium will affect the way you present dialogue. In a print text, you will present dialogue through written words. In an oral or electronic text, you might include actual recorded dialogue.

68–70

IF YOU NEED MORE HELP

See also the guidelines on **INTERVIEWING EXPERTS** for advice on setting up and recording interviews and those on **QUOTING**, **PARAPHRASING**, and **SUMMARIZING** for help deciding how to integrate dialogue into your text.

463–64
478–90

42 Explaining Processes

When you explain a process, you tell how something is (or was) done—how a bill becomes a law, how an embryo develops—or you tell someone how to do something—how to throw a curve ball, how to write a memoir. This chapter focuses on those two kinds of explanations, offering examples and guidelines for explaining a process in a way that works for your rhetorical situation.

Explaining a Process Clearly

Whether the process is simple or complex, you'll need to identify its key stages or steps and explain them one by one, in order. The sequence matters because it allows readers to follow your explanation; it is especially important when you're explaining a process that others are going to follow. Most often you'll explain a process chronologically, from start to finish. **TRANSITIONS**—words like *first*, *next*, *then*, and so on—are often necessary, therefore, to show readers how the stages of a process relate to one another and to indicate time sequences. Finally, you'll find that verbs matter; they indicate the actions that take place at each stage of the process.

349 ◆

Explaining How Something Is Done

All processes consist of steps, and when you explain how something is done, you describe each step, generally in order, from first to last. Here, for example, is an explanation of how French fries are made, from an essay published in the *New Yorker*:

> Fast-food French fries are made from a baking potato like an Idaho russet, or any other variety that is mealy, or starchy, rather than waxy. The potatoes are harvested, cured, washed, peeled, sliced, and then blanched—cooked enough so that the insides have a fluffy texture but not so much that the fry gets soft and breaks. Blanching is followed by drying, and drying by a thirty-second deep fry, to give the potatoes a crisp shell. Then the fries are frozen until the moment of service, when they are deep-fried again, this time for somewhere around three minutes. Depending on the fast-food chain involved, there are other steps interspersed in this process. McDonald's fries, for example, are briefly dipped in a sugar solution, which gives them their golden-brown color; Burger King fries are dipped in a starch batter, which is what gives those fries their distinctive hard shell and audible crunch. But the result is similar. The potato that is first harvested in the field is roughly 80 percent water. The process of creating a French fry consists, essentially, of removing as much of that water as possible—through blanching, drying, and deep-frying—and replacing it with fat.
>
> —Malcolm Gladwell, "The Trouble with Fries"

Gladwell clearly explains the process of making French fries, showing us the specific steps—how the potatoes "are harvested, cured, washed, peeled, sliced," and so on—and using clear transitions—"followed by," "then," "until," "when"—and action verbs to show the sequence. His last sentence makes his stance clear, pointing out that the process of creating a French fry consists of removing as much of a potato's water as possible "and replacing it with fat."

Explaining How to Do Something

In explaining how to do something, you are giving instruction so that others can follow the process themselves. See how Martha Stewart explains the process of making French fries. She starts by listing the ingredients and then describes the steps:

4 medium baking potatoes
2 tablespoons olive oil
1$\frac{1}{2}$ teaspoons salt
$\frac{1}{4}$ teaspoon freshly ground pepper
malt vinegar (optional)

1. Heat oven to 400 degrees. Place a heavy baking sheet in the oven. Scrub and rinse the potatoes well, and then cut them lengthwise into $\frac{1}{2}$-inch-wide batons. Place the potato batons in a medium bowl, and toss them with the olive oil, salt, and pepper.

2. When baking sheet is hot, about 15 minutes, remove from the oven. Place prepared potatoes on the baking sheet in a single layer. Return to oven, and bake until potatoes are golden on the bottom, about 30 minutes. Turn potatoes over, and continue cooking until golden all over, about 15 minutes more. Serve immediately.

—Martha Stewart, *Favorite Comfort Food*

Coming from Martha Stewart, the explanation leaves out no details, giving a clear sequence of steps and descriptive verbs that tell us exactly what to do: "heat," "place," "scrub and rinse," and so on. After she gives the recipe, she even goes on to explain the process of *serving* the fries — "Serve these French fries with a bowl of malt vinegar" — and reminds us that "they are also delicious dipped in spicy mustard, mayonnaise, and, of course, ketchup."

Explaining a Process Visually

607–15

Some processes are best explained **VISUALLY**, with diagrams or photographs. See, for example, how a blogger explains one process of shaping dough into a bagel — giving the details in words and then showing us in photos how to do it:

academic literacies · rhetorical situations · genres · processes · strategies · research MLA / APA · media / design · readings

Roll each portion into a ball and place on prepared baking sheet. Cover with a damp towel and let rest for 20 minutes.

Roll balls into 6- to 7-inch ropes. If the dough resists, just let it rest for a few minutes and try rolling it again.

Wrap the dough around your palm and the back of your hand, overlapping the ends by an inch or two.

Press the overlapping edges against the countertop, rolling the bagel back and forth to seal the seam.

Place bagels back on baking sheet and cover with plastic wrap that has been coated with cooking spray.

—Maggie Lauer, *The Other Side of Fifty*

Considering the Rhetorical Situation

As always, you need to think about the message that you want to articulate, the audience you want to reach, and the larger context you are writing in.

PURPOSE   Your purpose for writing will affect the way you explain a process. If you're arguing that we should avoid eating fast food, you might explain the process by which chicken nuggets are made. But to give information about how to fry chicken, you would explain the process quite differently.

AUDIENCE   Whom are you trying to reach, and will you need to provide any special background information or to interest them in the process before you explain it?

GENRE   Does your genre require you to explain a process? In a lab report, for example, you'll need to explain processes used in the experiment. You might want to explain a process in a profile of an activity or a proposal for a solution.

STANCE   If you're giving practical directions for doing something, you'll want to take a straightforward "do this, then do that" perspective. If you're writing to entertain, you need to take a clever or amusing stance.

MEDIA / DESIGN   Your medium will affect the way you explain a process. In a print text, you can use both words and images. On the web, you may have the option of showing an animation of the process as well.

IF YOU NEED MORE HELP

See also **PROFILES** if you are writing about an activity that needs to be explained. See **NARRATING** for more advice on organizing an explanation chronologically. Sometimes you may be assigned to write a whole essay or report that explains a process; see **PROCESSES** for help drafting, revising, and so on.

Narrating **43**

▲ 156–82

Narratives are stories. As a writing strategy, a good narrative can lend support to most kinds of writing—in a **POSITION PAPER** arguing for Title IX compliance, for example, you might include a brief narrative about an Olympic sprinter who might never have had an opportunity to compete on a track-and-field team without Title IX. Or you can bring a **PROFILE** of a favorite coach to life with an anecdote about a pep talk he or she once gave before a championship track meet. Whatever your larger writing purpose, you need to make sure that any narratives you add support that purpose—they should not be inserted simply to tell an interesting story. You'll also need to compose them carefully—to put them in a clear *sequence*, include *pertinent detail*, and make sure they are appropriate to your particular rhetorical situation.

▲ 224–34

Sequencing

When we write a narrative, we arrange events in a particular sequence. Writers typically sequence narratives in chronological order, reverse chronological order, or as a flashback.

Use chronological order. Often you may tell the story chronologically, starting at the beginning of an event and working through to the end, as Maya Angelou does in this brief narrative from an essay about her high school graduation:

> The school band struck up a march and all classes filed in as had been rehearsed. We stood in front of our seats, as assigned, and on a signal from the choir director, we sat. No sooner had this been accomplished

419

than the band started to play the national anthem. We rose again and sang the song, after which we recited the pledge of allegiance. We remained standing for a brief minute before the choir director and the principal signaled to us, rather desperately I thought, to take our seats. —Maya Angelou, "Graduation"

Use reverse chronological order. You may also begin with the final action and work back to the first, as Aldo Leopold does in this narrative about cutting down a tree:

Now our saw bites into the 1890s, called gay by those whose eyes turn cityward rather than landward. We cut 1899, when the last passenger pigeon collided with a charge of shot near Babcock, two counties to the north; we cut 1898, when a dry fall, followed by a snowless winter, froze the soil seven feet deep and killed the apple trees; 1897, another drouth year, when another forestry commission came into being; 1896, when 25,000 prairie chickens were shipped to market from the village of Spooner alone; 1895, another year of fires; 1894, another drouth year; and 1893, the year of "the Bluebird Storm," when a March blizzard reduced the migrating bluebirds to near zero.

—Aldo Leopold, *A Sand County Almanac*

253–64 **RÉSUMÉS** are one genre where we generally use reverse chronological order, listing the most recent jobs or degrees first and then working backward. Notice, too, that we usually write these as narratives—telling what we have done rather than just naming positions we have held:

Sept. 2014–present	*Student worker*, Department of Information Management, Central State University, Wilberforce, OH. Compile data and format reports using Excel, Word, and university database.
June–Sept. 2014	*Intern*, QuestPro Corporation, West Louisville, KY. Assisted in development of software.
Sept. 2013–June 2014	*Bagger*, Ace Groceries, Elba, KY. Bagged customers' purchases.

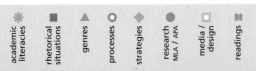

academic literacies • rhetorical situations • genres • processes • strategies • research MLA / APA • media / design • readings

Use a flashback. You can sometimes put a flashback in the middle of a narrative, to tell about an incident that illuminates the larger narrative. Terry Tempest Williams does this in an essay about the startling incidence of breast cancer in her family: she recalls a dinnertime conversation with her father right after her mother's death from cancer, when she learned for the first time what caused all of the cancer in her family:

> Over dessert, I shared a recurring dream of mine. I told my father that for years, as long as I could remember, I saw this flash of light in the night in the desert. That this image had so permeated my being, I could not venture south without seeing it again, on the horizon, illuminating buttes and mesas.
>
> "You did see it," he said.
>
> "Saw what?" I asked, a bit tentative.
>
> "The bomb. The cloud. We were driving home from Riverside, California. You were sitting on your mother's lap. She was pregnant. In fact, I remember the date, September 7, 1957. We had just gotten out of the Service. We were driving north, past Las Vegas. It was an hour or so before dawn, when this explosion went off. We not only heard it, but felt it. I thought the oil tanker in front of us had blown up. We pulled over and suddenly, rising from the desert floor, we saw it, clearly, this golden-stemmed cloud, the mushroom. The sky seemed to vibrate with an eerie pink glow. Within a few minutes, a light ash was raining on the car."
>
> I stared at my father. This was new information to me.
>
> —Terry Tempest Williams, "The Clan of the One-Breasted Women"

Williams could have simply announced this information as a fact—but see how much more powerful it is when told in narrative form.

Use time markers. Time markers help readers follow a sequence of events. The most obvious time markers are those that simply label the time, as the narrative entries in a diary, journal, or log might. For example, here is the final part of the narrative kept in a diary by a doomed Antarctic explorer:

WEDNESDAY, MARCH 21: Got within eleven miles of depot. Monday night; had to lay up all yesterday in severe blizzard. Today forlorn hope, Wilson and Bowers going to depot for fuel.

MARCH 22 and 23: Blizzard bad as ever—Wilson and Bowers unable to start—tomorrow last chance—no fuel and only one or two [days] of food left—must be near the end. Have decided it shall be natural—we shall march for the depot with or without our effects and die in our tracks.

THURSDAY, MARCH 29: Since the 21st we have had a continuous gale from W.S.W. and S.W. We had fuel to make two cups of tea apiece and bare food for two days on the 20th. Every day we have been ready to start for our depot eleven miles away, but outside the door of the tent it remains a scene of whirling drift. I do not think we can hope for any better things now. We shall stick it out to the end, but we are getting weaker, of course, and the end cannot be far. It seems a pity, but I do not think I can write more. . . .

Last Entry: For God's sake look after our people.

—Robert F. Scott, *Scott's Last Expedition: The Journals*

More often you will integrate time markers into the prose itself, as is done in this narrative about a woman preparing and delivering meals to workers at a cotton gin:

She made her plans meticulously and in secret. <u>One early evening</u> to see if she was ready, she placed stones in two five-gallon pails and carried them three miles to the cotton gin. She rested a little, and then, discarding some rocks, she walked in the darkness to the sawmill five miles farther along the dirt road. <u>On her way back</u> to her little house and her babies, she dumped the remaining rocks along the path.

    <u>That same night</u> she worked into the early hours boiling chicken and frying ham. She made dough and filled the rolled-out pastry with meat. <u>At last</u> she went to sleep.

    <u>The next morning</u> she left her house carrying the meat pies, lard, an iron brazier, and coals for a fire. <u>Just before lunch</u> she appeared in an empty lot behind the cotton gin. <u>As the dinner noon bell rang</u>, she

dropped the savors into boiling fat, and the aroma rose and floated over to the workers who spilled out of the gin, covered with white lint, looking like specters.

—Maya Angelou, *Wouldn't Take Nothing for My Journey Now*

Use transitions. Another way to help readers follow a narrative is with **TRANSITIONS**, words like *first, then, meanwhile, at last,* and so on. See how the following paragraphs from Langston Hughes's classic essay about meeting Jesus use transitions (and time markers) to advance the action:

349

<u>Suddenly</u> the whole room broke into a sea of shouting, <u>as</u> they saw me rise. Waves of rejoicing swept the place. Women leaped in the air. My aunt threw her arms around me. The minister took me by the hand and led me to the platform.

<u>When</u> things quieted down, in a hushed silence, punctuated by a few ecstatic "Amens," all the new young lambs were blessed in the name of God. <u>Then</u> joyous singing filled the room. <u>That night,</u> for the last time in my life but one—for I was a big boy twelve years old—I cried.
                                                      —Langston Hughes, "Salvation"

Including Pertinent Detail

When you include a narrative in your writing, you must decide which details you need—and which ones you don't need. For example, you don't want to include so much detail that the narrative distracts the reader from the larger text. You must also decide whether you need to include any background, to set the stage for the narrative. The amount of detail you include depends on your audience and purpose: How much detail does your audience need? How much detail do you need to make your meaning clear? In an essay on the suspicion African American men often face when walking at night, a journalist deliberately presents a story without setting the stage at all:

My first victim was a woman—white, well dressed, probably in her late twenties. I came upon her late one evening on a deserted street in Hyde Park, a relatively affluent neighborhood in an otherwise mean, impoverished section of Chicago. As I swung onto the avenue behind her, there seemed to be a discreet, uninflammatory distance between us. Not so. She cast back a worried glance. To her, the youngish black man—a broad six feet two inches with a beard and billowing hair, both hands shoved into the pockets of a bulky military jacket—seemed menacingly close. After a few more quick glimpses, she picked up her pace and was soon running in earnest. Within seconds she disappeared into a cross street. —Brent Staples, "Black Men and Public Space"

Words like *victim* and phrases like "came upon her" lead us to assume the narrator is scary and perhaps dangerous. We don't know why he is walking on the deserted street because he hasn't told us: he simply begins with the moment he and the woman encounter each other. For his purposes, that's all the audience needs to know at first, and details of his physical appearance that explain the woman's response come later, after he tells us about the encounter. Had he given us those details at the outset, the narrative would not have been nearly so effective. In a way, Staples lets the story sneak up on us, as the woman apparently felt he had on her.

Other times you'll need to provide more background information, as an MIT professor does when she uses an anecdote to introduce an essay about young children's experiences with electronic toys. First the writer tells us a little about Merlin, the computer tic-tac-toe game that the children in her anecdote play with. As you'll see, the anecdote would be hard to follow without the introduction:

Among the first generation of computational objects was Merlin, which challenged children to games of tic-tac-toe. For children who had only played games with human opponents, reaction to this object was intense. For example, while Merlin followed an optimal strategy for winning tic-tac-toe most of the time, it was programmed to make a slip every once in a while. So when children discovered strategies that allowed them to win and then tried these strategies a second time, they usually would not work. The machine gave the impression of not being "dumb enough" to let down its defenses twice. Robert,

academic literacies · rhetorical situations · genres · processes · strategies · research MLA / APA · media / design · readings

seven, playing with his friends on the beach, watched his friend Craig perform the "winning trick," but when he tried it, Merlin did not slip up and the game ended in a draw. Robert, confused and frustrated, threw Merlin into the sand and said, "Cheater. I hope your brains break." He was overheard by Craig and Greg, aged six and eight, who salvaged the by-now very sandy toy and took it upon themselves to set Robert straight. "Merlin doesn't know if it cheats," says Craig. "It doesn't know if you break it, Robert. It's not alive." Greg adds, "It's smart enough to make the right kinds of noises. But it doesn't really know if it loses. And when it cheats, it don't even know it's cheating." Jenny, six, interrupts with disdain: "Greg, to cheat you have to know you are cheating. Knowing is part of cheating."

—Sherry Turkle, "Cuddling Up to Cyborg Babies"

Opening and Closing with Narratives

Narratives are often useful as **BEGINNINGS** to essays and other kinds of writing. Everyone likes a good story, so an interesting or pithy narrative can be a good way to get your audience's attention. In the following introductory paragraph, a historian tells a gruesome but gripping story to attract our attention to a subject that might not otherwise merit our interest, bubonic plague:

331–38

In October 1347, two months after the fall of Calais, Genoese trading ships put into the harbor of Messina in Sicily with dead and dying men at the oars. The ships had come from the Black Sea port of Caffa (now Feodosiya) in the Crimea, where the Genoese maintained a trading post. The diseased sailors showed strange black swellings about the size of an egg or an apple in the armpits and groin. The swellings oozed blood and pus and were followed by spreading boils and black blotches on the skin from internal bleeding. The sick suffered severe pain and died quickly, within five days of the first symptoms. As the disease spread, other symptoms of continuous fever and spitting of blood appeared instead of the swellings or buboes. These victims coughed and sweated heavily and died even more quickly, within three days or less, sometimes in twenty-four hours. In both types everything that issued from the body—breath, sweat, blood from the buboes and lungs, bloody urine, and blood-blackened excrement—smelled foul. Depression and despair accompanied the physical symptoms, and before the end "death is seen seated on the face."

—Barbara Tuchman, "This Is the End of the World: The Black Death"

Imagine how different the preceding paragraph would be if it weren't in the form of a narrative. Imagine, for example, that Tuchman began by defining bubonic plague. Would that have gotten your interest? The piece was written for a general audience; how might it have been different if it had been written for scientists? Would they need (or appreciate) the story told here?

338–42 Narrative can be a good way of **ENDING** a text, too, by winding up a discussion with an illustration of the main point. Here, for instance, is a concluding paragraph from an essay on American values and Las Vegas weddings.

I sat next to one . . . wedding party in a Strip restaurant the last time I was in Las Vegas. The marriage had just taken place; the bride still wore her dress, the mother her corsage. A bored waiter poured out a few swallows of pink champagne ("on the house") for everyone but the bride, who was too young to be served. "You'll need something with more kick than that," the bride's father said with heavy jocularity to his new son-in-law; the ritual jokes about the wedding night had a certain Panglossian character, since the bride was clearly several months pregnant. Another round of pink champagne, this time not on the house, and the bride began to cry. "It was just as nice," she sobbed, "as I hoped and dreamed it would be."

—Joan Didion, "Marrying Absurd"

No doubt Didion makes her points about American values clearly and cogently in the essay. But concluding with this story lets us *see* (and hear) what she is saying about Las Vegas wedding chapels, which sell "'niceness,' the facsimile of proper ritual, to children who do not know how else to find it, how to make the arrangements, how to do it 'right.'"

Considering the Rhetorical Situation

As a writer or speaker, you need to think about the message that you want to articulate, the audience you want to reach, and the larger context you are writing in.

PURPOSE
Your purpose will affect the way you use narrative. For example, in an essay about seat belt laws, you might tell about the painful rehabilitation of a teenager who was not wearing a seat belt and was injured in an accident in order to persuade readers that seat belt use should be mandatory.
55–56

AUDIENCE
Whom do you want to reach, and do you have an anecdote or other narrative that will help them understand your topic or persuade them that your argument has merit?
57–60

GENRE
Does your genre require you to include narrative? A memoir about an important event might be primarily narrative, whereas a reflection about an event might focus more on the significance of the event than on what happened.
61–63

STANCE
What is your stance, and do you have any stories that would help you convey that stance? A funny story, for example, can help create a humorous stance.
64–67

MEDIA / DESIGN
In a print or spoken text, you will likely be limited to brief narratives, perhaps illustrated with photos or other images. In an electronic text, you might have the option of linking to full-length narratives or visuals available on the web.
68–70

IF YOU NEED MORE HELP

See also the **PROCESSES** chapters if you are assigned to write a narrative essay and need help drafting, revising, and so on. Two special kinds of narratives are **LAB REPORTS** (which use narrative to describe the steps in an experiment from beginning to end) and **RÉSUMÉS** (which essentially tell the story of the work we've done, at school and on the job).

279

Glossary
253–64

44 Taking Essay Exams

Essay exams present writers with special challenges. You must write quickly, on a topic presented to you on the spot, to show your instructor what you know about a specific body of information. This chapter offers advice on how to take essay exams.

Considering the Rhetorical Situation

55–56 **PURPOSE**
In an essay exam, your purpose is to show that you have mastered certain material and that you can analyze and apply it in an essay. You may need to make an argument or simply to convey information on a topic.

57–60 **AUDIENCE**
Will your course instructor be reading your exam, or a TA? Sometimes standardized tests are read by groups of trained readers. What specific criteria will your audience use to evaluate your writing?

61–63 **GENRE**
Does the essay question specify or suggest a certain genre? In a literature course, you may need to write a compelling literary analysis of a passage. In a history course, you may need to write an argument for the significance of a key historical event. In an economics course, you may need to contrast the economies of the North and South before the Civil War. If the essay question doesn't specify a genre, look for keywords such as *argue, evaluate,* or *explain,* which point to a certain genre.

64–67 **STANCE**
In an essay exam, your stance is usually unemotional, thoughtful, and critical.

academic literacies · rhetorical situations · genres · processes · strategies · research MLA / APA · media / design · readings

MEDIA/DESIGN Since essay exams are usually handwritten on lined paper or in an exam booklet, legible handwriting is a must.

68–70

Analyzing Essay Questions

Essay questions usually include key verbs that specify the kind of writing you'll need to do—argue a position, compare two texts, and so on. Following are some of the most common kinds of writing you'll be asked to do on an essay exam.

- *Analyze:* Break an idea, theory, text, or event into its parts and examine them. For example, a world history exam might ask you to **ANALYZE** European imperialism's effect on Africa in the late nineteenth century, and discuss how Africans responded.

94–128

- *Apply:* Consider how an idea or concept might work out in practice. For instance, a film studies exam might ask you to apply the concept of auteurism—a theory of film that sees the director as the primary creator, whose body of work reflects a distinct personal style—to two films by Clint Eastwood. An economics exam might ask you to apply the concept of opportunity costs to a certain supplied scenario.

- *Argue/prove/justify:* Offer reasons and evidence to support a position. A philosophy exam, for example, might ask you to **ARGUE** whether or not all stereotypes contain a "kernel of truth" and whether believing a stereotype is ever justified.

355–73

- *Classify:* Group something into categories. For example, a marketing exam might ask you to **CLASSIFY** shoppers in categories based on their purchasing behavior, motives, attitudes, or lifestyle patterns.

374–79

- *Compare/contrast:* Explore the similarities and/or differences between two or more things. An economics exam, for example, might ask you to **COMPARE** the effectiveness of patents and tax incentives in encouraging technological advances.

380–87

- *Critique:* **ANALYZE** and **EVALUATE** a text or argument, considering its strengths and weaknesses. For instance, an evolutionary biology exam might ask you to critique John Maynard Smith's assertion that "scientific theories say nothing about what is right but only about what is possible" in the context of the theory of evolution.

- *Define:* Explain what a word or phrase means. An art history exam, for example, might ask you to **DEFINE** negative space and discuss the way various artists use it in their work.

- *Describe:* Tell about the important characteristics or features of something. For example, a sociology exam might ask you to **DESCRIBE** Erving Goffman's theory of the presentation of self in ordinary life, focusing on roles, props, and setting.

- *Evaluate:* Determine something's significance or value. A drama exam, for example, might ask you to **EVALUATE** the setting, lighting, and costumes in a filmed production of *Macbeth*.

- *Explain:* Provide reasons and examples to clarify an idea, argument, or event. For instance, a rhetoric exam might ask you to explain the structure of the African American sermon and discuss its use in writings of Frederick Douglass and Martin Luther King Jr.

- *Summarize/review:* Give the major points of a text or idea. A political science exam, for example, might ask you to **SUMMARIZE** John Stuart Mill's concept of utilitarianism and its relation to freedom of speech.

- *Trace:* Explain a sequence of ideas or order of events. For instance, a geography exam might ask you to trace the patterns of international migration since 1970 and discuss how these patterns differ from those of the period between 1870 and World War I.

Some Guidelines for Taking Essay Exams

Before the exam

- *Read* over your class notes and course texts strategically, **ANNOTATING** them to keep track of details you'll want to remember.

- *Collaborate* by forming a **STUDY GROUP** to help one another master the course content.

285–86

- *Review* key ideas, events, terms, and themes. Look for common themes and **CONNECTIONS** in lecture notes, class discussions, and any readings—they'll lead you to important ideas.

473–75

- *Ask* your instructor about the form the exam will take: how long it will be, what kind of questions will be on it, how it will be evaluated, and so on. Working with a study group, write questions you think your instructor might ask, and then answer the questions together.

- *Warm up* just before the exam by **FREEWRITING** for ten minutes or so to gather your thoughts.

289–90

During the exam

- *Scan the questions* to determine how much each part of the test counts and how much time you should spend on it. For example, if one essay is worth 50 points and two others are worth 25 points each, you'll want to spend half your time on the 50-point question.

- *Read over* the entire test before answering any questions. Start with the question you feel most confident answering, which may or may not be the first question on the test.

- *Don't panic.* Sometimes when students first read an essay question, their minds go blank, but after a few moments they start to recall the information they need.

- *Plan.* Although you won't have much time for revising or editing, you still need to plan and allow yourself time to make some last-minute changes before you turn in the exam. So apportion your time. For a three-question essay test in a two-hour test period, you might divide your time like this:

Total Exam Time—120 minutes
Generating ideas—20 minutes (6–7 minutes per question)
Drafting—85 minutes (45 for the 50-point question,
            20 for each 25-point question)
Revising, editing, proofreading—15 minutes

Knowing that you have built in time at the end of the exam period can help you remain calm as you write, as you can use that time to fill in gaps or reconsider answers you feel unsure about.

- *Jot down the main ideas* you need to cover in answering the question on scratch paper or on the cover of your exam book, number those ideas in the order you think makes sense—and you have an outline for your essay. If you're worried about time, plan to write the most important parts of your answers early on. If you don't complete your answer, refer your instructor to your outline to show where you were headed.

- *Turn the essay question into your introduction,* like this:

    Question: How did the outcomes of World War II differ from those of World War I?

    Introduction: The outcomes of World War II differed from those of World War I in three major ways: World War II affected more of the world and its people than World War I, distinctions between citizens and soldiers were eroded, and the war's brutality made it impossible for Europe to continue to claim cultural superiority over other cultures.

358–67

- *State your thesis explicitly,* provide **REASONS** and **EVIDENCE** to support your thesis, and use transitions to move logically from one idea to the next. Restate your main point in your conclusion. You don't want to give what one professor calls a "garbage truck answer," dumping everything you know into a blue book and expecting the instructor to sort it all out.

- *Write on every other line* and only on one side of each page so that you'll have room to make additions or corrections. If you're typing on a computer, double space.

- *If you have time left, go over your exam,* looking for ideas that need elaboration as well as for grammatical and punctuation errors.

After the exam. If your instructor doesn't return your exam, consider asking for a conference to go over your work so you can learn what you did well and where you need to improve—important knowledge to take with you into your next exam.

academic literacies rhetorical situations genres processes strategies research MLA / APA media / design readings

part 6

Doing Research

We do research all the time, for many different reasons. We search the web for information about a new computer, ask friends about the best place to get coffee, try on several pairs of jeans before deciding which ones to buy. You have no doubt done your share of library research before now, and you probably have visited a number of schools' websites before deciding which college you wanted to attend. Research, in other words, is something you do every day. The following chapters offer advice on the kind of research you'll need to do for your academic work and, in particular, for research projects.

Doing Research

Developing a Research Plan 45

When you need to do research, it's sometimes tempting to jump in and start looking for information right away. To do research well, however — to find appropriate sources and use them wisely — you need to work systematically. You need a research plan. This chapter will help you establish such a plan and then get started.

Establishing a Schedule

Doing research is complex and time-consuming, so it's good to establish a schedule for yourself. Research-based writing projects usually require you to come up with a topic (or to analyze the requirements of an assigned topic) and then come up with a research question to guide your research efforts. Once you do some serious, focused research to find the information you need, you'll be ready to turn your research question into a tentative thesis and sketch out a rough outline. After doing whatever additional research you need to fill in your outline, you'll write a draft — and get some response to that draft. Perhaps you'll need to do additional research before revising. Finally, you'll need to edit and proofread. And so you'll want to start by creating a timeline for getting all this work done, perhaps using the form on the next page.

Getting Started

Once you have a schedule, you can get started. The sections that follow offer advice on considering your rhetorical situation, coming up with a topic, and doing preliminary research; developing a research question, a

academic literacies

rhetorical situations

genres

processes

strategies

research MLA / APA

media / design

readings

Scheduling a Research Project

Complete by:

Analyze your rhetorical situation.   _____
Choose a possible topic or analyze the assignment.   _____
Plan a research strategy and do   _____
   preliminary research.
Come up with a research question.   _____
Schedule interviews and other field research.   _____
Find sources.   _____
Read sources and take notes.   _____
Do any field research.   _____
Come up with a tentative thesis and outline.   _____
Write a draft.   _____
Get response.   _____
Do any additional research.   _____
Revise.   _____
Prepare a list of works cited.   _____
Edit.   _____
Proofread the final draft.   _____
Submit the final draft.   _____

tentative thesis, and a rough outline; and creating a working bibliography and keeping track of your sources. The chapters that follow offer guidelines for **FINDING SOURCES**, **EVALUATING SOURCES**, and **SYNTHESIZING IDEAS**.

445–68 ●
469–72
473–77

Considering the Rhetorical Situation

As with any writing task, you need to start by considering your purpose, your audience, and the rest of your rhetorical situation:

academic literacies
rhetorical situations
genres
processes
strategies
research MLA / APA
media / design
readings

PURPOSE   Is this project part of an assignment—and if so, does   ■ 55–56
it specify any one purpose? If not, what is your broad
purpose? To inform? argue? analyze? a combination?

AUDIENCE   To whom are you writing? What does your audience   ■ 57–60
likely know about your topic, and is there any back-
ground information you'll need to provide? What opinions or attitudes do your readers likely hold? What kinds
of evidence will they find persuasive? How do you want
them to respond to your writing?

GENRE   Are you writing to report on something? to compose a   ■ 61–63
profile? to make a proposal? an argument? What are the
requirements of your genre in terms of the number and
kind of sources you must use?

STANCE   What is your attitude toward your topic? What accounts   ■ 64–67
for your attitude? How do you want to come across?
Curious? Critical? Positive? Something else?

MEDIA / DESIGN What medium or media will you use? Print? Spoken? Elec-   ■ 68–70
tronic? Will you need to create any charts, photographs,
video, presentation software slides, or other visuals?

Coming Up with a Topic

If you need to choose a topic, consider your interests as they relate to the
course for which you're writing. What do you want to learn about? What
do you have questions about? What topics from the course have you found
intriguing? What community, national, or global issues do you care about?

If your topic is assigned, you need to make sure you understand
exactly what it asks you to do. Read the assignment carefully, looking for
keywords: does it ask you to **ANALYZE**, **COMPARE**, **EVALUATE**, **SUMMARIZE**,   ▲ 94–128
or **ARGUE**? If the assignment offers broad guidelines but allows you to   ◆ 380–87
choose within them, identify the requirements and the range of possible   ▲ 197–205
topics and define your topic within those constraints.   ● 486–87
                                                            ◆ 355–73

For example, in an American history course, your instructor might ask you to "discuss social effects of the Civil War." Potential but broad topics might include poverty among Confederate soldiers or former slaveholders, the migration of members of those groups to Mexico or Northern cities, the establishment of independent African American churches, or the spread of the Ku Klux Klan—to name only a few of the possibilities.

Narrow the topic. As you consider possible topics, look for ways to narrow your topic's focus to make it specific enough to discuss in depth. For example:

> **Too general:** fracking
>
> **Still too general:** fracking and the environment
>
> **Better:** the potential environmental effects of extracting natural gas through the process of hydraulic fracturing, or fracking

If you limit your topic, you can address it with specific information that you'll be more easily able to find and manage. In addition, a limited topic will be more likely to interest your audience than a broad topic that forces you to use abstract, general statements. For example, it's much harder to write well about "the environment" than it is to address a topic that explores a single environmental issue.

Think about what you know about your topic. Chances are you already know something about your topic, and articulating that knowledge can help you see possible ways to focus your topic or come up with potential 289–92 sources of information. **FREEWRITING**, **LISTING**, **CLUSTERING**, and **LOOPING** are all good ways of tapping your knowledge of your topic. Consider where you might find information about it: Have you read about it in a textbook? heard stories about it on the news? visited websites focused on it? Do you know anyone who knows about this topic?

Consulting with Librarians and Doing Preliminary Research

Consulting with a reference librarian at your school and doing some preliminary research in the library can save you time in the long run. Reference

librarians can direct you to the best scholarly sources for your topic and help you focus your topic by determining appropriate search terms and **KEYWORDS** — significant words that appear in the title, abstract, or text of potential sources and that you can use to search for information on your topic in library catalogs, in databases, and on the web. These librarians can also help you choose the most appropriate reference works, sources that provide general overviews of the scholarship in a field. General internet searches can be time-consuming, as they often result in thousands of possible sites — too many to weed out efficiently, either by revising your search terms or by going through the sites themselves, many of which are unreliable. Library databases, on the other hand, include only sources that already have been selected by experts, and searches in them usually present manageable numbers of results.

452–55

Wikipedia can often serve as a jumping-off point for preliminary research, but since its entries are written and edited by people who may not have expertise in the subject, it is not considered a reliable academic source. Specialized encyclopedias, however, usually present subjects in much greater depth and provide more scholarly references that might suggest starting points for your research. Even if you know a lot about a subject, doing preliminary research can open you to new ways of seeing and approaching it, increasing your options for developing and narrowing your topic.

Coming Up with a Research Question

Once you've surveyed the territory of your topic, you'll likely find that your understanding of the topic has become broader and deeper. You may find that your interests have changed and your research has led to surprises and additional research. That's okay: as a result of exploring avenues you hadn't anticipated, you may well come up with a better topic than the one you'd started with. At some point, though, you need to develop a research question—a specific question that you will then work to answer through your research.

53 ■ To write a research question, review your analysis of the **RHETORICAL SITUATION**, to remind yourself of any time constraints or length considerations. Generate a list of questions beginning with *What? When? Where? Who? How? Why? Would? Could?* and *Should?* Here, for example, are some questions about the tentative topic "the potential environmental effects of extracting natural gas through the process of hydraulic fracturing, or fracking":

> *What* are the environmental effects of fracking?
>
> *When* was fracking introduced as a way to produce natural gas?
>
> *Where* is fracking done, and how does this affect the surrounding people and environment?
>
> *Who* will benefit from increased fracking?
>
> *How* much energy does fracking use?
>
> *Why* do some environmental groups oppose fracking?
>
> *Would* other methods of extracting natural gas be safer?
>
> *Could* fracking cause earthquakes?
>
> *Should* fracking be expanded, regulated, or banned?

Select one question from your list that you find interesting and that suits your rhetorical situation. Use the question to guide your research.

Drafting a Tentative Thesis

345–47 ◆ Once your research has led you to a possible answer to your research question, try formulating that answer as a tentative **THESIS**. You need not be committed to the thesis; in fact, you should not be. The object of your research should be to learn about your topic, not to find information that simply supports what you already think you believe. Your tentative thesis may (and probably will) change as you learn more about your subject, consider the many points of view on it, and reconsider your topic and, perhaps, your goal: what you originally planned to be an argument for considering other points of view may become a call to action. However tentative, a thesis allows you to move forward by clarifying your purpose for doing research. Here are some tentative thesis statements on the topic of fracking:

Fracking is a likely cause of earthquakes in otherwise seismically stable regions of the country.

The federal government should strictly regulate the production of natural gas by fracking.

Fracking can greatly increase our supplies of natural gas, but other methods of producing energy should still be pursued.

As with a research question, a tentative thesis should guide your research efforts—but be ready to revise it as you learn still more about your topic. Research should be a process of **INQUIRY** in which you approach your topic with an open mind, ready to learn and possibly change. If you hold too tightly to a tentative thesis, you risk focusing only on evidence that supports your view, making your writing biased and unconvincing.

281–84

Creating a Rough Outline

After you've created a tentative thesis, write out a rough **OUTLINE** for your research project. Your outline can be a simple list of topics you want to explore, something that will help you structure your research efforts and organize your notes and other materials. As you read your sources, you can use your outline to keep track of what you need to find and where the information you do find fits into your argument. Then you'll be able to see if you've covered all the ideas you intended to explore—or whether you need to rethink the categories on your outline.

293–95

Keeping a Working Bibliography

A working bibliography is a record of all the sources you consult. You should keep such a record so that you can find sources easily when you need them and then cite any that you use. Your library likely offers tools to store source information you find in its databases and catalog, and software such as *Zotero* can also help you save, manage, and cite your sources.

Information for a Working Bibliography

FOR A BOOK

Library call number
Author(s) or editor(s)
Title and subtitle
Publication information: city, publisher, year of publication
Other information: edition, volume number, translator, and so on
If your source is an essay in a collection, include its author, title, and page numbers.

FOR A SOURCE FROM A DATABASE

Publication information for the source, as listed above
Name of database
DOI (digital object identifier) or URL of original source, such as the periodical in which an article was published. (for APA style)
Stable URL or permalink for database
Date you accessed source

FOR AN ARTICLE IN A PRINT PERIODICAL

Author(s)
Title and subtitle
Name of periodical
Volume number, issue number, date
Page numbers

FOR A WEB SOURCE

URL
Author(s) or editor(s) if available
Name of site
Sponsor of site
Date site was first posted or last updated
Date you accessed site
If the source is an article or book reprinted on the web, include its title, the title and publication information of the periodical or book, where it was first published, and any page numbers.

academic literacies · rhetorical situations · genres · processes · strategies · research MLA / APA · media / design · readings

You may find it useful to print out bibliographical data you find useful or to keep your working bibliography on index cards or in a notebook. However you decide to compile your working bibliography, include all the information you'll need later to document any sources you use; follow the **DOCUMENTATION** style you'll use when you write so that you won't need to go back to your sources to find the information. Some databases make this step easy by preparing rough-draft citations in several styles that you can copy, paste, and edit.

496–99

On the previous page is most of the basic information you'll want to include for each source in your working bibliography. Go to wwnorton.com/write/fieldguide for templates you can use to keep track of this information.

Keeping Track of Your Sources

- *Staple together photocopies and printouts.* It's easy for individual pages to get shuffled or lost on a desk or in a backpack. Keep a stapler handy, and fasten pages together as soon as you copy them or print them out.

- *Bookmark web sources* or save them using a free bookmark management tool. For database sources, use the DOI or stable URL, permalink, or document URL (the terms used by databases vary) — not the URL in the "Address" or "Location" box in your browser, which will expire after you end your online session.

- *Label everything.* Label your copies with the source's author and title.

- *Highlight sections you plan to use.* When you sit down to draft, your goal will be to find what you need quickly, so as soon as you decide you might use a source, highlight the paragraphs or sentences that you think you'll use. If your instructor wants copies of your sources to see how you used them, you've got them ready. If you're using PDF copies, you can highlight or add notes using *Adobe Reader*.

- *Use your rough outline to keep track of what you've got.* In the margin of each highlighted section, write the number or letter of the outline division to which the section corresponds. (It's a good idea to write it in the same place consistently so you can flip through a stack of copies and easily see what you've got.) Alternatively, attach sticky notes to each copy, using a different color for each main heading in your outline.

- *Keep everything in an online folder, file folder, or box.* Keep everything related to your research in one place. If you create online subfolders or create folders that correspond to your rough outline, you'll be able to organize your material, at least tentatively. And if you highlight, label, and use sticky notes, your material will be even better organized, making writing a draft easier. The folder or box will also serve you well if you are required to create a portfolio that includes your research notes, copies of sources, and drafts.

- *Use a reference management system.* Web-based reference or citation management systems allow you to create and organize a personal database of resources. You can import references from databases to a personal account, organize them, and draft citations in various formats. *RefWorks*, *EndNote*, *Mendeley*, *CiteULike*, and *Zotero* are five such systems; check with your librarian to see what system your library supports, or search online, as several of them are available for free. Be aware, though, that the citations generated are often inaccurate and need to be checked carefully for content and format. So treat them as rough drafts and plan to edit them.

445–68
469–72

IF YOU NEED MORE HELP

See the guidelines on **FINDING SOURCES** once you're ready to move on to in-depth research and those on **EVALUATING SOURCES** for help thinking critically about the sources you find.

Finding Sources **46**

To analyze media coverage of the 2012 Democratic National Convention, you examine news stories and blogs published at the time. To write an essay interpreting a poem by Maya Angelou, you study the poem and read several critical interpretations in literary journals. To write a report on career opportunities in psychology, you interview a graduate of your university who is working in a psychology clinic. In each of these cases, you go beyond your own knowledge to consult additional sources of information.

This chapter offers guidelines for locating a range of sources—print and online, general and specialized, published and firsthand. Keep in mind that as you do research, finding and **EVALUATING SOURCES** are two activities that usually take place simultaneously. So this chapter and the next one go hand in hand.

469–72

Kinds of Sources

Primary and secondary sources.   Your research will likely lead you to both primary and secondary sources. *Primary sources* include historical documents, literary works, eyewitness accounts, field reports, diaries, letters, and lab studies, as well as any original research you do through interviews, observation, experiments, or surveys. *Secondary sources* include scholarly books and articles, reviews, biographies, textbooks, and other works that interpret or discuss primary sources. Novels and films are primary sources; articles interpreting them are secondary sources. The Declaration of Independence is a primary historical document; a historian's description of the events surrounding the Declaration's writing is secondary. A published report of scientific findings is primary; a critique of that report is secondary.

Whether a work is considered primary or secondary sometimes depends on your topic and purpose. If you're analyzing a poem, a critic's article interpreting the poem is a secondary source—but if you're investigating that critic's work, the article would be a primary source for your own study and interpretation.

Secondary sources are often useful because they can help you understand and evaluate primary source material. Whenever possible, however, you should find and use primary sources, because secondary sources can distort or misrepresent the information in primary sources. For example, a seemingly reputable secondary source describing the 1948 presidential election asserted that the *New York Times* ran a headline reading, "Thomas E. Dewey's Election as President Is a Foregone Conclusion." But the actual article was titled "Talk Is Now Turning to the Dewey Cabinet," and it began by noting "[the] *popular view that* Gov. Thomas E. Dewey's election as President is a foregone conclusion." Here the secondary source got not only the headline wrong but also distorted the source's intended meaning by leaving out an important phrase. Your research should be as accurate and reliable as it can be; using primary sources whenever you can helps ensure that it is.

Scholarly and popular sources.   Scholarly sources are written by academic experts or scholars in a particular discipline and are *peer-reviewed* — evaluated by other experts in the same discipline for their factual accuracy and lack of bias. They are also written largely *for* experts in a discipline, as a means of sharing research, insights, and in-depth analysis with one another; that's why they must meet high standards of accuracy and objectivity and adhere to the discipline's accepted research methods, including its style for documenting sources. Scholarly articles are usually published in academic journals; scholarly books may be published by university presses or by other academically focused publishers.

academic literacies · rhetorical situations · genres · processes · strategies · research MLA / APA · media / design · readings

Popular sources include just about all other online and print publications, from websites to magazines to books written for nonspecialists. These sources generally explain or provide opinion on current events or topics of general interest; when they discuss scholarly research, they tend to simplify the concepts and facts, providing definitions, narratives, and examples to make them understandable to nonspecialist audiences. They are often written by journalists or other professional writers who may specialize in a particular area but who report or comment on the scholarship of others rather than doing any themselves. Their most important difference from scholarly sources is that popular sources are not reviewed by other experts in the field being discussed, although editors or fact-checkers review the writing before it's published.

In most of your college courses, you'll be expected to rely primarily on scholarly sources rather than popular ones. However, if you're writing about a very current topic or need to provide background information on a topic, a mix of scholarly and popular sources may be appropriate. To see how scholarly and popular sources differ in appearance, look at the Documentation Map for scholarly journals (p. 516) and at the illustrations on pages 448–49. Here's a guide to determining whether or not a potential source is scholarly:

IDENTIFYING SCHOLARLY SOURCES: WHAT TO LOOK FOR

- *Author.* Look for the author's scholarly credentials, including his or her affiliations with academic or other research-oriented institutions.

- *Peer review.* Look for a list of reviewers at the front of the journal or on the journal's or publisher's website. If you don't find one, the source is probably not peer-reviewed.

- *Source citations.* Look for a detailed list of works cited or references at the end of the source and citations either parenthetically within the text or in footnotes or endnotes. (Popular sources may include a reference list but seldom cite sources within the text, except in signal phrases.)

Scholarly Source

Published in an academic journal.

Includes an abstract.

Cites academic research with consistent documentation style.

Describes research methods, includes numerical data.

Multiple authors who are academics.

Includes complete references list.

Journal List > NIHPA Author Manuscripts > PMC2910808

NIH Public Access
Author Manuscript
Accepted for publication in a peer reviewed journal

About Author manuscripts   Submit a manuscript

PubReader format:
click here to try

J Res Pers. Author manuscript: available in PMC 2011 August 1.
Published in final edited form as:
J Res Pers. 2010 August 1; 44(4): 478–484.
doi: 10.1016/j.jrp.2010.06.001

PMCID: PMC2910808
NIHMSID: NIHMS210233

Sounds like a Narcissist: Behavioral Manifestations of Narcissism in Everyday Life

Nicholas S. Holtzman, Simine Vazire, and Matthias R. Mehl

Author information ▶ Copyright and License information ▶

See other articles in PMC that cite the published article.

Formats:
Article | PubReader | ePub (beta) | PDF (338K)

Related citations in PubMed
Impulsivity and the self-defeating behavior of narcissists.
[Pers Soc Psychol Rev. 2006]
Why are narcissists so charming at first sight? Decoding the narcissism-popularity link at zero acqu... [J Pers Soc Psychol. 2010]
The performance of narcissists rises and falls with perceived opportunity for glory.   [J Pers Soc Psychol. 2002]
An empirical typology of narcissism and mental health in late adolescence.   [J Adolesc. 2006]
Animal models of obsessive-compulsive disorder: rationale to understanding psychobiology and ... [Psychiatr Clin North Am. 2006]
See reviews...
See all...

Abstract
Go to: ☑

Little is known about narcissists' everyday behavior. The goal of this study was to describe how narcissism is manifested in everyday life. Using the Electronically Activated Recorder (EAR), we obtained naturalistic behavior from participants' everyday lives. The results suggest that the defining characteristics of narcissism that have been established from questionnaire and laboratory-based studies are borne out in narcissists' day-to-day behaviors. Narcissists did indeed behave in more extraverted and less agreeable ways than non-narcissists, skip class more (among narcissists high in exploitativeness/entitlement only), and use more sexual language. Furthermore, we found that the link between narcissism and disagreeable behavior is strengthened when controlling for self-esteem, thus extending prior questionnaire-based findings (Paulhus, Robins, Trzesniewski, & Tracy, 2004) to observed, real-world behavior.

Keywords: narcissism, behavior, personality traits, sexual behavior, language use

Cited by other articles in PMC
Evidence for the criterion validity and clinical utility of the Pathological Narcissism Inventory   [Assessment. 2012]
See all...

Links
MedGen
PubMed

Narcissists love attention. Lucky for them, they have recently received a considerable amount of it from academic psychologists, especially in laboratory settings (e.g., Back, Schmukle, & Egloff, 2010; Bushman & Baumeister, 1998; Campbell, Foster, & Finkel, 2002; Miller et al., 2009). This laboratory research has led to several wide-reaching theories about why narcissists do what they do (Holtzman & Strube, 2010; Morf & Rhodewalt, 2001; Twenge & Campbell, 2009; Vazire & Funder, 2006). Despite all this attention from researchers, however, we still know little about what narcissists actually do in their everyday lives. The aim of this paper is to help create an empirical basis for a more complete understanding of narcissism by exploring behavioral manifestations of narcissism in everyday life. Thus, we intend to answer a simple, yet largely unanswered question: What do narcissists do on a day-to-day basis?

Recent activity
Turn Off   Clear
Sounds like a Narcissist: Behavioral Manifestations of Narcissism in Everyday Li...   PMC
See more...

Does self-love lead to love for others? A story of narcissistic game playing.   [J Pers Soc Psychol. 2002]
Interpersonal and intrapsychic adaptiveness of trait self-enhancement: a mixed blessing?   [J Pers Soc Psychol. 1998]

Method
Go to: ☑

Participants

Participants were 80 undergraduate students at the University of Texas at Austin (79 provided valid EAR data), recruited mainly from introductory psychology courses and by flyers in the psychology department. The sample was 54% female, and the ethnic composition of the sample was 65% White, 21% Asian, 11% Latino, and 3% of another ethnicity. Participants ranged from 18 to 24 years old ($M = 18.7$, $SD = 1.4$). Participants were compensated $50. Data from this sample were also reported in Vazire and Mehl (2008), where further information can be found about the study.[1]

Narcissistic Personality Inventory (NPI)

The NPI is a 40-item test of narcissism that is reliable and well-validated (Raskin & Terry, 1988). The items on this forced-choice test contain pairs of statements such as "Sometimes I tell good stories" (non-narcissistic) versus "Everybody likes to hear my stories" (narcissistic). In our study, the NPI exhibited good reliability ($\alpha = .83$). As seen in Table 1, we also calculated means and reliabilities for four facets (Emmons, 1987).

Table 1
Means, Standard Deviations, Gender-Differences, and Reliabilities for the NPI and NPI Facets

Knowing me, knowing you: the accuracy and unique predictive validity of self-ratings and other-rating [J Pers Soc Psychol. 2008]

A principal-components analysis of the Narcissistic Personality Inventory and further evidence of its ... [J Pers Soc Psychol. 1988]
Narcissism: theory and measurement.
[J Pers Soc Psychol. 1987]

Contributor Information
Go to: ☑

Nicholas S. Holtzman, Washington University in St. Louis.

Simine Vazire, Washington University in St. Louis.

Matthias R. Mehl, University of Arizona.

References
Go to: ☑

1. Back MD, Schmukle SC, Egloff B. Why are narcissists so charming at first sight? Decoding the narcissism-popularity link at zero acquaintance. Journal of Personality and Social Psychology. 2010;98:132–145. [PubMed]
2. Baumeister RF, Vohs KD, Funder DC. Psychology as the science of self-reports and finger movements: Whatever happened to actual behavior? Perspectives on Psychological Science. 2007;2:396–403.

academic literacies • rhetorical situations • genres • processes • strategies • research MLA / APA • media / design • readings

Popular Source

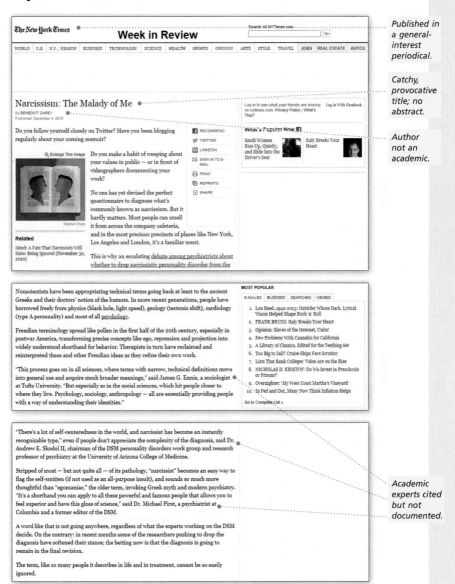

Published in a general-interest periodical.

Catchy, provocative title; no abstract.

Author not an academic.

Academic experts cited but not documented.

- *Publisher.* Look for publishers that are professional scholarly organizations, such as the Modern Language Association or the Organization of American Historians, that are affiliated with universities or colleges, or that have a stated academic mission.

- *Language and content.* Look for abstracts (one-paragraph summaries of the contents) at the beginning of articles and for technical or specialized language and concepts that readers are assumed to be familiar with.

- *Other clues.* Look for little or no advertising on websites or within the journal; for a plain design with few or no illustrations, especially in print sources; and for listing in academic databases when you limit your search to *academic, peer-reviewed,* or *scholarly sources.*

Print and online sources.   Some sources are available only in print; some are available only online. But many print sources are also available on the web. You'll find print sources in your school's library, but chances are that many reference books in your library will also be available online. In general, for academic writing it's best to try to find most of your online sources through the library's website rather than commercial search sites, which may lead you to unreliable sources and cause you to spend much more time sorting and narrowing search results. This chapter discusses four paths to finding sources you'll want to consult:

455–57

REFERENCE WORKS, for encyclopedias, bibliographies, and the like

457–58
THE LIBRARY CATALOG, for books

459–61
INDEXES AND DATABASES, for periodicals

462–63
SEARCH SITES AND SUBJECT DIRECTORIES, for material on the web

Searching in Academic Libraries

College and university libraries typically offer several ways to search their holdings. Take a look at this search box, from the homepage of the Houston Community College libraries:

academic literacies   rhetorical situations   genres   processes   strategies   research MLA / APA   media / design   readings

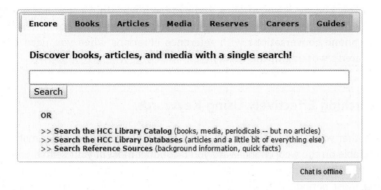

This box allows you to search through all the library's holdings at once an option that may be a good way to get started. You may already know, though, that you need to focus your search on one type of source, such as scholarly articles, leading you to choose the Articles tab.

This box lets you shape and limit your search in several ways: by selecting a specific database, by choosing to search only for full-text articles and only peer-reviewed articles, and by searching within a specific journal. The Chat button can be very useful; many libraries offer email, texting, and phone conversations with reference librarians when you need help but aren't working in the library.

Searching Effectively Using Keywords

Whether you're searching for books, articles in periodicals, or other material available on the web, chances are you'll conduct most of your search online. Most materials produced since the 1980s and most library catalogs are online, and most periodical articles can be found by searching electronic indexes and databases. In each case, you can search for authors, titles, or subjects.

To search online, you'll need to come up with keywords. The key to searching efficiently is to use keywords and combinations of them that will focus your searches on the information you need — but not too much of it. Often you'll start out with one general keyword that will yield far too many results; then you'll need to switch to more specific terms or combinations (*homeopathy* instead of *medicine* or *secondary education Japan* instead of *education Japan*).

Other times your keyword search won't yield enough sources; then you'll need to use broader terms or combinations (*education Japan* instead of *secondary education Japan*) or substitute synonyms (*home remedy* instead of *folk medicine*). Sometimes you'll need to learn terms used in academic disciplines or earlier in history for things you know by other names, such as *myocardial infarction* rather than *heart attack* or *the Great War* instead of *World War I*. Or look through the sources that turn up in response to other terms to see what keywords you might use in subsequent searches. Searching requires flexibility, in the words you use and the methods you try.

Finding keywords using word clouds. One way to find keywords to help you narrow and focus your topic is to create a word cloud, a visual representation of words used in a text; the more often a word is used, the larger it looks in the word cloud. Several websites, including *Tagxedo, Wordle,* and *TagCrowd,* let you create word clouds. Examining a word cloud

academic literacies   rhetorical situations   genres   processes   strategies   research MLA / APA   media / design   readings

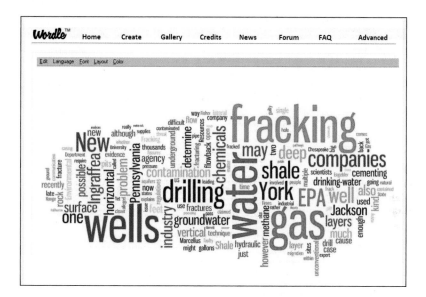

created from an article in a reference work may help you see what terms are used to discuss your topic — and may help you see new possible ways to narrow it. Here, for example, is a word cloud derived from an article in *Scientific American* discussing fracking. Many of the terms — *fracking, water, gas, wells, drilling* — are just what you'd expect. However, some terms — *Ingraffea, Marcellus, cementing* — may be unfamiliar and lead to additional possibilities for research. For instance, *Ingraffea* refers to an expert on fracking whose publications might be worth examining, while *cementing* refers to an important and controversial aspect of the hydraulic fracturing process.

Finding keywords using databases.   Once you've begun searching for and finding possible sources, you can expand your list of possible keywords by skimming the "detailed record" or "metadata" page for any scholarly articles you find, where full bibliographic information on the source may be found. A search for *fracking* resulted in this source:

Note the list of author-supplied keywords, which offers options for narrowing and focusing your topic. Each keyword is a link, so simply clicking on it will produce a new list of sources.

Advanced keyword searching.   Most search sites have "advanced search" options that will help you focus your research. Some allow you to ask questions in conversational language: *What did Thomas Jefferson write about slavery?* Others allow you to focus your search by using specific words or symbols. Here are some of the most common ones:

- Type quotation marks around words to search for an exact phrase— "Thomas Jefferson."
- Type AND to specify that more than one keyword must appear in sources: Jefferson AND Adams. Some search engines require a plus sign instead: +Jefferson +Adams.
- Type OR if you're looking for sources that include any of several terms: Jefferson OR Adams OR Madison.
- Type NOT to find sources *without* a certain word: Jefferson NOT Adams. Some search engines call for a minus sign (actually, a hyphen) instead: +Jefferson –Adams.
- Type an asterisk to search for words in different form. For example, teach* will yield sources containing *teacher* and *teaching*.

Reference Works

The reference section of your school's library is the place to find encyclopedias, dictionaries, atlases, almanacs, bibliographies, and other reference works in print. Many of these sources are also online and can be accessed from any computer that is connected to the internet. Others are available only in the library. Remember, though, that whether in print or online, reference works are only a starting point, a place where you can get an overview of your topic.

General reference works.   Consult encyclopedias for general background information on a subject, dictionaries for definitions of words, atlases for maps and geographic data, and almanacs for statistics and other data on current events. These are some works you might consult:

The New Encyclopaedia Britannica
The Columbia Encyclopedia
Webster's Third New International Dictionary
Oxford English Dictionary
National Geographic Atlas of the World

Statistical Abstract of the United States
The World Almanac and Book of Facts

Caution: *Wikipedia* is a popular online research tool, but since anyone can edit its entries, you can't be certain of its accuracy. Use it for general overviews, but look elsewhere — including *Wikipedia*'s own references and citations — for authoritative sources.

Specialized reference works. You can also go to specialized reference works, which provide in-depth information on a single field or topic. These may also include authoritative bibliographies, leading you to more specific works. A reference librarian can refer you to specialized encyclopedias in particular fields, but good places to start are online collections of many topic-specific reference works that offer overviews of a topic, place it in a larger context, and sometimes provide links to potential academic sources. Collections that are available through libraries include the following:

> *CQ Researcher* offers in-depth reports on topics in education, health, the environment, criminal justice, international affairs, technology, the economy, and social trends. Each report gives an overview of a particular topic, outlines of the differing positions on it, and a bibliography of resources on it.

> *Gale Virtual Reference Library* (GVRL) offers thousands of full-text specialized encyclopedias, almanacs, articles, and ebooks.

> *Oxford Reference Online* contains hundreds of dictionaries, encyclopedias, and other reference works on a wide variety of subjects, as well as timelines with links to each item mentioned on each timeline.

> *SAGE Reference Online* includes many encyclopedias and handbooks on topics in the social sciences.

Bibliographies. Bibliographies provide an overview of what has been published on a topic, listing published works along with the information you'll need to find each work. Some are annotated with brief summaries of each work's contents. You'll find bibliographies at the end of scholarly articles and books, and you can also find book-length bibliographies, both

academic literacies / rhetorical situations / genres / processes / strategies / research MLA / APA / media / design / readings

in the reference section of your library and online. Check with a reference librarian for bibliographies on your research topic.

Books / Searching the Library Catalog

The library catalog is your primary source for finding books. Almost all library catalogs are computerized and can be accessed through the library's website. You can search by author, title, subject, or keyword. The image below shows the result of a keyword search for material on art in Nazi Germany. This search of the library's catalog revealed forty items — print books, ebooks, and video recordings — on the topic; to access information on each one, the researcher must simply click on the title or thumbnail image. The image on the next page shows detailed information for one source: bibliographic data about author, title, and publication; related subject headings (which may lead to other useful materials in the library) — and more. Library catalogs also supply a call number, which identifies the book's location on the library's shelves.

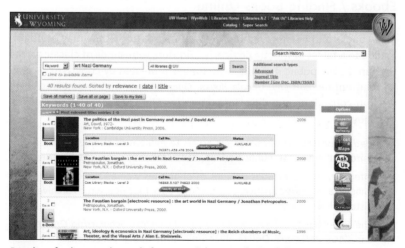

Results of a keyword search for material on art in Nazi Germany.

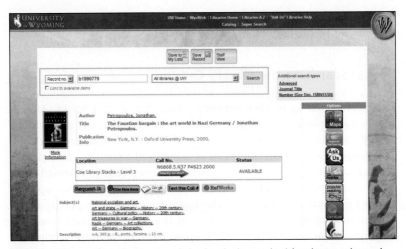

Detailed information about one of the books located with a keyword search.

Ebooks / Finding Books Online

Many books in the library catalog are available online. Some may be downloaded to a tablet or mobile device. In addition, thousands of classic works that are in the public domain — no longer protected by copyright — may be read online. *Bartleby*, *Google Books*, *Open Library*, and *Project Gutenberg* are four collections of public-domain works. Here are some other sources of ebooks:

> *Hathi Trust Digital Library* offers access to millions of ebooks, about a third of them in the public domain, contributed by university libraries.
>
> *Internet Archive* includes millions of ebooks as well as audio, moving images, a live music archive, and the Way Back Machine, which archives historical webpages.
>
> The *Gale Virtual Reference Library (GVRL)*, *Oxford Scholarship Online*, and *SAGE Reference Online* all contain large ebook collections.

Periodicals / Searching Indexes and Databases

To find journal, magazine, and newspaper articles, you will need to search periodical indexes and databases. Indexes provide listings of articles organized by topics; many databases provide the full texts. Some indexes are in print and can be found in the reference section of the library; most are online. Some databases are available for free; most of the more authoritative ones, however, are available only by subscription and so must be accessed through a library.

Many databases now include not only scholarly articles but also dissertations, theses, book chapters, book reviews, and conference proceedings. Dissertations and theses are formal works of scholarship done as requirements for graduate degrees; book reviews offer critical evaluations of scholarly and popular books; and conference proceedings are papers presented, usually orally, at scholarly meetings.

When you access a source through a database, the URL or link address is different each time you log in, so if you want to return to a source, look for a *stable URL*, *permalink*, or *document URL* option and choose it to copy and paste into your list of sources.

General indexes and databases. A reference librarian can help you determine which databases will be most helpful to you, but here are some useful ones:

Academic Search Complete is a multidisciplinary index and database containing the full text of articles in thousands of journals and indexing of even more, with abstracts of their articles.

EBSCOhost provides interlinked databases of abstracts and full-text articles from a variety of periodicals.

FirstSearch offers access to millions of full-text, full-image articles in dozens of databases covering many disciplines.

InfoTrac offers millions of full-text articles in a broad spectrum of disciplines and on a wide variety of topics from thousands of scholarly and popular periodicals, including the *New York Times*.

JSTOR archives scanned copies of entire publication runs of scholarly journals in many disciplines, but it does not include current issues of the journals.

LexisNexis contains full-text publications and articles from a large number of sources—newspapers, business and legal resources, medical texts, and reference sources such as *The World Almanac* and the Roper public opinion polls.

ProQuest Central provides access to full-text articles from thousands of books, scholarly journals, conference papers, magazines, newspapers, blogs, podcasts, and websites and a large collection of dissertations and theses.

Single-subject indexes and databases. The following are just a sample of what's available; check with a reference librarian for indexes and databases in the subject you're researching.

America: History and Life indexes scholarly literature on the history and culture of the United States and Canada.

BIOSIS Previews provides abstracts and indexes for thousands of sources on a wide variety of biological and medical topics.

ERIC is the U.S. Department of Education's Educational Resource Information Center database. It includes hundreds of journal titles as well as conference papers, technical reports, and other resources on education.

Historical Abstracts includes abstracts of articles on the history of the world, excluding the United States and Canada, since 1450.

Humanities International Index contains bibliographic references to more than 2,000 journals dealing with the humanities.

MLA International Bibliography indexes scholarly articles on modern languages, literature, folklore, and linguistics.

PsycINFO indexes scholarly literature in a number of disciplines relating to the behavioral sciences and mental health.

PubMed includes millions of citations for biomedical literature, many with links to full-text content.

Print indexes. You may need to consult print indexes to find articles published before the 1980s. Here are six useful ones:

academic literacies · rhetorical situations · genres · processes · strategies · research MLA / APA · media / design · readings

The Readers' Guide to Periodical Literature (print, 1900–; online, 1983–)

InfoTrac Magazine Index (print, 1988–; online, 1973–)

The New York Times Index (print and online, 1851–)

Humanities Index (print, 1974–; online, 1984–)

Social Sciences Index (print, 1974–; online, 1983–)

General Science Index (print, 1978–; online, 1984–)

Images, Sound, and More

Your library likely subscribes to various databases that allow you to find and download video, audio, and image files. Here is a sampling:

AP Images provides access to photographs taken for the Associated Press, the cooperative agency of thousands of newspapers and radio and television stations worldwide.

ArtStor provides images in the arts, architecture, humanities, and sciences.

Dance in Video offers hundreds of videos of dance productions and documentaries on dance.

Education in Video includes thousands of videos of teaching demonstrations, lectures, documentaries, and footage of students and teachers in their classrooms.

Naxos Music Library contains more than 100,000 classical, jazz, and world music recordings, as well as libretti and synopses of hundreds of operas and other background information.

Theatre in Video provides videos of more than 250 performances of plays and more than 100 film documentaries.

The following indexes and databases are freely available on the internet:

ipl2, the Internet Public Library, is a searchable, annotated subject directory of thousands of websites selected and evaluated by librarians for their usefulness to users of public libraries.

The WWW Virtual Library is a catalog of websites on a wide range of subjects, compiled by volunteers with expertise in particular subject areas.

CSA Discovery Guides provide comprehensive information on current issues in the arts and humanities, natural sciences, social sciences, and technology, with an overview of each subject, key citations with abstracts, and links to websites.

The Voice of the Shuttle, or *VOS,* offers information on subjects in the humanities, organized to mirror "the way the humanities are organized for research and teaching as well as the way they are adapting to social, cultural, and technological changes."

The Library of Congress offers online access to information on a wide range of subjects, including academic subjects, as well as prints, photographs, and government documents.

JURIST is a university-based online gateway to authoritative legal instruction, information, scholarship, and news.

Searching the Web

The web provides access to countless sites containing information posted by governments, educational institutions, organizations, businesses, and individuals. Such websites are different from other sources — including the kinds of online sources you access through indexes and databases — in two key ways: (1) their content varies greatly in its reliability and (2) they are not stable: what you see on a site today may be different (or gone) tomorrow. Anyone who wants to can post material on the web, so you need to evaluate carefully what you find there to eliminate sources that are not current, lack credibility, or are primarily advertisements or promotional in nature.

Because it is so vast and dynamic, finding what you need on the web for academic writing can be a challenge. The primary way of finding information on the web is with a search site. You may find the most suitable results for academic writing by using *Google Scholar,* a search site that finds scholarly literature, including peer-reviewed papers, technical reports, and abstracts. Here are other ways of searching the web:

- *Keyword searches. Google, Yahoo!, Bing,* and most other search sites all scan the web looking for keywords that you specify.

- *Subject directories.* *Google*, *Yahoo!*, and some other search sites offer directories that arrange information by topics, much like a library cataloging system. Such directories allow you to broaden or narrow your search if you need to — for example, a search for "birds" can be broadened to "animals" or narrowed to "blue-footed booby."

- *Metasearches.* *Yippy*, *Dogpile*, and *ZapMeta* are metasearch sites that allow you to use several search engines simultaneously. They are best for searching broadly; use a single search site for the most precise results.

- **Twitter searches.** In addition to *Twitter* Search, you can find *Twitter* content through search sites such as *Twazzup* and *Topsy*.

Each search site and metasearch site has its own protocols for searching; most have an "advanced search" option that will help you search more productively. Remember, though, that you need to be careful about EVALUATING SOURCES that you find on the web because the web is unregulated and no one independently verifies the information posted on its sites.

469–72

Doing Field Research

Sometimes you'll need to do your own research, to go beyond the information you find in published sources and gather data by doing field research. Three kinds of field research you might want to consider are interviews, observations, and questionnaires.

Interviewing experts.   Some kinds of writing — a profile of a living person, for instance — almost require that you conduct an interview. And sometimes you may just need to find information that you haven't been able to find in published sources. To get firsthand information on the experience of serving as a soldier in Afghanistan, you might interview your cousin who served a tour of duty there; to find current research on pesticide residues in food, you might need to interview a toxicologist. Whatever your goal, you can conduct interviews in person, using video-calling software such as *Skype* or *FaceTime*, by telephone, through email, or by mail. In general, you will want to use interviews to find information you can't find elsewhere. Below is some advice on planning and conducting an interview.

Before the interview

55–56

1. Once you identify someone you want to interview, email or phone to ask the person, stating your **PURPOSE** for the interview and what you hope to learn.

2. Once you've set up an appointment, send a note or email confirming the time and place. If you wish to record the interview, be sure to ask for permission to do so. If you plan to conduct the interview by mail or email, state when you will send your questions.

3. Write out questions. Plan questions that invite extended response and supporting details: "What accounts for the recent spike in gasoline prices?" forces an explanation, whereas "Is the recent spike in gas prices a direct result of global politics?" is likely to elicit only a yes or a no.

At the interview

4. Record the full name of the person you interview, along with the date, time, and place of the interview; you'll need this information to cite and document the interview accurately.

5. Take notes, even if you are recording the interview.

6. Keep track of time: don't take more than you agreed to beforehand unless both of you agree to keep talking. End by thanking your subject and offering to provide a copy of your final product.

After the interview

7. Flesh out your notes with details as soon as possible after the interview, while you still remember them. What did you learn? What surprised you? Summarize both the interviewee's words and your impressions.

8. Make sure you've reproduced quotations from the interview accurately and fairly. Avoid editing quotations in ways that distort the speaker's intended meaning.

9. Be sure to send a thank-you note or email.

Observation.   Some writing projects are based on information you get by observing something. For a sociology report, you may observe how students behave in large lectures. For an education course, you may observe one child's progress as a writer over a period of time. The following advice can help you conduct observations.

Before observing

1. Think about your research **PURPOSE**: What are you looking for? What do you expect to find? How will your presence as an observer affect what you observe? What do you plan to do with what you find?

   55–56

2. If necessary, set up an appointment. You may need to ask permission of the people you wish to observe and of your school as well. (Check with your instructor about your school's policy in this area.) Be honest and open about your goals and intentions; college students doing research assignments are often welcomed where others may not be.

While observing

3. If you're taking notes on paper, you may want to divide each page down the middle vertically and write only on the left side of the page, reserving the right side for information you will fill in later. If you're using a laptop, you can set up two columns or a split screen.

4. Note descriptive details about the setting. What do you see? What do you hear? Do you smell anything? Get down details about color, shape, size, sound, and so on. Consider photographing or making a sketch of what you see.

5. Who is there, and what are they doing? **DESCRIBE** what they look like, and make notes about what they say. Note any significant demographic details—about gender, race, occupation, age, dress, and so on.

   399–407

6. What is happening? Who's doing what? What's being said? Make note of these kinds of **NARRATIVE** details.

   419–27

After observing

7. As soon as possible after you complete your observations, use the right side of your notes to fill in gaps and include additional details.

94–128 ▲

8. **ANALYZE** your notes, looking for patterns. Did some things appear or happen more than once? Did anything stand out? surprise or puzzle you? What did you learn?

Questionnaires and surveys. Various kinds of questionnaires and surveys can provide information or opinions from a large number of people. For a political science course, you might conduct a survey to ask students who they plan to vote for. Or, for a marketing course, you might distribute a questionnaire asking what they think about an advertising campaign. The advice in this section will help you create useful questionnaires and surveys.

Define your goal. The goal of a questionnaire or survey should be limited and focused, so that every question will contribute to your research question. Also, people are more likely to respond to a brief, focused survey.

Define your sample. A survey gets responses from a representative sample of the whole group. The answers to these questions will help you define that sample:

1. Who should answer the questions? The people you contact should represent the whole population. For example, if you want to survey undergraduate students at your school, your sample should reflect your school's enrollment in terms of gender, year, major, age, ethnicity, and so forth as closely as possible.
2. How many people make up a representative sample? In general, the larger your sample, the more the answers will reflect those of the whole group. But if your population is small—200 students in a history course, for example—your sample must include a large percentage of that group.

Decide on a medium. Will you ask the questions face-to-face? over the phone? on a website such as *SurveyMonkey*? by mail? by email? Face-to-face questions work best for simple surveys or for gathering impersonal information. You're more likely to get responses to more personal questions with printed or online questionnaires, which should be neat and easy to read. Phone interviews may require well-thought-out scripts that anticipate possible answers and make it easy to record these answers.

Design good questions.   The way you ask questions will determine the usefulness of the answers you get, so take care to write questions that are clear and unambiguous. Here are some typical question types:

- *Multiple-choice*

  What is your current age?

  _____ 15–20   _____ 21–25   _____ 26–30   _____ 31–35   _____ Other

- *Rating scale*

  How would you rate the service at the campus bookstore?

  _____ Excellent   _____ Good   _____ Fair   _____ Poor

- *Agreement scale*

  How much do you agree with the following statements?

	Strongly Agree	Agree	Disagree	Strongly Disagree
The bookstore has sufficient numbers of textbooks available.	❐	❐	❐	❐

	Strongly Agree	Agree	Disagree	Strongly Disagree
Staff at the bookstore are knowledgeable.	❐	❐	❐	❐
Staff at the bookstore are courteous.	❐	❐	❐	❐

- *Open-ended*

  How often do you visit the campus bookstore?

  How can the campus bookstore improve its service?

Include all potential alternatives when phrasing questions to avoid biasing the answers. And make sure each question addresses only one issue — for example, "bookstore staff are knowledgeable and courteous" could lead to the response "knowledgeable, agree; courteous, disagree."

When arranging questions, place easier ones at the beginning and harder ones near the end (but if the questions seem to fall into a different natural order, follow it). Make sure each question asks for information you will need—if a question isn't absolutely necessary, omit it.

Include an introduction. Start by stating your survey's purpose and how the results will be used. It's also a good idea to offer an estimate of the time needed to complete the questions. Remind participants of your deadline.

Test the survey or questionnaire. Make sure your questions elicit the kinds of answers you need by asking three or four people who are part of your target population to answer them. They can help you find unclear instructions, questions that aren't clear or that lack sufficient alternatives, or other problems that you should correct to make sure your results are useful. But if you change the questionnaire as a result of their responses, don't include their answers in your total.

469–72 ⬤
478–80

IF YOU NEED MORE HELP

See **EVALUATING SOURCES** for help determining their usefulness. See also Chapter 49 for help **TAKING NOTES** on your sources.

academic literacies · rhetorical situations · genres · processes · strategies · research MLA / APA · media / design · readings

Evaluating Sources

Searching the *Health Source* database for information on the incidence of meningitis among college students, you find seventeen articles. A *Google* search on the same topic produces over 10,000 hits. How do you decide which sources to read? This chapter presents advice on evaluating sources—first to determine whether a source might be useful for your purposes and is worth looking at more closely and then to read with a critical eye the ones you choose.

Considering Whether a Source Might Be Useful

Think about your **PURPOSE**. Are you trying to persuade readers to believe or do something? to inform them about something? If the former, it will be especially important to find sources representing various positions; if the latter, you may need sources that are more factual or informative. Reconsider your **AUDIENCE**. What kinds of sources will they find persuasive? If you're writing for readers in a particular field, what counts as evidence in that field? Following are some questions that can help you judge whether a possible source you've found deserves your time and attention:

55–56

57–60

- *Is it reliable?* Is it **SCHOLARLY**? peer-reviewed? published in a reputable journal or magazine, or by a reputable publisher? Did you find it in a library database? on the web? Evaluating web-based texts may require more work than using results from library databases. But whatever kind of search you do, skim the results quickly to evaluate their reliability.

446–48

- *Is it relevant?* How does the source relate to your purpose? What will it add to your work? Look at the title and at any introductory material—a preface, abstract, or introduction—to see what the source covers.

- **What are the author's credentials?** How is the author qualified to write on the subject? Is he or she associated with a particular position on the issue? See whether the source mentions other works this author has written. In any case, you might do a web search to see what else you can learn about him or her.

64–67

- **What is the STANCE?** Consider whether a source covers various perspectives or advocates one particular point of view. Does its title suggest a certain slant? If it's online, you might check to see whether it includes links to other sites and, if so, what their perspectives are. You'll want to consult sources with a variety of viewpoints.

- **Who is the publisher or sponsor?** If it's a book, what kind of company published it; if an article, what kind of periodical did it appear in? Books published by university presses and articles in scholarly journals are reviewed by experts before they are published. Books and articles written for the general public typically do not undergo rigorous review—and they may lack the kind of in-depth discussion that is useful for research.

  If the source is online, is the site maintained by an organization? an interest group? a government agency? an individual? Look for clues in the URL: *edu* is used mostly by colleges and universities, *gov* by government agencies, *org* by nonprofit organizations, *mil* by the military, and *com* by commercial organizations. Evaluate the publisher's or sponsor's motives: to present information even-handedly? to promote a certain point of view, belief, or position? to sell something?

- **What is the level?** Can you understand the material? Texts written for a general audience might be easier to understand but not authoritative enough for academic work. Texts written for scholars will be more authoritative but may be hard to comprehend.

- **When was it published?** See when books and articles were published. Check to see when online sources were created and last updated. (If the site lists no date, see if links to other sites still work.) Recent does not necessarily mean better — some topics may require very current information whereas others may call for older sources.

- *Is it available?* Is it a source you can get hold of? If it's a book and your school's library doesn't have it, can you get it through interlibrary loan?

- *Does it include other useful information?* Is there a bibliography that might lead you to other sources? How current are the sources it cites?

Once you've decided that a source should be examined more closely, use the following questions to give it critical scrutiny.

Reading Sources with a Critical Eye

- *What ARGUMENTS does the author make?* Does the author present a number of different positions, or does he or she argue for a particular position? Do you need to ANALYZE THE ARGUMENT?

  ▲ 156–82
  ✳ 29–30

- *How persuasive do you find the argument?* What reasons and evidence does the author provide in support of any position(s)? Are there citations or links — and if so, are they credible? Is any evidence presented without citations? Do you find any of the author's assumptions questionable? How thoroughly does he or she consider opposing arguments?

- *What is the author's STANCE?* Does the author strive for objectivity, or does the content or language reveal a particular bias? Does the author consider opposing views and treat them fairly?

  ■ 64–67

- *Do you recognize ideas you've run across in other sources?* Does the source leave out any information or perspective that other sources include — or include any that other sources leave out?

- *Does this source support or challenge your own position—or does it do both?* Does it support your thesis? Offer a different argument altogether? Does it represent a position you may need to ACKNOWLEDGE or REFUTE? Don't reject a source just because it challenges your views; your sources should reflect a variety of views on your topic, showing that you've considered the subject thoroughly.

  ▲ 176
  ▲ 177

- *What can you tell about the intended AUDIENCE and PURPOSE?* Is the author writing to a general audience, to a subset of that audience, to

  ■ 57–60
  ■ 55–56

specialists in a particular field? Are you a member of that audience? If not, does that affect the way you interpret what you read? Is the main purpose to inform readers about a topic or to argue a certain point?

IF YOU NEED MORE HELP

478–90 See **QUOTING, PARAPHRASING, AND SUMMARIZING** for help in taking notes on
491–95 your sources and deciding how to use them in your writing. See also **ACKNOWLEDGING SOURCES, AVOIDING PLAGIARISM** for advice on giving credit to the sources you use.

---

academic literacies
rhetorical situations
genres
processes
strategies
research MLA / APA
media / design
readings

To **ANALYZE** the works of a poet, you show how she uses similar images in three different poems to explore a recurring concept. To solve a crime, a detective studies several eyewitness accounts to figure out who did it. To trace the history of photojournalism, a professor **COMPARES** the uses of photography during the Civil War and during the Vietnam War. These are all cases where someone *synthesizes*—brings together material from two or more sources in order to generate new information or to support a new perspective. When you do research, you need to go beyond what your sources say; you need to use what they say to inspire and support *what you want to say*. This chapter focuses on how to synthesize ideas you find in other sources as the basis for your own ideas.

▲ 94–128

◆ 380–87

Reading for Patterns and Connections

Your task as a writer is to find as much information as you can on your topic—and then to sift through all that you have found to determine and support what you yourself will write. In other words, you'll need to synthesize ideas and information from the sources you've consulted to figure out first what arguments *you* want to make and then to provide support for those arguments.

When you synthesize, you group similar bits of information together, looking for patterns or themes or trends and trying to identify the key points. For example, in researching the effectiveness of the SAT writing exam, you find several sources showing that scores correlate directly with length and that a majority of U.S. colleges and universities have decided not to count the results of the test in their admission decisions. You can infer from that pattern of research results that the test is not yet seen as an effective measure of writing ability. Here are some tips for reading to identify patterns and connections:

- Read all your sources with an open mind. Withhold judgment, even of sources that seem wrong-headed or implausible. Don't jump to conclusions.

486–87
- Take notes and write a brief **SUMMARY** of each source to help you see relationships, patterns, and connections among your sources. Take notes on your own thoughts, too.

289–92
293–95
- Pay attention to your first reactions. You'll likely have many ideas to work with, but your first thoughts can often lead somewhere that you will find interesting. Try **FREEWRITING**, **CLUSTERING**, or **LISTING** to see where they lead. How do these thoughts and ideas relate to your topic? Where might they fit into your rough **OUTLINE**?

- Try to think creatively, and pay attention to thoughts that flicker at the edge of your consciousness, as they may well be productive.

- Be playful. Good ideas sometimes come when we let our guard down or take ideas to extremes just to see where they lead.

Ask yourself these questions about your sources:

- What sources make the strongest arguments? What makes them so strong?

- Do some arguments recur in several sources?

- Which arguments do you agree with? disagree with? Of those you disagree with, which ones seem strong enough that you need to **ACKNOWLEDGE** them in your text?

368
- Are there any disagreements among your sources?

- Are there any themes you see in more than one source?

- Are any data—facts, statistics, examples—or experts cited in more than one source?

- Do several of your sources use the same terms? Do they use the terms similarly, or do they use them in different ways?

- What have you learned about your topic? How have your sources affected your thinking on your topic? Do you need to adjust your **THESIS**? If so, how?

◆ 345–47

- Have you discovered new questions you need to investigate?

- Keep in mind your **RHETORICAL SITUATION** — have you found the information you need that will achieve your purpose, appeal to your audience, and suit your genre and medium?

■ 53

What is likely to emerge from this questioning is a combination of big ideas, including new ways of understanding your topic and insights into recent scholarship about it, and smaller ones, such as how two sources agree with each other but not completely and how the information in one source supports or undercuts the argument of another. These ideas and insights will become the basis for your own ideas and for what *you* have to say about the topic.

Synthesizing Ideas Using Notes

You may find that identifying connections among your sources is easier if you examine them together rather than reading them one by one. For example, taking notes on note cards and then laying the cards out on a desk or table (or on the floor) lets you see passages that seem related. Doing the same with photocopies or printouts of your sources can help you identify similarities as well.

In doing research for an essay arguing that the sale of assault weapons should be banned, you might find several sources that address the scope of U.S. citizens' right to bear arms. On the next page are notes taken on three such sources: Joe Klein, a journalist writing in *Time.com*; Antonin Scalia, a U.S. Supreme Court justice, quoted in an online news article; and Drew Westen, a professor of psychology writing in a blog sponsored by the *New York Times*. Though the writers hold very different views, juxtaposing these notes and highlighting certain passages shows a common thread running through the sources. In this example, all three sources might be used to support the thesis that restrictions on the owning of weapons — but not an outright ban — are both constitutional and necessary.

Source 1

Limits of gun ownership

Although the U. S. Constitution includes the right to bear arms, that right is not absolute. "No American has the right to own a stealth bomber or a nuclear weapon. Armor-piercing bullets are forbidden. The question is where you draw a reasonable bright line."
—Klein, "How the Gun Won" — quote

Source 4

Limits of gun ownership

Supreme Court Justice Antonin M. Scalia has noted that when the Constitution was written and ratified, some weapons were barred. So limitations could be put on owning some weapons, as long as the limits are consistent with those in force in 1789.
—Scalia, quoted in Woods — paraphrase

Source 3

Limits of gun ownership

Westen's "message consulting" research has shown that Americans are ambivalent about guns but react very positively to a statement of principle that includes both the right to own guns and restrictions on their ownership, such as prohibiting large ammunition clips and requiring all gun purchasers to undergo background checks for criminal behavior or mental illness.
—Westen — paraphrase

academic literacies • rhetorical situations • genres • processes • strategies • research MLA / APA • media / design • readings

Synthesizing Information to Support Your Own Ideas

If you're doing research to write a **REPORT**, your own ideas will be communicated primarily through which information you decide to include from the sources you cite and how you organize that information. If you're writing a **TEXTUAL ANALYSIS**, your synthesis may focus on the themes, techniques, or other patterns you find. If you're writing a research-based **ARGUMENT**, on the other hand, your synthesis of sources must support the position you take in that argument. No matter what your genre, the challenge is to synthesize information from your research to develop ideas about your topic and then to support those ideas.

▲ 129–55

▲ 94–128

▲ 156–82

Entering the Conversation

As you read and think about your topic, you will come to an understanding of the concepts, interpretations, and controversies relating to your topic — and you'll become aware that there's a larger conversation going on. When you begin to find connections among your sources, you will begin to see your own place in that conversation, to discover your own ideas and your own stance on your topic. This is the exciting part of a research project, for when you write out your own ideas on the topic, you will find yourself entering that conversation. Remember that your **STANCE** as an author needs to be clear: simply stringing together the words and ideas of others isn't enough. You need to show readers *how* your source materials relate to one another and to your thesis.

■ 64–67

> **IF YOU NEED MORE HELP**
>
> See Chapter 49, **QUOTING, PARAPHRASING, AND SUMMARIZING,** for help in integrating source materials into your own text. See also Chapter 50 on **ACKNOWLEDGING SOURCES, AVOIDING PLAGIARISM** for advice on giving credit to the sources you cite.

● 478–90
491–95

49 Quoting, Paraphrasing, and Summarizing

In an oral presentation about the rhetoric of Abraham Lincoln, you quote a memorable line from the Gettysburg Address. For an essay on the Tet Offensive in the Vietnam War, you paraphrase arguments made by several commentators and summarize some key debates about that war. When you work with the ideas and words of others, you need to clearly distinguish those ideas and words from your own and give credit to their authors. This chapter will help you with the specifics of quoting, paraphrasing, and summarizing source materials that you use in your writing.

Taking Notes

When you find material you think will be useful, take careful notes. How do you determine how much to record? You need to write down enough information so that when you refer to it later, you will be reminded of its main points and have a precise record of where it comes from.

- *Use a computer file, note cards, or a notebook,* labeling each entry with the information that will allow you to keep track of where it comes from—author, title, and the pages or the URL (or DOI [digital object identifier]). You needn't write down full bibliographic information (you can abbreviate the author's name and title) since you'll include that information in your **WORKING BIBLIOGRAPHY**.

- *Take notes in your own words, and use your own sentence patterns.* If you make a note that is a detailed **PARAPHRASE**, label it as such so that you'll know to provide appropriate **DOCUMENTATION** if you use it.

441–43

483–86
496–99

academic literacies · rhetorical situations · genres · processes · strategies · research MLA / APA · media / design · readings

- *If you find wording that you'd like to quote,* be sure to enclose it in quotation marks to distinguish your source's words from your own. Double-check your notes to be sure any quoted material is accurately quoted—and that you haven't accidentally **PLAGIARIZED** your sources.

491–95

- *Label each note with a number to identify the source and a subject heading* to relate the note to a subject, supporting point, or other element in your essay. Doing this will help you to sort your notes easily and match them up with your rough outline. Restrict each note to a single subject.

Here are a few examples of one writer's notes on a source discussing synthetic dyes, bladder cancer, and the use of animals to determine what causes cancers. Each note includes a subject heading and brief source information and identifies whether the source is quoted or paraphrased.

Source 3

<u>Synthetic dyes</u>

The first synthetic dye was mauve, invented in 1854 and derived from coal. Like other coal-derived dyes, it contained aromatic amines.
Steingraber, "Pesticides," 976 —paraphrase

Source 3

<u>Synthetic dyes & cancer</u>

Bladder cancer was common among textile workers who used dyes. Steingraber: "By the beginning of the twentieth century, bladder cancer rates among this group of workers had skyrocketed."
Steingraber, "Pesticides," 976 — paraphrase and quote

> **Source 3**
>
> <u>Synthetic dyes & cancer</u>
>
> In 1938, Wilhelm Hueper exposed dogs to aromatic amines and showed that the chemical caused bladder cancer.
> Steingraber, "Pesticides," 976 —paraphrase

Deciding Whether to Quote, Paraphrase, or Summarize

298–300

480–83

When it comes time to **DRAFT**, you'll need to decide *how* to use any source you want to include—in other words, whether to quote, paraphrase, or summarize it. You might follow this rule of thumb: **QUOTE** texts when the wording is worth repeating or makes a point so well that no rewording will do it justice, when you want to cite the exact words of a known authority on your topic, when an authority's opinions challenge or disagree with those of others, or

483–86

486–87

when the source is one you want to emphasize. **PARAPHRASE** sources that are not worth quoting but contain details you need to include. **SUMMARIZE** longer passages whose main points are important but whose details are not.

Quoting

Quoting a source is a way of weaving someone else's exact words into your text. You need to reproduce the source exactly, though you can modify it to omit unnecessary details (with ellipses) or to make it fit smoothly into your text (with brackets). You also need to distinguish quoted material from

487–90

your own by enclosing short quotations in quotation marks, setting off longer quotes as a block, and using appropriate **SIGNAL PHRASES**.

MLA 500–548

Incorporate short quotations into your text, enclosed in quotation marks. If you are following **MLA STYLE**, short quotations are defined as four typed

lines or fewer; if using **APA STYLE**, as below, short means fewer than forty words.

APA 549–89

> Gerald Graff (2003) has argued that colleges make the intellectual life seem more opaque than it needs to be, leaving many students with "the misconception that the life of the mind is a secret society for which only an elite few qualify" (p. 1).

If you are quoting three lines or fewer of poetry, run them in with your text, enclosed in quotation marks. Separate lines with slashes, leaving one space on each side of the slashes.

> Emma Lazarus almost speaks for the Statue of Liberty with the words inscribed on its pedestal: "Give me your tired, your poor, / Your huddled masses yearning to breathe free, / The wretched refuse of your teeming shore" (58).

Set off long quotations block style.   If you are using MLA style, set off quotations of five or more typed lines by indenting the quote one-half inch (or five spaces) from the left margin. If you are using APA style, indent quotations of forty or more words one-half inch (or five spaces) from the left margin. In either case, do not use quotation marks, and put any parenthetical documentation *after* any end punctuation.

> Nonprofit organizations such as Oxfam and Habitat for Humanity rely on visual representations of the poor. What better way to get our attention, asks rhetorician Diana George:
>
> > In a culture saturated by the image, how else do we convince Americans that—despite the prosperity they see all around them—there is real need out there? The solution for most nonprofits has been to show the despair. To do that they must represent poverty as something that can be seen and easily recognized: fallen down shacks and trashed out public housing, broken windows, dilapidated porches, barefoot kids with stringy hair, emaciated old women and men staring out at the camera with empty eyes. (210)

If you are quoting four or more lines of poetry, they need to be set off block style in the same way.

Indicate any omissions with ellipses. You may sometimes delete words from a quotation that are unnecessary for your point. Insert three ellipsis marks (leaving a space before the first and after the last one) to indicate the deletion. If you omit a sentence or more in the middle of a quotation, put a period before the three ellipsis dots. Be careful not to distort the source's meaning, however.

> Faigley points out that Gore's "Information Superhighway" metaphor "associated the economic prosperity of the 1950s and . . . 1960s facilitated by new highways with the potential for vast . . . commerce to be conducted over the Internet" (253).

> According to Welch, "Television is more acoustic than visual. . . . One can turn one's gaze away from the television, but one cannot turn one's ears from it without leaving the area where the monitor leaks its aural signals into every corner" (102).

Indicate additions or changes with brackets. Sometimes you'll need to change or add words in a quotation — to make the quotation fit grammatically within your sentence, for example, or to add a comment. In the following example, the writer changes the passage "one of our goals" to clarify the meaning of "our."

> Writing about the dwindling attention among some composition scholars to the actual teaching of writing, Susan Miller notes that "few discussions of writing pedagogy take it for granted that one of [writing teachers'] goals is to teach how to write" (480).

Here's an example of brackets used to add explanatory words to a quotation:

> Barbosa observes that Buarque's lyrics have long included "many a metaphor of *saudades* [yearning] so characteristic of *fado* music" (207).

Use punctuation correctly with quotations. When you incorporate a quotation into your text, you have to think about the end punctuation in the quoted material and also about any punctuation you need to add when you insert the quote into your own sentence.

Periods and commas. Put periods or commas *inside* closing quotation marks, except when you have parenthetical documentation at the end, in which case you put the period or comma after the parentheses.

> "Country music," Tichi says, "is a crucial and vital part of the American identity" (23).

After long quotations set off block style with no quotation marks, however, the period goes *before* the documentation, as in the example on page 481.

Question marks and exclamation points. These go *inside* closing quotation marks if they are part of the quoted material but *outside* when they are not. If there's parenthetical documentation at the end of the quotation, any punctuation that's part of your sentence comes after it.

> Speaking at a Fourth of July celebration in 1852, Frederick Douglass asked, "What have I, or those I represent, to do with your national independence?" (35).

> Who can argue with W. Charisse Goodman's observation that media images persuade women that "thinness equals happiness and fulfill-ment" (53)?

Colons and semicolons. These always go *outside* closing quotation marks.

> It's hard to argue with W. Charisse Goodman's observation that media images persuade women that "thinness equals happiness and fulfillment"; nevertheless, American women today are more overweight than ever (53).

Paraphrasing

When you paraphrase, you restate information from a source in your own words, using your own sentence structures. Paraphrase when the source material is important but the original wording is not. Because it includes all the main points of the source, a paraphrase is usually about the same length as the original.

Here is a paragraph about synthetic dyes and cancer, followed by two paraphrases of it that demonstrate some of the challenges of paraphrasing:

ORIGINAL SOURCE

In 1938, in a series of now-classic experiments, exposure to synthetic dyes derived from coal and belonging to a class of chemicals called aromatic amines was shown to cause bladder cancer in dogs. These results helped explain why bladder cancers had become so prevalent among dyestuffs workers. With the invention of mauve in 1854, synthetic dyes began replacing natural plant-based dyes in the coloring of cloth and leather. By the beginning of the twentieth century, bladder cancer rates among this group of workers had skyrocketed, and the dog experiments helped unravel this mystery. The International Labor Organization did not wait for the results of these animal tests, however, and in 1921 declared certain aromatic amines to be human carcinogens. Decades later, these dogs provided a lead in understanding why tire-industry workers, as well as machinists and metalworkers, also began falling victim to bladder cancer: aromatic amines had been added to rubbers and cutting oils to serve as accelerants and antirust agents.

—Sandra Steingraber, "Pesticides, Animals, and Humans"

The following paraphrase borrows too much of the language of the original or changes it only slightly, as the highlighted words and phrases show:

UNACCEPTABLE PARAPHRASE: WORDING TOO CLOSE

Now-classic experiments in 1938 showed that when dogs were exposed to aromatic amines, chemicals used in synthetic dyes derived from coal, they developed bladder cancer. Similar cancers were prevalent among dyestuffs workers, and these experiments helped to explain why. Mauve, a synthetic dye, was invented in 1854, after which cloth and leather manufacturers replaced most of the natural plant-based dyes with synthetic dyes. By the early twentieth century, this group of workers had skyrocketing rates of bladder cancer, a mystery the dog experiments helped to unravel. As early as 1921, though, before the test results proved the connection, the International Labor Organization had labeled certain aromatic amines carcinogenic. Even so, decades later many metalworkers, machinists, and tire-industry workers began developing bladder cancer. The animal tests helped researchers understand that rubbers and cutting oils contained aromatic amines as accelerants and antirust agents (Steingraber 976).

The next paraphrase uses original language but follows the sentence structure of Steingraber's text too closely:

UNACCEPTABLE PARAPHRASE: SENTENCE STRUCTURE TOO CLOSE

In 1938, several pathbreaking experiments showed that being exposed to synthetic dyes that are made from coal and belong to a type of chemicals called aromatic amines caused dogs to get bladder cancer. These results helped researchers identify why cancers of the bladder had become so common among textile workers who worked with dyes. With the development of mauve in 1854, synthetic dyes began to be used instead of dyes based on plants in the dyeing of leather and cloth. By the end of the nineteenth century, rates of bladder cancer among these workers had increased dramatically, and the experiments using dogs helped clear up this oddity. The International Labor Organization anticipated the results of these tests on animals, though, and in 1921 labeled some aromatic amines carcinogenic. Years later these experiments with dogs helped researchers explain why workers in the tire industry, as well as metalworkers and machinists, also started dying of bladder cancer: aromatic amines had been put into rubbers and cutting oils as rust inhibitors and accelerants (Steingraber 976).

Patchwriting, a third form of unacceptable paraphrase, combines the other two. Composition researcher Rebecca Moore Howard defines it as "copying from a source text and then deleting some words, altering grammatical structures, or plugging in one-for-one synonym-substitutes." Here is a patchwrite of the first two sentences of the original source: (The source's exact words are shaded in yellow; paraphrases are in blue.)

PATCHWRITE

Scientists have known for a long time that chemicals in the environment can cause cancer. For example, in 1938, in a series of important experiments, being exposed to synthetic dyes made out of coal and belonging to a kind of chemicals called aromatic amines was shown to cause dogs to develop bladder cancer. These experiments explain why this type of cancer had become so common among workers who handled dyes.

Here is an acceptable paraphrase of the entire passage:

ACCEPTABLE PARAPHRASE

Biologist Sandra Steingraber explains that pathbreaking experiments in 1938 demonstrated that dogs exposed to aromatic amines (chemicals used in coal-derived synthetic dyes) developed cancers of the bladder that were similar to cancers common among dyers in the textile industry. After mauve, the first synthetic dye, was invented in 1854, leather and cloth manufacturers replaced most natural dyes made from plants with synthetic dyes, and by the early 1900s textile workers had very high rates of bladder cancer. The experiments with dogs proved the connection, but years before, in 1921, the International Labor Organization had labeled some aromatic amines carcinogenic. Even so, years later many metal-workers, machinists, and workers in the tire industry started to develop unusually high rates of bladder cancer. The experiments with dogs helped researchers understand that the cancers were caused by aromatic amines used in cutting oils to inhibit rust and in rubbers as accelerants (976).

Some guidelines for paraphrasing

- *Use your own words and sentence structure.* It is acceptable to use some words from the original, but as much as possible, the phrasing and sentence structures should be your own.

487–90
- *Introduce paraphrased text with* **SIGNAL PHRASES**.

- *Put in quotation marks any of the source's original phrasing that you use.*

- *Indicate the source.* Although the wording may be yours, the ideas and information come from another source; be sure to name the author and include **DOCUMENTATION** to avoid the possibility of **PLAGIARISM**.

MLA 503–37
APA 552–75
491–95

Summarizing

A summary states the main ideas in a source concisely and in your own words. Unlike a paraphrase, a summary does *not* present all the details, and it is generally as brief as possible. Summaries may boil down an entire

academic literacies · rhetorical situations · genres · processes · strategies · research MLA / APA · media / design · readings

book or essay into a single sentence, or they may take a paragraph or more to present the main ideas. Here, for example, is a one-sentence summary of the Steingraber paragraph:

> Steingraber explains that experiments with dogs demonstrated that aromatic amines, chemicals used in synthetic dyes, cutting oils, and rubber, cause bladder cancer (976).

In the context of an essay, the summary might take this form:

> Medical researchers have long relied on experiments using animals to expand understanding of the causes of disease. For example, biologist and ecologist Sandra Steingraber notes that in the second half of the nineteenth century, the rate of bladder cancer soared among textile workers. According to Steingraber, experiments with dogs demonstrated that synthetic chemicals in dyes used to color the textiles caused the cancer (976).

Some guidelines for summarizing

- *Include only the main ideas; leave out the details.* A summary should include just enough information to give the reader the gist of the original. It is always much shorter than the original, sometimes even as brief as one sentence.

- *Use your own words.* If you quote phrasing from the original, enclose the phrase in quotation marks.

- *Indicate the source.* Although the wording may be yours, the ideas and information come from another source. Name the author, either in a signal phrase or parentheses, and include an appropriate **IN-TEXT CITATION** to avoid the possibility of **PLAGIARISM**.

MLA 503–9
APA 552–75
491–95

Introducing Source Materials Using Signal Phrases

You need to introduce quotations, paraphrases, and summaries clearly, usually letting readers know who the author is—and, if need be, something about his or her credentials. Consider this sentence:

> Professor and textbook author Elaine Tyler May argues that many high school history books are too bland to interest young readers (531).

The beginning ("Professor and textbook author Elaine Tyler May argues") functions as a *signal phrase*, telling readers who is making the assertion and why she has the authority to speak on the topic—and making clear that everything between the signal phrase and the parenthetical citation comes from that source. Since the signal phrase names the author, the parenthetical citation includes only the page number; had the author not been identified in the signal phrase, she would have been named in the parentheses:

> Even some textbook authors believe that many high school history books are too bland to interest young readers (May 531).

MLA and APA have different conventions for constructing signal phrases. In MLA, the language you use in a signal phrase can be neutral — like *X says* or *Y thinks* or *according to Z*. Or it can suggest something about the **STANCE** — the source's or your own. The example above referring to the textbook author uses the verb *argues*, suggesting that what she says is open to dispute (or that the writer believes it is). How would it change your understanding if the signal verb were *observes* or *suggests*?

64–67

In addition to the names of sources' authors, signal phrases often give readers information about institutional affiliations and positions authors have, their academic or professional specialties, and any other information that lets readers judge the credibility of the sources. You should craft each signal phrase you use so as to highlight the credentials of the author. Here are some examples:

> A study done by Anthony M. Armocida, professor of psychology at Duke University, showed that . . .

The signal phrase identifies the source's author, his professional position, and his university affiliation, emphasizing his title.

> Science writer Isaac McDougal argues that . . .

This phrase acknowledges that the source's author may not have scholarly credentials but is a published writer; it's a useful construction if the source doesn't provide much information about the writer.

academic literacies　rhetorical situations　genres　processes　strategies　research MLA / APA　media / design　readings

Writing in *Psychology Today*, Amanda Chao-Fitz notes that . . . .

This is the sort of signal phrase you use if you have no information on the author; you establish credibility on the basis of the publication in which the source appears.

If you're writing using APA style, signal phrases are typically briefer, giving only the author's last name and the date of publication:

According to Benzinger (2010), . . .

Quartucci (2011) observed that . . .

SOME COMMON SIGNAL VERBS

acknowledges	claims	disagrees	observes
admits	comments	disputes	points out
advises	concludes	emphasizes	reasons
agrees	concurs	grants	rejects
argues	confirms	illustrates	reports
asserts	contends	implies	responds
believes	declares	insists	suggests
charges	denies	notes	thinks

Verb tenses. MLA and APA also have different conventions regarding the tenses of verbs in signal phrases. MLA requires present-tense verbs (*writes, asserts, notes*) in signal phrases to introduce a work you are quoting, paraphrasing, or summarizing.

In *Poor Richard's Almanack*, Benjamin Franklin <u>notes</u>, "He that cannot obey, cannot command" (739).

If, however, you are referring to the act of writing or saying something rather than simply quoting someone's words, you might not use the present tense. The writer of the following sentence focuses on the year in which the source was written—therefore, the verb is necessarily in the past tense:

Back in 1941, Kenneth Burke <u>wrote</u> that "the ethical values of work are in its application of the competitive equipment to cooperative ends" (316).

If you are following APA style, use the past tense or present-perfect tense to introduce sources composed in the past.

Dowdall, Crawford, and Wechsler (1998) <u>observed</u> that women attending women's colleges are less likely to engage in binge drinking than are women who attend coeducational colleges (p. 713).

APA requires the present tense, however, to discuss the results of an experiment or to explain conclusions that are generally agreed on.

The findings of this study <u>suggest</u> that excessive drinking has serious consequences for college students and their institutions.

The authors of numerous studies <u>agree</u> that smoking and drinking among adolescents are associated with lower academic achievement.

IF YOU NEED MORE HELP

491–95 ●
MLA 539–48 ●
APA 578–89
33–44 ✳

See Chaper 50 for help **ACKNOWLEDGING SOURCES** and giving credit to the sources you use. See also the **SAMPLE RESEARCH PAPERS** to see how sources are cited in MLA and APA styles. And see Chapter 3 if you're writing a **SUMMARY/ RESPONSE** essay.

 academic literacies
 rhetorical situations
 genres
 processes
 strategies
● research MLA / APA
□ media / design
▌ readings

Acknowledging Sources, Avoiding Plagiarism

50

Whenever you do research-based writing, you find yourself entering a conversation — reading what many others have had to say about your topic, figuring out what you yourself think, and then putting what you think in writing — "putting in your oar," as the rhetorician Kenneth Burke once wrote. As a writer, you need to *acknowledge* any words and ideas that come from others — to give credit where credit is due, to recognize the various authorities and many perspectives you have considered, to show readers where they can find your sources, and to situate your own arguments in the ongoing conversation. Using other people's words and ideas without acknowledgment is *plagiarism,* a serious academic and ethical offense. This chapter will show you how to acknowledge the materials you use and avoid plagiarism.

Acknowledging Sources

When you insert in your text information that you've obtained from others, your reader needs to know where your source's words or ideas begin and end. Therefore, you should usually introduce a source by naming the author in a **SIGNAL PHRASE** and then provide brief **DOCUMENTATION** of the specific material from the source in a parenthetical reference following the material. (Sometimes you can put the author's name in the parenthetical reference as well.) You need only brief documentation of the source here, since your readers will find full bibliographic information about it in your list of **WORKS CITED** or **REFERENCES**.

487–90
MLA 503–9
APA 552–56

MLA 510–38
APA 557–75

Sources that need acknowledgment. You almost always need to acknowledge any information that you get from a specific source. Material you should acknowledge includes the following:

- *Direct quotations.* Unless they are well known (see p. 494 for some examples), any quotations from another source must be enclosed in quotation marks, cited with brief bibliographic information in parentheses, and usually introduced with a signal phrase that tells who wrote or said it and provides necessary contextual information, as in the following sentence:

  > In a dissenting opinion on the issue of racial preferences in college admissions, Supreme Court justice Ruth Bader Ginsburg argues, "The stain of generations of racial oppression is still visible in our society, and the determination to hasten its removal remains vital" (*Gratz v. Bollinger*).

- *Arguable statements and information that may not be common knowledge.* If you state something about which there is disagreement or for which arguments can be made, cite the source of your statement. If in doubt about whether you need to give the source of an assertion, provide it. As part of an essay on "fake news" programs, for example, you might make the following assertion:

  > The satire of *The Daily Show* complements the conservative bias of FOX News, since both have abandoned the stance of objectivity maintained by mainstream news sources, contends Michael Hoyt, executive editor of the *Columbia Journalism Review* (43).

Others might argue with the contention that the FOX News Channel offers biased reports of the news, so the source of this assertion needs to be acknowledged. In the same essay, you might present information that should be cited because it's not widely known, as in this example:

  > According to a report by the Pew Research Center, 12 percent of Americans under thirty got information about the 2012 presidential campaign primarily from "fake news" and comedy shows like *The Daily Show* and *Saturday Night Live* (2).

- *The opinions and assertions of others.* When you present the ideas, opinions, and assertions of others, cite the source. You may have rewritten the concept in your own words, but the ideas were generated by someone else and must be acknowledged, as they are here:

  > David Boonin, writing in the *Journal of Social Philosophy*, asserts that, logically, laws banning marriage between people of different races are not discriminatory since everyone of each race is affected equally by them. Laws banning same-sex unions are discriminatory, however, since they apply only to people with a certain sexual orientation (256).

- *Any information that you didn't generate yourself.* If you did not do the research or compile the data yourself, cite your source. This goes for interviews, statistics, graphs, charts, visuals, photographs — anything you use that you did not create. If you create a chart using data from another source, you need to cite that source.

- *Collaboration with and help from others.* In many of your courses and in work situations, you'll be called on to work with others. You may get help with your writing at your school's writing center or from fellow students in your writing courses. Acknowledging such collaboration or assistance, in a brief informational note, is a way of giving credit—and saying thank you. See guidelines for writing notes in the **MLA** and **APA** sections of this book.

⬤ MLA 509–10
APA 557

Sources that don't need acknowledgment. Widely available information and common knowledge do not require acknowledgment. What constitutes common knowledge may not be clear, however. When in doubt, provide a citation, or ask your instructor whether the information needs to be cited. You generally do not need to cite the following:

- *Information that most readers are likely to know.* You don't need to acknowledge information that is widely known or commonly accepted as fact. For example, in a literary analysis, you wouldn't cite a source saying that Harriet Beecher Stowe wrote *Uncle Tom's Cabin*; you can assume your readers already know that. On the other hand, you should cite the source from which you got the information that the book was

first published in installments in a magazine and then, with revisions, in book form, because that information isn't common knowledge. As you do research in areas you're not familiar with, be aware that what constitutes common knowledge isn't always clear; the history of the novel's publication would be known to Stowe scholars and would likely need no acknowledgment in an essay written for them. In this case, too, if you aren't sure whether to acknowledge information, do so.

- *Information and documents that are widely available.* If a piece of information appears in several sources or reference works or if a document has been published widely, you needn't cite a source for it. For example, the date when astronauts Neil Armstrong and Buzz Aldrin landed a spacecraft on the moon can be found in any number of reference works. Similarly, the Declaration of Independence and the Gettysburg Address are reprinted in thousands of sources, so the ones where you found them need no citation.

- *Well-known quotations.* These include such famous quotations as Lady Macbeth's "Out, damned spot!" and John F. Kennedy's "Ask not what your country can do for you; ask what you can do for your country." Be sure, however, that the quotation is correct. Winston Churchill is said to have told a class of schoolchildren, "Never, ever, ever, ever, ever, ever, ever give up. Never give up. Never give up. Never give up." His actual words, however, are much different and begin "Never give in."

- *Material that you created or gathered yourself.* You need not cite photographs that you took, graphs that you composed based on your own findings, or data from an experiment or survey that you conducted—though you should make sure readers know that the work is yours.

A good rule of thumb: *when in doubt, cite your source.* You're unlikely to be criticized for citing too much—but you may invite charges of plagiarism by citing too little.

Avoiding Plagiarism

When you use the words or ideas of others, you need to acknowledge who and where the material came from; if you don't credit those sources, you are guilty of plagiarism. Plagiarism is often committed unintentionally — as when a writer paraphrases someone else's ideas in language that is too close to the original. It is essential, therefore, to know what constitutes plagiarism: (1) using another writer's words or ideas without acknowledging the source, (2) using another writer's exact words without quotation marks, and (3) paraphrasing or summarizing someone else's ideas using language or sentence structures that are too close to theirs.

To avoid plagiarizing, take careful **NOTES** as you do your research, clearly labeling as quotations any words you quote directly and being careful to use your own phrasing and sentence structures in paraphrases and summaries. Be sure you know what source material you must **DOCUMENT**, and give credit to your sources, both in the text and in a list of **REFERENCES** or **WORKS CITED**.

475–76

496–99
APA 557–75
MLA 510–38

Be aware that it's easy to plagiarize inadvertently when you're working with online sources, such as full-text articles, that you've downloaded or cut and pasted into your notes. Keep careful track of these materials, since saving copies of your sources is so easy. Later, be sure to check your draft against the original sources to make sure your quotations are accurately worded — and take care, too, to include quotation marks and document the source correctly. Copying online material right into a document you are writing and forgetting to put quotation marks around it or to document it (or both) is all too easy to do. You must acknowledge information you find on the web just as you must acknowledge all other source materials.

And you must recognize that plagiarism has consequences. Scholars' work will be discredited if it too closely resembles another's. Journalists found to have plagiarized lose their jobs, and students routinely fail courses or are dismissed from their school when they are caught cheating—all too often by submitting as their own essays that they have purchased from online "research" sites. If you're having trouble completing an assignment, seek assistance. Talk with your instructor, or if your school has a writing center, go there for advice on all aspects of your writing, including acknowledging sources and avoiding plagiarism.

51 Documentation

In everyday life, we are generally aware of our sources: "I read it on Megan McArdle's blog." "Amber told me it's your birthday." "If you don't believe me, ask Mom." Saying how we know what we know and where we got our information is part of establishing our credibility and persuading others to take what we say seriously.

The goal of a research project is to study a topic, combining what we learn from sources with our own thinking and then composing a written text. When we write up the results of a research project, we cite the sources we use, usually by quoting, paraphrasing, or summarizing, and we acknowledge those sources, telling readers where the ideas came from. The information we give about sources is called documentation, and we provide it not only to establish our credibility as researchers and writers but also so that our readers, if they wish to, can find the sources themselves.

Understanding Documentation Styles

The Norton Field Guide covers the documentation styles of the Modern Language Association (MLA) and the American Psychological Association (APA). MLA style is used chiefly in the humanities; APA is used mainly in the social sciences. Both are two-part systems, consisting of (1) brief in-text parenthetical documentation for quotations, paraphrases, or summaries and (2) more-detailed documentation in a list of sources at the end of the text. MLA and APA require that the end-of-text documentation provide the following basic information about each source you cite:

- author, editor, or creator of the source
- title of source (and of publication or site where it appears)
- place of publication (for print sources; APA only)
- name of publisher
- date of publication
- retrieval information (for online sources)

MLA and APA are by no means the only documentation styles. Many other publishers and organizations have their own style, among them the University of Chicago Press and the Council of Science Editors. We focus on MLA and APA here because those are styles that college students are often required to use. On the following page are examples of how the two parts—the brief parenthetical documentation in your text and the more detailed information at the end—correspond in each of these systems.

The examples here and throughout this book are color-coded to help you see the crucial parts of each citation: brown for author and editor, yellow for title, and gray for publication information: place of publication, name of publisher, date of publication, page number(s), and so on.

As the examples of in-text documentation show, in either MLA or APA style you should name the author either in a signal phrase or in parentheses following the source information. But there are several differences between the two styles in the details of the documentation. In MLA, the author's full name is used in a signal phrase; in APA, only the last name is used. In APA, the abbreviation *p.* is used with the page number, which is provided only for a direct quotation; in MLA, a page number (if there is one) is always given, but with no abbreviation before it. Finally, in APA the date of publication always appears just after the author's name.

Comparing the MLA and APA styles of listing works cited or references also reveals some differences: MLA includes an author's first name while APA gives only initials; MLA puts the date near the end while APA places it right after the author's name; APA requires the place of publication while MLA usually does not; MLA capitalizes most of the words in a book's title and subtitle while APA capitalizes only the first words and proper nouns and proper adjectives in each.

MLA Style

IN-TEXT DOCUMENTATION

As Lester Faigley puts it, "The world has become a bazaar from which to shop for an individual 'lifestyle' " (12).

As one observer suggests, "The world has become a bazaar from which to shop for an individual 'lifestyle' " (Faigley 12).

WORKS-CITED DOCUMENTATION

Faigley, Lester. *Fragments of Rationality: Postmodernity and the Subject of Composition.* U of Pittsburgh P, 1992.

APA Style

IN-TEXT DOCUMENTATION

As Faigley (1992) suggested, "The world has become a bazaar from which to shop for an individual 'lifestyle'" (p. 12).

As one observer has noted, "The world has become a bazaar from which to shop for an individual 'lifestyle'" (Faigley, 1992, p. 12).

REFERENCE-LIST DOCUMENTATION

Faigley, L. (1992). *Fragments of rationality: Postmodernity and the subject of composition.* Pittsburgh, PA: University of Pittsburgh Press.

author   title   publication

Some of these differences are related to the nature of the academic fields in which the two styles are used. In humanities disciplines, the authorship of a text is emphasized, so both first and last names are included in MLA documentation. Scholarship in those fields may be several years old but still current, so the publication date doesn't appear in the in-text citation. In APA style, as in many documentation styles used in the sciences, education, and engineering, emphasis is placed on the date of publication because in these fields, more recent research is usually preferred over older studies. However, although the elements are arranged differently, both MLA and APA — and other documentation styles as well — require similar information about author, title, and publication.

52 MLA Style

MLA style calls for (1) brief in-text documentation and (2) complete bibliographic information in a list of works cited at the end of your text. The models and examples in this chapter draw on the eighth edition of the *MLA Handbook*, published by the Modern Language Association in 2016. For additional information, visit style.mla.org.

A DIRECTORY TO MLA STYLE

In-Text Documentation   503

Formatting a Research Paper   538

Sample Research Paper   539

Throughout this chapter, you'll find models and examples that are color coded to help you see how writers include source information in their texts and in their lists of works cited: tan for author, editor, translator, and other contributors; yellow for titles; gray for publication information—date of publication, page number(s) or other location information, and so on.

IN-TEXT DOCUMENTATION

Brief documentation in your text makes clear to your reader what you took from a source and where in the source you found the information.

In your text, you have three options for citing a source: **QUOTING**, **PARAPHRASING**, and **SUMMARIZING**. As you cite each source, you will need to decide whether or not to name the author in a signal phrase—"as Toni Morrison writes"—or in parentheses—"(Morrison 24)."

478–90

The first examples below show basic in-text documentation of a work by one author. Variations on those examples follow. The examples illustrate the MLA style of using quotation marks around titles of short works and italicizing titles of long works.

1. AUTHOR NAMED IN A SIGNAL PHRASE

If you mention the author in a **SIGNAL PHRASE**, put only the page number(s) in parentheses. Do not write *page* or *p*.

487–90

> McCullough describes John Adams's hands as those of someone used to manual labor (18).

2. AUTHOR NAMED IN PARENTHESES

If you do not mention the author in a signal phrase, put his or her last name in parentheses along with the page number(s). Do not use punctuation between the name and the page number(s).

> Adams is said to have had "the hands of a man accustomed to pruning his own trees, cutting his own hay, and splitting his own firewood" (McCullough 18).

Whether you use a signal phrase and parentheses or parentheses only, try to put the parenthetical documentation at the end of the sentence or as close as possible to the material you've cited—without awkwardly interrupting the sentence. Notice that in the example above, the parenthetical reference comes after the closing quotation marks but before the period at the end of the sentence.

3. TWO OR MORE WORKS BY THE SAME AUTHOR

If you cite multiple works by one author, include the title of the work you are citing either in the signal phrase or in parentheses. Give the full title if it's brief; otherwise, give a short version.

> Kaplan insists that understanding power in the Near East requires "Western leaders who know when to intervene, and do so without illusions" (*Eastward* 330).

Put a comma between author and title if both are in the parentheses.

> Understanding power in the Near East requires "Western leaders who know when to intervene, and do so without illusions" (Kaplan, *Eastward* 330).

4. AUTHORS WITH THE SAME LAST NAME

Give the author's first and last names in any signal phrase, or add the author's first initial in the parenthetical reference.

author   title   publication

Imaginative applies not only to modern literature but also to writing of all periods, whereas *magical* is often used in writing about Arthurian romances (A. Wilson 25).

5. TWO OR MORE AUTHORS

For a work with two authors, name both, either in a signal phrase or in parentheses.

> Carlson and Ventura's stated goal is to introduce Julio Cortázar, Marjorie Agosín, and other Latin American writers to an audience of English-speaking adolescents (v).

For a work by three or more authors, name the first author followed by *et al.*

> One popular survey of American literature breaks the contents into sixteen thematic groupings (Anderson et al. A19-24).

6. ORGANIZATION OR GOVERNMENT AS AUTHOR

Acknowledge the organization either in a signal phrase or in parentheses. It's acceptable to shorten long names.

> The US government can be direct when it wants to be. For example, it sternly warns, "If you are overpaid, we will recover any payments not due you" (Social Security Administration 12).

7. AUTHOR UNKNOWN

If you don't know the author, use the work's title or a shortened version of the title in the parenthetical reference.

> A powerful editorial in last week's paper asserts that healthy liver donor Mike Hurewitz died because of "frightening" faulty postoperative care ("Every Patient's Nightmare").

8. LITERARY WORKS

When referring to literary works that are available in many different editions, give the page numbers from the edition you are using, followed by information that will let readers of any edition locate the text you are citing.

NOVELS. Give the page and chapter number, separated by a semicolon.

> In *Pride and Prejudice*, Mrs. Bennet shows no warmth toward Jane and Elizabeth when they return from Netherfield (105; ch. 12).

VERSE PLAYS. Give act, scene, and line numbers, separated with periods.

> Macbeth continues the vision theme when he says, "Thou hast no speculation in those eyes / Which thou dost glare with" (3.3.96-97).

POEMS. Give the part and the line numbers (separated by periods). If a poem has only line numbers, use the word *line(s)* only in the first reference.

> Whitman sets up not only opposing adjectives but also opposing nouns in "Song of Myself" when he says, "I am of old and young, of the foolish as much as the wise, / . . . a child as well as a man" (16.330-32).

> One description of the mere in *Beowulf* is "not a pleasant place" (line 1372). Later, it is labeled "the awful place" (1378).

9. WORK IN AN ANTHOLOGY

Name the author(s) of the work, not the editor of the anthology—either in a signal phrase or in parentheses.

> "It is the teapots that truly shock," according to Cynthia Ozick in her essay on teapots as metaphor (70).

> In *In Short: A Collection of Creative Nonfiction*, readers will find both an essay on Scottish tea (Hiestand) and a piece on teapots as metaphors (Ozick).

author   title   publication

10. ENCYCLOPEDIA OR DICTIONARY

Acknowledge an entry in an encyclopedia or dictionary by giving the author's name, if available. For an entry without an author, give the entry's title in parentheses. If entries are arranged alphabetically, no page number is needed.

> According to *Funk & Wagnall's New World Encyclopedia*, early in his career Kubrick's main source of income came from "hustling chess games in Washington Square Park" ("Kubrick, Stanley").

11. LEGAL AND HISTORICAL DOCUMENTS

For legal cases and acts of law, name the case or act in a signal phrase or in parentheses. Italicize the name of a legal case.

> In 2005, the Supreme Court confirmed in *MGM Studios, Inc. v. Grokster, Ltd.* that peer-to-peer file sharing is copyright infringement.

Do not italicize the titles of laws, acts, or well-known historical documents such as the Declaration of Independence. Give the title and any relevant articles and sections in parentheses. It's fine to use common abbreviations such as *art.* or *sec.* and to abbreviate well-known titles.

> The president is also granted the right to make recess appointments (US Const., art. 2, sec. 2).

12. SACRED TEXT

When citing a sacred text such as the Bible or the Qur'an for the first time, give the title of the edition, and in parentheses give the book, chapter, and verse (or their equivalent), separated by periods. MLA recommends abbreviating the names of the books of the Bible in parenthetical references. Later citations from the same edition do not have to repeat its title.

> The wording from *The New English Bible* follows: "In the beginning of creation, when God made heaven and earth, the earth was without form and void, with darkness over the face of the abyss, and a mighty wind that swept over the surface of the waters" (Gen. 1.1-2).

13. MULTIVOLUME WORK

If you cite more than one volume of a multivolume work, each time you cite one of the volumes, give the volume *and* the page number(s) in parentheses, separated by a colon and a space.

> Sandburg concludes with the following sentence about those paying last respects to Lincoln: "All day long and through the night the unbroken line moved, the home town having its farewell" (4: 413).

If your works cited list includes only a single volume of a multivolume work, give just the page number in parentheses.

14. TWO OR MORE WORKS CITED TOGETHER

If you're citing two or more works closely together, you will sometimes need to provide a parenthetical reference for each one.

> Tanner (7) and Smith (viii) have looked at works from a cultural perspective.

If you include both in the same parentheses, separate the references with a semicolon.

> Critics have looked at both *Pride and Prejudice* and *Frankenstein* from a cultural perspective (Tanner 7; Smith viii).

15. SOURCE QUOTED IN ANOTHER SOURCE

When you are quoting text that you found quoted in another source, use the abbreviation *qtd. in* in the parenthetical reference.

> Charlotte Brontë wrote to G. H. Lewes: "Why do you like Miss Austen so very much? I am puzzled on that point" (qtd. in Tanner 7).

16. WORK WITHOUT PAGE NUMBERS

For works without page numbers, including many online sources, identify the source using the author or other information either in a signal phrase or in parentheses.

> Studies show that music training helps children to be better at multitask-ing later in life ("Hearing the Music").

If the source has chapter, paragraph, or section numbers, use them with the abbreviations *ch.*, *par.*, or *sec.*: ("Hearing the Music," par. 2). Alternatively, you can refer to a heading on a screen to help readers locate text.

> Under the heading "The Impact of the Railroad," Rawls notes that the transcontinental railroad was called an iron horse and a greedy octopus.

For an audio or a video recording, give the hours, minutes, and seconds (separated by colons) as shown on the player: (00:05-08:30).

17. AN ENTIRE WORK OR A ONE-PAGE ARTICLE

If you cite an entire work rather than a part of it, or if you cite a single-page article, there's no need to include page numbers.

> Throughout life, John Adams strove to succeed (McCullough).

NOTES

Sometimes you may need to give information that doesn't fit into the text itself — to thank people who helped you, to provide additional details, to refer readers to other sources, or to add comments about sources. Such information can be given in a *footnote* (at the bottom of the page) or an *endnote* (on a separate page with the heading *Notes* just before your works cited list). Put a superscript number at the appropriate point in your text, signaling to readers to look for the note with the corresponding number. If you have multiple notes, number them consecutively throughout your paper.

TEXT

> This essay will argue that small liberal arts colleges should not recruit athletes and, more specifically, that giving student athletes preferential treatment undermines the larger educational goals.[1]

NOTE

　　1. I want to thank all those who have contributed to my thinking on this topic, especially my classmates and my teacher Marian Johnson.

LIST OF WORKS CITED

A works cited list provides full bibliographic information for every source cited in your text. See page 539 for guidelines on formatting this list and page 547 for a sample works cited list.

Core Elements

The new MLA style provides a list of "core elements" for documenting sources, advising writers to list as many of them as possible in the order that MLA specifies. We've used these general principles to provide templates and examples for documenting 53 kinds of sources college writers most often need to cite, and the following general guidelines for how to treat each of the core elements.

AUTHORS AND OTHER CONTRIBUTORS

- If there is one author, list the name last name first: Morrison, Toni.

- If there are two authors, list the first author last name first and the second one first name first: Lunsford, Andrea, and Lisa Ede. Put their names in the order given in the work.

- If there are three or more authors, give the first author's name followed by *et al.*: Rose, Mike, et al.

- Include any middle names or initials: Heath, Shirley Brice; Toklas, Alice B.

- If you're citing an editor, translator, or others who are not authors, specify their role. For works with multiple contributors, put the one whose work you wish to highlight before the title, and list any others you want to mention after the title. For contributors named before the title, put the label after the name: Fincher, David, director. For those named after the title, specify their role first: directed by David Fincher.

TITLES

- Include any subtitles and capitalize all the words in titles and subtitles except for articles (*a, an, the*), prepositions (*to, at, from,* and so on), and coordinating conjunctions (*and, but, for, or, nor, yet*)—unless they are the first or last word of a title or subtitle.
- Italicize the titles of books, periodicals, and other long whole works (*Pride and Prejudice, Wired*), even if they are part of a larger work.
- Enclose in quotation marks the titles of short works and sources that are part of larger works: "Letter from Birmingham Jail."
- To document a source that has no title, describe it without italics or quotation marks: Letter to the author, Review of doo wop concert.

PUBLICATION INFORMATION

- Write publishers' names in full, but omit words like *Company* or *Inc.*
- For university presses, use *U* for "University" and *P* for "Press": Princeton UP, U of California P.

DATES

- Whether to give just the year or to include the month and day depends on the source. Give the full date that you find there.
- For books, give the year of publication: 1948. If a book lists more than one date, use the most recent one.
- Periodicals may be published annually, monthly, seasonally, weekly, or daily. Give the full date that you find in the periodical: 2011, Apr. 2011, Spring 2011, 16 Apr. 2011.
- Abbreviate the months except for May, June, and July: Jan., Feb., Mar., Apr., Aug., Sept., Oct., Nov., Dec.
- Because online sources often change or even disappear, provide the date on which you accessed them: Accessed 6 June 2015.

- If an online source includes the time when it was posted or modified, include the time along with the date: 18 Oct. 2005, 9:20 a.m.

LOCATION

- For most print articles and other short works, help readers locate the source by giving a page number or range of pages: p. 24, pp. 24-35. For those that are not on consecutive pages, give the first page number with a plus sign: pp. 24+.
- For online sources, give the URL, omitting *http://* or *https://*. If a source has a permalink, give that.
- For sources found in a database, give the DOI for any that have one. Otherwise, give the URL.
- For physical objects that you find in a museum, archive, or some other place, give the name of the place and its city: Menil Collection, Houston. Omit the city if it's part of the place's name: Boston Public Library.
- For performances or other live presentations, name the venue and its city: Mark Taper Forum, Los Angeles. Omit the city if it's part of the place's name: Berkeley Repertory Theatre.

PUNCTUATION

- Use a period after the author name(s) that start an entry (Morrison, Toni.) and the title of the source you're documenting (*Beloved*.)
- Use a comma between the author's last and first names: Morrison, Toni.
- Sometimes you'll need to provide information about more than one work for a single source—for instance, when you cite an article from a periodical that you access through a database. MLA refers to the periodical and database (or any other entity that holds a source) as "containers." Use commas between elements within each container and put a period at the end of each container. For example:

> Semuels, Alana. "The Future Will Be Quiet." *The Atlantic,* Apr. 2016,
> pp. 19-20. *ProQuest,* search.proquest.com/docview/
> 1777443553?accountid+42654. Accessed 5 Apr. 2016.

author   title   publication

The guidelines below should help you document kinds of sources you're likely to use. The first section shows how to acknowledge authors and other contributors and applies to all kinds of sources—print, online, or others. Later sections show how to treat titles, publication information, location, and access information for many specific kinds of sources. In general, provide as much information as possible for each source—enough to tell readers how to find a source if they wish to access it themselves.

Authors and Other Contributors

When you name authors and other contributors in your citations, you are crediting them for their work and letting readers know who's in on the conversation. The following guidelines for citing authors and other contributors apply to all sources you cite: in print, online, or in some other media.

1. ONE AUTHOR

Author's Last Name, First Name. *Title*. Publisher, Date.

Anderson, Curtis. *The Long Tail: Why the Future of Business Is Selling Less of More.* Hyperion, 2006.

2. TWO AUTHORS

1st Author's Last Name, First Name, and 2nd Author's First and Last Names. *Title*. Publisher, Date.

Lunsford, Andrea, and Lisa Ede. *Singular Texts/Plural Authors: Perspectives on Collaborative Writing*. Southern Illinois UP, 1990.

3. THREE OR MORE AUTHORS

1st Author's Last Name, First Name, et al. *Title*. Publisher, Date.

Sebranek, Patrick, et al. *Writers INC: A Guide to Writing, Thinking, and Learning*. Write Source, 1990.

4. TWO OR MORE WORKS BY THE SAME AUTHOR

Give the author's name in the first entry, and then use three hyphens in the author slot for each of the subsequent works, listing them alphabetically by the first important word of each title.

> Author's Last Name, First Name. *Title That Comes First Alphabetically.*
> Publisher, Date.
>
> - - -. *Title That Comes Next Alphabetically.* Publisher, Date.
>
> Kaplan, Robert D. *The Coming Anarchy: Shattering the Dreams of the Post Cold War.* Random House, 2000.
>
> - - -. *Eastward to Tartary: Travels in the Balkans, the Middle East, and the Caucasus.* Random House, 2000.

5. AUTHOR AND EDITOR OR TRANSLATOR

> Author's Last Name, First Name. *Title.* Role by First and Last Names,
> Publisher, Date.
>
> Austen, Jane. *Emma.* Edited by Stephen M. Parrish, W. W. Norton, 2000.
>
> Dostoevsky, Fyodor. *Crime and Punishment.* Translated by Richard Pevear and Larissa Volokhonsky, Vintage Books, 1993.

Start with the editor or translator if you are focusing on their contribution rather than the author's.

> Pevear, Richard, and Larissa Volokhonsky, translators. *Crime and Punishment.* By Fyodor Dostoevsky, Vintage Books, 1993.

6. NO AUTHOR OR EDITOR

When there's no known author or editor, start with the title.

> *The Turner Collection in the Clore Gallery.* Tate Publications, 1987.
>
> "Being Invisible Closer to Reality." *The Atlanta Journal-Constitution,* 11 Aug. 2008, p. A3.

author   title   publication

7. ORGANIZATION OR GOVERNMENT AS AUTHOR

> Organization Name. *Title.* Publisher, Date.

> Diagram Group. *The Macmillan Visual Desk Reference.* Macmillan, 1993.

For a government publication, give the name of the government first, followed by the names of any department and agency.

> United States, Department of Health and Human Services, National
> Institute of Mental Health. *Autism Spectrum Disorders.*
> Government Printing Office, 2004.

When the organization is both author and publisher, start with the title and list the organization only as the publisher.

> *Stylebook on Religion 2000: A Reference Guide and Usage Manual.*
> Catholic News Service, 2002.

Articles and Other Short Works

Articles, essays, reviews, and other shorts works are found in journals, magazines, newspapers, other periodicals, and books—all of which you may find in print, online, or in a database. For most short works, you'll need to provide information about the author, the titles of both the short work and the longer work, any page numbers, and various kinds of publication information, all explained below.

8. ARTICLE IN A JOURNAL

PRINT

> Author's Last Name, First Name. "Title of Article." *Name of Journal,*
> Volume, Issue, Date, Pages.

Documentation Map (MLA)

Article in a Print Journal

Marge Simpson, Blue-Haired Housewife: ← **Title of article**
Defining Domesticity on *The Simpsons*

JESSAMYN NEUHAUS ← **Author**

MORE THAN TWENTY SEASONS AFTER ITS DEBUT AS A SHORT ON *THE Tracy Ullman Show* in 1989, pundits, politicians, scholars, journalists, and critics continue to discuss and debate the meaning and relevance of *The Simpsons* to American society. For academics and educators, the show offers an especially dense pop culture text, inspiring articles and anthologies examining *The Simpsons* in light of American religious life, the representation of homosexuality in cartoons, and the use of pop culture in the classroom, among many other topics (Dennis; Frank; Henry "The Whole World's Gone Gay"; Hobbs; Kristiansen). Philosophers and literary theorists in particular are intrigued by the quintessentially postmodern self-aware form and content of *The Simpsons* and the questions about identity, spectatorship, and consumer culture it raises (Alberti; Bybee and Overbeck; Glynn; Henry "The Triumph of Popular Culture"; Herron; Hull; Irwin et al.; Ott; Parisi).

Simpsons observers frequently note that this TV show begs one of the fundamental questions in cultural studies: can pop culture ever provide a site of individual or collective resistance or must it always ultimately function in the interests of the capitalist dominant ideology? Is *The Simpsons* a brilliant satire of virtually every cherished American myth about public and private life, offering dissatisfied Americans the opportunity to critically reflect on contemporary issues (Turner 435)? Or is it simply another TV show making money for the Fox Network? Is *The Simpsons* an empty, cynical, even nihilistic view of the world, lulling its viewers into laughing hopelessly at the pointless futility of

Volume ──────────────┐ ┌────── **Issue**

Name of journal → *The Journal of Popular Culture*, Vol. 43, No. 4, 2010 ← **Year**
© 2010, Wiley Periodicals, Inc.

515–23 ⬤
for more
on citing
articles
MLA style

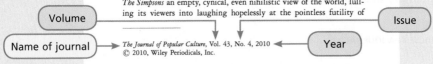

Neuhaus, Jessamyn. "Marge Simpson, Blue-Haired Housewife: Defining Domesticity on *The Simpsons*." *The Journal of Popular Culture*, vol. 43, no. 4, 2010, pp. 761-81.

Cooney, Brian C. "Considering *Robinson Crusoe*'s 'Liberty of Conscience' in an Age of Terror." *College English,* vol. 69, no. 3, Jan. 2007, pp. 197-215.

ONLINE

Author's Last Name, First Name. "Title of Article." *Name of Journal,* Volume, Issue, Date, Pages (if any), URL. Accessed Day Month Year.

Gleckman, Jason. "Shakespeare as Poet or Playwright? The Player's Speech in *Hamlet.*" *Early Modern Literary Studies,* vol. 11, no. 3, Jan. 2006, purl.oclc.org/emls/11-3/glechaml.htm. Accessed 31 Mar. 2015.

9. ARTICLE IN A MAGAZINE

PRINT

Author's Last Name, First Name. "Title of Article." *Name of Magazine,* Date, Pages.

Neyfakh, Leon. "The Future of Getting Arrested." *The Atlantic,* Jan.-Feb. 2015, pp. 26+.

ONLINE

Author's Last Name, First Name. "Title of Article." *Name of Magazine,* Date on web, Pages (if any), URL. Accessed Day Month Year.

Khazan, Olga. "Forgetting and Remembering Your First Language." *The Atlantic,* 24 July 2014, www.theatlantic.com/international/ archive/2014/07/learning-forgetting-and-remembering-your-first-language/374906/. Accessed 2 Apr. 2015.

10. ARTICLE IN A NEWSPAPER

PRINT

Author's Last Name, First Name. "Title of Article." *Name of Newspaper,*
Date, Pages.

Saulny, Susan, and Jacques Steinberg. "On College Forms, a Question of
Race Can Perplex." *The New York Times,* 14 June 2011, p. A1.

To document a particular edition of a newspaper, list the edition (*late ed.,*
natl. ed., and so on) after the date. If a section of the newspaper is numbered, put that detail after the edition information.

Burns, John F., and Miguel Helft. "Under Pressure, YouTube Withdraws
Muslim Cleric's Videos." *The New York Times,* 4 Nov. 2010, late ed.,
sec. 1, p. 13.

ONLINE

Author's Last Name, First Name. "Title of Article." *Name of Newspaper,*
Date on web, URL. Accessed Day Month Year.

Banerjee, Neela. "Proposed Religion-Based Program for Federal Inmates
Is Canceled." *The New York Times,* 28 Oct. 2006, www.nytimes.
com/2006/10/28/us/28prison.html?_r=0. Accessed 4 Apr. 2015.

11. ARTICLE ACCESSED THROUGH A DATABASE

Author's Last Name, First Name. "Title of Article." *Name of Periodical,*
Volume, Issue, Date, Pages. *Name of Database,* DOI or URL.
Accessed Day Month Year.

Stalter, Sunny. "Subway Ride and Subway System in Hart Crane's 'The
Tunnel.'" *Journal of Modern Literature,* vol. 33, no. 2, Jan. 2010,
pp. 70-91. *JSTOR,* doi: 10.2979/jml.2010.33.2.70. Accessed 30 Mar.
2015.

Documentation Map (MLA)

Article in an Online Magazine

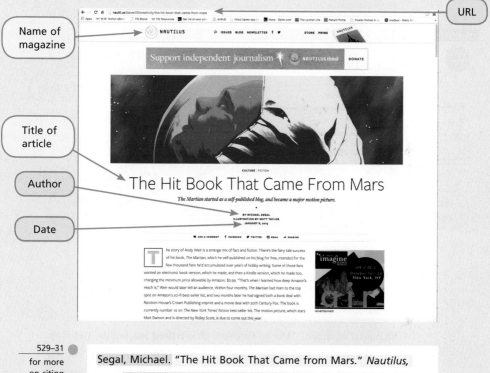

URL

Name of
magazine

Title of
article

Author

Date

529–31
for more
on citing
websites
MLA style

Segal, Michael. "The Hit Book That Came from Mars." *Nautilus*,
8 Jan. 2015, nautil.us/issue/20/creativity/the-hit-book-that-
came-from-mars. Accessed 10 Oct. 2016.

Documentation Map (MLA)

Journal Article Accessed through a Database

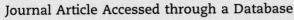

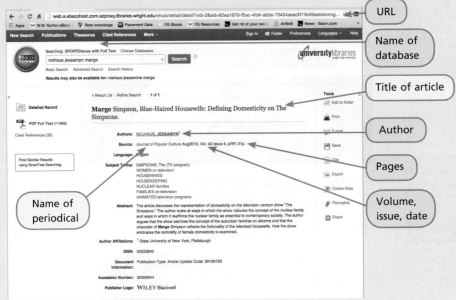

URL

Name of database

Title of article

Author

Pages

Name of periodical

Volume, issue, date

Neuhaus, Jessamyn. "Marge Simpson, Blue-Haired Housewife: Defining Domesticity on *The Simpsons*." *Journal of Popular Culture*, vol. 43, no. 4, Aug. 2010, pp. 761-81. *SPORT Discus with Full Text*, ezproxy. libraries.wright.edu/login?url=http://search.ebscohost.com/login.aspx? direct=true&db=a9h&AN=52300944&site=ehost-live. Accessed 24 Mar. 2016.

12. ENTRY IN A REFERENCE WORK

PRINT

Author's Last Name, First Name (if any). "Title of Entry." *Title of Reference Book,* edited by Editor's First and Last Names (if any), Edition number, Publisher, Date, Pages.

"California." *The New Columbia Encyclopedia*, edited by William H. Harris and Judith S. Levey, 4th ed., Columbia UP, 1975, pp. 423-24.

"Feminism." *Longman Dictionary of American English*, Longman, 1983, p. 252.

If there's no author given, start with the title of the entry.

ONLINE

Document online reference works the same as print ones, adding the URL and access date after the date of publication.

"Baseball." *The Columbia Electronic Encyclopedia,* edited by Paul Lagassé, 6th ed., Columbia UP, 2012. www.infoplease.com/encyclopedia. Accessed 25 May 2016.

13. EDITORIAL

PRINT

"Title of Editorial." Editorial. *Name of Periodical,* Date, Page.

"Gas, Cigarettes Are Safe to Tax." Editorial. *The Lakeville Journal,* 17 Feb. 2005, p. A10.

ONLINE

"Title of Editorial." Editorial. *Name of Periodical,* Date on web, URL. Accessed Day Month Year.

"Keep the Drinking Age at 21." Editorial. *Chicago Tribune*, 28 Aug. 2008, articles.chicagotribune.com/2008-08-26/news/0808250487_1_ binge-drinking-drinking-age-alcohol-related-crashes. Accessed 26 Apr. 2015.

14. LETTER TO THE EDITOR

Author's Last Name, First Name. "Title of Letter (if any)." Letter. *Name of Periodical,* Date on web, URL. Accessed Day Month Year.

Pinker, Steven. "Language Arts." Letter. *The New Yorker,* 4 June 2012, www.newyorker.com/magazine/2012/06/04/language-arts-2. Accessed 6 Apr. 2015.

15. REVIEW

PRINT

Reviewer's Last Name, First Name. "Title of Review." Review of *Title,* by Author's First and Last Names. *Name of Periodical,* Date, Pages.

Frank, Jeffrey. "Body Count." Review of *The Exception,* by Christian Jungersen. *The New Yorker,* 30 July 2007, pp. 86-87.

If a review has no author or title, start with what's being reviewed:

Review of *Ways to Disappear,* by Idra Novey. *The New Yorker,* 28 Mar. 2016, p. 79.

ONLINE

Reviewer's Last Name, First Name. "Title of Review." Review of *Title,* by Author's First and Last Names. *Name of Periodical,* Date, URL. Accessed Day Month Year.

Donadio, Rachel. "Italy's Great, Mysterious Storyteller." Review of *My Brilliant Friend,* by Elena Ferrante. *The New York Review of Books,* 18 Dec. 2014, www.nybooks.com/articles/2014/ 12/18/italys-great-mysterious-storyteller. Accessed 28 Sept. 2015.

16. COMMENT ON AN ONLINE ARTICLE

Commenter. Comment on "Title of Article." *Name of Periodical,* Date posted, Time posted, URL. Accessed Day Month Year.

Nick. Comment on "The Case for Reparations." *The Atlantic,* 22 May 2014, 3:04 p.m., www.theatlantic.com/business/archive/2014/05/ how-to-comment-on-reparations/371422/#article-comments. Accessed 8 May 2015.

Books and Parts of Books

For most books, you'll need to provide information about the author, the title, the publisher, and the year of publication. If you found the book inside a larger volume, a database, or some other work, be sure to specify that as well.

Documentation Map (MLA)
Print Book

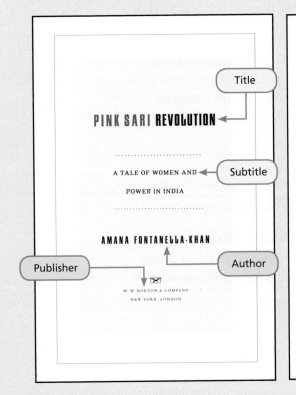

523–29
for more
on citing
books
MLA style

Fontanella-Khan, Amana. *Pink Sari Revolution: A Tale of Women and Power in India.* W. W. Norton, 2013.

17. BASIC ENTRIES FOR A BOOK

PRINT

Author's Last Name, First Name. *Title.* Publisher, Year of publication.

Watson, Brad. *Miss Jane.* W. W. Norton, 2016.

EBOOK

Document an ebook as you would a print book, but add information about the ebook—or the type of ebook if you know it.

Watson, Brad. *Miss Jane.* Ebook, W. W. Norton, 2016.

Watson, Brad. *Miss Jane.* Kindle ed., W. W. Norton, 2016.

IN A DATABASE

Author's Last Name, First Name. *Title.* Publisher, Year of publication. *Name of Database,* DOI or URL. Accessed Day Month Year.

Anderson, Sherwood. *Winesburg, Ohio.* B. W. Huebsch, 1919. *Bartleby.com,* www.bartleby.com/156/. Accessed 8 Apr. 2015.

18. ANTHOLOGY

Last Name, First Name, editor. *Title.* Publisher, Year of publication.

Hall, Donald, editor. *The Oxford Book of Children's Verse in America.* Oxford UP, 1985.

19. WORK(S) IN AN ANTHOLOGY

Author's Last Name, First Name. "Title of Work." *Title of Anthology,* edited by First and Last Names, Publisher, Year of publication, Pages.

Achebe, Chinua. "Uncle Ben's Choice." *The Seagull Reader: Literature,* edited by Joseph Kelly, W. W. Norton, 2005, pp. 23-27.

TWO OR MORE WORKS FROM ONE ANTHOLOGY

Prepare an entry for each selection by author and title, followed by the anthology editors' last names and the pages of the selection. Then include an entry for the anthology itself (see no. 18).

Author's Last Name, First Name. "Title of Work." Anthology Editors' Last Names, Pages.

Hiestand, Emily. "Afternoon Tea." Kitchen and Jones, pp. 65-67.

Ozick, Cynthia. "The Shock of Teapots." Kitchen and Jones, pp. 68-71.

20. MULTIVOLUME WORK

ALL VOLUMES

Author's Last Name, First Name. *Title of Work.* Publisher, Year(s) of publication. Number of vols.

Churchill, Winston. *The Second World War.* Houghton Mifflin, 1948-53. 6 vols.

SINGLE VOLUME

Author's Last Name, First Name. *Title of Work.* Vol. number, Publisher, Year of publication. Number of vols.

Sandburg, Carl. *Abraham Lincoln: The War Years.* Vol. 2, Harcourt, Brace & World, 1939. 4 vols.

21. BOOK IN A SERIES

Author's Last Name, First Name. *Title of Book.* Edited by First and Last Names, Publisher, Year of publication. Series Title.

Walker, Alice. *Everyday Use.* Edited by Barbara T. Christian, Rutgers UP, 1994. Women Writers: Texts and Contexts.

author   title   publication

22. GRAPHIC NARRATIVE

Author's Last Name, First Name. *Title.* Publisher, Year of publication.

Bechdel, Alison. *Fun Home: A Family Tragicomedy.* Houghton Mifflin, 2006.

If the work has both an author and an illustrator, start with the one whose work is more relevant to your research, and label the role of anyone who's not an author.

Pekar, Harvey. *Bob & Harv's Comics.* Illustrated by R. Crumb, Running Press, 1996.

Crumb, R., illustrator. *Bob & Harv's Comics.* By Harvey Pekar, Running Press, 1996.

23. SACRED TEXT

If you cite a specific edition of a religious text, you need to include it in your works cited list.

The New English Bible with the Apocrypha. Oxford UP, 1971.

The Torah: A Modern Commentary. Edited by W. Gunther Plaut, Union of American Hebrew Congregations, 1981.

24. EDITION OTHER THAN THE FIRST

Author's Last Name, First Name. *Title.* Name or number of edition, Publisher, Year of publication.

Fowler, H. W. *A Dictionary of Modern English.* 2nd ed., Oxford UP, 1965.

25. REPUBLISHED WORK

Author's Last Name, First Name. *Title.* Year of original publication. Current publisher, Year of republication.

Bierce, Ambrose. *Civil War Stories.* 1909. Dover, 1994.

26. FOREWORD, INTRODUCTION, PREFACE, OR AFTERWORD

Part Author's Last Name, First Name. Name of Part. *Title of Book,*
by Author's First and Last Names, Publisher, Year of publication,
Pages.

Tanner, Tony. Introduction. *Pride and Prejudice*, by Jane Austen, Penguin,
1972, pp. 7-46.

27. PUBLISHED LETTER

Letter Writer's Last Name, First Name. Letter to First and Last
Names. Day Month Year. *Title of Book,* edited by First and Last
Names, Publisher, Year of publication, Pages.

White, E. B. Letter to Carol Angell. 28 May 1970. *Letters of E. B. White,*
edited by Dorothy Lobarno Guth, Harper & Row, 1976, p. 600.

28. PAPER AT A CONFERENCE

PAPER PUBLISHED IN CONFERENCE PROCEEDINGS

Author's Last Name, First Name. "Title of Paper." *Title of Published
Conference Proceedings,* edited by First and Last Names, Publisher,
Year of publication, Pages.

Flower, Linda. "Literate Action." *Composition in the Twenty-first Century:
Crisis and Change,* edited by Lynn Z. Bloom et al., Southern Illinois
UP, 1996, pp. 249-60.

PAPER HEARD AT A CONFERENCE

Author's Last Name, First Name. "Title of Paper." *Title of Conference,*
Day Month Year, Location, City.

Hern, Katie. "Inside an Accelerated Reading and Writing Classroom."
Conference on Acceleration in Developmental Education, 15 June
2016, Sheraton Inner Harbor Hotel, Baltimore.

author   title   publication

29. DISSERTATION

> Author's Last Name, First Name. *Title*. Diss. Institution, Year, Publisher, Year of publication.

> Goggin, Peter N. *A New Literacy Map of Research and Scholarship in Computers and Writing*. Diss. Indiana U of Pennsylvania, 2000, University Microfilms International, 2001.

For an unpublished dissertation, put the title in quotation marks, and end with the institution and the year.

> Kim, Loel. "Students Respond to Teacher Comments: A Comparison of Online Written and Voice Modalities." Diss. Carnegie Mellon U, 1998.

Websites

Many sources are available in multiple media—for example, a print periodical that is also on the web and contained in digital databases—but some are published only on websites. This section covers the latter.

30. ENTIRE WEBSITE

> Last Name, First Name, role. *Title of Site*. Publisher, Date, URL. Accessed Day Month Year.

> Zalta, Edward N., principal editor. *Stanford Encyclopedia of Philosophy*. Metaphysics Research Lab, Center for the Study of Language, Stanford U, 1995-2015, plato.stanford.edu/index.html. Accessed 21 Apr. 2015.

PERSONAL WEBSITE

> Author's Last Name, First Name. *Title of Site*. Date, URL. Accessed Day Month Year.

> Heath, Shirley Brice. *Shirley Brice Heath*. 2015, shirleybriceheath.net. Accessed 6 June 2015.

Documentation Map (MLA)

Work on a Website

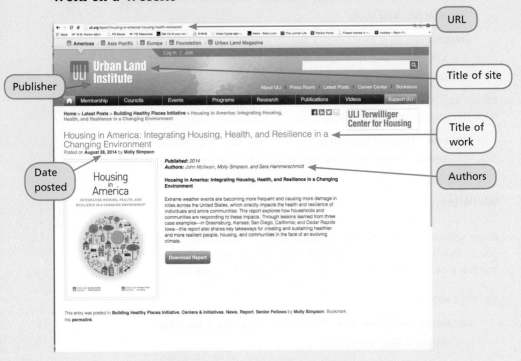

McIlwain, John, et al. "Housing in America: Integrating Housing, Health, and Resilience in a Changing Environment." *Urban Land Institute*, Urban Land Institute, 28 Aug. 2014, uli.org/report/housing-in-america-housing-health-resilience. Accessed 17 Sept. 2015.

31. WORK ON A WEBSITE

> Author's Last Name, First Name (if any). "Title of Work." *Title of Site,* Publisher, Date, URL. Accessed Day Month Year.

> "Global Minnesota: Immigrants Past and Present." *Immigration History Research Center,* U of Minnesota, 2015, cla.umn.edu.ihrc. Accessed 25 May 2016.

32. BLOG ENTRY

> Author's Last Name, First Name. "Title of Blog Entry." *Title of Blog,* Date, URL. Accessed Day Month Year.

> Hollmichel, Stefanie. "Bringing Up the Bodies." *So Many Books,* 10 Feb. 2014, somanybooksblog.com/2014/02/10/bring-up-the-bodies/. Accessed 12 Feb. 2014.

Document a whole blog as you would an entire website (no. 30) and a comment on a blog as you would a comment on an online article (no. 16).

33. WIKI

> "Title of Entry." *Title of Wiki,* Publisher, Date, URL. Accessed Day Month Year.

> "Pi." *Wikipedia,* Wikimedia Foundation, 28 Aug. 2013, en.wikipedia.org/wiki/Pi. Accessed 25 Oct. 2013.

Personal Communication and Social Media

34. PERSONAL LETTER

> Sender's Last Name, First Name. Letter to the author. Day Month Year.

> Quindlen, Anna. Letter to the author. 11 Apr. 2013.

35. EMAIL

> Sender's Last Name, First Name. "Subject Line." Received by First and Last Names, Day Month Year.

Smith, William. "Teaching Grammar—Some Thoughts." Received by
Richard Bullock, 19 Nov. 2013.

36. TEXT MESSAGE

Sender's Last Name, First Name. Text message. Received by First and Last
Names, Day Month Year.

Douglass, Joanne. Text message. Received by Kim Yi, 4 June 2015.

37. POST TO AN ONLINE FORUM

Author. "Subject line" or "Full text of short untitled post." *Name of
Forum,* Day Month Year, URL.

@somekiryu. "What's the hardest part about writing for you?" *Reddit,*
22 Apr. 2016, redd.it/4fyni0.

38. POST TO *TWITTER, FACEBOOK,* OR OTHER SOCIAL MEDIA

Author. "Full text of short untitled post" or "Title" or Descriptive label.
Name of Site, Day Month Year, Time, URL.

@POTUS (Barack Obama). "I'm proud of the @NBA for taking a stand
against gun violence. Sympathy for victims isn't enough—change
requires all of us speaking up." *Twitter,* 23 Dec. 2015, 1:21 p.m.,
twitter.com/POTUS/status/679773729749078016.

Black Lives Matter. "Rise and Grind! Did you sign this petition yet?
We now have a sign on for ORGANIZATIONS to lend their
support." *Facebook,* 23 Oct. 2015, 11:30 a.m., www.facebook.com/
BlackLivesMatter/photos/a.294807204023865.1073741829.
180212755483311/504711973033386/?type=3&theater.

@quarterlifepoetry. Illustrated poem about girl at Target. *Instagram,*
22 Jan. 2015, www.instagram.com/p/yLO6fSurRH/.

Audio, Visual, and Other Sources

39. ADVERTISEMENT

PRINT

Name of Product or Company. Advertisement or Description of ad. *Title of Periodical,* Date, Page.

Cal Alumni Association. Sports Merchandise ad. *California,* Spring 2016, p. 3.

AUDIO OR VIDEO

Name of Product or Company. Advertisement or Description of ad. Date. *Name of Host Site,* URL. Accessed Day Month Year.

Chrysler. Super Bowl commercial. 6 Feb. 2011. *YouTube,* www.youtube.com/watch?v=SKLZ254Y_jtc. Accessed 1 May 2015.

40. ART

ORIGINAL

Artist's Last Name, First Name. *Title of Art.* Year created, Site, City.

Van Gogh, Vincent. *The Potato Eaters.* 1885, Van Gogh Museum, Amsterdam.

REPRODUCTION

Artist's Last Name, First Name. *Title of Art.* Year created. *Title of Book,* by First and Last Names, Publisher, Year of publication, Page.

Van Gogh, Vincent. *The Potato Eaters.* 1885. *History of Art: A Survey of the Major Visual Arts from the Dawn of History to the Present Day,* by H. W. Janson, Prentice-Hall/Harry N. Abrams, 1969, p. 508.

ONLINE

Artist's Last Name, First Name. *Title of Art.* Year created. *Name of Site,* URL. Accessed Day Month Year.

Warhol, Andy. *Self-portrait.* 1979. *J. Paul Getty Museum,* www.getty. edu/art/collection/objects/106971/andy-warhol-self-portrait-american-1979/. Accessed 20 Jan. 2015.

41. CARTOON

PRINT

Author's Last Name, First Name. "Title of Cartoon."*Title of Periodical,*
Date, Page.

Chast, Roz. "The Three Wise Men of Thanksgiving." *The New Yorker,*
1 Dec. 2003, p. 174.

ONLINE

Author's Last Name, First Name. "Title of Cartoon." *Title of Site,*
Date, URL. Accessed Day Month Year.

Munroe, Randall. "Up Goer Five." *xkcd,* 12 Nov. 2012, xkcd.com/1133/.
Accessed 22 Apr. 2015.

42. SUPREME COURT CASE

First Plaintiff v. First Defendant. *United States Reports* citation. Name of
Court, Year of decision, URL. Accessed Day Month Year.

District of Columbia v. Heller. 554 US 570. Supreme Court of the US, 2008,
www.lawcornell.edu/supct/html/07-290.ZS.html. Accessed 3 June 2016.

43. FILM

Name individuals based on the focus of your project—the director, the
screenwriter, the cinematographer, or someone else.

Title of Film. Role by First and Last Names, Production Studio, Date.

Breakfast at Tiffany's. Directed by Blake Edwards, Paramount, 1961.

STREAMING

Title of Film. Role by First and Last Names, Production Studio,
Date. *Streaming Service,* URL. Accessed Day Month Year.

Interstellar. Directed by Christopher Nolan, Paramount, 2014. *Amazon
Prime Video,* www.amazon.com/Interstellar-Matthew-McConaughey/
dp/B00TU9UFTS. Accessed 2 May 2015.

author   title   publication

44. INTERVIEW

If the interview has a title, put it in quotation marks following the subject's name.

BROADCAST

> Subject's Last Name, First Name. Interview or "Title of Interview."
>> *Title of Program,* Network, Day Month Year.

Gates, Henry Louis, Jr. Interview. *Fresh Air,* NPR, 9 Apr. 2002.

PUBLISHED

> Subject's Last Name, First Name. Interview or "Title of Interview." *Title*
>> *of Publication,* Date, Pages.

Stone, Oliver. Interview. *Esquire,* Nov. 2004, pp. 170-71.

PERSONAL

> Subject's Last Name, First Name. Personal interview. Day Month Year.

Roddick, Andy. Personal interview. 17 Aug. 2013.

45. MAP

> "Title of Map." Publisher, URL. Accessed Day Month Year.

"National Highway System." US Department of Transportation Federal
> Highway Administration, www.fhwa.dot.gov/planning/images/nhs.pdf.
> Accessed 10 May 2015.

46. MUSICAL SCORE

> Composer's Last Name, First Name. *Title of Composition.* Year of
> composition. Publisher, Year of publication.

Stravinsky, Igor. *Petrushka*. 1911. W. W. Norton, 1967.

47. ONLINE VIDEO

> Author's Last Name, First Name. *Title. Name of Host Site,* Date, URL.
> Accessed Day Month Year.

Westbrook, Adam. *Cause/Effect: The Unexpected Origins of Terrible Things.* *Vimeo*, 9 Sept. 2014, vimeo.com/105681474. Accessed 20 Dec. 2015.

48. ORAL PRESENTATION

Presenter's Last Name, First Name. "Title of Presentation." Sponsoring Institution, Date, Location.

Cassin, Michael. "Nature in the Raw—The Art of Landscape Painting." Berkshire Institute for Lifelong Learning, 24 Mar. 2005, Clark Art Institute, Williamstown.

49. PODCAST

If you accessed a podcast online, give the URL and date of access; if you accessed it through a service such as *iTunes* or *Spotify*, indicate that instead.

Last Name, First Name, role. "Title of Episode." *Title of Program,* season, episode, Sponsor, Date, URL. Accessed Day Month Year.

Koenig, Sarah, host. "DUSTWUN." *Serial,* season 2, episode 1, WBEZ, 10 Dec. 2015, serialpodcast.org/season-two/1/dustwun. Accessed 23 Apr. 2016.

Foss, Gilad, writer and performer. "Aquaman's Brother-in-Law." *Superhero Temp Agency,* season 1, episode 1, 16 Apr. 2015. *iTunes.*

50. RADIO PROGRAM

Last Name, First Name, role. "Title of Episode." *Title of Program,* Station, Day Month Year of broadcast, URL. Accessed Day Month Year.

Glass, Ira, host. "In Defense of Ignorance." *This American Life,* WBEZ, 22 Apr. 2016, thisamericanlife.org/radio-archives/episode/585/ in-defense-of-ignorance. Accessed 2 May 2016.

51. SOUND RECORDING

ONLINE

Last Name, First Name. "Title of Work." *Title of Album,* Distributor, Date. *Name of Audio Service.*

Simone, Nina. "To Be Young, Gifted and Black." *Black Gold*, RCA Records, 1969. *Spotify.*

CD

Last Name, First Name. "Title of Work." *Title of Album,* Distributor, Date.

Brown, Greg. "Canned Goods." *The Live One,* Red House, 1995.

52. TV SHOW

ORIGINAL BROADCAST

"Title of Episode." *Title of Show,* role by First and Last Names, season, episode, Network, Day Month Year.

"The Silencer." *Criminal Minds,* written by Erica Messer, season 8, episode 1, NBC, 26 Sept. 2012.

DVD

"Title of Episode." Broadcast Year. *Title of DVD,* role by First and Last Names, season, episode, Production Studio, Release Year, disc number.

"The Pants Tent." 2003. *Curb Your Enthusiasm: Season One*, performance by Larry David, season 1, episode 1, HBO Video, 2006, disc 1.

ONLINE

"Title of Episode." *Title of Show,* season, episode, role by First and Last Names (if any), Production Studio, Day Month Year. *Name of Host Site,* URL. Accessed Day Month Year.

"Shadows in the Glass." *Marvel's Daredevil*, season 1, episode 8, Netflix, 10 Apr. 2015. *Netflix*, www.netflix.com/watch/80018198?trackId =13752289&tctx=0%2C7%2Cbcfd6259-6e64-4d51-95ab-2a9f747e-abf0-158552415. Accessed 3 Nov. 2015.

53. VIDEO GAME

Last Name, First Name, role. *Title of Game.* Distributor, Date of release. Gaming System or Platform.

Metzen, Chris, and James Waugh, writers. *StarCraft II: Legacy of the Void*. Blizzard Entertainment, 2015. OS X.

FORMATTING A RESEARCH PAPER

Name, course, title. MLA does not require a separate title page. In the upper left-hand corner of your first page, include your name, your professor's name, the name of the course, and the date. Center the title of your paper on the line after the date; capitalize it as you would a book title.

Page numbers. In the upper right-hand corner of each page, one-half inch below the top of the page, include your last name and the page number. Number pages consecutively throughout your paper.

Font, spacing, margins, and indents. Choose a font that is easy to read (such as Times New Roman) and that provides a clear contrast between regular and italic text. Double-space the entire paper, including your works cited list. Set one-inch margins at the top, bottom, and sides of your text; do not justify your text. The first line of each paragraph should be indented one-half inch from the left margin.

Long quotations. When quoting more than three lines of poetry, more than four lines of prose, or dialogue between characters in a drama, set off the quotation from the rest of your text, indenting it one-half inch (or five spaces) from the left margin. Do not use quotation marks, and put any parenthetical documentation *after* the final punctuation.

> In *Eastward to Tartary*, Kaplan captures ancient and contemporary Antioch for us:
>> At the height of its glory in the Roman-Byzantine age, when it had an amphitheater, public baths, aqueducts, and sewage pipes, half a million people lived in Antioch. Today the population is only 125,000. With sour relations between Turkey and Syria, and unstable politics throughout the Middle East, Antioch is now a backwater—seedy and tumbledown, with relatively few tourists. I found it altogether charming. (123)

author　　　title　　　publication

In the first stanza of Arnold's "Dover Beach," the exclamations make clear that the speaker is addressing someone who is also present in the scene:

> Come to the window, sweet is the night air!
> Only, from the long line of spray
> Where the sea meets the moon-blanched land,
> Listen! You hear the grating roar
> Of pebbles which the waves draw back, and fling. (6-10)

Be careful to maintain the poet's line breaks. If a line does not fit on one line of your paper, put the extra words on the next line. Indent that line an additional quarter inch (or two spaces).

Illustrations.   Insert illustrations close to the text that discusses them. For tables, provide a number (*Table* 1) and a title on separate lines above the table. Below the table, provide a caption and information about the source. For graphs, photos, and other figures, provide a figure number (*Fig.* 1), caption, and source information below the figure. If you give only brief source information (such as a parenthetical note), or if the source is cited elsewhere in your text, include it in your list of works cited. Be sure to make clear how any illustrations relate to your point.

List of Works Cited.   Start your list on a new page, following any notes. Center the title and double-space the entire list. Begin each entry at the left margin, and indent subsequent lines one-half inch (or five spaces). Alphabetize the list by authors' last names (or by editors' or translators' names, if appropriate). Alphabetize works with no author or editor by title, disregarding *A*, *An*, and *The*. To cite more than one work by a single author, list them as in no. 4 on page 514.

SAMPLE RESEARCH PAPER

The following report was written by Dylan Borchers for a first-year writing course. It's formatted according to the guidelines of the MLA (style.mla.org).

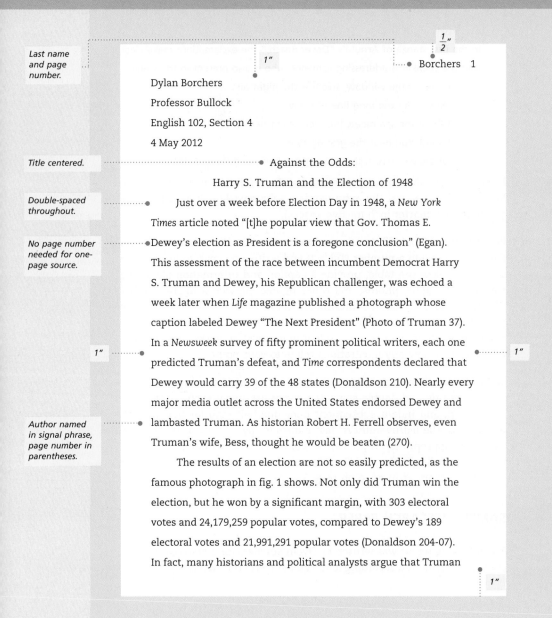

Last name and page number.

Dylan Borchers

Professor Bullock

English 102, Section 4

4 May 2012

Title centered.

Against the Odds:

Harry S. Truman and the Election of 1948

Double-spaced throughout.

Just over a week before Election Day in 1948, a *New York Times* article noted "[t]he popular view that Gov. Thomas E.

No page number needed for one-page source.

Dewey's election as President is a foregone conclusion" (Egan). This assessment of the race between incumbent Democrat Harry S. Truman and Dewey, his Republican challenger, was echoed a week later when *Life* magazine published a photograph whose caption labeled Dewey "The Next President" (Photo of Truman 37). In a *Newsweek* survey of fifty prominent political writers, each one predicted Truman's defeat, and *Time* correspondents declared that Dewey would carry 39 of the 48 states (Donaldson 210). Nearly every major media outlet across the United States endorsed Dewey and lambasted Truman. As historian Robert H. Ferrell observes, even

Author named in signal phrase, page number in parentheses.

Truman's wife, Bess, thought he would be beaten (270).

The results of an election are not so easily predicted, as the famous photograph in fig. 1 shows. Not only did Truman win the election, but he won by a significant margin, with 303 electoral votes and 24,179,259 popular votes, compared to Dewey's 189 electoral votes and 21,991,291 popular votes (Donaldson 204-07). In fact, many historians and political analysts argue that Truman

Borchers 2

Fig. 1. President Harry S. Truman holds up an edition of the *Chicago Daily Tribune* that mistakenly announced "Dewey Defeats Truman" (Rollins).

Illustration is positioned close to the text to which it relates, with figure number, caption, and parenthetical documentation.

would have won by an even greater margin had third-party Progressive candidate Henry A. Wallace not split the Democratic vote in New York State and Dixiecrat Strom Thurmond not won four states in the South (McCullough 711). Although Truman's defeat was heavily predicted, those predictions themselves, Dewey's passiveness as a campaigner, and Truman's zeal turned the tide for a Truman victory.

In the months preceding the election, public opinion polls predicted that Dewey would win by a large margin. Pollster Elmo Roper stopped polling in September, believing there was no reason to continue, given a seemingly inevitable Dewey landslide. Although the margin narrowed as the election drew near, the other pollsters

No signal phrase; author and page number in parentheses.

predicted a Dewey win by at least 5 percent (Donaldson 209). Many historians believe that these predictions aided the president in the long run. First, surveys showing Dewey in the lead may have prompted some of Dewey's supporters to feel overconfident about their candidate's chances and therefore to stay home from the polls on Election Day. Second, these same surveys may have energized Democrats to mount late get-out-the-vote efforts ("1948 Truman-Dewey Election"). Other analysts believe that the overwhelming predictions of a Truman loss also kept at home some Democrats who approved of Truman's policies but saw a Truman loss as inevitable. According to political analyst Samuel Lubell, those Democrats may have saved Dewey from an even greater defeat (Hamby, *Man* 465). Whatever the impact on the voters, the polling numbers had a decided effect on Dewey.

Paragraphs indented ½ inch or 5 spaces.

Historians and political analysts alike cite Dewey's overly cautious campaign as one of the main reasons Truman was able to achieve victory. Dewey firmly believed in public opinion polls. With all indications pointing to an easy victory, Dewey and his staff believed that all he had to do was bide his time and make no foolish mistakes. Dewey himself said, "When you're leading, don't talk" (Smith 30). Each of Dewey's speeches was well crafted and well rehearsed. As the leader in the race, he kept his remarks faultlessly positive, with the result that he failed to deliver a solid message or even mention Truman or any of Truman's policies. Eventually, Dewey began to be perceived as aloof and stuffy. One observer compared him to the plastic groom on top of a wedding cake (Hamby, "Harry S. Truman"), and others noted his stiff, cold demeanor (McCullough 671–74).

> Two works cited within the same sentence.

As his campaign continued, observers noted that Dewey seemed uncomfortable in crowds, unable to connect with ordinary people. And he made a number of blunders. One took place at a train stop when the candidate, commenting on the number of children in the crowd, said he was glad they had been let out of school for his arrival. Unfortunately for Dewey, it was a Saturday ("1948: The Great Truman Surprise"). Such gaffes gave voters the feeling that Dewey was out of touch with the public.

> Title used when there's no known author.

Again and again through the autumn of 1948, Dewey's campaign speeches failed to address the issues, with the candidate declaring that he did not want to "get down in the gutter" (Smith 515). When told by fellow Republicans that he was losing ground, Dewey insisted that his campaign not alter its course. Even *Time* magazine, though it endorsed and praised him, conceded that his speeches were dull (McCullough 696). According to historian Zachary Karabell, they were "notable only for taking place, not for any specific message" (244). Dewey's numbers in the polls slipped in the weeks before the election, but he still held a comfortable lead over Truman. It would take Truman's famous whistle-stop campaign to make the difference.

Few candidates in US history have campaigned for the presidency with more passion and faith than Harry Truman. In

Borchers   5

the autumn of 1948, he wrote to his sister, "It will be the greatest campaign any President ever made. Win, lose, or draw, people will know where I stand" (91). For thirty-three days, Truman traveled the nation, giving hundreds of speeches from the back of the *Ferdinand Magellan* railroad car. In the same letter, he described the pace: "We made about 140 stops and I spoke over 147 times, shook hands with at least 30,000 and am in good condition to start out again tomorrow for Wilmington, Philadelphia, Jersey City, Newark, Albany and Buffalo" (91). McCullough writes of Truman's campaign:

> No President in history had ever gone so far in quest of support from the people, or with less cause for the effort, to judge by informed opinion. . . . As a test of his skills and judgment as a professional politician, not to say his stamina and disposition at age sixty-four, it would be like no other experience in his long, often difficult career, as he himself understood perfectly. More than any other event in his public life, or in his presidency thus far, it would reveal the kind of man he was. (655)

He spoke in large cities and small towns, defending his policies and attacking Republicans. As a former farmer and relatively late bloomer, Truman was able to connect with the public. He developed an energetic style, usually speaking from notes rather than from a prepared speech, and often mingled with the crowds that met his train. These crowds grew larger as the campaign

Quotations of more than 4 lines indented $\frac{1}{2}$ inch (5 spaces) and double-spaced.

Parenthetical reference after final punctuation.

progressed. In Chicago, over half a million people lined the streets as he passed, and in St. Paul the crowd numbered over 25,000. When Dewey entered St. Paul two days later, he was greeted by only 7,000 supporters ("1948 Truman-Dewey Election"). Reporters brushed off the large crowds as mere curiosity seekers wanting to see a president (McCullough 682). Yet Truman persisted, even if he often seemed to be the only one who thought he could win. By going directly to the American people and connecting with them, Truman built the momentum needed to surpass Dewey and win the election.

The legacy and lessons of Truman's whistle-stop campaign continue to be studied by political analysts, and politicians today often mimic his campaign methods by scheduling multiple visits to key states, as Truman did. He visited California, Illinois, and Ohio 48 times, compared with 6 visits to those states by Dewey. Political scientist Thomas M. Holbrook concludes that his strategic campaigning in those states and others gave Truman the electoral votes he needed to win (61, 65).

The 1948 election also had an effect on pollsters, who, as Elmo Roper admitted, "couldn't have been more wrong." *Life* magazine's editors concluded that pollsters as well as reporters and commentators were too convinced of a Dewey victory to analyze the polls seriously, especially the opinions of undecided voters (Karabell 256). Pollsters assumed that undecided voters would vote in the same proportion as decided voters—and that turned out to be a false assumption (Karabell 257). In fact, the lopsidedness of the polls might have led voters who supported Truman to call themselves undecided out of an unwillingness to associate themselves with the losing side, further skewing the polls' results (McDonald et al. 152). Such errors led pollsters to change their methods significantly after the 1948 election.

Work by 3 or more authors is shortened using et al.

After the election, many political analysts, journalists, and historians concluded that the Truman upset was in fact a victory for the American people, who, the *New Republic* noted, "couldn't be ticketed by the polls, knew its own mind and had picked the rather unlikely but courageous figure of Truman to carry its banner" (T.R.B. 3). How "unlikely" is unclear, however; Truman biographer Alonzo Hamby notes that "polls of scholars consistently rank Truman among the top eight presidents in American history" (*Man* 641). But despite Truman's high standing, and despite the fact that the whistle-stop campaign is now part of our political landscape, politicians have increasingly imitated the style of the Dewey campaign, with its "packaged candidate who ran so as not to lose, who steered clear of controversy, and who made a good show of appearing presidential" (Karabell 266). The election of 1948 shows that voters are not necessarily swayed by polls, but it may have presaged the packaging of candidates by public relations experts, to the detriment of public debate on the issues in future presidential elections.

1"   Borchers 8

Works Cited

Donaldson, Gary A. *Truman Defeats Dewey*. UP of Kentucky, 1999.

Egan, Leo. "Talk Is Now Turning to the Dewey Cabinet." *The
 New York Times*, 20 Oct. 1948, p. 8E, www.nytimes.com/
 timesmachine/1948/10/26/issue.html. Accessed 18 Apr. 2012.

Ferrell, Robert H. *Harry S. Truman: A Life*. U of Missouri P, 1994.

Hamby, Alonzo L., editor. "Harry S. Truman: Campaigns and
 Elections." *American President*, Miller Center, U of Virginia,
 11 Jan. 2012, millercenter.org/president/biography/truman-
 campaigns-and-elections. Accessed 17 Mar. 2012.

- - -. *Man of the People: A Life of Harry S. Truman*. Oxford UP, 1995.

Holbrook, Thomas M. "Did the Whistle-Stop Campaign Matter?" PS:
 Political Science and Politics, vol. 35, no. 1, Mar. 2002, pp. 59-66.

Karabell, Zachary. *The Last Campaign: How Harry Truman Won the
 1948 Election*. Alfred A. Knopf, 2000.

McCullough, David. *Truman*. Simon and Schuster, 1992.

McDonald, Daniel G., et al. "The Spiral of Silence in the 1948
 Presidential Election." *Communication Research*, vol. 28, no. 2,
 Apr. 2001, pp. 139-55.

"1948: The Great Truman Surprise." *The Press and the Presidency*,
 Dept. of Political Science and International Affairs, Kennesaw
 State U, 29 Oct. 2003, kennesaw.edu/pols.3380/pres/1984.html.
 Accessed 10 Apr. 2012.

Heading centered.

Double-spaced.

Alphabetized by authors' last names.

Each entry begins at the left margin; subsequent lines are indented.

Multiple works by a single author listed alphabetically by title. For second and subsequent works, replace author's name with three hyphens.

Sources beginning with numerals are alphabetized as if the number were spelled out.

"1948 Truman-Dewey Election." *American Political History*, Eagleton
Institute of Politics, Rutgers, State U of New Jersey,
1995-2012, www.eagleton.rutgers.edu/research/
americanhistory/ap_trumandewey.php. Accessed 18 Apr. 2012.

Photo of Truman in San Francisco. *Life*, 1 Nov. 1948, p. 37. *Google
Books*, books.google.com/books?id=ekoEAAAAMBAJ&printsec=
frontcover#v=onepage&q&f=false. Accessed 20 Apr. 2012.

Rollins, Byron. "President Truman with *Chicago Daily Tribune*
Headline of 'Dewey Defeats Truman.'" Associated Press,
4 Nov. 1948. *Harry S. Truman Library & Museum*, www.
trumanlibrary.org/photographs/view.php?id=25248. Accessed
20 Apr. 2012.

Roper, Elmo. "Roper Eats Crow; Seeks Reason for Vote Upset."
Evening Independent, 6 Nov. 1948, p. 10. *Google News*, news.
google.com/newspapers?nid=PZE8UkGerEcC&dat=19481106&
printsec=frontpage&hl=en. Accessed 13 Apr. 2012.

Smith, Richard Norton. *Thomas E. Dewey and His Times*. Simon and
Schuster, 1982.

T.R.B. "Washington Wire." *The New Republic*, 15 Nov. 1948, pp. 3-4.
EBSCOhost, search.ebscohost.com/login.aspx?direct=true&db
=tsh&AN=14779640&site=ehost-live. Accessed 20 Apr. 2012.

Truman, Harry S. "Campaigning, Letter, October 5, 1948." *Harry S.
Truman*, edited by Robert H. Ferrell, CQ P, 2003, p. 91.

A range of
dates is given
for web projects
developed over a
period of time.

Every source
used is in the list
of works cited.

American Psychological Association (APA) style calls for (1) brief documentation in parentheses near each in-text citation and (2) complete documentation in a list of references at the end of your text. Throughout this chapter, you'll find models and examples that are color-coded to help you see how writers include source information in their texts and reference lists: brown for author or editor, yellow for title, gray for publication information: place of publication, publisher, date of publication, page number(s), and so on. These models and examples draw on the *Publication Manual of the American Psychological Association*, 6th edition (2009). Additional information is available at www.apastyle.org.

A DIRECTORY TO APA STYLE

In-Text Documentation   552

IN-TEXT DOCUMENTATION

Brief documentation in your text makes clear to your reader precisely what you took from a source and, in the case of a quotation, precisely where (usually, on which page) in the source you found the text you are quoting.

478–90

PARAPHRASES and **SUMMARIES** are more common than **QUOTATIONS** in APA-style projects. As you cite each source, you will need to decide whether to name the author in a signal phrase—"as McCullough (2001) wrote"— or in parentheses—"(McCullough, 2001)." Note that APA requires you to use the past tense or present perfect tense for verbs in **SIGNAL PHRASES** : "Moss (2003) argued," "Moss (2003) has argued."

487–90

1. AUTHOR NAMED IN A SIGNAL PHRASE

If you are quoting, you must give the page number(s). You are not required to give the page number(s) with a paraphrase or a summary, but APA encourages you to do so, especially if you are citing a long or complex work; most of the models in this chapter do include page numbers.

AUTHOR QUOTED

Put the date in parentheses right after the author's name; put the page in parentheses as close to the quotation as possible.

> McCullough (2001) described John Adams as having "the hands of a man accustomed to pruning his own trees, cutting his own hay, and splitting his own firewood" (p. 18).

Notice that in this example, the parenthetical reference with the page number comes *after* the closing quotation marks but *before* the period at the end of the sentence.

AUTHOR PARAPHRASED OR SUMMARIZED

Put the date in parentheses right after the author's name; follow the date with the page.

John Adams's hands were those of a laborer, according to McCullough (2001, p. 18).

2. AUTHOR NAMED IN PARENTHESES

If you do not mention an author in a signal phrase, put his or her name, a comma, and the year of publication in parentheses as close as possible to the quotation, paraphrase, or summary.

AUTHOR QUOTED

Give the author, date, and page in one parenthesis, or split the information between two parentheses.

One biographer (McCullough, 2001) has said John Adams had "the hands of a man accustomed to pruning his own trees, cutting his own hay, and splitting his own firewood" (p. 18).

AUTHOR PARAPHRASED OR SUMMARIZED

Give the author, date, and page in one parenthesis toward the beginning or the end of the paraphrase or summary.

John Adams's hands were those of a laborer (McCullough, 2001, p. 18).

3. AUTHORS WITH THE SAME LAST NAME

If your reference list includes more than one person with the same last name, include initials in all documentation to distinguish the authors from one another.

Eclecticism is common in contemporary criticism (J. M. Smith, 1992, p. vii).

4. TWO AUTHORS

Always mention both authors. Use *and* in a signal phrase, but use an ampersand (&) in parentheses.

Carlson and Ventura (1990) wanted to introduce Julio Cortázar, Marjorie Agosín, and other Latin American writers to an audience of English-speaking adolescents (p. v).

According to the Peter Principle, "In a hierarchy, every employee tends to rise to his level of incompetence" (Peter & Hull, 1969, p. 26).

5. THREE OR MORE AUTHORS

In the first reference to a work by three to five persons, name all contributors. Use *and* in a signal phrase, but use an ampersand (&) in parentheses. In subsequent references, name the first author followed by *et al.*, Latin for "and others." Whenever you refer to a work by six or more contributors, name only the first author, followed by *et al.* (See no. 4.)

Faigley, George, Palchik, and Selfe (2004) have argued that where there used to be a concept called *literacy*, today's multitude of new kinds of texts has given us *literacies* (p. xii).

Peilen et al. (1990) supported their claims about corporate corruption with startling anecdotal evidence (p. 75).

6. ORGANIZATION OR GOVERNMENT AS AUTHOR

If an organization has a long name that is recognizable by its abbreviation, give the full name and the abbreviation the first time you cite the source. In subsequent references, use only the abbreviation. If the organization does not have a familiar abbreviation, always use its full name.

FIRST REFERENCE

(American Psychological Association [APA], 2008)

SUBSEQUENT REFERENCES

(APA, 2008)

7. AUTHOR UNKNOWN

Use the complete title if it is short; if it is long, use the first few words of the title under which the work appears in the reference list.

> *Webster's New Biographical Dictionary* (1988) identifies William James as "American psychologist and philosopher" (p. 520).

> A powerful editorial asserted that healthy liver donor Mike Hurewitz died because of "frightening" faulty postoperative care ("Every Patient's Nightmare," 2007).

8. TWO OR MORE WORKS CITED TOGETHER

If you cite multiple works in the same parenthesis, place them in the order that they appear in your reference list, separated by semicolons.

> Many researchers have argued that what counts as "literacy" is not necessarily learned at school (Heath, 1983; Moss, 2003).

9. TWO OR MORE WORKS BY AN AUTHOR IN THE SAME YEAR

If your list of references includes more than one work by the same author published in the same year, order them alphabetically by title, adding lowercase letters ("a," "b," and so on) to the year.

> Kaplan (2000a) described orderly shantytowns in Turkey that did not resemble the other slums he visited.

10. SOURCE QUOTED IN ANOTHER SOURCE

When you cite a source that was quoted in another source, let the reader know that you used a secondary source by adding the words *as cited in*.

> During the meeting with the psychologist, the patient stated repeatedly that he "didn't want to be too paranoid" (as cited in Oberfield & Yasik, 2004, p. 294).

11. WORK WITHOUT PAGE NUMBERS

Instead of page numbers, some electronic works have paragraph numbers, which you should include (preceded by the abbreviation *para.*) if you are referring to a specific part of such a source. In sources with neither page nor paragraph numbers, refer readers to a particular part of the source if possible, perhaps indicating a heading and the paragraph under the heading.

> Russell's dismissals from Trinity College at Cambridge and from City College in New York City have been seen as examples of the controversy that marked his life (Irvine, 2006, para. 2).

12. AN ENTIRE WORK

You do not need to give a page number if you are directing readers' attention to an entire work.

> Kaplan (2000) considered Turkey and Central Asia explosive.

When you are citing an entire website, give the URL in the text. You do not need to include the website in your reference list. To cite part of a website, see no. 20 on page 566.

> Beyond providing diagnostic information, the website for the Alzheimer's Association includes a variety of resources for family and community support of patients suffering from Alzheimer's disease (http://www.alz.org).

13. PERSONAL COMMUNICATION

Document email, telephone conversations, interviews, personal letters, messages from nonarchived discussion sources, and other personal texts as *personal communication*, along with the person's initial(s), last name, and the date. You do not need to include such personal communications in your reference list.

> L. Strauss (personal communication, December 6, 2013) told about visiting Yogi Berra when they both lived in Montclair, New Jersey.

NOTES

You may need to use content notes to give an explanation or information that doesn't fit into your text. To signal a content note, place a superscript numeral at the appropriate point in your text. If you have multiple notes, number them consecutively throughout your text. Put the notes themselves on a separate page with the heading *Notes*, after your reference list. Here is an example from *In Search of Solutions: A New Direction in Psychotherapy* (2003).

TEXT WITH SUPERSCRIPT

An important part of working with teams and one-way mirrors is taking the consultation break, as at Milan, BFTC, and MRI.[1]

CONTENT NOTE

[1]It is crucial to note here that while working within a team is fun, stimulating, and revitalizing, it is not necessary for successful outcomes. Solution-oriented therapy works equally well when working solo.

REFERENCE LIST

A reference list provides full bibliographic information for every source cited in your text with the exception of entire websites and personal communications. See page 578 for guidelines on preparing such a list; for a sample reference list see pages 588–89.

Print Books

For most books, you'll need to provide the author, the publication date, the title and any subtitle, and the place of publication and publisher.

IMPORTANT DETAILS FOR DOCUMENTING PRINT BOOKS

- **AUTHORS**: Use the author's last name, but replace the first and middle names with initials (D. Kinder for Donald Kinder).

- **DATES**: If more than one year is given, use the most recent one.

- **TITLES**: Capitalize only the first word and proper nouns and proper adjectives in titles and subtitles.

- **PUBLICATION PLACE**: Give city followed by state (abbreviated) or country, if outside the United States (for example, Boston, MA; London, England; Toronto, Ontario, Canada). If more than one city is given, use the first. Do not include the state or country if the publisher is a university whose name includes that information.

- **PUBLISHER**: Use a shortened form of the publisher's name (Little, Brown for Little, Brown and Company), but retain *Association*, *Books*, and *Press* (American Psychological Association, Princeton University Press).

1. ONE AUTHOR

Author's Last Name, Initials. (Year of publication). *Title*. Publication City, State or Country: Publisher.

Louis, M. (2003). *Moneyball: The art of winning an unfair game*. New York, NY: Norton.

2. TWO OR MORE WORKS BY THE SAME AUTHOR

If the works were published in different years, list them chronologically.

Lewis, B. (1995). *The Middle East: A brief history of the last 2,000 years*. New York, NY: Scribner.

Lewis, B. (2003). *The crisis of Islam: Holy war and unholy terror*. New York, NY: Modern Library.

If the works were published in the same year, list them alphabetically by title, adding "a," "b," and so on to the year (see p. 560).

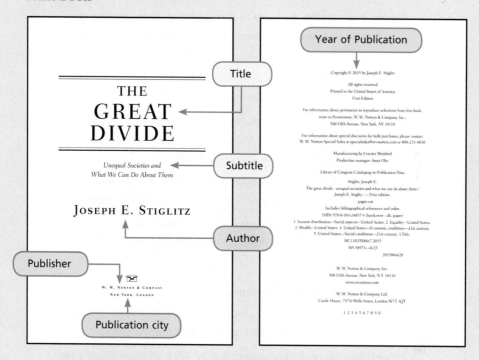

Documentation Map (APA)
Print Book

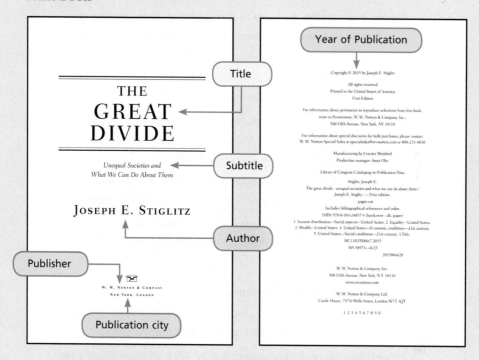

Stiglitz, J. E. (2015). *The great divide: Unequal societies and what we can do about them.* New York, NY: Norton.

557–63
for more on
citing books
APA style

Kaplan, R. D. (2000a). *The coming anarchy: Shattering the dreams of the post cold war.* New York, NY: Random House.

Kaplan, R. D. (2000b). *Eastward to Tartary: Travels in the Balkans, the Middle East, and the Caucasus.* New York, NY: Random House.

3. TWO OR MORE AUTHORS

For two to seven authors, include all names.

First Author's Last Name, Initials, Next Author's Last Name, Initials, & Final Author's Last Name, Initials. (Year of publication). *Title.* Publication City, State or Country: Publisher.

Leavitt, S. D., & Dubner, S. J. (2005). *Freakonomics: A rogue economist explores the hidden side of everything.* New York, NY: Morrow.

For a work by eight or more authors, name just the first six authors, followed by three ellipsis points, and end with the final author (see no. 21 for an example from a magazine article).

4. ORGANIZATION OR GOVERNMENT AS AUTHOR

Sometimes an organization or a government agency is both author and publisher. If so, use the word *Author* as the publisher.

Organization Name or Government Agency. (Year of publication). *Title.* Publication City, State or Country: Publisher.

Catholic News Service. (2002). *Stylebook on religion 2000: A reference guide and usage manual.* Washington, DC: Author.

5. AUTHOR AND EDITOR

Author's Last Name, Initials. (Year of edited edition). *Title.* (Editor's Initials Last Name, Ed.). Publication City, State or Country: Publisher. (Original work[s] published year[s])

author   title   publication

Dick, P. F. (2008). *Five novels of the 1960s and 70s.* (J. Lethem, Ed.). New York, NY: Library of America. (Original works published 1964-1977)

6. EDITED COLLECTION

First Editor's Last Name, Initials, Next Editor's Last Name, Initials, & Final Editor's Last Name, Initials. (Eds.). (Year of edited edition). *Title.* Publication City, State or Country: Publisher.

Raviv, A., Oppenheimer, L., & Bar-Tal, D. (Eds.). (1999). *How children understand war and peace: A call for international peace education.* San Francisco, CA: Jossey-Bass.

7. WORK IN AN EDITED COLLECTION

Author's Last Name, Initials. (Year of publication). Title of article or chapter. In Initials Last Name (Ed.), *Title* (pp. pages). Publication City, State or Country: Publisher.

Harris, I. M. (1999). Types of peace education. In A. Raviv, L. Oppenheimer, & D. Bar-Tal (Eds.), *How children understand war and peace: A call for international peace education* (pp. 46-70). San Francisco, CA: Jossey-Bass.

8. UNKNOWN AUTHOR

Title. (Year of publication). Publication City, State or Country: Publisher.

Webster's new biographical dictionary. (1988). Springfield, MA: Merriam-Webster.

If the title page of a work lists the author as *Anonymous*, treat the reference-list entry as if the author's name were Anonymous, and alphabetize it accordingly.

9. EDITION OTHER THAN THE FIRST

Author's Last Name, Initials. (Year). *Title* (name or number ed.). Publication City, State or Country: Publisher.

Burch, D. (2008). *Emergency navigation: Find your position and shape your course at sea even if your instruments fail* (2nd ed.). Camden, ME: International Marine/McGraw-Hill.

10. TRANSLATION

Author's Last Name, Initials. (Year of publication). *Title* (Translator's Initials Last Name, Trans.). Publication City, State or Country: Publisher. (Original work published Year)

Hugo, V. (2008). *Les misérables* (J. Rose, Trans.). New York, NY: Modern Library. (Original work published 1862)

11. MULTIVOLUME WORK

Author's Last Name, Initials. (Year). *Title* (Vols. numbers). Publication City, State or Country: Publisher.

Nastali, D. P., & Boardman, P. C. (2004). *The Arthurian annals: The tradition in English from 1250 to 2000* (Vols. 1-2). New York, NY: Oxford University Press USA.

ONE VOLUME OF A MULTIVOLUME WORK

Author's Last Name, Initials. (Year). *Title of whole work (Vol. number).* Publication City, State or Country: Publisher.

Spiegelman, A. (1986). *Maus* (Vol. 1). New York, NY: Random House.

12. ARTICLE IN A REFERENCE BOOK

UNSIGNED

Title of entry. (Year). In *Title of reference book* (Name or number ed., Vol. number, pp. pages). Publication City, State or Country: Publisher.

Macrophage. (2003). In *Merriam-Webster's collegiate dictionary* (11th ed., p. 745). Springfield, MA: Merriam-Webster.

author   title   publication

SIGNED

Author's Last Name, Initials. (Year). Title of entry. In *Title of reference book* (Vol. number, pp. pages). Publication City, State or Country: Publisher.

Wasserman, D. E. (2006). Human exposure to vibration. In *International encyclopedia of ergonomics and human factors* (Vol. 2, pp. 1800-1801). Boca Raton, FL: CRC.

Print Periodicals

For most articles, you'll need to provide information about the author; the date; the article title and any subtitle; the periodical title; and any volume or issue number and inclusive page numbers.

IMPORTANT DETAILS FOR DOCUMENTING PRINT PERIODICALS

- **AUTHORS**: List authors as you would for a book (see pp. 558–60).
- **DATES**: For journals, give year only. For magazines and newspapers, give year followed by a comma and then month or month and day.
- **TITLES**: Capitalize article titles as you would for a book. Capitalize the first and last words and all principal words of periodical titles. Do not capitalize *a*, *an*, *the*, or any prepositions or coordinating conjunctions unless they begin the title of the periodical.
- **VOLUME AND ISSUE**: For journals and magazines, give volume or volume and issue, depending on the journal's pagination method. For newspapers, do not give volume or issue.
- **PAGES**: Use *p.* or *pp.* for a newspaper article but not for a journal or magazine article. If an article does not fall on consecutive pages, give all the page numbers (for example, 45, 75-77 for a journal or magazine; pp. C1, C3, C5-C7 for a newspaper).

13. ARTICLE IN A JOURNAL PAGINATED BY VOLUME

> Author's Last Name, Initials. (Year). Title of article. *Title of Journal,*
> *volume*, pages.

> Gremer, J. R., Sala, A., & Crone, E. E. (2010). Disappearing plants: Why
> they hide and how they return. *Ecology, 91*, 3407-3413.

14. ARTICLE IN A JOURNAL PAGINATED BY ISSUE

> Author's Last Name, Initials. (Year). Title of article. *Title of Journal,*
> *volume*(issue), pages.

> Weaver, C., McNally, C., & Moerman, S. (2001). To grammar or not to
> grammar: That is *not* the question! *Voices from the Middle, 8*(3),
> 17-33.

15. ARTICLE IN A MAGAZINE

If a magazine is published weekly, include the day and the month. If there
are a volume number and an issue number, include them after the magazine title.

> Author's Last Name, Initials. (Year, Month Day). Title of article. *Title of*
> *Magazine, volume*(issue), page(s).

> Gregory, S. (2008, June 30). Crash course: Why golf carts are more
> hazardous than they look. *Time, 171*(26), 53.

If a magazine is published monthly, include the month(s) only.

16. ARTICLE IN A NEWSPAPER

If page numbers are consecutive, separate them with a hyphen. If not,
separate them with a comma.

> Author's Last Name, Initials. (Year, Month Day). Title of article. *Title of*
> *Newspaper*, p(p). page(s).

> Schneider, G. (2005, March 13). Fashion sense on wheels. *The Washington*
> *Post*, pp. F1, F6.

author   title   publication

17. ARTICLE BY AN UNKNOWN AUTHOR

> Title of article. (Year, Month Day). *Title of Periodical*, *volume*(issue),
> page(s) or p(p). page(s).

> Hot property: From carriage house to family compound. (2004,
> December). *Berkshire Living*, *1*(1), 99.

> Clues in salmonella outbreak. (2008, June 21). *New York Times*, p. A13.

18. BOOK REVIEW

> Reviewer's Last Name, Initials. (Date of publication). Title of review
> [Review of by the book *Title of Work*, by Author's Initials Last Name].
> *Title of Periodical*, *volume*(issue), page(s).

> Brandt, A. (2003, October). Animal planet [Review of the book
> *Intelligence of apes and other rational beings*, by D. R. Rumb
> & D. A. Washburn]. *National Geographic Adventure*, *5*(10), 47.

If the review does not have a title, include the bracketed information about
the work being reviewed, immediately after the date of publication.

19. LETTER TO THE EDITOR

> Author's Last Name, Initials. (Date of publication). Title of letter [Letter to
> the editor]. *Title of Periodical*, *volume*(issue), page(s) or p(p). page(s).

> Hitchcock, G. (2008, August 3). Save our species [Letter to the editor].
> *San Francisco Chronicle*, p. P-3.

Online Sources

Not every online source gives you all the data that APA would like to see
in a reference entry. Ideally, you will be able to list author's or editor's
name; date of first electronic publication or most recent revision; title of
document; information about print publication if any; and retrieval information: DOI (digital object identifier, a string of letters and numbers that

identifies an online document) or URL. In some cases, additional information about electronic publication may be required (title of site, retrieval date,
name of sponsoring institution).

IMPORTANT DETAILS FOR DOCUMENTING ONLINE SOURCES

- **AUTHORS**: List authors as you would for a print book or periodical.

- **TITLES**: For websites and electronic documents, articles, or books, capitalize titles and subtitles as you would for a book; capitalize periodical
  titles as you would for a print periodical.

- **DATES**: After the author, give the year of the document's original
  publication on the web or of its most recent revision. If neither of
  those years is clear, use *n.d.* to mean "no date." For undated content
  or content that may change (for example, a wiki entry), include
  the month, day, and year that you retrieved the document. You
  don't need to include the retrieval date for content that's unlikely
  to change.

- **DOI OR URL**: Include the DOI instead of the URL in the reference
  whenever one is available. If no DOI is available, provide the URL of the
  home page or menu page. If you do not identify the sponsoring institution, you do not need a colon before the URL or DOI. Don't include any
  punctuation at the end of the URL or DOI. When a URL won't fit on the
  line, break the URL before most punctuation, but do not break *http://*.

20. WORK FROM A NONPERIODICAL WEBSITE

> Author's Last Name, Initials. (Date of publication). Title of work. *Title of
> site*. DOI or Retrieved Month Day, Year [if necessary], from URL

> Cruikshank, D. (2009, June 15). Unlocking the secrets and powers of the
> brain. *National Science Foundation*. Retrieved from http://www.nsf.gov
> /discoveries/disc_summ.jsp?cntn_id=114979&org=NSF

When citing an entire website, include the URL in parentheses within the
text. Do not include the website in your list of references.

author　　　　title　　　　publication

Documentation Map (APA)

Work from a Website

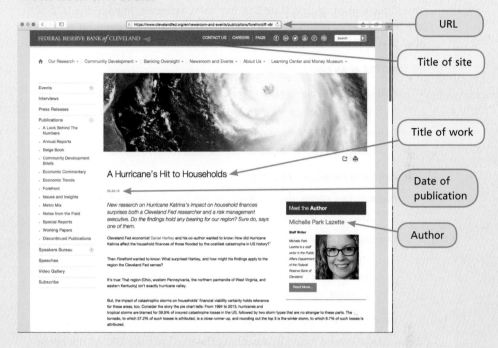

URL

Title of site

Title of work

Date of publication

Author

565–73 for more on citing websites APA style

Lazette, M. P. (2015, February 25). A hurricane's hit to households. *Federal Reserve Bank of Cleveland.* Retrieved from https://www.clevelandfed .org/en/Newsroom%20and%20Events/Publications/Forefront /Katrina.aspx

21. ARTICLE IN AN ONLINE PERIODICAL

When available, include the volume number and issue number as you would for a print source. If no DOI has been assigned, provide the URL of the homepage or menu page of the journal or magazine, even for articles that you access through a database.

ARTICLE IN AN ONLINE JOURNAL

Author's Last Name, Initials. (Year). Title of article. *Title of Journal, volume*(issue), pages. DOI or Retrieved from URL

Corbett, C. (2007). Vehicle-related crime and the gender gap. *Psychology, Crime & Law, 13*, 245-263. doi:10.1080/10683160600822022

ARTICLE IN AN ONLINE MAGAZINE

Author's Last Name, Initials. (Year, Month Day). Title of article. *Title of Magazine, volume*(issue). DOI or Retrieved from URL

Barreda, V. D., Palazzesi, L., Tellería, M. C., Katinas, L., Crisci, J. N., Bromer, K., . . . Bechis, F. (2010, September 24). Eocene Patagonia fossils of the daisy family. *Science, 329*, 1621. doi:10.1126/science .1193108

ARTICLE IN AN ONLINE NEWSPAPER

If the article can be found by searching the site, give the URL of the home page or menu page.

Author's Last Name, Initials. (Year, Month Day). Title of article. *Title of Newspaper.* Retrieved from URL

Collins, G. (2012, September 12). Game time. *The New York Times.* Retrieved from http://www.nytimes.com

22. ARTICLE AVAILABLE ONLY THROUGH A DATABASE

Some sources, such as an out-of-print journal or rare book, can be accessed only through a database. When no DOI is provided, give either the name of the database or its URL. (See p. 571 for a template and example.)

Documentation Map (APA)

Article in a Journal with DOI

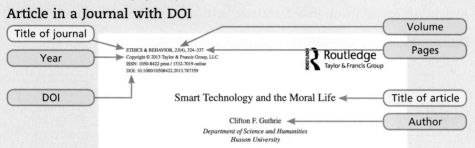

Title of journal

Year

DOI

Volume

Pages

Title of article

Author

ETHICS & BEHAVIOR, 23(4), 324–337
Copyright © 2013 Taylor & Francis Group, LLC
ISSN: 1050-8422 print / 1532-7019 online
DOI: 10.1080/10508422.2013.787359

Routledge
Taylor & Francis Group

Smart Technology and the Moral Life

Clifton F. Guthrie
Department of Science and Humanities
Husson University

Smart technology is recording and nudging our intuitive and behavioral reactions in ways that are not fully shaped by our conscious ethical reasoning and so are altering our social and moral worlds. Beyond reasons to worry, there are also reasons to embrace this technology for nudging human behavior toward prosocial activity. This article inquires about four ways that smart technology is shaping the individual moral life: the persuasive effect of promptware, our newly evolving experiences of embodiment, our negotiations with privacy, and our experiences of risk and serendipity.

Keywords: persuasive technology, morality, ethics, virtue

PERSUASIVE TECHNOLOGY

For some time, cars have worked to shape our behaviors, beeping to warn us when a door is unlocked or a seat belt unfastened, or giving us fuel efficiency feedback. These straightforward but persuasive sensor systems nudge us toward a repertoire of safe driving behaviors, and we often cannot override them even if we want to. Newer cars include an increasing number of smart technologies that interact with us more intelligently. Some detect the presence of electronic keys and make it impossible for drivers to lock themselves out. Others use sensors to monitor approaching obstacles or lane boundaries and give warnings or even apply the brakes. We are seeing the emergence of street intersections that communicate directly with cars and cars that can communicate with one another (Dean, Fletcher, Porges, & Ulrich, 2012). These are so-called smart technologies because they draw data from the environment and from us, and often make decisions on our behalf. A leading researcher in automated driving noted, "The driver is still in control. But if the driver is not doing the right thing, the technology takes over" (Markoff & Sengupta, 2013).

As cars become smarter they are helping to lead us into what technologists describe as a pervasive, ambient, or calm computing environment. In 1991, Mark Weiser of the Palo Alto Research Center presciently called it "ubiquitous computing" or "ubicomp" in a much-quoted article from *Scientific American*, in which he outlined what has come to be accepted as a standard interpretation of the history of human interaction with computers. This is the age in which computers are increasingly liberated from manual input devices like laptops and cell phones to become an invisible, interactive, computational sensorium. Early examples include motion sensors, smart

Correspondence should be addressed to Clifton F. Guthrie, Department of Science and Humanities, Husson University, 1 College Circle, Bangor, ME 04401. E-mail: cfguthrie@gmail.com

563–65, 568
for more
on citing
journals
APA style

566
for more
on DOIs

Guthrie, C. F. (2013). Smart Technology and the Moral Life. *Ethics & Behavior, 23*, 324-337. doi: 10.1080/10508422.2013.787359

Documentation Map (APA)

Article Accessed through a Database with DOI

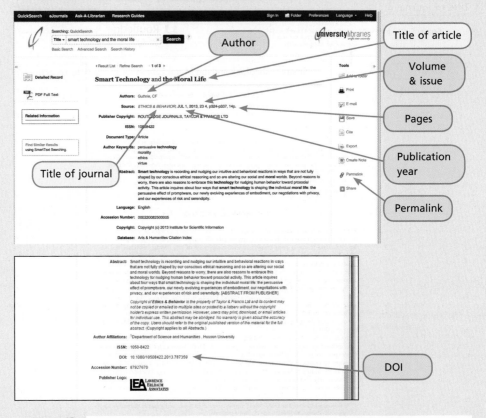

568, 571
for more
on citing an
article in a
database
APA style

Guthrie, C. F. (2013). Smart technology and the moral life. *Ethics & Behavior 23*(4), 324-337. doi:10.1080/10508422.2013.787359

author   title   publication

Author's Last Name, Initials. (Year). Title of article. *Title of Journal,*
volume(issue), pages. DOI or Retrieved from Name of database
or URL

Simpson, M. (1972). Authoritarianism and education: A comparative
approach. *Sociometry, 35*(2), 223-234. Retrieved from http://www.jstor
.org/stable/2786619

23. ARTICLE OR CHAPTER IN A WEB DOCUMENT OR ONLINE REFERENCE WORK

For a chapter in a web document or an article in an online reference
work, give the URL of the chapter or entry if no DOI is provided.

Author's Last Name, Initials. (Year). Title of entry. In Initials Last Name
(Ed.), *Title of reference work*. DOI or Retrieved from URL

Korfmacher, C. (2006). Personal identity. In J. Fieser & B. Dowden (Eds.),
Internet encyclopedia of philosophy. Retrieved from http://www.iep
.utm.edu/person-i/

24. ELECTRONIC BOOK

Author's Last Name, Initials. (Year). *Title of book*. DOI or Retrieved from URL

TenDam, H. (n.d.). *Politics, civilization & humanity*. Retrieved from http://
onlineoriginals.com/showitem.asp?itemID=46&page=2

For an ebook based on a print version, include a description of the digital
format in brackets after the book title.

Blain, M. (2009). *The sociology of terror: Studies in power, subjection,*
and victimage ritual [Adobe Digital Editions version]. Retrieved
from http://www.powells.com/sub/AdobeDigitalEditionsPolitics
.html?sec_big_link=1

25. WIKI ENTRY

Give the entry title and the date of posting, or *n.d.* if there is no date. Then
include the retrieval date, the name of the wiki, and the URL for the entry.

Title of entry. (Year, Month Day). Retrieved Month Day, Year, from Title
of wiki: URL

Discourse. (n.d.). Retrieved November 8, 2013, from Psychology Wiki:
http://psychology.wikia.com/wiki/Discourse

26. ONLINE DISCUSSION SOURCE

If the name of the list to which the message was posted is not part of the
URL, include it after *Retrieved from*. The URL you provide should be for the
archived version of the message or post.

Author's Last Name, Initials. (Year, Month Day). Subject line of message
[Descriptive label]. Retrieved from URL

Baker, J. (2005, February 15). Re: Huffing and puffing [Electronic
mailing list message]. Retrieved from American Dialect Society
electronic mailing list: http://listserv.linguistlist.org/cgi-bin
/wa?A2=ind0502C&L=ADS-L&P=R44

Do not include email or other nonarchived discussions in your list of
references. Simply give the sender's name in your text. See no. 13 on
page 556 for guidelines on identifying such sources in your text.

27. BLOG ENTRY

Author's Last Name, Initials. (Year, Month Day). Title of post [Blog post].
Retrieved from URL

Collins, C. (2009, August 19). Butterfly benefits from warmer springs?
[Blog post]. Retrieved from http://www.intute.ac.uk/blog
/2009/08/19/butterfly-benefits-from-warmer-springs/

28. ONLINE VIDEO

Last Name, Initials (Writer), & Last Name, Initials (Producer). (Year, Month
Day posted). *Title* [Descriptive label]. Retrieved from URL

Coulter, J. (Songwriter & Performer), & Booth, M. S. (Producer). (2006, September 23). *Code Monkey* [Video file]. Retrieved from http:// www.youtube.com/watch?v=v4Wy7gRGgeA

29. PODCAST

Writer's Last Name, Initials. (Writer), & Producer's Last Name, Initials. (Producer). (Year, Month Day). Title of podcast. *Title of site or program* [Audio podcast]. Retrieved from URL

Britt, M. A. (Writer & Producer). (2009, June 7). Episode 97: Stanley Milgram study finally replicated. *The Psych Files Podcast* [Audio podcast]. Retrieved from http://www.thepsychfiles.com/

Other Kinds of Sources

30. FILM, VIDEO, OR DVD

Last Name, Initials (Producer), & Last Name, Initials (Director). (Year). *Title* [Motion picture]. Country: Studio.

Wallis, H. B. (Producer), & Curtiz, M. (Director). (1942). *Casablanca* [Motion picture]. United States: Warner.

31. MUSIC RECORDING

Composer's Last Name, Initials. (Year of copyright). Title of song. On *Title of album* [Medium]. City, State or Country: Label.

Veloso, C. (1997). Na baixado sapateiro. On *Livros* [CD]. Los Angeles, CA: Nonesuch.

32. PROCEEDINGS OF A CONFERENCE

Author's Last Name, Initials. (Year of publication). Title of paper. In *Proceedings Title* (pp. pages). Publication City, State or Country: Publisher.

Heath, S. B. (1997). Talking work: Language among teens. In *Symposium about Language and Society—Austin* (pp. 27-45). Austin: Department of Linguistics at the University of Texas.

33. TELEVISION PROGRAM

Last Name, Initials (Writer), & Last Name, Initials (Director). (Year). Title of episode [Descriptive label]. In Initials Last Name (Producer), *Series title*. City, State or Country: Network.

Dunkle, R. (Writer), & Lange, M. (Director). (2012). Hit [Television series episode]. In E. A. Bernero (Executive Producer), *Criminal minds*. New York, NY: NBC.

34. SOFTWARE OR COMPUTER PROGRAM

Title and version number [Computer software]. (Year). Publication City, State or Country: Publisher.

Elder Scrolls V: Skyrim [Computer software]. (2011). Rockwood, MD: Bethesda.

35. GOVERNMENT DOCUMENT

Government Agency. (Year of publication). *Title*. Publication City, State or Country: Publisher.

U.S Department of Health and Human Services, Centers for Disease Control and Prevention. (2009). *Fourth national report on human exposure to environmental chemicals*. Washington, DC: Government Printing Office.

ONLINE GOVERNMENT DOCUMENT

Government Agency. (Year of publication). *Title* (Publication No. [if any]). Retrieved from URL

U.S Department of Health and Human Services, National Institutes of
Health, National Institute of Mental Health. (2006). *Bipolar disorder*
(NIH Publication No. 06-3679). Retrieved from http://www.nimh.nih
.gov/health/publications/bipolar-disorder/nimh-bipolar-adults.pdf

36. DISSERTATION

Include the database name and accession number for dissertations that
you retrieve from a database.

Author's Last Name, Initials. (Year). *Title of dissertation* (Doctoral
dissertation). Retrieved from Name of database. (accession number)

Knapik, M. (2008). *Adolescent online trouble-talk: Help-seeking in
cyberspace* (Doctoral dissertation). Retrieved from ProQuest
Dissertation and Theses database. (AAT NR38024)

For a dissertation that you access on the web, include the name of institution
after *Doctoral dissertation.* For example: (Doctoral dissertation, University of
North Carolina). End your documentation with *Retrieved from* and the URL.

37. TECHNICAL OR RESEARCH REPORT

Author's Last Name, Initials. (Year). *Title of report* (Report number).
Publication City, State or Country: Publisher.

Elsayed, T., Namata, G., Getoor, L., & Oard, D. W. (2008). *Personal name
resolution in email: A heuristic approach* (Report No. LAMP-TR-150).
College Park: University of Maryland.

Sources Not Covered by APA

To document a source for which APA does not provide guidelines, look at
models similar to the source you have cited. Give any information readers
will need in order to find it themselves — author; date of publication; title;
publisher; information about electronic retrieval (DOI or URL); and any
other pertinent information. You might want to try your reference note
yourself, to be sure it will lead others to your source.

FORMATTING A PAPER

Title page.　APA generally requires a title page. At the upper left-hand corner of the page, include "Running head:" and a shortened version of your title in capital letters. The page number (1) should go in the upper right-hand corner. Center the full title of the paper, your name, and the name of your school on separate lines about halfway down the page. You may add an "Author Note" at the bottom of the page to provide course information, acknowledgments, or contact information.

Page numbers.　Use a shortened title in capital letters in the upper left-hand corner of each page; place the page number in the upper right-hand corner. Number pages consecutively throughout your paper.

Fonts, spacing, margins, and indents.　Use a serif font (such as Times New Roman or Bookman) for the text, and a sans serif font (such as Calibri or Verdana) for figure labels. Double-space the entire paper, including any notes and your list of references. Leave one-inch margins at the top, bottom, and sides of your text; do not justify the text. Paragraphs should be indented one-half inch (or five to seven spaces) from the left margin. APA recommends using two spaces after end-of-sentence punctuation.

Headings.　Though they are not required in APA style, headings can help readers follow your organization. The first level of heading should be bold, centered, and capitalized as you would any other title; the second level of heading should be bold and flush with the left margin; the third level should be bold and indented, with only the first letter and proper nouns capitalized and with a period at the end of the heading, with the text following on the same line.

First Level Heading

Second Level Heading

　　Third level heading.

Long quotations.   Indent quotations of more than forty words to one-half inch (or five to seven spaces) from the left margin. Do not use quotation marks, and place page number(s) in parentheses after the end punctuation.

> Kaplan (2000) captured ancient and contemporary Antioch for us:
>
>> At the height of its glory in the Roman-Byzantine age, when it had an amphitheater, public baths, aqueducts, and sewage pipes, half a million people lived in Antioch. Today the population is only 125,000. With sour relations between Turkey and Syria, and unstable politics throughout the Middle East, Antioch is now a backwater—seedy and tumbledown, with relatively few tourists. (p. 123)
>
> Antioch's decline serves as a reminder that the fortunes of cities can change drastically over time.

Illustrations.   For each table, provide a number (*Table* 1) and a descriptive title on separate lines above the table; below the table, include a note with information about the source. For figures — charts, diagrams, graphs, photos, and so on — include a figure number (*Figure* 1) and information about the source in a note below the figure. Number tables and figures

Table 1
Hours of Instruction Delivered per Week

	American classrooms	Japanese classrooms	Chinese classrooms
First grade			
Language arts	10.5	8.7	10.4
Mathematics	2.7	5.8	4.0
Fifth grade			
Language arts	7.9	8.0	11.1
Mathematics	3.4	7.8	11.7

Note. Adapted from "Peeking Out from Under the Blinders: Some Factors We Shouldn't Forget in Studying Writing," by J. R. Hayes, 1991, National Center for the Study of Writing and Literacy (Occasional Paper No. 25). Retrieved from National Writing Project website: http://www.nwp.org/

separately, and be sure to refer to any illustrations in your text and clarify how they relate to the rest of your text.

Abstract.   An abstract is a concise summary of your paper that briefly introduces readers to your topic and main points. Most scholarly journals require an abstract; check with your instructor about his or her preference. Put your abstract on the second page, with the word *Abstract* centered at the top. Unless your instructor specifies a length, limit your abstract to 250 words or fewer.

List of references.   Start your list on a new page after the text but before any endnotes. Center the title and double-space the entire list. Each entry should begin at the left margin, and subsequent lines should be indented one-half inch (or five to seven spaces). Alphabetize the list by authors' last names (or by editors' names, if appropriate). Alphabetize works that have no author or editor by title, disregarding *A*, *An*, and *The*. Be sure every source listed is cited in the text; don't include sources that you consulted but didn't cite.

SAMPLE RESEARCH PAPER

Carolyn Stonehill wrote the following paper for a first-year writing course. It is formatted according to the guidelines of the *Publication Manual of the American Psychological Association*, 6th edition (2009). While APA guidelines are used widely in linguistics and the social sciences, exact requirements may vary from discipline to discipline and course to course. If you're unsure about what your instructor wants, ask for clarification.

Running head: IT'S IN OUR GENES   1

Page number.

"Running head:" and shortened title.

It's in Our Genes:

The Biological Basis of Human Mating Behavior

Carolyn Stonehill

Wright State University

Title, name, and school name.

IT'S IN OUR GENES   2

Abstract

While cultural values and messages certainly play a part in
the process of mate selection, the genetic and psychological
predispositions developed by our ancestors play the biggest role in
determining to whom we are attracted. Women are attracted to
strong, capable men with access to resources to help rear children.
Men find women attractive based on visual signs of youth, health,
and, by implication, fertility. While perceptions of attractiveness
are influenced by cultural norms and reinforced by advertisements
and popular media, the persistence of mating behaviors that have
no relationship to societal realities suggests that they are part of our
biological heritage.

Heading centered.

Limited to 250 words or fewer.

Two spaces after end punctuation.

It's in Our Genes:

The Biological Basis of Human Mating Behavior

Consider the following scenario: It's a sunny afternoon on campus, and Jenny is walking to her next class. Out of the corner of her eye, she catches sight of her lab partner, Joey, parking his car. She stops to admire how tall, muscular, and stylishly dressed he is, and she does not take her eyes off him as he walks away from his shiny new BMW. As he flashes her a pearly white smile, Jenny melts, then quickly adjusts her skirt and smooths her hair.

This scenario, while generalized, is familiar: Our attraction to people—or lack of it—often depends on their physical traits. But why this attraction? Why does Jenny respond the way she does to her handsome lab partner? Why does she deem him handsome at all? Certainly Joey embodies the stereotypes of physical attractiveness prevalent in contemporary American society. Advertisements, television shows, and magazine articles all provide Jenny with signals telling her what constitutes the ideal American man. Yet she is also attracted to Joey's new sports car even though she has a new car herself. Does Jenny find this man striking because of the influence of her culture, or does her attraction lie in a more fundamental part of her constitution? Evolutionary psychologists, who apply principles of evolutionary biology to research on the human mind, would say that Jenny's responses in this situation are due largely to mating strategies developed by her prehistoric ancestors. Driven by the need to reproduce and

Title centered.

Double-spaced throughout.

Paragraphs indent 5 to 7 spaces ($\frac{1}{2}$ inch).

1″

1″

1″

propagate the species, these ancestors of ours formed patterns of mate selection so effective in providing for their needs and those of their offspring that they are mimicked even in today's society. While cultural values and messages clearly play a part in the process of mate selection, the genetic and psychological predispositions developed by our ancestors play the biggest role in determining to whom we are attracted.

Women's Need to Find a Capable Mate

Pioneering evolutionary psychologist R. Trivers (as cited in Allman, 1993) observed that having and rearing children requires women to invest far more resources than men because of the length of pregnancy, the dangers of childbirth, and the duration of infants' dependence on their mothers (p. 56). According to H. Fisher (as cited in Frank, 2001), one of the leading advocates of this theory, finding a capable mate was a huge preoccupation of all prehistoric reproductive women, and for good reason: "A female couldn't carry a baby in one arm and sticks and stones in the other arm and still feed and protect herself on the very dangerous open grasslands, so she began to need a mate to help her rear her young" (p. 85). So because of this it became advantageous for the woman to find a strong, capable man with access to resources, and it became suitable for the man to find a healthy, reproductively sound woman to bear and care for his offspring. According to evolutionary psychologists, these are the bases upon which modern mate selection is founded, and there are many examples of this phenomenon to be found in our own society.

First-level headings boldface, centered.

Authors referred to by last name.

Source quoted in another source; secondary source and date in first parentheses, page number in second parentheses.

IT'S IN OUR GENES   5

    One can see now why Jenny might be attracted by Joey's display of resources—his BMW. In our society, men with good job prospects, a respected social position, friends in high places, or any combination thereof have generally been viewed as more desirable mates than those without these things because they signal to women that the men have resources (Buss & Schmitt, 1993, p. 226). Compared with males, females invest more energy in bearing and raising children, so it is most advantageous for females to choose mates with easy access to resources, the better to provide for their children.

Men's Need to Find a Healthy Mate

    For men, reproductive success depends mainly on the reproductive fitness of their female counterpart: No amount of available resources can save a baby miscarried in the first month of gestation. Because of this need for a healthy mate, men have evolved a particular attraction "radar" that focuses on signs of a woman's health and youth, markers that are primarily visual (Weiten, 2001, p. 399). Present-day attractiveness ratings are based significantly on this primitive standard: "Some researchers have suggested that cross-cultural standards of beauty reflect an evolved preference for physical traits that are generally associated with youth, such as smooth skin, good muscle tone, and shiny hair" (Boyd & Silk, 2000, p. 625). This observation would explain why women of our time are preoccupied with plastic surgery, makeup, and—in Jenny's case—a quick hair check as a potential date

Author names in parentheses when no signal phrase is used.

Ampersands used in parenthetical references, and used in signal phrases.

Author named in a signal phrase, publication date in parentheses after the name.

approaches. As Cunningham, Roberts, Barbee, Druen, and Wu (1995) noted, "A focus on outer beauty may have stemmed from a need for desirable inner qualities," such as health, strength, and fertility, and "culture may build on evolutionary dynamics by specifying grooming attributes that signal successful adaptation" (pp. 262-263).

The Influence of the Media on Mate Selection

There is, however, a good deal of opposition to evolutionary theory. Some critics say that the messages fed to us by the media are a larger influence on the criteria of present-day mate selection than any sort of ancestral behavior. Advertisements and popular media have long shown Americans what constitutes a physically ideal mate: In general, youthful, well-toned, symmetrical features are considered more attractive than aging, flabby, or lopsided ones. Evolutionary psychologists argue that research has not determined what is cause and what is effect. Cosmides and Tooby (1997) offered the following analogy to show the danger of assigning culture too powerful a causal role:

Quotations of 40+ words indented 5 to 7 spaces.

For example, people think that if they can show that there is information in the culture that mirrors how people behave, then *that* is the cause of their behavior. So if they see that men on TV have trouble crying, they assume that their example is *causing* boys to be afraid to cry. But which is cause and which effect? Does the fact that men don't cry much on TV *teach* boys to not cry, or does it merely *reflect* the way boys normally develop? In the absence of research on the particular topic,

IT'S IN OUR GENES   7

there is no way of knowing. ("Nature and Nurture: An

Adaptationist Perspective," para. 16)

We can hypothesize, then, that rather than media messages

determining our mating habits, our mating habits determine the

media messages. Advertisers rely on classical conditioning to

interest consumers in their products. For instance, by showing an

image of a beautiful woman while advertising a beauty product,

advertisers hope that consumers will associate attractiveness

with the use of that particular product (Weiten, 2001). In order

for this method to be effective, however, the images depicted in

conjunction with the beauty product must be ones the general

public already finds attractive, and an image of a youthful, clear-

skinned woman would, according to evolutionary psychologists, be

attractive for reasons of reproductive fitness. In short, what some

call media influence is not an influence at all but merely a mirror in

which we see evidence of our ancestral predispositions.

If Not Media, Then What?

Tattersall (2001), a paleoanthropologist at the American

Museum of Natural History, offered another counterargument to

the evolutionary theory of mate selection. First, he argued that the

behavior of organisms is influenced not only by genetics, but also

by economics and ecology working together (p. 663). Second, he

argued that no comparisons can be made between modern human

behavior and that of our evolutionary predecessors because the

appearance of *Homo sapiens* presented a sudden, qualitative change

Major heading and paragraph number cited for quote from unpaginated work from a website.

from the Neanderthals—not a gradual evolution of behavioral traits:

> As a cognitive and behavioral entity, our species is truly unprecedented. Our consciousness is an emergent quality, not the result of eons of fine-tuning of a single instrument. And, if so, it is to this recently acquired quality of uniqueness, not to the hypothetical "ancestral environments," that we must look in the effort to understand our often unfathomable behaviors. (p. 665)

End punctuation before parentheses in block quotations.

The key to Tattersall's argument is this "emergent quality" of symbolic thought; according to his theories, the ability to think symbolically is what separates modern humans from their ancestors and shows the impossibility of sexual selection behaviors having been passed down over millions of years. Our sexual preferences, Tattersall said, are a result of our own recent and species-specific development and have nothing whatsoever to do with our ancestors.

Opponents of the evolutionary theory, though, fail to explain how "unfathomable" mating behaviors can exist in our present society for no apparent or logical reason. Though medicine has advanced to the point where fertility can be medically enhanced, Singh (1993) observed that curvy women are still viewed as especially attractive because they are perceived to possess greater fertility—a perception that is borne out by several studies of female fertility, hormone levels, and waist-to-hip ratio (p. 304). Though

IT'S IN OUR GENES   9

more and more women are attending college and achieving high-paying positions, women are still "more likely than men to consider economic prospects a high priority in a mate" (Sapolsky, 2001-2002, p. 18). While cultural norms and economic conditions influence our taste in mates, as Singh (1993) showed in observing that "the degree of affluence of a society or of an ethnic group within a society may, to a large extent, determine the prevalence and admiration of fatness [of women]" (pp. 304-305), we still react to potential mates in ways determined in Paleolithic times. The key to understanding our mating behavior does not lie only in an emergent modern quality, nor does it lie solely in the messages relayed to us by society; rather, it involves as well the complex mating strategies developed by our ancestors.

Heading centered.

Alphabetized by authors' last names.

All lines after the first line of each entry indented.

References

Allman, W. F. (1993, July 19). The mating game. *U.S. News & World Report,* 115(3), 56-63.

Boyd, R., & Silk, J. B. (2000). *How humans evolved* (2nd ed.). New York, NY: Norton.

Buss, D. M., & Schmitt, D. P. (1993). Sexual strategies theory: An evolutionary perspective on human mating. *Psychological Review,* 100(2), 204-232.

Cosmides, L., & Tooby, J. (1997). Evolutionary psychology: A primer. Center for Evolutionary Psychology. Retrieved April 30, 2013, from http://www.psych.ucsb.edu/research/cep/primer.html

Cunningham, M. R., Roberts, A. R., Barbee, A. P., Druen, P. B., & Wu, C.-H. (1995). "Their ideas of beauty are, on the whole, the same as ours": Consistency and variability in the cross-cultural perception of female physical attractiveness. *Journal of Personality and Social Psychology,* 68, 261-279.

Frank, C. (2001, February). Why do we fall in—and out of—love? Dr. Helen Fisher unravels the mystery. *Biography,* 85-87, 112.

Sapolsky, R. M. (2001-2002, December-January). What do females want? *Natural History,* 18-21.

Singh, D. (1993). Adaptive significance of female physical attractiveness: Role of waist-to-hip ratio. *Journal of Personality and Social Behavior,* 65, 293-307.

IT'S IN OUR GENES   11

Tattersall, I. (2001). Evolution, genes, and behavior. *Zygon: Journal of Religion & Science, 36,* 657-666. doi:10.1111/0591=2835.00389

Weiten, W. (2001). *Psychology: Themes & variations* (5th ed.). San Bernardino, CA: Wadsworth.

All sources cited in the text are listed.

part 7

Media / Design

Consciously or not, we design all the texts we write, choosing typefaces, setting up text as lists or charts, deciding whether to add headings—and then whether to center them or align them on the left. Sometimes our genre calls for certain design elements—essays begin with titles, letters begin with salutations ("Dear Auntie Em"). Other times we design texts to meet the demands of particular audiences, formatting documentation in MLA or APA or some other style, setting type larger for young children, and so on. And our designs always depend upon our medium. A memoir might take the form of an essay in a book, be turned into a bulleted list for a slide presentation, or include links to images or other pages if presented on a website. The chapters in this part offer advice for CHOOSING MEDIA; working with DESIGN, IMAGES, and SOUND; WRITING ONLINE; and GIVING PRESENTATIONS.

Media / Design

Consciously or not, we design all the texts we write,
choosing typefaces, setting up text as lists of items or
running text, creating charts or graphs, incorporating
photographs, adding sound, and so on. And our designs
always depend upon our medium. A memoir might take
the form of an essay in a book, be turned into a bulleted
list for a slide presentation, include links to images or
other pages if presented on a website. The chapters
in this part offer advice for working with these media
and design.

Choosing Media 54

USA Today reports on contract negotiations between automakers and auto-workers with an article that includes a large photo and a colorful graph; the article on the same story on *nytimes.com* includes a video of striking workers. In your economics class, you give a presentation about the issue that includes *Prezi* slides.

These examples show how information about the same events can be delivered using three different media: print (*USA Today*), electronic (*nytimes.com*), and spoken (the main medium for your class presentation). They also show how different media offer writers different modes of expressing meaning, ranging from words to images to sounds and hyperlinks. A print text can include written words and still visuals; online, the same text can also incorporate links to moving images and sound as well as to other written materials. A presentation with slides can include both spoken and written words, can incorporate video and audio elements — and can also include print handouts.

In college writing, the choice of medium often isn't up to you: your instructor may require a printed essay or a classroom talk, a website, or some combination of media. Sometimes, though, you'll be the one deciding. Because your medium will play a big part in the way your audience receives and reacts to your message, you'll need to think hard about what media best suits your audience, purpose, and message. This chapter will help you choose media when the choice is yours.

Print

When you have a choice of medium, print has certain advantages over spoken and electronic text in that it's more permanent and doesn't depend on audience access to technology. Depending on your own access to technology, you can usually insert photos or other visuals and can present data and other information as graphs or charts. Obviously, though, print documents are more work than electronic ones to update or change, and they don't allow for sound, moving images, or hyperlinks to other materials.

Electronic

Online writing is everywhere: on course learning platforms and class websites; in virtual discussion groups and wikis; in emails, text messages, tweets, and other social media. And when you're taking an online course, you are, by definition, always using an electronic medium. Remember that this medium has advantages as well as limitations and potential pitfalls. You can add audio, video, and hyperlinks — but your audience may not have the same access to technology that you do. These are just some of the things you'll need to keep in mind when deciding, say, whether to include or to link to videos or a site that has restricted access.

Spoken

If you deliver your text orally, as a speech or presentation, you have the opportunity to use your tone of voice, gestures, and physical bearing to establish credibility. But you must write your text so that it's easy to understand when it is heard rather than read. The spoken medium can be used alone with a live, face-to-face audience, but it's often combined with print, in the form of handouts, or with electronics, in the form of presentation software like *PowerPoint* or *Prezi*, or designed for remote audiences in formats like webcasts, webinars, podcasts, or video-calling services such as *Skype*.

academic literacies   rhetorical situations   genres   processes   strategies   research MLA / APA   media / design   readings

Multimedia

It's increasingly likely that you'll be assigned to create a multimedia text, one that includes some combination of print, oral, and electronic elements. It's also possible that you'll have occasion to write a multimodal text, one that uses more than one mode of expression: words, images, audio, video, hyperlinks, and so on. The words *multimedia* and *multimodal* are often used interchangeably, but *multimodal* is the term that's used most often in composition classes, whereas *multimedia* is the one used in other disciplines and in industry. In composition classes, the word generally refers to writing that includes more than just words.

For example, let's say that in a U.S. history class you're assigned to do a project about the effects of the Vietnam War on American society. You might write an essay using words alone to discuss such effects as increased hostility toward the military and government, generational conflict within families and society at large, and increased use of recreational drugs. But you could also weave such a text together with many other materials to create a multimodal composition.

If you're using print, for example, you could include photographs from the Vietnam era, such as of antiwar protests or military funerals. Another possibility might be a time line that puts developments in the war in the context of events going on simultaneously elsewhere in American life, such as in fashion and entertainment or in the feminist and civil rights movements. If you're posting your project online, you might also incorporate video clips of TV news coverage of the war and clips from films focusing on it or its social effects, such as *Apocalypse Now* or *Easy Rider*. Audio elements could include recorded interviews with veterans who fought in the war, people who protested against it, or government officials who were involved in planning or overseeing it. Many of these elements could be inserted into your document as hyperlinks.

If your assignment specifies that you give an oral presentation, you could play some of the music of the Vietnam era, show videos of government officials defending the war and demonstrators protesting it, maybe hang some psychedelic posters from the era.

Considering the Rhetorical Situation

55–56 **PURPOSE** What's your purpose, and what media will best suit that purpose? A text or email may be appropriate for inviting a friend to lunch, but neither would be ideal for demonstrating to a professor that you understand a complex historical event; for that, you'd likely write a report, either in print or online — and you might include photos or maps or other such texts to provide visual context.

57–60 **AUDIENCE** What media are your audience likely to expect — and be able to access? A blog may be a good way to reach people who share your interest in basketball or cupcakes, but to reach your grandparents, you may want to put a handwritten note in the mail. Some employers require applicants to submit résumés and applications online, while others prefer to receive them in print form.

61–63 **GENRE** Does your genre require a particular medium? If you're giving an oral presentation, you'll often be expected to include slides. Academic essays are usually formatted to be printed out, even if they are submitted electronically. An online essay based on field research might include audio files of those you've interviewed, but if your essay were in print, you'd need to quote (or paraphrase or summarize) what they said.

64–67 **STANCE** If you have a choice of media, think about whether a particular medium will help you convey your stance. A print document in MLA format, for instance, will make you seem scholarly and serious. Tweeting or blogging, however, might work better for a more informal stance. Presenting data in charts will sometimes help you establish your credibility as a knowledgeable researcher.

Once you decide on the media and modes of expression you're using, you'll need to design your text to take advantage of their possibilities and to deal with their limitations. The next chapters will help you do that.

Designing Text 55

You're trying to figure out why a magazine ad you're looking at is so funny, and you realize that the font used for the text is deliberately intended to make you laugh. In giving an assignment for a research paper, your psychology professor specifies that you are to follow APA format. Your classmates complain that the *PowerPoint* slides you use for a presentation are hard to read, and one of them suggests that it's because there's not enough contrast between the colors of the words and the background. Whether you're putting together your résumé, creating a website for your intramural soccer league, or writing a research essay for a class, you need to think about how you design what you write.

Sometimes you can rely on established conventions: in academic writing using MLA and APA style, for example, there are specific guidelines for margins, headings, and the use of single-, double-, or triple-spaced lines of text. But often you'll have to make design decisions on your own — and not just about words and spacing. If what you're writing includes photos, charts, tables, graphs, or other visuals, you'll need to figure out how to integrate these with your written text in the most attractive and effective way; online, you may also need to decide where and how to include video clips and hyperlinks. You might even use scissors, glue, and staples to attach objects to a poster or create pop-ups in a brochure.

No matter what your text includes, its design will influence how your audience responds to it and therefore how well it achieves your purpose. This chapter offers general advice on designing print and online texts to suit your purpose, audience, genre, and stance.

Considering the Rhetorical Situation

As with all writing tasks, your rhetorical situation should affect the way you design a text. Here are some points to consider:

55–56 **PURPOSE**   How can you design your text to help achieve your purpose? If you're reporting information, for instance, you may want to present statistical data in a chart or table rather than in the main text to help readers grasp it more quickly. If you're trying to get readers to care about an issue, a photo or pull quote—a brief selection of text "pulled out" and reprinted in a larger font—might help you do so.

57–60 **AUDIENCE**   How can you make your design appeal to your intended audience? By using a certain font style or size to make your text look hip, serious, or easy to read? What kind of headings — big and bold, simple and restrained? — would your readers expect or find helpful? What colors would appeal to them?

61–63 **GENRE**   Are you writing in a genre that has design conventions, such as an annotated bibliography, a lab report, or a résumé? Do you need to follow a format such as those prescribed in MLA or APA style?

64–67 **STANCE**   How can your design reflect your attitude toward your audience and subject? Do you need a businesslike font or a playful one? Would tables and graphs help you establish your credibility? How can illustrations help you convey a certain tone?

Some Basic Principles of Design

Be consistent. To keep readers oriented while reading documents or browsing multiple webpages, any design elements should be used consistently. In a print academic essay, that task may be as simple as using the same font throughout for your main text and using boldface or italics for headings. If you're writing for the web, navigation buttons and other major elements should be in the same place on every page. In a presentation, each slide should use the same background and the same font unless there's a good reason to introduce differences.

Keep it simple.   One of your main design goals should be to help readers see quickly — even intuitively — what's in your text and how to find specific information. Adding headings to help readers see the parts, using consistent colors and fonts to help them recognize key elements, setting off steps in lists, using white space to set off blocks of text or to call attention to certain elements, and (especially) resisting the temptation to fill pages with fancy graphics or unnecessary animations: these are all ways of making your text simple to read.

Look, for example, at a furniture store's simple, easy-to-understand webpage design on page 600. This webpage contains considerable information: a row of links across the top, directing readers to various products; a search option; a column down the right side that provides details about the chair shown in the wide left-hand column; thumbnail photos below the chair, showing its various options; and suggestions across the bottom for furniture to go with it. Despite the wealth of content, the site's design is both easy to figure out and, with the generous amount of white space, easy on the eyes.

Aim for balance.   On the webpage on page 600, the photo takes up about a quarter of the screen and is balanced by a narrower column of text, and the "Matching Products" and "More POÄNG series" sections across the page bottom balance the company logo and links bar across the top. For a page without images, balance can be created through the use of margins, headings, and spacing. In the journal page shown on page 516, notice how using white space around the article title and the author's name, as well as setting both in larger type and the author's name in all capital letters, helps to balance them vertically against the large block of text below.

The large initial letter of the text also helps to balance the mass of smaller type that follows. MLA and APA styles have specific design guidelines for academic research papers that cover these elements. A magazine

page might create a sense of balance by using pull quotes and illustrations to break up dense vertical columns of text.

Use color and contrast carefully.　Academic readers usually expect black text on a white background, with perhaps one other color for headings. Presentation slides and webpages are most readable with a plain, light-colored background and dark text that provides contrast. Remember that not everyone can see all colors and that an online text that includes several colors might be printed out and read in black and white; make sure your audience will be able to distinguish any color variations well enough to grasp your meaning. Colored lines on a graph, for example, should be distinguishable even if readers cannot see the colors. Red-green contrasts are especially hard to see and should be avoided.

Use available templates.　Good design takes time, and most of us do not have training as designers. If you're pressed for time or don't feel up to the challenge of designing your own text, take advantage of the many templates available. In *Microsoft Word*, for example, you can customize "styles" to specify the font, including its size and color; single- or double-spacing; paragraph indentations; and several other features that will then automatically apply to your document. Websites that host personal webpages and blogs offer dozens of templates that you can use or modify to suit your needs. And presentation software offers many templates that can simplify creating slides.

Some Elements of Design

Fonts.　You can usually choose from among many fonts, and the one you choose will affect how well the audience can read your text and how they will perceive your **TONE**. Times Roman will make a text look businesslike or academic; *Comic Sans* will make it look playful. For most academic writing,

65

you'll want to use a font size between 10 and 12 points and a serif font (such as Times Roman or Bookman) rather than a sans serif font (such as Arial, Verdana, or Calibri) because serif fonts are generally easier to read. Reserve sans serif for headings and parts of the text that you want to highlight. Decorative fonts (such as *Magneto*, *Amaze*, Chiller, and Jokerman) should be used sparingly and only when they're appropriate for your audience, purpose, and the rest of your **RHETORICAL SITUATION**. If you use more than one font in a text, use each one consistently: one for **HEADINGS**, one for captions, one for the main body of your text. And don't go overboard—you won't often have reason to use more than two or, at most, three fonts in any one text.

53
604–5

Every font has regular, **bold**, and *italic* forms. In general, choose regular for the main text and lower-level headings, bold for major headings, and italic within the main text to indicate titles of books and other long works and, occasionally, to emphasize words or brief phrases. Avoid italicizing or boldfacing entire sentences or paragraphs, especially in academic writing. If you are following **MLA**, **APA**, or some other style format, be sure your use of fonts conforms to its requirements.

MLA 500–548
APA 549–90

Finally, consider the line spacing of your text. Generally, academic writing is double-spaced, whereas **JOB LETTERS** and **RÉSUMÉS** are usually single-spaced. Some kinds of **REPORTS** may call for single-spacing; check with your instructor if you're not sure. You'll often need to add extra space to set off parts of a text—items in a list, for instance, or headings.

253–64
129–55

Layout.   Layout is the way text is arranged on a page. An academic essay, for example, will usually have a title centered at the top, one-inch margins all around, and double-spacing. A text can be presented in paragraphs— or in the form of **LISTS**, **TABLES**, **CHARTS**, **GRAPHS**, and so on. Sometimes you'll need to include other elements as well: headings, images and other graphics, captions, lists of works cited.

603
609–11

Paragraphs.   Dividing text into paragraphs focuses information for readers and helps them process the information by dividing it into manageable chunks. If you're writing a story for a print newspaper with narrow columns, for example, you'll divide your text into shorter paragraphs

than you would if you were writing an academic essay. In general, indent paragraphs five to seven spaces (one-half inch) when your text is double-spaced; either indent or skip a line between paragraphs that are single-spaced.

Lists.   Put information into list form that you want to set off and make easily accessible. Number the items in a list when the sequence matters (in instructions, for example); use bullets when the order is not important. Set off lists with an extra line of space above and below, and add extra space between the items on a list if necessary for legibility. Here's an example:

> Darwin's theory of how species change through time derives from three postulates, each of which builds on the previous one:
>
> 1. The ability of a population to expand is infinite, but the ability of any environment to support populations is always finite.
> 2. Organisms within populations vary, and this variation affects the ability of individuals to survive and reproduce.
> 3. The variations are transmitted from parents to offspring.
>
> —Robert Boyd and Joan B. Silk, *How Humans Evolved*

Do not set off text as a list unless there's a good reason to do so, however. Some lists are more appropriately presented in paragraph form, especially when they give information that is not meant to be referred to more than once. In the following example, there is no reason to highlight the information by setting it off in a list—and bad news is softened by putting it in paragraph form:

> I regret to inform you that the Scholarship Review Committee did not approve your application for a Board of Rectors scholarship for the following reasons: your grade-point average did not meet the minimum requirements; your major is not among those eligible for consideration; and the required letter of recommendation was not received before the deadline.

Presented as a list, that information would be needlessly emphatic.

Headings.   Headings make the structure of a text easier to follow and help readers find specific information. Some genres require standard headings — announcing an **ABSTRACT**, for example, or a list of **WORKS CITED**. Other times you will want to use headings to provide an overview of a section of text. You may not need any headings in brief texts, but when you do, you'll probably want to use one level at most, just to announce major topics. Longer texts, information-rich genres such as brochures or detailed **REPORTS**, and websites may require several levels of headings. If you decide to include headings, you will need to decide how to phrase them, what fonts to use, and where to position them.

183–87 ▲
539 ●

129–56 ▲

Phrase headings concisely.   Make your headings succinct and parallel in structure. You might make all the headings nouns (**Mushrooms**), noun phrases (**Kinds of Mushrooms**), gerund phrases (**Recognizing Kinds of Mushrooms**), or questions (**How Do I Identify Mushrooms?**). Whatever form you decide on, use it consistently for each heading. Sometimes your phrasing will depend on your purpose. If you're simply helping readers find information, use brief phrases:

HEAD	**Forms of Social Groups among Primates**
SUBHEAD	*Solitary Social Groups*
SUBHEAD	*Monogamous Social Groups*

If you want to address your readers directly with the information in your text, consider writing your headings as questions:

How can you identify morels?
Where can you find morels?
How can you cook morels?

Make headings visible.   Headings need to be visible, so if you aren't following an academic style like MLA or APA, consider making them larger than the regular text, putting them in **bold** or *italics*, or using <u>underlining</u> — or a different font. For example, you could make your main text a serif font like Times Roman and your headings in a sans serif font like Arial. On the web, consider making headings a different color from the body text.

academic literacies · rhetorical situations · genres · processes · strategies · research MLA / APA · media / design · readings

When you have several levels of headings, use capitalization, bold, and italics to distinguish among the various levels:

First-Level Head
Second-Level Head
Third-level head

APA format requires that each level of heading appear in a specific style: centered bold uppercase and lowercase for the first level, flush-left bold uppercase and lowercase for the second level, and so on.

576

Position headings appropriately. If you're following APA format, center first-level headings. If you are not following a prescribed format, you get to decide where to position your headings: centered, flush with the left margin, or even alongside the text in a wide left-hand margin. Position each level of head consistently throughout your text. Generally, online headings are positioned flush left.

White space. Use white space to separate the various parts of a text. In general, use one-inch margins for the text of an essay or report. Unless you're following MLA or APA format, include space above headings, above and below lists, and around photos, graphs, and other visuals. See the two **SAMPLE RESEARCH PAPERS** in this book for examples of the formats required by MLA and APA.

MLA 539–48
APA 578–89

Evaluating a Design

Does the design suit your PURPOSE? Does the overall look of the design help convey the text's message, support its argument, or present information?

55–56

How well does the design meet the needs of your AUDIENCE? Will the overall appearance of the text appeal to the intended readers? Is the font large enough for them to read? Are there headings to help them find their way through the text? Does the design help readers find the information they need?

55–56

61–63 ▪
How well does the text meet any GENRE requirements? Can you tell by looking at the text that it is an academic essay, a lab report, a résumé, a blog? Do its fonts, margins, headings, and page layout meet the require-

MLA 538–39 ●
APA 576–79
ments of **MLA**, **APA**, or whatever style is being followed?

64–67 ▪
How well does the design reflect your STANCE? Do the page layout and fonts convey the appropriate tone — serious, playful, adventuresome, con-servative, or whatever other tone you intended?

academic literacies ✳
rhetorical situations ▪
genres ▲
processes ○
strategies ◆
research MLA / APA ●
media / design ▫
readings ◗

For an art history class, you write an essay comparing two paintings by Willem de Kooning. For an engineering class project, you design a model of a bridge and give an in-class presentation explaining the structures and forces involved, which you illustrate with slides. For a psychology assignment, you interview several people who've suffered foreclosures on their homes in recent years about how the experience affected them and how they've tried to cope with the resulting stress — and then create an online text weaving together a slideshow of photos of the people outside their former homes, a graph of foreclosure rates, video and audio clips from the interviews, and your own insights.

All of these writing tasks require you to incorporate and sometimes to create visuals and sound. Many kinds of visuals can be included in print documents: photos, diagrams, graphs, charts, and more. And with writing that's delivered online or as a spoken presentation, your choices expand to include audio and video, voice-over narration, and links to other materials.

Visuals and sound aren't always appropriate, however, or even possible — so think carefully before you set out to include them. But they can help you make a point in ways that words alone cannot. Election polling results are easier to see in a bar graph than the same information would be in a paragraph; an audio clip can make a written analysis of an opera easier to understand. This chapter provides some tips for using visuals and incorporating sound in your writing.

Considering the Rhetorical Situation

Use visuals that are appropriate for your audience, purpose, and the rest of your **RHETORICAL SITUATION**. If you're trying to persuade voters in your

53

607

town to back a proposal on an issue they don't know or care much about, for example, you might use dramatic pictures just to get their attention. But when it's important to come across as thoughtful and objective, maybe you need a more subdued look — or to make your points with written words alone. A newspaper article on housing prices might include a bar graph or line graph and also some photos. A report on the same topic for an economics class would probably have graphs with no photos; a community website might have graphs, links to related sites, and a video interview with a home owner.

In your academic writing, especially, be careful that any visuals you use support your main point — and don't just serve to decorate the text. (Therefore, avoid clip art, which is primarily intended as decoration.) Images should support what you say elsewhere with written words and add information that words alone can't provide as clearly or easily.

Using Visuals

Photos, videos, tables, pie charts, bar graphs: these are many kinds of visuals you could use.

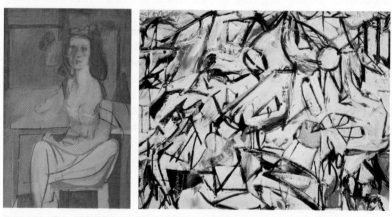

An essay discussing the work of Willem de Kooning might contrast one of his more representational works (such as the one on the left) with one that's more abstract (right).

academic literacies · rhetorical situations · genres · processes · strategies · research MLA / APA · media / design · readings

Photographs.   Photos can support an **ARGUMENT**, illustrate **NARRATIVES** and **PROCESSES**, present other points of view, and help readers "place" your information in time and space. You may use photos you take yourself, or you can download photos and other images from the internet — within limits. Most downloadable photos are copyrighted, meaning that you can use them without obtaining permission from the copyright owner only if you are doing so for academic purposes, to fulfill an assignment. If you are going to publish your text, either in print or on the web, you must have permission. Consider, too, the file size of digital images; large files can clog readers' email in-boxes, take a long time to display on their screens, or be hard for you to upload in the first place, so you may have to compress an image or reduce its resolution (which can diminish its sharpness).

355–73
419–27
414–18

Videos.   If you're writing online, you can include video clips for readers to play. If you're using a video already available online, such as on *YouTube*, you can show the opening image with an arrow for readers to click on to start the video, or you can simply copy the video's URL and paste it into your text as a **LINK**. In either case, you need to introduce the video in your text with a **SIGNAL PHRASE**. As with any other source, you need to provide an in-text citation and full documentation.

613–14
487–90

If you want to include a video you made yourself, you can edit it using such programs as *iMovie* or *Windows Movie Maker*. Once you're ready to insert it into your document, the easiest way is to first upload it to *You-Tube*, choosing the Private setting so only those you authorize may view it, and then create a link in your document.

Graphs, charts, and tables.   Statistical and other numerical information is often best presented in graphs, charts, and tables. If you can't find the right one for your purpose, you can create your own, as long as it's based on sound data from reliable sources. To do so, you can use various spreadsheet programs or online chart and graph generators.

In any case, remember to follow basic design principles: be **CONSISTENT**, label all parts clearly, and **KEEP THE DESIGN SIMPLE**, so readers can focus on the information and not be a distracted by a needlessly complex design. In particular, use color and contrast wisely to emphasize what's

598–99

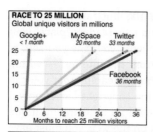

RACE TO 25 MILLION
Global unique visitors in millions

Line graphs are a good way of showing changes in data over time. Each line here represents a different social networking site. Plotting the lines together allows readers to compare the data at different points in time. Be sure to label the *x* and *y* axes and limit the number of lines to four at the most.

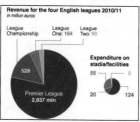

REVENUE
In billion euros

Bar graphs are useful for comparing quantitative data, measurements of how much or how many. The bars can be horizontal or vertical. This graph shows IKEA's earnings between 2000 and 2011. Some software offers 3-D and other special effects, but simple graphs are often easier to read.

Revenue for the four English leagues 2010/11
in million euros

Pie charts can be used to show how a whole is divided into parts or how parts of a whole relate to one another. The segments in a pie should always add up to 100 percent, and each segment should be clearly labeled.

ECONOMY WATCH
A snapshot of key figures for the world's largest economies.

Tables are useful for displaying numerical information concisely, especially when several items are being compared. Presenting information in columns and rows permits readers to find data and identify relationships among them.

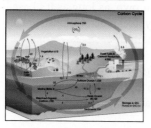

Diagrams and flowcharts are ways of showing relationships and processes. This diagram shows how carbon moves between the Earth and its atmosphere. Flowcharts can be made using widely available templates; diagrams, on the other hand, can range from simple drawings to works of art. Some simple flowcharts may be found in the Genre chapters (for example, p. 252).

 academic literacies   rhetorical situations   genres   processes   strategies   research MLA / APA   media / design   readings

most significant. Choose **COLORS** that are easy to distinguish from one another — and that remain so if the graph or chart is printed out in black and white. (Using gradations of color from light to dark will show in black and white.) Some common kinds of graphs, charts, and tables are shown on the facing page.

601

SOME TIPS FOR USING VISUALS

- Position images as close as possible to the discussion to which they relate. In *Microsoft Word*, simply position your cursor where you want to insert an image; click Picture on the Insert tab; choose the appropriate image from your files; and click Insert. You may then need to adjust the way the text flows or wraps around the image: in the Page Layout tab, choose the appropriate option in Wrap Text.

- In academic writing, number all images, using separate sequences of numbers for figures (photos, graphs, diagrams, video clips, and drawings) and tables: Fig. 1, Fig. 2; Table 1, Table 2.

- Explain in your written text whatever information you present in an image — don't expect it to speak for itself. Refer to the image before it appears, identifying it and summarizing its point. For example: "As Table 1 shows, Italy's economic growth rate has been declining for thirty years."

- Provide a title or caption for each image to identify it and explain its significance for your text. For example: "Table 1: Italy's Economic Growth Rate, 1985–2015."

- Label the parts of visuals clearly to ensure that your audience will understand what they show. For example, label each section of a pie chart to show what it represents.

- Cite the source of any images you don't create yourself. You need not document visuals you create, based on data from your own experimental or field research, but if you use data from a source to create a graph or chart, **CITE THE SOURCE** of the data.

491–94

- In general, you may use visuals created by someone else in your academic writing as long as you include full **DOCUMENTATION**. If you post your writing online, however, you must first obtain permission from the copyright owner.

496–99

Incorporating Sound

Audio clips, podcasts, and other sound files can serve various useful purposes in online writing. Music, for example, can create a mood for your text, giving your audience hints about how to interpret the meaning of your words and images or what emotional response you're evoking. Other types of sound effects — such as background conversations, passing traffic, birdsongs, crowd noise at sports events — can provide a sense of immediacy, of being part of the scene or event you're describing. Spoken words can serve as the primary way you present an online text or as an enhancement of or even a counterpoint to a written text. (And if your audience includes visually impaired people, an audio track can allow or help them to follow the text.)

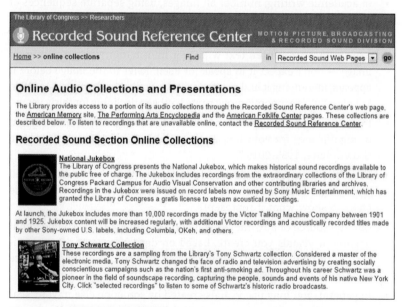

The Library of Congress is a good source for online recordings of music, speeches, and radio broadcasts.

You can download or link to various spoken texts online, or you can record voice and music as podcasts using programs such as *GarageBand* and *Audacity*. Remember to provide an **IN-TEXT CITATION** and full **DOCUMENTATION** of any sound material you obtain from another source.

496–99

Adding Links

If you're writing an online text in which you want to include images, video, or sound material available on the web, it's often easier and more effective to create links to them within the text than to embed them by copying and pasting. Such links allow readers to see the materials' original context and to explore it if they wish.

The example below shows a blog post from the Archives of American Art with links to additional detail and documentation.

John Singer Sargent

This lively caricature from the <u>Francis Davis Millet and Millet family papers</u> features an artist fervently painting his subject, just in the background. Most likely it is John Singer Sargent at work on his painting <u>*Carnation, Lily, Lily, Rose*</u>. His posture and the expression on his face suggest an exuberance that matches the action of the paint dripping and splashing as it prepares to meet the canvas with energetic strokes.

<u>Caricature of an artist painting vigorously</u>, ca. 1885-1886. <u>Francis Davis Millet and Millet family papers, Archives of American Art</u>, Smithsonian Institution.

SOME TIPS FOR CREATING LINKS

487–90

- Indicate links with underlining and color (most often blue), and introduce them with a **SIGNAL PHRASE**.

- Don't include your own punctuation in a link. In the example on page 613, the period is not part of the link.

- Try to avoid having a link open in a new browser window. Readers expect links to open in the same window.

Editing Carefully — and Ethically

You may want to edit a photograph, cropping to show only part of it or using *Photoshop* or similar programs to enhance the colors or otherwise alter it. Similarly, you may want to edit a video, podcast, or other audio file to shorten it or remove irrelevant parts. If you are considering making a change of this kind, however, be sure not to do so in a way that misrepresents the content. If you alter a photo, be sure the image still represents the subject accurately; if you alter a recording of a speech or interview, be sure the edited version maintains the speaker's intent. Whenever you alter an image, a video, or a sound recording, tell your readers how you have changed it.

The same goes of editing charts and graphs. Changing the scale on a bar graph, for example, can change the effect of the comparison, making the quantities being compared seem very similar or very different, as shown in the two bar graphs of identical data in Figures 1 and 2.

Because of the different fund-raising goals implied by the graphs ($800 or $5,000) and the different increments of the dollars raised ($200 or $1,000), the graphs send very different messages, though the dollars raised by each fund-raiser remain the same. Just as you shouldn't edit a quotation or a photograph in a way that might misrepresent its meaning, you should not present statistical data in a way that could mislead readers.

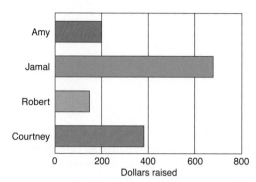

Fig. 1. Fund-raising results for the class gift.

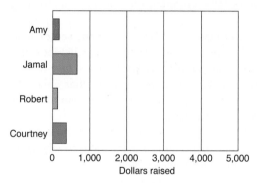

Fig. 2. Fund-raising results for the class gift.

57 Writing Online

Email. *Facebook*. Texts. Tweets. It may seem as if almost all writing is done online now. In college courses, you may still be required to turn in some writing assignments on paper, but more and more writing is not only done online but submitted that way too. And many classes are being taught online, with little or no face-to-face communication between instructors and students.

Online, your instructor and classmates usually cannot see or hear you — and that matters more than you might think. A puzzled look or a smile of recognition can start an important conversation in a face-to-face class, but in an online environment, your audience usually has only your written words to respond to. Therefore, you need to express your thoughts and feelings as clearly as you can *in writing*.

So it's useful to think about how the electronic medium affects the way we write — and how we can express ourselves most effectively when we write online. This chapter provides some advice.

Online Genres

For most of us, email, texting, and social networking sites like *Facebook* are already parts of everyday life. But using them for academic purposes may require some careful attention. Following are some guidelines.

Email. When emailing faculty members and school administrators, you are writing in an academic context, so your messages should reflect it: use an appropriate salutation ("Dear Professor Hagzanian"); write clearly and concisely in complete sentences; use standard capitalization and punctuation; proofread; and sign your full name. If you're writing about a specific

academic literacies ❋ rhetorical situations ■ genres ▲ processes ○ strategies ◆ research MLA / APA ● media / design ▢ readings ᛞ

course or group work, identify the course or group explicitly. Also, craft a specific subject line; instead of writing "Question about paper," be specific: "Profile organization question." If you change topics, change your subject line as well rather than simply replying to an old email. And be careful before you hit Send — you want to be good and sure that your email neither says something you'll regret later (don't send an email when you're angry!) nor includes anything you don't want the whole world reading (don't put confidential or sensitive information in email).

Texts.   Texting is inherently informal and often serves as an alternative to a phone call. Since texting often takes place as a conversation in real time (and phone keyboards can be hard to use), those who write texts often use acronyms, shorthand, and emoticons — ROTFL (rolling on the floor laughing), OST (on second thought), 2nite (tonight), 10Q (thank you), :) (happy) — to get their meaning across quickly and efficiently. If you use these abbreviations, though, be sure your readers will understand them!

Social media.   You may take a course that involves using *Facebook* or another social media site as a way for class members to communicate or as part of a **LEARNING MANAGEMENT SYSTEM**. If so, you need to consider your rhetorical situation to make sure your course postings represent you as a respectful (and respectable) member of the class. Also, remember that many employers routinely check job applicants' social media pages, so don't post writing or photos that you wouldn't want a potential employer to see.

⬚ 622–24

Websites.   Websites are groups of webpages organized around a homepage and connected to one another (and to other websites) through hyperlinks, which take users automatically from one page to another. While it's possible to create your own websites from scratch, free website builders such as *Weebly*, *Google Sites*, or *Wix* make it easy to create a site by providing templates for homepages, page designs, and navigation systems.

One key element in a website is the use of links to bring material from other sources into your text. You can link to the definition of a key term, for instance, rather than defining it yourself, or you can summarize a

The homepage of Discover History, the National Park Service cultural resource program, provides a navigation menu on the left that leads to various sections of the site. Links embedded within the introductory text connect to Park Service pages outside the program.

source and link to the full text rather than quoting or paraphrasing it. Providing links lets readers decide whether they need or want to see more detailed information — or not.

Blogs. Blogs are websites that generally focus on a single topic — politics, celebrities, gaming, baseball, you name it. They're maintained and updated regularly by individuals or groups who post opinions, reflections, information, and more — with writing, photos, video and audio files, and links to other sites. Blogs are an easy way to share your writing with others — and to invite response. Free blog hosting sites such as *WordPress*, *Tumblr*, or *Blogger* offer templates that let you create a blog and post to it easily, and some learning management systems include blogging capability as well.

This blog, hosted by the Smithsonian Institution, focuses on marine biology and includes video, audio, slideshows, and written narratives. Readers can interact with and respond to the text by clicking on icons for Facebook, Twitter, and other social networking sites.

If your blog is public, anyone can read it, including potential employers, so just as with *Facebook* and other social media, you'll want to be careful about how you present yourself and avoid posting anything that others could see as offensive. (Think twice before posting when you're angry or upset.) You may want to activate privacy settings that let you restrict access to some of the content or that make your blog unsearchable by *Google* and other search tools. Also, assume that what you post in a blog is permanent: your friends, family, employer — anyone — may read a posting years in the future, even if the blog is no longer active.

Wikis.   Wikis are websites that allow a group to work collaboratively, with all users free to add, edit, and delete content. *Wikipedia*, the online encyclopedia, is one of the most famous wikis: its content is posted and edited by people all over the world. You may be asked to contribute to a class wiki, such as the one below from a writing course at Bloomsburg University of Pennsylvania. Students post their work to the wiki, and everyone in the class has access to everyone else's writing and can comment on or revise it. When contributing to a wiki, you should be careful to write precisely, edit carefully, and make sure your research is accurate and appropriately cited — others may be quick to question and rewrite your work if it's sloppy or inaccurate. Free wiki apps include *MediaWiki*, *Tiki Wiki*, and *DokuWiki*.

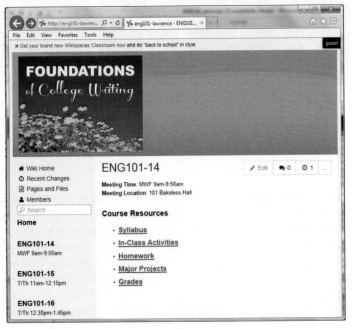

A writing-course wiki from Bloomsburg University of Pennsylvania.

academic literacies
rhetorical situations
genres
processes
strategies
research MLA / APA
media / design
readings

Managing Online Course Work

Because so much of your college work will be done online — at the very least, you'll do most of your writing on a computer and submit some assignments via email — it's important to set up some procedures for yourself. In a single writing course, for example, you may write three or four drafts of four essays — that's twelve to sixteen documents. To keep track of your files, you'll need to create folders, establish consistent file names, and back up your work.

Creating folders. Create a folder for each course, and name it with the course title or number and the academic term: ENG 101 Fall 2016. Within each course folder, create a folder for each major assignment. Save your work in the appropriate folder, so you can always find it.

Saving files. Your word processor likely saves documents to a specific format identified by a three- or four-letter ending automatically added to the file name: .doc, .docx, .txt, and so on. However, this default format may not be compatible with other programs. If you're not sure what format you'll need, use the Save As command to save each document in Rich Text Format, or .rtf, which most word processors can read.

Naming files. If you are expected to submit files electronically, your instructor may ask you to name them in a certain way. If not, devise a system that will let you easily find the files, including multiple drafts of your writing. For example, you might name your files using *Your last name + Assignment + Draft number + Date:* Jones Evaluation Draft 2 10-5-2013.docx. You'll then be able to find a particular file by looking for the assignment, the draft number, or the date. Saving all your drafts as separate files will make it easy to include them in a portfolio; also, if you lose a draft, you'll be able to use the previous one to reconstruct it.

Backing up your work. Hard drives fail, laptops and tablets get dropped, flash drives are left in public computers. Because files stored in computers can be damaged or lost, you should save your work in several places: on your computer, on a flash drive or portable hard drive, in space supplied by your school, or online. You can also ensure that an extra copy of your work exists by emailing a copy to yourself.

Finding Basic Course Information

You'll need to learn some essential information about any online courses you take:

- *The phone number for the campus help desk* or technology center. Check the hours of operation, and keep the number handy.

- *The syllabus,* list of assignments, and calendar with deadlines.

622–24

- *Where to find tutorials* for your school's **LEARNING MANAGEMENT SYSTEM** and other programs you may need help with.

- *How and when you can contact your instructor* — in person during office hours? by phone or email? — and how soon you can expect a response.

- *What file format you should use* to submit assignments — .doc, .docx, .rtf, .pdf, something else? — and how to submit them.

- *How to use the spellcheck function* on your word processor or learning management system.

- *How to participate in online discussions* — will you use a discussion board? a chat function in a learning management system? a blog? a social network? something else?

Using Learning Management Systems

Whether you're in a face-to-face, hybrid, or online class, you may be asked to do some or all of your classwork online using a learning management system (LMS) such as *Blackboard* or *Desire2Learn.* An LMS is a web-based educational tool that brings together all the course information your

academic literacies · rhetorical situations · genres · processes · strategies · research MLA / APA · media / design · readings

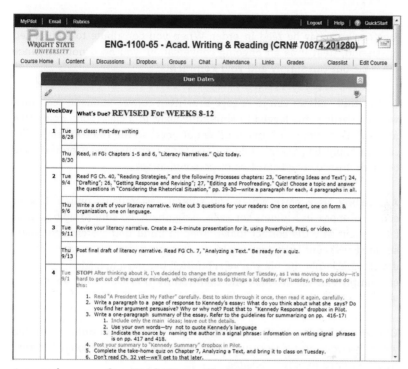

A course homepage from Wright State's Pilot LMS.

instructor wants you to have, along with features that allow you to participate in the class in various ways. Your school's LMS likely includes the following features that you'll be expected to use:

A course homepage   contains posts from your instructor; a calendar with due dates for assignments; and links to the course syllabus, other course content, and additional features available on the site.

A discussion board   allows you to communicate with classmates even if everyone isn't logged in to the board at the same time. These conversations may be organized in "threads" so that posts on a particular topic appear together and may be read in order. When you contribute to a threaded discussion, treat it as an ongoing conversation: you need not introduce the topic but can simply add your comments.

A chat tool allows you to engage in written conversations in real time, with all participants logged in simultaneously. In a classroom, doing this may be like texting with many others at once, so the rules for class discussion apply: be patient while waiting for a response; focus on the topic being discussed; avoid sarcasm or personal attacks.

A dropbox is a place where you submit assignments online. If your course dropbox has folders for each assignment, be sure to upload your assignment into the correct folder. Keep in mind that systems go down, so don't wait until the last minute to submit a file. It's a good idea to double-check that the file you've submitted has been uploaded; often you can simply exit the dropbox and then return to it to see that your file is where it should be.

Online portfolios. Many LMSs allow you to create an online portfolio where you may post your coursework as well as photos, personal information, and links to other websites.

Additional features. An LMS may also include email; a space to keep a journal; a whiteboard for posting images, graphics, and presentations; a gradebook; a social network (sometimes called a Ning) for class members only; and other features that can help you keep track of your work in a class.

Giving Presentations 58

In a marketing class, you give a formal presentation that includes slides and handouts as part of a research project on developing brand loyalty to clothing labels among college students. As a candidate for student government, you deliver several speeches to various campus groups that are simultaneously broadcast over the web. At a good friend's wedding, after you make a toast to the married couple, another friend who couldn't attend in person toasts them remotely using *Skype*; a third guest records both toasts on his cell phone and uploads them to *Facebook*. Whether or not you include electronic and print media, whenever you are called on to give a spoken presentation, you need to make your points clear and memorable. This chapter offers guidelines to help you prepare and deliver effective presentations. We'll start with two good examples.

ABRAHAM LINCOLN

Gettysburg Address

Given by the sixteenth president of the United States, at the dedication of the Gettysburg battlefield as a memorial to those who died in the Civil War, this is one of the most famous speeches ever delivered in the United States.

Four score and seven years ago our fathers brought forth on this continent, a new nation, conceived in Liberty, and dedicated to the proposition that all men are created equal.

Now we are engaged in a great civil war, testing whether that nation, or any nation so conceived and so dedicated, can long endure.

We are met on a great battle-field of that war. We have come to dedi-cate a portion of that field, as a final resting place for those who here gave their lives that that nation might live. It is altogether fitting and proper that we should do this.

But, in a larger sense, we can not dedicate — we can not consecrate — we can not hallow — this ground. The brave men, living and dead, who struggled here, have consecrated it, far above our poor power to add or detract. The world will little note, nor long remember what we say here, but it can never forget what they did here. It is for us the living, rather, to be dedicated here to the unfinished work which they who fought here have thus far so nobly advanced. It is rather for us to be here dedicated to the great task remaining before us — that from these honored dead we take increased devotion to that cause for which they gave the last full measure of devotion — that we here highly resolve that these dead shall not have died in vain — that this nation, under God, shall have a new birth of freedom — and that government of the people, by the people, for the people, shall not perish from the earth.

You won't likely be called on to deliver such an address, but the techniques Lincoln used — brevity, rhythm, recurring themes — are ones you can use in your own spoken texts. The next example represents the type of spoken text we are sometimes called on to deliver at important occasions in the lives of our families.

JUDY DAVIS

Ours Was a Dad . . .

This short eulogy was given at the funeral of the writer's father, Walter Boock. Judy Davis lives in Davis, California, where she was for many years the prin-cipal of North Davis Elementary School.

Elsa, Peggy, David, and I were lucky to have such a dad. Ours was a dad who created the childhood for us that he did not have for himself.

academic literacies • rhetorical situations • genres • processes • strategies • research MLA/APA • media/design • readings

The dad who sent us airborne on the soles of his feet, squealing with delight. The dad who built a platform in the peach tree so we could eat ourselves comfortably into peachy oblivion. The dad who assigned us chores and then did them with us. The dad who felt our pain when we skinned our knees.

Ours was the dad who took us camping, all over the U.S. and Canada, but most of all in our beloved Yosemite. The one who awed us with his ability to swing around a full pail of water without spilling a drop and let us hold sticks in the fire and draw designs in the night air with hot orange coals.

Our dad wanted us to feel safe and secure. On Elsa's eighth birthday, we acquired a small camping trailer. One very blustery night in Minnesota, Mom and Dad asleep in the main bed, David suspended in the hammock over them, Peggy and Elsa snuggled in the little dinette bed, and me on an air mattress on the floor, I remember the most incredible sense of well-being: our family all together, so snug, in that little trailer as the storm rocked us back and forth. It was only in the morning that I learned about the tornado warnings. Mom and Dad weren't sleeping: they were praying that when morning came we wouldn't find ourselves in the next state.

Ours was the dad who helped us with homework at the round oak table. He listened to our oral reports, taught us to add by looking for combinations of 10, quizzed us on spelling words, and when our written reports sounded a little too much like the *World Book* encyclopedia, he told us so.

Ours was a dad who believed our round oak table that seated twelve when fully extended should be full at Thanksgiving. Dad called the chaplain at the airbase, asked about homesick boys, and invited them to join our family. Or he'd call International House in Berkeley to see if someone from another country would like to experience an American Thanksgiving. We're still friends with the Swedish couple who came for turkey forty-five years ago. Many people became a part of our extended family around that table. And if twelve around the table was good, then certainly fourteen would be better. Just last fall, Dad commissioned our neighbor Randy to make yet another leaf for the table. There were fourteen around the table for Dad's last Thanksgiving.

Ours was a dad who had a lifelong desire to serve. He delivered Meals on Wheels until he was eighty-three. He delighted in picking up the day-old doughnuts from Mr. Rollen's shop to give those on his route an extra treat. We teased him that he should be receiving those meals himself! Even after walking became difficult for him, he continued to drive and took along an able friend to carry the meals to the door.

Our family, like most, had its ups and downs. But ours was a dad who forgave us our human failings as we forgave him his. He died in peace, surrounded by love. Elsa, Peggy, David, and I were so lucky to have such a dad.

This eulogy, in honor of the writer's father, provides concrete and memorable details that give the audience a clear image of the kind of man he was. The repetition of the phrase "ours was a dad" provides a rhythm and unity that moves the text forward, and the use of short, conventional sentences makes the text easy to understand — and deliver.

Key Features / Spoken Presentations

A clear structure.   Spoken texts need to be clearly organized so that your audience can follow what you're saying. The **BEGINNING** needs to engage their interest, make clear what you will be talking about, and perhaps forecast the central parts of your talk. The main part of the text should focus on a few main points — only as many as your listeners can be expected to absorb and retain. (Remember, they can't go back to reread!) The **ENDING** is especially important: it should leave your audience with something, to remember, think about, or do. Davis ends as she begins, saying that she and her sisters and brother "were so lucky to have such a dad." Lincoln ends with a dramatic resolution: "that government of the people, by the people, for the people, shall not perish from the earth."

331–38

338–42

Signpost language to keep your audience on track.   You may need to provide cues to help your listeners follow your text, especially **TRANSITIONS** that lead them from one point to the next. Sometimes you'll also want to stop and **SUMMARIZE** a complex point to help your audience keep track of your ideas and follow your development of them.

349

486–87

A tone to suit the occasion. Lincoln spoke at a serious, formal event, the dedication of a national cemetery, and his address is formal and even solemn. Davis's eulogy is more informal in **TONE**, as befits a speech given for friends and loved ones. In a presentation to a panel of professors, you probably would want to take an academic tone, avoiding too much slang and speaking in complete sentences. If you had occasion to speak on the very same topic to a neighborhood group, however, you would likely want to speak more casually.

◾ 65

Repetition and parallel structure. Even if you're never called on to deliver a Gettysburg Address, you will find that repetition and parallel structure can lend power to a presentation, making it easier to follow — and more likely to be remembered. "We can not dedicate — we can not consecrate — we can not hallow": the repetition of "we can not" and the parallel forms of the three verbs are one reason these words stay with us more than 150 years after they were written and delivered. These are structures any writer can use. See how the repetition of "ours was a dad" in Davis's eulogy creates a rhythm that engages listeners and at the same time unifies the text.

Slides and other media. Depending on the way you deliver your presentation, you will often want or need to use other media — *PowerPoint*, *Prezi*, or other presentation slides, video and audio clips, handouts, flip charts, whiteboards, and so on — to present certain information and to highlight key points.

Considering the Rhetorical Situation

As with any writing, you need to consider your rhetorical situation when preparing a presentation:

PURPOSE Consider what your primary purpose is. To inform? persuade? entertain? evoke another kind of emotional response?

◾ 55–56

57–60 **AUDIENCE** Think about whom you'll be addressing and how well you know them. Will they be interested, or will you need to get them interested? Are they likely to be friendly? How can you get and maintain their attention, and how can you establish common ground with them? How much will they know about your subject — will you need to provide background or define any terms?

61–63 **GENRE** The genre of your text will affect the way you structure and present it. If you're making an argument, for instance, you'll need to consider counterarguments — and, depending on the way you're giving the presentation, perhaps to allow for questions and comments from members of the audience who hold other opinions. If you're giving a report, you may have reasons to prepare handouts with detailed information you don't have time to cover in your spoken text, or links to online documents or websites.

64–67 **STANCE** Consider the attitude you want to express. Is it serious? thoughtful? passionate? well informed? humorous? something else? Choose your words and any other elements of your presentation accordingly. Whatever your attitude, your presentation will be received better by your listeners if they perceive you as comfortable and sincere.

A Brief Guide to Writing Presentations

Whether you're giving a poster presentation at a conference or an oral report in class, what you say will differ in important ways from what you might write for others to read. Here are some tips for composing an effective presentation.

Budget your time.   A five-minute presentation calls for about two and a half double-spaced pages of writing, and ten minutes means only four or five pages. Your introduction and conclusion should each take about one-tenth of the total time available; time for questions (if the format allows for them) should take about one-fifth; and the body of the talk, the rest. In a ten-minute presentation, then, allot one minute for your introduction, one minute for your conclusion, and two minutes for questions, leaving six minutes for the body of your talk.

Organize and draft your presentation.   Readers can go back and reread if they don't understand or remember something the first time through a text. Listeners can't. Therefore, it's important that you structure your presentation so that your audience can follow your text — and remember what you say.

- *Craft an introduction* that engages your audience's interest and tells them what to expect. Depending on your rhetorical situation, you may want to **BEGIN** with humor, with an anecdote, or with something that reminds them of the occasion for your talk or helps them see the reason for it. In any case, you always need to summarize your main points, provide any needed background information, and outline how you'll proceed.

  ◆ 331–38

- *In the body of your presentation,* present your main points in more detail and support them with **REASONS** and **EVIDENCE**. As you draft, you may well find that you have more material than you can present in the time available, so you'll need to choose the most important points to focus on and leave out the rest.

  ◆ 359–67

- *Let your readers know you're concluding* (but try to avoid saying "in conclusion"), and then use your remaining time to restate your main points and to explain why they're important. End by saying "thank you" and offering to answer questions or take comments if the format allows for them.

Consider whether to use visuals.   You may want or need to include some visuals to help listeners follow what you're saying. Especially when you're presenting complex information, it helps to let them see it as well as hear it. Remember, though, that visuals should be a means of conveying information, not mere decoration.

DECIDING ON THE APPROPRIATE VISUALS

- *Slides* are useful for listing main points and for projecting illustrations, tables, and graphs.

- *Videos, animations, and sounds* can add additional information to your presentations.

- *Flip charts, whiteboards, or chalkboards* allow you to create visuals as you speak or to keep track of comments from your audience.

- *Posters* sometimes serve as the main part of a presentation, providing a summary of your points. You then offer only a brief introduction and answer any questions.

- *Handouts* can provide additional information, lists of works cited, or copies of any slides you show.

What visual tools (if any) you decide to use is partly determined by how your presentation will be delivered. Will you be speaking to a crowd or a class, delivering your presentation through a podcast, or creating an interactive presentation for a web conference? Make sure that any necessary equipment and programs are available — and that they work. If at all possible, check out any equipment in the place where you'll deliver your presentation before you go live. If you bring your own equipment for a live presentation, make sure you can connect to the internet if you need to and that electrical outlets are in reach of your power cords. Also, make sure that your visuals can be seen. You may have to rearrange the furniture or the screen to make sure everyone can see.

And finally, have a backup plan. Computers fail; projector bulbs burn out; marking pens run dry. Whatever your plan is, have an alternative in case any problems occur.

Presentation software.   *PowerPoint, Keynote,* and other presentation soft-ware can include images, video, and sound in addition to displaying writ-ten text. They are most useful for linear presentations that move audiences along one slide at a time. Cloud-based programs like *Prezi* also allow you to arrange words or slides in various designs, group related content together, and zoom in and out. Here are some tips for writing and design-ing slides:

- *Use* LISTS *or images, not paragraphs.* Use slides to emphasize your main points, not to reproduce your talk onscreen: keep your audi-ence's attention focused on what you're saying. A list of brief points, presented one by one, reinforces your words. An image can provide additional information that your audience can take in quickly.

603

- *Make your text easy for your audience to read.* FONTS should be at least 18 points, and larger than that for headings. Projected slides are easier to read in sans serif fonts like Arial, Helvetica, and Tahoma than in serif fonts like Times New Roman. And avoid using all capital letters, which can be hard to read.

601–2

- *Choose colors carefully.* Your text and any illustrations must contrast with the background. Dark content on a light background is easier to read than the reverse. And remember that not everyone sees all colors; be sure your audience doesn't need to be able to see particular colors or contrasts in order to get your meaning. Red-green and blue-yellow contrasts are especially hard for some people to see and should be avoided.

- *Use bells and whistles sparingly, if at all.* Presentation software offers lots of decorative backgrounds, letters that fade in and out or dance across the screen, and sound effects. These features can be more distracting than helpful; use them only if they help to make your point.

- *Mark your text.* In your notes or prepared text, mark each place where you need to click a mouse to call up the next slide.

This Prezi presentation rotates, includes audio and video, and zooms in and out to let viewers take a closer look.

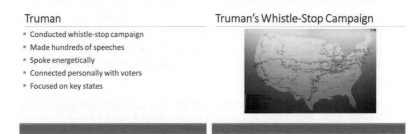

Two PowerPoint slides on the U.S. presidential election of 1948. The slide on the left outlines the main points; the one on the right shows a map of Truman's whistle-stop campaign, providing a graphic illustration of the miles he traveled as he campaigned to be president.

Handouts.   When you want to give your audience information they can refer to later — reproductions of your visuals, bibliographic information about your sources, printouts of your slides — do so in the form of handouts. Refer to the handouts in your presentation, but unless they include material your audience needs to consult before or as you talk, wait until you are finished to distribute them so as not to distract listeners. Clearly label everything you give out, including your name and the date and title of the presentation.

Delivering a Presentation

The success of a presentation often hinges on how you deliver it. As you work on your spoken texts, bear in mind the following points:

Practice.   Practice, practice, and then practice some more. The better you know your talk, the more confident you will be, and your audience will respond positively to that confidence. If you're reading a prepared text, try to write it as if you were talking. Then practice by recording it as you read it; listen for spots that sound as if you're reading, and work on your delivery to sound more relaxed. As you practice, pay attention to keeping within your time limit. If possible, rehearse your talk with a small group of friends to test their response and to get used to speaking in front of an audience.

Speak clearly.   When you're giving a spoken presentation, your first goal is to be understood by your audience. If listeners miss important words or phrases because you don't pronounce them distinctly, your talk will not succeed. Make sure, too, that your pace matches your audience's needs. Often you'll need to make yourself speak more slowly than usual to explain complex material (or to compensate for nerves); sometimes you may need to speed up to keep your audience's attention. In general, though, strive for a consistent pace throughout, one that ensures you don't have to rush at the end.

Pause for emphasis.   In writing, you have white space and punctuation to show readers where an idea or discussion ends. When speaking, you need to pause to signal the end of a thought, to give listeners a moment to consider something you've said, or to get them ready for a surprising or amusing statement.

Stand up (or sit up) straight and look at your audience.   If you're in the same physical space as your audience, try to maintain some eye contact with them. If that's uncomfortable, fake it: pick a spot on the wall just above the head of a person in the back of the room, and focus on it. You'll appear as if you're looking at your audience even if you're not looking them in the eye. And if you stand or sit up straight, you'll project the sense that you have confidence in what you're saying. If you appear to believe in your words, others will, too. If you're speaking via an online forum like *Skype*, look at the computer's camera — not at the screen. Also, make sure the camera is positioned at your eye level, so you aren't looking down at it (and showing your viewers the ceiling behind you!).

Use gestures for emphasis.   If you're not used to speaking in front of a group, you may let your nervousness show by holding yourself stiffly, elbows tucked in. To overcome some of that nervousness, take some deep breaths, try to relax, and move your arms and the rest of your body as you would if you were talking to a friend. Use your hands for emphasis: most public speakers use one hand to emphasize specific points and both hands to make larger gestures. Watch politicians on C-SPAN to see how people who speak on a regular basis use gestures as part of their overall delivery.

academic literacies | rhetorical situations | genres | processes | strategies | research MLA / APA | media / design | readings

part 8

Readings

"Read, read, read. Read everything — trash, classics, good and bad, and see how they do it." So said the American writer William Faulkner, and on the following pages you will find an anthology of readings that shows how Amy Tan, Lynda Barry, David Sedaris, Nicholas Carr, Judith Ortiz Cofer, and many other writers "do it." Read on, and pay attention to how these writers use the KEY FEATURES and STRATEGIES that you yourself are learning to use. The anthology includes readings in ten GENRES and a chapter of readings that mix genres; you'll find a menu of readings in the back of the book.

Readings

Literacy Narratives **59**

DANIEL FELSENFELD

Rebel Music

Daniel Felsenfeld (b. 1970) is a composer of classical music and a writer for NewMusicBox, *a multimedia publication "dedicated to the music of American composers and improvisers and their champions." He has composed in many different genres: orchestral music, opera, chamber music, solo music for piano and violin, and vocal music. Felsenfeld is author or coauthor of several books on music, including* Benjamin Britten and Samuel Barber: Their Lives and Their Music *(2005), and of several listening guides that accompany CDs. In this essay, which originally appeared in 2010 in* Opinionator, *a commentary blog of the* New York Times, *he explores his journey of becoming literate in classical music.*

MUSIC MAY BE THE UNIVERSAL LANGUAGE, but those of us who spend our lives with it are expected to know it in depth, from early on. Many composers, whether traditional or experimental, have been steeped in Western classical music from the cradle. That was not the case with me.

My primal time was the middle of the '80's in Orange County, Calif. I was 17 years old. The O.C. was billed as the ideal suburban community, but when you are raised in a palm-tree lined Shangri-La as I was, it is hard to grasp what's missing without that crucial glimpse beyond. Now I realize: even though we had enough water to keep the manicured lawns just so, I was experiencing a personal drought, an arid lack of culture of all kinds, especially music.

I was by no means unmusical, though any talent I have remains a mystery, coming as I do from perhaps the least musical of families (who would be the first to admit this). To her credit, my mother signed me up for the de rigueur piano lessons. Each week I dazzled poor Ms. Shimizu with either an astonishing performance of a Mozart sonata or a heretofore unseen level of ill-preparedness. I slogged my way through Chopin Preludes, culminating my high school piano study with a middling performance of Beethoven's "Pathétique" sonata. Probably not unlike most kids' first encounter with formal music study: uninspiring.

academic literacies   rhetorical situations   genres   processes   strategies   research MLA / APA   media / design   readings

Eventually I quit lessons, but had developed chops enough to work in both piano bars (an underage piano man, traveling with my own snifter) and community theater orchestra pits. The music was dull, or at least had a dulling effect on me — it didn't sparkle, or ask questions. I took a lot of gigs, but at 17 I was already pretty detached. I was attracted to music for some reason I lacked vocabulary to explain, and neither *Oklahoma!* nor *Annie* offered answers.

That might have been it — working my way through junior college 5 playing in pits or at Nordstrom's, settling into some career or other — a piano studio, weddings, writing songs for mild amusement. Thankfully, it was not.

Some afternoons I would go to my friend Mike's house at the end of my cul-de-sac to listen to tapes of bands a lot of my friends were listening to: General Public, Howard Jones, the Thompson Twins (or David Bowie, Bauhaus and The Clash in our edgier moments). One day, bored with the music, Mike flipped his double-decked cassette case over to reveal rows of hidden tapes in a concealed compartment.

"Want to hear something really wild?" he said.

"But of course."

At 17, rebellion was of course a staple in my life. The smartest kids I knew took the route of dolling themselves up in anti-establishment finery — goth, punk, straight edge — forming bands, going to clubs in Los Angeles, spouting manifestos. I had auditioned this mode, joining a band (whose name escapes me) and, in one of my great (mercifully unphotographed) late high school moments, taking a long, throbbing solo at a school assembly on one of those bygone over-the-shoulder keyboards.

It seems implausible now, but the "something really wild" Mike 10 held was not goth, metal, or punk. It was a neatly hand-labeled tape of Beethoven's Ninth Symphony. He put it on, and I listened. I think it was then I actually heard music for the first time.

Was this the same Beethoven to whose sonata I had done such violence? It unrolled from the small speakers, this big, gorgeous, unruly beast of a thing, contemporary, horrifying, a juggernaut that moved from the dark to unbearable brightness, soaring and spitting, malingering and dancing wildly, the Most Beautiful Thing I Ever Heard. This "symphony" by this Beethoven had a drug-like effect on me. At my insistence we listened again. And again. I wished it would just keep going.

Mike, who was just a kid in the neighborhood with odd — evolved? sophisticated? — taste, had dozens more tapes: Brahms, Mozart, Bach, Prokofiev, Tchaikovsky, Sibelius, Rachmaninoff, Strauss. I may have known that this kind of music was called classical, but I certainly did not understand that it was considered "great" or that it was revered as the foundation of musical culture in the West. I just loved it more than anything I'd heard before, and I must have sensed it was also miles away from Orange County, exactly as far as my adolescent self longed to be. I dubbed Mike's tapes, and listened to them in secret. Driving to school with Beethoven blaring, I'd switch to KROQ as I entered the parking lot, swerving into my spot believing I'd put one over on people again.

> The symphony unrolled from the small speakers — a big, gorgeous, unruly beast of a thing. Was this the same Beethoven to whose sonata I had done such violence?

My passion for this "other" kind of music felt like the height of rebellion: I was the lone Bolshevik in my army. I loved this new (to me) music, but loved my abstract role in it even more. Rebels sought to break the mold, to do something that was exclusively "theirs," to be weird by way of self-expression. And since I was the only one I knew listening to symphonies and concerti, operas and string quartets, I felt I was the weirdest of them all; it served my adolescent need to be misunderstood. And so I decided, with little prior experience or interest, to become a composer.

Little did I know, right?

All too soon, I came to understand what hard work this was. I studied scores, read biographies, got a serious piano teacher and logged hours a day practicing, traded up Mike's cassettes for the then-novel compact discs, and boarded the spaceship bound for planet New York once or twice (always returning, at least then, to warmer climes). After signing up for theory classes at Fullerton Junior College, I met my first living composers: Brent Pierce taught me counterpoint and harmony (one summer I wrote a daily fugue), and Lloyd Rodgers was my private teacher (who encouraged me to copy out the entire "Well Tempered

15

academic literacies · rhetorical situations · genres · processes · strategies · research MLA / APA · media / design · readings

Clavier" by hand). In the meantime, I heard my first examples of what is called "New Music," that is, classical music written more recently than the 19th century.

Of course, some of my illusions vanished as soon as I realized there were composers I could actually meet. I was no longer a rebellion of one, but this halcyon innocence was traded for the ability to interact with artists who were always taking on the obscene challenge of creating music that was totally new, completely theirs.

Now I live far from the O.C., in New York, having long ago colonized this distant planet and gone native, an active member of a community I once admired from what seemed an impossible distance. And while there are moments I lament not having been raised in a musical family, or my late and clumsy start, I also strive to make my less-than-ideal origins an asset. I've learned I do my best work when I remove myself and try to return to that Age of Wonder when I first heard the gorgeous dissonances of pieces like Samuel Barber's *Hermit Songs* or *Prayers of Kierkegaard*, Elliott Carter's Second String Quartet, Michael Nyman's The Kiss, George Crumb's *Black Angels*, Arnold Schoenberg's *Pierrot Lunaire*, Benjamin Britten's *Turn of the Screw*, John Corigliano's First Symphony, and Stephen Sondheim's *Sweeney Todd*, and took them to be the *same* dissonances, not contrasting sides of a sometimes-contentious or politicized art world. When I am composing, I try to return to that time and place of inexperience when I was knocked sideways by dangerous sounds. Why else write? Why else listen?

Engaging with the Text

1. What is the **SIGNIFICANCE** to Daniel Felsenfeld of his literacy narrative? Where in the essay does he make the significance clear?

   ▲ 88

2. What **STANCE** does Felsenfeld assume toward his stated topic of "rebel music"? Where does this stance become clear in the essay? By the end of the essay, what are we meant to understand about why he uses the phrase "rebel music"?

   ■ 64–67

3. This essay details some of Felsenfeld's journey to becoming literate in music so that he could become a composer. How is music literacy similar to literacy in the sense of reading and writing? What does the latter prepare you to do in the world?

607–15 □

4. If you were asked to choose or design a **VISUAL** to accompany this essay, what would it show or look like? What point(s) about the essay would you want the visual to highlight?

5. *For Writing.* As this essay shows, there are many literacies people develop in life: math literacy, music literacy, art literacy, body building literacy, knitting literacy, and so on. In addition to the ability to read and write essays, what other literacies have you developed?

419–27 ◆

Write a **NARRATIVE** about one of those literacies, including specific details about how you developed it.

academic literacies
rhetorical situations
genres
processes
strategies
research MLA / APA
media / design
readings

TANYA MARIA BARRIENTOS

Se Habla Español

Tanya Maria Barrientos (b. 1960) is director of executive communications for the Robert Wood Johnson Foundation, a former columnist and feature writer for the Philadelphia Inquirer, *and the author of two novels. The following essay appeared in* Latina, *a bilingual magazine published by and for Latinas. It was adapted from an essay of the same title that was published in* Border-Line Personalities: A New Generation of Latinas Dish on Sex, Sass, and Cultural Shifting *(2004). In this piece, Barrientos recounts her struggles as a Latina who is not fluent in Spanish. She takes her title from a phrase often seen in store windows, announcing that "Spanish is spoken" there.*

THE MAN ON THE OTHER END of the phone line is telling me the classes I've called about are first-rate: native speakers in charge, no more than six students per group. I tell him that will be fine and yes, I've studied a bit of Spanish in the past. He asks for my name and I supply it, rolling the double "r" in "Barrientos" like a pro. That's when I hear the silent snag, the momentary hesitation I've come to expect at this part of the exchange. Should I go into it again? Should I explain, the way I have to half a dozen others, that I am Guatemalan by birth but *pura gringa* by circumstance?

This will be the sixth time I've signed up to learn the language my parents speak to each other. It will be the sixth time I've bought workbooks and notebooks and textbooks listing 501 conjugated verbs in alphabetical order, in hopes that the subjunctive tense will finally take root in my mind. In class I will sit across a table from the "native speaker," who will wonder what to make of me. "Look," I'll want to say (but never do). "Forget the dark skin. Ignore the obsidian eyes. Pretend I'm a pink-cheeked, blue-eyed blonde whose name tag says 'Shannon.'" Because that is what a person who doesn't innately know the difference between *corre, corra,* and *corrí* is supposed to look like, isn't it?

I came to the United States in 1963 at age 3 with my family and immediately stopped speaking Spanish. College-educated and seamlessly bilingual when they settled in west Texas, my parents (a psychology professor and an artist) wholeheartedly embraced the notion of the American melting pot. They declared that their two children would speak nothing but *inglés*. They'd read in English, write in English, and fit into Anglo society beautifully.

It sounds politically incorrect now. But America was not a hyphenated nation back then. People who called themselves Mexican Americans or Afro-Americans were considered dangerous radicals, while law-abiding citizens were expected to drop their cultural baggage at the border and erase any lingering ethnic traits.

To be honest, for most of my childhood I liked being the brown girl   5 who defied expectations. When I was 7, my mother returned my older brother and me to elementary school one week after the school year had already begun. We'd been on vacation in Washington, D.C., visiting the Smithsonian, the Capitol, and the home of Edgar Allan Poe. In the Volkswagen on the way home, I'd memorized "The Raven," and I would recite it with melodramatic flair to any poor soul duped into sitting through my performance. At the school's office, the registrar frowned when we arrived.

"You people. Your children are always behind, and you have the nerve to bring them in late?"

"My children," my mother answered in a clear, curt tone, "will be at the top of their classes in two weeks."

The registrar filed our cards, shaking her head.

I did not live in a neighborhood with other Latinos, and the public school I attended attracted very few. I saw the world through the clear, cruel vision of a child. To me, speaking Spanish translated into being poor. It meant waiting tables and cleaning hotel rooms. It meant being left off the cheerleading squad and receiving a condescending smile from the guidance counselor when you said you planned on becoming a lawyer or a doctor. My best friends' names were Heidi and Leslie and Kim. They told me I didn't seem "Mexican" to them, and I took it as a compliment. I enjoyed looking into the faces of Latino store clerks and waitresses and, yes, even our maid and saying "Yo *no hablo español*." It made me feel superior. It made me feel American. It made me feel white. I thought if I stayed away from Spanish, stereotypes would stay away from me.

Then came the backlash. During the two decades when I'd worked 10
hard to isolate myself from the stereotype I'd constructed in my own
head, society shifted. The nation changed its views on ethnic identity.
College professors started teaching history through African American
and Native American eyes. Children were told to forget about the melting pot and picture America as a multicolored quilt instead. Hyphens
suddenly had muscle, and I was left wondering where I fit in.

The Spanish language was supposedly the glue that held the new
Latino community together. But in my case it was what kept me apart.
I felt awkward among groups whose conversations flowed in and out
of Spanish. I'd be asked a question in Spanish
and I'd have to answer in English, knowing this   **If I stayed away**
raised a mountain of questions. I wanted to   **from Spanish,**
call myself Latina, to finally take pride, but it **stereotypes would**
felt like a lie. So I set out to learn the language **stay away from me.**
that people assumed I already knew.

After my first set of lessons, I could function in the present tense. "*Hola,
Paco. ¿Qué tal? ¿Qué color es tu cuaderno? El mío es azul.*" My vocabulary built
quickly, but when I spoke, my tongue felt thick inside my mouth — and
if I needed to deal with anything in the future or the past, I was sunk. I
enrolled in a three-month submersion program in Mexico and emerged able
to speak like a sixth-grader with a solid C average. I could read Gabriel Gar-
cía Márquez with a Spanish-English dictionary at my elbow, and I could follow 90 percent of the melodrama on any given telenovela. But true speakers
discover my limitations the moment I stumble over a difficult construction,
and that is when I get the look. The one that raises the wall between us.
The one that makes me think I'll never really belong. Spanish has become
a litmus test showing how far from your roots you've strayed.

My bilingual friends say I make too much of it. They tell me that my
Guatemalan heritage and unmistakable Mayan features are enough to legiti-
mize my membership in the Latin American club. After all, not all Poles speak
Polish. Not all Italians speak Italian. And as this nation grows more and more
Hispanic, not all Latinos will share one language. But I don't believe them.

There must be other Latinas like me. But I haven't met any. Or,
I should say, I haven't met any who have fessed up. Maybe they are

secretly struggling to fit in, the same way I am. Maybe they are hiring tutors and listening to tapes behind locked doors, just like me. I wish we all had the courage to come out of our hiding places and claim our rightful spot in the broad Latino spectrum. Without being called hopeless gringas. Without having to offer apologies or show remorse.

If it will help, I will go first.   15

Aquí estoy. Spanish-challenged and *pura* Latina.

Engaging with the Text

344–45

1. Tanya Maria Barrientos gives her essay a Spanish **TITLE**. How does this prepare you for the subject of the essay? What does this title lead you to believe about Barrientos's feelings about Spanish? Is that impression supported by the rest of the essay? Why or why not?

331–38

2. Barrientos **BEGINS** her essay with an anecdote about signing up for a Spanish class. What is the effect of beginning with this anecdote? Does it attract your interest? Why or why not? How does it prepare you for the rest of the essay?

88

3. Barrientos tells of learning to read and write in Spanish. One key feature of a literacy narrative is an indication of the narrative's **SIGNIFICANCE**. For her, what is the significance of learning that language? Why is it so important to her?

64–67

4. Barrientos peppers her essay with Spanish words and phrases, without offering any English translation. What does this tell you about her **STANCE**? Would her stance seem different if she'd translated the Spanish? Why or why not?

245–52

5. *For Writing.* As Barrientos notes, language plays a big part in her identity. Think about the languages you speak. If you speak only English, think about what kind of accent you have. (If you think you don't have one, consider how you might sound to someone from a different region or social class.) Does the language you speak or accent you have change according to the situation? Does it change according to how you perceive yourself? Write an essay **REFLECTING** on the way you speak and how it affects (or is affected by) your identity.

academic literacies   rhetorical situations   genres   processes   strategies   research MLA / APA   media / design   readings

AMY TAN

Mother Tongue

Amy Tan (b. 1952) is the author of novels, children's books, essays, and a memoir. Her work has appeared in McCall's, the Atlantic, the New Yorker, and other magazines. She is best known for her novel The Joy Luck Club (1989), which examines the lives of and the relationships between four Chinese American daughters and their mothers. The following selection was first delivered as a talk at a symposium on language in San Francisco in 1989.

I AM NOT A SCHOLAR OF ENGLISH OR LITERATURE. I cannot give you much more than personal opinions on the English language and its variations in this country or others.

I am a writer. And by that definition, I am someone who has always loved language. I am fascinated by language in daily life. I spend a great deal of my time thinking about the power of language — the way it can evoke an emotion, a visual image, a complex idea, or a simple truth. Language is the tool of my trade. And I use them all — all the Englishes I grew up with.

Recently, I was made keenly aware of the different Englishes I do use. I was giving a talk to a large group of people, the same talk I had already given to half a dozen other groups. The nature of the talk was about my writing, my life, and my book, *The Joy Luck Club*. The talk was going along well enough, until I remembered one major difference that made the whole talk sound wrong. My mother was in the room. And it was perhaps the first time she had heard me give a lengthy speech, using the kind of English I have never used with her. I was saying things like, "The intersection of memory upon imagination" and "There is an aspect of my fiction that relates to thus-and-thus" — a speech filled with carefully wrought grammatical phrases, burdened, it suddenly seemed to me, with nominalized forms, past perfect tenses, conditional phrases, all the forms of standard English that I had learned in school and through books, the forms of English I did not use at home with my mother.

Just last week, I was walking down the street with my mother, and I again found myself conscious of the English I was using, the English I do use with her. We were talking about the price of new and used furniture and I heard myself saying this: "Not waste money that way." My husband was with us as well, and he didn't notice any switch in my English. And then I realized why. It's because over the twenty years we've been together I've often used the same kind of English with him, and sometimes he even uses it with me. It has become our language of intimacy, a different sort of English that relates to family talk, the language I grew up with.

So you'll have some idea of what this family talk I heard sounds   5
like, I'll quote what my mother said during a recent conversation which I videotaped and then transcribed. During this conversation, my mother was talking about a political gangster in Shanghai who had the same last name as her family's, Du, and how the gangster in his early years wanted to be adopted by her family, which was rich by comparison. Later, the gangster became more powerful, far richer than my mother's family, and one day showed up at my mother's wedding to pay his respects. Here's what she said in part:

"Du Yusong having business like fruit stand. Like off the street kind. He is Du like Du Zong — but not Tsung-ming Island people. The local people call putong, the river east side, he belong to that side local people. That man want to ask Du Zong father take him in like become own family. Du Zong father wasn't look down on him, but didn't take seriously, until that man big like become a mafia. Now important person, very hard to inviting him. Chinese way, came only to show respect, don't stay for dinner. Respect for making big celebration, he shows up. Mean gives lots of respect. Chinese custom. Chinese social life that way. If too important won't have to stay too long. He come to my wedding. I didn't see, I heard it. I gone to boy's side, they have YMCA dinner. Chinese age I was nineteen."

You should know that my mother's expressive command of English belies how much she actually understands. She reads the *Forbes* report, listens to *Wall Street Week*, converses daily with her stockbroker, reads all of Shirley MacLaine's books with ease — all kinds of things I can't

begin to understand. Yet some of my friends tell me they understand 50 percent of what my mother says. Some say they understand 80 to 90 percent. Some say they understand none of it, as if she were speaking pure Chinese. But to me, my mother's English is perfectly clear, perfectly natural. It's my mother tongue. Her language, as I hear it, is vivid, direct, full of observation and imagery. That was the language that helped shape the way I saw things, expressed things, made sense of the world.

Lately, I've been giving more thought to the kind of English my mother speaks. Like others, I have described it to people as "broken" or "fractured" English. But I wince when I say that. It has always bothered me that I can think of no way to describe it other than "broken," as if it were damaged and needed to be fixed, as if it lacked a certain wholeness and soundness. I've heard other terms used, "limited English," for example. But they seem just as bad, as if everything is limited, including people's perceptions of the limited English speaker.

I know this for a fact, because when I was growing up, my mother's "limited" English limited my perception of her. I was ashamed of her English. I believed that her English reflected the quality of what she had to say. That is, because she expressed them imperfectly her thoughts were imperfect. And I had plenty of empirical evidence to support me: the fact that people in department stores, at banks, and at restaurants did not take her seriously, did not give her good service, pretended not to understand her, or even acted as if they did not hear her.

My mother has long realized the limitations of her English as well. 10 When I was fifteen, she used to have me call people on the phone to pretend I was she. In this guise, I was forced to ask for information or even to complain and yell at people who had been rude to her. One time it was a call to her stockbroker in New York. She had cashed out her small portfolio and it just so happened we were going to go to New York the next week, our very first trip outside California. I had to get on the phone and say in an adolescent voice that was not very convincing, "This is Mrs. Tan."

And my mother was standing in the back whispering loudly, "Why he don't send me check, already two weeks late. So mad he lie to me, losing me money."

And then I said in perfect English, "Yes, I'm getting rather concerned. You had agreed to send the check two weeks ago, but it hasn't arrived."

Then she began to talk more loudly. "What he want, I come to New York tell him front of his boss, you cheating me?" And I was trying to calm her down, make her be quiet, while telling the stockbroker, "I can't tolerate any more excuses. If I don't receive the check immediately, I am going to have to speak to your manager when I'm in New York next week." And sure enough, the following week there we were in front of this astonished stockbroker, and I was sitting there red-faced and quiet, and my mother, the real Mrs. Tan, was shouting at his boss in her impeccable broken English.

We used a similar routine just five days ago, for a situation that was far less humorous. My mother had gone to the hospital for an appointment, to find out about a benign brain tumor a CAT scan had revealed a month ago. She said she had spoken very good English, her best English, no mistakes. Still, she said, the hospital did not apologize when they said they had lost the CAT scan and she had come for nothing. She said they did not seem to have any sympathy when she told them she was anxious to know the exact diagnosis, since her husband and son had both died of brain tumors. She said they would not give her any more information until the next time and she would have to make another appointment for that. So she said she would not leave until the doctor called her daughter. She wouldn't budge. And when the doctor finally called her daughter, me, who spoke in perfect English — lo and behold — we had assurances the CAT scan would be found, promises that a conference call on Monday would be held, and apologies for any suffering my mother had gone through for a most regrettable mistake.

I think my mother's English almost had an effect on limiting my 15 possibilities in life as well. Sociologists and linguists probably will tell you that a person's developing language skills are more influenced by peers. But I do think that the language spoken in the family, especially in immigrant families which are more insular, plays a large role in shaping the language of the child. And I believe that it affected my results on achievement tests, IQ tests, and the SAT. While my English skills were never judged as poor, compared to math, English could not be considered

academic literacies   rhetorical situations   genres   processes   strategies   research MLA / APA   media / design   readings

my strong suit. In grade school I did moderately well, getting perhaps B's, sometimes B-pluses, in English and scoring perhaps in the sixtieth or seventieth percentile on achievement tests. But those scores were not good enough to override the opinion that my true abilities lay in math and science, because in those areas I achieved A's and scored in the ninetieth percentile or higher.

This was understandable. Math is precise; there is only one correct answer. Whereas, for me at least, the answers on English tests were always a judgment call, a matter of opinion and personal experience. Those tests were constructed around items like fill-in-the-blank sentence completion, such as, "Even though Tom was _____, Mary thought he was _____." And the correct answer always seemed to be the most bland combinations of thoughts, for example, "Even though Tom was shy, Mary thought he was charming," with the grammatical structure "even though" limiting the correct answer to some sort of semantic opposites, so you wouldn't get answers like, "Even though Tom was foolish, Mary thought he was ridiculous." Well, according to my mother, there were very few limitations as to what Tom could have been and what Mary might have thought of him. So I never did well on tests like that.

The same was true with word analogies, pairs of words in which you were supposed to find some sort of logical, semantic relationship — for example, "*Sunset* is to *nightfall* as _____ is to _____." And here you would be presented with a list of four possible pairs, one of which showed the same kind of relationship: *red* is to *stoplight*, *bus* is to *arrival*, *chills* is to *fever*, *yawn* is to *boring*. Well, I could never think that way. I knew what the tests were asking, but I could not block out of my mind the images already created by the first pair, "*sunset* is to *nightfall*" — and I would see a burst of colors against a darkening sky, the moon rising, the lowering of a curtain of stars. And all the other pairs of words — red, bus, stoplight, boring — just threw up a mass of confusing images, making it impossible for me to sort out something as logical as saying: "A sunset precedes nightfall" is the same as "a chill precedes a fever." The only way I would have gotten that answer right would have been to imagine an associative situation, for example, my being disobedient and staying out past sunset, catching a chill at

night, which turns into feverish pneumonia as punishment, which indeed did happen to me.

I have been thinking about all this lately, about my mother's English, about achievement tests. Because lately I've been asked, as a writer, why there are not more Asian Americans represented in American literature. Why are there few Asian Americans enrolled in creative writing programs? Why do so many Chinese students go into engineering? Well, these are broad sociological questions I can't begin to answer. But I have noticed in surveys — in fact, just last week — that Asian students, as a whole, always do significantly better on math achievement tests than in English. And this makes me think that there are other Asian-American students whose English spoken in the home might also be described as "broken" or "limited." And perhaps they also have teachers who are steering them away from writing and into math and science, which is what happened to me.

Fortunately, I happen to be rebellious in nature and enjoy the challenge of disproving assumptions made about me. I became an English major my first year in college, after being enrolled as pre-med. I started writing nonfiction as a freelancer the week after I was told by my former boss that writing was my worst skill and I should hone my talents toward account management.

But it wasn't until 1985 that I finally began to write fiction. And at first   20
I wrote using what I thought to be wittily crafted sentences, sentences that would finally prove I had mastery over the English language. Here's an example from the first draft of a story that later made its way into *The Joy Luck Club*, but without this line: "That was my mental quandary in its nascent state." A terrible line, which I can barely pronounce.

Fortunately, for reasons I won't get into today, I later decided I should envision a reader for the stories I would write. And the reader I decided upon was my mother, because these were stories about mothers. So with this reader in mind — and in fact she did read my early drafts — I began to write stories using all the Englishes I grew up with: the English I spoke to my mother, which for lack of a better term might be described as "simple"; the English she used with me, which for lack of a better term might be described as "broken"; my translation of her Chinese, which could certainly be described as "watered down"; and what I imagined to be her translation of her Chinese if she could speak in perfect English, her internal language, and for that I sought to preserve the essence, but neither an English nor a Chinese structure. I wanted to capture what language ability tests can never reveal: her intent, her passion, her imagery, the rhythms of her speech and the nature of her thoughts.

Apart from what any critic had to say about my writing, I knew I had succeeded where it counted when my mother finished reading my book and gave me her verdict: "So easy to read."

Engaging with the Text

1. A literacy narrative needs **VIVID DETAIL** to bring it to life. What main kind of detail does Amy Tan use in her essay? Point to two of her details that strike you as especially interesting and revealing, and explain why they do.

   ▲ 84

2. Tan **BEGINS** by announcing, "I am not a scholar of English. . . . I cannot give you much more than personal opinions on the English language and its variations in this country or others." How does this opening set up your expectations for the rest of the essay? Why do you think Tan chose to begin by denying her own authority?

   ◆ 331–38

3. Tan writes about the different "Englishes" she speaks. What categories does she **DIVIDE** English into? Why are these divisions important to Tan? How does she say they affect her as a writer?

   ◆ 375–76

4. How does writing for an academic **AUDIENCE** affect the language Tan primarily uses in the essay? What kind of English do you think she believes her audience speaks? Why? Support your answer with quotations from the text.

   ■ 57–60

5. *For Writing.* Explore the differences between the language you speak at home and the languages you use with friends, teachers, employers, and so on. Write an essay that **REFLECTS** on the various languages you speak. If you speak only one language, consider the variations in the ways you speak it — at home, at work, at school, at church, wherever.

   ▲ 245–52

LYNDA BARRY

Lost and Found

Lynda Barry (b. 1956) is an award-winning cartoonist and author. Well known for her weekly comic strip Ernie Pook's Comeek, *Barry is the author of nineteen books, the latest of which is* Syllabus: Notes from an Accidental Professor *(2014). As the title suggests, Barry teaches workshops around the country on comic writing. Her graphic novel* What It Is *(2008) received the comics industry's 2009 Eisner Award for Best Reality-Based Work. This work is part memoir; Barry often writes about her life, as she does in* One! Hundred! Demons! *(2002), from which this excerpt is taken.*

AFTER I LEARNED TO READ, I LOVED GETTING HOME FROM SCHOOL AND WAITING FOR THE AFTERNOON PAPER. WE DIDN'T HAVE BOOKS IN THE HOUSE, BUT THE PAPER GAVE ME PLENTY TO WORK WITH.

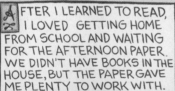

THE FIRST SECTION I TURNED TO WAS THE CLASSIFIEDS. I ALWAYS READ THE 'LOST AND FOUND' ADS, TRYING TO MEMORIZE DESCRIPTIONS OF DOGS AND CATS WHO WERE OUT THERE ALONE AND SCARED.

2 YR OLD M BRN + WHT CHIHUAHUA MIX. RD COLLAR. ANS TO "HENRY." REWARD.

"JINGLES" LOST 10/2. F GRAY TABBY. BLIND RT EYE NEEDS MEDICATION.

POOR JINGLES.

WHEN I CAME FORWARD WITH THE SOLUTION TO THESE CRIMES, AT FIRST NO ONE WOULD BELIEVE ME. I EXPECTED THAT. I WATCHED A LOT OF MOVIES. NO ONE EVER BELIEVES KIDS AT FIRST. YOU HAVE TO WAIT UNTIL ALMOST THE END. YOU HAVE TO WAIT 'TIL YOUR LIFE IS IN DANGER.

CALLING ALL CARS! THAT KID WAS RIGHT ABOUT THE WANT ADS!

BUT NOW THE CRYPT-VAMPIRE AND THE WEDDING DRESS-ZOMBIE HAVE HER IN THEIR CLUTCHES! WE WERE SO STUPID! REPEAT! VERY STUPID!

MOSTLY I DIED IN MY CLAS-SIFIED STORIES. EVEN THEN I LOVED TRAGIC ENDINGS. PEO-PLE WOULD BE CRYING SO HARD. THEY'D COVER MY COFFIN WITH FILL DIRT, VERY CLEAN. THE PARTY PIANIST WOULD PLAY.

CHERISH IS THE WORD I USE TO DIS-CRI-IBE...

WHEN I READ ABOUT WRITER'S LIVES, THERE ARE USUALLY STORIES ABOUT WRITING FROM THE TIME THEY WERE LITTLE. I NEVER WROTE ANYTHING UN-TIL I WAS A TEENAGER, AND THEN IT WAS ONLY A DIARY THAT SAID THE SAME THING OVER AND OVER.

I thought Bill liked me but turns out he doesn't. I'm so depressed about Bill. He didn't call me. I can't stop thinking about Bill.

WRITERS TALK ABOUT ALL THE BOOKS THEY LOVED WHEN THEY WERE CHILDREN. CLASSIC STORIES I NEVER READ, BUT I LIED ABOUT BECAUSE I WAS SCARED IT WAS PROOF I WASN'T REALLY A WRITER.

AND WIND IN THE WILLOWS?

AMAZING.

"THE LION, THE WITCH AND THE WARDROBE?"

INCREDIBLE. SAME WITH "WATER HEAD DOWN"

YOU MEAN "WATERSHIP"

UH, YEAH.

AH, YES

SUPER DRAMATICALLY EDUCATED... KNOWS ABOUT "STORY STRUC-TURE" AND "ARC." AND "PLOT POINTS"

JIVE-ASS FAKER WHO CAN'T SPELL AND HAS NO IDEA WHAT "STORY STRUCTURE" EVEN MEANS

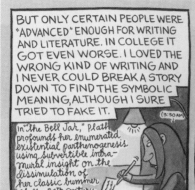

BUT ONLY CERTAIN PEOPLE WERE "ADVANCED" ENOUGH FOR WRITING AND LITERATURE. IN COLLEGE IT GOT EVEN WORSE. I LOVED THE WRONG KIND OF WRITING AND I NEVER COULD BREAK A STORY DOWN TO FIND THE SYMBOLIC MEANING, ALTHOUGH I SURE TRIED TO FAKE IT.

(3:30 AM)

In "The Bell Jar," Plath profounds her enumerated existential parthenogenesis using subvertible intra-mural insight on the dissimulation of her classic bummer of the 20th Century.

MY TROUBLE ENDED WHEN I STARTED MAKING COMIC-STRIPS. IT'S NOT SOMETHING A PERSON HAS TO BE VERY "ADVANCED" TO DO. AT LEAST NOT IN THE MINDS OF LITERARY TYPES.

SO YOU'RE A CARTOONIST! HOW ADORABLE!

POLITICAL? NO. HUMOROUS? KINDA. WE'RE BOTH WRITERS.

SAY, MAYBE WE COULD COLLABORATE! WE WRITE IT AND YOU DRAW IT! HOW FUN!

NOBODY FEELS THE NEED TO PROVIDE DEEP CRITICAL IN-SIGHT TO SOMETHING WRITTEN BY HAND. MOSTLY THEY KEEP IT AS SHORT AS A WANT AD. THE WORST I GET IS, "TOO MANY WORDS. NOT FUNNY. DON'T GET THE JOKE." I CAN LIVE WITH THAT.

GALS, EVER FELT SO intimidated by the IDEA OF writing THAT you've never even given it a try? Think writing is only FOR "writers"? Sure IS common!

ESPECIALLY BECAUSE I'M SURE THAT THE NINE-YEAR-OLD VERSION OF ME WHO MADE UP ALL THOSE "CLASSI-FIED STORIES" WOULD THINK THAT THIS ONE HAD A VERY HAPPY ENDING.

(and YES, Gals - the first thing, I read in the paper is still the "lost and found")

LOST. SOMEWHERE AROUND PUBERTY. ABILITY TO MAKE UP STORIES. HAPPINESS DEPENDS ON IT. PLEASE WRITE.

Engaging with the Text

1. Lynda Barry uses both text and images to provide **VIVID DETAILS** in her narrative. Choose two details that include both an image and verbal text, and explain how Barry makes these two modes of expression work together effectively.

2. In a number of places, Barry uses (or invents) **DIALOGUE** between herself and various other people, including another writer, the creative-writing teacher "Mrs. Snobaroo," and people at a party who find out that Barry is a cartoonist. How does this dialogue — which seems to focus on the lack of connection or understanding between Barry and the people she's talking with — help Barry **SUPPORT** the larger point she's making in her narrative?

3. How would you describe the **STANCE** Barry takes toward her early experiences with literacy? What other kind of stance might she have taken? What would have been the advantages and disadvantages, if any, of that other stance versus the one she actually takes?

4. Given that we know Barry is a highly successful author and cartoonist, why do you suppose she wrote about her lack of success in getting into creative writing classes and dealing with literature classes in high school and college? What point is she making by recalling these failures?

5. *For Writing.* Select an early memory of reading and/or writing that continues to feel relevant and important for you today. Create a cartoon strip about this experience, telling the story by drawing pictures and writing supporting text (or writing the text first and drawing pictures to illustrate it). If possible, choose a title related to what you were reading or writing about during this experience, as Barry does with "Lost and Found."

academic literacies · rhetorical situations · genres · processes · strategies · research MLA / APA · media / design · readings

Textual Analyses 60

LAUREL THATCHER ULRICH

Well-Behaved Women Seldom Make History

Laurel Thatcher Ulrich (b. 1938) is a professor of history at Harvard University, where she was appointed the 300th Anniversary University Professor. She is author and editor of a half-dozen books, including Good Wives: Image and Reality in the Lives of Women in Northern New England, 1650–1759 *(1982),* The Age of Homespun: Objects and Stories in the Creation of an American Myth *(2001), and* Well-Behaved Women Seldom Make History *(2007) from which the following essay was taken. Ulrich introduced the phrase "well-behaved women seldom make history" in a 1976 journal article titled "Vertuous Women Found: New England Ministerial Literature, 1668–1735," about how women were characterized in Puritan funeral sermons. Much to Ulrich's surprise, the phrase generated an explosion of cultural interest and now appears on greeting cards, T-shirts, bumper stickers, mugs, and plaques, among other places.*

SOME TIME AGO a former student e-mailed me from California: "You'll be delighted to know that you are quoted frequently on bumpers in Berkeley." Through a strange stroke of fate I've gotten used to seeing my name on bumpers. And on T-shirts, tote bags, coffee mugs, magnets, buttons, greeting cards, and websites.

I owe this curious fame to a single line from a scholarly article I published in 1976. In the opening paragraph, I wrote: "Well-behaved women seldom make history." That sentence, slightly altered, escaped into popular culture in 1995, when journalist Kay Mills used it as an epigraph for her informal history of American women, *From Pocahontas to Power Suits.* Perhaps by accident, she changed the word *seldom* to *rarely.* Little matter. According to my dictionary, *seldom* and *rarely* mean the same thing: "Well-behaved women *infrequently,* or on *few occasions,* make history." This may be one of those occasions. My original article

academic literacies | rhetorical situations | genres | processes | strategies | research MLA / APA | media / design | readings

was a study of the well-behaved women celebrated in Puritan funeral sermons.

In 1996, a young woman named Jill Portugal found the "rarely" version of the quote in her roommate's copy of *The New Beacon Book of Quotations by Women*. She wrote me from Oregon asking permission to print it on T-shirts. I was amused by her request and told her to go ahead; all I asked was that she send me a T-shirt. The success of her enterprise surprised both of us. A plain white shirt with the words "Well-behaved women rarely make history" printed in black roman type became a best-selling item. Portugal calls her company "one angry girl designs." Committed to "taking over the world, one shirt at a time," she fights sexual harassment, rape, pornography, and what she calls "fascist beauty standards."

Her success inspired imitators, only a few of whom bothered to ask permission. My runaway sentence now keeps company with anarchists, hedonists, would-be witches, political activists of many descriptions, and quite a few well-behaved women. It has been featured in *CosmoGirl*, the *Christian Science Monitor*, and *Creative Keepsake Scrapbooking Magazine*. According to news reports, it was a favorite of the pioneering computer scientist Anita Borg. The Sweet Potato Queens of Jackson, Mississippi, have adopted it as an "official maxim," selling their own pink-and-green T-shirt alongside another that reads "Never Wear Panties to a Party."

My accidental fame has given me a new perspective on American 5 popular culture. While some women contemplate the demise of feminism, others seem to have only just discovered it. A clerk in the Amtrak ticket office in D.C.'s Union Station told a fellow historian that all the women in her office wore the button. "I couldn't resist telling her that I was acquainted with you, and she just lit right up, and made me promise to tell you that the women at the Amtrak office thank you for all your 'words of wisdom.'"

. . .

The "well-behaved women" quote works because it plays into longstanding stereotypes about the invisibility and the innate decorum of the female sex. Many people think women are less visible in history than men because their bodies impel them to nurture. Their job is to bind the wounds, stir the soup, and bear the children of those whose mission it is to fight wars, rule nations, and define the cosmos. Not all those who make this argument consider women unimportant — on the contrary, they often revere the contributions of women as wives, mothers, and caregivers — or at least they say so. But they also assume that domestic roles haven't changed much over the centuries, and that women who perform them have no history. A New Hampshire pastor captured this notion when he wrote in his commonplace book in 1650, "Woman's the center & lines are men." If women occupy the fixed center of life, and if history is seen as a linear progression of public events, a changing panorama of wars and kingdoms, then only those who through outrageous behavior, divine intervention, or sheer genius step into the stream of public consequence have a history.

The problem with this argument is not only that it limits women. It also limits history. Good historians are concerned not only with famous people and public events but with broad transformations in human behavior, things like falling death rates or transatlantic migration. Here seemingly small actions by large numbers of people can bring about profound change. But this approach runs up against another imperative of history — its reliance on written sources. Until recent times most women (and a great many men) were illiterate. As a consequence their activities were recorded, if at all, in other people's writing. People who caused trouble might show up in court records, newspapers, or their masters' diaries. Those who quietly went about their lives were either forgotten, seen at a distance, or idealized into anonymity. Even today, publicity favors those who make — or break — laws.

But the difficulty is bigger than that. History is an account of the past based on surviving sources, but it is also a way of making sense out of the present. In the heat and confusion of events, people on all sides of an issue mine old stories for inspiration, enlightenment, or confirmation. Their efforts add to the layers of understanding attached to the original events, shaping what later generations know and care about. Scholars sometimes call these popular reconstructions of the past "memory" to distinguish them from formal history. But serious history is also forged

academic literacies   rhetorical situations   genres   processes   strategies   research MLA / APA   media / design   readings

in the tumult of change. History is not just what happened in the past. It is what later generations choose to remember.

. . .

Historians don't own history. But we do have a lot of experience sifting through competing evidence. Historical research is a bit like detective work. We re-create past events from fragments of information, trying hard to distinguish credible accounts from wishful thinking. One of our jobs is to explore the things that get left out when a person becomes an icon. Recent scholarship on the Sweet Potato Queens' heroine, Mae West, is a good example. There is no question about West's reputation for misbehavior. She said it herself: "When I'm bad, I'm better." Beginning her stage career at the age of six, she moved from playing the saintly Little Eva in *Uncle Tom's Cabin* to shimmying her way to fame. In uptight Boston, theater owners cut off the lights "with West's first ripple." But in New York she was the darling of urban sophisticates who wanted

Mae West, *photographed in the 1930s.*

to explore the seamy side of life without leaving their theater seats. When she moved to Hollywood in the 1930s, censors tried to clean up her scripts, but she knew how to fill even the blandest lines with sexual innuendo. *Variety* complained that "Mae couldn't sing a lullaby without making it sexy."

That is how Mae West made history. But what sort of history did she make? Some recent studies focus on her debts to the male homosexuals whose outrageous impersonations defined *camp* in the 1920s. Others claim that her largest debt was to African American entertainers. West's shimmy, for example, ultimately derived from West African traditions adapted in rural dance halls, or "jooks." Her ballad "Honey let yo' drawers hang down low" (which may have inspired the Sweet Potato Queens' "Never Wear Panties to a Party") was a favorite in southern jooks. In the early twentieth century, West, the sexually active, streetwise girl from Brooklyn, gave middle-class audiences a glimpse of worlds that both fascinated and repelled. Like the legendary Godiva,* she allowed people to imagine the unimaginable. Because she was also a savvy businesswoman, she was able to live off other people's fantasies.

A first-year student at a California university told me that to make history, people need to do the unexpected. She offered the example of civil rights activist Rosa Parks, "who would not leave her seat." I like her emphasis on the unexpected. It not only captures the sense of history as the study of how things change, it offers a somewhat more complex way of understanding the contribution of a woman like Parks.

Was Parks a well-behaved woman? The Montgomery, Alabama, bus company did not think so. As the student from California recognized, Parks made history precisely because she dared to challenge both social norms and the law. Her refusal to obey the statute that required her to give up her seat to a white passenger sparked the 361-day-long boycott that thrust Martin Luther King into the public eye and led to a historic Supreme Court decision outlawing segregation on public transportation.

10

Godiva: Lady Godiva, an eleventh-century Anglo-Saxon noblewoman who reportedly rode naked through the streets of Coventry, England, to protest taxes imposed by her husband. [Editor's note]

academic literacies   rhetorical situations   genres   processes   strategies   research MLA / APA   media / design   readings

Yet Parks became an icon for the civil rights movement not only for her courage but because the media identified her as a hard-working seamstress who simply got tired of moving to the back of the bus. Few people outside Montgomery knew her as the politically conscious secretary of the local NAACP, nor understood how many years she and her husband had been working for social justice before that fateful day on the bus. In 1954 and 1955, Parks had attended workshops on desegregation sponsored by the radical Highlander Folk School in Tennessee, a public education project that Mississippi's Senator James Eastland excoriated as a "front for a conspiracy to overthrow this country."

Nor has popular history recorded the names of other Montgomery women — teenagers — whose arrests that year for refusing to give up their seats failed to ignite a movement. Years later, E. D. Nixon, president of the Montgomery NAACP, explained why he hadn't chosen any of these other women to make a historic stand against segregation. "OK, the case of Louise Smith. I found her daddy in front of his shack, barefoot, drunk. Always drunk. Couldn't use her. In that year's second case, the girl, very brilliant but she'd had an illegitimate baby. Couldn't use her. The last case before Rosa was the daughter of a preacher who headed a reform school for years. My interview of her convinced me that she wouldn't stand up to pressure. She were even afraid of me. When Rosa Parks was arrested, I thought, 'This is it!' 'Cause she's morally clean, she's reliable, nobody had nothing on her, she had the courage of her convictions." Parks's publicly acknowledged good behavior helped to justify her rebellion and win support for her cause. As one friend recalled, she "was too sweet to even say 'damn' in anger."

After Parks's death in the fall of 2005, the airways were filled with tributes celebrating the life of the "humble seamstress," the "simple woman" who sparked a revolution because her feet were tired. Reviewing these eulogies, syndicated columnist Ellen Goodman asked, "Is it possible we prefer our heroes to be humble? Or is it just our heroines?" She wondered if it wasn't time Americans got over the notion that women are "accidental heroines," unassuming creatures thrust into the public eye by circumstances beyond their control. Goodman noted that Parks and her compatriots spent years preparing for just such an opportunity.

Rosa Parks's mug shot, taken shortly after her arrest on December 1, 1955, for refusing to obey a bus driver's order to give up her seat to a white passenger.

She concluded: "Rosa Parks was 'unassuming' — except that she rejected all the assumptions about her place in the world. Rosa Parks was a 'simple woman' — except for a mind made up and fed up. She was 'quiet' — except, of course, for one thing. Her willingness to say 'no' changed the world."

The California student said that in contrast to Parks a "well-behaved 15 woman" is "a quiet, subservient, polite, indoors, cooking, cleaning type of girl who would never risk shame by voicing her own opinion." There is a delicious irony in this part of her definition. Notice that it associates a particular kind of work — cooking and cleaning — with subservience and passivity. Yet the boycott that made Parks famous was sustained by hundreds of African American domestic servants — cooks and maids — who walked to work rather than ride segregated buses. They too did the unexpected.*

Serious history talks back to slogans. But in the contest for public attention, slogans usually win. Consider my simple sentence. It sat quietly for years in the folds of a scholarly journal. Now it honks its ambiguous wisdom from coffee mugs and tailgates.

. . .

In my scholarly work, my form of misbehavior has been to care about things that other people find predictable or boring. My second book is a case in point. At a distance, the life of Martha Moore Ballard was the stuff from which funeral sermons were made. She was a "good wife" in every sense of the word, indistinguishable from all the self-sacrificing and pious women celebrated in Puritan eulogies. In conventional terms,

---

*Awele Makeba's powerful one-woman show, "Rage Is Not a 1-Day Thing," dramatizes the lives of sixteen little-known participants, male and female, black and white. For details see her website, http://www.awele.com/programs.htm. For a list of resources prepared for the fiftieth anniversary of the boycott in 2005, see http://www .teachingforchange.org/busboycott/busboycott.htm. Additional documents can be found in Stewart Burns, ed., *Daybreak of Freedom: The Montgomery Bus Boycott* (Chapel Hill and London: University of North Carolina Press, 1997). Herbert Kohl, *She Would Not Be Moved: How We Tell the Story of Rosa Parks and the Montgomery Bus Boycott* (New York and London: The New Press, 2005), urges teachers to move from the theme "Rosa Was Tired" to the more historically accurate concept "Rosa Was Ready."

she did not make history. She cherished social order, respected authority, and abhorred violence. As a midwife and healer, she relied on home-grown medicines little different from those found in English herbals a century before her birth. Her religious sentiments were conventional; her reading was limited to the Bible, edifying pamphlets, and newspapers. Although she lived through the American Revolution, she had little interest in politics. She was a caregiver and a sustainer rather than a mover and shaker.

Ballard made history by performing a methodical and seemingly ordinary act — writing a few words in her diary every day. Through the diary we know her as a pious herbalist whose curiosity about the human body led her to observe and record autopsies as well as nurse the sick, whose integrity allowed her to testify in a sensational rape trial against a local judge who was her husband's employer, and whose sense of duty took her out of bed at night not only to deliver babies but to care for the bodies of a wife and children murdered by their own husband and father. The power of the diary is not only in its sensational stories, however, but in its patient, daily recording of seemingly inconsequential events, struggles with fatigue and discouragement, conflicts with her son, and little things — like the smell of a room where a dead body lay. In Ballard's case, the drama really was in the humdrum. The steadiness of the diary provided the frame for everything else that happened.

. . .

Although I have received mail addressed to Martha Ballard and have been identified on at least one college campus as a midwife, I am only a little bit like my eighteenth-century subject. Like her, I was raised to be an industrious housewife and a self-sacrificing and charitable neighbor, but sometime in my thirties I discovered that writing about women's work was a lot more fun than doing it. I remember thinking one winter day how ironic it was that I was wrapped in a bathrobe with the heat of a wood stove rising toward my loft as I wrote about a courageous woman who braved snowstorms and crossed a frozen river on a cake of ice to care for mothers in labor. I felt selfish, pampered, and decadent. But I did not stop what I was doing. I did not know why I needed to write Martha's story, and I could not imagine that anybody else would ever want to follow me through my meandering glosses on her diary. I was astonished at the reception of the book. Even more important than the prizes was the discovery of how important this long-dead midwife's story was to nurses, midwives, and anonymous caregivers dealing with quite different circumstances today. These readers helped me to see that history is more than an engaging enterprise. It is a primary way of creating meaning. The meaning I found in Martha Ballard's life had something to do with my own life experience, but perhaps a lot more to do with the collective experiences of a generation of Americans coping with dramatic changes in their own lives.

When I wrote that "well-behaved women seldom make history," 20 I was making a commitment to help recover the lives of otherwise obscure women. I had no idea that thirty years later, my own words would come back to me transformed. While I like some of the uses of the slogan more than others, I wouldn't call it back even if I could. I applaud the fact that so many people — students, teachers, quilters, nurses, newspaper columnists, old ladies in nursing homes, and mayors of western towns — think they have the right to make history.

Some history-making is intentional; much of it is accidental. People make history when they scale a mountain, ignite a bomb, or refuse to move to the back of the bus. But they also make history by keeping diaries, writing letters, or embroidering initials on linen sheets. History is a conversation and sometimes a shouting match between present and past, though often the voices we most want to hear are barely audible. People make history by passing on gossip, saving old records, and by naming rivers, mountains, and children. Some people leave only their bones, though bones too make history when someone notices.

Historian Gerda Lerner has written: "All human beings are practicing historians. . . . We live our lives; we tell our stories. It is as natural as breathing." But if no one cares about these stories, they do not survive. People do not only make history by living their lives, but by creating records and by turning other people's lives into books or slogans.

Engaging with the Text

55–56

1. What is the **PURPOSE** of Laurel Thatcher Ulrich's textual analysis of her slogan? What point is she trying to make with the analysis? How does her point relate to her purpose?

331–38
338–42

2. How does Ulrich **BEGIN** her essay? How does the opening relate to how the essay **ENDS**? How effective is her beginning in drawing the reader to her analysis of the slogan "Well-behaved women seldom make history"?

3. Ulrich discusses the ambiguity of her slogan, noting that some read it as referring to the lack of women in histories or the lack of histories about women, whereas others read it as meaning that only by "misbehaving" do women make history. How does she relate this ambiguity to the broader issue of how history in general is written? Identify two examples she provides to illustrate the complexities of writing history.

111

4. What kind of **SUPPORT** does Ulrich offer as evidence of the points she makes? Select three pieces of evidence in the essay and discuss how effective each is in supporting the point it is intended to support.

94–128

5. *For Writing.* Do a web search for "well-behaved women seldom [or rarely] make history" to identify three objects on which the slogan appears, and write an essay **ANALYZING** how its meaning might be understood by those who purchase them. Describe the objects and those — whether businesses, organizations, or individuals — who are promoting them. What meaning do you think the promoters assume potential buyers will perceive? How closely does that meaning relate to the point Ulrich originally made with this phrase? What does your analysis reveal about the role of slogans in history?

DIANA GEORGE

Changing the Face of Poverty
Nonprofits and the Problem of Representation

Diana George (b. 1948) is a professor of English at Virginia Polytechnic Institute and State University. She has written widely on culture, writing, and visual representation. She is the editor of Kitchen Cooks, Plate Twirlers, and Troubadours *(1999), a collection of essays by writing program administrators, and a coauthor of* Reading Culture *(with John Trimbur, 2006) and* Picturing Texts *(with Lester Faigley, Anna Palchik, and Cynthia Selfe, 2004). The following analysis comes from* Popular Literacy: Studies in Cultural Practices and Poetics *(2001). The endnotes are presented according to* The Chicago Manual of Style, *as they appeared in the original publication.*

> Constructively changing the ways the poor are represented in every aspect of life is one progressive intervention that can challenge everyone to look at the face of poverty and not turn away.
> — BELL HOOKS, OUTLAW CULTURE

AS I WRITE THIS, Thanksgiving is near. I am about to go out and fill a box with nonperishables for the annual St. Vincent de Paul food drive. Christmas lights already outline some porches. Each day my mailbox is stuffed with catalogs and bills and with appeals from the Native American Scholarship Fund, the Salvation Army, WOJB — Voice of the Anishinabe, the Navaho Health Foundation, the Barbara Kettle Gundlach Shelter Home for Abused Women, Little Brothers Friends of the Elderly, Habitat for Humanity, and more. One *New Yorker* ad for Children, Inc. reads, "You don't have to leave your own country to find third-world poverty." Underneath the ad copy, from a black-and-white photo, a young girl in torn and ill-fitting clothes looks directly at the viewer. The copy continues, "In Appalachia, sad faces of children, like Mandy's, will haunt you. There

> **ENCLOSED:** No Address Labels to Use Up.
> No Calendars to Look At.
> No Petitions to Sign.
>
> And No Pictures of Starving Children.

Text from the outer envelope of a 1998 Oxfam appeal.

are so many children like her — children who are deprived of the basic necessities right here in America."*

The Oxfam promise that I quote above — to use no pictures of starving children — is surely an attempt to avoid the emotional overload of such images as the one Children, Inc. offers. Still, those pictures — those representations of poverty — have typically been one way nonprofits have kept the poor before us. In a culture saturated by the image, how else do we convince Americans that — despite the prosperity they see all around them — there is real need out there? The solution for most nonprofits has been to show the despair. To do that they must represent poverty as something that can be seen and easily recognized: fallen down shacks and trashed out public housing, broken windows, dilapidated porches, barefoot kids with stringy hair, emaciated old women and men staring out at the camera with empty eyes. In such images, poverty is dirt and rags and helplessness. In mail, in magazines, and in newspapers, ads echoing these appeals must vie for our time, attention, and dollars with Eddie Bauer, Nordstrom's, The Gap, and others like them whose polished and attractive images fill our days.

In the pages that follow . . . I examine a particular representation of poverty — publicity videos produced by Habitat for Humanity — in order to suggest that reliance on stereotypes of poverty can, in fact, work against the aims of the organization producing them. . . .

---

*The copy here has been revised, with the author's permission, to reflect the more recent Children, Inc., ad. [Editor's note]

An ad for Children, Inc.

Habitat for Humanity: A Case in Point

I have chosen Habitat for Humanity publicity videos for my focus because Habitat is a popular and far-reaching nonprofit with affiliates not only in the United States but throughout the world. Its goal is not a modest one: Habitat for Humanity aims to eliminate poverty housing from the globe. More than that, Habitat puts housing into the hands of the people who will be housed — into the hands of the homeowners and their neighbors. This is not another program aimed at keeping people in what has become known as the poverty or welfare cycle.

To be very clear, then, I am not criticizing the work of Habitat for Humanity. It is an organization that has done an amazing job of addressing what is, as cofounder Millard Fuller tells us again and again, a worldwide problem. What I would draw attention to, however, is how that problem of inadequate housing and its solution are represented, especially in publicity material produced and distributed by the organization, and how those representations can feed into the troubles that Habitat continues to have as it attempts to change the ways Americans think of helping others. What's more, the kinds of visual arguments Habitat and other nonprofits use to advocate for action or change have become increasingly common tools for getting the message to the public, and yet, I would argue, these messages too often fail to overturn cultural commonplaces that represent poverty as an individual problem that can be addressed on an individual basis. Habitat's catch phrase — A Hand Up, Not a Hand-Out — appeals to a nation that believes anyone can achieve economic security with just the right attitude and set of circumstances.

Habitat's basic program has a kind of elegance. Applicants who are chosen as homeowners put in sweat equity hours to build their home and to help build the homes of others chosen by Habitat. The organization then sells the home to the applicant at cost (that cost held down through Habitat's ability to provide volunteer labor and donated materials) and charges a small monthly mortgage that includes no interest. Unlike public assistance, which is raised or lowered depending on the recipient's circumstances, most Habitat affiliates do not raise mortgage

payments when homeowners get better jobs or find themselves in better financial shape. And once the house is paid for, it belongs to the homeowner.

Obviously, in order to run a program like this one, Habitat must produce publicity appeals aimed at convincing potential donors to give time, money, and material. Print ads, public service television and radio spots, commercial appeals linked to products like Maxwell House coffee, and publicity videos meant to be played for churches, volunteer organizations, and even in-flight video appeals on certain airlines are common media for Habitat.

Habitat publicity videos are typically configured as problem-solution arguments. The problem is that too many people have inadequate shelter. The solution is community involvement in a program like Habitat for Humanity. The most common setup for these productions is an opening sequence of images — a visual montage — in which we see black-and-white shots of rural shacks, of men and women clearly in despair, and of thin children in ragged clothing. The voice-over narrative of one such montage tells us the story:

> Poverty condemns millions of people throughout the world to live in deplorable and inhuman conditions. These people are trapped in a cycle of poverty, living in places offering little protection from the rain, wind, and cold. Terrible sanitary conditions make each day a battle with disease and death. And, for this, they often pay over half their income in rent because, for the poor, there are no other choices. Daily, these families are denied a most basic human need: a decent place to live. The reasons for this worldwide tragedy are many. They vary from city to city, country to country, but the result is painfully the same whether the families are in New York or New Delhi.[1]

It is a compelling dilemma.

Organizations like Habitat for Humanity, in order to convey the seriousness of this struggle and, of course, to raise funds and volunteer support for their efforts in addressing it, must produce all sorts of publicity. And in that publicity they must tell us quickly what the problem is and what we can do to help. To do that, Habitat gives us a visual representation of poverty, a representation that mirrors the most common understandings of poverty in America.

Now, there is nothing inherently wrong with that representation 10 unless, of course, what you want to do (as Habitat does) is convince the American people to believe in the radical idea that those who have must care for the needs of others, not just by writing a check, but by enabling an entirely different lifestyle. For Americans, it is truly radical to think that our poorer neighbors might actually be allowed to buy a home at no interest and with the donated time and materials of others. It is a radical notion that such a program means that these neighbors then own that house and aren't obliged to do more than keep up with payments in order to continue owning it. And it is a radical idea that Habitat does this work not only in our neighborhoods (not isolated in low-income housing developments) but throughout the world. Habitat International truly believes that we are all responsible for partnering with our neighbors throughout the world so that everyone might eventually have, at least, a simple decent place to live. Like the philosophy behind many nonprofits, Habitat's is not a mainstream notion.

Still, that representation of poverty — clinging as it does to commonplaces drawn from FSA photographs in this century, from Jacob Riis's nineteenth-century photos of urban poverty, and from documentaries of Third World hunger — has serious limitations, which must be obvious to those who remember the moment that the Bush administration* confidently announced that, after looking everywhere, they had discovered no real hunger in the United States. And that myth that poverty cannot/does not actually exist in the heart of capitalism has once again been reinforced in the 1998 Heritage Foundation report in which Robert Rector echoed the perennial argument that there is little true poverty in this country ("Myth").[2] Heritage Foundation's finding comes despite figures

---

*Bush administration: the administration of George H. W. Bush (1989–93). FSA: the Farm Security Administration, a federal agency that hired such prominent photographers as Walker Evans and Dorothea Lange to document rural poverty in the 1930s. Jacob Riis (1849–1914): Danish American social reformer. [Editor's note]

academic literacies · rhetorical situations · genres · processes · strategies · research MLA / APA · media / design · readings

from the National Coalition for the Homeless ("Myths and Facts About Homelessness"), which tell us that in 1997 nearly one in five homeless people in twenty-nine cities across the United States was employed in a full- or part-time job.[3]

In her call for a changed representation of poverty in America, bell hooks argues that in this culture poverty "is seen as synonymous with depravity, lack and worthlessness." She continues, "I talked with young black women receiving state aid, who have not worked in years, about the issue of representation. They all agree that they do not want to be identified as poor. In their apartments they have the material possessions that indicate success (a VCR, a color television), even if it means that they do without necessities and plunge into debt to buy these items."[4] Hers is hardly a noble image of poverty, but it is a true one and one that complicates the job of an organization like Habitat that must identify "worthy" applicants. This phenomenon of poverty in the center of wealth, in a country with its national mythology of hearty individuals facing the hardness of the Depression with dignity and pride, is certainly a part of what Manning Marable challenges when he asks readers not to judge poverty in the United States by the standards of other countries. Writing of poverty among black Americans, Marable reminds us that "the process of impoverishment is profoundly national and regional."[5] It does little good to compare the impoverished of this country with Third World poverty or, for that matter, with Depression Era poverty.

The solution in these Habitat videos is just as visible and compelling a representation as is the problem. The solution, it seems, is a modern-day barn raising. In clip after clip, Habitat volunteers are shown lined up to raise walls, to hammer nails, to cut boards, to offer each other the "hand up not a hand out," as these publicity messages tell us again and again. Like the barn-raising scene from Peter Weir's *Witness*, framed walls come together against blue skies. People who would normally live in very different worlds come together to help a neighbor. It is all finished in record time: a week, even a day. Volunteers can come together quickly. Do something. Get out just as quickly.

The real trouble with Habitat's representation, then, is twofold: it tells us that the signs of poverty are visible and easily recognized. And it suggests that one of the most serious results of poverty (inadequate shelter) can be addressed quickly with volunteer efforts to bring individuals up and out of the poverty cycle.

Of course, if Habitat works, what could be wrong with the representation? It is an organization so popular that it receives support from diametrically opposed camps. Newt Gingrich and Jesse Jackson have both pounded nails and raised funds for Habitat. This is what Millard Fuller calls the "theology of the hammer." People might not agree on political parties and they might not agree on how to worship or even what to worship, Fuller says, but they can all agree on a hammer. All can come together to build houses. Or, can they?

As successful as Habitat has been, it is an organization that continues to struggle with such issues as who to choose for housing, how to support potential homeowners, and how to convince affiliates in the United States to tithe a portion of their funds to the real effort of Habitat: eliminating poverty housing throughout the world, not just in the United States. And, even in the United States, affiliates often have trouble identifying "deserving" applicants or convincing local residents to allow Habitat homes to be built in their neighborhoods. There are certainly many cultural and political reasons for these problems, but I would suggest that the way poverty continues to be represented in this country and on tapes like those videos limits our understanding of what poverty is and how we might address it.

That limitation holds true for those caught in poverty as well as those wanting to help. What if, as a potential Habitat applicant, you don't recognize yourself or you refuse to recognize yourself in those representations? As Stanley Aronowitz points out in *The Politics of Identity*, that can happen very easily as class identities, in particular, have become much more difficult to pin down since World War II, especially with an expansion of consumer credit that allowed class and social status to be linked to consumption rather than to professions or even wages. In his discussion of how electronic media construct the *social imaginary*, Aronowitz talks of the working class with few media representations available to them as having fallen into a kind of "cultural homelessness."[6] How much more true is that of the impoverished in this country who

may be neither homeless nor ragged, but are certainly struggling every day to feed their families, pay rent, and find jobs that pay more than what it costs for daycare?

I have been particularly interested in this last question because of a difficulty I mentioned earlier, that of identifying appropriate applicants for Habitat homes or even getting some of the most needy families of a given affiliate to apply for Habitat homes. When I showed the video *Building New Lives* to Kim Puuri, a Copper Country Habitat for Humanity homeowner and now member of the affiliate's Homeowner Selection Committee, and asked her to respond, she was very clear in what she saw as the problem:

> When I see those pictures I usually think of Africa or a third-world country and NOT the U.S. It's not that they can't be found here, it's just that you don't publicly see people that bad off other than street people. If they could gear the publicity more to the geographical areas, it may make more of an impact or get a better response from people. It would mean making several videos. It may not be so much of a stereotype, but an association between Habitat and the people they help. People viewing the videos and pictures see the conditions of the people and feel that their own condition may not be that bad and feel they probably wouldn't qualify.[7]

What this Habitat homeowner has noticed is very close to what Stuart Hall describes. That is, the problem with this image, this representation, is not that it is not real enough. The problem has nothing to do with whether or not these are images of poverty as it exists in the world. There is no doubt that this level of poverty does exist in this country and elsewhere despite the Heritage Foundation's attempts to demonstrate otherwise. The problem is that this representation of poverty is a narrow one and functions to narrow the ways we might respond to the poor who do not fit this representation.

The representation I have been discussing is one that insists on constructing poverty as an individual problem that can be dealt with by volunteers on an individual basis. That is the sort of representation common in this country, the sort of representation Paul Wellstone objects to in a recent call to action when he says "We can offer no single description of American poverty." What it takes to break through such a representation is first, as Hall suggests, to understand it as a representation, to understand it as a way of imparting meaning. And the only way to contest that representation, to allow for other meanings, other descriptions, is to know more about the many dimensions of poverty in America. "More than 35 million Americans — one out of every seven of our fellow citizens — are officially poor. More than one in five American children are poor. And the poor are getting poorer," Wellstone writes.[8] But we can be certain that much of that poverty is not the sort pictured in those black-and-white images. And if it doesn't look like poverty, then how do we address it? How do we identify those "deserving" our help?

Indeed, as Herbert Gans has suggested, the labels we have chosen   20 to place on the poor in this country often reveal more than anything "an ideology of undeservingness," by which we have often elided poverty and immorality or laziness or criminality. "By making scapegoats of the poor for fundamental problems they have not caused nor can change," Gans argues, "Americans can also postpone politically difficult and divisive solutions to the country's economic ills and the need to prepare the economy and polity for the challenges of the twenty-first century."[9] These are tough issues to confront and certainly to argue in a twenty-minute video presentation aimed at raising funds and volunteer support, especially when every piece of publicity must make a complex argument visible.

Notes

1. *Building New Lives* (Americus, Ga.: Habitat for Humanity International). This and other Habitat videos are directed primarily at potential volunteers for the organization or might be used to inform local residents about the work of Habitat.

2. Robert Rector, "The Myth of Widespread American Poverty," *The Heritage Foundation Backgrounder* (18 Sept. 1998), no. 1221. This publication is available on-line at <http://www.heritage.org/library/backgrounder/bg1221es.html>.

academic literacies | rhetorical situations | genres | processes | strategies | research MLA / APA | media / design | readings

3. Cited in Barbara Ehrenreich, "Nickel and Dimed: On (Not) Getting By in America," *Harper's* (January 1999), 44. See also Christina Coburn Herman's *Poverty Amid Plenty: The Unfinished Business of Welfare Reform*, NETWORK, A National Social Justice Lobby (Washington, D.C., 1999), from NETWORK's national Welfare Reform Watch Project, which reports that most studies of welfare use telephone surveys even though a substantial percentage of those needing aid do not have phone service (41 percent in the NETWORK survey had no operative phone) and, therefore, are not represented in most welfare reform reports. This report is available on-line at <http://www.network-lobby.org>.

4. bell hooks, "Seeing and Making Culture: Representing the Poor," *Outlaw Culture: Resisting Representations* (New York: 1994), 169.

5. Manning Marable, *How Capitalism Underdeveloped Black America* (Boston: South End Press, 1983), 54.

6. Stanley Aronowitz, *The Politics of Identity: Class, Culture, Social Movements* (New York: Routledge, 1992), 201.

7. Kim Puuri, personal correspondence with author.

8. Paul Wellstone, "If Poverty Is the Question," *Nation* (14 April 1997), 15.

9. Herbert J. Gans, *The War Against the Poor* (New York: Basic Books, 1995), 6–7.

Engaging with the Text

1. How, according to Diana George, is poverty represented by nonprofit agencies such as Habitat for Humanity? What problems does George identify as a result of such representation?

2. George opens her analysis with a bell hooks quote, followed by descriptions of how frequently she encounters charities near Thanksgiving. How do the quote and the description appeal to different **AUDIENCES**?

   57–60

3. The Children, Inc. ad that George refers to is reprinted here on page 677. What does George mean by the "emotional overload" of this image? Why do you think the Oxfam envelope promises not to include images like this?

55–56

4. What main **PURPOSE** is George's textual analysis intended to serve? Where is that purpose made explicit? What other purposes might her essay serve?

94–128

5. *For Writing.* Identify a print, TV, or web ad aimed at influencing your opinion on a political or social issue. **ANALYZE** the visuals (drawings, pictures, photographs) and the accompanying words in the ad to describe how the issue is represented. How effectively does the ad meet its goals? Can you identify any problems with how the issue is represented that might undermine those goals?

SASHA FRERE-JONES

Weirdly Popular

Sasha Frere-Jones (b. 1967) is the executive editor of Genius, *a website that provides a forum for annotating texts ranging from rap music to restaurant menus. Previously, he was the* New Yorker's *pop music critic for eleven years and a columnist for newyorker.com. He has also written for* Slate, Slant, Spin, *and other publications. The following music review appeared in the* New Yorker *in 2014.*

DO PEOPLE ENJOY "WEIRD AL" YANKOVIC because he's funny or because he's not that funny? The comedian, who specializes in song parodies, just released his fourteenth studio album, *Mandatory Fun*, which features his class-clown mangling of hits by Lorde, Iggy Azalea, and Pharrell Williams, among others. It débuted at No. 1, selling more than a hundred thousand copies in its first week. Considering the post-digital slump in music sales — a hit album a decade ago could sell as many as a million copies in a week; this year, Sia's *1000 Forms of Fear* entered the charts at No. 1 by selling only fifty-two thousand copies — this might be the biggest first week for a comedy album ever. But what is it that Weird Al actually does? I don't laugh at his songs, yet I'm delighted by his presence in the world of pop culture. With his parodic versions of hit songs, this somehow ageless fifty-four-year-old has become popular not because he is immensely clever — though he can be — but because he embodies how many people feel when confronted with pop music: slightly too old and slightly too square. That feeling never goes away, and neither has Al, who has sold more than twelve million albums since 1979.

Anxiety starts early for pop audiences. For decades, I have had twenty-somethings tell me that they don't know what's on the charts, haven't listened to any new artists since college, and don't "know anything about music." They feel confused by how quickly the value of their knowledge of what's current fades. Weird Al's songwriting process,

academic
literacies

rhetorical
situations

genres

processes

strategies

research
MLA / APA

media /
design

readings

almost without exception, is to confront that anxiety and to celebrate it. Yankovic will take a mysterious and masterful song and turn it into something mundane and universal. He makes the grand aspirational concerns of teen-agers in Lorde's "Royals" into a story that includes a lesson about the hygienic advantage of taking food home in aluminum foil. (You'll see the rhyme there.) Charli XCX's boast of being "classic, expensive, you don't get to touch," in Azalea's "Fancy," becomes an ad for a handyman who can resurface your patio in Yankovic's "Handy."

The opening lyrics of "Smells Like Nirvana," Yankovic's 1992 version of Nirvana's "Smells Like Teen Spirit," are as close to a mission statement as he has: "What is this song all about? Can't figure any lyrics out. How do the words to it go? I wish you'd tell me, I don't know." Weird Al has been cool for so long because pop makes everybody feel uncool; that he is the only one to admit it has made him a pop star. What's strange is how frequently the musicians whom Weird Al parodies feel blessed, as if some kind of comic Pope had waved at them. Williams, for instance, told Yankovic that he was "honored" to give him permission to do a take on his hit "Happy."

Yankovic grew up in Lynwood, a suburb of Los Angeles, and learned the accordion as a child, playing polka and other genres. Inspired by satirists like Tom Lehrer and Allan Sherman — the previous No. 1 comedy album was Sherman's *My Son, the Nut*, in 1963 — Yankovic began to create his own parodies. As his Twitter bio succinctly says, he's "the Eat It guy." In 1984, his version of Michael Jackson's "Beat It" seemed almost as popular as Jackson's original and, on MTV, made a star out of a goofball with bad glasses, curly hair (longer now, but still not gray), and a taste for Hawaiian shirts. Jackson sang about the pointlessness of violence; Yankovic used the handiest rhyme available and turned "Beat It" into a song about finishing your dinner. His video re-creates Jackson's famous red-leather style and adds gang members armed with utensils, which was sufficient to push Yankovic's song up to No. 12 on the *Billboard* singles chart and earn him a Grammy.

Musical verisimilitude is part of what Yankovic provides — it's a 5 form of comfort that's slightly different from comedy. With his producers and musicians, Yankovic comes up with songs that can function, in a pinch, as stand-ins for the original. He was as good at re-creating Jackson and Quincy Jones's dance-rock production (itself a slightly out-of-touch reading of the rock music of the era) as he is at mimicking the minimal beat made by the Invisible Men and the Arcade for Azalea's "Fancy." For those who feel ashamed to play a chart hit, or possibly even hate the chart hit, Yankovic offers an opportunity to have your cake and eat it. None of these parodies would work with weak songs; he chooses ones with strong melodies and distinct personalities. If you feel out of your element listening to a hip-hop song about flying around the world and cleaning out minibars, you can still enjoy the shape of Azalea's song by listening to "Handy." You're probably not going to do this publicly if you're over the age of ten, but then no song will sell this many copies in one week to pre-teens alone. There are many people listening to Weird Al on headphones at work, which makes sense, because Yankovic is never disrespectful of the music; what he's sending up is the idea that he would ever be cool enough to live in the world the music came from.

He did, however, come close to transcendent coolness when he released videos for all the songs on *Mandatory Fun*, as Beyoncé did last year with her self-titled, out-of-the-blue album; several writers pointed out the parallel. In fact, Yankovic had done that before, for *Alpocalypse*, from 2011. The only real similarity with Beyoncé is that each video has obviously been carefully planned and has its own, distinct tone. The videos have been a core part of his approach from the beginning, and this album is no different. In fact, I often find that I encounter Weird Al's music through videos rather than through singles on the radio or through full-length albums.

The video for "Word Crimes," which has been viewed more than twelve million times on YouTube, is a good example of another appealing aspect of Yankovic's work: a soft and goofy sweetness. The original song, Robin Thicke's "Blurred Lines," was a huge hit in 2013, despite the suspicion that the music was a shameless rip-off of Marvin Gaye's "Got to Give It Up." (Litigation is ongoing.) Thicke's lyrics centered on his deciding for an unnamed woman that "I know you want it," which, if not criminally coercive, sounded extremely creepy. Yankovic's video turned the video for

Thicke's song, a display of barely clad models, into an animated lesson on avoiding grammatical crudeness. Brackets and exclamation points dance as Yankovic defines contractions and counsels against using "c" to mean "see." But Yankovic never comes off as a scold. Every aspect of his art is enthusiastic and cheerful, a throwback to an earlier era of comedy and pop culture, when lightness had validity. Now every fairy-tale princess and superhero has to be drenched in blood, watching a city collapse in a fake orgasm of C.G.I. overload. Standup comedians these days are more likely to plumb the depths of their emotional dysfunction than they are to wear trick costumes or do imitations. Yankovic is comforting in the way of Bugs Bunny, or early Steve Martin.

Or in the way of *The Dr. Demento Show*, which I listened to as a kid, and on which Yankovic first aired his parodies, in the seventies. Working in a wild and wacky tone that made me cringe even then, the syndicated late-night d.j. who called himself Dr. Demento played comedy acts like the Firesign Theatre and parodies like Yankovic's. Though I eventually left behind what felt like kid stuff, kid stuff is another way of describing a thing that we know, that feels familiar and unthreatening. In a time of complete unrest, even the darkest and most grownup person will reach for something sweet and unchallenging. Funny voices and kazoos and accordions and polka serve not to entertain or delight us so much as to reassure us. Thank God, then, for the medley on Yankovic's new album, which folds in hits by anxiety-provoking young acts like Miley Cyrus and One Direction: "Now That's What I Call Polka!"

Engaging with the Text

1. According to Sasha Frere-Jones's analysis, why are Weird Al Yankovic's song parodies still so popular?

2. What **SUPPORT** does Frere-Jones offer for his analysis of Yankovic's popularity? How convincing do you find this support? Why? ▲ 111

3. How does Frere-Jones **DEFINE** "kid stuff"? How does this definition help you understand the appeal of Yankovic's music? ◆ 388–98

4. Frere-Jones refers to Bugs Bunny, early Steve Martin, and being a child of the 1970s. Given these references and other clues, how would you describe his intended **AUDIENCE**? How might the essay have been different if intended for an audience of teenagers?

57–60 ▪

94–128 ▲

5. *For Writing.* Locate one of Weird Al's music videos and do a **TEXTUAL ANALYSIS** of the song and visuals he uses. Carefully listen to the words and watch the images. What kind of listeners do you think the lyrics and video are targeted toward — what age, personality type, and so on? What effect do the lyrics and video have on you? What effect would you expect they would have on other people you know?

WILLIAM SAFIRE

A Spirit Reborn

William Safire (1929–2009) became an award-winning author and syndicated columnist after working as a speechwriter for President Richard Nixon and Vice President Spiro Agnew. His awards included a Pulitzer Prize for one of his political columns in 1978 and the Presidential Medal of Freedom in 2006, given by President George W. Bush. His last book, The Right Word in the Right Place at the Right Time *(2004), was a compilation of his weekly* On Language *columns published in the* New York Times Magazine. *For the first anniversary of the terrorist attacks of September 11, 2001, Safire published the following essay in the* Times, *analyzing what the Gettysburg Address meant to Americans after 9/11.*

ABRAHAM LINCOLN'S WORDS AT THE DEDICATION of the Gettysburg cemetery will be the speech repeated at the commemoration of September 11 by the governor of New York and by countless other speakers across the nation.

The lips of many listeners will silently form many of the famous phrases. "Four score and seven years ago" — a sonorous way of recalling the founding of the nation eighty-seven years before he spoke — is a phrase many now recite by rote, as is "the last full measure of devotion."

But the selection of this poetic political sermon as the oratorical centerpiece of our observance need not be only an exercise in historical evocation, nonpolitical correctness, and patriotic solemnity. What makes this particular speech so relevant for repetition on this first anniversary of the worst bloodbath on our territory since Antietam Creek's waters ran red is this: now, as then, a national spirit rose from the ashes of destruction.

Here is how to listen to Lincoln's all-too-familiar speech with new ears.

In those 236 words, you will hear the word *dedicate* five times. The first 5 two times refer to the nation's dedication to two ideals mentioned in the Declaration of Independence, the original ideal of "liberty" and the ideal that became central to the Civil War: "that all men are created equal."

The third, or middle, *dedication* is directed to the specific consecration of the site of the battle of Gettysburg: "to dedicate a portion of that field as a final resting place." The fourth and fifth times Lincoln repeated *dedicate* reaffirmed those dual ideals for which the dead being honored fought: "to the unfinished work" and then "to the great task remaining before us" of securing freedom and equality.

Those five pillars of dedication rested on a fundament of religious metaphor. From a president not known for his piety — indeed, often criticized for his supposed lack of faith — came a speech rooted in the theme of national resurrection. The speech is grounded in conception, birth, death, and rebirth.

Consider the barrage of images of birth in the opening sentence. The nation was "conceived in liberty" and "brought forth" — that is, delivered into life — by "our fathers" with all "created" equal. (In the nineteenth century, both "men" and "fathers" were taken to embrace women and mothers.) The nation was born.

Then, in the middle dedication, to those who sacrificed themselves, come images of death: "final resting place" and "brave men, living and dead."

Finally, the nation's spirit rises from this scene of death: "that this   10
nation, under God, shall have a new birth of freedom." Conception, birth, death, rebirth. The nation, purified in this fiery trial of war, is resurrected. Through the sacrifice of its sons, the sundered nation would be reborn as one.

An irreverent aside: All speechwriters stand on the shoulders of orators past. Lincoln's memorable conclusion was taken from a fine oration by the Reverend Theodore Parker at an 1850 Boston antislavery convention. That social reformer defined the transcendental "idea of freedom" to be "a government of all the people, by all the people, for all the people."

Lincoln, thirteen years later, dropped the "alls" and made the phrase his own. (A little judicious borrowing by presidents from previous orators shall not perish from the earth.) In delivering that final note, the Union's defender is said to have thrice stressed the noun "people" rather than the prepositions "of," "by," and "for." What is to be emphasized is

not rhetorical rhythm but the reminder that our government's legitimacy springs from America's citizens; the people, not the rulers, are sovereign. Not all nations have yet grasped that.

Do not listen on September 11 only to Lincoln's famous words and comforting cadences. Think about how Lincoln's message encompasses but goes beyond paying "fitting and proper" respect to the dead and the bereaved. His sermon at Gettysburg reminds "us the living" of our "unfinished work" and "the great task remaining before us" — to resolve that this generation's response to the deaths of thousands of our people leads to "a new birth of freedom."

Engaging with the Text

1. William Safire's main point in his textual analysis is that after 9/11, as after the "bloodbath" of the Battle of Gettysburg, "a national spirit rose from the ashes of destruction." On the basis of your memories and experiences, do you agree with this point? Why or why not?

2. Who is the intended **AUDIENCE** for this analysis? Are they expected to be familiar with the Gettysburg Address? How can you tell? How did the intended audience affect how Safire wrote this essay?

   57–60

3. Of the ending of the Gettysburg Address, Safire observes that it is "the reminder that our government's legitimacy springs from America's citizens; the people, not the rulers, are sovereign." What **EVIDENCE** does Safire offer about the use of the word *dedicate* to support this conclusion?

   359–67

4. Safire ends his analysis by declaring that Lincoln's address "reminds 'us the living' of our 'unfinished work' and 'the great task remaining before us' — to resolve that this generation's response to the deaths of thousands of our people leads to 'a new birth of freedom.'" How do you react to this ending? Has Americans' response to 9/11 led to greater freedom? How, or why not? What "unfinished work," if any, remains?

5. *For Writing.* Famous speeches live on for a reason — for what they say, how they say it, or often both. Choose one that interests you, such as Julia Gillard's "Misogyny Speech," Barack Obama's "A More Perfect Union," Hillary Clinton's "Women's Rights Are Human Rights," or John F. Kennedy's Inaugural Address, and **ANALYZE** it as Safire has the Gettysburg Address. Look at how the speaker used particular language or rhetorical **STRATEGIES** to convey a message memorably.

94–128 ▲

329 ◆

Reports **61**

697

ADAM PIORE

Why We Keep Playing the Lottery

Adam Piore (b. 1970) is a freelance journalist who focuses on science, international business, and travel. A former correspondent and editor for Newsweek, *he has also written for* Bloomberg Business, GQ, *and* Scientific American, *among other magazines. Piore is the author of* The Accidental Terrorist: A California Accountant's Coup d'Etat *(2012). The following report appeared in 2014 in* Nautilus, *which calls itself a "different kind of science magazine."*

To GRASP HOW UNLIKELY IT WAS for Gloria C. MacKenzie, an 84-year-old Florida widow, to have won the $590 million Powerball lottery in May, Robert Williams, a professor of health sciences at the University of Lethbridge in Alberta, offers this scenario: head down to your local convenience store, slap $2 on the counter, and fill out a six-numbered Powerball ticket. It will take you about 10 seconds. To get your chance of winning down to a coin toss, or 50 percent, you will need to spend 12 hours a day, every day, filling out tickets for the next 55 years. It's going be expensive. You will have to plunk down your $2 at least 86 million times.

Williams, who studies lotteries, could have simply said the odds of winning the $590 million jackpot were 1 in 175 million. But that wouldn't register. "People just aren't able to grasp 1 in 175 million," Williams says. "It's just beyond our experience — we have nothing in our evolutionary history that prepares us or primes us, no intellectual architecture, to try and grasp the remoteness of those odds." And so we continue to play. And play. People in 43 states bought a total of 232 million Powerball tickets for the lottery won by MacKenzie. In fact, the lottery in the United States is so exceedingly popular that it was one of the few consumer products where spending held steady and, in some states, increased, during the recent recession. That's still the case. About 57 percent of

Americans reported buying tickets in the last 12 months, according to a recent Gallup study. And for the 2012 fiscal year, U.S. lottery sales totaled about $78 billion, according to the North American Association of State and Provincial Lotteries.

It may seem easy to understand why we keep playing. As one trademarked lottery slogan goes, "Hey, you never know." Somebody has to win. But to really understand why hundreds of millions of people play a game they will never win, a game with serious social consequences, you have to suspend logic and consider it through an alternate set of rules — rules written by neuroscientists, social psychologists, and economists. When the odds are so small that they are difficult to conceptualize, the risk we perceive has less to do with outcomes than with how much fear or hope we are feeling when we make a decision, how we "frame" and organize sets of logical facts, and even how we perceive ourselves in relation to others. Once you know the alternate set of rules, plumb the literature, and speak to the experts, the popularity of the lottery suddenly makes a lot more sense. It's a game where reason and logic are rendered obsolete, and hope and dreams are on sale. And nobody knows how to sell hope and dreams better than Rebecca Paul Hargrove.

On most days in a nondescript office park on the outskirts of Nashville, Tennessee, you will find Hargrove reclining in a purple executive chair behind a massive desk. She occupies a corner office in the Tennessee Education State Lottery Corporation, where she serves as president.

Hargrove is a lottery legend. In the 1980s and '90s she built the state 5 lotteries in Georgia and Florida from scratch, constructing multibillion-dollar empires that soon surpassed many lotteries that had been around far longer. After two years of Hargrove's leadership, Florida was outselling every other lottery in the nation, including California, which had a population twice Florida's size. When Hargrove left Georgia for Tennessee in 2003, Georgia Lt. Gov. Mark Taylor commented, "Now I know how the Boston Red Sox fans felt. Babe Ruth has been traded to the Yankees." Hargrove, he said, was "the premier lottery executive in the country."

On a sweltering morning in June, I was ushered into Hargrove's second floor corner office. She greeted me warmly, dressed in a pink T-shirt, khaki pants, and a button-down sweater. With a mass of snowy white hair swept back in a loose bun, and a pair of glasses perched precariously on the bridge of her nose, Hargrove came across as a folksy Fairy Godmother, with a gift for schmooze. Within minutes of my arrival, she was spinning out anecdotes about her hairdresser's predilection for cat-themed instant game tickets and the little old lady who lives down the block from her mother and won $56 million.

> It's a game where reason and logic are rendered obsolete, and hope and dreams are on sale.

Hargrove has an intuitive understanding of what drives her customers to play the game. She has a preternatural sense of where their psychological buttons are located and how to push them. She responded in a flash to my comment about the logical futility of playing the lottery. "If you made a logical investment choice, you'd play a different game," she said, leaning forward for emphasis. "It's not an investment. It's entertainment. For a very small amount of money you might *change your life*. For $2 you can spend the day dreaming about what you would do with half a billion dollars — half a billion dollars!"

In 1985, when Illinois Governor James Thompson tapped Hargrove to head the state lottery, she didn't know much about the business. But

academic literacies | rhetorical situations | genres | processes | strategies | research MLA / APA | media / design | readings

the former beauty queen (Miss Indiana 1972, Miss America finalist 1973) did know a thing or two about selling a product. After winning a TV job doing the weekend weather at an ABC affiliate in her hometown of Indianapolis, she moved to Springfield, Illinois, to work for an NBC affiliate. In Springfield, she recruited her own TV advertisers and produced her own commercials, demonstrating a natural talent for marketing. She got involved in politics and rose to Illinois Republican State Party Chairwoman, before taking over the Illinois lottery.

In her new job, Hargrove did what any savvy marketer would do: She sat down and thought about her own motivations. "I played the lotto when I was caught up in the frenzy of a $40 million jackpot," she said. "And I thought, 'What made me play?' What made me play was the thought of what I would do with $40 million. You pay $1 and then for three days you can think about that question. Would I share with my brother-in-law? No! I don't like that brother-in-law. But I would share with my neighbor's nephew."

With that simple insight, Hargrove struck marketing gold. More than 10 200 ads went up on billboards across the state. "How to Get from Washington Boulevard to Easy Street," read one in a poor Chicago neighborhood, displaying a picture of a tantalizing pile of lotto money. Hargrove also pushed for larger, attention grabbing jackpots. In 1987, she played a key role in creating a multistate lottery, consisting of nine states and the District of Columbia, so that jackpots could balloon to as much as $80 million. The excitement generated by the eye-popping jackpots, she figured, would generate more excitement than any one state could create on its own. "The more the jackpot is, the more tickets you sell," she said. "It feeds the dreaming."

From her first days in the lottery business, Hargrove learned to make the lottery fantasy tangible by making sure that winning, on a smaller scale, is something people experience. "If you play a lot and you play for three years and you never win, you're not going to keep playing," Hargrove said.

In Illinois, Hargrove experimented with smaller prizes, which had better odds of winning than the big state lottos. When she introduced a second weekly lotto drawing, she saw an immediate 5 percent spike in sales. To prevent player burnout, Hargrove pioneered games with different prices, designs, and themes. She might trot a game where you scratch off cute cats for cat lovers, and a game with footballs for Bears fans. She might sell four leaf clovers on St. Patrick's Day, and reindeer-themed tickets around Christmas. The odds of winning may remain remote, but keeping it "fresh" and "exciting" added a sense of possibility and made it more fun, she said. Hargrove knew that game cards were impulse buys, so she emphasized point-of-purchase advertising. She pushed to make the cards as ubiquitous as "bubble gum."

Sitting in her Tennessee office, her energy never flagging, Hargrove stressed the lottery raised millions to fund educational programs for the state's children, and that was something that should always be apparent. The direct link to education "affects everything — it affects how the legislators feel, it affects how the playing public feels about it, it affects how the press feels about you," she said. "All those things add up to a positive experience buying a lottery ticket."

While Hargrove's feel-good marketing goes a long way toward explaining why we keep playing the lottery, scientists are increasingly making it clear how lottery marketing taps into our brains and impacts our communities.

Selling the lottery dream is possible because, paradoxically, the probabilities of winning are so infinitesimal they become irrelevant. Our brains didn't evolve to calculate complex odds. In our evolutionary past, the ability to distinguish between a region with a 1 percent or 10 percent chance of being attacked by a predator wouldn't have offered much of an advantage. An intuitive and coarse method of categorization, such as "doesn't happen," "happen sometimes," "happens most of time," "always happens," would have sufficed, explains Jane L. Risen, an associate professor of Behavioral Science at the University of Chicago, Booth School of Business, who studies decision-making. Despite our advances in reason and mathematics, she says, we still often rely on crude calculations to make decisions, especially quick decisions like buying a lottery ticket.

In the conceptual vacuum created by incomprehensible odds, people are likely to experience magical thinking or superstition, play a hunch, or simply throw reason out the window all together, says George Loewenstein, a professor of economics and psychology at Carnegie Mellon. "Most of the weird stuff that you see with decision-making and risk happens with small probabilities," he says.

> Selling the lottery dream is possible because, paradoxically, the probabilities of winning are so infinitesimal they become irrelevant.

One reason may be that uncertainty activates a network of brain areas that push us reflexively to find a resolution. Uncertainty for the brain is a negative state, and so it screams, "'I don't know what to do, I don't know how to act, my organism is at risk,'" says Giorgio Coricelli, an associate professor of economics and psychology at University of Southern California. "To make the choice, your brain automatically looks for suggestions, searches for more information, and if there is little information, we can make strange associations, assume something is realistic, even if it is superstitious."

There is plenty of historical research to correlate the rise of religion and superstition with uncertainty, Coricelli says. In the same way, he adds, when there is little we can do to raise a probability, we are just as likely to play the lucky number 7 or insist on buying our lottery ticket at a certain time of day to raise our chance of winning.

Our proclivity for fantasy makes us an easy target for advertising. Lottery commercials depict winners in stretch limousines, counting stacks of money, dressed in evening gowns and tuxedos, sipping champagne.

The commercials hit home because fantasizing about winning the lottery activates the same parts of our brains that would be activated if we actually won, notes Daniel Levine, professor of psychology at the University of Texas at Arlington, and an expert on decision theory and neural networks. Picturing ourselves in a limo activates visual areas of the brain, while imagining the clink of champagne glasses lights up the auditory cortex. These areas have links to the brain regions involved in emotion, decision-making, and motivation. "The motivational areas of the brain can be heavily influenced by vivid daydreaming," Levine says.

20

"Just like seeing something can activate the emotional system, so can envisioning it."

But even fantasy will drop its hold on us if we always lose — a point Hargrove grasped from the start. Research has shown that positive reinforcement is a key in virtually all of the successful lotteries, notes the University of Lethbridge's Williams. Lotteries that allow players to choose combinations of four or five numbers from a total of 60 numbers are popular, he says, because many players experience "the near miss," which creates the illusion that they came close to winning the multimillion-dollar jackpot. Most players don't realize, however, that "near-miss" is an illusion. The odds of winning get worse with each successive match.

academic literacies
rhetorical situations
genres
processes
strategies
research MLA / APA
media / design
readings

Another important factor comes into play as we step up to the cash register at the convenience store: self-image. Lottery sales, it turns out, are heavily influenced by the way we are thinking about the purchase, and the way we perceive ourselves in relation to others when we do.

Carnegie Mellon's Loewenstein and colleagues demonstrated it's possible to change how many lottery tickets people will buy by making them think — or not think — about their purchase in a larger context. The researchers gave one group of study participants $1 at a time, five times, and asked them if they wanted to buy a lottery ticket. They gave a second group $5 and asked how many tickets they wanted, while a third group received $5 and was told they had only two choices: they could spend it all on tickets or not buy any tickets at all. The people in the first group purchased twice as many tickets as those asked explicitly what percentage of the $5 they wanted to spend on tickets. Members of the all or nothing group opted for no tickets 87 percent of the time.

One of the things the experiment shows is that lottery players are often "thinking myopically," says Romel Mostafa, who co-authored the 2008 study with Loewenstein, and is now an Assistant Professor of Business, Economics, and Public Policy at Ivey Business School, Western University. "We think about these purchases in one or two at a time. But when the decisions aggregate over time, it adds up. And if I were to bracket the spending over a longer period of time, I would not have bought it in the first place."

This same "framing" phenomenon also helps explain our misper-   25
ception of the risk. Most people "frame" the lottery as "Boy, I could win $100 million," rather than considering what they might lose, says Princeton economist Hank Farber. "To them a dollar seems inconsequential," he says.

It's not just the way we frame the odds in the lottery that can affect how likely we are to play the game. It turns out that the way we frame our own economic status can also play a role in our decision to play the lottery.

Mostafa, Loewenstein, and colleagues designed a study to examine the influence that "feeling poor" has on the decision to play the lottery. They approached people at the Pittsburgh Greyhound Bus Depot (who had an average income of $29,228) and asked them to fill out a questionnaire about "community issues." Much of the survey was just window dressing. The only thing researchers cared about were two different versions of multiple choice answers offered for a single question, "How much money do you make." Half received questionnaires with the categories: "less than $10,000, less than $20,000, less than $30,000." The other half were presented with choices designed to make them feel poor. The categories included "less than $100,000," "less than $200,000," and "less than $300,000."

After completing the questionnaires, the participants were paid $5 and asked if they wanted to use any of the money to buy lottery tickets. Those who had been made to feel poor bought twice as many lottery tickets as those in the control group, the authors wrote in a 2008 study published in the *Journal of Behavioral Decision Making*.

> The commercials hit home because fantasizing about winning the lottery activates the same parts of our brains that would be activated if we actually won.

"The lottery is a way to raise the ceiling on what can happen to you," says Loewenstein. "So if you are reminded of your poverty, it makes the idea of lifting the poverty a more salient motive. Lottery tickets become that much more attractive at that moment."

For many poor people, he adds, there is "no scenario they can come up with in which they are suddenly going to get very rich." To them, the lottery may be a low probability event — but so is getting a job that pays six figures.

That point is driven home by a 2006 Consumer Federation of America study, which surveyed 1,000 adult Americans about their personal views on wealth. The survey found that 21 percent of Americans — 38 percent of whom had incomes below $25,000 — thought that winning the lottery represented the "most practical" way for them to accumulate several hundred thousand dollars.

"A lot of people say that the lottery is a regressive tax, which is true," Loewenstein says, referring to taxes that aren't pegged to income, and take a larger proportion of income from those who can least afford it. (A person who makes $15,000 a year and buys $1,500 worth of lottery tickets has spent 10 percent of his income, while a person who makes

$150,000 and buys $1,500 has spent only 1 percent.) "It is true that poor people spend a substantially higher fraction of their income on lottery tickets" than the affluent, he notes. "But I don't think it is necessarily irrational. Buying lottery tickets is a fairly inexpensive way of raising the ceiling on what can happen to you economically." In other words, when your economic prospects are dim, buying hope makes sense.

How we perceive ourselves in relation to others also shapes our decision to play the lottery — a lever the industry consistently pulls. A salient example is the "Postcode Lottery" in the Netherlands. Weekly it awards a "Street Prize" to one postal code, the Dutch equivalent of a zip code, chosen at random. When a postal code (usually about 25 houses on a street) is drawn, everybody who has played the lottery in that code wins about

> "There is no scenario that poor people can come up with in which they are suddenly going to get very rich."

$12,500 or more. Those living there who neglected to buy a ticket prior to the drawing win nothing — except the chance to watch their neighbors celebrate. In secondary drawings, many of those who purchased tickets in the winning postcode win BMWs, and are eligible to win as much as $14 million — $7 million for one lucky winner picked from within the winning postcode, and $7 million for their immediate neighbors who bought tickets.

In a 2003 study, researchers in the Departments of Economic and Social Psychology, and Marketing at Tilbrug University in the Netherlands, noted fear of regret played a significantly larger role in the Postcode Lottery than in a regular lottery. It was not the chance of winning that drove the players to buy tickets, the researchers found, it was the idea that they might be forced to sit on the sidelines contemplating missed opportunity. The promoters of the postcode lottery seemed well aware of that. One mailer read: "Sour, that is how it feels when you miss an amount of at least 2 million by just an inch. Because seeing a multimillion prize fall on your own address, but winning nothing since you did not buy a ticket, that is something that you do not want to experience."

"The brain is very sensitive to loss — even low probability losses," 35 explains USC's Coricelli. "So if you frame something as a loss, biologically there is a compulsion to avoid it. We have an aversion to it."

In fact, says Levine of the University of Texas, we are hardwired to evaluate gains or losses based not on their own terms, but in comparison with other people. "If you don't see anybody in a limo, you can be perfectly happy with your Honda Civic," Levine says. "But if you do, you might feel less happy with what you have. It is a comparison. You can manipulate people into potentially feeling regret when they see other people getting more than they have."

In the end, fear and regret are the flipsides of hope and dreams — all are powerful emotions that when tapped can cause us to relinquish rationality, to act on instinct, even to make decisions that might not be in our best interest. As I left Hargrove's office and drove along the Tennessee Interstate toward the airport, I scanned the highway for the giant Powerball billboards that she had touted as the best marketing tool in her arsenal. She didn't need many words to get her message across, as the billboard that week trumpeted, in 10-foot-high digital numbers, a $100 million jackpot. I couldn't help but think, as I drove along, "What would I do with that much money?"

Engaging with the Text

1. What, according to Adam Piore, makes playing the lottery so attractive? If you play, why do you? If not, why not?

2. What kind of **RESEARCH** does Piore offer to support his claims in this report? Do you find these kinds of research to be trustworthy? Why or why not? If he had also interviewed lottery winners or people who regularly play the lottery, how would these primary sources have affected his report? What if he had relied only on such interviews?

3. Reports typically avoid giving an opinion on their subject, yet Piore's opinion on playing the lottery seems rather clear. How would you describe his **STANCE** toward his subject? Identify at least one passage where it is clear.

433

64–67

academic literacies | rhetorical situations | genres | processes | strategies | research MLA / APA | media / design | readings

4. Piore turns to neuroscientists, social psychologists, and economists to explore why people play the lottery despite the dismal odds of winning. What are two of the specific **CAUSES AND EFFECTS** that Piore identifies as contributing to lotteries' popularity? Do these causal analyses make sense to you? Why or why not? Did any of them surprise you?

   350–54

5. *For Writing.* Why do we do what we do? This is a timeless question. Consider why you or your friends do something: listen to a certain kind of music, eat a certain food, use a certain technology, or wear a certain fashion. Research the topic by interviewing several people who do the same thing, and search the web for studies on it. (You might also speak with a professor in psychology or sociology about the reasons.) Then write a **REPORT** on what you find.

   129–55

ELEANOR J. BADER

Homeless on Campus

Eleanor J. Bader is a freelance writer and an instructor in the English Department at Kingsborough Community College in Brooklyn, New York. She is also the coauthor of Targets of Hatred: Anti-Abortion Terrorism *(2001). The following report appeared in the* Progressive, *a liberal political magazine, in 2004. As you read, notice how Bader effectively incorporates specific examples to support the information she reports.*

AESHA IS A TWENTY-YEAR-OLD at Kingsborough Community College in Brooklyn, New York. Until the fall of 2003, she lived with five people — her one-year-old son, her son's father, her sister, her mother, and her mother's boyfriend — in a three-bedroom South Bronx apartment. Things at home were fine until her child's father became physically abusive. Shortly thereafter, Aesha realized that she and her son had to leave the unit.

After spending thirty days in a temporary shelter, they landed at the city's emergency assistance unit (EAU). "It was horrible," Aesha says. "We slept on benches, and it was very crowded. I was so scared I sat on my bag and held onto the stroller day and night, from Friday to Monday." Aesha and her son spent several nights in the EAU before being sent to a hotel. Sadly, this proved to be a temporary respite. After a few days, they were returned to the EAU, where they remained until they were finally moved to a family shelter in Queens.

Although Aesha believes that she will be able to stay in this facility until she completes her associate's degree, the ordeal of being homeless has taken a toll on her and her studies. "I spend almost eight hours a day on the trains," she says. "I have to leave the shelter at 5:00 a.m. for the Bronx where my girlfriend watches my son for me. I get to her house around 7:00. Then I have to travel to school in Brooklyn — the last stop on the train followed by a bus ride — another two hours away."

Reluctantly, Aesha felt that she had no choice but to confide in teachers and explain her periodic absences. "They've all said that as long as I keep up with the work I'll be OK," she says. But that is not easy for Aesha or other homeless students.

Adriana Broadway lived in ten places, with ten different families, during high school. A native of Sparks, Nevada, Broadway told the LeTendre Education Fund for Homeless Children, a scholarship program administered by the National Association for the Education of Homeless Children and Youth, that she left home when she was thirteen. "For five years, I stayed here and there with friends," she wrote on her funding application. "I'd stay with whoever would take me in and allow me to live under their roof."

Johnny Montgomery also became homeless in his early teens. He told LeTendre staffers that his mother threw him out because he did not get along with her boyfriend. "She chose him over me," he wrote. "Hard days and nights have shaped me." Much of that time was spent on the streets.

Asad Dahir has also spent time on the streets. "I've been homeless more than one time and in more than one country," Dahir wrote on his scholarship application. Originally from Somalia, he and his family fled their homeland due to civil war and ended up in a refugee camp in neighboring Kenya. After more than a year in the camp, he and his thirteen-year-old brother were resettled, first in Atlanta and later in Ohio. There, high housing costs once again rendered the pair homeless.

Broadway, Montgomery, and Dahir are three of the forty-four homeless students from across the country who have been awarded LeTendre grants since 1999. Thanks, in part, to these funds, all three have been attending college and doing well.

But few homeless students are so lucky. "Each year at our national conference, homeless students come forward to share their stories," says Jenn Hecker, the organizing director of the National Student Campaign Against Hunger and Homelessness. "What often comes through is shame. Most feel as though they should be able to cover their costs." Such students usually try to blend in and are reluctant to disclose either their poverty or homelessness to others on campus, she says. Hecker blames rising housing costs for the problem and cites a 2003 survey that found the median wage needed to pay for a two-bedroom apartment in the United States to be $15.21, nearly three times the federal minimum.

Even when doubled up, students in the most expensive states — Massachusetts, California, New Jersey, New York, and Maryland — are scrambling. "In any given semester, there are four or five families where the head of household is in college," says Beth Kelly, a family service counselor at the Clinton Family Inn, a New York City transitional housing program run by Homes for the Homeless. 10

Advocates for the homeless report countless examples of students sleeping in their cars and sneaking into a school gym to shower and change clothes. They speak of students who couch surf or camp in the woods — bicycling or walking to classes — during temperate weather. Yet, for all the anecdotes, details about homeless college students are hazy.

"I wish statistics existed on the number of homeless college students," says Barbara Duffield, executive director of the National Association for the Education of Homeless Children and Youth. "Once state and federal responsibility to homeless kids stops — at the end of high school — it's as if they cease to exist. They fall off the map."

Worse, they are neither counted nor attended to.

"Nobody has ever thought about this population or collected data on them because nobody thinks they are a priority to study," says Martha Burt, principal research associate at the Urban Institute.

Critics say colleges are not doing enough to meet — or even recognize — the needs of this group. 15

"The school should do more," says Aesha. "They have a child care center on my campus, but they only accept children two and up. It would have helped if I could've brought my son to day care at school." She also believes that the college should maintain emergency housing for homeless students.

"As an urban community college, our students are commuters," responds Uda Bradford, interim dean of student affairs at Kingsborough Community College. "Therefore, our student support services are developed within that framework."

"As far as I know, no college has ever asked for help in reaching homeless students," says Mary Jean LeTendre, a retired Department of

academic literacies   rhetorical situations   genres   processes   strategies   research MLA / APA   media / design   readings

Education administrator and creator of the LeTendre Education Fund. "Individual colleges have come forward to help specific people, but there is nothing systematic like there is for students in elementary and high school."

"There is a very low awareness level amongst colleges," Duffield adds. "People have this 'you can pull yourself up by your bootstraps' myth about college. There is a real gap between the myth and the reality for those who are trying to overcome poverty by getting an education."

Part of the problem is that the demographics of college attendance 20 have changed. "Most educational institutions were set up to serve fewer, less diverse, more privileged students," says Andrea Leskes, a vice president with the Association of American Colleges and Universities. "As a result, we are not successfully educating all the students who come to college today. This means that nontraditional students — the older, returning ones as well as those from low income or other disenfranchised communities — often receive inadequate support services."

"It's not that colleges are not concerned, but attention today is not on serving the poor," says Susan O'Malley, chair of the faculty senate at the City University of New York. "It's not in fashion. During the 1960s, people from all over the country were going to Washington and making a lot of noise. The War on Poverty was influenced by this noise. Now the poor are less visible."

Mary Gesing, a counselor at Kirkwood Community College in Cedar Rapids, Iowa, agrees. "Nothing formal exists for this population, and the number of homeless students on campus is not tracked," she says. Because of this statistical gap, programs are not devised to accommodate homeless students or address their needs.

Despite these programmatic shortfalls, Gesing encounters two to three homeless students — often single parents — each semester. Some became homeless when they left an abuser. Others lost their housing because they could no longer pay for it due to a lost job, the termination of unemployment benefits, illness, the cessation of child support, or drug or alcohol abuse.

Kirkwood's approach is a "patchwork system," Gesing explains, and homeless students often drop out or fail classes because no one knows of their plight. "When people don't know who to come to for help they just fade away," she says.

"Without housing, access to a workspace, or access to a shower, 25 students' lives suffer, their grades suffer, and they are more likely to drop classes, if not withdraw entirely from school. I've seen it happen," says Amit Rai, an English professor at a large, public university in Florida. "If seen from the perspective of students, administrators would place affordable housing and full access to health care at the top of what a university should provide."

Yet for all this, individual teachers — as well as administrators and counselors — can sometimes make an enormous difference.

B.R., a faculty member who asked that neither her name nor school be disclosed, has allowed several homeless students to sleep in her office during the past decade. "Although there is no institutional interest or involvement in keeping these students enrolled, a few faculty members really care about the whole student and don't shy away from helping," she says.

One of the students she sheltered lived in the space for three months, whenever she couldn't stay with friends. Like Aesha, this student was fleeing a partner who beat her. Another student had been kicked out of the dorm because her stepfather never paid the bill. She applied for financial assistance to cover the cost, but processing took months. "This student stayed in my office for an entire semester," B.R. says.

A sympathetic cleaning woman knew what was going on and turned a blind eye to the arrangement. "Both students showered in the dorms and kept their toothbrushes and cosmetics in one of the two department bathrooms which I gave them keys to," B.R. adds. "The administration never knew a thing. Both of the students finished school and went on to become social workers. They knew that school would be their saving grace, that knowledge was the only thing that couldn't be snatched."

Engaging with the Text

1. This piece reports on the general topic of homeless college students. What is Eleanor J. Bader's specific point? How do you know? How else could she have made her point explicit?

2. Bader's **PURPOSE** in this report is to make visible college students who are homeless and to report on some of the causes. How does this purpose affect the way the report is written? Point to specific examples from the text in your response.

   ■ 55–56

3. Bader **ENDS** her essay with a powerful quote from a teacher she calls B.R.: "[The students] knew that school would be their saving grace, that knowledge was the only thing that couldn't be snatched." What does B.R. mean by this observation? In what ways can an education help such students, and in what ways might it be misleading to think that an education alone will solve all of their problems?

   ◆ 338–42

4. Consider the number of **NARRATIVES** in this report. Why do you think Bader includes so many? What other kinds of **WELL-RESEARCHED INFORMATION** does she include, if any? What additional kinds of information might she have used to help accomplish her purpose?

   ◆ 419–27
   ▲ 145

5. *For Writing.* You may not be aware of some student services that are readily available on your campus. Choose one service your school provides, and do some research to learn who uses it and whether they're satisfied with it or think it could be improved. Write a **REPORT** on your findings. As an alternative, you may want to deliver your report as a website.

   ▲ 129–55

JONATHAN KOZOL

Fremont High School

*An educator, activist, and award-winning writer, Jonathan Kozol (b. 1936)
is known for his work as an advocate for social justice and public educa-
tion. He is the author of over a dozen books, including* Fire in the Ashes:
Twenty-Five Years among the Poorest Children in America *(2012) and*
The Shame of the Nation: The Restoration of Apartheid Schooling in
America *(2005), from which the following selection is taken. In this piece,
Kozol reports on one of the many schools he studied to write this book.*

FREMONT HIGH SCHOOL IN LOS ANGELES enrolls almost 5,000 students
on a three-track schedule, with about 3,300 in attendance at a given
time. The campus "sprawls across a city block, between San Pedro Street
and Avalon Boulevard in South Central Los Angeles," the *Los Angeles
Times* observes. A "neighborhood fortress, its perimeter protected by an
eight-foot steel fence topped by spikes," the windows of the school are
"shielded from gunfire by thick screens." According to teachers at the
school, the average ninth grade student reads at fourth or fifth grade
level. Nearly a third read at third grade level or below. About two thirds
of the ninth grade students drop out prior to twelfth grade.

There were 27 homerooms for the first-year students, nine homerooms for seniors at the time I visited in spring of 2003. Thirty-five to
40 classrooms, nearly a third of all the classrooms in the school, were
located in portables. Some classes also took place in converted storage
closets — "windowless and nasty," said one of the counselors — or in converted shop rooms without blackboards. Class size was high, according
to a teacher who had been here for six years and who invited me into
her tenth grade social studies class. Nearly 220 classes had enrollments
ranging between 33 and over 40 students. The class I visited had 40 students, almost all of whom were present on the day that I was there.

Unlike the staggered luncheon sessions I observed at Walton High,
lunch was served in a single sitting to the students in this school. "It's
physically impossible to feed 3,300 kids at once," the teacher said. "The

The school's slogan at the front entrance projects a positive outlook.

line for kids to get their food is very long and the entire period lasts only 30 minutes. It takes them 15 minutes just to walk there from their classes and get through the line. They get 10 minutes probably to eat their meals. A lot of them don't try. You've been a teacher, so you can imagine what it does to students when they have no food to eat for an entire day. The schoolday here at Fremont is eight hours long."

For teachers, too, the schedule sounded punishing. "I have six classes every day, including my homeroom," she said. "I've had *more* than 40 students in a class some years. My average class this year is 36. I see more than 200 students every day. Classes start at seven-thirty. I don't usually leave until four or four-thirty. . . . "

High school students, when I meet them first, are often more reluc- 5 tant than the younger children are to open up their feelings and express their personal concerns; but hesitation on the part of students did not prove to be a problem in this class at Fremont High. The students knew

The perimeter is protected by an eight-foot steel fence topped by spikes.

I was a writer (they were told this by their teacher) and they took no time in getting down to matters that were on their minds.

"Can we talk about the bathrooms?" asked a student named Mireya.

In almost any classroom there are certain students who, by force of the directness or unusual sophistication of their way of speaking, tend to capture your attention from the start. Mireya later spoke insightfully of academic problems, at the school, but her observations on the physical and personal embarrassments she and her schoolmates had to undergo cut to the heart of questions of essential dignity or the denial of such dignity that kids in squalid schools like this one have to deal with.

Fremont High School, as court papers document, has "15 fewer bathrooms than the law requires." Of the limited number of bathrooms that are working in the school, "only one or two . . . are open and unlocked for girls to use." Long lines of girls are "waiting to use the bathrooms," which are generally "unclean" and "lack basic supplies," including toilet paper. Some of the classrooms "do not have air-conditioning," so that students

"become red-faced and unable to concentrate" during "the extreme heat of summer." The rats observed by children in their elementary schools proliferate at Fremont High as well. "Rats in eleven . . . classrooms," maintenance records of the school report. "Rat droppings" are recorded "in the bins and drawers" of the high school's kitchen. "Hamburger buns" are being "eaten off [the] bread-delivery rack," school records note.

No matter how many times I read these tawdry details in court filings and depositions, I'm always surprised again to learn how often these unsanitary physical conditions are permitted to continue in a public school even after media accounts describe them vividly. But hearing of these conditions in Mireya's words was even more unsettling, in part because this student was so fragile-seeming and because the need even to speak of these indignities in front of me and all the other students seemed like an additional indignity.

"The problem is this," she carefully explained. "You're not allowed to 10 use the bathroom during lunch, which is a 30-minute period. The only time that you're allowed to use it is between your classes." But "this is a huge building," she went on. "It has long corridors. If you have one class at one end of the building and your next class happens to be way down at the other end, you don't have time to use the bathroom and still get to class before it starts. So you go to your class and then you ask permission from your teacher to go to the bathroom and the teacher tells you, 'No. You had your chance between the periods. . . . '

"I feel embarrassed when I have to stand there and explain it to a teacher."

"This is the question," said a wiry-looking boy named Edward, leaning forward in his chair close to the door, a little to the right of where I stood. "Students are not animals, but even animals need to relieve themselves sometimes. We're in this building for eight hours. What do they think we're supposed to do?"

"It humiliates you," said Mireya, who went on to make the interesting statement that "the school provides solutions that don't actually work," and this idea was taken up by other students in describing course requirements within the school. A tall black student, for example, told me that she hoped to be a social worker or a doctor but was programmed into "Sewing Class" this year. She also had to take another course, called

"Life Skills," which she told me was a very basic course — "a retarded class," to use her words — that "teaches things like the six continents," which she said she'd learned in elementary school.

When I asked her why she had to take these courses, she replied that she'd been told they were required, which reminded me of the response the sewing teacher I had met at Roosevelt Junior High School gave to the same question. As at Roosevelt, it turned out that this was not exactly so. What was required was that high school students take two courses in an area of study that was called "the Technical Arts," according to the teacher. At schools that served the middle class or upper middle class, this requirement was likely to be met by courses that had academic substance and, perhaps, some relevance to college preparation. At Beverly Hills High School, for example, the technical arts requirement could be fulfilled by taking subjects such as residential architecture, the designing of commercial structures, broadcast journalism, advanced computer graphics, a sophisticated course in furniture design, carving and sculpture, or an honors course in engineering research and design. At Fremont High, in contrast, this requirement was far more likely to be met by courses that were basically vocational.

Mireya, for example, who had plans to go to college, told me that she 15 had to take a sewing class last year and now was told she'd been assigned to take a class in hair-dressing as well. When I asked the teacher why Mireya could not skip these subjects and enroll in classes that would help her to pursue her college aspirations, she replied, "It isn't a question of what students want. It's what the school may have available. If all the other elective classes that a student wants to take are full, she has to take one of these classes if she wants to graduate."

A very small girl named Obie who had big blue-tinted glasses tilted up across her hair interrupted then to tell me with a kind of wild gusto that she took hair-dressing *twice*! When I expressed surprise that this was possible, she said there were two levels of hair-dressing offered here at Fremont High. "One is in hair-styling," she said. "The other is in braiding."

Mireya stared hard at this student for a moment and then suddenly began to cry. "I don't *want* to take hair-dressing. I did not need sewing

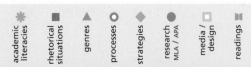

academic literacies · rhetorical situations · genres · processes · strategies · research MLA / APA · media / design · readings

either. I knew how to sew. My mother is a seamstress in a factory. I'm trying to go to college. I don't need to sew to go to college. My mother sews. I hoped for something else."

"What would you rather take?" I asked.

"I wanted to take an AP class," she answered.

Mireya's sudden tears elicited a strong reaction from one of the boys 20 who had been silent up to now. A thin and dark-eyed student, named Fortino, with long hair down to his shoulders who was sitting on the left side of the classroom, he turned directly to Mireya.

"Listen to me," he said. "The owners of the sewing factories need laborers. Correct?"

"I guess they do," Mireya said.

"It's not going to be their own kids. Right?"

"Why not?" another student said.

"So they can grow beyond themselves," Mireya answered quietly. 25 "But we remain the same."

"You're ghetto," said Fortino, "so we send you to the factory." He sat low in his desk chair, leaning on one elbow, his voice and dark eyes loaded with a cynical intelligence. "You're ghetto — so you sew!"

"There are higher positions than these," said a student named Samantha.

"You're ghetto," said Fortino unrelentingly to her. "So sew!"

Mireya was still crying.

Several students spoke then of a problem about frequent substitute 30 teachers, which was documented also in court papers. One strategy for staffing classes in these three- and four-track schools when substitutes could not be found was to assign a teacher who was not "on track" — that is, a teacher who was on vacation — to come back to school and fill in for the missing teacher. "Just yesterday I was subbing [for] a substitute who was subbing for a teacher who never shows up," a teacher told the ACLU lawyers. "That's one scenario. . . . "

Obie told me that she stopped coming to class during the previous semester because, out of her six teachers, three were substitutes. "Come on now! Like — hello? We live in a rich country? Like the richest country in the world? Hello?"

The teacher later told me that three substitutes in one semester, if the student's words were accurate, would be unusual. But "on average, every student has a substitute teacher in at least one class. Out of 180 teacher-slots, typically 25 or so cannot be filled and have to be assigned to substitutes."

Hair-dressing and sewing, it turned out, were not the only classes students at the school were taking that appeared to have no relevance to academic education. A number of the students, for example, said that they were taking what were known as "service classes" in which they would sit in on an academic class but didn't read the texts or do the lessons or participate in class activities but passed out books and did small errands for the teachers. They were given half-credits for these courses. Students received credits, too, for jobs they took outside of school, in fast-food restaurants for instance, I was told. How, I wondered, was a credit earned or grade determined for a job like this outside of school? "Best behavior and great customer service," said a student who was working in a restaurant, as she explained the logic of it all to ACLU lawyers in her deposition.

The teacher gave some other examples of the ways in which the students were shortchanged in academic terms. The year-round calendar, she said, gave these students 20 fewer schooldays than the students who attended school on normal calendars receive. In compensation, they attended classes for an extra hour, up until three-thirty, and students in the higher grades who had failed a course and had to take a make-up class remained here even later, until six, or sometimes up to nine.

"They come out of it just totally glassed-over," said the teacher, and, 35 as one result, most teachers could not realistically give extra homework to make up for fewer days of school attendance and, in fact, because the kids have been in school so long each day, she said, "are likely to give less."

Students who needed to use the library to do a research paper for a class ran into problems here as well, because, as a result of the tight scheduling of classes, they were given no free time to use the library except at lunch, or for 30 minutes after school, unless a teacher chose to bring a class into the library to do a research project during a class period. But this was frequently impossible because the library was often closed when it was being

academic literacies rhetorical situations genres processes strategies research MLA / APA media / design readings

used for other purposes such as administration of examinations, typically for "make-up tests," as I was told. "It's been closed now for a week because they're using it for testing," said Samantha.

"They were using it for testing last week also," said Fortino, who reported that he had a research paper due for which he had to locate 20 sources but had made no progress on it yet because he could not get into the library.

"You have to remember," said the teacher, "that the school's in session all year long, so if repairs need to be made in wiring or something like that in the library, they have to do it while the kids are here. So at those times the library is closed. Then, if there's testing taking place in there, the library is closed. And if an AP teacher needs a place to do an AP prep, the library is closed. And sometimes when the teachers need a place to meet, the library is closed." In all, according to the school librarian, the library is closed more than a quarter of the year.

During a meeting with a group of teachers later in the afternoon, it was explained to me in greater detail how the overcrowding of the building limited course offerings for students. "Even when students *ask* to take a course that interests them and teachers want to teach it," said one member of the faculty — she gave the example of a class in women's studies she said she would like to teach — "the physical shortages of space repeatedly prevent this." Putting students into service classes, on the other hand, did not require extra space. So, instead of the enrichment students might have gained from taking an elective course that had some academic substance, they were obliged to sit through classes in which they were not enrolled and from which they said that they learned virtually nothing.

Mireya had asked her teacher for permission to stay in the room   40
with us during my meeting with the other teachers and remained right to the end. At five p.m., as I was about to leave the school, she stood beside the doorway of the classroom as the teacher, who was giving me a ride, assembled all the work she would be taking home.

"Why is it," she asked, "that students who do not need what we need get so much more? And we who need it so much more get so much less?"

I told her I'd been asking the same question now for nearly 40 years and still had no good answer. She answered, maturely, that she did not think there was an answer.

Engaging with the Text

344–45

1. The **TITLE** of the book in which this essay appears is *The Shame of the Nation: The Restoration of Apartheid Schooling in America.* How does this piece illuminate and support the book title? Based on your reading of Jonathan Kozol's report, what is the "shame of the nation," and how is "apartheid schooling" taking place in the United States even though schools were legally desegregated over forty years ago?

55–56

2. What is the **PURPOSE** of Kozol's report? What do you think Kozol hopes will happen because of it? Given this purpose, who is the most important audience for this piece?

145
359–67

3. How does Kozol demonstrate that his information is **ACCURATE** and **WELL RESEARCHED**? What kinds of **EVIDENCE** does he use to support his points? To what degree do you find his information accurate?

338–42

4. Reread the final three paragraphs of Kozol's report. How effective is this **ENDING**? Do you think Kozol believes there is no answer to Mireya's question? Why or why not?

463–64

5. *For Writing.* Research a public high school near where you live — the school you attended or one near your college. Get permission from the school principal to **INTERVIEW** several teachers and students about their experiences with the curriculum, recreation facilities, lunch room, school library, and class sizes. Locate any recent newspaper accounts or school reports to supplement and verify the information you obtain from your interviews. Write a **REPORT** that **COMPARES** what

129–55
380–87

you find out about the high school you researched with what Kozol reports about Fremont High. In what ways are the problems similar and in what ways are they different?

※ academic literacies   ■ rhetorical situations   ▲ genres   ○ processes   ◆ strategies   ● research MLA / APA   ▢ media / design   ▌ readings

ALINA TUGEND

Multitasking Can Make You Lose . . . Um . . . Focus

Alina Tugend (b. 1959) is a columnist for the Business section of the New York Times *and the author of* Better by Mistake: The Unexpected Benefits of Being Wrong *(2011). Her work has also appeared in the* Los Angeles Times, *the* Atlantic, Family Circle, *and other publications. This report on multitasking was published in the* New York Times *in 2008.*

AS YOU ARE READING THIS ARTICLE, are you listening to music or the radio? Yelling at your children? If you are looking at it online, are you e-mailing or instant-messaging at the same time? Checking stocks?

Since the 1990s, we've accepted multitasking without question. Virtually all of us spend part or most of our day either rapidly switching from one task to another or juggling two or more things at the same time.

While multitasking may seem to be saving time, psychologists, neuroscientists and others are finding that it can put us under a great deal of stress and actually make us less efficient.

Although doing many things at the same time — reading an article while listening to music, switching to check e-mail messages and talking on the phone — can be a way of making tasks more fun and energizing, "you have to keep in mind that you sacrifice focus when you do this," said Edward M. Hallowell, a psychiatrist and author of *CrazyBusy: Overstretched, Overbooked, and About to Snap!* (Ballantine, 2006). "Multitasking is shifting focus from one task to another in rapid succession. It gives the illusion that we're simultaneously tasking, but we're really not. It's like playing tennis with three balls."

Of course, it depends what you're doing. For some people, listening 5 to music while working actually makes them more creative because they are using different cognitive functions.

But despite what many of us think, you cannot simultaneously e-mail and talk on the phone. I think we're all familiar with what

Dr. Hallowell calls "e-mail voice," when someone you're talking to on the phone suddenly sounds, well, disengaged.

"You cannot divide your attention like that," he said. "It's a big illusion. You can shift back and forth."

We all know that computers and their spawn, the smartphone and cellphone, have created a very different world from several decades ago, when a desk worker had a typewriter, a phone and an occasional colleague who dropped into the office.

Think even of the days before the cordless phone. Those old enough can remember when talking on the telephone, which was stationary, meant sitting down, putting your feet up and chatting — not doing laundry, cooking dinner, sweeping the floor and answering the door.

That is so far in the past. As we are required, or feel required, to do 10 more and more things in a shorter period of time, researchers are trying to figure out how the brain changes attention from one subject to another.

A pedestrian walking and texting.

academic literacies   rhetorical situations   genres   processes   strategies   research MLA / APA   media / design   readings

Earl Miller, the Picower professor of neuroscience at the Massachusetts Institute of Technology, explained it this way: human brains have a very large prefrontal cortex, which is the part of the brain that contains the "executive control" process. This helps us switch and prioritize tasks.

In humans, he said, the prefrontal cortex is about one-third of the entire cortex, while in dogs and cats, it is 4 or 5 percent and in monkeys about 15 percent.

"With the growth of the prefrontal cortex, animals become more and more flexible in their behavior," Professor Miller said.

We can do a couple of things at the same time if they are routine, but once they demand more cognitive process, the brain has "a severe bottleneck," he said.

Professor Miller conducted studies where electrodes were attached   15 to the head to monitor participants performing different tasks.

He found that "when there's a bunch of visual stimulants out there in front of you, only one or two things tend to activate your neurons, indicating that we're really only focusing on one or two items at a time."

David E. Meyer, a professor of psychology at the University of Michigan, and his colleagues looked at young adults as they performed tasks that involved solving math problems or classifying geometric objects.

Their 2001 study, published in *The Journal of Experimental Psychology*, found that for all types of tasks, the participants lost time when they had to move back and forth from one undertaking to another, and that it took significantly longer to switch between the more complicated tasks.

Although the time it takes for our brains to switch tasks may be only a few seconds or less, it adds up. If we're talking about doing two jobs that can require real concentration, like text-messaging and driving, it can be fatal.

The RAC Foundation, a British nonprofit organization that focuses   20 on driving issues, asked 17 drivers, age 17 to 24, to use a driving simulator to see how texting affects driving.

The reaction time was around 35 percent slower when writing a text message — slower than driving drunk or stoned.

All right, there are definitely times we should not try to multitask. But, we may think, it's nice to say that we should focus on one thing at a time, but the real world doesn't work that way. We are constantly interrupted.

A 2005 study, "No Task Left Behind? Examining the Nature of Fragmented Work," found that people were interrupted and moved from one project to another about every 11 minutes. And each time, it took about 25 minutes to circle back to that same project.

Interestingly, a study published last April, "The Cost of Interrupted Work: More Speed and Stress," found that "people actually worked faster in conditions where they were interrupted, but they produced less," said Gloria Mark, a professor of informatics at the University of California at Irvine and a co-author of both studies. And she also found that people were as likely to self-interrupt as to be interrupted by someone else.

"As observers, we'll watch, and then after every 12 minutes or so, for no apparent reasons, someone working on a document will turn and call someone or e-mail," she said. As I read that, I realized how often I was switching between writing this article and checking my e-mail.

Professor Mark said further research needed to be done to know why people work in these patterns, but our increasingly shorter attention spans probably have something to do with it.

Her study found that after only 20 minutes of interrupted performance, people reported significantly higher stress, frustration, workload, effort and pressure.

"I also argue that it's bad for innovation," she said. "Ten and a half minutes on one project is not enough time to think in-depth about anything."

Dr. Hallowell has termed this effort to multitask "attention deficit trait." Unlike attention deficit disorder, which he has studied for years and has a neurological basis, attention deficit trait "springs entirely from the environment," he wrote in a 2005 *Harvard Business Review* article, "Overloaded Circuits: Why Smart People Underperform."

"As our minds fill with noise — feckless synaptic events signifying nothing — the brain gradually loses its capacity to attend fully and gradually to anything," he wrote. Desperately trying to keep up with a multitude of jobs, we "feel a constant low level of panic and guilt."

academic literacies / rhetorical situations / genres / processes / strategies / research MLA / APA / media / design / readings

But Dr. Hallowell says that despite our belief that we cannot control how much we're overloaded, we can.

"We need to recreate boundaries," he said. That means training yourself not to look at your BlackBerry every 20 seconds, or turning off your cellphone. It means trying to change your work culture so such devices are banned at meetings. Sleeping less to do more is a bad strategy, he says. We are efficient only when we sleep enough, eat right and exercise.

So the next time the phone rings and a good friend is on the line, try this trick: Sit on the couch. Focus on the conversation. Don't jump up, no matter how much you feel the need to clean the kitchen. It seems weird, but stick with it. You, too, can learn the art of single-tasking.

Engaging with the Text

1. According to Alina Tugend's research, what are the **EFFECTS** of multitasking? Tugend doesn't say much about the causes of this practice. Why do you think she doesn't? What do you think are the causes?

   350–54

2. How well does Tugend maintain a **TIGHT FOCUS** on her topic in this report? Given the claim she makes in her title, why might a tightly focused topic be especially important for helping readers understand the issue?

   145

3. Tugend **DEFINES** several terms in her report. Locate one or more of these, and discuss what the definitions contribute to the report.

   388–98

4. What is Tugend's **STANCE** toward multitasking? Point out specific phrases that reveal her attitude. How appropriate is her stance, given her subject matter?

   64–67

5. *For Writing.* Undertake your own study of multitasking. Spend time observing students, faculty, and staff in common spaces on your campus — the library, the student union, the dorms, and so on — to see how much multitasking occurs. In addition, discuss with classmates, friends, and relatives their habits regarding multitasking. Write a **REPORT** on what you observe and what folks say about how beneficial or how detrimental multitasking can be.

   129–55

62 Arguments

academic
literacies

rhetorical
situations

genres

processes

strategies

research
MLA / APA

media /
design

readings

ALEX WEISS

Should Gamers Be Prosecuted for Virtual Stealing?

Alex Weiss (b. 1990) was a student at Arizona State University when he wrote this essay as a blog posting for his Work and Play in Contemporary Fiction/Digital Narrative class. The online magazine Slate *published it in a section titled* Future Tense, *a partnership among* Slate, *Arizona State, and the New America Foundation. The purpose of this partnership, as noted by* Future Tense, *is "to explore emerging technologies and their transformative effects on society and public policy."*

THE MASSIVELY MULTIPLAYER ONLINE VIDEO GAME *RuneScape* was the site of a "virtual theft."

Last week, the Dutch Supreme Court made a curious ruling: It convicted a teenage gamer of stealing something that doesn't exist. The defendant stole two virtual items while playing *RuneScape*, a free massively multiplayer online [MMO] video game. According to the Associated Press, the defendant's attorney argued that the stolen amulet and shield "were neither tangible nor material and, unlike for example electricity, had no economic value." The court, however, disagreed, ruling that the time the 13-year-old victim spent in the game trying to earn the objects gave them value.

As a reformed online-gaming thief, this ruling makes no sense to me. It places too much value on the time people spend playing video games. Video games are not work or investments for which people should be compensated; they are escapism.

During my disappointing teenage years, I played an MMO set in space-capitalist hell titled *EVE Online. EVE* is the rat race imploded upon itself, a game that brings out the worst of its subscribers' humanity. In *EVE*, players can spend months working toward a goal, anything from starting a small in-game business to the production of a massive ship that requires billions of *EVE*'s in-game currency and months of man-hours.

The massively multiplayer online video game RuneScape *was the site of a "virtual theft."*

These projects may seem foolish to those outside of the gaming world, but they represent a great deal to their creators. And these hopes and dreams can be destroyed rapidly by another player who just wants to be a jerk. That's the whole point, actually.

EVE is one of the few MMOs that encourage players to use real money to purchase in-game currency, called "isk," which in turn is used to build highly desirable objects in the virtual world. It is also the only game that actively allows thievery in the context of the game world. In fact, player satisfaction in EVE is based on taking chances and risking everything you've spent time building up. For instance, as *Kotaku* details, in 2010 pirates destroyed a ship that another player had filled with six years' worth of in-game subscription renewals. At the time, the six years' worth of play was valued at more than $1,000 in real money through EVE's rather complicated financial system.

A few years ago, I could have been one of those pirates. In *EVE*, I enjoyed messing with people, making fake investments, engaging in corporation thievery, and even having an extended e-relationship with someone who thought I was a girl. I'd join corporations, running rainmaker scams by convincing the leadership that an antagonistic group was out to destroy everything we had built. Sometimes I even hired decoys to disrupt our supply lines just enough so that the monetary loss got their attention. After receiving the "bribe" money, they'd go away while I reaped the rewards of a now-trustworthy member of the target organization. After I had taken all I needed to take, I either blocked them or kept their enraged messages for posterity.

RuneScape, the game [the] Dutch minor was playing, is a bit different from both *EVE*, whose point is to engage in Bernie Madoff–esque shenanigans, and the more well-known *World of Warcraft*. *WoW* has a very strict policy against scamming, thievery, and even harsh language; violators can be banned, and victims' lost goods are refunded. The developers of *RuneScape*, however, didn't explicitly state that the thief couldn't do what he did, nor did they refund the victim his item. So here, we have a real-world court attempting to punish someone for behavior permitted within the realm. The real and virtual laws conflict, and it seems unfair to penalize the teenager for this. Reportedly, the player also beat up his victim, for which he should, of course, be punished. But attempting to bring real-world law into virtual realms — and putting monetary value on time spent immersed in a virtual world — seems dangerous.

Engaging with the Text

1. The **THESIS** of Alex Weiss's argument is "Video games are not work or investments for which people should be compensated; they are escapism." What **REASONS** and **EVIDENCE** does he offer to support this thesis? Do you agree with him? Why or why not?

 345–47

 358–59
359–67

2. At the end of his essay, Weiss writes that "attempting to bring real-world law into virtual realms — and putting monetary value on time

spent immersed in a virtual world — seems dangerous." Given the ruling in the case at the Dutch Supreme Court, what policies and issues regarding behavior in online games need to be legally ironed out in the next few years? Who should be involved in the debates over how online games are policed?

64–67 ■
3. What is Weiss's **STANCE** toward gaming in this argument? How does he reveal his stance?

344–45 ◆
4. Weiss titles his argument "Should Gamers Be Prosecuted for Virtual Stealing?" How does the **TITLE** function in this argument? How would you respond to the question it poses?

5. *For Writing.* In an essay, explore one of the issues that emerging technologies (such as social media, gaming, texting, and Skyping) are giving 355–73 ◆ rise to. Explain the issue and take a stand on it, **ARGUING** for how it should be addressed and who should be included in the debate. Be sure to pro169–70 ▲vide **CONVINCING EVIDENCE** (for which you need to do some research), to adopt **A TRUSTWORTHY TONE**, and to **CONSIDER OTHER POSSIBLE POSITIONS** on the issue.

NICHOLAS CARR

Is Google Making Us Stupid?

Nicholas Carr (b. 1959) has written widely on technology, business, and culture. His books include The Big Switch: Rewiring the World, from Edison to Google *(2008),* The Shallows: What the Internet Is Doing to Our Brains *(2010), and* The Glass Cage: Automation and Us *(2014). In addition to his blog* Rough Type, *in which he makes observations about the latest technologies and related issues, he regularly contributes to several periodicals. The following piece has been widely debated since its appearance as a cover article of the* Atlantic *in 2008. As you read, notice how Carr mixes in genres such as report and reflection to support his argument about the effects of the Internet on literacy, cognition, and culture.*

"**D**ave, stop. Stop, will you?" Stop, Dave. Will you stop, Dave?" So the supercomputer HAL pleads with the implacable astronaut Dave Bowman in a famous and weirdly poignant scene toward the end of Stanley Kubrick's *2001: A Space Odyssey.* Bowman, having nearly been sent to a deep-space death by the malfunctioning machine, is calmly, coldly disconnecting the memory circuits that control its artificial "brain." "Dave, my mind is going," HAL says, forlornly. "I can feel it. I can feel it."

I can feel it, too. Over the past few years I've had an uncomfortable sense that someone, or something, has been tinkering with my brain, remapping the neural circuitry, reprogramming the memory. My mind isn't going — so far as I can tell — but it's changing. I'm not thinking the way I used to think. I can feel it most strongly when I'm reading. Immersing myself in a book or a lengthy article used to be easy. My mind would get caught up in the narrative or the turns of the argument, and I'd spend hours strolling through long stretches of prose. That's rarely the case anymore. Now my concentration often starts to drift after two or three pages. I get fidgety, lose the thread, begin looking for something else to do. I feel as if I'm always dragging my wayward brain back to the text. The deep reading that used to come naturally has become a struggle.

Dave (Keir Dullea) removes HAL's "brain" in 2001: A Space Odyssey.

I think I know what's going on. For more than a decade now, I've been spending a lot of time online, searching and surfing and sometimes adding to the great databases of the Internet. The Web has been a godsend to me as a writer. Research that once required days in the stacks or periodical rooms of libraries can now be done in minutes. A few *Google* searches, some quick clicks on hyperlinks, and I've got the telltale fact or pithy quote I was after. Even when I'm not working, I'm as likely as not to be foraging in the Web's info-thickets reading and writing e-mails, scanning headlines and blog posts, watching videos and listening to podcasts, or just tripping from link to link to link. (Unlike footnotes, to which they're sometimes likened, hyperlinks don't merely point to related works; they propel you toward them.)

For me, as for others, the Net is becoming a universal medium, the conduit for most of the information that flows through my eyes and ears and into my mind. The advantages of having immediate access to such an incredibly rich store of information are many, and they've been widely described and duly applauded. "The perfect recall of silicon memory," *Wired's* Clive Thompson has written, "can be an enormous boon to thinking." But that boon comes at price. As the media theo-rist Marshall McLuhan pointed out in the 1960s, media are not just passive channels of information. They supply the stuff of thought, but they also shape the process of thought. And what the Net seems to be doing is chipping away my capacity for concentration and con-templation. My mind now expects to take in information the way the Net distributes it: in a swiftly moving stream of particles. Once I was a scuba diver in the sea of words. Now I zip along the surface like a guy on a Jet Ski.

I'm not the only one. When I mention my troubles with reading to   5 friends and acquaintances — literary types, most of them — many say they're having similar experiences. The more they use the Web, the more they have to fight to stay focused on long pieces of writing. Some of the bloggers I follow have also begun mentioning the phenomenon. Scott Karp, who writes a blog about online media, recently confessed that he has stopped reading books altogether. "I was a lit major in college, and used to be [a] voracious book reader," he wrote. "What happened?" He speculates on the answer: "What if I do all my reading on the web not so much because the way I read has changed, i.e. I'm just seeking convenience, but because the way I THINK has changed?"

Bruce Friedman, who blogs regularly about the use of computers in medicine, also has described how the Internet has altered his mental habits. "I now have almost totally lost the ability to read and absorb a longish article on the web or in print," he wrote earlier this year. A pathologist who has long been on the faculty of the University of Michi-gan Medical School, Friedman elaborated on his comment in a telephone conversation with me. His thinking, he said, has taken on a "staccato" quality, reflecting the way he quickly scans short passages of text from many sources online. "I can't read *War and Peace* anymore," he admitted. "I've lost the ability to do that. Even a blog post of more than three or four paragraphs is too much to absorb. I skim it."

Anecdotes alone don't prove much. And we still await the long-term neurological and psychological experiments that will provide a definitive picture of how Internet use affects cognition. But a recently published study of online research habits, conducted by scholars from University

College London, suggests that we may well be in the midst of a sea change in the way we read and think. As part of the five-year research program, the scholars examined computer logs documenting the behavior of visitors to two popular research sites, one operated by the British Library and one by a U.K. educational consortium, that provide access to journal articles, e-books, and other sources of written information. They found that people using the sites exhibited "a form of skimming activity," hopping from one source to another and rarely returning to any source they'd already visited. They typically read no more than one or two pages of an article or book before they would "bounce" out to another site. Sometimes they'd save a long article, but there's no evidence that they ever went back and actually read it. The authors of the study report:

> It is clear that users are not reading online in the traditional sense; indeed there are signs that new forms of "reading" are emerging as users "power browse" horizontally through titles, contents pages and abstracts going for quick wins. It almost seems that they go online to avoid reading in the traditional sense.

Thanks to the ubiquity of text on the Internet, not to mention the popularity of text-messages on cell phones, we may well be reading more today than we did in the 1970s or 1980s, when television was our medium of choice. But it's a different kind of reading, and behind it lies a different kind of thinking — perhaps even a new sense of the self. "We are not only *what* we read," says Maryanne Wolf, a developmental psychologist at Tufts University and the author of *Proust and the Squid: The Story and Science of the Reading Brain.* "We are *how* we read." Wolf worries that the style of reading promoted by the Net, a style that puts "efficiency" and "immediacy" above all else, may be weakening our capacity for the kind of deep reading that emerged when an earlier technology, the printing press, made long and complex works of prose commonplace. When we read online, she says, we tend to become "mere decoders of information." Our ability to interpret text, to make the rich mental connections that form when we read deeply and without distraction, remains largely disengaged.

Reading, explains Wolf, is not an instinctive skill for human beings. It's not etched into our genes the way speech is. We have to teach our minds how to translate the symbolic characters we see into the language we understand. And the media or other technologies we use in learning and practicing the craft of reading play an important part in shaping the neural circuits inside our brains. Experiments demonstrate that readers of ideograms, such as the Chinese, develop a mental circuitry for reading that is very different from the circuitry found in those of us whose written language employs an alphabet. The variations extend across many regions of the brain, including those that govern such essential cognitive functions as memory and the interpretation of visual and auditory stimuli. We can expect as well that the circuits woven by our use of the Net will be different from those woven by our reading of books and other printed works.

Sometime in 1882, Friedrich Nietzsche* bought a typewriter — a Malling-Hansen Writing Ball, to be precise. His vision was failing, and keeping his eyes focused on a page had become exhausting and painful, often bringing on crushing headaches. He had been forced to curtail his writing, and he feared that he would soon have to give it up. The typewriter rescued him, at least for a time. Once he had mastered touch-typing, he was able to write with his eyes closed, using only the tips of his fingers. Words could once again flow from his mind to the page.   10

But the machine had a subtler effect on his work. One of Nietzsche's friends, a composer, noticed a change in the style of his writing. His already terse prose had become even tighter, more telegraphic. "Perhaps you will through this instrument even take to a new idiom," the friend wrote in a letter, noting that, in his own work, his "'thoughts' in music and language often depend on the quality of pen and paper."

---

*Friedrich Nietzsche (1844–1900): nineteenth-century German philosopher whose work has been influential in several disciplines, including philosophy, literary studies, rhetoric, and linguistics. [Editor's note]

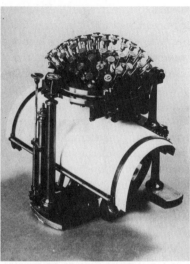

Friedrich Nietzsche and his Malling-Hansen Writing Ball.

"You are right," Nietzsche replied, "our writing equipment takes part in the forming of our thoughts." Under the sway of the machine, writes the German media scholar Friedrich A. Kittler, Nietzsche's prose "changed from arguments to aphorisms, from thoughts to puns, from rhetoric to telegram style."

The human brain is almost infinitely malleable. People used to think that our mental meshwork, the dense connections formed among the 100 billion or so neurons inside our skulls, was largely fixed by the time we reached adulthood. But brain researchers have discovered that that's not the case. James Olds, a professor of neuroscience who directs the Krasnow Institute for Advanced Study at George Mason University, says that even the adult mind "is very plastic." Nerve cells routinely break old connections and form new ones. "The brain," according to Olds, "has the ability to reprogram itself on the fly, altering the way it functions."

As we use what the sociologist Daniel Bell has called our "intellectual technologies" — the tools that extend our mental rather than our physical capacities — we inevitably begin to take on the qualities of those technologies. The mechanical clock, which came into common use in the 14th century, provides a compelling example. In *Technics and Civilization*, the historian and cultural critic Lewis Mumford described how the clock "disassociated time from human events and helped create the belief in an independent world of mathematically measurable sequences." The "abstract framework of divided time" became "the point of reference for both action and thought."

The clock's methodical ticking helped bring into being the scientific 15 mind and the scientific man. But it also took something away. As the late MIT computer scientist Joseph Weizenbaum observed in his 1976 book, *Computer Power and Human Reason: From Judgment to Calculation*, the conception of the world that emerged from the widespread use of timekeeping instruments "remains an impoverished version of the older one, for it rests on a rejection of those direct experiences that formed the basis for, and indeed constituted, the old reality." In deciding when to eat, to work, to sleep, to rise, we stopped listening to our senses and started obeying the clock.

The process of adapting to new intellectual technologies is reflected in the changing metaphors we use to explain ourselves to ourselves. When the mechanical clock arrived, people began thinking of their brains as operating "like clockwork." Today, in the age of software, we have come to think of them as operating "like computers." But the changes, neuroscience tells us, go much deeper than metaphor. Thanks to our brain's plasticity, the adaptation occurs also at a biological level.

The Internet promises to have particularly far-reaching effects on cognition. In a paper published in 1936, the British mathematician Alan Turing proved that a digital computer, which at the time existed only as a theoretical machine, could be programmed to perform the function of any other information-processing device. And that's what we're seeing today. The Internet, an immeasurably powerful computing system, is subsuming most of our other intellectual technologies. It's becoming our map and our clock, our printing press and our typewriter, our calculator and our telephone, and our radio and TV.

When the Net absorbs a medium, that medium is re-created in the Net's image. It injects the medium's content with hyperlinks, blinking ads, and other digital gewgaws, and it surrounds the content with the content of all the other media it has absorbed. A new e-mail message, for instance, may announce its arrival as we're glancing over the latest headlines at a newspaper's site. The result is to scatter our attention and diffuse our concentration.

The Net's influence doesn't end at the edges of a computer screen, either. As people's minds become attuned to the crazy quilt of Internet media, traditional media have to adapt to the audience's new expectations. Television programs add text crawls and pop-up ads, and magazines and newspapers shorten their articles, introduce capsule summaries, and crowd their pages with easy-to-browse info-snippets. When, in March of this year, the *New York Times* decided to devote the second and third pages of every edition to article abstracts, its design director, Tom Bodkin, explained that the "shortcuts" would give harried readers a quick "taste" of the day's news, sparing them the "less efficient" method of actually turning the pages and reading the articles. Old media have little choice but to play by the new-media rules.

Never has a communications system played so many roles in our 20 lives — or exerted such broad influence over our thoughts — as the Internet does today. Yet, for all that's been written about the Net, there's been little consideration of how, exactly, it's reprogramming us. The Net's intellectual ethic remains obscure.

About the same time that Nietzsche started using his typewriter, an earnest young man named Frederick Winslow Taylor carried a stopwatch into the Midvale Steel plant in Philadelphia and began a historic series of experiments aimed at improving the efficiency of the plant's machinists. With the approval of Midvale's owners, he recruited a group of factory hands, set them to work on various metalworking machines, and recorded and timed their every movement as well as the operations of the machines. By breaking down every job into a sequence of small,

A testing engineer (possibly Taylor) observes a Midvale Steel worker c. 1885.

discrete steps and then testing different ways of performing each one, Taylor created a set of precise instructions — an "algorithm," we might say today — for how each worker should work. Midvale's employees grumbled about the strict new regime, claiming that it turned them into little more than automatons, but the factory's productivity soared.

More than a hundred years after the invention of the steam engine, the Industrial Revolution had at last found its philosophy and its philosopher. Taylor's tight industrial choreography — his "system," as he liked to call it — was embraced by manufacturers throughout the country and, in time, around the world. Seeking maximum speed, maximum efficiency, and maximum output, factory owners used time-and-motion studies to organize their work and configure the jobs of their workers. The goal, as Taylor defined it in his celebrated 1911 treatise, *The Principles of Scientific Management*, was to identify and adopt, for every job, the "one best method" of work and thereby to effect "the gradual substitution of science for rule of thumb throughout the mechanic arts." Once his system was applied to all acts of manual labor, Taylor assured his followers, it would bring about a restructuring not only of industry but of society, creating a utopia of perfect efficiency. "In the past the man has been first," he declared; "in the future the system must be first."

Taylor's system is still very much with us; it remains the ethic of industrial manufacturing. And now, thanks to the growing power that computer engineers and software coders wield over our intellectual lives, Taylor's ethic is beginning to govern the realm of the mind as well. The Internet is a machine designed for the efficient and automated collection, transmission, and manipulation of information, and its legions of programmers are intent on finding the "one best method" — the perfect algorithm — to carry out every mental movement of what we've come to describe as "knowledge work."

Google's headquarters, in Mountain View, California — the Googleplex — is the Internet's high church, and the religion practiced inside its walls is Taylorism. Google, says its chief executive, Eric Schmidt, is "a company that's founded around the science of measurement," and it is striving to "systematize everything" it does. Drawing on the terabytes of behavioral data it collects through its search engine and other sites, it carries out thousands of experiments a day, according to the *Harvard Business Review*, and it uses the results to refine the algorithms that increasingly control how people find information and extract meaning from it. What Taylor did for the work of the hand, Google is doing for the work of the mind.

The company has declared that its mission is "to organize the world's information and make it universally accessible and useful." It seeks to develop "the perfect search engine," which it defines as something that "understands exactly what you mean and gives you back exactly what you want." In Google's view, information is a kind of commodity, a utilitarian resource that can be mined and processed with industrial efficiency. The more pieces of information we can "access"

25

The Googleplex.

and the faster we can extract their gist, the more productive we become as thinkers.

Where does it end? Sergey Brin and Larry Page, the gifted young men who founded Google while pursuing doctoral degrees in computer science at Stanford, speak frequently of their desire to turn their search engine into an artificial intelligence, a HAL-like machine that might be connected directly to our brains. "The ultimate search engine is something as smart as people — or smarter," Page said in a speech a few years back. "For us, working on search is a way to work on artificial intelligence." In a 2004 interview with *Newsweek*, Brin said, "Certainly if you had all the world's information directly attached to your brain, or an artificial brain that was smarter than your brain, you'd be better off." Last year, Page told a convention of scientists that Google is "really trying to build artificial intelligence and to do it on a large scale."

Such an ambition is a natural one, even an admirable one, for a pair of math whizzes with vast quantities of cash at their disposal and a small army of computer scientists in their employ. A fundamentally scientific enterprise, Google is motivated by a desire to use technology, in Eric Schmidt's words, "to solve problems that have never been solved before," and artificial intelligence is the hardest problem out there. Why wouldn't Brin and Page want to be the ones to crack it?

Still, their easy assumption that we'd all "be better off" if our brains were supplemented, or even replaced, by an artificial intelligence is unsettling. It suggests a belief that intelligence is the output of a mechanical process, a series of discrete steps that can be isolated, measured, and optimized. In Google's world, the world we enter when we go online, there's little place for the fuzziness of contemplation. Ambiguity is not an opening for insight but a bug to be fixed. The human brain is just an outdated computer that needs a faster processor and a bigger hard drive.

The idea that our minds should operate as high-speed data-processing machines is not only built into the workings of the Internet, it is the network's reigning business model as well. The faster we surf across the Web — the more links we click and pages we view — the more opportunities Google and other companies gain to collect information about us and to feed us advertisements. Most of the proprietors of the commercial Internet have a financial stake in collecting the crumbs of data we leave behind as we flit from link to link — the more crumbs, the better. The last thing these companies want is to encourage leisurely reading or slow, concentrated thought. It's in their economic interest to drive us to distraction.

Maybe I'm just a worrywart. Just as there's a tendency to glorify techno-   30
logical progress, there's a countertendency to expect the worst of every new tool or machine. In Plato's *Phaedrus*, Socrates bemoaned the development of writing. He feared that, as people came to rely on the written word as a substitute for the knowledge they used to carry inside their heads, they would, in the words of one of the dialogue's characters, "cease to exercise their memory and become forgetful." And because they would be able to "receive a quantity of information without proper instruction," they would "be thought very knowledgeable when they are for the most part quite ignorant." They would be "filled with the conceit of wisdom instead of real wisdom." Socrates wasn't wrong — the new technology did often have the effects he feared — but he was short-sighted. He couldn't foresee the many ways that writing and reading would serve to spread information, spur fresh ideas, and expand human knowledge (if not wisdom).

academic literacies

rhetorical situations

genres

processes

strategies

research MLA / APA

media / design

readings

The arrival of Gutenberg's printing press,* in the 15th century, set off another round of teeth gnashing. The Italian humanist Hieronimo Squarciafico worried that the easy availability of books would lead to intellectual laziness, making men "less studious" and weakening their minds. Others argued that cheaply printed books and broadsheets would undermine religious authority, demean the work of scholars and scribes, and spread sedition and debauchery. As New York University professor Clay Shirky notes, "Most of the arguments made against the printing press were correct, even prescient." But, again, the doomsayers were unable to imagine the myriad blessings that the printed word would deliver.

So, yes, you should be skeptical of my skepticism. Perhaps those who dismiss critics of the Internet as Luddites or nostalgists will be proved correct, and from our hyperactive, data-stoked minds will spring a golden age of intellectual discovery and universal wisdom. Then again, the Net isn't the alphabet, and although it may replace the printing press, it produces something altogether different. The kind of deep reading that a sequence of printed pages promotes is valuable not just for the knowledge we acquire from the author's words but for the intellectual vibrations those words set off within our own minds. In the quiet spaces opened up by the sustained, undistracted reading of a book, or by any other act of contemplation, for that matter, we make our own associations, draw our own inferences and analogies, foster our own ideas. Deep reading, as Maryanne Wolf argues, is indistinguishable from deep thinking.

If we lose those quiet spaces, or fill them up with "content," we will sacrifice something important not only in our selves but in our culture. In a recent essay, the playwright Richard Foreman eloquently described what's at stake:

> I come from a tradition of Western culture, in which the ideal
> (my ideal) was the complex, dense and "cathedral-like" structure

---

Johannes Gutenberg (1398–1468): a German goldsmith and printer credited with the invention of the printing press and the first mechanically printed Bible. [Editor's note]

of the highly educated and articulate personality — a man or woman who carried inside themselves a personally constructed and unique version of the entire heritage of the West. [But now] I see within us all (myself included) the replacement of complex inner density with a new kind of self — evolving under the pressure of information overload and the technology of the "instantly available."

As we are drained of our "inner repertory of dense cultural inheritance," Foreman concluded, we risk turning into "'pancake people' — spread wide and thin as we connect with that vast network of information accessed by the mere touch of a button."

I'm haunted by that scene in 2001. What makes it so poignant, and so weird, is the computer's emotional response to the disassembly of its mind: its despair as one circuit after another goes dark, its childlike pleading with the astronaut — "I can feel it. I can feel it. I'm afraid" — and its final reversion to what can only be called a state of innocence. HAL's outpouring of feeling contrasts with the emotionlessness that characterizes the human figures in the film, who go about their business with an almost robotic efficiency. Their thoughts and actions feel scripted, as if they're following the steps of an algorithm. In the world of 2001, people have become so machinelike that the most human character turns out to be a machine. That's the essence of Kubrick's dark prophecy: as we come to rely on computers to mediate our understanding of the world, it is our own intelligence that flattens into artificial intelligence.

Engaging with the Text

359–67

1. According to Nicholas Carr, what has been the effect of the Internet on the way we read, think, and live? What **EVIDENCE** does he offer to support his claims? How does his discussion of the changes wrought by other technologies help him make his argument?

academic literacies   rhetorical situations   genres   processes   strategies   research MLA / APA   media / design   readings

2. Sergey Brin has noted, "Some say Google is God. Others say Google is Satan. But if they think Google is too powerful, remember that with search engines, unlike other companies, all it takes is a single click to go to another search engine." How does Carr's essay support or challenge this assertion? Why do you think this topic elicits such strong responses?

3. Where in his argument does Carr **INCORPORATE OTHER VIEWPOINTS**? How successfully does he deal with them?

◆ 368–69

4. Why does Carr **BEGIN** and **END** by referring to HAL from the film 2001: *A Space Odyssey*? How do the quotes he chooses from the film help him appeal to his **AUDIENCE**?

◆ 331–42

■ 57–60

5. *For Writing.* What is your view of how technology is affecting the way we think, read, write, and live? Write an **ARGUMENT** in which you support or challenge Carr's conclusion that "as we come to rely on computers to mediate our understanding of the world, it is our own intelligence that flattens into artificial intelligence." Consider mixing in some **REFLECTION** on your own use of computers to help make your argument.

▲ 156–82

▲ 245–52

JEREMY ADAM SMITH

Our Fear of Immigrants

Jeremy Adam Smith (b. 1970) is founder of the fathering blog Daddy Dialectic; *editor of* Shareable.net, *which he helped to launch; publisher of* Dollars and Sense *magazine; and contributing editor of* Greater Good *magazine. His writing on parenting, politics, popular culture, and urban life has also been published in* Mothering, *the* Nation, Utne, *and many other forums. Smith is the author of* The Daddy Shift *(2009) and co-editor of two other books,* The Compassionate Instinct *(2010) and* Are We Born Racist? *(2010). The following argument appeared in 2014 in* Pacific Standard: The Science of Society, *a publication that focuses on issues related to justice, education, economics, and the environment.*

RODRIGO GUZMAN'S DESK was empty.

It was January 2013 and Christmas break was over. As the fourth graders took their seats at Jefferson Elementary School in Berkeley, California, teacher Barbara Wenger noted Rodrigo's absence in her attendance book.

But he wasn't back the next day, or the day after that. His family had come to the United States on a tourist visa, now long expired, when Rodrigo was just 16 months old. As they tried to go home to Berkeley from their Christmas vacation, the family was detained in Houston, Texas — and then sent back to Mexico.

After Wenger explained why Rodrigo would not return, the class of 10-year-olds, many of whom had known him since kindergarten, was shocked. "How is that fair?" she says they asked. "That's ridiculous!" The kids "tried to make Rodrigo feel better" by making him a video and sending him a Valentine in February — and their parents helped the kids to write to their Congressmen and speak out in the media.

More and more children like Rodrigo are crossing the border, many 5 without parents or guardians. During the past nine months, 57,000

> "When shaping immigration policy, we should be holding in the front of our minds that we're talking about real families, real kids, who have hopes and incredible stories."

unaccompanied minors have been caught trying to cross the border, double what it was during the same period last year.

In the face of this humanitarian crisis — which experts blame on Central American drug wars — many native-born Americans have reacted with fear and revulsion.

Earlier this month in Murrieta, California, angry protesters blocked buses full of undocumented children and women on their way to a holding facility. "Send the illegals back," read a typical sign. GOP policy backs the protesters: The only immigration-related bill passed by the House is an amendment that would revoke a program that has given 600,000 youth legal status and deportation protection. All other efforts to reform the immigration system have been blocked by the GOP and a small number of Democratic allies.

Why do immigrants provoke such strong feelings of both empathy and revulsion, a polarization that pits fourth graders in Berkeley against the citizens of Murrieta? What characteristics and qualities do Rodrigo's classmates possess that the bus-stoppers do not? These are questions that psychologists and sociologists have been exploring for years — and their answers suggest how we can reduce the revulsion and foster a stronger sense of empathy with newcomers.

Why Do We Fear Immigrants?

Princeton psychologist Susan Fiske has traveled around the world to explore the nature of prejudice, looking specifically at how different groups — from housewives and Christians to the elderly and immigrants — are regarded as being competent and emotionally warm.

"I've found that the outlines of both blatant prejudice and subtle unexamined forms of prejudice are identical in Europe and in the United States," she says. "We've now done our warmth-by-competence map in three dozen countries, and the results amaze me: It's the same everywhere."   10

Immigrants, Fiske finds, are especially reviled in the countries she studied. So the protesters of Murrieta are not outliers in the human family — and when a trait like prejudice against outsiders is so universal, that suggests to scientists that it might contain some evolutionary advantage.

In fact, the research suggests that immigrant rights advocates face many, many psychological barriers in pursuit of their goals. Fear of foreigners might well be the most intractable of all human prejudices because it is so tightly linked to survival and natural selection.

"At the end of the day, we're motivated by resource-distribution," says University of California–Berkeley psychology professor Rodolfo Mendoza-Denton, who studies stereotypes and intergroup relations. When newcomers arrive in the midst of a stable population that's already worked out who gets what, "the most common human reaction is to hog resources, not to share."

It's a problem that arises from one of our best, most unique qualities: Human beings are extremely social animals that are very dependent on our group membership for food, shelter, and security. "We care deeply about our in-groups," Fiske says. "But the downside is that you're then excluding people who are not in the in-group."

This is a social pattern that can be mapped in our bodies, down   15
to a molecular level. Threat centers in the brain light up on perceiving an out-group member, while neurotransmitters like oxytocin seem to facilitate both in-group bonding and out-group exclusion.

The biological architecture of prejudice also hints at the fear that immigrants bring disease — people from faraway ecologies may carry different pathogens, activating knee-jerk disgust, as Mark Schaller and colleagues at the University of British Columbia have documented.

That's why many American cities are excluding immigrants based on health concerns. As Mayor Alan Long of Murrieta, who led the protests to stop the buses, recently said in an interview, "you don't ship people that are ill and contagious all over the country." His fellow protesters held signs reading "Save our children from diseases."

A Threat to Native Hierarchies

In these ways, we're built by evolution for in-group cooperation and out-group exclusion — but the real threat posed by immigrants may lie in their ability to upset the power hierarchies of the in-group.

"Any newcomer represents a threat to the person who has power," says University of California–Berkeley psychologist Dacher Keltner, who studies the impact of power differences on human relationships. "People with wealth and at the top of hierarchies aren't thinking as carefully about what other individuals can offer and contribute — and this leads them to embrace stereotypes."

> "There are ways to conceptualize immigration, not on a deficit model, but as bringing in skills and resources that grow the economy, potentially growing the pool of what goes around."

The stereotypes can then be used to jus-[20] tify abuse and exploitation. "Part of the reason why people get placed in the low-warmth/low-competence dimension is to justify or motivate mistreatment toward those groups," Mendoza-Denton says. In other words, it becomes so much easier to hand undocumented immigrants substandard housing or dangerous jobs if we call them "illegals" and categorize them as lazy and shiftless.

Mendoza-Denton points out that under the umbrella of "foreigners," different groups will be perceived differently at different times, often to motivate specific behavior. "Groups seen as high-competence, low-warmth [like the Japanese or Chinese] are classified as enemies; people are classed as low-competence, low-warmth to facilitate abuse or neglect." Out-groups are sorted into categories in order to motivate different kinds of negative behavior against them, from violence to economic exploitation to exclusion from good housing.

The discrimination is enabled by power differences between immigrants and the native-born — which in turn reinforces those differences. "Powerful people are more likely to see other people as means to their ends," Keltner says. "I think the deeper point to me is that people in power have this status quo bias. They want the system to stay the same — but healthy social systems are dynamic."

This is why immigration policy debates in America put liberals and conservatives on opposite sides. Liberals as a group tend to favor dynamic social systems and social change while conservatives, philosophically, try to conserve in-group resources and keep things as steady as possible.

Of course, both groups will claim to be compassionate — but conservatives will tend to see compassion as a limited resource, to be rationed for the in-group. Indeed, the final barrier to empathy with the new wave of refugees may lie in its magnitude: Horror over tens of thousands of children crossing the border without their parents transmutes into fear and repulsion, because many native-born Americans despair of being unable to help them.

"My lab has found that people are more likely to respond with 25 disgust — and to dehumanize — such extreme out-groups when they anticipate that compassion for those groups will be emotionally overwhelming and exhausting," says Daryl Cameron, a psychologist at the University of Iowa.

Can We Tame Xenophobia?

If xenophobia has such deep evolutionary and psychological roots, what explains Ms. Wenger's fourth-grade class, which rallied to support their friend Rodrigo after he was sent back to Mexico?

Both liberals and conservatives have claimed that the most important fact of the Berkeley case is that they are children. For some liberal commentators, Wenger's class stands as proof that children are born without prejudice, and that hate must be taught. Conservatives have a different take, suggesting that the embrace of an undocumented immigrant in their midst is just the result of an inexperienced, childish perspective. "That's what I want a bunch of fourth graders making legislation," wrote one commentator on the right-wing site *newsbuster.com*. "MACARONI AND CHEESE EVERY DAY FOR SUPPER!!!!"

But both groups are wrong, the research suggests.

academic literacies　rhetorical situations　genres　processes　strategies　research MLA / APA　media / design　readings

From a very young age, children start sorting themselves into in-groups and out-groups, so the potential for prejudice is there before social conditioning takes hold, contrary to what many liberals believe. But in this case, says the research, their age is not as important as the fact that many of them had *sat in the same classroom as Rodrigo for almost five years*, in one of the most racially integrated and culturally diverse school districts in the nation.

> "People with wealth and at the top of hierarchies aren't thinking as carefully about what other individuals can offer and contribute — and this leads them to embrace stereotypes."

This is what social scientists call the con-   30 tact hypothesis — the simple idea that contact between groups facilitates tolerance and cooperation. Research finds that its effects are deep and long lasting, which is why conservatives are wrong to malign Rodrigo's classmates as childish: They'll likely take that multicultural perspective into adulthood.

Many studies have found that the brain stops going into high alert when exposed to out-group faces if steps are taken to make the faces familiar. Researchers also find that our definition of who is part of the in-group is extremely malleable. This is often simply a matter of giving two different groups the same goal, as Muzafer Sherif discovered 50 years ago in his famed "Robbers Cave" experiment. Nothing binds children of different races together more quickly than needing to dissect a frog together in science class.

Later studies by Thomas Pettigrew and Linda Tropp elaborated on this insight. In addition to having common goals, they found kids need to be treated as equals and to have non-competitive interactions with one another. That last bit — cooperation over competition — turns out to be rather important. "In our research, we talk about warmth and competence dimensions," Fiske says. "And the warmth dimension is completely predicted by cooperative or competitive intent." As Mendoza-Denton says, "There are ways to conceptualize immigration, not on a deficit model, but as bringing in skills and resources that grow the economy, potentially growing the pool of what goes around."

The fourth graders of Berkeley are different in another way from the citizens of Murrieta: the values of the people leading their communities.

In Murrieta, the town's mayor led the anti-immigrant protests. In Berkeley, teachers and administrators never lose an opportunity to talk about the value of diversity. As the district's website says, "Berkeley Unified School District believes that diversity in our student population enriches the educational experiences of students." The leadership's framing emphasizes that newcomers strengthen the community with new ideas and energy, as opposed to threatening its integrity.

"The views and messages from authorities really matter," Mendoza-Denton says. "Because difficult intergroup situations are ambiguous — and in ambiguous situations people look to leaders to set the tone. That's got to be really consistent across different levels of leadership." As part of that leadership, people need to hear solutions, to mitigate the fear that compassion will lead to feeling overwhelmed. 35

Keltner also says it helps for native-born people to be conscious of their power over newcomers:

> A lot of great leaders, like Abraham Lincoln, had this very disciplined approach to the ethics of power — you have to be humble, you have to listen, you have to serve — because the forces of power push us in the opposite direction. Ultimately, you have to find a cause that's about other people — otherwise, you're Justin Bieber.

That may be the final difference between the fourth graders of Berkeley and the protesters of Murrieta: They had a cause that was about someone else, not themselves. "It isn't fair," one classmate told the website *Berkeleyside*. "All of his classmates and all of his friends miss him and he misses Berkeley." In contrast, the slogans of Murrieta — e.g., "We have no money for you" — were uniformly negative and self-centered.

Thus the prescription for increasing empathy with immigrants contains a one-two punch: One punch is emotional and social, to overcome innate fear of outsiders; the other is cognitive and educational, to correct for irrational fears like the one of disease. "If you're talking about cognitive-behavioral therapy for depression, there's a very strong

education component where you try to persuade the person to empirically examine their own beliefs," says Mendoza-Denton.

These are ideas that Wenger put to work in her fourth-grade class. As a teacher, she says she understands that sometimes a rule is a rule, and that rules must be followed. She explained to her class that Rodrigo's parents broke the law. But the education doesn't stop there for Wenger, because you must also ask *why* the family broke the law — and if the law applies equally to everyone.

"When shaping immigration policy, we should be holding in the front of our minds that we're talking about real families, real kids, who have hopes and incredible stories," she says. "If we can't hold those real people at the forefront of any discussion around immigration policy, then we just fall into rhetoric. We end up just saying 'A rule's a rule' or 'We have something that other people shouldn't be able to get' or 'We're going to be damaged because of these hordes of people coming through.'"

Wenger's advice to the protesters of Murrieta? "Sit down and have supper with immigrants," she says. "Ask them their stories."

It would be a start.

Engaging with the Text

1. What is the central point that Jeremy Adam Smith is making in this argument? Does he state this point explicitly? If so, where?

2. Smith clearly takes a sympathetic **STANCE** toward immigrants even as he discusses the complexities of the issue. Identify three phrases that signal his stance, and discuss what each contributes to his argument or why it weakens it.

12–15

3. A successful argument needs solid **EVIDENCE**. Smith offers quotations from liberal and conservative politicians as well as scholars in psychology and biology who have done studies on human attitudes toward those seen as outsiders. He also uses an extended anecdote about children's reaction to the deportation of a classmate. Is this evidence trustworthy? Why or why not? What would happen to his argument if he focused only on anecdotes?

359–67

604–5

4. Three **HEADINGS** appear in this essay. Apart from breaking up the text visually, what function are they meant to serve? Are they effective? Why or why not?

5. *For Writing*. Immigration also raises issues less sweeping than deporting immigrants without legal status or giving them a path to citizenship. For example, debates at the state and local level have involved such issues as drivers' licenses and in-state college tuition for undocumented immigrants and "English-only" language policies in government agencies. Choose one such issue, either in your state or locality

156–82

or elsewhere, and write an essay making an **ARGUMENT** about it. In researching your topic, you may want to interview some immigrants or a political scientist or other instructor who has studied the issue.

GRANT PENROD

Anti-Intellectualism: Why We Hate the Smart Kids

Grant Penrod (b. 1985) wrote the following essay for a first-year composition course at Arizona State University. It won second place in the Printer's Devil Contest, an annual competition open to all students enrolled in writing classes at the university.

T HE FOOTBALL TEAM FROM MOUNTAIN VIEW HIGH SCHOOL won the Arizona state championship last year. Again. Unbeknownst to the vast majority of the school's student body, so did the Science Bowl Team, the Speech and Debate Team, and the Academic Decathlon team. The football players enjoyed the attentions of an enthralled school, complete with banners, assemblies, and even video announcements in their honor, a virtual barrage of praise and downright deification. As for the three champion academic teams, they received a combined total of around ten minutes of recognition, tacked onto the beginning of a sports assembly. Nearly all of the graduating seniors will remember the name and escapades of their star quarterback; nearly none of them will ever even realize that their class produced Arizona's first national champion in Lincoln-Douglas Debate. After all, why should they? He and his teammates were "just the nerds."

This instance finds plentiful company in the experiences of everyday life; intellectuals constantly see their efforts trivialized in the rush to lavish compliments elsewhere. However, such occurrences present only a faint silhouette of true anti-intellectualism; trivialization seems insignificant when compared with the outright disdain for the educated harbored by much of society. That academia's proponents provoke the wrath of the populace is certain. As an illustration, a commentator under the screen name ArCaNe posted the following quote on *TalkingCock.com*, an online discussion board: "Man how I hate nerds . . . if I ever had a tommygun with me . . . I would most probably blow each one of their . . . heads off." Were this statement alone in its extremism, it could be written off a joke. Unfortunately, it represents just one statement along countless similar sites and postings, a veritable cornucopia of evidence attesting to society's distaste for intellectuals. The question, then, is not whether anti-intellectualism exists, but rather why it exists. Several factors seem to contribute to the trend, including social stereotypes, public examples, and monetary obsession. Any or all of these factors can contribute to anti-intellectualism, and the result is a crushing disregard for the lives and achievements of fellow human beings.

Perhaps the most obvious cause of anti-intellectualist tendencies, harmful social stereotypes begin to emerge as early as in high school. The idea of the "geek" or "nerd" of the class is a familiar one to most students, and it is not a pleasant one. One online venter, Dan6erous, describes the image well: "A+ this and . . . got a 1600 on my SAT and got all AP class[es] next year woohoo. That's all these people care about don't they have lives damn nerds." In this respect, the trend to dislike intellectuals stems at least in part from an inescapable perception that concern for grades and test scores excludes the coexistence of normal social activities. Sadly, this becomes somewhat of a self-fulfilling prophecy; "nerds" are excluded from social activity because of their label, and that label in turn intensifies through the resulting lack of social contact. The cycle seems unbreakable. Of course, not all "nerds" are socially excluded; most high school students could readily name a few intelligent people with at least a degree of popularity. The point, though, is that the *image* of intellectualism is disliked as anti-social, and the harms of even a fallacious perception to this effect spread to all of the intelligentsia.

This argument, however, merely accounts for the perpetuation of anti-intellectual feelings. Those feelings must also *originate* somewhere, possibly in the examples set by public figures. Certainly the image presented by modern celebrities suggests that intellectualism has no ties to success and social legitimacy. As an illustration, a Web site hosted by *Angelfire.com* features a compilation of the names of famous high school dropouts. With such well-known cultural icons as Christina Aguilera, Kid Rock, L. L. Cool J., and Sammy Sosa qualifying for such a list, any drive toward intelligence or education becomes laughable in the eyes of media-inundated young people ("Noted High School and Elementary School Dropouts"). Thus, intellectualism loses the respect that its rigor would

otherwise tend to earn it. Uneducated success extends far beyond just singers and sports stars, too; even the current President of the United States* presents the image of the success of nonintellectualism. His reputation as a "C" student is widely touted, and his public speeches hardly exonerate his intellectual image. The fact that such a vital public figure can get away with saying things like "It's clearly a budget. It's got a lot of numbers in it," and "There needs to be a wholesale effort against racial profiling, which is illiterate children" reflects rather poorly on the regard in which most Americans hold intelligence (Lewis).

Sadly, the aforementioned examples of uneducated success are even further entrenched by the prodigious wealth of the celebrities involved. For example, Sammy Sosa earned an intimidating eighteen million dollars during the year 2002 ("Celebrity 100"). Indeed, as a writer for *The Carillon* put it, "In more than a few cases athletes' incomes surpass the gross national product of some third-world countries" (Brejak). In the eyes of an ever-watchful public, just the existence of such amazingly affluent yet strikingly uneducated individuals would seem to call into question the necessity and even legitimacy of intellectualism. Certainly, most of the people affected by these media images are teenagers, but these budding young anti-intellectuals carry the sentiments of education-bashing on into their adult lives as well. As an illustration, Robert T. Kiyosaki (no longer a teenager) claims in his book *If You Want to Be Rich and Happy, Don't Go to School?* that education is now merely an archaic institution that continues to cling to obsolete practices (Review). The tendency to forgo enlightenment for "success" even leaks into the college community now: a recent article by Ethan Bronner states that "in the survey . . . 74.9 percent of freshmen chose being well off as an essential goal while only 40.8 percent" selected "developing a philosophy" as a similar goal. Indeed, Americans seem enamored with wealth at the expense of intellectualism. Unfortunately for them, this supposed negative correlation between brains and buying power doesn't even exist: "People holding doctorate degrees earned more than twice the salary of high school graduates" in the year 2000 ("Census 2000").

———————————

President: George W. Bush was president at the time of this essay. [Editor's note]

Regardless of the causes of anti-intellectualism, the effects are clear and devastating; society looks down on those individuals who help it to progress, ostracizing its best and brightest. Some may blame television or general societal degradation for the fall of the educated, but at heart the most disturbing issue involved is the destruction of promising personalities; ignoring intellectuals both in school and later on in life crushes its victims, as illustrated in the following lines:

> My loud and bitter screams aren't being heard
> No one is there to hear them or to care
> They do not come cuz I'm a nerd
> Dealing with this pain is a lot to bear. (Casey F.)

For the sake of the smart kids, we all need to "lay off" a little.

Works Cited

ArCaNe. "Re: A Gifted Student." *TalkingCock.com*, 2 Sept. 2001, www.talkingcock.com/html/article.php?sid_416. Accessed 21 Apr. 2009.

Brejak, Matt. "Money, Contracts and Switzerland." *The Carillon,* 28 Oct. 1999, ursu.uregina.ca/_carillon/99.10.28/sports/money.html. Accessed 24 Apr. 2009.

Bronner, Ethan. "College Freshmen Aiming for High Marks in Income." *The New York Times,* 12 Jan. 1998, www.nytimes.com/1998/01/12/us/college-freshmen-aiming-for-high-marks-in-income.html. Accessed 28 Apr. 2009.

Casey F. "My loud and bitter screams aren't being heard." *TeenMag.com,* 9 Apr. 2002, www.teenmag.com/allaboutyou/poetry/poetry_040902_8.html. Accessed 25 Apr. 2009.

"The Celebrity 100—Jocks." *Forbes,* 20 June 2002, www.forbes.com/2002/06/20/celebjockslide_12.html. Accessed 15 Apr. 2009.

"Census 2000: Education." *The Bermuda Sun,* 18 Dec. 2002, www.bermudasun.org/archives/2002-12-18/01News13/. Accessed 21 Apr. 2009.

Dan6erous. Online posting. *Chilax,* 31 Aug. 2003, chilax.com/forum/index.php?showtopic_1331&st_60. Accessed 14 Apr. 2009.

Review of *If You Want to Be Rich and Happy, Don't Go to School?* by Robert T. Kiyosaki. *EducationReformBooks.net,* World Prosperity, www.educationreformbooks.net/richandhappy.htm. Accessed 28 Apr. 2009.

academic literacies   rhetorical situations   genres   processes   strategies   research MLA / APA   media / design   readings

Lewis, Jone Johnson, comp. "Bushisms Quotes." *Wisdom Quotes*, 2009,
www.wisdomquotes.com/topics/bushisms. Accessed 28 Apr. 2009.

"Noted High School and Elementary School Dropouts." *Angelfire*,
14 Apr. 2009, www.angelfire.com/stars4/lists/dropouts.html.
Accessed 28 Apr. 2009.

Engaging with the Text

1. Grant Penrod claims that the effects of anti-intellectualism are "clear and devastating," arguing that society "ostracizes its best and brightest." What **REASONS** and **EVIDENCE** does he provide to support his claim? Do you find his argument persuasive? Why or why not?

   358–67

2. What does Penrod's **TITLE** tell us about his intended **AUDIENCE**? What values do you think he assumes they hold? How does he **APPEAL** to these readers? How successful do you think he is?

   344–45
57–60
170

3. Penrod suggests that intellectuals are disliked in part because of the "perception that concern for grades and test scores excludes the coexistence of normal social activities" — and that this becomes a "self-fulfilling prophecy; 'nerds' are excluded from social activity because of their label, and that label in turn intensifies through the resulting lack of social contact." Do you agree? Why or why not?

4. To support his claim that anti-intellectualism is fueled in part by the media, Penrod names celebrities from sports, music, and politics who became successful without the benefit of an education. Do you agree that the success of these celebrities is partly responsible for anti-intellectualism? Why or why not? What **EVIDENCE** could be offered to **REFUTE** this argument?

   359–67
369

5. *For Writing.* Penrod identifies "nerds" as one stereotypical high school group. "Jocks" are another familiar stereotype. How were students **CLASSIFIED** into stereotyped groups at your high school? Were the classifications fair? Who did the classifying? What were the consequences for members of the group and for other students? Write an essay about one of these groups that **ARGUES A POSITION** on what factors motivated the stereotyping. You'll need to support your argument with reasons and evidence, such as facts, statistics, and anecdotes.

   355–73
156–82

63 Evaluations

See also:

ALI HEINEKAMP
Juno: Not Just Another
Teen Movie   198

764

academic
literacies

rhetorical
situations

genres

processes

strategies

research
MLA / APA

media /
design

readings

DANAH BOYD

Wikipedia *as a Site of Knowledge Production*

danah boyd (b. 1977) is a professor at New York University, a principal researcher at Microsoft Research, and a founder of the Data & Society Research Institute. An award-winning researcher, boyd is author of Hanging Out, Messing Around, and Geeking Out: Kids Living and Learning with New Media *(2009) and* It's Complicated: The Social Lives of Networked Teens *(2014). She blogs both on DML Central blog and on her own site, Apophenia, which means "seeing patterns or meaning in apparently random or meaningless data." The following evaluation is taken from* It's Complicated.

WIKIPEDIA HAS A BAD RAP in American K–12 education. The de facto view among many educators is that a free encyclopedia that anyone can edit must be filled with inaccuracies and misleading information. Students' tendency to use the service as their first and last source for information only reinforces their doubts. Ignoring the educational potential of *Wikipedia*, teachers consistently tell students to stay clear of *Wikipedia* at all costs. I heard this sentiment echoed throughout the United States.

In Massachusetts, white fifteen-year-old Kat told me that "*Wikipedia* is a really bad thing to use because they don't always cite their sources. . . . You don't know who's writing it." Brooke, a white fifteen-year-old from Nebraska, explained that "[teachers] tell us not to [use *Wikipedia*] because a lot of — some of the information is inaccurate." These comments are nearly identical to the sentiments I typically hear from parents and teachers. Although it is not clear whether students are reproducing their teachers' beliefs or have come to the same conclusion independently, students are well aware that most teachers consider *Wikipedia* to have limited accuracy.

When people dismiss *Wikipedia*, they almost always cite limited trust and credibility, even though analyses have shown that *Wikipedia*'s content is just as credible as, if not more reliable than, more traditional resources like *Encyclopaedia Britannica*.[1] Teachers continue to prefer familiar, formally recognized sources. Educators encourage students to go to the library. When they do recommend digital sources, they view some as better than others without explaining why.[2] As Aaron, a white fifteen-year-old from Texas explained, "A lot of teachers don't want you to use [Wikipedia] as a source in a bibliography because it's not technically accredited. And they'd rather you use a university professor's website or something." Although Aaron didn't know what it meant for a source to be accredited, he had a mental model of which sources his teachers viewed as legitimate and which they eschewed. Similarly, Heather, a white sixteen-year-old from Iowa, explained, "Our school says not to use *Wikipedia* as our main source. You can use it as like a second or third source but not as a main source. They say *MSN Encarta*. . . . They say to use that because it's more reliable." When I asked students why they should prefer sites like *Encarta* and professors' webpages, they referenced trust and credibility, even though students couldn't explain what made those particular services trustworthy.

Although nearly every teenager I met told me stories about teachers who had forbidden them from using *Wikipedia* for schoolwork, nearly all of them used the site anyhow. Some used the site solely as a starting point for research, going then to Google to find sources they could cite that their teachers considered more respectable. Others knowingly violated their teachers' rules and worked to hide their reliance on *Wikipedia*. In Boston, I met a teen boy who told me that his teachers never actually checked the sources, so he used *Wikipedia* to get information he needed. When he went to list citations, he said they came from more credible sources like *Encarta,* knowing that his teachers would never check to see whether a particular claim *actually* came from *Encarta*. In other words, he faked his sources because he believed his teachers wouldn't check. Although he had found a way of working around his teachers' rules, he had failed to learn why they wanted citations in the first place. All he had learned was that his teachers' restrictions on using *Wikipedia* were "stupid."

Because many adults assume that youth are digitally savvy — and because they themselves do not understand many online sources — they

5

often end up giving teens misleading or inaccurate information about what they see online. A conflict emerges as teens turn to *Wikipedia* with uncritical eyes while teachers deride the site without providing a critical lens with which to look at the information available.

Wikipedia can be a phenomenal educational tool, but few educators I met knew how to use it constructively. Unlike other sources of information, including encyclopedias and books by credible authors, the entire history of how users construct a *Wikipedia* entry is visible. By looking at the "history" of a page, a viewer can see when someone made edits, who did the editing, and what that user edited. By looking at the discussion, it's possible to read the debates that surround the edits. *Wikipedia* isn't simply a product of knowledge; it's also a record of the process by which people share and demonstrate knowledge.

In most educational institutions, publishers and experts vet much of the content that teens encounter and there is no discussion about why something is accurate or not. Some teachers deem certain publications trustworthy and students treat that content as fact. Reading old history books and encyclopedias can be humorous — or depressing, depending on the content and your point of view — because of what the writers assumed to be accurate at one point in time or in one cultural context. Just like today, past students who were given those materials were also taught that all of the information they were receiving was factual.

Although many students view textbooks as authoritative material, the content is neither neutral nor necessarily accurate. Textbooks often grow outdated more quickly than schools can replace them. The teens I interviewed loved finding inaccuracies in their own textbooks, such as lists of planets that included Pluto. Of course, not all inaccuracies are the product of mistakes or outdated facts. Some writers insert biases into texts because they reinforce certain social or political beliefs. In the United States, Texas is notorious for playing a significant role in shaping the content of textbooks in all states.[3] So when educators in Texas insist on asserting that America's "founding fathers" were all Christian, it creates unease among historians who do not believe this to be accurate. What goes into a textbook is highly political.

History, in particular, differs depending on perspective. I grew up hearing examples of this in my own family. Born to a British father and a Canadian mother, my mother moved to New York as a young girl. She recalls her confusion when my grandfather complained about her American history lessons and threatened to destroy her textbook. Compared to the British narratives my patriotic British veteran grandfather had learned, the American origin story was outright offensive. American and British high schools teach events like the American Revolutionary War very differently — and rarely do schools in either country consider such things as the role of women or the perspectives of slaves or Native Americans. This is a topic of deep interest to historians and the driving force behind books like Howard Zinn's *A People's History of the United States*, which tells American history through the perspective of those who "lost." Although many people believe that the winner gets to control the narrative, accounts also diverge when conflicting stories don't need to be resolved. When countries like the United States and the United Kingdom produce their own textbooks, they don't need to arrive at mutually agreeable narratives. However, when people like my mother cross the ocean and must face conflicting perspectives, there's often little room for debating these perspectives. In my mother's childhood household, there was a right history and a wrong history. According to my grandfather, my mother's textbook was telling the wrong history.

Wikipedia often, but not always, forces resolution of conflicting 10 accounts. Critics may deride *Wikipedia* as a crowdsourced, user-generated collection of information of dubious origin and accuracy, but the service also provides a platform for seeing how knowledge evolves and is contested. The *Wikipedia* entry on the American Revolution is a clear product of conflicting ideas of history, with information that stems from British and American textbooks interwoven and combined with information on the role of other actors that have been historically marginalized in standard textbooks.

What makes the American Revolution *Wikipedia* entry interesting is not simply the output in the form of a comprehensive article but the extensive discussion pages and edit history. On the history pages, those who edit *Wikipedia* entries describe why they made a change.

On discussion pages, participants debate how to resolve conflicts between editors. There's an entire section on the American Revolution discussion page dedicated to whether colonists should be described as "patriots" — the American term — or "insurgents" — the British term. In the discussion, one user suggests a third term: "revolutionaries." Throughout the *Wikipedia* entry, the editors collectively go to great lengths to talk about "American patriots" or use terms like "revolutionaries" or simply describe the colonists as "Americans." The American Revolution discussion page on *Wikipedia* is itself a lesson about history. Through archived debate, the editors make visible just how contested simple issues are, forcing the reader to think about why writers present information in certain ways. I learned more about the different viewpoints surrounding the American Revolution by reading the *Wikipedia* discussion page than I learned in my AP American history class.

Although most teens that I met who used the internet knew of *Wikipedia* and most of those who had visited the site knew it was editable, virtually none knew about the discussion page or the history of edits. No one taught them to think of *Wikipedia* as an evolving document that reveals how people produce knowledge. Instead they determined whether an article was "good" or "bad" based on whether they thought that their teachers could be trusted when they criticized *Wikipedia*. This is a lost opportunity. *Wikipedia* provides an ideal context for engaging youth to interrogate their sources and understand how information is produced.

Wikipedia is, by both its nature and its commitments, a work in progress. The content changes over time as users introduce new knowledge and raise new issues. The site has its share of inaccuracies, but the community surrounding *Wikipedia* also has a systematic approach to addressing them. At times, people actively and intentionally introduce false information, either as a hoax or for personal gain. *Wikipedia* acknowledges these problems and maintains a record for observers. *Wikipedia* even maintains a list of hoaxes that significantly affected the site.[4]

Many digital technologies undermine or destabilize institutions of authority and expertise, revealing alternative ways of generating and curating content.[5] Crowdsourced content — such as what is provided to *Wikipedia* — is not necessarily better, more accurate, or more comprehensive than expert-vetted content, but it can, and often does, play a valuable role in making information accessible and providing a site for reflection on the production of knowledge. The value of *Wikipedia* would be minimal if it weren't for sources that people could use in creating entries. Many of *Wikipedia*'s history articles, for example, rely heavily on content written by historians. What *Wikipedia* does well is combine and present information from many sources in a free, publicly accessible, understandable way while also revealing biases and discussions that went into the production of that content. Even with their limitations and weaknesses, projects like *Wikipedia* are important for educational efforts because they make the production of knowledge more visible. They also highlight a valuable way of using technology to create opportunities for increased digital literacy.

Notes

1. Jim Giles, "Special Report: Internet Encyclopaedias Go Head to Head," *Nature* 438 (2005): 900–901.

2. Although educators often dismiss *Wikipedia* over issues of credibility, they also tend to downplay the educational value of using the service. In "Writing, Citing, and Participatory Media: Wikis as Learning Environments in the High School Classroom" (*International Journal of Learning and Media* 1, no. 4 [2010]: 23–44), Andrea Forte and Amy Bruckman found that engaging with wikis was a learning-rich experience for high school students that contributed to both writing and information assessment skills.

3. Texas's undue influence on the US textbook market is discussed in Gail Collins, "How Texas Inflicts Bad Textbooks on Us," *New York Review of Books*, June 21, 2012. For examples of how Texan Christianity shapes textbooks, see Michael Birnbaum, "Historians Speak Out Against Proposed Texas Textbook Changes," *Washington Post*, March 18, 2010.

4. See http://en.wikipedia.org/wiki/Wikipedia:List_of_hoaxes_on_Wikipedia.241.

5. The potential of social media and other recent technologies for helping address issues in information flow and curation — including crowd-sourcing, classification, and cooperation — has been the topic of numerous books in recent years. See David Weinberger, *Everything Is Miscellaneous: The Power of the New Digital Disorder* (New York: Holt, 2007); Clay Shirky, *Cognitive Surplus: Creativity and Generosity in a Connected Age* (New York: Penguin, 2010); and Yochai Benkler, *The Penguin and the Leviathan: How Cooperation Triumphs over Self-Interest* (New York: Crown, 2011).

Engaging with the Text

1. Why does danah boyd think *Wikipedia*'s "bad rap in American K–12 education" is undeserved? What crucial advantage does she think the site provides? How much had you thought about this issue before you read this essay? Do you agree with boyd about its importance? Why or why not?

2. The primary **AUDIENCE** for boyd's evaluation is teachers, though parents and students would also benefit from it. Is her evaluation effective for this audience? Why or why not? How might it change if she were targeting students instead, or parents who don't want their children "confused" by conflicting interpretations of historical events?   57–60

3. Boyd does not **BEGIN** with her own assessment of *Wikipedia*. Instead, she starts out with its general reputation and only gradually leads up to her own judgment, stating it most fully in her **ENDING** paragraph. What are the advantages of this strategy? What might be the disadvantages? Was it a good choice for this topic? Why or why not?   331–38   338–42

4. A strong evaluation requires a **BALANCED AND FAIR** assessment of a subject. Is boyd's assessment of *Wikipedia* balanced and fair? Identify two passages that support your answer, and explain how.   202

5. *For Writing.* Select an information website other than *Wikipedia* that offers definitions or encyclopedic information. Compare and contrast several entries on that site with their counterparts on *Wikipedia*, and offer an **EVALUATION** of the site based on that comparison.   197–205

CONSUMER REPORTS

Fast Food: Four Big Names Lose

36,733 Readers Rate the Food, Value, Staff, and Speed at 53 Chains

The following report appeared in the August 2011 issue of Consumer Reports, *a magazine dedicated to testing products and services and reporting the results of such tests to consumers so they can make informed choices. In this case,* Consumer Reports *relied on the ratings in a survey of 36,733 readers. As you read, notice the criteria the writer uses to evaluate the subject — fast-food restaurants.*

NEXT TIME YOU HAVE A CRAVING FOR FAST FOOD, think twice about slowing down for Burger King, KFC, McDonald's, or Taco Bell.

In our first major survey of quick-service restaurants (industry-speak for fast-food chains), subscribers who made a total of more than 98,000 visits to 53 chains said those four biggies were worse than many others. The main reason: the uninspiring food, though they also had so-so service. Readers said those chains, which boast of supersized value, don't even offer much bang for the buck. Other major chains with relatively low scores: sandwich shops Arby's and Quiznos and pizza joints Domino's and Pizza Hut.

By contrast, our survey revealed good deals and even better meals at dozens of less-ubiquitous fast-food restaurants. Readers gave 21 of them especially high marks for food; 11 stood out for value. In-N-Out Burger (264 restaurants in Arizona, California, Nevada, Texas, and Utah), Chipotle Mexican Grill (1,100 nationwide), Chick-fil-A (1,536 nationwide), and Papa Murphy's Take 'N' Bake Pizza (1,250 in 37 states and Canada) ranked at the top of their type, and offered speedy and solicitous service that the industry giants couldn't match. (Most restaurant counts are approximate.)

Our survey's other key findings:

Diners want better food. Many restaurants scored higher for service — 5
specifically, speed and politeness — than for food. At chains with the highest scores for food, 42 to 54 percent of patrons called the fare excellent, but at Burger King, KFC, McDonald's, and Taco Bell, no more than 11 percent of patrons did. In fact, 15 to 19 percent of respondents who ate at one of those chains thought the food was fair, poor, or very poor. At Sbarro, an international Italian chain trying to emerge from bankruptcy, 27 percent of patrons judged the food fair, poor, or very poor.

Cheap food may not be a bargain. Fifty-four percent of those surveyed cited low prices as a reason for picking a particular fast-food restaurant, and savvy shoppers can often score discounts by downloading coupons and other perks from a chain's website and social-media pages. But despite the low prices, just 19 percent of all respondents said they got excellent value for their money. In-N-Out Burger, Papa Murphy's, and CiCi's Pizza offered the best value; Sbarro, Round Table Pizza, and KFC, the worst.

Who makes the best fries?

By Wendy's own reckoning, its spuds were sort of duds. Ken Calwell, the chain's chief marketing officer before being named Papa Murphy's Pizza president, conceded that Wendy's never enjoyed McDonald's reputation for tasty french fries. So Wendy's went back to the kitchen and came out with a revamped fry, made from russet potatoes, with the skin on for added flavor and texture, cooked in trans-fat-free oil, and dusted with sea salt.

Wendy's says its new fries are so good that they beat McDonald's by a wide margin in a recent independent consumer taste test. To see for ourselves, we had two sensory experts taste fries from those two chains and from Burger King, Five Guys, Fuddruckers, and KFC in the New York tristate area.

Bottom line. Wendy's has the right to brag, and we scored its fries Very Good. Our experts gave Wendy's a slight edge over McDonald's because its fries were "a bit more potato-y." The others were close too, except Burger King; its fries tasted fatty, had less-intense potato flavor, and rated only Good.

Wendy's: Distinct potato flavor enhanced by browned and earthy taste of skins. Crispy outside, moist inside. Quality somewhat inconsistent.

Five Guys: Big baked-potato flavor complemented by oil and salt. Crispness and doneness were variable.

McDonald's: Moderate potato and browned flavors with crispy texture.

KFC: Flavorful seasoned wedges with extra-crispy coating and peppery kick. Very soft interior.

Fuddruckers: Spicy wedges with garlic, black pepper, salt, and paprika, sometimes distributed unevenly. Interiors slightly dry and mealy; edges lightly crisped. Some earthy skin flavor and bitterness.

Burger King: Relatively low in flavor; coating detracts from quality. Fatty taste has about the same intensity as potato flavor.

Diners want a better experience. Whether they ordered cafeteria-style, at a counter, or at a drive-thru, or had food delivered, readers were much less pleased overall with fast-food restaurants than with casual full-service eateries like Cracker Barrel, Outback Steakhouse, and Red Lobster. Sixty percent of respondents said they were completely or very satisfied with their fast-food dining experiences vs. 68 percent of casual-restaurant patrons.

Sometimes fast food isn't. The slowest places to get fast food were KFC, Popeyes, and Pizza Hut.

Consumers talk thin but eat fat. Despite their reputation for blowing a diet to smithereens, fast-food restaurants offer plenty of healthful options. Hardee's (1,900 in 30 states and nine countries) and Carl's Jr. (1,100 worldwide) recently started selling charbroiled turkey burgers; Subway (34,679 in 98 countries), egg-white omelets; and Little Caesars (thousands from coast to coast), pizza crust and sauce with no animal products.

Trouble is, there aren't many takers. "Indulgence wins over healthfulness every time," says Darren Tristano, executive vice president of Technomic, a food-service research and consulting firm in Chicago. When asked if they had eaten a healthful meal during their most recent visit to a fast-food restaurant, only 13 percent of those surveyed said yes. At pizza chains, just 4 percent said they'd ordered something healthful. 10

Subway, with a "Fresh Fit" menu . . . , had the most diet-conscious eaters: Almost half of respondents who ate there said they chose a nutritious meal. But not all sandwiches are created equal, even at Subway, where the footlong Italian B.M.T. sub packs 900 calories and 40 grams of fat.

Winners and Losers

Are some of the biggest and best-known chains low-rated because of the Walmart syndrome, in which the public enjoys taking potshots at the 800-pound gorilla? Not according to Tristano. "The large chains are consistent and they're everywhere, but they do get lower scores for their

Sinking sub!

Subway is known for its healthful menu offerings, notably low-fat subs like the Turkey Breast & Black Forest Ham sandwich pictured below. But not every choice at Subway is a smart one. The footlong Italian B.M.T., with cheese, ham, pepperoni, salami, and veggies, is packed with more than a day's worth of sodium and more than half of a day's recommended fat allotment.

SIX-INCH Turkey Breast & Black Forest Ham
on nine-grain wheat bread: 280 calories, 4 grams of fat, and 820 milligrams of sodium

FOOTLONG Italian B.M.T.
on nine-grain wheat bread: 900 calories, 40 grams of fat, and 3,000 milligrams of sodium

overall experience," he says. "It's not high quality that's driving traffic, it's good value, drive-thru, and convenience."

Fortunately, if you like fast food of any type, there are plenty of good choices.

For burger fans, the best restaurants include In-N-Out Burger, rated highest of all 53 chains, Burgerville (39 in Oregon and Washington), Five Guys Burgers and Fries (750 nationwide and in Canada), Culver's (428 mainly in the Midwest), and Back Yard Burgers (120 mostly in the South and East).

For Mexican food, Chipotle, Rubio's Fresh (180 in the West), Qdoba (500 nationally), and Baja Fresh (255 in 24 states and Dubai) earned high marks for food and service.

15

academic literacies | rhetorical situations | genres | processes | strategies | research MLA / APA | media / design | readings

FAST-FOOD FACT

A better burger? Thirty-six percent of Burgerville diners in our survey said they ordered a healthful meal. No other burger joint came close. Though its burgers are about as nutritious as the rest, the chain may benefit from a "halo" effect from what it calls its "fresh, local, sustainable" food and reliance on "pastured, vegetarian-fed, and antibiotic-free" beef.

One chicken chain topped the rest: Chick-fil-A. (It has come under criticism, but not for its food: A franchisee ruffled feathers earlier this year by donating food for events by a group reportedly opposing gay marriage, prompting company president and chief operating officer Dan Cathy to respond in a video. "Providing food to these events," he said in part, "is not an endorsement.")

Crave a top-notch wedge, hero, hoagie, or sub served quickly with a smile on the side? Try Jason's Deli (200 in 28 states), Firehouse Subs (426 in 24 states), Jersey Mike's Sub (500 nationwide), Potbelly Sandwich Shop (200 in 11 states and Washington, D.C.), Jimmy John's Gourmet Sandwiches (1,000 nationwide), or Schlotzsky's (327 nationwide).

The single standout for pizza: Papa Murphy's Take 'N' Bake Pizza, which has an unconventional concept: Patrons order a pizza to bake at home.

The Big Picture

On average, our survey respondents bought lunch or dinner at a fast-food chain four times a month; 13 percent did so 10 or more times. Although three-quarters said the sagging economy didn't affect how often they ate fast food, 22 percent said they eat out at fast-food restaurants less often than they used to because of financial concerns.

Still, fast-food restaurants have weathered the recession better than white-tablecloth and casual restaurants, many of which were forced to offer discounts such as smaller portions at lower prices. "The restaurant industry is immediately affected by how flush consumers feel, so the recession had a huge impact," says Robin Lee Allen, executive editor of *Nation's Restaurant News,* a trade publication. But things are picking up. After three dismal years, the National Restaurant Association,

How good are the chains' main dishes?

We asked 25,079 subscribers who recently bought the pizza chains' pizza, chicken chains' grilled or roasted chicken, sandwich chains' subs, and Mexican chains' tacos and burritos this question: On a scale of 1 to 10, from least delicious to most delicious you've ever eaten, how would you rate the taste?

The tables reveal that some house specialties came close to our readers' standards for excellence, but CiCi's Pizza, Del Taco, Little Caesars, Sbarro, and Taco Bell earned significantly lower scores than most chains for the foods that best define them. Domino's, which with fanfare changed its core recipe in December 2009, seeking a better pie, came in fifth place, behind Papa Murphy's and other pizza joints. KFC chicken was rated less tasty than chicken from most rival chains.

Among burger chains (which we covered in October), burgers at In-N-Out Burger and Five Guys Burgers and Fries were standouts. Burger King and Wendy's fared better than McDonald's, whose burgers ranked lowest of all.

Mexican food	Taste
Chipotle Mexican Grill	7.7
Rubio's Fresh Mexican Grill	7.5
Qdoba Mexican Grill	7.4
Moe's Southwest Grill	7.3
Baja Fresh Mexican Grill	7.2
Taco John's	6.6
Del Taco	6.1
Taco Bell	6.0

Chicken	Taste
Chick-fil-A	7.6
Boston Market	7.4
Popeyes Louisiana Kitchen	7.4
El Pollo Loco	7.4
Zaxby's	7.2
Bojangles' Famous Chicken 'n Biscuits	7.1
Church's Chicken	7.0
KFC	6.6

Sandwiches and subs	Taste
Firehouse Subs	8.0
Jason's Deli	7.8
Jersey Mike's Subs	7.7
Schlotzsky's	7.7
Jimmy John's Gourmet Sandwiches	7.6
Potbelly Sandwich Shop	7.4
Togo's	7.4
McAlister's Deli	7.2
Quiznos	7.1
Subway	6.8
Arby's	6.8

Pizza	Taste
Papa Murphy's Take 'N' Bake Pizza	7.8
Round Table Pizza	7.3
Papa John's	6.9
Pizza Hut	6.6
Domino's Pizza	6.1
CiCi's Pizza	5.8
Little Caesars	5.7
Sbarro	5.7

academic literacies   rhetorical situations   genres   processes   strategies   research MLA / APA   media / design   readings

a trade group, forecasts that restaurant sales will grow by an estimated 3.6 percent this year, to $604 billion. Twenty-seven percent of that total is expected to be spent at fast-food restaurants. Their food is relatively inexpensive to begin with, and they've attracted new customers determined to keep eating out but on a tighter budget.

Many chains keep customers coming back with limited-time promotions like Whataburger's Chop House Cheddar Burger and super-cheap options such as Domino's pizza-and-chicken-wing package, $5.99 each. The tactic of mixing low-price choices (think Dollar Menu), patented specialties (McDonald's Big Mac), and some pricier items (Burger King's A1 Steakhouse XT burger) is called barbell or tiered pricing. Its goal is to lure customers with a few heavily advertised loss leaders, then tempt them to buy more profitable items.

FAST-FOOD FACT

Pizza snobs? In the Boston-to-New York corridor and in Chicago, you're likely to find a mom-and-pop pizza shop on almost every corner. Readers who live in these areas gave pizza chains much lower scores than those who live in the rest of the U.S.

That's effective, but experts wonder whether rising commodity and fuel costs will lead to price hikes that cause a double whammy: fewer cars at the drive-thru and fewer customers buying profitable fare.

To enhance the customer experience (and the perception of value), many chains are upgrading their facilities. McDonald's, for instance, is replacing its classic yellow-and-red interiors with muted yellows, greens, and oranges and exchanging its fiberglass chairs for wood and faux-leather ones. In addition, most franchises will add a second drive-thru window; some will also add a TV or two.

Besides remodeling, some chains are allowing customers to place orders online for pickup; expanding their selection of snacks and breakfast items; adding grilled items; reducing fat and sodium; and catering to customers with diabetes or gluten intolerance.

How to Avoid Temptation

Some states and towns have passed or are considering regulations 25 requiring restaurants to display nutrition information at the point of sale, so it's in your face when you order. Does that keep diners from overindulging? A handful of small studies show mixed results.

Researchers at Yale University reported in a 2009 study that they observed 303 adults in New Haven, Connecticut, and found that a group that saw calorie counts before ordering consumed 14 percent fewer calories than a group that didn't. A study by New York University researchers who analyzed the ordering habits of consumers in low-income areas suggested that those who were exposed to calorie counts before ordering didn't make healthier choices.

Another recent study by researchers at Duke–National University of Singapore Graduate Medical School focused on one fast-food chain in King County, Washington, where local legislation requires calorie counts. It found that the labeling had no effect on consumer behavior in the year after the law's implementation.

A provision in the Patient Protection and Affordable Care Act of 2010 requires consistent calorie labeling of menus at food establishments with 20 or more locations. But that part of the legislation is progressing slowly. In April the Food and Drug Administration issued guidelines on implementing the rule, and it's awaiting comments. Allen of *Nation's Restaurant News* says the final rule is expected to be published by year's end and to go into effect six months later.

Even before the rule takes effect, there are plenty of ways for you to ensure that healthfulness wins over indulgence:

Visit websites. Many fast-food chains post figures for fat, calories, 30 and sodium.

Have it your way. Many chains will hold the mayo or cheese, go easy on sauces, substitute skim milk for whole, or serve dressings on the side. Being able to customize was a key reason many respondents visited sandwich shops.

Ratings: Fast-food chains

in order of reader score

BETTER < < < < > > > WORSE

Restaurant	Reader score (0–100)	Survey results (Food, Value, Staff, Speed)
BURGERS		
In-N-Out Burger	88	
Burgerville	83	
Five Guys Burgers and Fries	83	
Culver's	82	
Back Yard Burgers	82	
Whataburger	80	
Fuddruckers	80	
White Castle	78	
Checkers	77	
Hardee's	76	
Sonic	76	
Krystal	75	
Carl's Jr.	75	
Wendy's	75	
Jack in the Box	74	
A&W Restaurants	74	
Burger King	71	
McDonald's	71	
MEXICAN		
Chipotle Mexican Grill	82	
Rubio's Fresh Mexican Grill	80	
Qdoba Mexican Grill	79	
Baja Fresh Mexican Grill	78	
Moe's Southwest Grill	77	
Taco John's	73	
Taco Bell	72	
Del Taco	71	
CHICKEN		
Chick-fil-A	83	
El Pollo Loco	76	
Boston Market	76	
Zaxby's	76	
Bojangles' Famous Chicken 'n Biscuits	76	
Popeyes Louisiana Kitchen	73	
Church's Chicken	72	
KFC	67	
SANDWICHES AND SUBS		
Jason's Deli	83	
Firehouse Subs	83	
Jersey Mike's Subs	82	
Potbelly Sandwich Shop	81	
Jimmy John's Gourmet Sandwich Shop	81	
Schlotzsky's	80	
Togo's	78	
Subway	77	
McAlister's Deli	77	
Arby's	73	
Quiznos	73	
PIZZA		
Papa Murphy's Take 'N' Bake Pizza	86	
Round Table Pizza	75	
Little Caesars	74	
Papa John's	74	
CiCi's Pizza	73	
Pizza Hut	70	
Domino's Pizza	68	
Sbarro	63	

Guide to the Ratings

Ratings are based on a survey of 36,733 *Consumer Reports* subscribers who told us about 98,253 dining experiences at 53 hamburger, pizza, chicken, sandwich, and Mexican fast-food chains from April 2009 to June 2010. Respondents are not necessarily representative of the national population. Reader score is a measure of overall satisfaction. A score of 100 would mean all respondents were completely satisfied with their experience; 80 means they were very well satisfied on average; 60, fairly well satisfied. Differences of 5 points are meaningful. Other results reflect how well each chain did compared with the rest in **food** quality, perceived **value**, politeness of **staff**, and **speed** of service.

Beware of certain words. When you see "battered," "creamy," "crispy," "crusted," "sautéed," or "stuffed," read "fattening." Look for roasted, broiled, baked, grilled, charbroiled, steamed, poached, or blackened food.

Summon your willpower. Don't supersize unless you plan to feed the entire family. Opt for a single patty instead of a double- or triple-decker, the standard soft drink rather than the Bunyonesque option, and a turkey or veggie burger instead of beef. More chains carry unsweetened tea, flavored water, and coffee as alternatives to sodas. Try a side salad with low-fat dressing, and for dessert, try sliced apples with a fat-free caramel sauce instead of a vanilla shake. At Sonic, the apples and sauce are 110 calories, vs. 480 calories for the shake.

Engaging with the Text

201–2

1. What **CLEARLY DEFINED CRITERIA** did *Consumer Reports* use to evaluate quick-service restaurants? Are these appropriate ones to use? Are there additional criteria you would have included?

609–11

2. Examine the **CHARTS** on page 778 and at the end of the evaluation on page 781. How helpful are the charts in summarizing the evaluations in the text? How well do the data they present match any experience you have had at the restaurants listed?

3. The article ends with the section "How to Avoid Temptation." Why do you think *Consumer Reports* included these suggestions? Can you think of any others that would be useful?

604–5

4. How does *Consumer Reports* use **HEADINGS** to help readers throughout the article? How do the headings function?

197–207

5. **For Writing.** Create your own survey to **EVALUATE** student hangout spots. Have students in your class, your dorm, or your program fill out the survey, rating various spots for criteria such as food, music, atmosphere, and decor. Tabulate the results and decide which are the most popular spots and which are less favored and why. Write an essay that presents the survey results for students on your campus to help them identify good places to go.

NATALIE STANDIFORD

The Tenacity of Hope

Natalie Standiford (b. 1961) is author of numerous books for children and young adults, including How to Say Goodbye in Robot *(2010),* The Boy on the Bridge *(2013), and* The Secret Tree *(2012), which the* New York Times *named a Notable Children's Book of 2012. She worked as an assistant editor in the children's book division of the publisher Random House before leaving to become a full-time writer. Standiford is also a musician, playing bass with fellow authors in the band Tiger Beat. The following book review appeared in the* New York Times *in 2012.*

"I AM NOT A MATHEMATICIAN, BUT I KNOW THIS," says Hazel Grace Lancaster, the narrator of *The Fault in Our Stars*, the latest novel by John Green, a Michael L. Printz medalist and author of several best-selling novels for young adults. "There are infinite numbers between zero and one. There's .1 and .12 and .112 and an infinite collection of others." The trouble, she says, is, "I want more numbers than I'm likely to get."

This is a problem faced by the heroines in both *The Fault in Our Stars* and *The Probability of Miracles,* two young adult novels about 16-year-old girls who have cancer: their days are numbered. At the outset, the two books are remarkably similar. Both begin by bluntly describing the harsh realities of life as a cancer patient through the wry sensibility of a smart, sarcastic teenage girl. They are both surprisingly funny and entertaining, given the subject matter, and both are at heart teenage love stories. About halfway through, though, *The Probability of Miracles* veers off in one direction — toward the miracles of the title — while *The Fault in Our Stars* stays the course of tragic realism. And that's where the difference lies.

Campbell Cooper, the heroine of Wendy Wunder's first novel, is a child of Disney World: her parents were both fire dancers in the "Spirit of Aloha" show at the Polynesian Hotel. Growing up in a manufactured fantasy world has made Cam understandably cynical. When her doctor reports that her cancer has spread and medical science has done all it can, Cam resigns herself to dying.

Then she comes across a "Flamingo List" she made a year earlier, a list of everything she wants to do before she dies, things she imagines to be part of a normal adolescence, like "Lose my virginity at a keg party," "Kill my little sister's dreams" and "Experiment with petty shoplifting." It's time to start crossing things off the Flamingo List, and so she starts with the easiest one: shoplifting.

Cam has accepted that she's going to die. But her mother and little   5
sister want her to keep fighting, to believe in miracles. Hoping Cam will learn to "trust how the universe unfolds," her mother insists on a road trip to Promise, Me., a mystical town known for its healing powers.

Promise, a sparkling New England village, is as much of a fantasy — if a less plasticized version — as the world Cam left behind in Florida. Upon their arrival, a handsome boy named Asher invites her and her family to stay in his gorgeous mansion overlooking the ocean. And though Cam resists the idea, Promise does appear to be full of miracles. The sunsets last for hours. Orcas improbably leap out of the bay in the evening. There are purple dandelions, a rainbow at night, snow in July and an unlikely flock of flamingoes. And Cam feels better. She can eat again; she has energy. Though she is "hope-resistant," that begins to change.

Cam has setbacks, but eventually she succumbs to the spell of Promise and Asher, a hunky football star who reads James Joyce for fun. Even Cam says, "A person can be too perfect, you know." By the end of the summer, she has crossed everything off her Flamingo List. Meanwhile, her sarcasm has lost its edge, and alas, so has the book. When Cam's story, which starts out so gritty and real, devolves into fantasy, the sense of what dying young of cancer is really like is lost.

The grim reality is always present, however, in Hazel Lancaster, the heroine of *The Fault in Our Stars,* who narrates her story in a hip, angry, funny tone similar to Cam's. Hazel has thyroid cancer that has spread calamitously to her lungs when she meets Augustus Waters, a former basketball player who has lost a leg to osteosarcoma, at a support group for cancer kids in Indianapolis. Augustus lends Hazel his favorite book, *The Price of Dawn,* the "brilliant and haunting novelization of my favorite video game," so she lends him hers: *An Imperial Affliction* by Peter Van

academic literacies · rhetorical situations · genres · processes · strategies · research MLA / APA · media / design · readings

Houten, about a girl who has cancer. Van Houten ends his novel abruptly in the middle of a sentence, and Hazel is obsessed with finding out what happened to the characters. Augustus, too, becomes riveted by *An Imperial Affliction,* and uses his "wish" from "The Genie Foundation," an organization devoted to the cheering up of sick children, to send himself and Hazel to Amsterdam to meet Van Houten.

At first Augustus, like Asher, seems too good to be true. He's sexy and smart, and he appears to want nothing more than to do nice things for Hazel. But we come to understand how Gus's illness has forced him to confront the big questions of life and death. Over the course of the narrative, his appealing exterior breaks down; his flaws, fears and humiliations are exposed, yet he is all the more lovable for his frailty and heartbreaking humanity.

Like *The Probability of Miracles,* this is a love story, but it is also a book   10
by John Green, author of *Looking for Alaska* and *Paper Towns,* and it is written in his signature tone, a blend of melancholy, sweet, philosophical and funny. When Hazel decides to give away her childhood swing set because the sight of it depresses her, she considers this headline for the Craigslist ad: "Lonely, Vaguely Pedophilic Swing Set Seeks the Butts of Children." Green's characters may be improbably witty, but even under the direst circumstances they are the kind of people you wish you knew.

If the story takes a grimmer turn than that of *The Probability of Miracles,* the characters compel the reader to stick with them. *The Fault in Our Stars* is all the more heart-rending for its bluntness about the medical realities of cancer. There are harrowing descriptions of pain, shame, anger and bodily fluids of every type. It is a narrative without rainbows or flamingoes; there are no magical summer snowstorms. Instead, Hazel has to lug a portable oxygen tank with her wherever she goes, and Gus has a prosthetic leg. Their friend Isaac is missing an eye and later goes blind. These unpleasant details do nothing to diminish the romance; in Green's hands, they only make it more moving. He shows us true love — two teenagers helping and accepting each other through the most humiliating physical and emotional ordeals — and it is far more romantic than any sunset on the beach.

As Hazel and Gus often remind each other, the world is not a wish-granting factory. Nevertheless, "a forever within the numbered days" can be found, and as Hazel shows us, maybe that's all we can ask for.

Engaging with the Text

1. At first, Natalie Standiford seems to maintain the same objective **STANCE** toward both novels she is reviewing. When she begins to give a negative evaluation of one and a positive evaluation of the other, does her stance — as reflected in her tone — change accordingly? Why do you think she does or does not shift her tone in this way?

12–15 ■

2. A writer of an evaluation must offer a **KNOWLEDGEABLE** discussion of her subject. How does Standiford reveal she is knowledgeable about the books she is reviewing? Point to one passage that makes clear that she knows what she is writing about — not only these books but others by their authors as well.

202 ▲

3. On the basis of what **CRITERIA** does Standiford compare and contrast the two novels? Are her criteria appropriate? Why or why not? What other criteria might she have used?

201–2 ▲

4. Standiford uses **TRANSITIONS** between her paragraphs to connect the ideas. For example, she refers back to the subject of the last sentence of the previous paragraph, as in "This is a problem . . ." and "Promise . . ."; she also links ideas chronologically using "Then" and "At first" and by comparison using "Like." Are these transitions clear and effective? Why or why not? How else might Standiford have helped readers move from one paragraph to another?

349 ◆

5. *For Writing.* Different writers often deal with the same subject from different perspectives. Select two short stories or brief nonfiction narratives (such as newspaper stories) that deal with the same subject. **COMPARE AND CONTRAST** the presentation of the storylines, the characters, and the settings in the two works, and write an **EVALUATION** that explains which you found more successful and why (or why both failed or succeeded equally).

380–87 ◆
197–205 ▲

✳ academic literacies ■ rhetorical situations ▲ genres ○ processes ◆ strategies ● research MLA / APA ▢ media / design 📖 readings

CHRIS SUELLENTROP

Where Wordplay Trumps Swordplay

Chris Suellentrop (b. 1975) is a freelance contributor to the New York Times, *where in 2006 he founded the blog* Opinionator *and became the first writer paid by the Times to blog. His writing has also been published in the* Boston Globe, Slate, *and the* Washington Post, *among other publications. In 2011, Suellentrop was awarded the National Magazine Award for profile writing. The following video game review appeared in the* New York Times *in 2014.*

T O A VIEWER OF PRESTIGE CABLE, *Iron From Ice*, the first episode of the new *Game of Thrones* video game, might seem inferior to HBO's *Game of Thrones* in nearly every way imaginable. The writing is worse. The acting is worse. The scenery and cinematography — animated instead of captured with a camera — are less gorgeous. There is no frequent, graphic sex to punctuate the conniving and the swordplay.

And yet, judged by this installment in a projected six-episode series, *Game of Thrones* is going to be a good video game, possibly even great. That's because the designers at Telltale Games have gotten the interactive elements right. What matters most in a video game, unlike in a TV drama, is the choosing.

A good shooter game forces a player to make countless small decisions under threat of virtual death. Those choices lead to what players call immersion, the sense of falling into another world. *Game of Thrones* isn't a shooter. (Its snooze-worthy action scenes, in fact, allow the player only one choice: Respond properly to an on-screen prompt, or die.) But its immersive appeal is similar. Here, the intensity and pressure occur not during firefights but during conversations.

And your words matter, because, as everyone knows, in *Game of Thrones*, everyone is at risk of death, all the time.

Telltale's masterpiece is *The Walking Dead* video game, which over the 5 course of 10 episodes and a little more than two years has proved itself more involving and affecting than the television show of the same name. (Each episode, like *Iron From Ice*, takes roughly two hours to play.) *The Walking*

Dead — the TV show and the video game — each take their inspiration from and are created under license from comic books by Robert Kirkman. Although the source material is the same, the characters and stories are different.

Iron From Ice owes much to *The Walking Dead* game, but it also faces, in some ways, a stiffer challenge. This game is adapted less from *A Song of Ice and Fire*, the fantasy series by George R. R. Martin, than from the *Game of Thrones* TV version, which HBO has licensed to Telltale. *Iron From Ice* begins outside the so-called Red Wedding, the climax of the show's third season, and the events of the game occur in the background of the show's fourth season. (Season 5 is slated for 2015.)

The game benefits in certain ways from this arrangement: We hear and see the voices and likenesses of the actors who play Lannisters and Tyrells and other Westeros plotters, including Peter Dinklage as Tyrion. But I was often drawn out of the fiction when a prominent visage from television appeared in Telltale's game, because I began comparing the game unfavorably with the show.

Unlike Telltale's *The Walking Dead*, *Game of Thrones* feels supplementary to the television show rather than competitive with it. Still, the main characters in the game are entirely new. The player is given a shifting perspective in the House of Forrester, a hitherto obscure Westeros family apparently mentioned in *A Dance With Dragons*, the fifth of Mr. Martin's novels.

The Forresters are an ersatz Stark clan, the heroic family that most *Game of Thrones* viewers root for. In *Iron From Ice*, you play as a squire who is banished to the Wall (much like Jon Snow), a handmaiden navigating the treacherous politics of King's Landing (much like Sansa Stark), and a young lord learning how to rule after his father's death (a mixture of Robb and Bran Stark).

The perspectives and the politicking help to make the game's conversations feel more like strategy and less like self-expression. The player must persuade others — through trickery, lies, bluffs, threats and even well-chosen truths — rather than just blurt out whatever option comports with how the game makes you feel at the moment. Can you convince Cersei Lannister that your loyalties are with the king? Should you get Margaery Tyrell to appeal on your behalf to King Joffrey? 10

No matter what you choose, I suspect that the plot remains largely the same, except with different characters taking similar actions. That trick is

academic literacies   rhetorical situations   genres   processes   strategies   research MLA / APA   media / design   readings

how Telltale has kept its previous games from branching too widely. Some players argue that this means the decisions in Telltale's games don't matter, because they don't open into practically limitless vistas of possibility.

But if it doesn't matter to you if someone in a story rises or falls, or lives or dies, then the failing is not one of choice or plotting but of character. And *Game of Thrones*, like the television show whose name it shares, is a game with characters worth caring about.

Engaging with the Text

1. When Chris Suellentrop **BEGINS** his review, it appears that he will offer a negative evaluation of his subject. Yet, he goes on to say, "*Game of Thrones* is going to be a good video game, possibly even great." Is this kind of reversal an effective way to grab the reader's attention? Why or why not?

331–38

2. A successful evaluation makes clear the writer's **CRITERIA**. What central criterion does Suellentrop apply in his evaluation? Do you also see this criterion as the key one for a video game? Why or why not? Sometimes the appropriate criteria depend on the **AUDIENCE**. How would you describe Suellentrop's intended audience for this review?

201–2

57–60

3. Does Suellentrop offer a **BALANCED AND FAIR ASSESSMENT** of his subject? Identify two passages that reveal his assessment and discuss whether they are balanced and fair.

202

4. Suellentrop **DEFINES** "immersion" in a video game as having to make many small but crucial choices that give "the sense of falling into another world." How does this definition help the reader understand the term? How is this sensation similar to — or different from — "immersion" in another kind of activity, such as reading, playing a sport, or listening to music?

388–98

5. *For Writing.* How do people decide whether to play a particular game? Select a recently released video or board game and write an **EVALUATION** of it for an audience who know little or nothing about it. What information would the audience need to help them decide whether or not to play this game? Make sure your evaluation is balanced and fair and is based on clearly defined criteria for what makes a good game.

197–205

64 Literary Analyses

See also:

academic literacies · rhetorical situations · genres · processes · strategies · research MLA / APA · media / design · readings

WILLOW D. CRYSTAL

"One of us . . . "
Concepts of the Private and the Public in "A Rose for Emily"

The following essay was written by Willow D. Crystal, a student at Harvard, as a model paper for The Norton Introduction to Literature. *As you read it, notice how Crystal draws on scholarly research to support her claims about the tensions between private and public constructs in Faulkner's "A Rose for Emily." See page 803 if you want to read the story.*

THROUGHOUT "A ROSE FOR EMILY," William Faulkner introduces a tension between what is private, or belongs to the individual, and what is public, or the possession of the group. "When Miss Emily Grierson died," the tale begins, "our whole town went to her funeral: the men through a sort of respectful affection for a fallen monument, the women mostly out of curiosity to see the inside of her house . . ." (803). The men of the small town of Jefferson, Mississippi, are motivated to attend Miss Emily's funeral for public reasons; the women, to see "the inside of her house," that private realm which has remained inaccessible for "at least ten years" (803).

This opposition of the private with the public has intrigued critics of Faulkner's tale since the story was first published. Distinctions between the private and the public are central to Lawrence R. Rodgers's argument in his essay "'We all said, "She will kill herself"': The Narrator/Detective in William Faulkner's 'A Rose for Emily.'" The very concept of the detective genre demands that "there must be concealed facts that . . . must become clear in the end" (119), private actions which become public knowledge. In her feminist tribute, "A Rose for 'A Rose for Emily,'" Judith Fetterley uses the private-public dichotomy to demonstrate the "grotesque reality" (34) of the patriarchal social system in Faulkner's story. According to Fetterley, Miss Emily's "private life becomes a public document that the town folk feel free to interpret at will" (36). Thus, while critics such as

Rodgers and Fetterley offer convincing — if divergent — interpretations of "A Rose for Emily," it is necessary first to understand in Faulkner's eerie and enigmatic story the relationship between the public and the private, and the consequences of this relationship within the story and for the reader.

The most explicit illustration of the opposition between the public and the private occurs in the social and economic interactions between the town of Jefferson, represented by the narrator's "our" and "we," and the reclusive Miss Emily. "Alive," the narrator explains, "Miss Emily had been a tradition, a duty, and a care; a sort of hereditary obligation upon the town, dating from that day in 1894 when Colonel Sartoris, the mayor, . . . remitted her taxes, the dispensation dating from the death of her father on into perpetuity" (803–4). Ironically (and this is one of the prime examples of the complexity of the relationship of private and public in the story), the price of privacy for Miss Emily becomes the loss of that very privacy. Despite — or perhaps because of — her refusal to buy into the community, the citizens of Jefferson determine that it is their "duty," their "hereditary obligation," to oversee her activities. When, for example, Miss Emily's house begins to emit an unpleasant smell, the town officials decide to solve the problem by dusting her property with lime. When she refuses to provide a reason why she wants to buy poison, the druggist scrawls "For rats" (809) across the package, literally and protectively overwriting her silence.

Arguably, the townspeople's actions serve to protect Miss Emily's privacy — by preserving her perceived gentility — as much as they effectively destroy it with their intrusive zeal. But in this very act of protection they reaffirm the town's proprietary relation to the public "monument" that is Miss Emily and, consequently, reinforce her inability to make decisions for herself.

While the communal narrator and Miss Emily appear to be polar opposites — one standing for the public while the other fiercely defends her privacy — the two are united when an outsider such as Homer Barron appears in their midst. If Miss Emily serves as a representation — an icon, an inactive figure in a "tableau," an "idol" — of traditional antebellum southern values, then Homer represents all that is new and different. 5

A "day laborer" (808) from the North, Homer comes to Jefferson to pave the side walks, a task which itself suggests the modernization of the town.

The secret and destructive union between these two representational figures implies a complex relationship between the private and the public. When Miss Emily kills Homer and confines his remains to a room in her attic, where, according to Rodgers, "she has been allowed to carry on her illicit love affair in post-mortem privacy" (119), this grotesque act ironically suggests that she has capitulated to the code of gentility that Jefferson imagines her to embody. This code demands the end of a romantic affair which some residents deemed "a disgrace to the town and a bad example to the young people" (809), thus placing tradition and the good of the community above Miss Emily's own wishes. Through its insistence on Miss Emily's symbolic relation to a bygone era, the town — via the narrator — becomes "an unknowing driving force behind Emily's crime" (Rodgers 120). Her private act is both the result of and a support for public norms and expectations.

At the same time, however, the act of murder also marks Miss Emily's corruption of that very code. By killing Homer in private, Miss Emily deliberately flouts public norms, and by eluding explicit detection until after her own death, she asserts the primacy of the private. The murder of the outsider in their midst thus leads Miss Emily to achieve paradoxically both a more complete privacy — a marriage of sorts without a husband — and a role in the preservation of the community.

Yet the elaborate relationship between Jefferson and Miss Emily is not the only way in which Homer's murder may be understood as a casualty of the tension between the public and the private. When Miss Emily kills Homer, Rodgers contends, "from the town's point of view, it was the best thing. . . . Homer represents the kind of unwelcomed resident and ineligible mate the town wants to repel if it is to preserve its traditional arrangements" (125). The people of Jefferson and Miss Emily join in a struggle to "repel" the outside and to ensure a private, inner order and tradition. This complicity creates intriguing parallels between the illicit, fatal union of Homer and Miss Emily and the reunion of the North and the South following the Civil War. In this reformulation of the private and the public, Miss Emily becomes, as Fetterley notes, a "metaphor and mirror for the town of Jefferson" (43). Miss Emily's honor is the townspeople's honor, her preservation their preservation.

Finally, the parallels between Miss Emily's secretive habits and the narrator's circuitous presentation of the story lead to a third dimension of the negotiations between the private and the public in "A Rose for Emily," a dimension in which Faulkner as author and the collective "we" as narrator confront their public consumers, the readers. Told by the anonymous narrator as if retrospectively, "A Rose for Emily" skips forward and back in time, omitting details and deferring revelations to such a degree that many critics have gone to extreme lengths to establish reliable chronologies for the tale. The much-debated "we" remains anonymous and unreachable throughout the tale — maintaining a virtually unbreachable privacy — even as it invites the public (the reader) to participate in the narrator's acts of detection and revelation. Rodgers observes:

> The dramatic distance on display here provides an ironic layer to the narrative. As the observers of the conflict between the teller-of-tale's desire to solve the curious mysteries that surround Emily's life — indeed, his complicity in shaping them — and his undetective-like detachment from her crimes, readers occupy the tantalizing position of having insight into unraveling the mystery which the narrator lacks. (120–21)

The reader is thus a member of the communal "we" — party to the narrator's investigation and Jefferson's voyeuristic obsession with Miss Emily — but also apart, removed to a plane from which "insight" into and observation of the narrator's own actions and motives become possible. The reader, just like Miss Emily, Homer, and the town of Jefferson itself, becomes a crucial element in the tension between the public and the private.

Thus, public and private are, in the end, far from exclusive categories.   10 And for all of its literal as well as figurative insistence on opposition and either/or structures, Faulkner's "A Rose for Emily" enacts the provocative idea of being "[o]ne of us" (812), of being both an individual and a member of a community, both a private entity and a participant in the public sphere.

academic literacies   rhetorical situations   genres   processes   strategies   research MLA / APA   media / design   readings

Works Cited

Faulkner, William. "A Rose for Emily." *The Norton Field Guide to Writing, with Readings.* 4th ed. Edited by Richard Bullock and Maureen Daly Goggin. W. W. Norton, 2016, pp. 803–12.

Fetterley, Judith. "A Rose for 'A Rose for Emily.'" *The Resisting Reader: A Feminist Approach to American Fiction,* Indiana UP, 1978, pp. 34–45.

Rodgers, Lawrence R. "'We all said, "She will kill her self"': The Narrator/Detective in William Faulkner's 'A Rose for Emily.'" *Clues: A Journal of Detection,* vol. 16, no. 1, Spring/Summer 1995, pp. 117–29.

Engaging with the Text

1. What is Willow D. Crystal's **THESIS**? Restate it in your own words. Read "A Rose for Emily" (on pp. 803–12) yourself. Do you agree with Crystal's analysis? Why or why not?

   345–47

2. Crystal focuses on three examples of the tensions between concepts of public and private. What do these examples contribute to her **ANALYSIS**?

   94–128
   64–67

3. How would you characterize Crystal's **STANCE** toward Faulkner's story? Identify specific language in her essay that reveals that stance.

4. How does Crystal **SYNTHESIZE OTHER SCHOLARSHIP** on Faulkner's story in her analysis? How does she use this synthesis to support her own analysis?

   473–77

5. *For Writing.* **ANALYZE** a literary work that intrigues you. You may base a literary analysis on your own reading and thinking about a text. However, your analysis may be enriched by knowing what others have written about the text as well. **RESEARCH** scholarship on the literary piece to see what other scholars may have said about it. Write an essay that both presents your own analysis and also responds to what others say about the same work. You can agree with what they say, disagree, or both; the important thing is to think about what others say, and to **QUOTE**, **PARAPHRASE**, or **SUMMARIZE** their views in your text.

   94–128
   433
   478–90

IRENE MORSTAN

"They'll See How Beautiful I Am": "I, Too" and the Harlem Renaissance

Irene Morstan wrote the following essay as a model paper for The Norton Introduction to Literature *while she was a student at the University of Nevada, Las Vegas. As you read her analysis of Langston Hughes's poem "I, Too," notice how Morstan draws on primary and secondary sources to place Hughes within the context of the Harlem Renaissance.*

LANGSTON HUGHES BEGINS HIS 1926 ESSAY "The Negro Artist and the Racial Mountain" with a statement made to him by another black poet: "I want to be a poet — not a Negro poet." Hughes takes this to mean that the poet wishes he were a white poet, and pities the poet for this. He believes that the black poet should accept his blackness. The goal for black poets should not be to sound like white poets but to celebrate and embrace their black identity.

Hughes was a central figure in a movement called the Harlem Renaissance, which was "a period of ten or fifteen years in the early twentieth century when an extraordinarily talented group of people came together [. . .] to celebrate and embody the awakening of a new African American consciousness" (Mays, "Cultural" 1031). *The Norton Introduction to Literature* states, "The Harlem Renaissance represented powerful assertions: that America had to include the voices of black Americans in order to find its own full definition and, equally, that artistic creativity [. . .] was essential to black Americans' realization and assertion of their full humanity" (Mays, "Cultural" 1031). Hughes speaks to both of those assertions in his poem "I, Too." He insists upon the place of the black poet, and person, at the American "table" and upon the power of the black poet to "sing."

The opening of "I, Too" is a declaration of the black man as a poet, despite being historically excluded from such a title. In the first line of the poem "I, too, sing America," Hughes indicates that the speaker is a poet.

academic literacies · rhetorical situations · genres · processes · strategies · research MLA / APA · media / design · readings

Hughes related poetry to music, suggesting that Hughes thinks music-making and writing poetry are related. Not only is the speaker a poet, but he is a black poet. By the second line of the poem the race of the speaker is clear; he refers to himself as the "darker brother." The "too" in the first line implies that the speaker has been set apart from another group of people, that he has been excluded from "sing[ing] America." However, the speaker is responding to this exclusion with an affirmative statement that he is both a black poet and part of the American family, despite being set aside by white people.

Refusing to be set aside was an important part of the Harlem Renaissance. James Weldon Johnson, in his preface to *The Book of American Negro Poetry*, says black poets moved away from writing in dialect to keep white people from thinking of them as "a happy-go-lucky, singing, shuffling, banjo-picking being or as a more or less pathetic figure" (1049). Black poets in the Harlem Renaissance did not want to be stereotyped by whites; they did not want to be Jim from *Adventures of Huckleberry Finn*. Such stereotypes made black people easy to overlook because they were represented as caricatures of people. These figures did not accurately represent the black person as a complex human being capable of artistic achievement. Not all Harlem Renaissance poets responded to this in the same way. The author of "Literature of the Harlem Renaissance" states, "Countee Cullen insisted that the Black poet is a part of the universal community of all poets, while Langston Hughes asserted his unique racial qualities." While Hughes, in "The Negro Artist and the Racial Mountain," says that he does not believe that black people should give up any of the things associated with black identity, including writing in dialect, he does explore the dismissal of the black poet by the white audience through "I, Too."

This theme of black exclusion surfaces in the second stanza where 5 the speaker talks about how "They send me to eat in the kitchen / When company comes" (lines 3–4). Here "they" refers to white people who dismiss the black poet from the "table" (line 9). These lines suggest that the white people are perhaps ashamed of "the darker brother" and do not want him to be present in front of the other white guests, the "company." Maybe they don't even see him as a brother, just a servant. This reflects the place of the black artist in the 1920s and 1930s. While the black artist might occasionally be present, he was meant to be a source of entertainment for white people, not an equal. Rudolph Fisher discusses the white interest in Harlem in *The Caucasian Storms Harlem*, where he notes, "White people have always more or less sought Negro entertainment as diversion" (1057). Despite being suspicious of white peoples' impulses to go to Harlem nightclubs, Fisher hopes that this white interest in black artistry will be the beginning of "finer things" and that "Maybe they are at last learning to speak our language" (1058).

The speaker of "I, Too" also sees that "finer things" are on the horizon. Even though he has been sent to the kitchen, a place reminiscent of the institution of slavery where black slaves worked to feed their white masters, the speaker of the poem says, "I laugh, / And eat well, / And grow strong" (lines 5–7). This dismissal has not crushed his spirit, and "Tomorrow, / I'll sit at the table" (lines 8–9). Hughes's speaker anticipates the time when the black poet will no longer be cast aside. Because of his strength and his spirit he is undeniable. In the future,

> Nobody'll dare
> Say to me,
> "Eat in the kitchen" (lines 11–13)

And the black spirit was undeniable during the Harlem Renaissance. The number of notable black authors and artists gathered in one place was incredible. During the 1920s and 1930s writers like Claude McKay, Countee Cullen, Zora Neale Hurston, Jean Toomer, Angelina Grimké, as well as Langston Hughes, were all in Harlem. This was one of the first times that black people from all over America were in one place together, as "more than 100,000 blacks migrated to Harlem during the 1920s" (Mays, "Cultural" 1034). Alain Locke, author of *The New Negro*, saw this as a turning point in black history and in the history of America, even arguing that it created a real black "race." In 1925, he wrote,

> Hitherto, it must be admitted that American Negroes have been a race more in name than in fact, or to be exact, more in sentiment than experience. The chief bond between them has been that of a common condition rather than a common consciousness; a

problem in common rather than a life in common. In Harlem, Negro
life is seizing upon its first chances for group expression and self-
determination. (1050)

The Harlem Renaissance was a movement where black writers, even
though they may have had some differences, joined together to create
black art according to their own rules, not the rules of white people. Black
artists had "grow[n] strong," and it is this strength that the speaker of
"I, Too" sees as causing change between blacks and whites.

However, as hopeful as the speaker is, he acknowledges that this
has not yet happened. By placing "then" on its own line and at the end
of the sentence (line 14), Hughes highlights that these actions are yet
to come. The "then" in the poem sounds wistful, as if the speaker gets
very excited about the prospect of being acknowledged and respected,
only to remember the difficulties that lie between the current state of
affairs and the one dreamt of for the future. Racial inequality was still
prevalent at the time of the Harlem Renaissance, and the situation did
not improve for some time. During the 1920s and 1930s segregation
was still normal. (Langston Hughes said that an African American who
moved to New York "had to live in Harlem, for rooms were hardly to be
found elsewhere unless one could pass for white or Mexican or Eurasian"
[The Big Sea 1065], and Fisher says that blacks like him were surprisingly
even excluded from some Harlem clubs [1057].) On the other hand, the
isolation of the "then" on its own line also could be read as being firmly
insistent that a positive change will come. This echoes the goal of the
writers of the Harlem Renaissance, "to [raise] the aspirations of American
blacks of all backgrounds and abilities" (Mays, "Cultural" 1038). In this
reading, "then" is both a statement of faith about the future and a call
to action about now.

These two readings reflect two different black views of Harlem literature. Some people were cynical and did not believe that change had
come or would. Langston Hughes recounts that "[a]bout the future of
Negro literature [Wallace] Thurman was very pessimistic. He thought the
Negro vogue had made us all too conscious of ourselves, had flattered
and spoiled us, and had provided too many easy opportunities for some

of us to drink gin and more gin, on which he thought we would always be drunk" (*The Big Sea* 1065). In contrast to this dark view of the Harlem Renaissance is novelist Zora Neale Hurston's view of the position of black people in 1920s America. In "How It Feels to Be Colored Me," she states, "I am not tragically colored. There is no great sorrow dammed up in my soul nor lurking behind my eyes. . . . I do not belong to the sobbing school of Negrohood who hold that nature somehow has given them a lowdown dirty deal. . . . I do not weep at the world — I am too busy sharpening my oyster knife" (1060). Here Hurston is expressing that she is not brought down by the slavery of the past, but is making herself ready to make the world hers. Her view is the positive one found in Hughes's poem.

Just as the writers of the Harlem Renaissance wanted their creative   10
abilities to be appreciated, so they also wanted black people and culture to be appreciated and embraced by the American public. The speaker of "I, Too" makes this apparent at the end of the poem when he says,

> Besides,
> They'll see how beautiful I am
> And be ashamed —
> I, too, am America. (lines 15–18)

The speaker is asserting that being black is being beautiful and that people who have discriminated against blacks will be ashamed of their behavior when they really see what black people are like. Not only are black people beautiful, they are part of America. The speaker of the poem makes this clear when he says that he is America. This "darker brother" is just as much a part of America as a white person (line 2), so he should not be excluded, either physically or literarily. Hughes, like many other writers of the Harlem Renaissance, is insisting that all Americans recognize the place of black people, both culturally and creatively, in the American identity.

Hughes speaks not only to white people in "I, Too" but also to other writers during the Harlem Renaissance. As is illustrated in the opening anecdote, Hughes was insistent about honoring blackness and common black life. He thought that all aspects of black life were worth celebrating,

academic literacies   rhetorical situations   genres   processes   strategies   research MLA / APA   media / design   readings

and "[u]nlike other notable black poets of the period — Claude McKay, Jean Toomer, and Countee Cullen — Hughes refused to differentiate between his personal experience and the common experience of black America. He wanted to tell the stories of his people in ways that reflected their actual culture, including both their suffering and their love of music, laughter, and language itself" ("Langston Hughes"). Hughes's references to race and beauty throughout "I, Too" show that he was committed to representing black life in a positive way.

Langston Hughes and the writers of the Harlem Renaissance are an important part of American history and have had a lasting impact on American literature. The quality of their works and power of their message shaped American culture. Through creative pieces like "I, Too," Hughes shows audiences how black literature and black people were valuable parts of the American identity.

Works Cited

Fisher, Rudolph. "From *The Caucasian Storms Harlem*." Mays, Norton, pp. 1054–58.

Hughes, Langston. "From *The Big Sea*." Mays, Norton, pp. 1062–66.

———. "I, Too." Mays, Norton, p. 1045.

———. "The Negro Artist and the Racial Mountain." 1926. *Poetry Foundation*, www.poetryfoundation.org/resources/learning/essays/detail/69395. Accessed 14 Apr. 2015.

Hurston, Zora Neale. "How It Feels to Be Colored Me." Mays, Norton, pp. 1059–62.

Johnson, James Weldon. "From the Preface to *The Book of American Negro Poetry*." Mays, Norton, pp. 1048–50.

"Langston Hughes." *Poets.org*, Academy of American Poets, www.poets.org/poetsorg/poet/langston-hughes. Accessed 14 Apr. 2015.

"Literature of the Harlem Renaissance." *Twentieth-Century Literary Criticism*, edited by Thomas J. Schoenberg and Lawrence J. Trudeau, vol. 218, Gale/Cengage Learning, 2009, pp. 260–376. *Literature Criticism Online*, go.galegroup.com/ps/i.do?id=GALE%7CJNYDPC

279809920&v=2.1&u= dayt38887&it=r&p=LCO&sw=w. Accessed 14 Apr. 2015.

Locke, Alain. "From *The New Negro*." Mays, *Norton*, pp. 1050–54.

Mays, Kelly J. "Cultural and Historical Contexts: The Harlem Renaissance." Mays, *Norton*, pp. 1031–40.

———, editor. *The Norton Introduction to Literature*. Shorter 12th ed., W. W. Norton, 2016.

Engaging with the Text

345–47
1. Irene Morstan states her **THESIS** at the end of the second paragraph: in his poem "I, Too," Langston Hughes "insists upon the place of the black poet, and person, at the American 'table,' and upon the power of 111 the black poet to 'sing.'" How does she **SUPPORT** this **ARGUABLE** main 355–73 point? Identify two places where she gives evidence for this claim.

2. Morstan discusses Hughes as part of the Harlem Renaissance. What features of the Harlem Renaissance does she discuss? How do these features help establish Hughes as one of the poets of that time and place?

57–60
3. For what **AUDIENCE** is Morstan writing this essay? What in her essay makes clear who she expects will read this piece?

445–68
4. How effectively does Morstan use her **SOURCES**? Would additional sources contribute anything to her essay? Why or why not?

5. *For Writing:* Select one of the Harlem Renaissance authors whose view on African American writers in America contrasted with that of Hughes, and analyze a piece of writing by him or her that expresses 209 this contrasting perspective. Be sure to pay **CAREFUL ATTENTION TO THE LANGUAGE OF THE TEXT** as you do a close reading and as you write your analysis. Consider in your analysis what this alternative viewpoint contributed to American literature.

academic literacies | rhetorical situations | genres | processes | strategies | research MLA / APA | media / design | readings

WILLIAM FAULKNER

A Rose for Emily

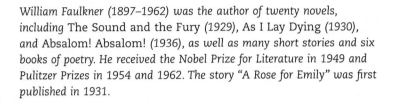

William Faulkner (1897–1962) was the author of twenty novels, including The Sound and the Fury *(1929),* As I Lay Dying *(1930), and* Absalom! Absalom! *(1936), as well as many short stories and six books of poetry. He received the Nobel Prize for Literature in 1949 and Pulitzer Prizes in 1954 and 1962. The story "A Rose for Emily" was first published in 1931.*

WHEN MISS EMILY GRIERSON DIED, our whole town went to her funeral: the men through a sort of respectful affection for a fallen monument, the women mostly out of curiosity to see the inside of her house, which no one save an old man-servant — a combined gardener and cook — had seen in at least ten years.

It was a big, squarish frame house that had once been white, decorated with cupolas and spires and scrolled balconies in the heavily lightsome style of the seventies,* set on what had once been our most select street. But garages and cotton gins had encroached and obliterated even the august names of that neighborhood; only Miss Emily's house was left, lifting its stubborn and coquettish decay above the cotton wagons and the gasoline pumps — an eyesore among eyesores. And now Miss Emily had gone to join the representatives of those august names where they lay in the cedar-bemused cemetery among the ranked and anonymous graves of Union and Confederate soldiers who fell at the battle of Jefferson.

Alive, Miss Emily had been a tradition, a duty, and a care; a sort of hereditary obligation upon the town, dating from that day in 1894 when Colonel Sartoris, the mayor — he who fathered the edict that no Negro woman should appear on the streets without an apron — remitted

---

*Seventies: the 1870s, the decade after the Civil War (1861–65). [Editor's note]

her taxes, the dispensation dating from the death of her father on into perpetuity. Not that Miss Emily would have accepted charity. Colonel Sartoris invented an involved tale to the effect that Miss Emily's father had loaned money to the town, which the town, as a matter of business, preferred this way of repaying. Only a man of Colonel Sartoris' generation and thought could have invented it, and only a woman could have believed it.

When the next generation, with its more modern ideas, became mayors and aldermen, this arrangement created some little dissatisfaction. On the first of the year they mailed her a tax notice. February came, and there was no reply. They wrote her a formal letter, asking her to call at the sheriff's office at her convenience. A week later the mayor wrote her himself, offering to call or to send his car for her, and received in reply a note on paper of an archaic shape, in a thin, flowing calligraphy in faded ink, to the effect that she no longer went out at all. The tax notice was also enclosed, without comment.

They called a special meeting of the Board of Aldermen. A deputa- 5 tion waited upon her, knocked at the door through which no visitor had passed since she ceased giving china-painting lessons eight or ten years earlier. They were admitted by the old Negro into a dim hall from which a stairway mounted into still more shadow. It smelled of dust and disuse — a close, dank smell. The Negro led them into the parlor. It was furnished in heavy, leather-covered furniture. When the Negro opened the blinds of one window, a faint dust rose sluggishly about their thighs, spinning with slow motes in the single sun-ray. On a tarnished gilt easel before the fireplace stood a crayon portrait of Miss Emily's father.

They rose when she entered — a small, fat woman in black, with a thin gold chain descending to her waist and vanishing into her belt, leaning on an ebony cane with a tarnished gold head. Her skeleton was small and spare; perhaps that was why what would have been merely plumpness in another was obesity in her. She looked bloated, like a body long submerged in motionless water, and of that pallid hue. Her eyes, lost in the fatty ridges of her face, looked like two small pieces of coal pressed into a lump of dough as they moved from one face to another while the visitors stated their errand.

academic literacies   rhetorical situations   genres   processes   strategies   research MLA / APA   media / design   readings

She did not ask them to sit. She just stood in the door and listened quietly until the spokesman came to a stumbling halt. Then they could hear the invisible watch ticking at the end of the gold chain.

Her voice was dry and cold. "I have no taxes in Jefferson. Colonel Sartoris explained it to me. Perhaps one of you can gain access to the city records and satisfy yourselves."

"But we have. We are the city authorities, Miss Emily. Didn't you get a notice from the sheriff, signed by him?"

"I received a paper, yes," Miss Emily said. "Perhaps he considers   10
himself the sheriff. . . . I have no taxes in Jefferson."

"But there is nothing on the books to show that, you see. We must go by the —"

"See Colonel Sartoris. I have no taxes in Jefferson."

"But, Miss Emily — "

"See Colonel Sartoris." (Colonel Sartoris had been dead almost ten years.) "I have no taxes in Jefferson. Tobe!" The Negro appeared. "Show these gentlemen out."

II

So she vanquished them, horse and foot, just as she had vanquished   15
their fathers thirty years before about the smell. That was two years after her father's death and a short time after her sweetheart — the one we believed would marry her — had deserted her. After her father's death she went out very little; after her sweetheart went away, people hardly saw her at all. A few of the ladies had the temerity to call, but were not received, and the only sign of life about the place was the Negro man — a young man then — going in and out with a market basket.

"Just as if a man — any man — could keep a kitchen properly," the ladies said; so they were not surprised when the smell developed. It was another link between the gross, teeming world and the high and mighty Griersons.

A neighbor, a woman, complained to the mayor, Judge Stevens, eighty years old.

"But what will you have me do about it, madam?" he said.

"Why, send her word to stop it," the woman said. "Isn't there a law?"

"I'm sure that won't be necessary," Judge Stevens said. "It's probably   20
just a snake or a rat that nigger of hers killed in the yard. I'll speak to
him about it."

The next day he received two more complaints, one from a man
who came in diffident deprecation. "We really must do something about
it, Judge. I'd be the last one in the world to bother Miss Emily, but we've
got to do something." That night the Board of Aldermen met — three
gray-beards and one younger man, a member of the rising generation.

"It's simple enough," he said. "Send her word to have her place
cleaned up. Give her a certain time to do it in, and if she don't . . ."

"Dammit, sir," Judge Stevens said, "will you accuse a lady to her face
of smelling bad?"

So the next night, after midnight, four men crossed Miss Emily's
lawn and slunk about the house like burglars, sniffing along the base of
the brickwork and at the cellar openings while one of them performed
a regular sowing motion with his hand out of a sack slung from his
shoulder. They broke open the cellar door and sprinkled lime there, and
in all the outbuildings. As they recrossed the lawn, a window that had
been dark was lighted and Miss Emily sat in it, the light behind her, and
her upright torso motionless as that of an idol. They crept quietly across
the lawn and into the shadow of the locusts that lined the street. After
a week or two the smell went away.

That was when people had begun to feel really sorry for her. People   25
in our town, remembering how old lady Wyatt, her great-aunt, had gone
completely crazy at last, believed that the Griersons held themselves a
little too high for what they really were. None of the young men were
quite good enough for Miss Emily and such. We had long thought of
them as a tableau; Miss Emily a slender figure in white in the background, her father a spraddled silhouette in the foreground, his back to
her and clutching a horsewhip, the two of them framed by the back-flung
front door. So when she got to be thirty and was still single, we were
not pleased exactly, but vindicated; even with insanity in the family
she wouldn't have turned down all of her chances if they had really
materialized.

academic literacies   rhetorical situations   genres   processes   strategies   research MLA / APA   media / design   readings

When her father died, it got about that the house was all that was left to her; and in a way, people were glad. At last they could pity Miss Emily. Being left alone, and a pauper, she had become humanized. Now she too would know the old thrill and the old despair of a penny more or less.

The day after his death all the ladies prepared to call at the house and offer condolence and aid, as is our custom. Miss Emily met them at the door, dressed as usual and with no trace of grief on her face. She told them that her father was not dead. She did that for three days, with the ministers calling on her, and the doctors, trying to persuade her to let them dispose of the body. Just as they were about to resort to law and force, she broke down, and they buried her father quickly.

We did not say she was crazy then. We believed she had to do that. We remembered all the young men her father had driven away, and we knew that with nothing left, she would have to cling to that which had robbed her, as people will.

III

She was sick for a long time. When we saw her again, her hair was cut short, making her look like a girl, with a vague resemblance to those angels in colored church windows — sort of tragic and serene.

The town had just let the contracts for paving the sidewalks, and in the summer after her father's death they began to work. The construction company came with niggers and mules and machinery, and a foreman named Homer Barron, a Yankee — a big, dark, ready man, with a big voice and eyes lighter than his face. The little boys would follow in groups to hear him cuss the niggers, and the niggers singing in time to the rise and fall of picks. Pretty soon he knew everybody in town. Whenever you heard a lot of laughing anywhere about the square, Homer Barron would be in the center of the group. Presently we began to see him and Miss Emily on Sunday afternoons driving in the yellow-wheeled buggy and the matched team of bays from the livery stable.

At first we were glad that Miss Emily would have an interest, because the ladies all said, "Of course a Grierson would not think serously of a

Northerner, a day laborer." But there were still others, older people, who said that even grief could not cause a real lady to forget *noblesse oblige* — without calling it *noblesse oblige*.* They just said, "Poor Emily. Her kinsfolk should come to her." She had some kin in Alabama; but years ago her father had fallen out with them over the estate of old lady Wyatt, the crazy woman, and there was no communication between the two families. They had not even been represented at the funeral.

And as soon as the old people said, "Poor Emily," the whispering began. "Do you suppose it's really so?" they said to one another. "Of course it is. What else could . . ." This behind their hands; rustling of craned silk and satin behind jalousies† closed upon the sun of Sunday afternoon as the thin, swift clop-clop-clop of the matched team passed: "Poor Emily."

She carried her head high enough — even when we believed that she was fallen. It was as if she demanded more than ever the recognition of her dignity as the last Grierson; as if it had wanted that touch of earthiness to reaffirm her imperviousness. Like when she bought the rat poison, the arsenic. That was over a year after they had begun to say "Poor Emily," and while the two female cousins were visiting her.

"I want some poison," she said to the druggist. She was over thirty then, still a slight woman, though thinner than usual, with cold, haughty black eyes in a face the flesh of which was strained across the temples and about the eyesockets as you imagine a lighthouse-keeper's face ought to look. "I want some poison," she said.

"Yes, Miss Emily. What kind? For rats and such? I'd recom — "   35

"I want the best you have. I don't care what kind."

The druggist named several. "They'll kill anything up to an elephant. But what you want is — "

"Arsenic," Miss Emily said. "Is that a good one?"

"Is . . . arsenic? Yes ma'am. But what you want — "

"I want arsenic."   40

---

*Noblesse oblige: the traditional obligation of the nobility to treat the lower classes with respect and generosity (French). [Editor's note]

†*Jalousies*: slatted window blinds. [Editor's note]

The druggist looked down at her. She looked back at him, erect, her face like a strained flag. "Why, of course," the druggist said. "If that's what you want. But the law requires you to tell what you are going to use it for."

Miss Emily just stared at him, her head tilted back in order to look him eye for eye, until he looked away and went and got the arsenic and wrapped it up. The Negro delivery boy brought her the package; the druggist didn't come back. When she opened the package at home there was written on the box, under the skull and bones: "For rats."

IV

So the next day we all said, "She will kill herself"; and we said it would be the best thing. When she had first begun to be seen with Homer Barron, we had said, "She will marry him." Then we said, "She will persuade him yet," because Homer himself had remarked — he liked men, and it was known that he drank with the younger men in the Elk's Club — that he was not a marrying man. Later we said, "Poor Emily," behind the jalousies as they passed on Sunday afternoon in the glittering buggy, Miss Emily with her head high and Homer Barron with his hat cocked and a cigar in his teeth, reins and whip in a yellow glove.

Then some of the ladies began to say that it was a disgrace to the town and a bad example to the young people. The men did not want to interfere, but at last the ladies forced the Baptist minister — Miss Emily's people were Episcopal — to call upon her. He would never divulge what happened during that interview, but he refused to go back again. The next Sunday they again drove about the streets, and the following day the minister's wife wrote to Miss Emily's relations in Alabama.

So she had blood-kin under her roof again and we sat back to watch 45 developments. At first nothing happened. Then we were sure that they were to be married. We learned that Miss Emily had been to the jeweler's and ordered a man's toilet set in silver, with the letters H. B. on each piece. Two days later we learned that she had bought a complete outfit of men's clothing, including a nightshirt, and we said, "They are married." We were really glad. We were glad because the two female cousins were even more Grierson than Miss Emily had ever been.

So we were not surprised when Homer Barron — the streets had been finished some time since — was gone. We were a little disappointed that there was not a public blowing-off, but we believed that he had gone on to prepare for Miss Emily's coming, or to give her a chance to get rid of the cousins. (By that time it was a cabal, and we were all Miss Emily's allies to help circumvent the cousins.) Sure enough, after another week they departed. And, as we had expected all along, within three days Homer Barron was back in town. A neighbor saw the Negro man admit him at the kitchen door at dusk one evening.

And that was the last we saw of Homer Barron. And of Miss Emily for some time. The Negro man went in and out with the market basket, but the front door remained closed. Now and then we would see her at a window for a moment, as the men did that night when they sprinkled the lime, but for almost six months she did not appear on the streets. Then we knew that this was to be expected too; as if that quality of her father which had thwarted her woman's life so many times had been too virulent and too furious to die.

When we next saw Miss Emily, she had grown fat and her hair was turning gray. During the next few years it grew grayer and grayer until it attained an even pepper-and-salt iron-gray, when it ceased turning. Up to the day of her death at seventy-four it was still that vigorous iron gray, like the hair of an active man.

From that time on her front door remained closed, save for a period of six or seven years, when she was about forty, during which she gave lessons in china-painting. She fitted up a studio in one of the downstairs rooms, where the daughters and grand-daughters of Colonel Sartoris' contemporaries were sent to her with the same regularity and in the same spirit that they were sent on Sundays with a twenty-five cent piece for the collection plate. Meanwhile her taxes had been remitted.

Then the newer generation became the backbone and the spirit of 50 the town, and the painting pupils grew up and fell away and did not send their children to her with boxes of color and tedious brushes and pictures cut from the ladies' magazines. The front door closed upon the

last one and remained closed for good. When the town got free postal delivery Miss Emily alone refused to let them fasten the metal numbers above her door and attach a mailbox to it. She would not listen to them.

Daily, monthly, yearly we watched the Negro grow grayer and more stooped, going in and out with the market basket. Each December we sent her a tax notice, which would be returned by the post office a week later, unclaimed. Now and then we would see her in one of the downstairs windows — she had evidently shut up the top floor of the house — like the carven torso of an idol in a niche, looking or not looking at us, we could never tell which. Thus she passed from generation to generation — dear, inescapable, impervious, tranquil, and perverse.

And so she died. Fell ill in the house filled with dust and shadows, with only a doddering Negro man to wait on her. We did not even know she was sick; we had long since given up trying to get any information from the Negro. He talked to no one, probably not even to her, for his voice had grown harsh and rusty, as if from disuse.

She died in one of the downstairs rooms, in a heavy walnut bed with a curtain, her gray head propped on a pillow yellow and moldy with age and lack of sunlight.

V

The Negro met the first of the ladies at the front door and let them in, with their hushed, sibilant voices and their quick, curious glances, and then he disappeared. He walked right through the house and out the back and was not seen again.

The two female cousins came at once. They held the funeral on the second day, with the town coming to look at Miss Emily beneath a mass of bought flowers, with the crayon face of her father musing profoundly above the bier and the ladies sibilant and macabre; and the very old men — some in their brushed Confederate uniforms — on the porch and the lawn, talking of Miss Emily as if she had been a contemporary of theirs, believing that they had danced with her and courted her perhaps, confusing time with its mathematical progression, as the old do, to whom all the past is not a diminishing road, but, instead, a

huge meadow which no winter ever quite touches, divided from them now by the narrow bottleneck of the most recent decade of years.

Already we knew that there was one room in that region above stairs which no one had seen in forty years, and which would have to be forced. They waited until Miss Emily was decently in the ground before they opened it.

The violence of breaking down the door seemed to fill this room with pervading dust. A thin, acrid pall as of the tomb seemed to lie everywhere upon this room decked and furnished as for a bridal: upon the valance curtains of faded rose color, upon the rose-shaded lights, upon the dressing table, upon the delicate array of crystal and the man's toilet things backed with tarnished silver, silver so tarnished that the monogram was obscured. Among them lay a collar and tie, as if they had just been removed, which, lifted, left upon the surface a pale crescent in the dust. Upon a chair hung the suit, carefully folded; beneath it the two mute shoes and the discarded socks.

The man himself lay in the bed.

For a long while we just stood there, looking down at the profound and fleshless grin. The body had apparently once lain in the attitude of an embrace, but now the long sleep that outlasts love, that conquers even the grimace of love, had cuckolded him. What was left of him, rotted beneath what was left of the nightshirt, had become inextricable from the bed in which he lay; and upon him and upon the pillow beside him lay that even coating of the patient and biding dust.

Then we noticed that in the second pillow was the indentation of a 60 head. One of us lifted something from it, and leaning forward, that faint and invisible dust dry and acrid in the nostrils, we saw a long strand of iron-gray hair.

JAMES BALDWIN
Sonny's Blues

James Baldwin (1924–1987) was an award-winning African American author of novels, essays, plays, and poems. Among his best known works are his first novel, Go Tell It on the Mountain (1953), and his first collection of essays, Notes of a Native Son (1955). He went on to become a prominent public figure during the civil rights movement of the 1960s. In 1986, Baldwin, who lived in France for much of his adult life, was awarded the French government's highest honor, the Légion D'Honneur. His short story "Sonny's Blues" was published in 1957.

I **READ ABOUT IT IN THE PAPER,** in the subway, on my way to work. I read it, and I couldn't believe it, and I read it again. Then perhaps I just stared at it, at the newsprint spelling out his name, spelling out the story. I stared at it in the swinging lights of the subway car, and in the faces and bodies of the people, and in my own face, trapped in the darkness which roared outside.

It was not to be believed and I kept telling myself that, as I walked from the subway station to the high school. And at the same time I couldn't doubt it. I was scared, scared for Sonny. He became real to me again. A great block of ice got settled in my belly and kept melting there slowly all day long, while I taught my classes algebra. It was a special kind of ice. It kept melting, sending trickles of ice water all up and down my veins, but it never got less. Sometimes it hardened and seemed to expand until I felt my guts were going to come spilling out or that I was going to choke or scream. This would always be at a moment when I was remembering some specific thing Sonny had once said or done.

When he was about as old as the boys in my classes his face had been bright and open, there was a lot of copper in it; and he'd had wonderfully direct brown eyes, and great gentleness and privacy. I wondered what he looked like now. He had been picked up, the evening before, in a raid on an apartment downtown, for peddling and using heroin.

I couldn't believe it: but what I mean by that is that I couldn't find any room for it anywhere inside me. I had kept it outside me for a long time. I hadn't wanted to know. I had had suspicions, but I didn't name them, I kept putting them away. I told myself that Sonny was wild, but he wasn't crazy. And he'd always been a good boy, he hadn't ever turned hard or evil or disrespectful, the way kids can, so quick, so quick, especially in Harlem. I didn't want to believe that I'd ever see my brother going down, coming to nothing, all that light in his face gone out, in the condition I'd already seen so many others. Yet it had happened and here I was, talking about algebra to a lot of boys who might, every one of them for all I knew, be popping off needles every time they went to the head.* Maybe it did more for them than algebra could.

I was sure that the first time Sonny had ever had horse,† he couldn't 5 have been much older than these boys were now. These boys, now, were living as we'd been living then, they were growing up with a rush and their heads bumped abruptly against the low ceiling of their actual possibilities. They were filled with rage. All they really knew were two darknesses, the darkness of their lives, which was now closing in on them, and the darkness of the movies, which had blinded them to that other darkness, and in which they now, vindictively, dreamed, at once more together than they were at any other time, and more alone.

When the last bell rang, the last class ended, I let out my breath. It seemed I'd been holding it for all that time. My clothes were wet — I may have looked as though I'd been sitting in a steam bath, all dressed up, all afternoon. I sat alone in the classroom a long time. I listened to the boys outside, downstairs, shouting and cursing and laughing. Their laughter struck me for perhaps the first time. It was not the joyous laughter which — God knows why — one associates with children. It was mocking and insular, its intent was to denigrate. It was disenchanted, and in this, also, lay the authority of their curses. Perhaps I was listening to them because I was thinking about my brother and in them I heard my brother. And myself.

One boy was whistling a tune, at once very complicated and very simple, it seemed to be pouring out of him as though he were a bird, and

---

*The head: toilet. [Editor's note]
†Horse: heroin. [Editor's note]

it sounded very cool and moving through all that harsh, bright air, only just holding its own through all those other sounds.

I stood up and walked over to the window and looked down into the courtyard. It was the beginning of the spring and the sap was rising in the boys. A teacher passed through them every now and again, quickly, as though he or she couldn't wait to get out of that courtyard, to get those boys out of their sight and off their minds. I started collecting my stuff. I thought I'd better get home and talk to Isabel.

The courtyard was almost deserted by the time I got downstairs. I saw this boy standing in the shadow of a doorway, looking just like Sonny. I almost called his name. Then I saw that it wasn't Sonny, but somebody we used to know, a boy from around our block. He'd been Sonny's friend. He'd never been mine, having been too young for me, and, anyway, I'd never liked him. And now, even though he was a grown-up man, he still hung around that block, still spent hours on the street corners, was always high and raggy. I used to run into him from time to time and he'd often work around to asking me for a quarter or fifty cents. He always had some real good excuse, too, and I always gave it to him. I don't know why.

But now, abruptly, I hated him. I couldn't stand the way he looked at 10 me, partly like a dog, partly like a cunning child. I wanted to ask him what the hell he was doing in the school courtyard.

He sort of shuffled over to me, and he said, "I see you got the papers. So you already know about it."

"You mean about Sonny? Yes, I already know about it. How come they didn't get you?"

He grinned. It made him repulsive and it also brought to mind what he'd looked like as a kid. "I wasn't there. I stay away from them people."

"Good for you." I offered him a cigarette and I watched him through the smoke. "You come all the way down here just to tell me about Sonny?"

"That's right." He was sort of shaking his head and his eyes looked 15 strange, as though they were about to cross. The bright sun deadened his damp dark brown skin and it made his eyes look yellow and showed up the dirt in his kinked hair. He smelled funky.* I moved a little away from

---

*Funky: unwashed. [Editor's note]

him and I said, "Well, thanks. But I already know about it and I got to get home."

"I'll walk you a little ways," he said. We started walking. There were a couple of kids still loitering in the courtyard and one of them said good-night to me and looked strangely at the boy beside me.

"What're you going to do?" he asked me. "I mean, about Sonny?"

"Look. I haven't seen Sonny for over a year, I'm not sure I'm going to do anything. Anyway, what the hell *can* I do?"

"That's right," he said quickly, "ain't nothing you can do. Can't much help old Sonny no more, I guess."

It was what I was thinking and so it seemed to me he had no right to   20
say it.

"I'm surprised at Sonny, though," he went on — he had a funny way of talking, he looked straight ahead as though he were talking to himself — "I thought Sonny was a smart boy, I thought he was too smart to get hung."

"I guess he thought so too," I said sharply, "and that's how he got hung. And how about you? You're pretty goddamn smart, I bet."

Then he looked directly at me, just for a minute. "I ain't smart," he said. "If I was smart, I'd have reached for a pistol a long time ago."

"Look. Don't tell *me* your sad story, if it was up to me, I'd give you one." Then I felt guilty — guilty, probably, for never having supposed that the poor bastard *had* a story of his own, much less a sad one, and I asked, quickly, "What's going to happen to him now?"

He didn't answer this. He was off by himself some place.   25

"Funny thing," he said, and from his tone we might have been discussing the quickest way to get to Brooklyn, "when I saw the papers this morning, the first thing I asked myself was if I had anything to do with it. I felt sort of responsible."

I began to listen more carefully. The subway station was on the corner, just before us, and I stopped. He stopped, too. We were in front of a bar and he ducked slightly, peering in, but whoever he was looking for didn't seem to be there. The juke box was blasting away with something black and bouncy and I half watched the barmaid as she danced her way from the juke box to her place behind the bar. And I watched her face as she laugh-ingly responded to something someone said to her, still keeping time to

the music. When she smiled one saw the little girl, one sensed the doomed, still-struggling woman beneath the battered face of the semi-whore.

"I never *give* Sonny nothing," the boy said finally, "but a long time ago I come to school high and Sonny asked me how it felt." He paused, I couldn't bear to watch him, I watched the barmaid, and I listened to the music which seemed to be causing the pavement to shake. "I told him it felt great." The music stopped, the barmaid paused and watched the juke box until the music began again. "It did."

All this was carrying me some place I didn't want to go. I certainly didn't want to know how it felt. It filled everything, the people, the houses, the music, the dark, quicksilver barmaid, with menace; and this menace was their reality.

"What's going to happen to him now?" I asked again.   30

"They'll send him away some place and they'll try to cure him." He shook his head. "Maybe he'll even think he's kicked the habit. Then they'll let him loose" — he gestured, throwing his cigarette into the gutter. "That's all."

"What do you mean, that's *all*?"

But I knew what he meant.

"I *mean*, that's *all*." He turned his head and looked at me, pulling down the corners of his mouth. "Don't you know what I mean?" he asked, softly.

"How the hell *would* I know what you mean?" I almost whispered it,   35 I don't know why.

"That's right," he said to the air, "how would *he* know what I mean?" He turned toward me again, patient and calm, and yet I somehow felt him shaking, shaking as though he were going to fall apart. I felt that ice in my guts again, the dread I'd felt all afternoon; and again I watched the barmaid, moving about the bar, washing glasses, and singing. "Listen. They'll let him out and then it'll just start all over again. That's what I mean."

"You mean — they'll let him out. And then he'll just start working his way back in again. You mean he'll never kick the habit. Is that what you mean?"

"That's right," he said, cheerfully. "*You* see what I mean."

"Tell me," I said at last, "why does he want to die? He must want to die, he's killing himself, why does he want to die?"

He looked at me in surprise. He licked his lips. "He don't want to die. 40
He wants to live. Don't nobody want to die, ever."

Then I wanted to ask him — too many things. He could not have
answered, or if he had, I could not have borne the answers. I started walking. "Well, I guess it's none of my business."

"It's going to be rough on old Sonny," he said. We reached the subway
station. "This is your station?" he asked. I nodded. I took one step down.
"Damn!" he said, suddenly. I looked up at him. He grinned again. "Damn
it if I didn't leave all my money home. You ain't got a dollar on you, have
you? Just for a couple of days, is all."

All at once something inside gave and threatened to come pouring
out of me. I didn't hate him any more. I felt that in another moment I'd
start crying like a child.

"Sure," I said. "Don't sweat." I looked in my wallet and didn't have a
dollar, I only had a five. "Here," I said. "That hold you?"

He didn't look at it — he didn't want to look at it. A terrible, closed look 45
came over his face, as though he were keeping the number on the bill a
secret from him and me. "Thanks," he said, and now he was dying to see
me go. "Don't worry about Sonny. Maybe I'll write him or something."

"Sure," I said. "You do that. So long."

"Be seeing you," he said. I went on down the steps.

And I didn't write Sonny or send him anything for a long time. When I
finally did, it was just after my little girl died, and he wrote me back a
letter which made me feel like a bastard.

Here's what he said:

> Dear brother,
>
> You don't know how much I needed to hear from you. I wanted
> to write you many a time but I dug how much I must have hurt you
> and so I didn't write. But now I feel like a man who's been trying to
> climb up out of some deep, real deep and funky hole and just saw
> the sun up there, outside. I got to get outside.
>
> I can't tell you much about how I got here. I mean I don't know
> how to tell you. I guess I was afraid of something or I was trying to
> escape from something and you know I have never been very strong
> in the head (smile). I'm glad Mama and Daddy are dead and can't

see what's happened to their son and I swear if I'd known what I was doing I would never have hurt you so, you and a lot of other fine people who were nice to me and who believed in me.

I don't want you to think it had anything to do with me being a musician. It's more than that. Or maybe less than that. I can't get anything straight in my head down here and I try not to think about what's going to happen to me when I get outside again. Sometime I think I'm going to flip and *never* get outside and sometime I think I'll come straight back. I tell you one thing, though, I'd rather blow my brains out than go through this again. But that's what they all say, so they tell me. If I tell you when I'm coming to New York and if you could meet me, I sure would appreciate it. Give my love to Isabel and the kids and I was sure sorry to hear about little Gracie. I wish I could be like Mama and say the Lord's will be done, but I don't know it seems to me that trouble is the one thing that never does get stopped and I don't know what good it does to blame it on the Lord. But maybe it does some good if you believe it.

Your brother,
Sonny

Then I kept in constant touch with him and I sent him whatever I 50 could and I went to meet him when he came back to New York. When I saw him many things I thought I had forgotten came flooding back to me. This was because I had begun, finally, to wonder about Sonny, about the life that Sonny lived inside. This life, whatever it was, had made him older and thinner and it had deepened the distant stillness in which he had always moved. He looked very unlike my baby brother. Yet, when he smiled, when we shook hands, the baby brother I'd never known looked out from the depths of his private life, like an animal waiting to be coaxed into the light.

"How you been keeping?" he asked me.

"All right. And you?"

"Just fine." He was smiling all over his face. "It's good to see you again."

"It's good to see you."

The seven years' difference in our ages lay between us like a chasm: I 55 wondered if these years would ever operate between us as a bridge. I was remembering, and it made it hard to catch my breath, that I had been there when he was born; and I had heard the first words he had ever spoken. When he started to walk, he walked from our mother straight to me. I caught him just before he fell when he took the first steps he ever took in this world.

"How's Isabel?"

"Just fine. She's dying to see you."

"And the boys?"

"They're fine, too. They're anxious to see their uncle."

"Oh, come on. You know they don't remember me."　　60

"Are you kidding? Of course they remember you."

He grinned again. We got into a taxi. We had a lot to say to each other, far too much to know how to begin.

As the taxi began to move, I asked, "You still want to go to India?"

He laughed. "You still remember that. Hell, no. This place is Indian enough for me."

"It used to belong to them," I said.　　65

And he laughed again. "They damn sure knew what they were doing when they got rid of it."

Years ago, when he was around fourteen, he'd been all hipped on the idea of going to India. He read books about people sitting on rocks, naked, in all kinds of weather, but mostly bad, naturally, and walking barefoot through hot coals and arriving at wisdom. I used to say that it sounded to me as though they were getting away from wisdom as fast as they could. I think he sort of looked down on me for that.

"Do you mind," he asked, "if we have the driver drive alongside the park? On the west side—I haven't seen the city in so long."

"Of course not," I said. I was afraid that I might sound as though I were humoring him, but I hoped he wouldn't take it that way.

So we drove along, between the green of the park and the stony, life-　　70 less elegance of hotels and apartment buildings, toward the vivid, killing streets of our childhood. These streets hadn't changed, though housing projects jutted up out of them now like rocks in the middle of a boiling sea. Most of the houses in which we had grown up had vanished, as had the stores from which we had stolen, the basements in which we had first tried sex, the rooftops from which we had hurled tin cans and bricks. But houses exactly like the houses of our past yet dominated the landscape,

boys exactly like the boys we once had been found themselves smothering in these houses, came down into the streets for light and air and found themselves encircled by disaster. Some escaped the trap, most didn't. Those who got out always left something of themselves behind, as some animals amputate a leg and leave it in the trap. It might be said, perhaps, that I had escaped, after all, I was a school teacher; or that Sonny had, he hadn't lived in Harlem for years. Yet, as the cab moved uptown through streets which seemed, with a rush, to darken with dark people, and as I covertly studied Sonny's face, it came to me that what we both were seeking through our separate cab windows was that part of ourselves which had been left behind. It's always at the hour of trouble and confrontation that the missing member aches.

We hit 110th Street and started rolling up Lenox Avenue. And I'd known this avenue all my life, but it seemed to me again, as it had seemed on the day I'd first heard about Sonny's trouble, filled with a hidden menace which was its very breath of life.

"We almost there," said Sonny.

"Almost." We were both too nervous to say anything more.

We live in a housing project. It hasn't been up long. A few days after it was up it seemed uninhabitably new. Now, of course, it's already rundown. It looks like a parody of the good, clean, faceless life — God knows the people who live in it do their best to make it a parody. The beat-looking grass lying around isn't enough to make their lives green, the hedges will never hold out the streets, and they know it. The big windows fool no one, they aren't big enough to make space out of no space. They don't bother with the windows, they watch the TV screen instead. The playground is most popular with the children who don't play at jacks, or skip rope, or roller skate, or swing, and they can be found in it after dark. We moved in partly because it's not too far from where I teach, and partly for the kids; but it's really just like the houses in which Sonny and I grew up. The same things happen, they'll have the same things to remember. The moment Sonny and I started into the house I had the feeling that I was simply bringing him back into the danger he had almost died trying to escape.

Sonny has never been talkative. So I don't know why I was sure he'd 75 be dying to talk to me when supper was over the first night. Everything went fine, the oldest boy remembered him, and the youngest boy liked him, and Sonny had remembered to bring something for each of them; and Isabel, who is really much nicer than I am, more open and giving, had gone to a lot of trouble about dinner and was genuinely glad to see him. And she's always been able to tease Sonny in a way that I haven't. It was nice to see her face so vivid again and to hear her laugh and watch her make Sonny laugh. She wasn't, or, anyway, she didn't seem to be, at all uneasy or embarrassed. She chatted as though there were no subject which had to be avoided and she got Sonny past his first, faint stiffness. And thank God she was there, for I was filled with that icy dread again. Everything I did seemed awkward to me, and everything I said sounded freighted with hidden meaning. I was trying to remember everything I'd heard about dope addiction and I couldn't help watching Sonny for signs. I wasn't doing it out of malice. I was trying to find out something about my brother. I was dying to hear him tell me he was safe.

"Safe!" my father grunted, whenever Mama suggested trying to move to a neighborhood which might be safer for children. "Safe, hell! Ain't no place safe for kids, nor nobody."

He always went on like this, but he wasn't, ever, really as bad as he sounded, not even on weekends, when he got drunk. As a matter of fact, he was always on the lookout for "something a little better," but he died before he found it. He died suddenly, during a drunken weekend in the middle of the war, when Sonny was fifteen. He and Sonny hadn't ever got on too well. And this was partly because Sonny was the apple of his father's eye. It was because he loved Sonny so much and was frightened for him, that he was always fighting with him. It doesn't do any good to fight with Sonny. Sonny just moves back, inside himself, where he can't be reached. But the principal reason that they never hit it off is that they were so much alike. Daddy was big and rough and loud-talking, just the opposite of Sonny, but they both had — that same privacy.

Mama tried to tell me something about this, just after Daddy died. I was home on leave from the army.

This was the last time I ever saw my mother alive. Just the same, this picture gets all mixed up in my mind with pictures I had of her when she was younger. The way I always see her is the way she used to be on a Sunday afternoon, say, when the old folks were talking after the big Sunday

dinner. I always see her wearing pale blue. She'd be sitting on the sofa. And my father would be sitting in the easy chair, not far from her. And the living room would be full of church folks and relatives. There they sit, in chairs all around the living room, and the night is creeping up outside, but nobody knows it yet. You can see the darkness growing against the windowpanes and you hear the street noises every now and again, or maybe the jangling beat of a tambourine from one of the churches close by, but it's real quiet in the room. For a moment nobody's talking, but every face looks darkening, like the sky outside. And my mother rocks a little from the waist, and my father's eyes are closed. Everyone is looking at something a child can't see. For a minute they've forgotten the children. Maybe a kid is lying on the rug, half asleep. Maybe somebody's got a kid in his lap and is absentmindedly stroking the kid's head. Maybe there's a kid, quiet and big-eyed, curled up in a big chair in the corner. The silence, the darkness coming, and the darkness in the faces frighten the child obscurely. He hopes that the hand which strokes his forehead will never stop — will never die. He hopes that there will never come a time when the old folks won't be sitting around the living room, talking about where they've come from, and what they've seen, and what's happened to them and their kinfolk.

But something deep and watchful in the child knows that this is bound 80 to end, is already ending. In a moment someone will get up and turn on the light. Then the old folks will remember the children and they won't talk any more that day. And when light fills the room, the child is filled with darkness. He knows that every time this happens he's moved just a little closer to that darkness outside. The darkness outside is what the old folks have been talking about. It's what they've come from. It's what they endure. The child knows that they won't talk any more because if he knows too much about what's happened to *them,* he'll know too much too soon, about what's going to happen to *him.*

The last time I talked to my mother, I remember I was restless. I wanted to get out and see Isabel. We weren't married then and we had a lot to straighten out between us.

There Mama sat, in black, by the window. She was humming an old church song, *Lord, you brought me from a long ways off.* Sonny was out somewhere. Mama kept watching the streets.

"I don't know," she said, "if I'll ever see you again, after you go off from here. But I hope you'll remember the things I tried to teach you."

"Don't talk like that," I said, and smiled. "You'll be here a long time yet."

She smiled, too, but she said nothing. She was quiet for a long time. And I said, "Mama, don't you worry about nothing. I'll be writing all the time, and you be getting the checks. . . ." 85

"I want to talk to you about your brother," she said, suddenly. "If anything happens to me he ain't going to have nobody to look out for him."

"Mama," I said, "ain't nothing going to happen to you *or* Sonny. Sonny's all right. He's a good boy and he's got good sense."

"It ain't a question of his being a good boy," Mama said, "nor of his having good sense. It ain't only the bad ones, nor yet the dumb ones that gets sucked under." She stopped, looking at me. "Your Daddy once had a brother," she said, and she smiled in a way that made me feel she was in pain. "You didn't never know that, did you?"

"No," I said, "I never knew that," and I watched her face.

"Oh, yes," she said, "your Daddy had a brother." She looked out of the window again. "I know you never saw your Daddy cry. But *I* did — many a time, through all these years." 90

I asked her, "What happened to his brother? How come nobody's ever talked about him?"

This was the first time I ever saw my mother look old.

"His brother got killed," she said, "when he was just a little younger than you are now. I knew him. He was a fine boy. He was maybe a little full of the devil, but he didn't mean nobody no harm."

Then she stopped and the room was silent, exactly as it had sometimes been on those Sunday afternoons. Mama kept looking out into the streets.

"He used to have a job in the mill," she said, "and, like all young folks, he just liked to perform on Saturday nights. Saturday nights, him and your father would drift around to different places, go to dances and things like that, or just sit around with people they knew, and your father's brother would sing, he had a fine voice, and play along with himself on his guitar. Well, this particular Saturday night, him and your father was coming home from some place, and they were both a little drunk and there was a moon that night, it was bright like day. Your father's brother was feeling kind of 95

academic literacies · rhetorical situations · genres · processes · strategies · research MLA / APA · media / design · readings

good, and he was whistling to himself, and he had his guitar slung over his shoulder. They was coming down a hill and beneath them was a road that turned off from the highway. Well, your father's brother, being always kind of frisky, decided to run down this hill, and he did, with that guitar banging and clanging behind him, and he ran across the road, and he was making water behind a tree. And your father was sort of amused at him and he was still coming down the hill, kind of slow. Then he heard a car motor and that same minute his brother stepped from behind the tree, into the road, in the moonlight. And he started to cross the road. And your father started to run down the hill, he says he don't know why. This car was full of white men. They was all drunk, and when they seen your father's brother they let out a great whoop and holler and they aimed the car straight at him. They was having fun, they just wanted to scare him, the way they do sometimes, you know. But they was drunk. And I guess the boy, being drunk, too, and scared, kind of lost his head. By the time he jumped it was too late. Your father says he heard his brother scream when the car rolled over him, and he heard the wood of that guitar when it give, and he heard them strings go flying, and he heard them white men shouting, and the car kept on a-going and it ain't stopped till this day. And, time your father got down the hill, his brother weren't nothing but blood and pulp."

Tears were gleaming on my mother's face. There wasn't anything I could say.

"He never mentioned it," she said, "because I never let him mention it before you children. Your Daddy was like a crazy man that night and for many a night thereafter. He says he never in his life seen anything as dark as that road after the lights of that car had gone away. Weren't nothing, weren't nobody on that road, just your Daddy and his brother and that busted guitar. Oh, yes. Your Daddy never did really get right again. Till the day he died he weren't sure but that every white man he saw was the man that killed his brother."

She stopped and took out her handkerchief and dried her eyes and looked at me.

"I ain't telling you all this," she said, "to make you scared or bitter or to make you hate nobody. I'm telling you this because you got a brother. And the world ain't changed."

I guess I didn't want to believe this. I guess she saw this in my face. She 100
turned away from me, toward the window again, searching those streets.

"But I praise my Redeemer," she said at last, "that He called your
Daddy home before me. I ain't saying it to throw no flowers at myself, but,
I declare, it keeps me from feeling too cast down to know I helped your
father get safely through this world. Your father always acted like he was
the roughest, strongest man on earth. And everybody took him to be like
that. But if he hadn't had me there — to see his tears!"

She was crying again. Still, I couldn't move. I said, "Lord, Lord, Mama,
I didn't know it was like that."

"Oh, honey," she said, "there's a lot that you don't know. But you are
going to find out." She stood up from the window and came over to me.
"You got to hold on to your brother," she said, "and don't let him fall, no
matter what it looks like is happening to him and no matter how evil you
gets with him. You going to be evil with him many a time. But don't you
forget what I told you, you hear?"

"I won't forget," I said. "Don't you worry, I won't forget. I won't let
nothing happen to Sonny."

My mother smiled as though she was amused at something she saw 105
in my face. Then, "You may not be able to stop nothing from happening.
But you got to let him know you's *there*."

Two days later I was married, and then I was gone. And I had a lot of
things on my mind and I pretty well forgot my promise to Mama until I
got shipped home on a special furlough for her funeral.

And, after the funeral, with just Sonny and me alone in the empty
kitchen, I tried to find out something about him.

"What do you want to do?" I asked him.

"I'm going to be a musician," he said.

For he had graduated, in the time I had been away, from dancing to 110
the juke box to finding out who was playing what, and what they were
doing with it, and he had bought himself a set of drums.

"You mean, you want to be a drummer?" I somehow had the feeling
that being a drummer might be all right for other people but not for my
brother Sonny.

"I don't think," he said, looking at me very gravely, "that I'll ever be a
good drummer. But I think I can play a piano."

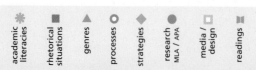

academic literacies   rhetorical situations   genres   processes   strategies   research MLA / APA   media / design   readings

I frowned. I'd never played the role of the oldest brother quite so seriously before, had scarcely ever, in fact, *asked* Sonny a damn thing. I sensed myself in the presence of something I didn't really know how to handle, didn't understand. So I made my frown a little deeper as I asked: "What kind of musician do you want to be?"

He grinned. "How many kinds do you think there are?"

"Be *serious*," I said. 115

He laughed, throwing his head back, and then looked at me. "I *am* serious."

"Well, then, for Christ's sake, stop kidding around and answer a serious question. I mean, do you want to be a concert pianist, you want to play classical music and all that, or — or what?" Long before I finished he was laughing again. "For Christ's *sake,* Sonny!"

He sobered, but with difficulty. "I'm sorry. But you sound so — *scared!*" and he was off again.

"Well, you may think it's funny now, baby, but it's not going to be so funny when you have to make your living at it, let me tell you *that.*" I was furious because I knew he was laughing at me and I didn't know why.

"No," he said, very sober now, and afraid, perhaps, that he'd hurt me, "I 120 don't want to be a classical pianist. That isn't what interests me. I mean" — he paused, looking hard at me, as though his eyes would help me to understand, and then gestured helplessly, as though perhaps his hand would help — "I mean, I'll have a lot of studying to do, and I'll have to study *everything,* but, I mean, I want to play *with* — jazz musicians." He stopped. "I want to play jazz," he said.

Well, the word had never before sounded as heavy, as real, as it sounded that afternoon in Sonny's mouth. I just looked at him and I was probably frowning a real frown by this time. I simply couldn't see why on earth he'd want to spend his time hanging around nightclubs, clowning around on bandstands, while people pushed each other around a dance floor. It seemed — beneath him, somehow. I had never thought about it before, had never been forced to, but I suppose I had always put jazz musicians in a class with what Daddy called "good-time people."

"Are you *serious?*"

"Hell, *yes,* I'm serious."

He looked more helpless than ever, and annoyed, and deeply hurt.

I suggested, helpfully: "You mean — like Louis Armstrong?"   125

His face closed as though I'd struck him. "No. I'm not talking about none of that old-time, down-home crap."

"Well, look, Sonny, I'm sorry, don't get mad. I just don't altogether get it, that's all. Name somebody — you know, a jazz musician you admire."

"Bird."

"Who?"

"Bird! Charlie Parker!* Don't they teach you nothing in the goddamn   130 army?"

I lit a cigarette. I was surprised and then a little amused to discover that I was trembling. "I've been out of touch," I said. "You'll have to be patient with me. Now. Who's this Parker character?"

"He's just one of the greatest jazz musicians alive," said Sonny, sullenly, his hands in his pockets, his back to me. "Maybe *the* greatest," he added, bitterly. "That's probably why *you* never heard of him."

"All right," I said, "I'm ignorant. I'm sorry. I'll go out and buy all the cat's records right away, all right?"

"It don't," said Sonny, with dignity, "make any difference to me. I don't care what you listen to. Don't do me no favors."

I was beginning to realize that I'd never seen him so upset before. With   135 another part of my mind I was thinking that this would probably turn out to be one of those things kids go through and that I shouldn't make it seem important by pushing it too hard. Still, I didn't think it would do any harm to ask: "Doesn't all this take a lot of time? Can you make a living at it?"

He turned back to me and half leaned, half sat, on the kitchen table. "Everything takes time," he said, "and — well, yes, sure, I can make a living at it. But what I don't seem to be able to make you understand is that it's the only thing I want to do."

"Well, Sonny," I said gently, "you know people can't always do exactly what they *want* to do —"

"No, I don't know that," said Sonny, surprising me. "I think people *ought* to do what they want to do, what else are they alive for?"

---

*Charlie "Bird" Parker (1920–1955): saxophone player for whom Birdland jazz club in New York was named; a founder of the new jazz, "bebop," that began to flourish in the 1940s. [Editor's note]

"You getting to be a big boy," I said desperately, "it's time you started thinking about your future."

"I'm thinking about my future," said Sonny, grimly. "I think about it all 140 the time."

I gave up. I decided, if he didn't change his mind, that we could always talk about it later. "In the meantime," I said, "you got to finish school." We had already decided that he'd have to move in with Isabel and her folks. I knew this wasn't the ideal arrangement because Isabel's folks are inclined to be dicty* and they hadn't especially wanted Isabel to marry me. But I didn't know what else to do. "And we have to get you fixed up at Isabel's."

There was a long silence. He moved from the kitchen table to the window. "That's a terrible idea. You know it yourself."

"Do you have a *better* idea?"

He just walked up and down the kitchen for a minute. He was as tall as I was. He had started to shave. I suddenly had the feeling that I didn't know him at all.

He stopped at the kitchen table and picked up my cigarettes. Looking 145 at me with a kind of mocking, amused defiance, he put one between his lips. "You mind?"

"You smoking already?"

He lit the cigarette and nodded, watching me through the smoke. "I just wanted to see if I'd have the courage to smoke in front of you." He grinned and blew a great cloud of smoke to the ceiling. "It was easy." He looked at my face. "Come on, now. I bet you was smoking at my age, tell the truth."

I didn't say anything but the truth was on my face, and he laughed. But now there was something very strained in his laugh. "Sure. And I bet that ain't all you was doing."

He was frightening me a little. "Cut the crap," I said. "We already decided that you was going to go and live at Isabel's. Now what's got into you all of a sudden?"

"*You* decided it," he pointed out. "I didn't decide nothing." He stopped in 150 front of me, leaning against the stove, arms loosely folded. "Look, brother. I

---

*Dicty: dictatorial, overbearing. [Editor's note]

don't want to stay in Harlem no more, I really don't." He was very earnest. He looked at me, then over toward the kitchen window. There was something in his eyes I'd never seen before, some thoughtfulness, some worry all his own. He rubbed the muscle of one arm. "It's time I was getting out of here."

"Where do you want to *go*, Sonny?"

"I want to join the army. Or the navy, I don't care. If I say I'm old enough, they'll believe me."

Then I got mad. It was because I was so scared. "You must be crazy. You goddamn fool, what the hell do you want to go and join the *army* for?"

"I just told you. To get out of Harlem."

"Sonny, you haven't even finished *school*. And if you really want to be   155
a musician, how do you expect to study if you're in the *army?*"

He looked at me, trapped, and in anguish. "There's ways. I might be able to work out some kind of deal. Anyway, I'll have the G.I. Bill* when I come out."

"*If* you come out." We stared at each other. "Sonny, please. Be reasonable. I know the setup is far from perfect. But we got to do the best we can."

"I ain't learning nothing in school," he said. "Even when I go." He turned away from me and opened the window and threw his cigarette out into the narrow alley. I watched his back. "At least, I ain't learning nothing you'd want me to learn." He slammed the window so hard I thought the glass would fly out, and turned back to me. "And I'm sick of the stink of these garbage cans!"

"Sonny," I said, "I know how you feel. But if you don't finish school now, you're going to be sorry later that you didn't." I grabbed him by the shoulders. "And you only got another year. It ain't so bad. And I'll come back and I swear I'll help you do *whatever* you want to do. Just try to put up with it till I come back. Will you please do that? For me?"

He didn't answer and he wouldn't look at me.   160

"Sonny. You hear me?"

He pulled away. "I hear you. But you never hear anything *I* say."

The G.I. Bill: the Servicemen's Readjustment Act of 1944, which provided a number of veterans' benefits, including tuition assistance. [Editor's note]

I didn't know what to say to that. He looked out of the window and then back at me. "OK," he said, and sighed. "I'll try."

Then I said, trying to cheer him up a little, "They got a piano at Isabel's. You can practice on it."

And as a matter of fact, it did cheer him up for a minute. "That's right," he said to himself. "I forgot that." His face relaxed a little. But the worry, the thoughtfulness, played on it still, the way shadows play on a face which is staring into the fire.

But I thought I'd never hear the end of that piano. At first, Isabel would write me, saying how nice it was that Sonny was so serious about his music and how, as soon as he came in from school, or wherever he had been when he was supposed to be at school, he went straight to that piano and stayed there until suppertime. And, after supper, he went back to that piano and stayed there until everybody went to bed. He was at the piano all day Saturday and all day Sunday. Then he bought a record player and started playing records. He'd play one record over and over again, all day long sometimes, and he'd improvise along with it on the piano. Or he'd play one section of the record, one chord, one change, one progression, then he'd do it on the piano. Then back to the record. Then back to the piano.

Well, I really don't know how they stood it. Isabel finally confessed that it wasn't like living with a person at all, it was like living with sound. And the sound didn't make any sense to her, didn't make any sense to any of them — naturally. They began, in a way, to be afflicted by this presence that was living in their home. It was as though Sonny were some sort of god, or monster. He moved in an atmosphere which wasn't like theirs at all. They fed him and he ate, he washed himself, he walked in and out of their door; he certainly wasn't nasty or unpleasant or rude, Sonny isn't any of those things; but it was as though he were all wrapped up in some cloud, some fire, some vision all his own; and there wasn't any way to reach him.

At the same time, he wasn't really a man yet, he was still a child, and they had to watch out for him in all kinds of ways. They certainly couldn't throw him out. Neither did they dare to make a great scene about that piano because even they dimly sensed, as I sensed, from so many thousands of miles away, that Sonny was at that piano playing for his life.

But he hadn't been going to school. One day a letter came from the school board and Isabel's mother got it — there had, apparently, been other letters but Sonny had torn them up. This day, when Sonny came in, Isabel's mother showed him the letter and asked where he'd been spending his time. And she finally got it out of him that he'd been down in Greenwich Village, with musicians and other characters, in a white girl's apartment. And this scared her and she started to scream at him and what came up, once she began — though she denies it to this day — was what sacrifices they were making to give Sonny a decent home and how little he appreciated it.

Sonny didn't play the piano that day. By evening, Isabel's mother had calmed down but then there was the old man to deal with, and Isabel herself. Isabel says she did her best to be calm but she broke down and started crying. She says she just watched Sonny's face. She could tell, by watching him, what was happening with him. And what was happening was that they penetrated his cloud, they had reached him. Even if their fingers had been a thousand times more gentle than human fingers ever are, he could hardly help feeling that they had stripped him naked and were spitting on that nakedness. For he also had to see that his presence, that music, which was life or death to him, had been torture for them and that they had endured it, not at all for his sake, but only for mine. And Sonny couldn't take that. He can take it a little better today than he could then but he's still not very good at it and, frankly, I don't know anybody who is.

The silence of the next few days must have been louder than the sound of all the music ever played since time began. One morning, before she went to work, Isabel was in his room for something and she suddenly realized that all of his records were gone. And she knew for certain that he was gone. And he was. He went as far as the navy would carry him. He finally sent me a postcard from some place in Greece and that was the first I knew that Sonny was still alive. I didn't see him any more until we were both back in New York and the war had long been over.

He was a man by then, of course, but I wasn't willing to see it. He came by the house from time to time, but we fought almost every time we met. I didn't like the way he carried himself, loose and dreamlike all

170

the time, and I didn't like his friends, and his music seemed to be merely an excuse for the life he led. It sounded just that weird and disordered.

Then we had a fight, a pretty awful fight, and I didn't see him for months. By and by I looked him up, where he was living, in a furnished room in the Village, and I tried to make it up. But there were lots of other people in the room and Sonny just lay on his bed, and he wouldn't come downstairs with me, and he treated these other people as though they were his family and I weren't. So I got mad and then he got mad, and then I told him that he might just as well be dead as live the way he was living. Then he stood up and he told me not to worry about him any more in life, that he *was* dead as far as I was concerned. Then he pushed me to the door and the other people looked on as though nothing were happening, and he slammed the door behind me. I stood in the hallway, staring at the door. I heard somebody laugh in the room and then the tears came to my eyes. I started down the steps, whistling to keep from crying, I kept whistling to myself, *You going to need me, baby, one of these cold, rainy days.*

I read about Sonny's trouble in the spring. Little Grace died in the fall. She was a beautiful little girl. But she only lived a little over two years. She died of polio and she suffered. She had a slight fever for a couple of days, but it didn't seem like anything and we just kept her in bed. And we would certainly have called the doctor, but the fever dropped, she seemed to be all right. So we thought it had just been a cold. Then, one day, she was up, playing, Isabel was in the kitchen fixing lunch for the two boys when they'd come in from school, and she heard Grace fall down in the living room. When you have a lot of children you don't always start running when one of them falls, unless they start screaming or something. And, this time, Gracie was quiet. Yet, Isabel says that when she heard that *thump* and then that silence, something happened to her to make her afraid. And she ran to the living room and there was little Grace on the floor, all twisted up, and the reason she hadn't screamed was that she couldn't get her breath. And when she did scream, it was the worst sound, Isabel says, that she'd ever heard in all her life, and she still hears it sometimes in her dreams. Isabel will sometimes wake me up with a low, moaning, strangling sound and I have to be quick to awaken her and hold her to me and where Isabel is weeping against me seems a mortal wound.

I think I may have written Sonny the very day that little Grace was 175
buried. I was sitting in the living room in the dark, by myself, and I suddenly thought of Sonny. My trouble made his real.

One Saturday afternoon, when Sonny had been living with us, or anyway, been in our house, for nearly two weeks, I found myself wandering
aimlessly about the living room, drinking from a can of beer, and trying
to work up courage to search Sonny's room. He was out, he was usually
out whenever I was home, and Isabel had taken the children to see their
grandparents. Suddenly I was standing still in front of the living room
window, watching Seventh Avenue. The idea of searching Sonny's room
made me still. I scarcely dared to admit to myself what I'd be searching
for. I didn't know what I'd do if I found it. Or if I didn't.

On the sidewalk across from me, near the entrance to a barbecue
joint, some people were holding an old-fashioned revival meeting. The
barbecue cook, wearing a dirty white apron, his conked* hair reddish and
metallic in the pale sun, and a cigarette between his lips, stood in the
doorway, watching them. Kids and older people paused in their errands
and stood there, along with some older men and a couple of very tough-
looking women who watched everything that happened on the avenue, as
though they owned it, or were maybe owned by it. Well, they were watching
this, too. The revival was being carried on by three sisters in black, and a
brother. All they had were their voices and their Bibles and a tambourine.
The brother was testifying† and while he testified two of the sisters stood
together, seeming to say, amen, and the third sister walked around with
the tambourine outstretched and a couple of people dropped coins into it.
Then the brother's testimony ended and the sister who had been taking
up the collection dumped the coins into her palm and transferred them to
the pocket of her long black robe. Then she raised both hands, striking the
tambourine against the air, and then against one hand, and she started to
sing. And the two other sisters and the brother joined in.

It was strange, suddenly, to watch, though I had been seeing these
meetings all my life. So, of course, had everybody else down there. Yet, they

---

*Conked: straightened and greased. [Editor's note]
†Testifying: proclaiming his religious belief. [Editor's note]

academic literacies   rhetorical situations   genres   processes   strategies   research MLA / APA   media / design   readings

paused and watched and listened and I stood still at the window. "'*Tis the old ship of Zion,*" they sang, and the sister with the tambourine kept a steady, jangling beat, "*it has rescued many a thousand!*" Not a soul under the sound of their voices was hearing this song for the first time, not one of them had been rescued. Nor had they seen much in the way of rescue work being done around them. Neither did they especially believe in the holiness of the three sisters and the brother, they knew too much about them, knew where they lived, and how. The woman with the tambourine, whose voice dominated the air, whose face was bright with joy, was divided by very little from the woman who stood watching her, a cigarette between her heavy, chapped lips, her hair a cuckoo's nest, her face scarred and swollen from many beatings, and her black eyes glittering like coal. Perhaps they both knew this, which was why, when, as rarely, they addressed each other, they addressed each other as Sister. As the singing filled the air the watching, listening faces underwent a change, the eyes focusing on something within; the music seemed to soothe a poison out of them; and time seemed, nearly, to fall away from the sullen, belligerent, battered faces, as though they were fleeing back to their first condition, while dreaming of their last. The barbecue cook half shook his head and smiled, and dropped his cigarette and disappeared into his joint. A man fumbled in his pockets for change and stood holding it in his hand impatiently, as though he had just remembered a pressing appointment further up the avenue. He looked furious. Then I saw Sonny, standing on the edge of the crowd. He was carrying a wide, flat notebook with a green cover, and it made him look, from where I was standing, almost like a schoolboy. The coppery sun brought out the copper in his skin, he was very faintly smiling, standing very still. Then the singing stopped, the tambourine turned into a collection plate again. The furious man dropped in his coins and vanished, so did a couple of the women, and Sonny dropped some change in the plate, looking directly at the woman with a little smile. He started across the avenue, toward the house. He has a slow, loping walk, something like the way Harlem hipsters walk, only he's imposed on this his own half-beat. I had never really noticed it before.

I stayed at the window, both relieved and apprehensive. As Sonny disappeared from my sight, they began singing again. And they were still singing when his key turned in the lock.

"Hey," he said.   180

"Hey, yourself. You want some beer?"

"No. Well, maybe." But he came up to the window and stood beside me, looking out. "What a warm voice," he said.

They were singing *If I could only hear my mother pray again!*

"Yes," I said, "and she can sure beat that tambourine."

"But what a terrible song," he said, and laughed. He dropped his note- 185 book on the sofa and disappeared into the kitchen. "Where's Isabel and the kids?"

"I think they went to see their grandparents. You hungry?"

"No." He came back into the living room with his can of beer. "You want to come some place with me tonight?"

I sensed, I don't know how, that I couldn't possibly say no. "Sure. Where?"

He sat down on the sofa and picked up his notebook and started leafing through it. "I'm going to sit in with some fellows in a joint in the Village."

"You mean, you're going to play, tonight?" 190

"That's right." He took a swallow of his beer and moved back to the window. He gave me a sidelong look. "If you can stand it." "I'll try," I said.

He smiled to himself and we both watched as the meeting across the way broke up. The three sisters and the brother, heads bowed, were singing *God be with you till we meet again.* The faces around them were very quiet. Then the song ended. The small crowd dispersed. We watched the three women and the lone man walk slowly up the avenue.

"When she was singing before," said Sonny, abruptly, "her voice reminded me for a minute of what heroin feels like sometimes — when it's in your veins. It makes you feel sort of warm and cool at the same time. And distant. And — and sure." He sipped his beer, very deliberately not look- ing at me. I watched his face. "It makes you feel — in control. Sometimes you've got to have that feeling."

"Do you?" I sat down slowly in the easy chair.

"Sometimes." He went to the sofa and picked up his notebook again. 195 "Some people do."

"In order," I asked, "to play?" And my voice was very ugly, full of contempt and anger.

"Well" — he looked at me with great, troubled eyes, as though, in fact, he hoped his eyes would tell me things he could never otherwise say — "they *think* so. And *if* they think so — !"

"And what do *you* think?" I asked.

He sat on the sofa and put his can of beer on the floor. "I don't know," he said, and I couldn't be sure if he were answering my question or pursuing his thoughts. His face didn't tell me. "It's not so much to *play*. It's to *stand* it, to be able to make it at all. On any level." He frowned and smiled: "In order to keep from shaking to pieces."

"But these friends of yours," I said, "they seem to shake themselves to pieces pretty goddamn fast." 200

"Maybe." He played with the notebook. And something told me that I should curb my tongue, that Sonny was doing his best to talk, that I should listen. "But of course you only know the ones that've gone to pieces. Some don't — or at least they haven't *yet* and that's just about all *any* of us can say." He paused. "And then there are some who just live, really, in hell, and they know it and they see what's happening and they go right on. I don't know." He sighed, dropped the notebook, folded his arms. "Some guys, you can tell from the way they play, they on something *all* the time. And you can see that, well, it makes something real for them. But of course," he picked up his beer from the floor and sipped it and put the can down again, "they *want* to, too, you've got to see that. Even some of them that say they don't — *some*, not all."

"And what about you?" I asked — I couldn't help it. "What about you? Do *you* want to?"

He stood up and walked to the window and I remained silent for a long time. Then he sighed. "Me," he said. Then: "While I was downstairs before, on my way here, listening to that woman sing, it struck me all of a sudden how much suffering she must have had to go through — to sing like that. It's *repulsive* to think you have to suffer that much."

I said: "But there's no way not to suffer — is there, Sonny?"

"I believe not," he said and smiled, "but that's never stopped anyone 205 from trying." He looked at me. "Has it?" I realized, with this mocking look, that there stood between us, forever, beyond the power of time or forgiveness, the fact that I had held silence — so long! — when he had needed human speech to help him. He turned back to the window. "No, there's no way not to suffer. But you try all kinds of ways to keep from drowning in it, to keep on top of it, and to make it seem — well, like *you*. Like you did something, all right, and now you're suffering for it. You know?" I said nothing. "Well you know," he said, impatiently, "why *do* people suffer? Maybe it's better to do something to give it a reason, *any* reason."

"But we just agreed," I said, "that there's no way not to suffer. Isn't it better, then, just to — take it?"

"But nobody just takes it," Sonny cried, "that's what I'm telling you! *Everybody* tries not to. You're just hung up on the *way* some people try — it's not *your* way!"

The hair on my face began to itch, my face felt wet. "That's not true," I said, "that's not true. I don't give a damn what other people do, I don't even care how they suffer. I just care how *you* suffer." And he looked at me. "Please believe me," I said, "I don't want to see you — die — trying not to suffer."

"I won't," he said flatly, "die trying not to suffer. At least, not any faster than anybody else."

"But there's no need," I said, trying to laugh, "is there? in killing yourself." 210

I wanted to say more, but I couldn't. I wanted to talk about will power and how life could be — well, beautiful. I wanted to say that it was all within; but was it? or, rather, wasn't that exactly the trouble? And I wanted to promise that I would never fail him again. But it would all have sounded — empty words and lies.

So I made the promise to myself and prayed that I would keep it.

"It's terrible sometimes, inside," he said, "that's what's the trouble. You walk these streets, black and funky and cold, and there's not really a living ass to talk to, and there's nothing shaking, and there's no way of getting it out — that storm inside. You can't talk it and you can't make love with it, and when you finally try to get with it and play it, you realize *nobody's* listening. So *you've* got to listen. You got to find a way to listen."

And then he walked away from the window and sat on the sofa again, as though all the wind had suddenly been knocked out of him. "Sometimes

you'll do *anything* to play, even cut your mother's throat." He laughed and looked at me. "Or your brother's." Then he sobered. "Or your own." Then: "Don't worry. I'm all right now and I think I'll *be* all right. But I can't forget — where I've been. I don't mean just the physical place I've been, I mean where I've *been*. And *what* I've been."

"What have you been, Sonny?" I asked. 215

He smiled — but sat sideways on the sofa, his elbow resting on the back, his fingers playing with his mouth and chin, not looking at me. "I've been something I didn't recognize, didn't know I could be. Didn't know anybody could be." He stopped, looking inward, looking helplessly young, looking old. "I'm not talking about it now because I feel *guilty* or anything like that — maybe it would be better if I did, I don't know. Anyway, I can't really talk about it. Not to you, not to anybody," and now he turned and faced me. "Sometimes, you know, and it was actually when I was most *out* of the world, I felt that I was in it, that I was *with* it, really, and I could play or I didn't really have to *play*, it just came out of me, it was there. And I don't know how I played, thinking about it now, but I know I did awful things, those times, sometimes, to people. Or it wasn't that I *did* anything to them — it was that they weren't real." He picked up the beer can; it was empty; he rolled it between his palms: "And other times — well, I needed a fix, I needed to find a place to lean, I needed to clear a space to *listen* — and I couldn't find it, and I — went crazy, I did terrible things to *me*, I was terrible *for* me." He began pressing the beer can between his hands, I watched the metal begin to give. It glittered, as he played with it like a knife, and I was afraid he would cut himself, but I said nothing. "Oh well. I can never tell you. I was all by myself at the bottom of something, stinking and sweating and crying and shaking, and I smelled it, you know? *my* stink, and I thought I'd die if I couldn't get away from it and yet, all the same, I knew that everything I was doing was just locking me in with it. And I didn't know," he paused, still flattening the beer can, "I didn't know, I still *don't* know, something kept telling me that maybe it was good to smell your own stink, but I didn't think that *that* was what I'd been trying to do — and — who can stand it?" and he abruptly dropped the ruined beer can, looking at me with a small, still smile, and then rose, walking to the window as though it were the lodestone rock. I watched his face, he watched the avenue. "I couldn't tell you when Mama died — but the reason I wanted to leave Harlem so bad was to get away from drugs. And then, when I ran away, that's what I was running from — really. When I came back, nothing had changed, I hadn't changed, I was just — older." And he stopped, drumming with his fingers on the windowpane. The sun had vanished, soon darkness would fall. I watched his face. "It can come again," he said, almost as though speaking to himself. Then he turned to me. "It can come again," he repeated. "I just want you to know that."

"All right," I said, at last. "So it can come again. All right."

He smiled, but the smile was sorrowful. "I had to try to tell you," he said.

"Yes," I said. "I understand that."

"You're my brother," he said, looking straight at me, and not smiling   220
at all.

"Yes," I repeated, "yes. I understand that."

He turned back to the window, looking out. "All that hatred down there," he said, "all that hatred and misery and love. It's a wonder it doesn't blow the avenue apart."

We went to the only nightclub on a short, dark street, downtown. We squeezed through the narrow, chattering, jampacked bar to the entrance of the big room, where the bandstand was. And we stood there for a moment, for the lights were very dim in this room and we couldn't see. Then, "Hello, boy," said the voice and an enormous black man, much older than Sonny or myself, erupted out of all that atmospheric lighting and put an arm around Sonny's shoulder. "I been sitting right here," he said, "waiting for you."

He had a big voice, too, and heads in the darkness turned toward us.

Sonny grinned and pulled a little away, and said, "Creole, this is my   225
brother. I told you about him."

Creole shook my hand. "I'm glad to meet you, son," he said, and it was clear that he was glad to meet me *there*, for Sonny's sake. And he smiled, "You got a real musician in *your* family," and he took his arm from Sonny's shoulder and slapped him, lightly, affectionately, with the back of his hand.

"Well. Now I've heard it all," said a voice behind us. This was another musician, and a friend of Sonny's, a coal-black, cheerful-looking man, built

close to the ground. He immediately began confiding to me, at the top of his lungs, the most terrible things about Sonny, his teeth gleaming like a lighthouse and his laugh coming up out of him like the beginning of an earthquake. And it turned out that everyone at the bar knew Sonny, or almost everyone; some were musicians, working there, or nearby, or not working, some were simply hangers-on, and some were there to hear Sonny play. I was introduced to all of them and they were all very polite to me. Yet, it was clear that, for them, I was only Sonny's brother. Here, I was in Sonny's world. Or, rather: his kingdom. Here, it was not even a question that his veins bore royal blood.

They were going to play soon and Creole installed me, by myself, at a table in a dark corner. Then I watched them, Creole, and the little black man, and Sonny, and the others, while they horsed around, standing just below the bandstand. The light from the bandstand spilled just a little short of them and, watching them laughing and gesturing and moving about, I had the feeling that they, nevertheless, were being most careful not to step into that circle of light too suddenly; that if they moved into the light too suddenly, without thinking, they would perish in flame. Then, while I watched, one of them, the small black man, moved into the light and crossed the bandstand and started fooling around with his drums. Then — being funny and being, also, extremely ceremonious — Creole took Sonny by the arm and led him to the piano. A woman's voice called Sonny's name and a few hands started clapping. And Sonny, also being funny and being ceremonious, and so touched, I think, that he could have cried, but neither hiding it nor showing it, riding it like a man, grinned, and put both hands to his heart and bowed from the waist.

Creole then went to the bass fiddle and a lean, very bright-skinned brown man jumped up on the bandstand and picked up his horn. So there they were, and the atmosphere on the bandstand and in the room began to change and tighten. Someone stepped up to the microphone and announced them. Then there were all kinds of murmurs. Some people at the bar shushed others. The waitress ran around, frantically getting in the last orders, guys and chicks got closer to each other, and the lights on the bandstand, on the quartet, turned to a kind of indigo. Then they all looked different there. Creole looked about him for the last time, as though he were making certain that all his chickens were in the coop, and then he — jumped and struck the fiddle. And there they were.

All I know about music is that not many people ever really hear it. And even then, on the rare occasions when something opens within, and the music enters, what we mainly hear, or hear corroborated, are personal, private, vanishing evocations. But the man who creates the music is hearing something else, is dealing with the roar rising from the void and imposing order on it as it hits the air. What is evoked in him, then, is of another order, more terrible because it has no words, and triumphant, too, for that same reason. And his triumph, when he triumphs, is ours. I just watched Sonny's face. His face was troubled, he was working hard, but he wasn't with it. And I had the feeling that, in a way, everyone on the bandstand was waiting for him, both waiting for him and pushing him along. But as I began to watch Creole, I realized that it was Creole who held them all back. He had them on a short rein. Up there, keeping the beat with his whole body, wailing on the fiddle, with his eyes half closed, he was listening to everything, but he was listening to Sonny. He was having a dialogue with Sonny. He wanted Sonny to leave the shoreline and strike out for the deep water. He was Sonny's witness that deep water and drowning were not the same thing — he had been there, and he knew. And he wanted Sonny to know. He was waiting for Sonny to do the things on the keys which would let Creole know that Sonny was in the water.

And, while Creole listened, Sonny moved, deep within, exactly like someone in torment. I had never before thought of how awful the relationship must be between the musician and his instrument. He has to fill it, this instrument, with the breath of life, his own. He has to make it do what he wants it to do. And a piano is just a piano. It's made out of so much wood and wires and little hammers and big ones, and ivory. While there's only so much you can do with it, the only way to find this out is to try; to try and make it do everything.

And Sonny hadn't been near a piano for over a year. And he wasn't on much better terms with his life, not the life that stretched before him now. He and the piano stammered, started one way, got scared, stopped; started another way, panicked, marked time, started again; then seemed

academic literacies rhetorical situations genres processes strategies research MLA / APA media / design readings

to have found a direction, panicked again, got stuck. And the face I saw on Sonny I'd never seen before. Everything had been burned out of it, and, at the same time, things usually hidden were being burned in, by the fire and fury of the battle which was occurring in him up there.

Yet, watching Creole's face as they neared the end of the first set, I had the feeling that something had happened, something I hadn't heard. Then they finished, there was scattered applause, and then, without an instant's warning, Creole started into something else, it was almost sardonic, it was *Am I Blue?** And, as though he commanded, Sonny began to play. Something began to happen. And Creole let out the reins. The dry, low, black man said something awful on the drums, Creole answered, and the drums talked back. Then the horn insisted, sweet and high, slightly detached perhaps, and Creole listened, commenting now and then, dry, and driving, beautiful and calm and old. Then they all came together again, and Sonny was part of the family again. I could tell this from his face. He seemed to have found, right there beneath his fingers, a damn brand-new piano. It seemed that he couldn't get over it. Then, for a while, just being happy with Sonny, they seemed to be agreeing with him that brand-new pianos certainly were a gas.

Then Creole stepped forward to remind them that what they were playing was the blues. He hit something in all of them, he hit something in me, myself, and the music tightened and deepened, apprehension began to beat the air. Creole began to tell us what the blues were all about. They were not about anything very new. He and his boys up there were keeping it new, at the risk of ruin, destruction, madness, and death, in order to find new ways to make us listen. For, while the tale of how we suffer, and how we are delighted, and how we may triumph is never new, it always must be heard. There isn't any other tale to tell, it's the only light we've got in all this darkness.

And this tale, according to that face, that body, those strong hands on 235 those strings, has another aspect in every country, and a new depth in every generation. Listen, Creole seemed to be saying, listen. Now these are Sonny's blues. He made the little black man on the drums know it, and the bright, brown man on the horn. Creole wasn't trying any longer to get Sonny in the

---

Am I Blue?: a jazz tune, by H. Akst and G. Clarke, from *On With the Show* (1929). [Editor's note]

water. He was wishing him Godspeed. Then he stepped back, very slowly, filling the air with the immense suggestion that Sonny speak for himself.

Then they all gathered around Sonny and Sonny played. Every now and again one of them seemed to say, amen. Sonny's fingers filled the air with life, his life. But that life contained so many others. And Sonny went all the way back, he really began with the spare, flat statement of the opening phrase of the song. Then he began to make it his. It was very beautiful because it wasn't hurried and it was no longer a lament. I seemed to hear with what burning he had made it his, and what burning we had yet to make it ours, how we could cease lamenting. Freedom lurked around us and I understood, at last, that he could help us to be free if we would listen, that he would never be free until we did. Yet, there was no battle in his face now, I heard what he had gone through, and would continue to go through until he came to rest in earth. He had made it his: that long line, of which we knew only Mama and Daddy. And he was giving it back, as everything must be given back, so that, passing through death, it can live forever. I saw my mother's face again, and felt, for the first time, how the stones of the road she had walked on must have bruised her feet. I saw the moonlit road where my father's brother died. And it brought something else back to me, and carried me past it, I saw my little girl again and felt Isabel's tears again, and I felt my own tears begin to rise. And I was yet aware that this was only a moment, that the world waited outside, as hungry as a tiger, and that trouble stretched above us, longer than the sky.

Then it was over. Creole and Sonny let out their breath, both soaking wet, and grinning. There was a lot of applause and some of it was real. In the dark, the girl came by and I asked her to take drinks to the bandstand. There was a long pause, while they talked up there in the indigo light and after awhile I saw a girl put a Scotch and milk on top of the piano for Sonny. He didn't seem to notice it, but just before they started playing again, he sipped from it and looked toward me, and nodded. Then he put it back on top of the piano. For me, then, as they began to play again, it glowed and shook above my brother's head like the very cup of trembling.*

---

*Cup of trembling: Isaiah 51:22: "I have taken out of thine hand the cup of trembling . . . thou shalt no more drink it again." [Editor's note]

ADRIENNE RICH

Aunt Jennifer's Tigers

Adrienne Rich (1929–2012) was among the most influential American feminists, poets, and essayists of the second half of the twentieth century. Among her best known works is her collection Diving into the Wreck: Poems 1971–1972 *(1973). Her collection* A Human Eye: Essays on Art in Society *(2009) secured her reputation as America's preeminent feminist intellectual. "Aunt Jennifer's Tigers" (1951) was written while Rich was a student at Radcliffe College.*

Aunt Jennifer's tigers prance across a screen,
Bright topaz denizens of a world of green.
They do not fear the men beneath the tree;
They pace in sleek chivalric certainty.

Aunt Jennifer's finger fluttering through her wool   5
Find even the ivory needle hard to pull.
The massive weight of Uncle's wedding band
Sits heavily upon Aunt Jennifer's hand.

When Aunt is dead, her terrified hands will lie
Still ringed with ordeals she was mastered by.   10
The tigers in the panel that she made
Will go on prancing, proud and unafraid.

WILLIAM SHAKESPEARE

Sonnet 29: When in disgrace with Fortune and men's eyes

William Shakespeare (1564–1616) penned 37 plays as well as 154 sonnets. While little is known of Shakespeare's life, his works continue to be performed, read, and revered throughout the world. Sonnet 29 appeared in 1609.

When in disgrace with Fortune and men's eyes,
I all alone beweep my outcast state,
And trouble deaf heaven with my bootless cries,
And look upon myself and curse my fate,
Wishing me like to one more rich in hope,   5
Featured like him, like him with friends possess'd,
Desiring this man's art, and that man's scope,
With what I most enjoy contented least.
Yet in these thoughts myself almost despising,
Haply I think on thee, and then my state,   10
Like to the lark at break of day arising
From sullen earth, sings hymns at heaven's gate;
For thy sweet love remember'd such wealth brings
That then I scorn to change my state with kings.

EMILY DICKINSON

A word is dead

Emily Dickinson (1830–86) wrote almost 1,800 poems but during her lifetime published only a few of them, remaining mostly secluded in her family home in Amherst, Massachusetts, and little known to the public. Through her family's and friends' efforts after her death, her work became widely read and celebrated, and today she is considered one of the most prominent nineteenth-century American poets. "A word is dead" was first published in 1894.

A word is dead
When it is said,
    Some say.
I say it just
Begins to live   5
    That day.

65 Memoirs

academic
literacies

rhetorical
situations

genres

processes

strategies

research
MLA / APA

media /
design

readings

DAVID SEDARIS

Us and Them

Humorist David Sedaris (b. 1956) is the author of several collections of personal essays and stories, including When You Are Engulfed in Flames *(2008),* Squirrel Seeks Chipmunk: A Modest Bestiary *(2010), and* Let's Explore Diabetes with Owls *(2013). A frequent contributor to the* New Yorker, *he is also a playwright whose works include* SantaLand Diaries & Seasons Greetings: 2 Plays *(1998), as well as works coauthored with his sister, Amy Sedaris. The following essay comes from Sedaris's book-length memoir* Dress Your Family in Corduroy and Denim *(2005).*

WHEN MY FAMILY FIRST MOVED to North Carolina, we lived in a rented house three blocks from the school where I would begin the third grade. My mother made friends with one of the neighbors, but one seemed enough for her. Within a year we would move again and, as she explained, there wasn't much point in getting too close to people we would have to say good-bye to. Our next house was less than a mile away, and the short journey would hardly merit tears or even good-byes, for that matter. It was more of a "see you later" situation, but still I adopted my mother's attitude, as it allowed me to pretend that not making friends was a conscious choice. I could if I wanted to. It just wasn't the right time.

Back in New York State, we had lived in the country, with no sidewalks or streetlights; you could leave the house and still be alone. But here, when you looked out the window, you saw other houses, and people inside those houses. I hoped that in walking around after dark I might witness a murder, but for the most part our neighbors just sat in their living rooms, watching TV. The only place that seemed truly different was owned by a man named Mr. Tomkey, who did not believe in television. This was told to us by our mother's friend, who dropped by one afternoon with a basketful of okra. The woman did not editorialize — rather, she just presented her information, leaving her listener to make of it what she might. Had my mother said, "That's the craziest thing I've ever heard in my life," I assume that the friend would have agreed, and had she said, "Three cheers for Mr. Tomkey," the friend likely would have agreed as well. It was a kind of test, as was the okra.

To say that you did not believe in television was different from saying that you did not care for it. Belief implied that television had a master plan and that you were against it. It also suggested that you thought too much. When my mother reported that Mr. Tomkey did not believe in television, my father said, "Well, good for him. I don't know that I believe in it, either."

"That's exactly how I feel," my mother said, and then my parents watched the news, and whatever came on after the news.

Word spread that Mr. Tomkey did not own a television, and you began 5 hearing that while this was all very well and good, it was unfair of him to inflict his beliefs upon others, specifically his innocent wife and children. It was speculated that just as the blind man develops a keener sense of hearing, the family must somehow compensate for their loss. "Maybe they read," my mother's friend said. "Maybe they listen to the radio, but you can bet your boots they're doing *something*."

I wanted to know what this something was, and so I began peering through the Tomkeys' windows. During the day I'd stand across the street from their house, acting as though I were waiting for someone, and at night, when the view was better and I had less chance of being discovered, I would creep into their yard and hide in the bushes beside their fence.

Because they had no TV, the Tomkeys were forced to talk during dinner. They had no idea how puny their lives were, and so they were not ashamed that a camera would have found them uninteresting. They did not know what attractive was or what dinner was supposed to look like or even what time people were supposed to eat. Sometimes they wouldn't sit down until eight o'clock, long after everyone else had finished doing the dishes. During the meal, Mr. Tomkey would occasionally pound the table and point at his children with a fork, but the moment he finished, everyone would start laughing. I got the idea that he was imitating someone else, and wondered if he spied on us while we were eating.

When fall arrived and school began, I saw the Tomkey children marching up the hill with paper sacks in their hands. The son was one grade lower than me, and the daughter was one grade higher. We never spoke, but I'd pass them in the halls from time to time and attempt to view the world through their eyes. What must it be like to be so ignorant and alone? Could a normal person even imagine it? Staring at an Elmer Fudd lunch box, I tried to divorce myself from everything I already knew: Elmer's inability to pronounce the letter *r*, his constant pursuit of an intelligent and considerably more famous rabbit. I tried to think of him as just a drawing, but it was impossible to separate him from his celebrity.

One day in class a boy named William began to write the wrong answer on the blackboard, and our teacher flailed her arms, saying, "Warning, Will. Danger, danger." Her voice was synthetic and void of emotion, and we laughed, knowing that she was imitating the robot in a weekly show about a family who lived in outer space. The Tomkeys, though, would have thought she was having a heart attack. It occurred to me that they needed a guide, someone who could accompany them through the course of an average day and point out all the things they were unable to understand. I could have done it on weekends, but friendship would have taken away their mystery and interfered with the good feeling I got from pitying them. So I kept my distance.

In early October the Tomkeys bought a boat, and everyone seemed greatly 10 relieved, especially my mother's friend, who noted that the motor was definitely secondhand. It was reported that Mr. Tomkey's father-in-law owned a house on the lake and had invited the family to use it whenever they liked. This explained why they were gone all weekend, but it did not make their absences any easier to bear. I felt as if my favorite show had been canceled.

Halloween fell on a Saturday that year, and by the time my mother took us to the store, all the good costumes were gone. My sisters dressed as witches and I went as a hobo. I'd looked forward to going in disguise to the Tomkey's door, but they were off at the lake, and their house was dark. Before leaving, they had left a coffee can full of gumdrops on the front porch, alongside a sign reading DON'T BE GREEDY. In terms of Halloween candy, individual gumdrops were just about as low as you could get. This was evidenced by the large number of them floating in an adjacent dog bowl. It was disgusting to think that this was what a gumdrop might look like in your stomach, and it was insulting to be told not to take too much of something you didn't really want in the first place. "Who do these Tomkeys think they are?" my sister Lisa said.

The night after Halloween, we were sitting around watching TV when the doorbell rang. Visitors were infrequent at our house, so while my father stayed behind, my mother, sisters, and I ran downstairs in a group, opening the door to discover the entire Tomkey family on our front stoop. The parents looked as they always had, but the son and daughter were dressed in costumes — she as a ballerina and he as some kind of a rodent with terry-cloth ears and a tail made from what looked to be an extension cord. It seemed they had spent the previous evening isolated at the lake and had missed the opportunity to observe Halloween. "So, well, I guess we're trick-or-treating *now,* if that's okay," Mr. Tomkey said.

I attributed their behavior to the fact that they didn't have a TV, but television didn't teach you everything. Asking for candy on Halloween was called trick-or-treating, but asking for candy on November first was called begging, and it made people uncomfortable. This was one of the things you were supposed to learn simply by being alive, and it angered me that the Tomkeys did not understand it.

"Why of course it's not too late," my mother said. "Kids, why don't you . . . run and get . . . the candy."

"But the candy is gone," my sister Gretchen said. "You gave it away last night." 15

"Not *that* candy," my mother said. "The other candy. Why don't you run and go get it?"

"You mean *our* candy?" Lisa said. "The candy that we *earned?*"

This was exactly what our mother was talking about, but she didn't want to say this in front of the Tomkeys. In order to spare their feelings, she wanted them to believe that we always kept a bucket of candy lying around the house, just waiting for someone to knock on the door and ask for it. "Go on, now," she said. "Hurry up."

academic literacies　rhetorical situations　genres　processes　strategies　research MLA / APA　media / design　readings

My room was situated right off the foyer, and if the Tomkeys had looked in that direction, they could have seen my bed and the brown paper bag marked MY CANDY. KEEP OUT. I didn't want them to know how much I had, and so I went into my room and shut the door behind me. Then I closed the curtains and emptied my bag onto the bed, searching for whatever was the crummiest. All my life chocolate has made me ill. I don't know if I'm allergic or what, but even the smallest amount leaves me with a blinding headache. Eventually, I learned to stay away from it, but as a child I refused to be left out. The brownies were eaten, and when the pounding began I would blame the grape juice or my mother's cigarette smoke or the tightness of my glasses — anything but the choco-late. My candy bars were poison but they were brand-name, and so I put them in pile no. 1, which definitely would not go to the Tomkeys.

Out in the hallway I could hear my mother straining for something 20 to talk about. "A boat!" she said. "That sounds marvelous. Can you just drive it right into the water?"

"Actually, we have a trailer," Mr. Tomkey said. "So what we do is back it into the lake."

"Oh, a trailer. What kind is it?"

"Well, it's a *boat* trailer," Mr. Tomkey said.

"Right, but is it wooden, or you know . . . I guess what I'm asking is what *style* trailer do you have?"

Behind my mother's words were two messages. The first and most 25 obvious was "Yes, I am talking about boat trailers, but also I am dying." The second, meant only for my sisters and me, was "If you do not imme-diately step forward with that candy, you will never again experience freedom, happiness, or the possibility of my warm embrace."

I knew that it was just a matter of time before she came into my room and started collecting the candy herself, grabbing indiscriminately, with no regard to my rating system. Had I been thinking straight, I would have hidden the most valuable items in my dresser drawer, but instead, panicked by the thought of her hand on my doorknob, I tore off the wrappers and began cramming the candy bars into my mouth, desper-ately, like someone in a contest. Most were miniature, which made them easier to accommodate, but still there was only so much room, and it was hard to chew and fit more in at the same time. The headache began immediately, and I chalked it up to tension.

My mother told the Tomkeys she needed to check on something, and then she opened the door and stuck her head inside my room. "What the *hell* are you doing?" she whispered, but my mouth was too full to answer. "I'll just be a moment," she called, and as she closed the door behind her and moved toward my bed, I began breaking the wax lips and candy necklaces pulled from pile no. 2. These were the second-best things I had received, and while it hurt to destroy them, it would have hurt even more to give them away. I had just started to mutilate a miniature box of Red Hots when my mother pried them from my hands, accidentally finishing the job for me. BB-size pellets clattered onto the floor, and as I followed them with my eyes, she snatched up a roll of Necco wafers.

"Not those," I pleaded, but rather than words, my mouth expelled chocolate, chewed chocolate, which fell onto the sleeve of her sweater. "Not those. Not those."

She shook her arm, and the mound of chocolate dropped like a horrible turd upon my bedspread. "You should look at yourself," she said. "I mean, *really* look at yourself."

Along with the Necco wafers she took several Tootsie pops and half a dozen caramels wrapped in cellophane. I heard her apologize to the Tomkeys for her absence, and then I heard my candy hitting the bottom of their bags.   30

"What do you say?" Mrs. Tomkey asked.

And the children answered, "Thank you."

While I was in trouble for not bringing my candy sooner, my sisters were in more trouble for not bringing theirs at all. We spent the early part of the evening in our rooms, then one by one we eased our way back upstairs, and joined our parents in front of the TV. I was the last to arrive, and took a seat on the floor beside the sofa. The show was a Western, and even if my head had not been throbbing, I doubt I would have had the wherewithal to follow it. A posse of outlaws crested a rocky hilltop, squinting at a flurry of dust advancing from the horizon,

and I thought again of the Tomkeys and of how alone and out of place they had looked in their dopey costumes. "What was up with that kid's tail?" I asked.

"Shhhh," my family said.

For months I had protected and watched over these people, but now, with one stupid act, they had turned my pity into something hard and ugly. The shift wasn't gradual, but immediate, and it provoked an uncomfortable feeling of loss. We hadn't been friends, the Tomkeys and I, but still I had given them the gift of my curiosity. Wondering about the Tomkey family had made me feel generous, but now I would have to shift gears and find pleasure in hating them. The only alternative was to do as my mother had instructed and take a good look at myself. This was an old trick, designed to turn one's hatred inward, and while I was determined not to fall for it, it was hard to shake the mental picture snapped by her suggestion: here is a boy sitting on a bed, his mouth smeared with chocolate. He's a human being, but also he's a pig, surrounded by trash and gorging himself so that others may be denied. Were this the only image in the world, you'd be forced to give it your full attention, but fortunately there were others. This stagecoach, for instance, coming round the bend with a cargo of gold. This shiny new Mustang convertible. This teenage girl, her hair a beautiful mane, sipping Pepsi through a straw, one picture after another, on and on until the news, and whatever came on after the news.

Engaging with the Text

1. David Sedaris **TITLES** his essay "Us and Them." Whom does this title refer to? Whom are we meant to sympathize with — "us" or "them"? How do you know?

   344–45

2. Successful memoirs tell a **GOOD STORY**. Do you think "Us and Them" meets that requirement? Why or why not? Refer to specific details from the text in your response.

   220

3. Sedaris describes two handwritten signs from Halloween night. The first is attached to a "coffee can full of gumdrops" telling trick or treaters "DON'T BE GREEDY." The second graces young Sedaris's bag of candy: "MY CANDY. KEEP OUT." What significance do these two signs have in the story? What do they tell us about Sedaris?

64–67

4. How would you characterize Sedaris's **STANCE**? What specific passages indicate his attitude about the events he recalls?

216–23
222–23
222

5. *For Writing.* Recall a time when a person or event taught you something about yourself, something that perhaps you could not fully understand until now. Write a **MEMOIR** that describes the person or narrates the event. Include **VIVID DETAIL** and be sure to make clear what **SIGNIFICANCE** the person or event had in your life.

ANDRE DUBUS III

My Father Was a Writer

Andre Dubus III (b. 1959), who teaches at the University of Massachusetts–Lowell, is a 2012 recipient of the American Academy of Arts and Letters Award in Literature. He is the author of five works of fiction, most recently Dirty Love *(2013). His novel* House of Sand and Fog *(1999) was turned into an Academy Award–nominated film released in 2003. The following is an excerpt from his nonfiction book,* Townie: A Memoir *(2011).*

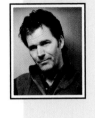

IT WAS THE SIX OF US: my young parents and all four of us kids born in a five year period beginning in 1958. We were each born on Marine bases, delivered by Marine doctors, Suzanne at Quantico in Virginia, me and Jeb on Camp Pendleton in California, and Nicole on Whidbey Island in Washington State. During these years, our father spent a lot of time aboard the USS *Ranger* off the coast of Japan. When we did see him, it was for brief stretches in cramped Marine base housing. His head was shaved, his face smooth and clean, but he was a man who didn't smile much, a man who seemed locked into a car on a road he didn't want to be on. But then my father's father died in 1963, and almost immediately after that Dad retired from the Marines as a captain and was accepted into the Iowa Writers' Workshop in Iowa City.

Though I didn't have words for it, I'd never seen him happier; he laughed often and loudly; he hugged and kissed our mother at every turn; he'd let his hair grow out long enough you could actually see some on his head, thick and brown. He'd grown a mustache, too. At night before bed, he'd sit me, my brother, and two sisters down at the kitchen table or on the couch in the living room and he'd tell us stories he made up himself — adventure stories where the hero and heroine were Indians defending their families and their people from the white man. One of them was Running Blue Ice Water, a kind and brave warrior who lingered in my imagination long after we'd been tucked in upstairs in a large room all four of us children shared.

My memory of that time is the memory of parties, though we were so broke we ate canned meat and big blocks of government cheese. Once a month Pop sold blood. But the parties went on. They happened at night, the house filled with talk and laughter and cigarette smoke. There were parties during the day, too. Blankets laid out on grass under the sun. Men and women eating sandwiches and sipping wine and reading poems out loud to each other.

Some parties were at the Vonneguts' house next door. All the Vonnegut kids were older than we were, but the father, Kurt, would walk down to our house every afternoon and sit with us four kids in the living room and watch *Batman* on the small black-and-white. He smoked one cigarette after the other. He laughed a lot and made jokes, and once he squinted down at me through the smoke and said: "Who's your favorite bad guy?"

"Um, False Face."

He smiled, his face a warm mix of mustache and round eyes and curly hair. "I like the Riddler."

5

In our bedroom floor was an air vent that overlooked the living room, and sometimes on party nights we kids would huddle around it and spy on our mother and father and their friends below, watch them dance and drink and argue and laugh, the men always louder than the women, their cigarette smoke curling up through the grate into our faces. I remember hearing a lot of dirty words then but also ones like *story, novel,* and *poem. Hemingway* and *Chekhov.*

In the morning we'd be up long before our parents. We'd get cereal and poke around in the party ruins, the table and floors of our small house littered with empty beer bottles, crushed potato chips, overflowing ashtrays, half the butts brushed with lipstick. If there was anything left in a glass, and if there wasn't a cigarette floating in it, Suzanne and I would take a few sips because we liked the taste of watered-down whiskey or gin. Once we found a carrot cake in the living room. Its sides were covered with white frosting, but the middle was nothing but a mashed crater. I remembered the cake from the night before, a mouthwatering three-layer with frosted writing on the top. I asked my mother who it

was for and she said it was for one of their friends who'd just sold his novel to a publisher; they were going to celebrate. And now the cake was unrecognizable, and when my mother came down that morning looking young and beautiful, probably in shorts and one of my father's shirts, smoking a cigarette, only twenty-five or -six, I asked her what had happened to the cake. She dug her finger into the frosting, then smiled at me. "Just your father and his crazy writer friends, honey." Did that mean he was a crazy writer, too? I wasn't sure.

It was another party at our house that confirmed it for me, though, one that began with jazz on the record player, a platter of cucumbers and carrots and horseradish dip on the kitchen table, glasses set out on the counter, and in his front room on his black wooden desk were two lit candles on either side of something rectangular and about two or three inches high covered with a black cloth. As my father's friends showed up one or two couples at a time, he'd walk them into his room with a drink or bottle of beer in his hand, and he'd point at what he told them was the failed novel he was holding a funeral for. He'd laugh and they'd laugh and one of his writer friends put his hand on his shoulder and squeezed, both of them looking suddenly pained and quite serious. I knew then my father was a writer too.

When our father's first book was published in 1967, he got a job 10 teaching at a small college in Massachusetts. We loaded up our rusted Chevrolet and drove east. For a year we lived in the woods of southern New Hampshire in a rented clapboard house on acres of pine and pasture. We had a swimming pool and a herd of sheep. There were fallen pine needles and a brook along whose banks Jeb and I found arrowheads, smooth pebbles, the bleached bones of rabbits or squirrels. We felt rich; we had all that land to play on, we had that big old house — its dark inviting rooms, its fireplaces, its fading wallpaper and floorboards fastened with square-cut nails from before the Civil War; we had that *pool*.

In 1968 we moved again, this time to a cottage on a pond on the Massachusetts-New Hampshire border. I was nine, and so it seemed like a house, but it was really a summer camp. Downstairs was the kitchen and its worn linoleum floor, the small living room with the black-and-white TV where we heard of the killing of Martin Luther King Jr.; it's where we saw X-ray photos of Robert Kennedy's brain and the .22 caliber bullet shot into it; it's where the following summer we watched a man walk on the moon, my mother sitting on the arm of the couch in shorts and one of Pop's button-down shirts, saying, "We're on the moon, you guys. We're on the fucking *moon*."

My father, thirty-two years old then, was earning seven thousand dollars a year teaching. He had a brown beard he kept trimmed, and he ran five miles a day, a ritual he had begun in the Marine Corps a few years earlier. My mother and father rarely had money to go out to a restaurant, but they still hosted a lot of parties at our house, usually on Friday or Saturday nights, sometimes both; my mother would set out saltine crackers and dip, sliced cheese and cucumbers and carrots; they'd open a jug of wine and a bucket of ice and wait for their friends to bring the rest: more wine, beer, bottles of gin and bourbon. Most of their friends came from the college where Pop taught: there was an art professor, a big man who wore black and had a clean-shaven handsome face and laughed loudly and looked to me like a movie actor; there were bearded poets and bald painters and women who taught pottery or literature or dance. There were students, too, mainly women, all of them beautiful, as I recall, with long shiny hair and straight white teeth, and they dressed in sleeveless sweaters or turtlenecks and didn't wear bras, their bell-bottoms hugging their thighs and flaring out widely over their suede boots.

The house would be filled with talk and laughter, jazz playing on the record player — a lot of Brubeck, Gerry Mulligan, and Buddy Rich. From my bed upstairs I could smell pot and cigarette smoke. I could hear music and the animated voices of my mother and father and their loud, intriguing friends. Sometimes there'd be yelling, and there'd be words like *Saigon*, *Viet Cong*, and *motherfucking Nixon*.

One weeknight on the news, there was a story about Marines killed in battle. I was lying on the floor under the coffee table as the camera panned over the bodies of soldiers lying on the ground, most of them on their stomachs, their arms splayed out beside them. Pop sat straight on the couch. His hands were on his knees, and his eyes were shining. "Pat, those are boys. Oh, goddamnit, those are eighteen-year-old *boys*."

Later, sleeping in the bed beside my brother's, there was a weight 15
on my chest and I woke to my father holding me, crying into the pillow
beside my ear. "My son, my son, oh, my son." He smelled like bourbon
and sweat. It was hard to breathe. I couldn't pull my arms free of the
blankets to hug Pop back. Then he was off me, crying over Jeb on his bed,
and there was my mother's whisper from the doorway, her shadowed
silhouette. Her arm reached for our father, and he stood and looked
down at us both a long while, then he was gone. The house was quiet,
my room dark and still. I lay awake and thought of all the good men
on TV who'd been shot in the head. I saw again the dead soldiers lying
on the ground, and until Pop had cried over us, I hadn't thought much
about Jeb and me having to go and fight, too. But in only nine years I'd
be as old as the dead, and it'd be my turn, wouldn't it?

But soldiers have to be brave, and I was not; I was a new kid in school
again, something I would be over and over for many years, trying to find
a solitary desk away from the others, dreading recess because everybody
knew everyone else and threw balls back and forth and chased after each
other grabbing and laughing, and I just didn't have the courage to jump
in. Then some kid would see me looking and yell, "What're you lookin'
at? You got a *problem?*"

Sometimes I'd get shoved and kicked and pushed to the ground. I
was still trying to figure out what I'd done to make them mad, I had not
yet learned that cruelty was cruelty and you don't ask why, just hit first
and hit hard.

There was more fighting at home. My parents must've tried to keep
it from us because it seemed to happen only late at night, both of them
screaming at each other, swearing, sometimes throwing things — pots
or pans, a plate or glass or ashtray, anything close by. When they fought,
their Southern accents were easier to hear, especially my mother's, "Goddamn you, you sonofa*bitch*." Pop's voice would get chest-deep and he'd
yell back at her as if she were a Marine under his command.

Many nights my brother and two sisters and I would listen from
the stairs in our pajamas, not because we enjoyed it but because it was
easier to bear when we weren't hearing it alone in our beds.

But by morning, the sun shone through the trees and most of the 20
thrown or broken dishes in the living room would be picked up, the
kitchen smelling like bacon and eggs, grits and toast and coffee, the
night before a bad dream already receding into the shadows where it
belonged. . . .

One sunlit afternoon in the early fall our parents sat us down in the
living room and told us they were getting separated. My father stood in
the kitchen doorway. My mother leaned against the wall on the other
side of the room. *Separated.* It was a word I'd never thought much about
before, but now I pictured them being cut one from the other with a big,
sharp knife. I sat in my father's chair, and I couldn't stop crying.

Then Pop was gone for weeks. One night, after Suzanne and Jeb and
Nicole were asleep, I lay in bed listening to my mother crying in her
room. It sounded like she was doing it into her pillow, but I could still
hear it, and I got up and walked down the creaking floorboards of the
hallway and knocked on her door. Her bedside lamp was on. She lifted
her head, wiped her eyes, and smiled at me. I asked her if she was all
right. She sat up and looked me up and down. She said, "I'm going to tell
you because you're old enough to hear it. Your father left me for Betsy
Armstrong. That's where he is right now, staying with her."

Betsy was one of the rich girls from the college. She had long straight
hair and a pretty face. I remembered her laughing once in the kitchen
with my mother. Now my mother got out of bed and leaned down and
hugged me. I hugged her back.

Then Pop was home again. I woke one morning and heard his voice
downstairs. I ran down there, and he hugged me. Later that day he was
in the bathroom shaving. I went in there just to watch. I was ten years
old, he was thirty-three. He turned from the mirror and said, "So you
know about Betsy then?"

The air in the room felt thicker somehow. "Yeah." 25

He reached into his wallet and pulled out a small photograph. He
handed it to me. "That's her."

It was of a girl I barely remembered seeing before, not the one I'd
thought she was. "She's pretty."

academic literacies | rhetorical situations | genres | processes | strategies | research MLA / APA | media / design | readings

"Yes, she is." Pop took the photo and slid it back into his wallet. I left the bathroom and walked straight to the kitchen where Mom stood at the sink washing dishes. I looked up at her face. She smiled down at me.

"Dad's girlfriend is prettier than you are, Mom." Her smile faded and she looked into the dishwater and kept scrubbing. I walked back to the bathroom and told my father what I'd said.

He was wiping shaving cream from his face with a towel. He stopped, 30 the towel still pressed to his cheek. "No, go apologize to her. Go tell her you're sorry right now."

I ran outside and into the woods. I don't remember ever apologizing to my mother, but Pop was back, girlfriend or not, and for a while things seemed to get back to normal, and there was less fighting than before. Each night when Pop came home from teaching, Mom would be cooking in the kitchen and they'd have cocktail hour, which meant none of us kids was allowed in there while they sipped Jim Beam and our father unwound and told Mom his day and she told him hers.

Soon the hour would be over, and the six of us would sit at the rickety table in that small, hot kitchen and we'd eat. We lived in New England, but at suppertime our house smelled like any in South Louisiana: Mom fried chicken, or simmered smothered breakfast steak or cheap cuts of pork, all served up with rice and gravy and baking powder biscuits. On the side there'd be collard greens or sliced tomatoes, cucumbers, and onions she'd put ice cubes on to keep crisp. She baked us hot tamale pies, and macaroni and cheese, or vegetable soup she'd cook for hours in a chicken stock, then serve in a hollowed-out crust of French bread, its top a steaming layer of melted cheddar. But while the food was wonderful, my mother and father hardly even looked at one another anymore and instead kept their attention on us, asking about school, about the tree fort Jeb and I were building out in the woods, about the Beatles album Suzanne listened to, the drawings Nicole did each afternoon. We rarely left the table hungry, but there was a hollowness in the air, a dark unspeakable stillness, one my father would soon drive into, and away.

It happened early on a Sunday in November. Pop was so much taller than the four of us, and we were following him down the porch stairs and along the path, Suzanne behind him in her cotton nightgown, then me and Jeb in our pajamas, Nicole last, her thick red hair and small face. We were eleven, ten, nine, and six. Ahead of us, there was the glint of frost on the gravel driveway and our car, the old Lancer, packed now with Pop's things: his clothes, his books, his shaving kit. The house was surrounded by tall pines and it was too cold to smell them, the air so clear and bright. Inside the house Mom was crying as if her pain were physical, as if someone were holding her down and doing something bad to her.

Daddy! Nicole ran past us over the gravel and she leapt and Pop turned, his eyes welling up, and he caught her, her arms around his neck, her face buried under his chin. I tried to ignore our mother's cries coming from the house. When my father looked down at me over Nicole's small shoulder, I stood as straight as I could and I hoped I looked strong.

Pop kissed Nicole's red hair. He lowered her to the gravel. His beard   35 was thick and dark, his cheeks and throat shaved clean. He was wearing a sweatshirt and corduroy pants, and he glanced up at our house. There was only the sound of our mother's cries, so maybe he would change his mind. Maybe he would stay.

Becoming a writer helped Andre Dubus III forge a relationship with his father, but making himself completely whole took more.

He looked down at us. "I'll see you soon. We'll go out to eat."

He hugged Suzanne, squeezed my shoulder. He tousled Jeb's hair, then he was in his car driving down the hill through the pines, blue exhaust coughing out its pipe. Jeb scooped up a handful of gravel and ran down the hill after him, "You bum! You bum! You bum!" He threw it all at once, the small rocks scattering across the road and into the woods like shrapnel.

Pop drove across the short bridge, then up a rise through more trees. Mom would need to be comforted now. Nicole too. There was food to think about. How to get it with no car. I tried to keep standing as straight as I could.

Engaging with the Text

1. How would you sum up what Andre Dubus III is saying in this memoir? Try to express in a sentence or two the **SIGNIFICANCE** to him of the events he relates.

   ▲ 222

2. Dubus's memoir is saturated in **VIVID DETAILS**. Select three paragraphs from different parts of the essay, and discuss what the details in them add to the story.

   ▲ 222–23

3. Dubus's **STANCE** toward his father in this memoir is respectful but somewhat distant. Identify two passages that make his stance clear. Is the stance appropriate for the story he is telling? Why or why not? What does his stance reveal about his feelings toward his father at the time he wrote the memoir?

   ■ 64–67

4. Dubus **TITLES** his memoir *My Father Was a Writer*. What is the significance of this title? Think of another title Dubus could have used, and explain what would be lost or gained by doing so.

   ◆ 344–45

5. *For Writing.* Write a **MEMOIR** about an event or several related events from your childhood that focuses on the significance of a particular person in your life. Use **VIVID DETAILS** to put your reader into the **NARRATIVE**.

   ▲ 216–23
   ▲ 222–23
   ◆ 419–27

PIPER KERMAN

#11187–424

Piper Kerman (b. 1969) is the author of Orange Is the New Black: My Year in a Women's Prison *(2010), from which the following memoir is taken. The book was turned into a TV show of the same name (minus the subtitle) that premiered on Netflix in 2013. Recipient of the 2014 Justice Trailblazer Award, Kerman serves on the board of the Women's Prison Association and is frequently invited to speak to audiences both inside and outside of prison.*

ON FEBRUARY 4, 2004, more than a decade after I had committed my crime, Larry drove me to the women's prison in Danbury, Connecticut. We had spent the previous night at home; Larry had cooked me an elaborate dinner, and then we curled up in a ball on our bed, crying. Now we were heading much too quickly through a drab February morning toward the unknown. As we made a right onto the federal reservation and up a hill to the parking lot, a hulking building with a vicious-looking triple-layer razor-wire fence loomed up. If that was minimum security, I was fucked.

Larry pulled into one of the parking areas. We looked at each other, saucer-eyed. Almost immediately a white pickup with police lights on its roof pulled in after us. I rolled down my window.

"There's no visiting today," the officer told me.

I stuck my chin out, defiance covering my fear. "I'm here to surrender."

"Oh. All right then." He pulled out and drove away. *Had he looked* 5 *surprised?* I wasn't sure.

In the car I stripped off all my jewelry — the seven gold rings; the diamond earrings Larry had given me for Christmas; the sapphire ring from my grandmother; the 1950s man's watch that was always around my wrist; all the earrings from all the extra holes that had so vexed my grandfather. I had on jeans, sneakers, and a long-sleeved T-shirt. With false bravado I said, "Let's do this."

We walked into the lobby. A placid woman in uniform was sitting behind the raised desk. There were chairs, some lockers, a pay phone, and a soda machine. It was spotless. "I'm here to surrender," I announced.

"Hold on." She picked up a phone and spoke to someone briefly. "Have a seat." We sat. For several hours. It got to be lunchtime. Larry handed me a foie gras sandwich that he had made from last night's leftovers. I wasn't hungry at all but unwrapped it from the tinfoil and munched every gourmet bite miserably. I am fairly certain that I was the first Seven Sisters grad to eat duck liver chased with a Diet Coke in the lobby of a federal penitentiary. Then again, you never know.

Finally, a considerably less pleasant-looking woman entered the lobby. She had a dreadful scar down the side of her face and neck. "Kerman?" she barked.

We sprang to our feet. "Yes, that's me."   10

"Who's this?" she said.

"This is my fiancé."

"Well, he's gotta leave before I take you in." Larry looked outraged. "That's the rule, it prevents problems. You have any personal items?"

I had a manila envelope in my hands, which I handed to her. It contained my self-surrender instructions from the U.S. Marshals, some of my legal paperwork, twenty-five photographs (an embarrassing number of my cats), lists of my friends' and family's addresses, and a cashier's check for $290 that I had been instructed to bring. I knew that I would need money in my prison account to make phone calls and buy . . . something? I couldn't imagine what.

"Can't take that," she said, handing the check to Larry.   15

"But I called last week, and they told me to bring it!"

"He has to send it to Georgia, then they'll process it," she said with absolute finality.

"*Where* do we send it?" I asked. I was suddenly furious.

"Hey, do you have that Georgia address?" the prison guard asked over her shoulder to the woman at the desk while poking through my envelope. "What are these, pictures? You got any nudie Judies in here?" She raised an eyebrow in her already-crooked face. Nudie Judies? Was she for real? She looked at me as if to ask, *Do I need to go through all these photos to see if you're a dirty girl?*

"No. No nudie Judies," I said. Three minutes into my self-surrender, and I already felt humiliated and beaten.

"Okay, are you ready?" I nodded. "Well, say goodbye. Since you're not married, it could be a while until he can visit." She took a symbolic step away from us, I guess to give us privacy.

I looked at Larry and hurled myself into his arms, holding on as tight as I could. I had no idea when I would see him again, or what would happen to me in the next fifteen months.

He looked as if he was going to cry; yet at the same time he was also furious. "I love you! I love you!" I said into his neck and his nice oatmeal sweater that I had picked for him. He squeezed me and told me he loved me too.

"I'll call you as soon as I can," I croaked.

"Okay."

"Please call my parents."

"Okay."

"Send that check immediately!"

"I know."

"I love you!"

And then he left the lobby, rubbing his eyes with the heel of his hand. He banged the doors hard and walked quickly to the parking lot.

The prison guard and I watched him get into the car. As soon as he was out of sight, I felt a surge of fear.

She turned to me. "You ready?" I was alone with her and whatever else was waiting for me.

"Yeah."

"Well, come on."

She led me out the door Larry had just exited from, turning right and walking along that vicious, towering fence. The fence had multiple layers; between each layer was a gate through which we had to be buzzed. She opened the gate, and I stepped in. I looked back over my shoulder at the free world. The next gate buzzed. I stepped through again, wire mesh and barbed metal soaring all around me. I felt fresh, rising panic.

This was not what I had expected. This was not how minimum-security camps had been described; this didn't look at all like "Club Fed." This was scaring the crap out of me.

We reached the door of the building and again were buzzed in. We walked through a small hallway into an institutional tiled room with harsh fluorescent light. It felt old, dingy, clinical, and completely empty. She pointed into a holding cell with benches bolted to the walls and metal screens over all visible sharp edges. "Wait in there." Then she walked through a door into another room.

I sat on a bench facing away from the door. I stared at the small high window through which I could see nothing but clouds. I wondered when I would see anything beautiful again. I meditated on the consequences of my long-ago actions and seriously questioned why I was not on the lam in Mexico. I kicked my feet. I thought about my fifteen-month sentence, which did nothing to quell my panic. I tried not to think about Larry. Then I gave up and tried to imagine what he was doing, with no success.

I had only the most tenuous idea of what might happen next, but I knew that I would have to be brave. Not foolhardy, not in love with risk and danger, not making ridiculous exhibitions of myself to prove that I wasn't terrified — really, genuinely brave. Brave enough to be quiet when quiet was called for, brave enough to observe before flinging myself into something, brave enough to not abandon my true self when someone else wanted to seduce or force me in a direction I didn't want to go, brave enough to stand my ground quietly. I waited an unquantifiable amount of time while trying to be brave.

"Kerman!" As I was unaccustomed to being called like a dog, it took 40 her a number of shouts before I realized that meant "Move." I jumped up and peered cautiously out of the holding cell. "Come on." The prison guard's rasp made it hard for me to understand what she was saying.

She led me into the next room, where her coworkers were lounging. Both were bald, male, and white. One of them was startlingly big, approaching seven feet tall; the other was very short. They both stared at me as if I had three heads. "Self-surrender," my female escort said to them by way of explanation as she started my paperwork. She spoke to me like I was an idiot yet explained nothing during the process. Every time I was slow to answer or asked her to repeat a question, Shorty would snort derisively, or worse, mimic my responses. I looked at him in disbelief. It was unnerving, as it was clearly intended to be, and it pissed me off, which was a welcome switch from the fear I was battling.

The female guard continued to bark questions and fill out forms. As I stood at attention and answered, I could not stop my eyes from turning toward the window, to the natural light outdoors.

"Come on."

I followed the guard toward the hallway outside the holding cell. She pawed through a shelf filled with clothing, then handed me a pair of granny panties; a cheap nylon bullet bra; a pair of elastic-waist khaki pants; a khaki top, like hospital scrubs; and tube socks. "What size shoe are you?" "Nine and a half." She handed me a little pair of blue canvas slippers like you would buy on the street in any Chinatown.

She indicated a toilet and sink area behind a plastic shower curtain. "Strip." I kicked off my sneakers, took off my socks, my jeans, my T-shirt, my bra, and my underpants, all of which she took from me. It was cold. "Hold your arms up." I did, displaying my armpits. "Open your mouth and stick out your tongue. Turn around, squat, spread your cheeks and cough." I would never get used to the cough part of this drill, which was supposed to reveal contraband hidden in one's privates — it was just so unnatural. I turned back around, naked. "Get dressed." 45

She put my own clothes in a box — they would be mailed back to Larry, like the personal effects of a dead soldier. The bullet bra, though hideous and scratchy, did fit. So in fact did all the khaki prison clothes, much to my amazement. She really had the eye. In minutes I was transformed into an inmate.

Now she seemed to soften toward me a bit. As she was fingerprinting me (a messy and oddly intimate process), she asked, "How long you been with that guy?"

"Seven years," I replied sullenly.

"He know what you were up to?"

Up to? What did she know! My temper flared again as I said defiantly, 50
"It's a ten-year-old offense. He had nothing to do with it." She seemed
surprised by this, which I took as a moral victory.

"Well, you're not married, so you probably won't be seeing him for
quite a while, not until he gets on your visitor list."

The horrifying reality that I had no idea when I would see Larry again
shut me right down. The prison guard was indifferent to the devastating
blow she had just dealt me.

She had been distracted by the fact that no one seemed to know
how to use the ID machine camera. Everyone took a turn poking at it,
until finally they produced a photo that made me look remarkably like
serial killer Aileen Wuornos. My chin was raised defiantly, and I looked
like hell. I later figured out that everyone looks either thuggish and
murderous or terrified and miserable in their prison ID photo. I'm proud
to say that, against all odds, I fell into the former category, though I felt
like the latter.

The ID card was red, with a bar code and the legend "U.S. Department of Justice Federal Bureau of Prisons — INMATE." In addition to the
unflattering photo, it also bore my new registration number in large
numerals: 11187–424. The last three numbers indicated my sentencing
district — Northern Illinois. The first five numbers were unique to me, my
new identity. Just as I had been taught to memorize my aunt and uncle's
phone number when I was six years old, I now silently tried to commit
my reg number to memory. 11187–424, 11187–424, 11187–424, 11187–424,
11187–424, 11187–424, 11187–424, 11187–424, 11187–424.

After the ID debacle, Ms. Personality said, "Mr. Butorsky's gonna 55
talk to you, but first go into medical." She pointed into another small
room.

Mr. Who? I went and stared out the window, obsessing about the razor
wire and the world beyond it from which I had been taken, until a medic
— a round Filipino man — came to see me. He performed the most basic
of medical interviews, which went quickly, as I have been blessed with
more or less perfect health. He told me he needed to perform a TB test,
for which I extended my arm. "Nice veins!" he said with very genuine
admiration. "No track marks!" Given his total lack of irony, I thanked him.

Mr. Butorsky was a compact, mustachioed fiftyish man, with watery, blinky blue eyes and, unlike the prison staff I had met so far, of discernible intelligence. He was leaning back in a chair, with paperwork spread out in front of him. It was my PSI — the presentencing investigation that the Feds do on people like me. It is supposed to document the basic facts of one's crime, one's prior offenses, one's family situation and children, one's history of substance abuse, work history, everything important.

"Kerman? Sit down," he gestured, looking at me in a way that I suspect was much practiced to be calculating, penetrating, and measuring. I sat. He regarded me for several seconds in silence. I kept my chin firm and didn't look at him. "How are you doing?" he asked.

It was startling to have anyone show the slightest interest in how, exactly, I was doing. I felt a flood of gratitude in spite of myself. "I'm okay."

"You are?"   60

I nodded, deciding this was a good situation for my tough act.

He looked out the window. "In a little bit I'm going to have them take you up to the Camp," he began.

My brain relaxed a bit and my stomach unclenched. I followed his gaze out the window, feeling profound relief that I wouldn't have to stay down here with evil Shorty.

"I'll be your counselor at the Camp. You know I've been reading your file." He gestured at my PSI on the desk. "Sort of unusual. Pretty big case."

Was it? I realized I had absolutely no idea if it was a big case or not.   65 If I was a big-time criminal, who exactly would my cellmates be?

"And it's been a long time since you were involved in all that," he continued. "That's pretty unusual. I can tell you've matured since then." He looked at me.

"Yeah, I guess so," I muttered.

"Well, look, I've been working up at that Camp for ten years. I run that Camp. It's my Camp, and there's nothing that goes on up there that I don't know about."

I was embarrassed by how relieved I felt: I didn't want to see this man, or any prison staffer, as my protector, but at the moment he was the closest thing to human I had encountered.

"We've got all types up there. What you really have to watch is the other inmates. Some of them are all right. No one's going to mess with you unless you let them. Now, women, they don't fight much. They talk, they gossip, they spread rumors. So they may talk about you. Some of these girls are going to think you think you're better than them. They're going to say, 'Oh, she's got money.'"

I felt uncomfortable. Was that how I came across? Was I going to be pegged as a snotty rich bitch?

"And there's lesbians up there. They're there, but they're not gonna bother you. Some are gonna try and be your friend, whatever — just stay away from them! I want you to understand, you do not have to have lesbian sex. I'm old-fashioned. I don't approve of any of that mess."

I tried very hard not to smirk. Guess he didn't read my file that closely. "Mr. Butorsky?"

"Yes?"

"I'm wondering when my fiancé and my mother can come to visit me?" I could not control the querulous tone in my voice.

"They're both in your PSI, right?" My PSI detailed all the members of my immediate family, including Larry, who had been interviewed by the probation department.

"Yes, they're all in there, and my father too."

"Anyone who's in your PSI is cleared to visit. They can come this weekend. I'll make sure the list is in the visiting room." He stood up. "You just keep to yourself, you're gonna be fine." He gathered up my paperwork and left.

I went out to retrieve my new creature comforts from the prison guard: two sheets, a pillowcase, two cotton blankets, a couple of cheap white towels, and a face cloth. These items were crammed into a mesh laundry bag. Add to that an ugly brown stadium coat with a broken zipper and a sandwich bag that contained a stubby mini-toothbrush, tiny packets of toothpaste and shampoo, and a rectangle of motel soap.

Heading out through the multiple gates of the monster fence, I felt elated that I would not be behind it, but now the mystery of the Camp was rushing toward me, unstoppable. A white minivan waited. Its driver, a middle-aged woman in army-issue-looking street clothes and sunglasses, greeted me warmly. She wore makeup and little gold hoops in her ears, and she looked like she could be a nice Italian-American lady called Ro from New Jersey. *The prison guards are getting friendlier*, I thought as I climbed into the passenger seat. She closed the door, and smiled encouragingly at me. She was chipper. I stared back at her.

She flipped up the sunglasses. "I'm Minetta. I'm an inmate too."

"Oh!" I was flabbergasted that she was a prisoner, and she was driving — and wearing makeup!

"What's your name — your last name? People go by their last names here."

"Kerman," I replied.

"Is this your first time down?"

"My first time here?" I was confused.

"Your first time in prison."

I nodded.

"You doin' okay, Kerman?" she asked as she guided the minivan up a small hill. "It's not so bad, you're going to be all right. We'll take care of you. Everyone's okay here, though you've gotta watch out for the stealing. How much time do you have?"

"How much time?" I bleated.

"How long is your sentence?"

"Oh! Fifteen months."

"That's not bad. That'll be over in no time."

We circled to the back entrance of a long, low building that resembled a 1970s elementary school. She pulled up next to a handicapped ramp and stopped the car. Clutching my laundry bag, I followed her toward the building, picking through patches of ice while the cold penetrated my thin rubber soles. Small knots of women wearing identical ugly brown coats were smoking in the February chill. They looked tough, and depressed, and they all had on big, heavy black shoes. I noticed that one of them was hugely pregnant. *What was a woman that pregnant doing in prison?*

"Do you smoke?" Minetta asked.

"No."

"Good for you! We'll just get you your bed assignment and get you settled. There's the dining hall." She gestured to her left down several

85

90

95

stairs. She was talking the entire time, explaining everything about Danbury Federal Prison Camp, none of which I was catching. I followed her up a couple of stairs and into the building.

". . . TV room. There's the education office, that's the CO's office. Hi, Mr. Scott! CO, that's the correctional officer. He's all right. Hey, Sally!" She greeted a tall white woman. "This is Kerman, she's new, self-surrender." Sally greeted me sympathetically with another "Are you okay?" I nodded, mute. Minetta pressed on. "Here's more offices, those are the Rooms up there, the Dorms down there." She turned to me, serious. "You're not allowed down there, it's out of bounds for you. You understand?"

I nodded, not understanding a thing.

Engaging with the Text

1. Piper Kerman's **PURPOSE** in this memoir is to offer a sense, from a first-person point of view, of what it is like to be stripped of one's identity in a prison environment. How does she make this purpose clear? How is the purpose related to the **SIGNIFICANCE** to her of her time in prison?

   55–56

   222

2. What does the **TITLE** refer to? How is it appropriate for this memoir?

   344–45

3. Kerman includes a good deal of **DIALOGUE** in her memoir. What part(s) of the dialogue do you find most interesting? Why? What difference would it make if there were no dialogue?

   408–13

4. A successful memoir offers a **GOOD STORY**. Is #11187–424 a good story? Why or why not? In your response, be sure to explain what makes a good story.

   220

5. *For Writing.* Write a brief **MEMOIR** about a time when you were caught doing something you weren't supposed to and received a punishment. Explain what you were doing, why you were doing it, how you got caught, and how you felt during the punishment (and perhaps before and after it as well).

   216–23

JUDITH ORTIZ COFER

The Myth of the Latin Woman

Judith Ortiz Cofer (1952–2016) retired in 2013 from the University of Georgia, where she was the Regents' and Franklin Professor of English and Creative Writing. She was a prolific writer, known as a poet, a short-story writer, a novelist, an essayist, and an autobiographer. Her works, some intended for a young-adult audience, include the novels The Meaning of Consuelo *(2003) and* If I Could Fly *(2011), the books of poems* Terms of Survival *(1987) and* Reaching for the Mainland *(1995), and the bilingual picture book* ¡A Bailar! Let's Dance! *(2011), to name just a few of her many book-length publications. The following essay comes from her memoir* The Latin Deli: Prose and Poetry *(1993).*

ON A BUS TRIP TO LONDON FROM OXFORD UNIVERSITY where I was earning some graduate credits one summer, a young man, obviously fresh from a pub, spotted me and as if struck by inspiration went down on his knees in the aisle. With both hands over his heart he broke into an Irish tenor's rendition of "María" from *West Side Story*. My politely amused fellow passengers gave his lovely voice the round of gentle applause it deserved. Though I was not quite as amused, I managed my version of an English smile: no show of teeth, no extreme contortions of the facial muscles — I was at this time of my life practicing reserve and cool. Oh, that British control, how I coveted it. But María had followed me to London, reminding me of a prime fact of my life: you can leave the Island, master the English language, and travel as far as you can, but if you are a Latina, especially one like me who so obviously belongs to Rita Moreno's gene pool, the Island travels with you.

This is sometimes a very good thing — it may win you that extra minute of someone's attention. But with some people, the same things can make *you* an island — not so much a tropical paradise as an Alcatraz, a place nobody wants to visit. As a Puerto Rican girl growing up in the United States and wanting like most children to "belong," I resented the stereotype that my Hispanic appearance called forth from many people I met.

Our family lived in a large urban center in New Jersey during the sixties, where life was designed as a microcosm of my parents' casas on the island. We spoke in Spanish, we ate Puerto Rican food bought at the bodega, and we practiced strict Catholicism complete with Saturday confession and Sunday mass at a church where our parents were accommodated into a one-hour Spanish mass slot, performed by a Chinese priest trained as a missionary for Latin America.

As a girl I was kept under strict surveillance, since virtue and modesty were, by cultural equation, the same as family honor. As a teenager I was instructed on how to behave as a proper señorita. But it was a conflicting message girls got, since the Puerto Rican mothers also encouraged their daughters to look and act like women and to dress in clothes our Anglo friends and their mothers found too "mature" for our age. It was, and is, cultural, yet I often felt humiliated when I appeared at an American friend's party wearing a dress more suitable to a semiformal than to a playroom birthday celebration. At Puerto Rican festivities, neither the music nor the colors we wore could be too loud. I still experience a vague sense of letdown when I'm invited to a "party" and it turns out to be a marathon conversation in hushed tones rather than a fiesta with salsa, laughter, and dancing — the kind of celebration I remember from my childhood.

I remember Career Day in our high school, when teachers told us to 5 come dressed as if for a job interview. It quickly became obvious that to the barrio girls, "dressing up" sometimes meant wearing ornate jewelry and clothing that would be more appropriate (by mainstream standards) for the company Christmas party than as daily office attire. That morning I had agonized in front of my closet, trying to figure out what a "career girl" would wear because, essentially, except for Marlo Thomas on TV, I had no models on which to base my decision. I knew how to dress for school: at the Catholic school I attended we all wore uniforms; I knew how to dress for Sunday mass, and I knew what dresses to wear for parties at my relatives' homes. Though I do not recall the precise details of my Career Day outfit, it must have been a composite of the above choices. But I remember a comment my friend (an Italian-American) made in later years that coalesced my impressions of that day. She said that at the business school she was attending the Puerto Rican girls always stood out for wearing "everything at once." She meant, of course, too much jewelry, too many accessories. On that day at school, we were simply made the negative models by the nuns who were themselves not credible fashion experts to any of us. But it was painfully obvious to me that to the others, in their tailored skirts and silk blouses, we must have seemed "hopeless" and "vulgar." Though I now know that most adolescents feel out of step much of the time, I also know that for the Puerto Rican girls of my generation that sense was intensified. The way our teachers and classmates looked at us that day in school was just a taste of the culture clash that awaited us in the real world, where prospective employers and men on the street would often misinterpret our tight skirts and jingling bracelets as a come-on.

Mixed cultural signals have perpetuated certain stereotypes — for example, that of the Hispanic woman as the "Hot Tamale" or sexual firebrand. It is a one-dimensional view that the media have found easy to promote. In their special vocabulary, advertisers have designated "sizzling" and "smoldering" as the adjectives of choice for describing not only the foods but also the women of Latin America. From conversations in my house I recall hearing about the harassment that Puerto Rican women endured in factories where the "boss men" talked to them as if sexual innuendo was all they understood and, worse, often gave them the choice of submitting to advances or being fired.

It is custom, however, not chromosomes, that leads us to choose scarlet over pale pink. As young girls, we were influenced in our decisions about clothes and colors by the women — older sisters and mothers who had grown up on a tropical island where the natural environment was a riot of primary colors, where showing your skin was one way to keep cool as well as to look sexy. Most important of all, on the island, women perhaps felt freer to dress and move more provocatively, since, in most cases, they were protected by the traditions, mores, and laws of a Spanish / Catholic system of morality and machismo whose main rule was: *You may look at my sister, but if you touch her I will kill you.* The extended family and church structure could provide a young woman with a circle of safety in her small pueblo on the island; if a man "wronged" a girl, everyone would close in to save her family honor.

academic literacies　rhetorical situations　genres　processes　strategies　research MLA / APA　media / design　readings

This is what I have gleaned from my discussions as an adult with older Puerto Rican women. They have told me about dressing in their best party clothes on Saturday nights and going to the town's plaza to promenade with their girlfriends in front of the boys they liked. The males were thus given an opportunity to admire the women and to express their admiration in the form of *piropos*: erotically charged street poems they composed on the spot. I have been subjected to a few piropos while visiting the Island, and they can be outrageous, although custom dictates that they must never cross into obscenity. This ritual, as I understand it, also entails a show of studied indifference on the woman's part; if she is "decent," she must not acknowledge the man's impassioned words. So I do understand how things can be lost in translation. When a Puerto Rican girl dressed in her idea of what is attractive meets a man from the mainstream culture who has been trained to react to certain types of clothing as a sexual signal, a clash is likely to take place. The line I first heard based on this aspect of the myth happened when the boy who took me to my first formal dance leaned over to plant a sloppy overeager kiss painfully on my mouth, and when I didn't respond with sufficient passion said in a resentful tone: "I thought you Latin girls were supposed to mature early" — my first instance of being thought of as a fruit or vegetable — I was supposed to *ripen*, not just grow into Womanhood like other girls.

It is surprising to some of my professional friends that some people, including those who should know better, still put others "in their place." Though rarer, these incidents are still commonplace in my life. It happened to me most recently during a stay at a very classy metropolitan hotel favored by young professional couples for their weddings. Late one evening after the theater, as I walked toward my room with my new colleague (a woman with whom I was coordinating an arts program), a middle-aged man in a tuxedo, a young girl in satin and lace on his arm, stepped directly into our path. With his champagne glass extended toward me, he exclaimed, "Evita!"

Our way blocked, my companion and I listened as the man half-recited, half-bellowed "Don't Cry for Me, Argentina." When he finished, the young girl said: "How about a round of applause for my daddy?"   10

We complied, hoping this would bring the silly spectacle to a close. I was becoming aware that our little group was attracting the attention of the other guests. "Daddy" must have perceived this too, and he once more barred the way as we tried to walk past him. He began to shout-sing a ditty to the tune of "La Bamba" — except the lyrics were about a girl named María whose exploits all rhymed with her name and gonorrhea. The girl kept saying "Oh, Daddy" and looking at me with pleading eyes. She wanted me to laugh along with the others. My companion and I stood silently waiting for the man to end his offensive song. When he finished, I looked not at him but at his daughter. I advised her calmly never to ask her father what he had done in the army. Then I walked between them and to my room. My friend complimented me on my cool handling of the situation. I confessed to her that I really had wanted to push the jerk into the swimming pool. I knew that this same man — probably a corporate executive, well educated, even worldly by most standards — would not have been likely to regale a white woman with a dirty song in public. He would perhaps have checked his impulse by assuming that she could be somebody's wife or mother, or at least *some-body* who might take offense. But to him, I was just an Evita or a María: merely a character in his cartoon-populated universe.

Because of my education and my proficiency with the English language, I have acquired many mechanisms for dealing with the anger I experience. This was not true for my parents, nor is it true for the many Latin women working at menial jobs who must put up with stereotypes about our ethnic group such as: "They make good domestics." This is another facet of the myth of the Latin woman in the United States. Its origin is simple to deduce. Work as domestics, waitressing, and factory jobs are all that's available to women with little English and few skills. The myth of the Hispanic menial has been sustained by the same media phenomenon that made "Mammy" from *Gone with the Wind* America's idea of the black woman for generations; María, the housemaid or counter girl, is now indelibly etched into the national psyche. The big and the little screens have presented us with the picture of the funny Hispanic maid, mispronouncing words and cooking up a spicy storm in a shiny California kitchen.

This media-engendered image of the Latina in the United States has been documented by feminist Hispanic scholars, who claim that such portrayals are partially responsible for the denial of opportunities for upward mobility among Latinas in the professions. I have a Chicana friend working on a Ph.D. in philosophy at a major university. She says her doctor still shakes his head in puzzled amazement at all the "big words" she uses. Since I do not wear my diplomas around my neck for all to see, I too have on occasion been sent to that "kitchen," where some think I obviously belong.

One such incident that has stayed with me, though I recognize it as a minor offense, happened on the day of my first public poetry reading. It took place in Miami in a boat-restaurant where we were having lunch before the event. I was nervous and excited as I walked in with my notebook in my hand. An older woman motioned me to her table. Thinking (foolish me) that she wanted me to autograph a copy of my brand new slender volume of verse, I went over. She ordered a cup of coffee from me, assuming that I was the waitress. Easy enough to mistake my poems for menus, I suppose. I know that it wasn't an intentional act of cruelty, yet of all the good things that happened that day, I remember that scene most clearly, because it reminded me of what I had to overcome before anyone would take me seriously. In retrospect I understand that my anger gave my reading fire, that I have almost always taken doubts in my abilities as a challenge — and that the result is, most times, a feeling of satisfaction at having won a convert when I see the cold, appraising eyes warm to my words, the body language change, the smile that indicates that I have opened some avenue for communication. That day I read to that woman and her lowered eyes told me that she was embarrassed at her little faux pas, and when I willed her to look up at me, it was my victory, and she graciously allowed me to punish her with my full attention. We shook hands at the end of the reading, and I never saw her again. She has probably forgotten the whole thing but maybe not.

Yet I am one of the lucky ones. My parents made it possible for me to acquire a stronger footing in the mainstream culture by giving me the chance at an education. And books and art have saved me from the harsher forms of ethnic and racial prejudice that many of my Hispanic *compañeras* have had to endure. I travel a lot around the United States, reading from my books of poetry and my novel, and the reception I most often receive is one of positive interest by people who want to know more about my culture. There are, however, thousands of Latinas without the privilege of an education or the entree into society that I have. For them life is a struggle against the misconceptions perpetuated by the myth of the Latina as whore, domestic, or criminal. We cannot change this by legislating the way people look at us. The transformation, as I see it, has to occur at a much more individual level. My personal goal in my public life is to try to replace the old pervasive stereotypes and myths about Latinas with a much more interesting set of realities. Every time I give a reading, I hope the stories I tell, the dreams and fears I examine in my work, can achieve some universal truth which will get my audience past the particulars of my skin color, my accent, or my clothes.

I once wrote a poem in which I called us Latinas "God's brown 15 daughters." This poem is really a prayer of sorts, offered upward, but also, through the human-to-human channel of art, outward. It is a prayer for communication, and for respect. In it, Latin women pray "in Spanish to an Anglo God / with a Jewish heritage," and they are "fervently hoping / that if not omnipotent / at least He be bilingual."

Engaging with the Text

222–23 ▲
345–47 ◆

1. A strong memoir includes **VIVID DETAILS** to bring the past back to life. How do the details Judith Ortiz Cofer includes support her **THESIS** that Latinas are poorly understood and grossly stereotyped? Identify two of these details and explain how they help her make her case.

338–42 ◆

2. How does Cofer **END** her essay? What is the significance of the ending?

55–56 ■

3. What is the **PURPOSE** of this memoir? What do you think Cofer hopes it to achieve? Where in the essay does she make that hope explicit?

4. Cofer explains that the way Puerto Rican women dress in Puerto Rico is "read" very differently by other people than when they dress in

the same way elsewhere in the United States. What is the difference between the two responses? What does she say to explain why in one place the young women are respected and revered and in the other are disrespected and treated rudely? What role do you think dress should play in how people read other people?

5. *For Writing.* Think about the way you dress. What image are you trying to create through your clothing and accessories? How do others *read* your image? Do they read it in ways you mean it to be read or in other ways that go against your intentions? Write a **MEMOIR**, one that reflects on both the past and the present, that addresses these questions.

▲ 216–23

66 Profiles

academic literacies

rhetorical situations

genres

processes

strategies

research MLA / APA

media / design

readings

JAMES HAMBLIN

Living Simply in a Dumpster

James Hamblin (b. 1983), a former radiologist at the UCLA Medical Center, left medical practice to join the Atlantic *as editor of its health channel. Today, he is a senior editor there, writing a health column and hosting a video series titled* If Our Bodies Could Talk *that he started in 2013. The following profile appeared in the* Atlantic *in 2014.*

TUCKED BEHIND THE WOMEN'S RESIDENCE HALLS in a back corner of Huston-Tillotson University's campus in Austin, Texas, sits a green dumpster. Were it not for the sliding pitched roof and weather station perched on top, a reasonable person might dismiss the box as "just another dumpster" — providing this person did not encounter the dean of the University College Jeff Wilson living inside.

The current exterior.

Professor Wilson went to the dumpster not just because he wished to live deliberately, and not just to teach his students about the environmental impacts of day-to-day life, and not just to gradually transform the dumpster into "the most thoughtfully-designed, tiniest home ever constructed." Wilson's reasons are a tapestry of these things.

Until this summer, the green dumpster was even less descript than it is now. There was no sliding roof; Wilson kept the rain out with a tarp. He slept on cardboard mats on the floor. It was essentially, as he called it, "dumpster camping." The goal was to establish a baseline experience of the dumpster without any accoutrements, before adding them incrementally.

Not long ago, Wilson was nesting in a 2,500-square-foot house. After going through a divorce ("nothing related to the dumpster," he told me, unsolicited), he spun into the archetypal downsizing of a newly minted bachelor. He moved into a 500-square-foot apartment. Then he began selling clothes and furniture on Facebook for almost nothing. Now he

Professor Wilson at home.

academic literacies

rhetorical situations

genres

processes

strategies

research MLA / APA

media / design

readings

says almost everything he owns is in his 36-square-foot dumpster, which is sanctioned and supported by the university as part of an ongoing sustainability-focused experiment called The Dumpster Project. "We could end up with a house under $10,000 that could be placed anywhere in the world," Wilson said at the launch, "[fueled by] sunlight and surface water, and people could have a pretty good life."

Wilson, known around town as Professor Dumpster, recounted in another recent interview that he now owns four pairs of pants, four shirts, three pairs of shoes, three hats, and, in keeping with his hipsteresque aesthetic, "eight or nine" bow ties. (That's an exceptional bow-tie-to-shirt ownership ratio.) He keeps all of this in cubbies under a recently installed false floor, along with some camping cooking equipment.

Customization of the space really began in July. Wilson asked Twitter what was the first thing he needed, and the response was almost unanimous: air conditioning. In the Austin heat, the dumpster was getting up to 130 degrees Fahrenheit during the day. On some nights it did not fall below the high 80s. So on his six-month anniversary of living in a human-sized convection oven, Wilson procured a modest air conditioner.

"We didn't want to make it too easy," Wilson said. "I wanted to see how elastic my sleeping habits would be relative to temperature and humidity. I found that I could actually get to sleep pretty well as long as I went to bed at about 11:00 p.m."

With the weather station now strapped to the top, Wilson tracks his personal climate in real time. Pulling up data on his computer from inside his centrally cooled office as we spoke, he announced that the dumpster was currently 104 degrees. During the spring, when Austin was a little cooler, he was able to pass some daytime hours in the dumpster. With the arrival of summer, that became unbearable. "But some interesting things happened because of that," he explained. He spent a lot more time out in the community, just walking around. "I almost feel like East Austin is my home and backyard," he said. He is constantly thinking about what sorts of things a person really needs in a house, and what can be more communal.

"What if everybody had to go to some sort of laundromat?" Wilson posited. "How would that shift how we have to, or get to, interact with others? I know I have met a much wider circle of people just from going to laundromats and wandering around outside of the dumpster when I would've been in there if I had a large flat screen and a La-Z-Boy."

Perks like insulation will come, allowing the small air conditioner to   10
keep pace with the Texas sun. The second phase of The Dumpster Project, which Wilson and collaborators call the "average American dumpster studio," will incorporate more amenities including a bed, a lamp, and a classic home-evoking pitched roof that will slide back and forth to allow ventilation, weather stripping, and locks (making this possibly the only dumpster in the world with interior locks). Eventually, the dumpster will have a dome to catch rainwater and provide shade, as well as a (tiny) sink and kitchen.

"Actually," he said as we spoke by phone, "it is starting to rain right now, and my roof's open on the dumpster."

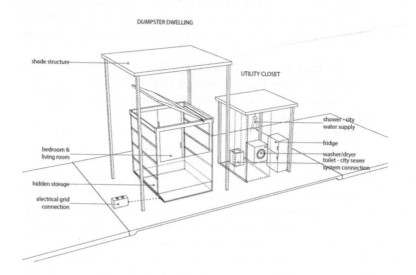

Phase two, currently in progress.

"Oh my god."

"Can I call you right back? It's a downpour. I'll be back in about a minute."

He called me back a minute later, sounding less distressed than one might expect from a person whose home had been drenched. The disposition that might make a person amenable to dumpster life is not one easily troubled by a little rain. His dumpster-home once looked like this:

The interior of the dumpster on Wilson's first night there.

He's also welcoming of anyone who wants to stop by the dumpster and talk sustainability any time. In addition to teaching courses in environmental change, global health and welfare, and environmental science at the college, Wilson describes The Dumpster Project primarily as an educational initiative that just happened to dovetail with his current life-downsizing. On some nights, Wilson will stay with a friend, and students from the ecology-focused campus group Green Is the New Black will get a night to stay in the dumpster.

"What does home look like in a world of 10 billion people?" the project's site implores, referring to the projected 40 percent increase in the human population by the end of the century. "How do we equip current and future generations with the tools they need for sustainable living practices?"

Unfortunately the site does not answer those questions in concrete terms. But with only 39 percent of Americans identifying as "believers" in global warming, just raising questions and promoting consciousness of sustainability might be a lofty enough aspiration.

Wilson's most anticipated upcoming boon is a toilet. "I'm not as concerned about the shower," he said, "but getting to the toilet some-times requires kind of a midnight run." Currently, he uses facilities at the university's gym. A toilet and shower will soon connect to the dumpster externally. "You don't really want to have a composting toilet inside of a closed-up 36 square feet," he explained.

In four months Wilson will enter the third phase of the project, the "uber dumpster home." That will involve installing solar panels and

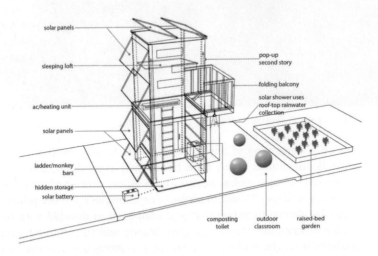

solar panels
sleeping loft
ac/heating unit
solar panels
ladder/monkey bars
hidden storage
solar battery

pop-up second story
folding balcony
solar shower uses roof-top rainwater collection

composting toilet
outdoor classroom
raised-bed garden

Phase three, beginning this winter.

academic literacies　　rhetorical situations　　genres　　processes　　strategies　　research MLA / APA　　media / design　　readings

unplugging from the energy grid, as well as completing aesthetic work that will essentially remove any semblance of dumpsterdom. "We kind of want to do the outside in a modern *Dwell* look," he said, including windows and reused lumber siding. "We want it basically to be such that if you were blindfolded and placed inside it, you'd just think you were in a very tiny house."

Wilson already goes around to local elementary and middle 20 schools recounting his experience in the context of talking about using less space, less energy, and less water, and creating less waste. There is a K–12 curriculum built around the dumpster experiment, and eventually the finished dumpster will be transported to these schools for display.

For Professor Dumpster, the undertaking is at once grand and diminutive, selfless and introspective, silly and gravely important, even dark. "We bring everything into the home these days," Wilson said. "You don't really need to leave the home for anything, even grocery shopping, anymore. What's interesting about this is it's really testing the limits of what you need in a home."

"The big hypothesis we're trying to test here is, can you have a pretty darn good life on much, much less?" He paused. "This is obviously an outlier experiment. But so far, I have, I'd say. A better life than I had before."

Engaging with the Text

1. James Hamblin's main point in this profile is that "Professor Wilson went to the dumpster not just because he wished to live deliberately, and not just to teach his students about the environmental impacts of day-to-day life, and not just to gradually transform the dumpster into 'the most thoughtfully-designed, tiniest home ever constructed.' Wilson's reasons are a tapestry of these things." How well does the rest of the profile support this thesis statement?

228

2. A good profile typically covers an **INTERESTING SUBJECT**. What caught your attention as you read this profile? How interesting did you find the subject?

3. Although downsizing one's home is becoming more common, especially among those concerned with sustainability, Wilson's 36-square-foot dumpster dwelling takes the trend to an extreme. How comfortable would you be in such a space? Explain how much space you believe you need to live a good life — either alone or as part of a multiperson household or both — and why.

607–15

4. **VISUALS** in a profile should be appropriate for the rhetorical situation. What do the visuals contribute to this profile, whose purpose is mainly informative? How well would you comprehend it without them? For this subject, what other visuals (including other kinds) might be helpful — or just interesting and engaging?

229

5. *For Writing.* Select an unusual subject — person, place, or thing — to profile. You will need a **FIRSTHAND ACCOUNT** of the subject, so it needs to be one you can easily visit, probably nearby your home or campus. If you are not profiling a person, try to speak with or research people involved with the subject to offer your readers a close-up view of it from a perspective besides your own.

ROB BAKER

Jimmy Santiago Baca: Poetry as Lifesaver

Rob Baker (b. 1979) is a freelance creative writer who was teaching English and creative writing at Barrington High School in Illinois when he wrote the following profile. It appeared in a 2008 issue of the Council Chronicle, *a monthly magazine published by the National Council of Teachers of English (NCTE). As you read, notice how Baker focuses his profile on the significance of poetry for Baca, using details from Baca's life to support his point.*

CHICANO POET JIMMY SANTIAGO BACA was born with rattlesnake poison in his blood. In January, 1952, just before his mother gave birth, she was bitten by a rattler. The healer who tended to her wound and then brought Baca into the world said that because of the venom Baca would be able to see in the dark and that he would change many times throughout his life, just as a snake sloughs its skin. And change many times he did.

As related in his award-winning autobiography, *A Place to Stand*, Baca's parents abandoned him when he was seven; he lived briefly with his grandparents and then in a series of detention centers from which he constantly ran away. He attended junior high, but dropped out after less than a year because he could not keep up academically nor mesh with the "normal" kids who had families. As a teenager, he lived a haphazard existence on the streets of Albuquerque, fighting, drinking, and doing drugs. He worked piecemeal jobs — loading food on planes, operating a vending machine route, a handyman business. Then, during stints in California and Arizona, he became a very successful drug dealer.

That he would morph into a renowned poet is perhaps the least likely change anyone would have predicted for Baca who, as a young adult, could barely read or write, who "hated books, hated reading," who had "never owned a book and had no desire to own one." And this change probably wouldn't have happened if Baca hadn't been sentenced, at age 21, to five to ten years in prison.

Jimmy Santiago Baca.

To read of Baca's prison years is to marvel at the human capacity for survival and renewal. In a place more reminiscent of Dante's *Inferno* than of an institution for rehabilitation, where blood was shed more often than light, and where the inmates' chronic lassitude, fear, and anger led to depression, murder, rape, and paranoia, Baca — remarkably — endured, and exited not only sane and alive, but as a poet.

Chance encounters catalyzed Baca's transformation. A couple years into his incarceration, Baca received a letter from a man as part of a church program to write to prisoners without families. As a result of their continued correspondence, Baca painstakingly taught himself to read and write, activities that helped bring purpose into his monotonous days. The man then put Baca in touch with a poet friend. Poetry changed Baca's life forever.

"I believe something in my brain or something in my nervous system was impacted by poetry, by the way the lines and the words were arranged," said Baca. "I was such an emotional animal and I had never read any poetry. When I read it, it just tolled so many bells in my head, it was like, 'Wow! I can actually communicate like this. There are actually people who talk like this and write like this.' I was just absorbed into it, into the vortex of this ecstasy."

Baca published poems while still in prison. His first collection, *Immigrants in Our Own Land* (Louisiana State University Press, 1979), came out just after his release.

Baca's writing explores his fractured family and personal life, his prison experiences, and his ethnicity. In addition to his autobiography, he has penned ten poetry collections, a book of short stories, and a screenplay, the 1993 film *Blood In, Blood Out*.

"Language gave me a way to keep the chaos of prison at bay and prevented it from devouring me," he wrote in his prologue to *A Place to Stand*. "It was a resource that allowed me to confront and understand my past . . . and it opened a way toward the future that was based not on fear or bitterness or apathy but on compassionate involvement."

In another life change, Baca ultimately morphed into a teacher. He began by working with gang members who regularly congregated near his home, though his initial contact with them seemed more likely to result in violence than poetry. One night, when the youths hanging out on his street were particularly raucous, Baca went outside in his pajamas, baseball bat in hand. He told them that they had awakened his baby and that they had to leave.

"They said, 'We ain't got no other place to go,'" Baca recounted. "So I said, 'All right, meet me at St. Anne's church tomorrow and I'll ask the priest if we can use the barracks there.' And you know what? They all met me there and I had my first workshop ever, and I realized with a sort of vague ignorance that I was really gifted at working with kids."

Baca now does many workshops a year and receives frequent visits from public school educators who come to observe his techniques. He says he's "very much into Latin American poets," but he also uses more frequently taught poets such as William Carlos Williams, Denise Levertov, Lawrence Ferlinghetti, and Walt Whitman.*

Baca encourages students to tell the stories no one else has: the stories of their own lives. He also encourages students to use poetry to discuss issues they might not normally talk about. "Most of the time there are subtle protocols you have to abide by. You're sitting at a table with friends, there are certain things you don't talk about. With these kids, ninety percent of their lived experience is stuff you don't talk about."

> Language gave me a way to keep the chaos of prison at bay and prevented it from devouring me. It was a resource that allowed me to confront and understand my past.

Baca believes poetry is able to reach the people he works with — people often considered by society to be "the worst of the worst" — because "there's nothing that is required for you to speak poetically from your heart."

To Baca, his mission as a teacher — and the role of poetry in general — is nothing less than to save lives. 15

"My job is simply to keep the light inside [my students] burning. That's it. My job is to make sure they do not fall into despair. And I guess

---

*William Carlos Williams (1883–1963), Denise Levertov (1923–97), Lawrence Ferlinghetti (b. 1919), and Walt Whitman (1819–92): American poets who composed in free verse. [Editor's note]

that's the answer to why I work with unwed mothers, I go to prisons, I work with homeless and gang kids, because their light's starting to go off, to dim, and I have to come in there and fire it up, and I do that with poetry, and I do that with commitment, and I do that with compassion."

Engaging with the Text

1. Rob Baker begins his profile of the poet Jimmy Santiago Baca with an **ANECDOTE**. How does this anecdote foreshadow the changes Baca experiences during his life? What role does language play in those changes?

   ◆ 337

2. What **ENGAGING DETAILS** does Baker provide in his profile to create an impression of Baca as someone who sees "his mission as a teacher — and the role of poetry in general — [as] nothing less than to save lives"?

   ▲ 229–30

3. This piece was published in a magazine for English teachers. How does Baker shape his profile of Baca to appeal to that **AUDIENCE**? How might his profile be different if he had written it for an audience of high school students? prison inmates?

   ■ 57–60

4. How much **BACKGROUND** on Baca does Baker provide in this profile? Why is this background important? How does it help the reader better understand who Baca is today?

   ▲ 229

5. *For Writing.* Identify someone with an interesting career, job, or hobby that has played a significant role in his or her life. Interview that person and write a **PROFILE** that demonstrates how that hobby or job has changed him or her. Use **DIALOGUE** and engaging details to help reveal your subject's character.

   ▲ 224–34
   ◆ 408–13

MARCIA F. BROWN

Maine's First Graffiti Artist

Marcia F. Brown (b. 1953), the current poet laureate for the city of Portland, Maine, is the author of four poetry collections: When We Invented Water *(2014),* What on Earth *(2010),* Home to Roost: Paintings and Poems of Belfast, Maine with Artist Archie Barnes *(2007), and* The Way Women Walk *(2006). Her poems and reviews have appeared in numerous journals and anthologies. The following profile was published in* Maine Home & Design *magazine in 2013.*

Just off Free Street in downtown Portland, the 1,500-square-foot PORTLAND mural sprawls across the back wall of the Asylum nightclub. A wry send-up of a vintage "Greetings from" postcard, the vibrant mural is the brainchild of South Portland artist Mike Rich, known as "TooRich" in graffiti circles. A team of eight artists (Rich, Learn, Turdl, MWM, Lerk, Esko, Lack, and Link) each took on a letter of the city's name, which swells beneath the iconic image of Portland Head Light. An aerosol paint can stands in for the lighthouse, rays of white radiating from its nozzle. A community fundraiser helped pay for the supplies, and it took the team a month to turn a scarred eyesore into what has become a popular local landmark.

Birthed on the tough streets and in the urban ghettos of America's big cities, graffiti art may finally be earning itself a seat at the table of contemporary art appreciation and debate. But to Mike Rich, self-proclaimed "Maine's first graffiti artist," that trend toward gentrification is a double-edged sword. "Graffiti is better than art," Rich posits. "The act in itself is important. It takes courage and planning. It's pure expression, and no one may ever know you created it. It requires sacrifice. I was making art when I was 11 — I started doing graffiti to get away from art."

To better understand the dichotomy of graffiti as both a demanding fringe art form and one increasingly embraced by community leaders

The Asylum's PORTLAND mural, designed by Rich and executed by eight artists.

and the arts establishment, I sat down with Mike Rich on a cold, sunny January morning to discuss his art as well as his lifestyle as a working carpenter, father, and professional graffiti artist.

It was 1983 when PBS aired the television special *Style Wars*, a documentary about graffiti art on subway cars. Rich remembers being enthralled by the streetwise artists, the quasi-military night maneuvers in the subways, the speed and stealth that produced the brilliant spray-painted graphics. "The outlaw image was very attractive to me," Rich admits, "but I also thought, Wow! They're making this beautiful art when they don't have to. No one knows them. They're gone, but it's there, in the morning." Rich loves the informality and the anonymity of the form. He likes that no one will review it. "You paint it and you may never see it again," he says approvingly. When the Howard C. Reiche Community School in Portland's West End held a graffiti competition, a young Rich saw teenage teams from New York and Boston "making awesome art." "They were like gods to me," Rich recalls. "I knew that's what I wanted to do."

At 38, Rich is in many ways as mercurial as the art form itself. 5 Wearing jeans and a zany graphic T-shirt that reveals arms covered with impressive tattoos, Rich moves around his small studio with a youthful, compressed energy. He's known for painting large surfaces fast. You get the feeling he doesn't sit still anywhere for long. At the same time, Rich is the father of two boys, Che (7) and Joe (12), and earns his living as a home builder, working through the Maine winters to allow himself time to paint outdoors during the summer months. He has lectured on graffiti art at the University of Southern Maine and at the Center for Maine Contemporary Art (CMCA), during his solo exhibition Spray Therapy. Constantly exploring new ideas and aspirations for his own work, he has developed deeply personal and complex theories on the role of graffiti art in modern society.

Graffiti's visual roots are derived from tagging — what Rich describes as "the art of vandalism." "The first time someone spray-painted letters and then outlined them in a second color — boom!" As more elaborate graphic elements were added, graffiti evolved into a recognizable style. Rich enjoys the narrative potential of graffiti and incorporates sly, often witty text and imagery in his murals. He has always been a style writer, exacting about the quality of his graphics. Rich says he never went for quantity of coverage or for property desecration. He celebrates the form as a kind of modern typography that can be traced back to hieroglyphics and cave painting. With its many styles of lettering and personal signatures, Rich thinks graffiti may well be the last bastion of handwriting.

As a kid, Rich says, he tagged "maybe just to have a voice, just to be seen." He thinks most adolescents who start tagging do so as a form of self-assertion, to put down a claim. "You paint your symbols — your tag — on something and it evokes a kind of ownership. It's the American dream for the disenfranchised."

Twenty years ago, Rich was living in the Munjoy South neighborhood of Portland when he slipped into an abandoned warehouse next door to paint its walls with 15-foot-tall images of his favorite group, the 80s hip-hop trio the Beastie Boys. The space ultimately became the hops and barley storage room for Shipyard Brewery, and on a recent tour of the factory, Rich was "blown away" to discover his mural still on the walls.

Mike Rich.

"It was incredibly validating to think that they saved it," Rich says. "The space is climate controlled, so my mural is sort of preserved in this giant sarcophagus." Shipyard's owners were equally pleased to meet the creator of their vintage graffiti and hired Rich to paint a company vehicle and a massive Shipyard mural at the Gridiron Restaurant and Sports Pub in Lewiston.

Rich concedes that much of his early work can't be attributed. For decades, graffiti has danced on the edges of the law. But times have changed, and communities are now inclined to sanction and assist talented muralists to create large-scale artwork in dedicated public spaces. Rich's friend and fellow artist Ryan Adams works with the Maine Center for Creativity (MCC) to identify wall spaces that are attractive candidates for artwork, and MCC tracks down the owners to ask their permission. According to CMCA director Suzette McAvoy, her organization's work with Rich led to the CMCA's sponsorship of a wall at Wynwood Walls in Miami. (Every year, Wynwood, a once-blighted warehouse district, becomes the canvas for a monumental display of street art and graffiti, transforming desolate street fronts into a vital arts hub.)

At this stage of his career, Rich wants to use his art for positive messaging. He has gained national attention for his involvement with the nonprofit "Dunk the Junk," a program for school kids that combines elements of street art, hip-hop, and basketball to combat childhood obesity. Rich leads an interactive school assembly during which he live-paints a customized mural that encourages kids to quit sugary drinks and junk food and instills awareness of good eating choices and nutrition. Dunk the Junk's founder, pediatrician Kevin Strong, says, "Mike is fast. Very fast. He can come up with a mural scheme and paint it in a few hours. His characters come alive, and his lettering is tight. Young audiences are fascinated by Mike's graffiti — how the colors explode on the wall — and, of course, graffiti's mystique of danger and rebellion. Mike is also passionate about the mission, and that is probably what makes his relationship with the kids so special."

Over 28 years, Rich has designed tattoos, T-shirts, cutouts, shadow boxes, new-age typography, logos, album covers, and book jackets.

He has painted murals — both brushed and sprayed — portraits, commercial trucks, signage, and residential decor. A "green wave" of rolling surf identifies a Maine Standard Biofuels tanker truck in Portland. Two boozy lobsters lounge in a "hot tub," cocktails in claw, on the Maine Lobsterbake Co. food truck in South Portland. Augusta's Migrant Health Program's mobile medical unit can be easily identified, in any language, by its colorful panel of farm workers in green fields of apples, blueberries, and potatoes. The art form has an astonishing range of applications. The front stairway of a private Camden residence boasts a stunning Rich design of bright ribbon-candy-striped risers sliced by glossy black treads. It makes going upstairs look like climbing a rainbow.

While graffiti art is migrating out of the shadows, some part of Mike Rich wants his art form to remain marginalized. He knows it's a delicate balancing act to uphold the anti-establishment roots of graffiti while reveling in the greater public acceptance, exposure, and purpose his art now enjoys. "It's not the easiest route I could have chosen as an artist," Rich says. "So much planning and strategy go into it. But when I can be a catalyst for change, or when this beautiful stuff appears where no one expects it — that's the magic. That's what keeps me going."

Engaging with the Text

1. What larger point would you say Marcia F. Brown is making in her profile of a specific graffiti artist? Do you agree with her point? Why or why not? What is your own perspective on graffiti? Is it art or vandalism? both? somewhere in between?

2. How would you describe the intended **AUDIENCE** for this profile? How does Brown's positive **STANCE** toward her subject help to make her targeted audience clear? Do a little online research on *Maine Home & Design*. How closely do you think the magazine's readership resembles this imagined audience?

57–60
64–67

380–87 ◆

3. This profile raises a number of issues involving **CONTRASTS** — between "fringe art" and "art," personal "tagging" and "positive messaging," youth and middle age. Brown says that Mike Rich is "known as 'TooRich' in graffiti circles"; how does that label relate to these issues? Rich **COMPARES** graffiti to hieroglyphics and cave painting and sees it as "the last bastion of handwriting." How do you react to these comparisons?

169 ▲

4. What **NECESSARY BACKGROUND INFORMATION** (not provided by the subject himself) does Brown offer about Rich? In what ways is it useful for readers? Is there other background that you would have liked her to include? If so, what is it?

5. *For Writing.* What is often called outsider art is all around us. Select an outsider art — such as tattooing, body piercing, a specific music genre, yarn bombing, or other activist art — or a specific artist in one

224–34 ▲

of these fields, and write a **PROFILE** that captures the art's or artist's characteristics and intentions.

TATIANA SCHLOSSBERG

At This Academy, the Curriculum Is Garbage

Tatiana Schlossberg (b. 1990) is an intern at the New York Times, *where this profile appeared in 2014. She previously wrote for the* Yale Herald, *an undergraduate newspaper at Yale University where she also served as editor, and the* Bergen Record, *a newspaper in northern New Jersey where she primarily covered crime and police work.*

ROSE-GOLD LIGHT WAS FALLING ONTO JAMAICA BAY and sea gulls passed overhead on another beautiful morning at Floyd Bennett Field in Brooklyn, a far reach of New York City mostly devoid of New Yorkers and cars.

It was a perfect setting, then, for learning how to drive a garbage truck, which is why some of the world's least graceful vehicles were groaning and screeching their way through a narrow trail of orange traffic cones. Nearby, where Sanitation Department trainees were learning how to both load the trucks and dump them, the air was filled with sounds familiar to any New Yorker — the crashing of cans and crushing of garbage in the early morning hours, so loud it might as well be happening inside one's bedroom.

"Hey!" an instructor called out to his students. "You have to make sure the hopper's closed before you drive off!"

Police academies are famous enough to have earned their own movie franchise, and stories about firefighters learning how to slide down a firehouse pole as a loyal Dalmatian watches nearby, and hop on a blaring truck are easy enough to imagine. But sanitation workers must be trained too — to pick up trash, recyclables and, now, compost every day; to sweep the streets and clear them after a snowstorm, and remove fallen trees after a hurricane; and to operate the half-dozen types of trucks needed to keep the city's streets and sidewalks tidy.

From the summer to the start of snow season, the Sanitation 5 Department will train 450 new workers at its academy, bringing the

Students practiced driving a garbage truck by navigating an obstacle course set up at the Sanitation Department academy at Floyd Bennett Field in Brooklyn.

force to 6,000 uniformed workers. A class of 125 that graduated on Friday is the first of four that will go through the four-week training this year.

On a recent day at the academy, after roll call and calisthenics, the trainees separated into groups. One learned about snow, though not a flake was around. Another practiced driving and dumping, and a third focused on changing tires, operating forklifts and washing the trucks.

At a session devoted to cleaning up litter, an instructor was teaching his students about one of the department's biggest occupational hazards: syringes in trash bags.

"Do you have X-ray vision?" he asked. He warned the trainees to hold the bags away from their bodies. "There could be needles in there!"

Another instructor showed his group how to line up the end of a snow chain with a forward-facing ridge on the tire, and then wind it

Without a flake to be seen, Edward Leccese, 36, and James Maggiore, 31, both from Staten Island, learned how to attach chains to the tires of snowplows.

around clockwise. He explained that once they went to work, the trainees would need to learn how to do it quickly, because hunching over the tire of a truck carrying 16 tons of salt "isn't somewhere you want to be for too long." His students practiced putting the chains on three more times.

No one was learning how to hang off the back of a truck. The department put a stop to the practice about four years ago after deciding it was too risky.   10

"I'm horrified when I see the private carters doing that," said Kathryn Garcia, the city's sanitation commissioner. "It's already a dangerous job."

To cut down on injuries further, Ms. Garcia has introduced a stretching program for workers to follow before heading out on their trucks in the morning.

The training does not cover how to deal with rats. When asked if he had any advice for avoiding rodent-related injuries, Steven Harbin, a department chief who runs the training academy, paused and then said, "Get a broom and tap the can."

The Sanitation Department's training academy was created in 1950, but there have been formal efforts to train new workers since the early 20th century, when the agency was known as the Department of Street Cleaning, said Robin Nagle, the department's resident anthropologist.

Picking up dead horses and stopping cholera are no longer concerns. More recently the department, which has a budget of $1.4 billion, has taken on a role as the city's environmental brigade, gathering up separated plastics, paper and food waste; and as the agency that redeems or bedevils the mayor, depending on how fast the streets are cleared of snow. ₁₅

Despite what some would consider drawbacks of the job, it is in high demand. Applicants must first pass a written exam, which was last given in 2007 because of hiring freezes. A new test is scheduled for the fall, a spokesman for the department said.

When new hires are finally called, but before they enter the academy, they must pass a physical evaluation, which mostly involves lifting and throwing garbage bags and cans of various weights in a specified amount of time. The physical test used to be harder and was widely known within the Civil Service as the "Superman" test for the number of feats of strength it entailed.

After criticism that the exam was unnecessarily difficult and an obstacle for women hoping to join the department, it was made somewhat easier — workers no longer had to try to vault over an eight-foot wall, for example — and in 1986, the city hired its first garbagewomen.

Now about 3 percent of the sanitation force, and five of the 125 current trainees, are women, including Valerie Albanese, a former school safety officer from Staten Island. Ms. Albanese, 43, said she had switched jobs because she liked physical labor.

"I'm also very excited to work with maggots," she joked. ₂₀

academic literacies · rhetorical situations · genres · processes · strategies · research MLA / APA · media / design · readings

Though most of the students in the current class said they considered the pay and benefits good, there was, not surprisingly, some envy of graduates of the police and fire academies, who earn more money and get all the glory.

After five and a half years, a sanitation worker can earn up to $69,933, not including overtime, about $20,000 less than police officers with the same experience. And sanitation veterans joke stoically that while the police get to ride their horses in parades, the garbage workers get to clean up after them.

"Maybe one day, when the New York Rangers are in the playoffs, we'll be able to have our honor guard standing behind them for the national anthem, instead of the Fire Department," said Patrick Siliato, 29, an academy instructor whose father is also a sanitation worker. (The Sanitation Department does indeed have an honor guard.)

The equipment that sanitation workers use, though, can be every bit as intricate as the gear on a fire engine. At the academy, one group of students was being trained in how to work a front-end loader, which is used to move heavy materials, like snow, salt, dirt and other debris. Operating the vehicle requires manipulating three pedals, two levers and a steering wheel that controls the body and front axle at once.

George Wilmer, a trainee from Crown Heights, Brooklyn, who was [25] eating an Italian combo sandwich during a midmorning break, was learning on the garbage truck. He said he used to work in shipping and receiving before finally getting the call from the Sanitation Department this year, seven years after taking the written test.

Mr. Wilmer, 43, said that he had knocked over a few cones when he was going through the obstacle course, but that it was "to be expected."

Another trainee, Anthony Olivieri, 27, a member of the New York National Guard whose mother is a sanitation worker, disagreed. He said he had not knocked over a single cone.

Mr. Wilmer said, "I used to have trucks like these ones under my Christmas tree when I was little.

"Now I get to play with the real thing."

Engaging with the Text

64–67

1. Tatiana Schlossberg maintains a lighthearted yet respectful **STANCE** toward her subject of garbage school. How is this stance appropriate given the subject? What other stance might she have taken?

344–45

2. The **TITLE** of Schlossberg's profile can be read in two ways: either the curriculum is bad or it is devoted to garbage. Newspapers often use clever headlines of this kind to draw readers into an article. Suggest two other ways the profile might be titled — one simply informative and the other using a play on words or some other form of humor, like the actual title.

480–83

3. Schlossberg includes many **QUOTATIONS**. Choose two of them that strike you as especially interesting, and explain what they add to the profile.

338–42

4. Schlossberg **ENDS** her profile with a quotation from one of the students: "Mr. Wilmer said, 'I used to have trucks like these ones under my Christmas tree when I was little. Now I get to play with the real thing.'" Is this an effective way to end? Why or why not? Why do you think Schlossberg chose to end this way?

5. *For Writing.* Schlossberg focuses on a subject that most of her readers have probably never thought about, namely, how sanitation workers are trained. Select a person whose job does not get much public notice yet is crucial to helping a community or an institution to function well, such as an administrator or an assistant at your school or a telephone repair person. Write a **PROFILE** on a day in the life of this worker that reveals how important the job is.

224–34

Proposals 67

MICHAEL CHABON

Kids' Stuff

Michael Chabon (b. 1963) has published a dozen books, about half of them novels, including The Yiddish Policemen's Union *(2007), the serialized novel* Gentlemen of the Road *(2007), and most recently* Telegraph Avenue *(2013). In 2001, he was awarded a Pulitzer Prize for Fiction for his novel* The Amazing Adventures of Kavalier & Clay, *which explores the lives of two Jewish comic-book artists in the 1940s. In addition to his novels, Chabon has written short-story and essay collections, newspaper serials, screenplays, children's and young-adult books, and comics. "Kids' Stuff" originated as a keynote speech at the 2004 Eisner Awards, known as the "Oscar awards of the comics industry."*

FOR AT LEAST THE FIRST FORTY YEARS OF THEIR EXISTENCE, from the Paleozoic pre-Superman era of *Famous Funnies* (1933) and *More Fun Comics* (1936), comic books were widely viewed, even by those who adored them, as juvenile: the ultimate greasy kids' stuff.* Comics were the literary equivalent of bubblegum cards, to be poked into the spokes of a young mind, where they would produce a satisfying — but entirely bogus — rumble of pleasure. But almost from the first, fitfully in the early days, intermittently through the fifties, and then starting in the mid-sixties with increasing vigor and determination, a battle has been waged by writers, artists, editors, and publishers to elevate the medium, to expand the scope of its subject matter and the range of its artistic styles, to sharpen and increase the sophistication of its language and visual grammar, to probe and explode the limits of the sequential panel, to give free rein to irony, tragedy, autobiography, and other grown-up-type modes of expression.

Also from the first, a key element — at times the central element — of this battle has been the effort to alter not just the medium itself but

---

*Greasy kids' stuff: a phrase used in 1960s advertisements for Vitalis, a men's hair-care product, to disparage competing brands. [Editor's note]

the public perception of the medium. From the late, great Will Eisner's lonely insistence, in an interview with the *Baltimore Sun* back in 1940 (1940!), on the artistic credibility of comics, to the nuanced and scholarly work of recent comics theorists, both practitioners and critics have been arguing passionately on behalf of comics' potential to please — in all the aesthetic richness of that term — the most sophisticated of readers.

The most sophisticated, that is, of *adult* readers. For the adult reader of comic books has always been the holy grail, the promised land, the imagined lover who will greet the long-suffering comic-book maker, at the end of the journey, with open arms, with acceptance, with approval.

A quest is often, among other things, an extended bout of inspired madness. Over the years this quest to break the chains of childish read-ership has resulted, like most bouts of inspired madness, in both folly and stunning innovation. Into the latter category we can put the work of Bernard Krigstein or Frank Miller, say, with their attempts to approximate, through radical attack on the conventions of panel layouts, the fragmenta-tion of human consciousness by urban life; or the tight, tidy, miniaturized madness of Chris Ware. Into the former category — the folly — we might put all the things that got Dr. Frederic Wertham so upset about EC Comics in the early fifties, the syringe-pierced eyeballs and baseball diamonds made from human organs; or the short-lived outfitting of certain Marvel titles in 1965 with a label that boasted "A Marvel Pop Art Production"; or the hypertrophied, tooth-gnashing, blood-letting quote unquote heroes of the era that followed Miller's *The Dark Knight Returns*. An excess of the desire to appear grown up is one of the defining characteristics of ado-lescence. But these follies were the inevitable missteps and overreaching in the course of a campaign that was, in the end, successful.

Because the battle has now, in fact, been won. Not only are comics 5 appealing to a wider and older audience than ever before, but the idea of comics as a valid art form on a par at least with, say, film or rock and roll is widely if not quite universally accepted. Comics and graphic novels are regularly reviewed and debated in *Entertainment Weekly*, the *New York Times Book Review*, even in the august pages of the *New York Review of Books*. Ben Katchor won a MacArthur Fellowship, and Art Spiegelman a Pulitzer Prize.

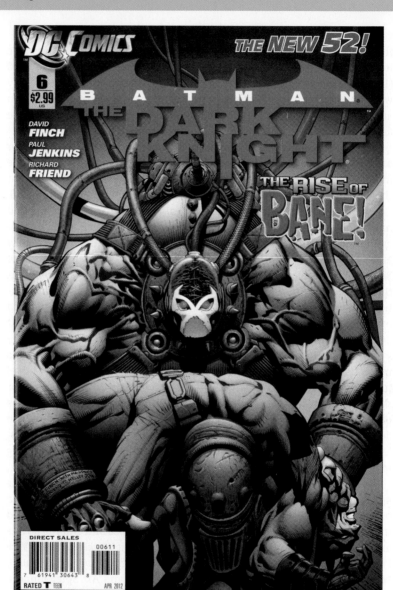

A *modern* Batman cover.

 academic literacies

 rhetorical situations

 genres

 processes

 strategies

 research MLA / APA

media / design

readings

A Batman *cover from the heyday of the child-focused audience.*

But the strange counterphenomenon to this indisputable rise in the reputation, the ambition, the sophistication, and the literary and artistic merit of many of our best comics over the past couple of decades is that over roughly the same period comics readership has declined. Some adults are reading better comics than ever before; but fewer people overall are reading any — far fewer, certainly, than in the great sales heyday of the medium, the early fifties, when by some estimates* as many as 650 million comic books were sold annually (compared to somewhere in the neighborhood of 80 million today). The top ten best-selling comic books in 1996, primarily issues making up two limited series, Marvel's *Civil Wars* and DC's *Infinite Crisis*, were all superhero books, and, like the majority of superhero books in the post–*Dark Knight*, post-*Watchmen* era, all of them dealt rather grimly, and in the somewhat hand-wringing fashion that has become obligatory, with the undoubtedly grown-up issues of violence, freedom, terrorism, vigilantism, political repression, mass hysteria, and the ambivalent nature of heroism. Among the top ten best-selling titles in 1960 (with an aggregate circulation, for all comics, of 400 million) one finds not only the expected *Superman* and *Batman* (decidedly sans ambivalence) but *Mickey Mouse*, *Looney Tunes*, and the classic sagas of *Uncle Scrooge*. And nearly the whole of the list for that year, from top to bottom, through *Casper the Friendly Ghost* (#14) and *Little Archie* (#25) to *Felix the Cat* (#47), is made up of kids' stuff, more or less greasy.

To recap — Days when comics were aimed at kids: huge sales. Days when comics are aimed at adults: not so huge sales, and declining.

The situation is more complicated than that, of course. Since 1960 there have been fundamental changes in a lot of things, among them the way comics are produced, licensed, marketed, and distributed. But maybe it is not too surprising that for a while now, fundamental changes and all, some people have been wondering: what if there were comic books for children?

---

*See, for example, www.comichron.com.

academic literacies · rhetorical situations · genres · processes · strategies · research MLA / APA · media / design · readings

Leaving aside questions of creator's rights, paper costs, retail consolidation, the explosive growth of the collector market, and direct-market sales, a lot of comic-book people will tell you that there is simply too much competition for the kid dollar these days and that, thrown into the arena with video games, special-effects-laden films, the Internet, iPods, etc., comics will inevitably lose out. I find this argument unconvincing, not to mention a cop-out. It is, furthermore, an example of our weird naïveté, in this generation, about how sophisticated we and our children have become vis-à-vis our parents and grandparents, of the misguided sense of retrospective superiority we tend to display toward them and their vanished world. As if in 1960 there was not a *ton* of cool stuff besides comic books on which a kid could spend his or her considerably less constricted time and considerably more limited funds. In the early days of comics, in fact, unlike now, a moderately adventuresome child could find all kinds of things to do that were not only fun (partly because they took place with no adult supervision or mediation), but absolutely free. The price of fun doesn't get any more competitive than that.

I also refuse to accept as explanation for anything the often- 10 tendered argument that contemporary children are more sophisticated, that the kind of comics that pleased a seven-year-old in 1960 would leave an ultracool kid of today snickering with disdain. Even if we accept this argument with respect to "old-fashioned" comics, it would seem to be invalidated by the increasing sophistication of comic books over the past decades. But I reject its very premise. The supposed sophistication — a better term would be *knowingness* — of modern children is largely, I believe, a matter of style, a pose which they have adapted from and modeled on the rampant pose of knowingness, of being wised up, that characterizes the contemporary American style, and has done at least since the late fifties–early sixties heyday of *Mad* magazine (a publication largely enjoyed, from the beginning, by children). Even in their irony and cynicism there is something appealingly insincere, maladroit, and, well, *childish* about children. What is more, I have found that even my own children, as knowing as they often like to present themselves, still take profound pleasure in the old comics that I have given them to read. My older son has still not quite recovered from the heartbreak he felt, when he was seven, reading an old "archive edition" of *Legion of Superheroes*, at the tragic death of Ferro Lad.

Children did not abandon comics; comics, in their drive to attain respect and artistic accomplishment, abandoned children. And for a long time the lovers and partisans of comics were afraid, after so many years of struggle and hard work and incremental gains, to pick up that old jar of greasy kid stuff again, and risk undoing all the labor of so many geniuses and revolutionaries and ordinary, garden-variety artists. Comics have always been an arriviste art form, and all upstarts are to some degree ashamed of their beginnings. But shame, anxiety, the desire to preserve hard-won gains — such considerations no longer serve to explain the disappearance of children's comics. The truth is that comic-book creators have simply lost the habit of telling stories to children. And how sad is that?

When commentators on comics address this question, in the hope of encouraging publishers, writers, and artists to produce new comic books with children in mind, they usually try formulating some version of the following simple equation: create more child readers now, and you will find yourselves with more adult readers later on. Hook them early, in other words. But maybe the equation isn't so simple after all. Maybe what we need, given the sophistication of children (if we want to concede that point) and the competition for their attention and their disposable income (which has always been a factor), is not simply *more* comics for kids, but more *great* comics for kids.

Easy, I suppose, for me to say. So although I am certain that there are many professional creators of comics — people with a good ear and a sharp eye for and a natural understanding of children and their enthusiasms — who would be able to do a far better job of it, having thrown down the finned, skintight gauntlet, I now feel obliged to offer, at the least, a few tentative principles and one concrete suggestion on how more great comics for kids might be teased into the marketplace, even by amateurs like me. I have drawn these principles, in part, from

my memories of the comics I loved when I was young, but I think they hold true as well for the best and most successful works of children's literature.

1) Let's not tell stories that we think "kids of today" might like. That is a route to inevitable failure and possible loss of sanity. *We should tell stories that we would have liked as kids.* Twist endings, the unexpected usefulness of unlikely knowledge, nobility and bravery where it's least expected, and the sudden emergence of a thread of goodness in a wicked nature, those were the kind of stories told by the writers and artists of the comic books that I liked.

2) Let's tell stories that, over time, build up an intricate, involved, involving mythology that is also accessible and comprehensible at any point of entry. The *intricacy*, the accretion of lore over time, should be both inventive and familiar, founded in old mythologies and fears but fully reinterpreted, reimagined. It will demand, it will ache, to be mastered by a child's mythology-mastering imagination. The *accessibility* will come from our making a commitment to tell a full, complete story, or a complete piece of a story, in every issue. This kind of layering of intricate lore and narrative completeness was a hallmark of the great "Superman-family" books (*Adventure, Jimmy Olsen, Superboy*) under the editorship of Mort Weisinger.

3) Let's cultivate an unflagging readiness as storytellers to retell the same stories *with endless embellishment.* Anybody who thinks that kids get bored by hearing the same story over and over again has never spent time telling stories to kids. The key, as in baroque music, is repetition with *variation.* Again the Mort Weisinger–edited *Superman* books, written by unflagging storytellers like Edmond Hamilton and Otto Binder, were exemplary in this regard. The proliferation of theme and variation there verges, at times, on sheer, splendid madness.

4) Let's blow their little minds. A mind is not blown, in spite of whatever Hollywood seems to teach, merely by action sequences, things exploding, thrilling planetscapes, wild bursts of speed. Those are all good things; but a mind is blown when something that you always feared but knew to be impossible turns out to be true; when the world turns out to be far vaster, far more marvelous or malevolent than you

15

ever dreamed; when you get proof that everything is connected to everything else, that everything you know is wrong, that you are both the center of the universe and a tiny speck sailing off its nethermost edge.

So much for my principles: here is my concrete suggestion. If it seems a little obvious, or has already been tried and failed, then I apologize. But I cannot help noticing that in the world of children's *literature*, an overwhelming preponderance of stories are stories *about* children. The same is true of films for children: the central characters are nearly always a child, or a pair or group of children. Comic books, however, even those theoretically aimed at children, are almost always about adults or teenagers. Doesn't that strike you as odd? I suggest that a publisher should try putting out a truly thrilling, honestly observed and remembered, richly imagined, involved and yet narratively straightforward comic book for children, *about children*.

My oldest son is ten now, and he likes comic books. In 1943, if you were a ten-year-old, you probably knew a dozen other kids your age who were into Captain Marvel and the Submariner and the Blue Beetle. When I was ten, in 1973, I knew three or four. But in his class, in his world, my son is all but unique; he's the only one he knows who reads them, studies them, seeks to master and be worthy of all the rapture and strangeness they still contain. Now, comic books are so important to me — I have thought, talked, and written about them so much — that if my son did not in fact like them, I think he would be obliged to loathe them. I have pretty much *forced* comics on my children. But those of us who grew up loving comic books can't afford to take this handcrafted, one-kid-at-a-time approach anymore. We have to sweep them up and carry them off on the flying carpets of story and pictures on which we ourselves, in entire generations, were borne aloft, on carpets woven by Curt Swan and Edmond Hamilton, Jack Kirby and Stan Lee, Chris Claremont and John Byrne. Those artists did it for us; we who make comics today have a solemn debt to pass it on, to weave bright carpets of our own. It's our duty, it's our opportunity, and I really do believe it will be our pleasure.

Engaging with the Text

1. Good proposals present a **WELL-DEFINED PROBLEM** so that readers understand the need for a solution. What problem does Michael Chabon present? How persuasively does he make the case for its existence and seriousness?

    ▲ 238

2. Chabon does not accept the argument made by comic-book people that the reason comic books today are being published more for adults than for children is that "there is simply too much competition for the kid dollar these days and that, thrown into the arena with video games, special-effects-laden films, the Internet, iPods, etc., comics will inevitably lose out." Why does he find this position unconvincing? What is your opinion on why the sales of comic books are declining and why so few are for children?

3. What are the four principles Chabon offers for creating great comics for kids? What **REASONS** does he offer for these principles?

    ◆ 358–59

4. What aspects of Chabon's proposal seem aimed particularly at his intended **AUDIENCE** — the kinds of "writers, artists, editors, and publishers" who attend the Eisner Awards? What parts might they find flattering? challenging? What parts might they be especially sympathetic to? Why?

    ■ 57–60

5. *For Writing.* Research some children's pastimes — such as card games, board games, or jigsaw puzzles — to identify one that has declined in popularity over the last fifty years. How would you propose bringing it back? What would it take to get kids interested in this pastime today? Write a **PROPOSAL** that outlines your ideas for reinvigorating the pastime.

    ▲ 235–44

DENNIS BARON

Don't Make English Official — Ban It Instead

Dennis Baron (b. 1944) is a professor of English and linguistics at the University of Illinois at Urbana-Champaign. His essays on the history of English usage, language legislation, and technology and literacy have been widely published in newspapers and magazines. His books include The English-Only Question: An Official Language for Americans? *(1992),* A Better Pencil: Reading, Writers, and the Digital Revolution *(2009), and* The Wit of William Shakespeare *(2012). He also serves as a consultant to policy makers, lawyers, and journalists on questions concerning language. The following proposal originally appeared in the* Washington Post *in 1996.*

CONGRESS IS CONSIDERING, and may soon pass, legislation making English the official language of the United States. Supporters of the measure say that English forms the glue that keeps America together. They deplore the dollars wasted translating English into other languages. And they fear a horde of illegal aliens adamantly refusing to acquire the most powerful language on earth.

On the other hand, opponents of official English remind us that without legislation we have managed to get over ninety-seven percent of the residents of this country to speak the national language. No country with an official language law even comes close. Opponents also point out that today's non-English-speaking immigrants are picking up English faster than earlier generations of immigrants did, so instead of official English, they favor "English Plus," encouraging everyone to speak both English and another language.

I would like to offer a modest proposal to resolve the language impasse in Congress. Don't make English official, ban it instead.

That may sound too radical, but proposals to ban English first surfaced in the heady days after the American Revolution. Anti-British sentiment was so strong in the new United States that a few superpatriots wanted to get rid of English altogether. They suggested replacing English with Hebrew, thought by many in the eighteenth century to be the world's first language, the one spoken in the garden of Eden. French was also considered, because it was thought at the time, and especially by the French, to be the language of pure reason. And of course there was Greek, the language of Athens, the world's first democracy. It's not clear how serious any of these proposals were, though Roger Sherman* of Connecticut supposedly remarked that it would be better to keep English for ourselves and make the British speak Greek.

Proposals to ban English first surfaced shortly after the American Revolution.

Even if the British are now our allies, there may be some benefit to 5 banning English today. A common language can often be the cause of strife and misunderstanding. Look at Ireland and Northern Ireland, the two Koreas, or the Union and the Confederacy. Banning English would prevent that kind of divisiveness in America today.

Also, if we banned English, we wouldn't have to worry about whose English to make official: the English of England or America? of Chicago or New York? of Ross Perot or William F. Buckley?†

We might as well ban English, too, because no one seems to read it much lately, few can spell it, and fewer still can parse it. Even English teachers have come to rely on computer spell checkers.

Another reason to ban English: it's hardly even English anymore. English started its decline in 1066, with the unfortunate incident at Hastings.‡ Since then it has become a polyglot conglomeration of French, Latin, Italian, Scandinavian, Arabic, Sanskrit, Celtic, Yiddish and Chinese, with an occasional smiley face thrown in.

More important, we should ban English because it has become a world language. Remember what happened to all the other world languages: Latin, Greek, Indo-European? One day they're on everybody's

---

Roger Sherman (1721–93): American revolutionary leader and signer of the Declaration of Independence and the U.S. Constitution. [Editor's note]

†*William F. Buckley Jr.* (1925–2008): conservative political commentator. *Ross Perot*: American industrialist and independent presidential candidate. [Editor's note]

‡*Hastings*: port on south coast of England, site of Saxon army's defeat by the invading Norman forces led by William of Normandy (c. 1028–87). [Editor's note]

tongue; the next day they're dead. Banning English now would save us that inevitable disappointment.

Although we shouldn't ban English without designating a replacement for it, there is no obvious candidate. The French blew their chance when they sold Louisiana. It doesn't look like the Russians are going to take over this country anytime soon — they're having enough trouble taking over Russia. German, the largest minority language in the U.S. until recently, lost much of its prestige after two world wars. Chinese is too hard to write, especially if you're not Chinese. There's always Esperanto, a language made up a hundred years ago that is supposed to bring about world unity. We're still waiting for that. And if you took Spanish in high school you can see that it's not easy to get large numbers of people to speak another language fluently. 10

> We might as well ban English . . . no one seems to read it much lately.

In the end, though, it doesn't matter what replacement language we pick, just so long as we ban English instead of making it official. Prohibiting English will do for the language what Prohibition did for liquor. Those who already use it will continue to do so, and those who don't will want to try out what has been forbidden. This negative psychology works with children. It works with speed limits. It even worked in the Garden of Eden.

Engaging with the Text

1. Dennis Baron signals that his proposal is meant as satire when he writes, "I would like to offer a modest proposal to resolve the language impasse in Congress. Don't make English official, ban it instead." Here Baron alludes to Jonathan Swift's "A Modest Proposal," an essay that is a tour de force of satire. If we aren't meant to take his proposal at face value — and we aren't — what is its **PURPOSE**? What, in other words, is the real argument Baron is making?

55–56

academic literacies · rhetorical situations · genres · processes · strategies · research MLA / APA · media / design · readings

2. Baron **BEGINS** his essay by presenting two views on whether or not English should be the official language of the United States. What is the central problem that both sides are trying to address? Is this an effective beginning? Why or why not? How else might he have begun?

331–38

3. Baron offers six **REASONS** for accepting his "solution." What are they? What is the central point that holds these different reasons together?

358–59

4. If Baron's purpose is not actually to propose banning English in America, why do you think he chose to use the proposal genre to put forth his argument? What other **GENRES** might he have used?

61–63

5. **For Writing.** Identify a current hotly debated issue in the country, your state, your town, or your school. **PROPOSE** an outlandish solution for the problem and provide a plausible, if ironic, argument for your solution. Be sure to anticipate — and respond to — possible objections to your proposed solution.

235–44

JONATHAN ZITTRAIN

The Case for Kill Switches in Military Weaponry

Jonathan Zittrain (b. 1969) is the George Bemis Professor of Internet Law and a professor of computer science at Harvard University. His research focuses on the intersections of the internet with law and public policy. Zittrain is the author of The Future of the Internet and How to Stop It *(2009) and coeditor of* Access Denied *(2008),* Access Controlled *(2009), and* Access Contested *(2011). The following proposal was published in* Scientific American *in 2014.*

THIS SUMMER THE INSURGENT GROUP **ISIS** captured the Iraqi city of Mosul — and along with it, three army divisions' worth of U.S.-supplied equipment from the Iraqi army, including Humvees, helicopters, antiaircraft cannons and M1 Abrams tanks. ISIS staged a parade with its new weapons and then deployed them to capture the strategic Mosul Dam from outgunned Kurdish defenders. The U.S. began conducting air strikes and rearming the Kurds to even the score against its own weaponry. As a result, even more weapons have been added to the conflict, and local arms bazaars have reportedly seen an influx of supply.

It is past time that we consider whether we should build in a way to remotely disable such dangerous tools in an emergency. Other technologies, including smartphones, already incorporate this kind of capability. The theft of iPhones plummeted this year after Apple introduced a remote "kill switch," which a phone's owner can use to make sure no one else can use his or her lost or stolen phone. If this feature is worth putting in consumer devices, why not embed it in devices that can be so devastatingly repurposed — including against their rightful owners, as at the Mosul Dam?

An immediate worry is that a kill switch might not work when it is supposed to. An even bigger concern is that it might work when it is not supposed to — for example, if it is hacked by an enemy. There is a reason tank operators start their vehicles with a switch requiring no ignition key or code — it is too easy to misplace or become

An M1 Abrams tank in Iraq.

separated from keys on a battlefield, even at the cost of unauthorized access.

But ignition keys represent the best technology of 1949. Today there are many more possibilities. At least one foreign policy analyst has suggested incorporating GPS limitations into Stinger surface-to-air missiles to assist the Free Syrian Army in its defenses against air attack while ensuring that the missiles are useless outside that theater of conflict. More simply, any device with onboard electronics, such as a Stinger or a modern tank, could have a timed expiration; the device could operate after the expiration date only if it receives a coded "renew" signal from any of a number of overhead satellites. The renewal would take effect as a matter of course — unless, say, the weapons were stolen. This fail-safe mechanism could be built using basic and well-tested digital signature-and-authentication technologies. One example is the permissive action link devices by which American nuclear weapons are secured so that they can be activated only when specific codes are shared. Another involves the protocols by which military drones are operated remotely and yet increasingly safeguarded against digital hijacking.

The simplest way to use a kill switch would be to place it in the 5 hands of the weapons' original recipients. With a kill switch, the current Iraqi government could disable the bristling trophies of ISIS's post-Mosul parade, or the embattled Libyan government could secure jetliners from taking off on terrorist missions from the overrun airport in Tripoli. A more radical use of a kill switch would be to leave it in the hands of the weapons-providing government. This would turn weaponry into a service rather than a product. Many arms purchasers would no doubt turn elsewhere, but others might find the U.S. to be the only willing source. Some arms deals, including deals between the U.S. and Israel, have already been subject to agreed-on limitations. A kill switch would represent a more powerful enforcement mechanism.

For those who believe the United Nations Security Council might have a meaningful role to play in advancing world security, imagine if a kill switch reposed there, capable of being triggered only if the Council voted to use it. In the most common case, a resolution to activate a kill switch would simply be vetoed by disagreeing states like China and Russia. But in those cases where world opinion is sufficiently unified — as with the current Security Council arms embargo against al Qaeda (and by explicit association, ISIS) — the Council's edict could have bite, with no military action necessary.

The past five years have occasioned a sea change in consumer technology: the code we run on our PCs, tablets, and smartphones, and the content that is available through them, are increasingly controllable from afar, by vendors with whom we must have a relationship rather than a mere transaction. And governments can in turn command those vendors. I've worried about that phenomenon, and why it is overkill to think of using tools such as kill switches for Kindle content to address concerns such as copyright infringement. But it is certainly worth considering them for battlefield tools of unprecedented power and sophistication.

Implementation is everything, and policy makers must reflect on the long-term consequences of using them. For example, because kill

switches could provide assurance that weapons can be controlled down the line, they could lead disquietly to more weapons transfers happening overall. If those kill switches then became easy to circumvent, we would be worse off than before.

Today, however, we are making a conscious choice to create and share medium and heavy weaponry while not restricting its use. This choice has very real impacts. If they can save even one innocent life at the end of a deactivated U.S. barrel, including the lives of our own soldiers, kill switches are worth a serious look.

Engaging with the Text

1. The thesis statement of Jonathan Zittrain's proposal is "If this feature [kill switches] is worth putting in consumer devices, why not embed it in devices that can be so devastatingly repurposed — including against their rightful owners, as at the Mosul Dam." Why do you think Zittrain frames his main point as a question rather than a statement? Why this particular kind of question? Does it set an **APPROPRIATE TONE** for his proposal?

   239

2. Zittrain **BEGINS** his proposal with an anecdote about the insurgent group ISIS capturing the Iraqi city of Mosul and U.S.-supplied military equipment. How does this beginning help **DEFINE THE PROBLEM** he proposes to solve?

   331–38
   238

3. In his third paragraph and then again in his next-to-last paragraph, Zittrain **RESPONDS TO ANTICIPATED QUESTIONS** his readers will have. How convincing do you find his responses? Can you think of other likely questions or objections that he did not address? If so, what are they?

   239

4. The wording of Zittrain's **CALLS TO ACTION** in the second paragraph ("It is past time that we consider whether we should . . .") and in the last sentence ("kill switches are worth a serious look") seems rather tentative, especially given his life-or-death topic. How does this kind of wording relate to his overall **STANCE** and **TONE** and to his **AUDIENCE** of *Scientific American* readers?

   64–67
   65–66
   57–60

5. *For Writing.* Zittrain proposes putting a device that is already avail-
    able for consumer use into battle use. Consider another feature that
    is already available in handheld devices (such as smartphones, iPads,
    or GPS) and propose using it for a different purpose. For example,
    how might the camera function of a smartphone be used for safety
    purposes? How might the place-tracking device of a GPS be used to
    locate children? Write a **PROPOSAL** to recommend implementation of
    your idea for expanding the function of the device.

235–44

PETER SINGER

The Singer Solution to World Poverty

Australian philosopher Peter Singer (b. 1946) is the Ira W. DeCamp professor of bioethics at Princeton University and the Laureate Professor in the Center for Applied Philosophy and Public Ethics at the University of Melbourne in Australia. The author of numerous books, among them Animal Liberation *(fourth edition 2009) and* The Life You Can Save: Acting Now to End World Poverty *(2009), he is considered one of the founders of the modern animal rights movement. The following proposal was first published in 1999 in the* New York Times Magazine.

IN THE BRAZILIAN FILM **C**ENTRAL **S**TATION, Dora is a retired schoolteacher who makes ends meet by sitting at the station writing letters for illiterate people. Suddenly she has an opportunity to pocket $1,000. All she has to do is persuade a homeless nine-year-old boy to follow her to an address she has been given. (She is told he will be adopted by wealthy foreigners.) She delivers the boy, gets the money, spends some of it on a television set, and settles down to enjoy her new acquisition. Her neighbor spoils the fun, however, by telling her that the boy was too old to be adopted — he will be killed and his organs sold for transplantation. Perhaps Dora knew this all along, but after her neighbor's plain speaking, she spends a troubled night. In the morning Dora resolves to take the boy back.

Suppose Dora had told her neighbor that it is a tough world, other people have nice new TVs too, and if selling the kid is the only way she can get one, well, he was only a street kid. She would then have become, in the eyes of the audience, a monster. She redeems herself only by being prepared to bear considerable risks to save the boy.

At the end of the movie, in cinemas in the affluent nations of the world, people who would have been quick to condemn Dora if she had not rescued the boy go home to places far more comfortable than her apartment. In fact, the average family in the United States spends almost one-third of its income on things that are no more necessary to them than Dora's new TV was to her. Going out to nice restaurants, buying new clothes because the old ones are no longer stylish, vacationing at beach resorts — so much of our income is spent on things not essential to the preservation of our lives and health. Donated to one of a number of charitable agencies, that money could mean the difference between life and death for children in need.

All of which raises a question: in the end, what is the ethical distinction between a Brazilian who sells a homeless child to organ peddlers and an American who already has a TV and upgrades to a better one — knowing that the money could be donated to an organization that would use it to save the lives of kids in need?

Of course, there are several differences between the two situations 5 that could support different moral judgments about them. For one thing, to be able to consign a child to death when he is standing right in front of you takes a chilling kind of heartlessness; it is much easier to ignore an appeal for money to help children you will never meet. Yet for a utilitarian philosopher like myself — that is, one who judges whether acts are right or wrong by their consequences — if the upshot of the American's failure to donate the money is that one more kid dies on the streets of a Brazilian city, then it is, in some sense, just as bad as selling the kid to the organ peddlers. But one doesn't need to embrace my utilitarian ethic to see that, at the very least, there is a troubling incongruity in being so quick to condemn Dora for taking the child to the organ peddlers while, at the same time, not regarding the American consumer's behavior as raising a serious moral issue.

In his 1996 book *Living High and Letting Die,* the New York University philosopher Peter Unger presented an ingenious series of imaginary examples designed to probe our intuitions about whether it is wrong to live well without giving substantial amounts of money to help people who are hungry, malnourished, or dying from easily treatable illnesses like diarrhea. Here's my paraphrase of one of these examples:

Bob is close to retirement. He has invested most of his savings in a very rare and valuable old car, a Bugatti, which he has not been able to insure. The Bugatti is his pride and joy. In addition to the pleasure he gets from driving and caring for his car, Bob knows that its rising

market value means that he will always be able to sell it and live comfortably after retirement. One day when Bob is out for a drive, he parks the Bugatti near the end of a railway siding and goes for a walk up the track. As he does so, he sees that a runaway train, with no one aboard, is running down the railway track. Looking farther down the track, he sees the small figure of a child very likely to be killed by the runaway train. He can't stop the train and the child is too far away to warn of the danger, but he can throw a switch that will divert the train down the siding where his Bugatti is parked. Then nobody will be killed — but the train will destroy his Bugatti. Thinking of his joy in owning the car and the financial security it represents, Bob decides not to throw the switch. The child is killed. For many years to come, Bob enjoys owning his Bugatti and the financial security it represents.

Bob's conduct, most of us will immediately respond, was gravely wrong. Unger agrees. But then he reminds us that we, too, have opportunities to save the lives of children. We can give to organizations like Unicef or Oxfam America. How much would we have to give one of these organizations to have a high probability of saving the life of a child threatened by easily preventable diseases? (I do not believe that children are more worth saving than adults, but since no one can argue that children have brought their poverty on themselves, focusing on them simplifies the issues.) Unger called up some experts and used the information they provided to offer some plausible estimates that include the cost of raising money, administrative expenses, and the cost of delivering aid where it is most needed. By his calculation, $200 in donations would help a sickly two-year-old transform into a healthy six-year-old — offering safe passage through childhood's most dangerous years. To show how practical philosophical argument can be, Unger even tells his readers that they can easily donate funds by using their credit card and calling one of these toll-free numbers: (800) 367-5437 for Unicef; (800) 693-2687 for Oxfam America.

> You shouldn't take that cruise, redecorate the house, or get that pricey new suit. After all, a $1,000 suit could save five children's lives.

Now you, too, have the information you need to save a child's life. How should you judge yourself if you don't do it? Think again about Bob and his Bugatti. Unlike Dora, Bob did not have to look into the eyes of the child he was sacrificing for his own material comfort. The child was a complete stranger to him and too far away to relate to in an intimate, personal way. Unlike Dora, too, he did not mislead the child or initiate the chain of events imperiling him. In all these respects, Bob's situation resembles that of people able but unwilling to donate to overseas aid and differs from Dora's situation.

If you still think that it was very wrong of Bob not to throw the 10
switch that would have diverted the train and saved the child's life, then it is hard to see how you could deny that it is also very wrong not to send money to one of the organizations listed above. Unless, that is, there is some morally important difference between the two situations that I have overlooked.

Is it the practical uncertainties about whether aid will really reach the people who need it? Nobody who knows the world of overseas aid can doubt that such uncertainties exist. But Unger's figure of $200 to save a child's life was reached after he had made conservative assumptions about the proportion of the money donated that will actually reach its target.

One genuine difference between Bob and those who can afford to donate to overseas aid organizations but don't is that only Bob can save the child on the tracks, whereas there are hundreds of millions of people who can give $200 to overseas aid organizations. The problem is that most of them aren't doing it. Does this mean that it is all right for you not to do it?

Suppose that there were more owners of priceless vintage cars — Carol, Dave, Emma, Fred and so on, down to Ziggy — all in exactly the same situation as Bob, with their own siding and their own switch, all sacrificing the child in order to preserve their own cherished car. Would that make it all right for Bob to do the same? To answer this question affirmatively is to endorse follow-the-crowd ethics — the kind of ethics that led many Germans to look away when the Nazi atrocities were being committed. We do not excuse them because others were behaving no better.

academic literacies | rhetorical situations | genres | processes | strategies | research MLA / APA | media / design | readings

We seem to lack a sound basis for drawing a clear moral line between Bob's situation and that of any reader of this article with $200 to spare who does not donate it to an overseas aid agency. These readers seem to be acting at least as badly as Bob was acting when he chose to let the runaway train hurtle toward the unsuspecting child. In the light of this conclusion, I trust that many readers will reach for the phone and donate that $200. Perhaps you should do it before reading further.

Now that you have distinguished yourself morally from people who 15 put their vintage cars ahead of a child's life, how about treating yourself and your partner to dinner at your favorite restaurant? But wait. The money you will spend at the restaurant could also help save the lives of children overseas! True, you weren't planning to blow $200 tonight, but if you were to give up dining out just for one month, you would easily save that amount. And what is one month's dining out, compared to a child's life? There's the rub. Since there are a lot of desperately needy children in the world, there will always be another child whose life you could save for another $200. Are you therefore obliged to keep giving until you have nothing left? At what point can you stop?

Hypothetical examples can easily become farcical. Consider Bob. How far past losing the Bugatti should he go? Imagine that Bob had got his foot stuck in the track of the siding, and if he diverted the train, then before it rammed the car it would also amputate his big toe. Should he still throw the switch? What if it would amputate his foot? His entire leg?

As absurd as the Bugatti scenario gets when pushed to extremes, the point it raises is a serious one: only when the sacrifices become very significant indeed would most people be prepared to say that Bob does nothing wrong when he decides not to throw the switch. Of course, most people could be wrong; we can't decide moral issues by taking opinion polls. But consider for yourself the level of sacrifice that you would demand of Bob, and then think about how much money you would have to give away in order to make a sacrifice that is roughly equal to that. It's almost certainly much, much more than $200. For most middle-class Americans, it could easily be more like $200,000.

Isn't it counterproductive to ask people to do so much? Don't we run the risk that many will shrug their shoulders and say that morality, so conceived, is fine for saints but not for them? I accept that we are unlikely to see, in the near or even medium-term future, a world in which it is normal for wealthy Americans to give the bulk of their wealth to strangers. When it comes to praising or blaming people for what they do, we tend to use a standard that is relative to some conception of normal behavior. Comfortably off Americans who give, say, 10 percent of their income to overseas aid organizations are so far ahead of most of their equally comfortable fellow citizens that I wouldn't go out of my way to chastise them for not doing more. Nevertheless, they should be doing much more, and they are in no position to criticize Bob for failing to make the much greater sacrifice of his Bugatti.

At this point various objections may crop up. Someone may say: "If every citizen living in the affluent nations contributed his or her share I wouldn't have to make such a drastic sacrifice, because long before such levels were reached, the resources would have been there to save the lives of all those children dying from lack of food or medical care. So why should I give more than my fair share?" Another, related objection is that the government ought to increase its overseas aid allocations, since that would spread the burden more equitably across all taxpayers.

Yet the question of how much we ought to give is a matter to be 20 decided in the real world — and that, sadly, is a world in which we know that most people do not, and in the immediate future will not, give substantial amounts to overseas aid agencies. We know, too, that at least in the next year, the United States government is not going to meet even the very modest United Nations–recommended target of 0.7 percent of gross national product; at a moment it lags far below that, at 0.09 percent, not even half of Japan's 0.22 percent or a tenth of Denmark's 0.97 percent. Thus, we know that the money we can give beyond that theoretical "fair share" is still going to save lives that would otherwise be lost. While the idea that no one need do more than his or her fair share is a powerful one, should it prevail if we know that others are not doing their fair share and that children will die preventable

academic literacies · rhetorical situations · genres · processes · strategies · research MLA / APA · media / design · readings

deaths unless we do more than our fair share? That would be taking fairness too far.

Thus, this ground for limiting how much we ought to give also fails. In the world as it is now, I can see no escape from the conclusion that each one of us with wealth surplus to his or her essential needs should be giving most of it to help people suffering from poverty so dire as to be life-threatening. That's right: I'm saying that you shouldn't buy that new car, take that cruise, redecorate the house, or get that pricey new suit. After all, a $1,000 suit could save five children's lives.

So how does my philosophy break down in dollars and cents? An American household with an income of $50,000 spends around $30,000 annually on necessities, according to the Conference Board, a nonprofit economic research organization. Therefore, for a household bringing in $50,000 a year, donations to help the world's poor should be as close as possible to $20,000. The $30,000 required for necessities holds for higher incomes as well. So a household making $100,000 could cut a yearly check for $70,000. Again, the formula is simple: Whatever money you're spending on luxuries, not necessities, should be given away.

Now, evolutionary psychologists tell us that human nature just isn't sufficiently altruistic to make it plausible that many people will sacrifice so much for strangers. On the facts of human nature, they might be right, but they would be wrong to draw a moral conclusion from those facts. If it is the case that we ought to do things that, predictably, most of us won't do, then let's face that fact head-on. Then, if we value the life of a child more than going to fancy restaurants, the next time we dine out we will know that we could have done something better with our money. If that makes living a morally decent life extremely arduous, well, then that is the way things are. If we don't do it, then we should at least know that we are failing to live a morally decent life — not because it is good to wallow in guilt but because knowing where we should be going is the first step toward heading in that direction.

When Bob first grasped the dilemma that faced him as he stood by that railway switch, he must have thought how extraordinarily unlucky he was to be placed in a situation in which he must choose between the life of an innocent child and the sacrifice of most of his savings. But he was not unlucky at all. We are all in that situation.

Engaging with the Text

55–56

1. What is the **PURPOSE** of Peter Singer's proposal? What is he actually proposing? What action does he want us to take? Point to passages where his purpose is made explicit.

363–64

2. Singer begins his essay with reference to the Brazilian film *Central Station* and follows it with a hypothetical **SCENARIO**. What role do the film and the scenario play in his proposal? What do they contribute to the persuasiveness of his argument? Do you find them effective? Why or why not?

3. Singer argues that "whatever money you're spending on luxuries, not necessities, should be given away." To what degree do you agree with this claim? How much faith in this claim does Singer himself appear to have?

239

4. What **QUESTIONS** does Singer anticipate? How does he address potential naysayers?

235–44

5. *For Writing.* Think of a large societal problem (for example, poverty, pollution, or unemployment) and how the actions of individuals might help alleviate it (volunteering at a food bank, recycling soda cans, restructuring a company to create more positions). Describe the problem and write a **PROPOSAL** for how you and other individuals can help to solve it.

academic literacies   rhetorical situations   genres   processes   strategies   research MLA / APA   media / design   readings

Reflections 68

DAVE BARRY

Guys vs. Men

Dave Barry (b. 1947) is a humorist who is the author of thirty books and countless columns. Two of his books — Dave Barry Turns 40 (1990) and Dave Barry's Greatest Hits (1988) — served as the basis for the TV sitcom Dave's World, which ran for four seasons from 1993 to 1997. In 1988, Barry was awarded a Pulitzer Prize for Commentary. Formerly a syndicated columnist, he has had writing published in over 500 newspapers in the United States and abroad. The following reflection is from his book Dave Barry's Complete Guide to Guys (1996).

MEN ITSELF IS A SERIOUS WORD, not to mention *manhood* and *manly*. Such words make being male sound like a very important activity, as opposed to what it primarily consists of, namely, possessing a set of minor and frequently unreliable organs.

But men tend to attach great significance to Manhood. This results in certain characteristically masculine, by which I mean stupid, behavioral patterns that can produce unfortunate results such as violent crime, war, spitting, and ice hockey. These things have given males a bad name.* And the "Men's Movement," which is supposed to bring out the more positive aspects of Manliness, seems to be densely populated with loons and goobers.

So I'm saying that there's another way to look at males: not as aggressive macho dominators; not as sensitive, liberated, hugging drummers; but as *guys.*

And what, exactly, do I mean by "guys"? I don't know. I haven't thought that much about it. One of the major characteristics of guyhood is that we guys don't spend a lot of time pondering our deep innermost feelings. There is a serious question in my mind about whether guys

---

*Specifically, "asshole."

actually *have* deep innermost feelings, unless you count, for example, loyalty to the Detroit Tigers, or fear of bridal showers.

But although I can't define exactly what it means to be a guy, I can 5 describe certain guy characteristics, such as:

Guys Like Neat Stuff

By "neat," I mean "mechanical and unnecessarily complex." I'll give you an example. Right now I'm typing these words on an *extremely* powerful computer. It's the latest in a line of maybe ten computers I've owned, each one more powerful than the last. My computer is chock-full of RAM and ROM and bytes and megahertzes and various other items that enable a computer to kick data-processing butt. It is probably capable of supervising the entire U.S. air-defense apparatus while simultaneously processing the tax return of every resident of Ohio. I use it mainly to write a newspaper column. This is an activity wherein I sit and stare at the screen for maybe ten minutes, then, using only my forefingers, slowly type something like:

Henry Kissinger looks like a big wart.

I stare at this for another ten minutes, have an inspiration, then amplify the original thought as follows:

Henry Kissinger looks like a big fat wart.

Then I stare at that for another ten minutes, pondering whether 10 I should try to work in the concept of "hairy."

This is absurdly simple work for my computer. It sits there, humming impatiently, bored to death, passing the time between keystrokes via brain-teaser activities such as developing a Unified Field Theory of the universe and translating the complete works of Shakespeare into rap.*

In other words, this computer is absurdly overqualified to work for me, and yet soon, I guarantee, I will buy an *even more powerful* one. I won't be able to stop myself. I'm a guy.

---

*To be or not? I got to *know*.
Might kill myself by the end of the *show*.

Probably the ultimate example of the fundamental guy drive to have neat stuff is the Space Shuttle. Granted, the guys in charge of this program *claim* it has a Higher Scientific Purpose, namely to see how humans function in space. But of course we have known for years how humans function in space: They float around and say things like: "Looks real good, Houston!"

No, the real reason for the existence of the Space Shuttle is that it is one humongous and spectacularly gizmo-intensive item of hardware. Guys can tinker with it practically forever, and occasionally even get it to work, and use it to place *other* complex mechanical items into orbit, where they almost immediately break, which provides a great excuse to send the Space Shuttle up *again*. It's Guy Heaven.

Other results of the guy need to have stuff are Star Wars, the 15 recreational boating industry, monorails, nuclear weapons, and wristwatches that indicate the phase of the moon. I am not saying that women haven't been involved in the development or use of this stuff. I'm saying that, without guys, this stuff probably would not exist; just as, without women, virtually every piece of furniture in the world would still be in its original position. Guys do not have a basic need to rearrange furniture. Whereas a woman who could cheerfully use the same computer for fifty-three years will rearrange her furniture on almost a weekly basis, sometimes in the dead of night. She'll be sound asleep in bed, and suddenly, at 2 A.M., she'll be awakened by the urgent thought: *The blue-green sofa needs to go perpendicular to the wall instead of parallel, and it needs to go there RIGHT NOW.* So she'll get up and move it, which of course necessitates moving other furniture, and soon she has rearranged her entire living room, shifting great big heavy pieces that ordinarily would require several burly men to lift, because there are few forces in Nature more powerful than a woman who needs to rearrange furniture. Every so often a guy will wake up to discover that, because of his wife's overnight efforts, he now lives in an entirely different house.

(I realize that I'm making gender-based generalizations here, but my feeling is that if God did not want us to make gender-based generalizations, She would not have given us genders.)

Guys Like a Really Pointless Challenge

Not long ago I was sitting in my office at the *Miami Herald*'s Sunday magazine, *Tropic*, reading my fan mail,* when I heard several of my guy coworkers in the hallway talking about how fast they could run the forty-yard dash. These are guys in their thirties and forties who work in journalism, where the most demanding physical requirement is the ability to digest vending-machine food. In other words, these guys have absolutely no need to run the forty-yard dash.

But one of them, Mike Wilson, was writing a story about a star high-school football player who could run it in 4.38 seconds. Now if Mike had written a story about, say, a star high-school poet, none of my guy coworkers would have suddenly decided to find out how well they could write sonnets. But when Mike turned in his story, they became *deeply* concerned about how fast they could run the forty-yard dash. They were so concerned that the magazine editor, Tom Shroder, decided that they should get a stopwatch and go out to a nearby park and find out. Which they did, a bunch of guys taking off their shoes and running around barefoot in a public park on company time.

This is what I heard them talking about, out in the hall. I heard Tom, who was thirty-eight years old, saying that his time in the forty had been 5.75 seconds. And I thought to myself: This is ridiculous. These are middle-aged guys, supposedly adults, and they're out there *bragging* about their performance in this stupid juvenile footrace. Finally I couldn't stand it anymore.

"Hey!" I shouted. "I could beat 5.75 seconds."   20

So we went out to the park and measured off forty yards, and the guys told me that I had three chances to make my best time. On the first try my time was 5.78 seconds, just three-hundredths of a second slower than Tom's, even though, at forty-five, I was seven years older than he. So I just *knew* I'd beat him on the second attempt if I ran really, really hard, which I did for a solid ten yards, at which point my left hamstring

---

*Typical fan letter: "Who cuts your hair? Beavers?"

muscle, which had not yet shifted into Spring Mode from Mail-Reading Mode, went, and I quote, "pop."

I had to be helped off the field. I was in considerable pain, and I was obviously not going to be able to walk right for weeks. The other guys were very sympathetic, especially Tom, who took the time to call me at home, where I was sitting with ice pack on my leg and twenty-three Advil in my bloodstream, so he could express his concern.

"Just remember," he said, "*you didn't beat my time.*"

There are countless other examples of guys rising to meet pointless challenges. Virtually all sports fall into this category, as well as a large part of U.S. foreign policy. ("I'll bet you can't capture Manuel Noriega!"* "Oh YEAH??")

Guys Do Not Have a Rigid and Well-Defined Moral Code

This is not the same as saying that guys are bad. Guys *are* capable of 25 doing bad things, but this generally happens when they try to be Men and start becoming manly and aggressive and stupid. When they're being just plain guys, they aren't so much actively *evil* as they are lost. Because guys have never really grasped the Basic Human Moral Code, which I believe was invented by women millions of years ago when all the guys were out engaging in some other activity, such as seeing who could burp the loudest. When they came back, there were certain rules that they were expected to follow unless they wanted to get into Big Trouble, and they have been trying to follow these rules ever since, with extremely irregular results. Because guys have never *internalized* these rules. Guys are similar to my small auxiliary backup dog, Zippy, a guy dog† who has been told numerous times that he is *not* supposed to (1) get into the kitchen garbage or (2) poop on the floor. He knows that these are the rules, but he has never really understood *why*, and sometimes he gets to thinking: Sure, I am *ordinarily* not supposed to get into

---

Manuel Noriega: former military dictator in Panama; he was removed from power by the United States in 1989. [Editor's note]

†I also have a female dog, Earnest, who *never* breaks the rules.

the garbage, but obviously this rule is not meant to apply when there are certain extenuating* circumstances, such as (1) somebody just threw away some perfectly good seven-week-old Kung Pao Chicken, and (2) I am home alone.

And so when the humans come home, the kitchen floor has been transformed into GarbageFest USA, and Zippy, who usually comes rushing up, is off in a corner disguised in a wig and sunglasses, hoping to get into the Federal Bad Dog Relocation Program before the humans discover the scene of the crime.

When I yell at him, he frequently becomes so upset that he poops on the floor.

Morally, most guys are just like Zippy, only taller and usually less hairy. Guys are *aware* of the rules of moral behavior, but they have trouble keeping these rules in the forefronts of their minds at certain times, especially the present. This is especially true in the area of faithfulness to one's mate. I realize, of course, that there are countless examples of guys being faithful to their mates until they die, usually as a result of being eaten by their mates immediately following copulation. Guys outside of the spider community, however, do not have a terrific record of faithfulness.

I'm not saying guys are scum. I'm saying that many guys who consider themselves to be committed to their marriages will stray if they are confronted with overwhelming temptation, defined as "virtually any temptation."

Okay, so maybe I *am* saying guys are scum. But they're not *mean-spirited* scum. And few of them — even when they are out of town on business trips, far from their wives, and have a clear-cut opportunity — will poop on the floor.

30

---

*I am taking some liberties here with Zippy's vocabulary. More likely, in his mind, he uses the term *mitigating*.

Engaging with the Text

1. Dave Barry claims that he isn't able to say what he means by the term "guys" because "one of the major characteristics of guyhood is that we guys don't spend a lot of time pondering our deep innermost feelings." Yet in this piece — indeed even this sentence — he identifies specific characteristics of "guys" that suggest he has indeed pondered this state of maleness thoroughly. How do you account for this contradiction?

2. Despite his assertion that he can't define the term, Barry essentially provides an **EXTENDED DEFINITION** of the term "guy," detailing several characteristics. What are they? Do you agree with his description of them? Why or why not? What other characteristics would you add, if any?

   390–94 ◆

3. Barry includes several **EXAMPLES** of the behavior he identifies as characteristic of guys. Identity several passages that include such examples and discuss what these contribute to his reflection.

   395 ◆

4. What is Barry's **STANCE** toward his topic? Point to specific passages that reveal that stance. Is this stance appropriate for Barry's **PURPOSE**? Why or why not?

   64–67 ■
   55–56 ■

5. *For Writing.* Identify a specific group of people, animals, things, or places, and reflect on what distinguishing characteristics are shared by its members. Write a **REFLECTION** on the group that identifies those major characteristics. Study Barry's reflection to see what techniques he uses to elicit a smile or chuckle. Try your hand at one or more of these.

   245–52 ▲

GEETA KOTHARI

If You Are What You Eat, Then What Am I?

Geeta Kothari (b. 1962) has published stories and essays in numerous newspapers, journals, and anthologies. She teaches writing at the University of Pittsburgh, where she is director of the Writing Center, and is the editor of Did My Mama Like to Dance? and Other Stories about Mothers and Daughters *(1994). The following reflection first appeared in 1999 in the* Kenyon Review, *a literary journal published at Kenyon College. As you read, notice how Kothari incorporates vivid anecdotes to illustrate the competing cultural experiences that complicate her sense of identity.*

> To belong is to understand the tacit codes of the people you live with.   —Michael Ignatieff, Blood and Belonging

THE FIRST TIME MY MOTHER and I open a can of tuna, I am nine years old. We stand in the doorway of the kitchen, in semidarkness, the can tilted toward daylight. I want to eat what the kids at school eat: bologna, hot dogs, salami — foods my parents find repugnant because they contain pork and meat byproducts, crushed bone and hair glued together by chemicals and fat. Although she has never been able to tolerate the smell of fish, my mother buys the tuna, hoping to satisfy my longing for American food.

Indians, of course, do not eat such things.

The tuna smells fishy, which surprises me because I can't remember anyone's tuna sandwich actually smelling like fish. And the tuna in those sandwiches doesn't look like this, pink and shiny, like an internal organ. In fact, this looks similar to the bad foods my mother doesn't want me to eat. She is silent, holding her face away from the can while peering into it like a half-blind bird.

"What's wrong with it?" I ask.

She has no idea. My mother does not know that the tuna everyone   5
else's mothers made for them was tuna *salad*.

"Do you think it's botulism?"

I have never seen botulism, but I have read about it, just as I have read about but never eaten steak and kidney pie.

There is so much my parents don't know. They are not like other parents, and they disappoint me and my sister. They are supposed to help us negotiate the world outside, teach us the signs, the clues to proper behavior: what to eat and how to eat it.

We have expectations, and my parents fail to meet them, especially my mother, who works full-time. I don't understand what it means, to have a mother who works outside and inside the home; I notice only the ways in which she disappoints me. She doesn't show up for school plays. She doesn't make chocolate-frosted cupcakes for my class. At night, if I want her attention, I have to sit in the kitchen and talk to her while she cooks the evening meal, attentive to every third or fourth word I say.

We throw the tuna away. This time my mother is disappointed. I go   10
to school with tuna eaters. I see their sandwiches, yet cannot explain the discrepancy between them and the stinking, oily fish in my mother's hand. We do not understand so many things, my mother and I.

When we visit our relatives in India, food prepared outside the house is carefully monitored. In the hot, sticky monsoon months in New Delhi and Bombay, we cannot eat ice cream, salad, cold food, or any fruit that can't be peeled. Definitely no meat. People die from amoebic dysentery, unexplained fevers, strange boils on their bodies. We drink boiled water only, no ice. No sweets except for jalebi, thin fried twists of dough in dripping hot sugar syrup. If we're caught outside with nothing to drink, Fanta, Limca, Thums Up (after Coca-Cola is thrown out by Mrs. Gandhi) will do. Hot tea sweetened with sugar, served with thick creamy buffalo milk, is preferable. It should be boiled, to kill the germs on the cup.

My mother talks about "back home" as a safe place, a silk cocoon frozen in time where we are sheltered by family and friends. Back home, my sister and I do not argue about food with my parents. Home is where they know all the rules. We trust them to guide us safely through the maze of city streets for which they have no map, and we trust them to feed and take care of us, the way parents should.

academic literacies   rhetorical situations   genres   processes   strategies   research MLA / APA   media / design   readings

Finally, though, one of us will get sick, hungry for the food we see our cousins and friends eating, too thirsty to ask for a straw, too polite to insist on properly boiled water.

At my uncle's diner in New Delhi, someone hands me a plate of aloo tikki, fried potato patties filled with mashed channa dal and served with a sweet and a sour chutney. The channa, mixed with hot chilies and spices, burns my tongue and throat. I reach for my Fanta, discard the paper straw, and gulp the sweet orange soda down, huge drafts that sting rather than soothe.

When I throw up later that day (or is it the next morning, when a   15 stomachache wakes me from deep sleep?), I cry over the frustration of being singled out, not from the pain my mother assumes I'm feeling as she holds my hair back from my face. The taste of orange lingers in my mouth, and I remember my lips touching the cold glass of the Fanta bottle.

At that moment, more than anything, I want to be like my cousins.

In New York, at the first Indian restaurant in our neighborhood, my father orders with confidence, and my sister and I play with the silverware until the steaming plates of lamb biryani arrive.

What is Indian food? my friends ask, their noses crinkling up.

Later, this restaurant is run out of business by the new Indo-Pak-Bangladeshi combinations up and down the street, which serve similar food. They use plastic cutlery and Styrofoam cups. They do not distinguish between North and South Indian cooking, or between Indian, Pakistani, and Bangladeshi cooking, and their customers do not care. The food is fast, cheap, and tasty. Dosa, a rice flour crepe stuffed with masala potato, appears on the same trays as chicken makhani.

Now my friends want to know, Do you eat curry at home?   20

One time my mother makes lamb vindaloo for guests. Like dosa, this is a South Indian dish, one that my Punjabi mother has to learn from a cookbook. For us, she cooks everyday food — yellow dal, rice, chapati, bhaji. Lentils, rice, bread, and vegetables. She has never referred to anything on our table as "curry" or "curried," but I know she has made chicken curry for guests. Vindaloo, she explains, is a curry too. I understand then

that curry is a dish created for guests, outsiders, a food for people who eat in restaurants.

I look around my boyfriend's freezer one day and find meat: pork chops, ground beef, chicken pieces, Italian sausage. Ham in the refrigerator, next to the homemade bolognese sauce. Tupperware filled with chili made from ground beef and pork.

He smells different from me. Foreign. Strange.

I marry him anyway.

He has inherited blue eyes that turn gray in bad weather, light brown hair, a sharp pointy nose, and excellent teeth. He learns to make chili with ground turkey and tofu, tomato sauce with red wine and portobello mushrooms, roast chicken with rosemary and slivers of garlic under the skin.

He eats steak when we are in separate cities, roast beef at his mother's house, hamburgers at work. Sometimes I smell them on his skin. I hope he doesn't notice me turning my face, a cheek instead of my lips, my nose wrinkled at the unfamiliar, musky smell.

I have inherited brown eyes, black hair, a long nose with a crooked bridge, and soft teeth with thin enamel. I am in my twenties, moving to a city far from my parents, before it occurs to me that jeera, the spice my sister avoids, must have an English name. I have to learn that haldi = turmeric, methi = fenugreek. What to make with fenugreek, I do not know. My grandmother used to make methi roti for our breakfast, cornbread with fresh fenugreek leaves served with a lump of homemade butter. No one makes it now that she's gone, though once in a while my mother will get a craving for it and produce a facsimile ("The cornmeal here is wrong") that only highlights what she's really missing: the smells and tastes of her mother's house.

I will never make my grandmother's methi roti or even my mother's unsatisfactory imitation of it. I attempt chapati; it takes six hours, three phone calls home, and leaves me with an aching back. I have to write translations down: jeera = cumin. My memory is unreliable. But I have always known garam = hot.

25

If I really want to make myself sick, I worry that my husband will one day leave me for a meat-eater, for someone familiar who doesn't sniff him suspiciously for signs of alimentary infidelity.

Indians eat lentils. I understand this as absolute, a decree from an unidentifiable authority that watches and judges me. 30

So what does it mean that I cannot replicate my mother's dal? She and my father show me repeatedly, in their kitchen, in my kitchen. They coach me over the phone, buy me the best cookbooks, and finally write down their secrets. Things I'm supposed to know but don't. Recipes that should be, by now, engraved on my heart.

Living far from the comfort of people who require no explanation for what I do and who I am, I crave the foods we have shared. My mother convinces me that moong is the easiest dal to prepare, and yet it fails me every time: bland, watery, a sickly greenish yellow mush. These imperfect limitations remind me only of what I'm missing.

But I have never been fond of moong dal. At my mother's table it is the last thing I reach for. Now I worry that this antipathy toward dal signals something deeper, that somehow I am not my parents' daughter, not Indian, and because I cannot bear the touch and smell of raw meat, though I can eat it cooked (charred, dry, and overdone), I am not American either.

I worry about a lifetime purgatory in Indian restaurants where I will complain that all the food looks and tastes the same because they've used the same masala.

Engaging with the Text

1. Geeta Kothari uses food as a way to explore the larger issue of cultural identity. How does she **DESCRIBE** Indian and American food? What **SPECIFIC DETAILS** does she include to help her readers understand the pulls of both American and Indian culture? 399–407 249

2. A good **TITLE** indicates what the piece is about and makes readers want to read it. How well does this title do those things? How does Kothari answer the question her title asks? 344–45

331–38

3. How does Kothari **BEGIN** her reflection? Is this an effective beginning? Why or why not? How does it signal to readers what Kothari will address in the rest of the piece?

4. For Kothari, cultural identity shapes, and is shaped by, the foods one eats and the ways one eats them. Her reflection reveals a struggle over two cultures — Indian and American — and she worries that she cannot locate herself fully in either. At the end of her text, she notes: "I worry that this antipathy toward dal signals something deeper, that somehow I am not my parents' daughter, not Indian, and because I cannot bear the touch and smell of raw meat . . . I am not American either." What does it mean to live on the border between two cultures in the ways Kothari describes?

5. *For Writing.* Think about the kinds of foods you grew up with and the ways they were similar or dissimilar to those of your peers. Write an essay **REFLECTING** on the role food has played in your own sense of your identity — whether it be your cultural heritage, your identification (or not) with your generation, your individual or family identity, or some other form.

245–52

PAULA MARANTZ COHEN

We Are All Quants Now

Paula Marantz Cohen (b. 1953) is Distinguished Professor of English at Drexel University and the author of four scholarly books, three novels, and numerous short stories and essays on literature, film, and culture. Her Silent Film and the Triumph of the American Myth *(2001) was selected as a Choice Outstanding Book for 2003. She is the coeditor of the* Journal of Modern Literature *and a regular contributor to the* (London) Times Literary Supplement. *The following reflection appeared in the* Wall Street Journal *in 2014.*

A YOUNG FRIEND OF MINE who babysits for children in hip areas of New York City recently reported having the following experience: One of her charges, a girl of about 7, was working on a drawing.

"That's good work," said my friend in encouraging fashion. "Are you proud of it?"

"I'm not sure," said the little girl, "I'll bring it to school and see how many 'likes' I get."

My friend, though in her 20s, is still old enough to remember a world before Facebook, and she reported this incident with some incredulity. For me, the effect is even stronger. I think that the child's response reflects a culturally significant trend.

For a 7-year-old to want to assess her drawing by the number of 5 "likes" it gets means that she understands her artwork in quantitative terms. It's the trickle-down effect of our culture of assessment and "big data" analysis. Not only are primary and secondary schools now instituting assessment testing at every grade and in every subject area, but the most elite universities that once prided themselves on delivering an ineffable "liberal education" are now seeking to quantify the value-added of four years on campus and tens of thousands of dollars in tuition. The same sorts of assessment tools drive the marketplace, as Netflix and Amazon quantify our buying habits and pitch us products based on our user profile. Is there any wonder that a young child would want to assess her artwork using the same sorts of tools?

This new twist in the culture has existential implications. It affects the shape of the self. It makes our judgments, values and tastes subject to a new context of evaluation. Who we are comes to mimic the tools that analyze us. This may explain why so many people, especially young adults, think that privacy doesn't matter. What do they have to hide? A surface, measurable self has replaced a deep, mysterious one.

My first impulse is to be put off by this. As the product of an old-fashioned liberal arts education and an old-fashioned idea of the self, I am inclined to see this new assessment-driven model as shallow and soulless. But I also wonder if my horror is misplaced — or at least narrow-minded. I am reminded of a cautionary statement from George Eliot's *Middlemarch*: "For we all of us, grave or light, get our thoughts entangled in metaphors, and act fatally on the strength of them." Are

notions of privacy, the unconscious and the soul metaphors in which I am entangled?

I want to be open-minded here and acknowledge that each paradigm, each master narrative that predominates at a particular point in culture, has its pros and cons. The cons of the assessment culture are that certain types of knowledge and certain kinds of pleasures and aesthetic experiences are lost.

But the new model has its advantages. Some of the difficulties in determining value, or "worth" in art and literature, can now be rectified by measuring the number of "likes" from its target audience. Where there is so much information coming at us with so much rapidity, a compilation of "likes" can simplify and clarify decision-making. Moreover, given the difficulties of finding friends or romantic partners in our fast-paced, nomadic society, the Internet's quantitative tools are enormously useful. The mounting statistics on divorce over the past half century say something about how badly a qualitative model has worked in this area.

The quantitative model associated with Internet dating and Internet-based interest groups may in fact be leading us back to a more traditional, pre-modern paradigm. By asking friends and family to assess a marital candidate, and then tallying the number of "likes" that the individual receives is to mimic the kind of assessment that used to prevail in the arrangement of a marriage by extended families or tribes. Where children are likely to be involved, such an approach seems to have some definite assets, helping to improve the chances of a sustained and sustaining family unit.

The trick, of course, is to calculate how many likes one needs to get in order to approximate love.

Engaging with the Text

1. Paula Marantz Cohen asserts that a cultural shift has taken place from qualitative, introspective, deep assessment to quantitative, objective, surface assessment. In other words, today the value of something is

judged by the results of statistical analysis or the sheer number of people who quickly react favorably to it, rather than by the carefully considered responses of those well qualified to judge. What do you see as the pros and cons of the two different assessment systems? Are there others besides the ones Cohen mentions? And has quantitative assessment really taken over our lives in recent years to the extent she claims? Has it perhaps long been dominant and is now simply more openly acknowledged? Are there areas where qualitative evaluation remains the norm or is even growing in importance?

64–67
57–60

2. Cohen takes a mixed negative and positive **STANCE** toward quantitative assessment, the subject of her reflection. Which stance would you expect her **AUDIENCE**, the business-minded readers of the *Wall Street Journal*, to identify with? How does the last sentence sum up her stance

250

and illustrate the **QUESTIONING, SPECULATIVE TONE** characteristic of reflections?

331–38
337

3. Cohen **BEGINS** her reflection with an **ANECDOTE** about a seven-year-old girl who will judge her artwork by the number of "likes" it receives from her classmates. What anecdote could you have used to begin a reflection on this subject?

248–49

4. How does Cohen signal that the topic of quants **INTRIGUES** her? Point to at least one passage where her interest in the topic is evident.

5. *For Writing.* Smartphones are becoming increasingly popular. Write a

245–52

REFLECTION on the use of smartphones today where selfies are easy to take, where people having meals together focus on their phones rather than one another, where moviegoers have to be asked to turn off their phones, where information about what menu a restaurant offers and how to get there is at one's fingertips. How have smartphones changed our lives both for bad and for good?

academic literacies · rhetorical situations · genres · processes · strategies · research MLA / APA · media / design · readings

TIM KREIDER

A Man and His Cat

Tim Kreider (b. 1967) is an author and a cartoonist who created the comic The Pain — When Will It End?, *which appeared in the* Baltimore City Paper *for over a decade. His comics have been collected in three books:* The Pain — When Will It End? *(2004),* Why Do They Kill Me? *(2005), and* Twilight of the Assholes *(2011); his most recent book,* We Learn Nothing *(2013), includes both essays and cartoons. Kreider has also written for the* Comics Journal, Film Quarterly, Men's Journal, *and the* New York Times, *in which the following reflection appeared in 2014.*

I LIVED WITH THE SAME CAT FOR 19 YEARS — by far the longest relationship of my adult life. Under common law, this cat was my wife. I fell asleep at night with the warm, pleasant weight of the cat on my chest. The first thing I saw on most mornings was the foreshortened paw of the cat retreating slowly from my face and her baleful crescent glare informing me that it was Cat Food Time. As I often told her, in a mellow, resonant, Barry White voice: "There is no *luuve* . . . like the *luuve* that exists . . . between a man . . . and his cat."

The cat was jealous of my attention; she liked to sit on whatever I was reading, walked back and forth and back and forth in front of my laptop's screen while I worked, and unsubtly interpolated herself between me and any woman I may have had over. She and my ex Kati Jo, who was temperamentally not dissimilar to the cat, instantly sized each other up as enemies. When I was physically intimate with a woman, the cat did not discreetly absent herself but sat on the edge of the bed with her back to me, facing rather pointedly away from the scene of debauch, quietly exuding disapproval, like your grandmother's ghost.

I realize that people who talk at length about their pets are tedious at best, and often pitiful or repulsive. They post photos of their pets online, tell little stories about them, speak to them in disturbing falsettos, dress

them in elaborate costumes and carry them around in handbags and BabyBjorns, have professional portraits taken of them and retouched to look like old master oil paintings. When people over the age of 10 invite you to a cat birthday party or a funeral for a dog, you need to execute a very deft etiquette maneuver, the equivalent of an Immelmann turn or triple axel, in order to decline without acknowledging that they are, in this area, insane.

This is especially true of childless people, like me, who tend to become emotionally overinvested in their animals and to dote on them in a way that gives onlookers the creeps. Often the pet seems to be a surrogate child, a desperate focus or joint project for a relationship that's lost any other raison d'être, like becoming insufferable foodies or getting

academic literacies rhetorical situations genres processes strategies research MLA / APA media / design readings

heavily into cosplay. When such couples finally have a child their cats or dogs are often bewildered to find themselves unceremoniously demoted to the status of pet; instead of licking the dinner plates clean and piling into bed with Mommy and Daddy, they're given bowls of actual dog food and tied to a metal stake in a circle of dirt.

I looked up how much Americans spend on pets annually and have 5 concluded that you do not want to know. I could tell you what I spent on my own cat's special kidney health cat food and kidney and thyroid medication, and periodic blood tests that cost $300 and always came back normal, but I never calculated my own annual spending, lest I be forced to confront some uncomfortable facts about me. What our mass spending on products to pamper animals who seem happiest while rolling in feces or eating the guts out of rodents — who don't, in fact, seem significantly less happy if they lose half their limbs — tells us about ourselves as a nation is probably also something we don't want to know. But it occurs to me that it may be symptomatic of the same chronic deprivation as are the billion-dollar industries in romance novels and porn.

I've speculated that people have a certain reservoir of affection that they need to express, and in the absence of any more appropriate object — a child or a lover, a parent or a friend — they will lavish that same devotion on a pug or a Manx or a cockatiel, even on something neurologically incapable of reciprocating that emotion, like a monitor lizard or a day trader or an aloe plant. Konrad Lorenz confirms this suspicion in his book "On Aggression," in which he describes how, in the absence of the appropriate triggering stimulus for an instinct, the threshold of stimulus for that instinct is gradually lowered; for instance, a male dove deprived of female doves will attempt to initiate mating with a stuffed pigeon, a rolled-up cloth or any vaguely bird-shaped object, and, eventually, with an empty corner of its cage.

Although I can clearly see this syndrome as pathological in others, I was its medical textbook illustration, the Elephant Man of the condition. I did not post photographs of my cat online or talk about her to people who couldn't be expected to care, but at home, alone with the cat, I behaved like some sort of deranged arch-fop. I made up dozens of nonsensical names for the cat over the years — The Quetzal, Quetzal Marie, Mrs. Quetzal Marie the Cat, The Inquetzulous Q'ang Marie. There was a litany I recited aloud to her every morning, a sort of daily exhortation that began, "Who knows, Miss Cat, what fantastical adventures the two of us will have today?" I had a song I sang to her when I was about to vacuum, a brassy Vegas showstopper called "That Thing You Hate (Is Happening Again)." We collaborated on my foot-pedal pump organ to produce The Hideous Cat Music, in which she walked back and forth at her discretion on the keyboard while I worked the pedals. The Hideous Cat Music resembled the work of the Hungarian composer Gyorgy Ligeti, with aleatory passages and unnervingly sustained tone clusters.

I never meant to become this person. My own cat turned up as a stray at my cabin on the Chesapeake Bay when I was sitting out on the deck eating leftover crabs. She was only a couple of months old then, small enough that my friend Kevin could fit her whole head in his mouth. She appeared from underneath the porch, piteously mewling, and I gave her some cold white crab meat. I did not know then that feeding a stray cat is effectively adopting that cat.

For a few weeks I was in denial about having a cat. My life at that time was not structured to accommodate the responsibility of returning home once every 24 hours to feed an animal. I posted fliers in the post office and grocery store with a drawing of the cat, hoping its owner would reclaim it. It seems significant in retrospect that I never entertained the possibility of taking the cat to the pound.

When I left for a long weekend for a wedding in another state, my friend Gabe explained to me that the cat clearly belonged to me now. I protested. This was a strictly temporary situation until I could locate a new home for the cat, I explained. I was not going to turn into some Cat Guy.

"How would you feel," he asked me, "if you were to get home from this weekend and that cat was gone?"

I moaned and writhed in the passenger seat.

"You're Cat Guy," he said in disgust.

It's amusing now to remember the strict limits I'd originally intended to place on the cat. One of the boundaries I meant to set was that the

10

academic literacies   rhetorical situations   genres   processes   strategies   research MLA / APA   media / design   readings

cat would not be allowed upstairs, where I slept. That edict was short-lived. It was not long before I became wounded when the cat declined to sleep with me.

"You're in *love* with that cat!" my then-girlfriend Margot once   15 accused me. To be fair, she was a very attractive cat. People would comment on it. My friend Ken described her as "a supermodel cat," with green eyes dramatically outlined in what he called "cat mascara" and bright pink "nose leather." Her fur, even at age 19, was rich and soft and pleasant to touch.

Biologists call cats "exploitive captives," an evocative phrase that might be used to describe a lot of relationships, not all of them interspecies. I made the mistake, early on, of feeding the cat first thing in the morning, forgetting that the cat could control when I woke up — by meowing politely, sitting on my chest and staring at me, nudging me insistently with her face, or placing a single claw on my lip. She refused to drink water from a bowl, coveting what she believed was the superior-quality water I drank from a glass. I attempted to demonstrate to the cat that the water we drank was the very same water by pouring it from my glass into her bowl right in front of her, but she was utterly unmoved, like a birther being shown Obama's long-form Hawaiian birth certificate. In the end I gave in and began serving her water in a glass tumbler, which she had to stick her whole face into to drink from.

Sometimes it would strike me that *an animal was living in my house*, and it seemed as surreal as if I had a raccoon or a kinkajou running loose in my house. Yet that animal and I learned, on some level, to understand each other. Although I loved to bury my nose in her fur when she came in from a winter day and inhale deeply of the Coldcat Smell, the cat did not like this one bit, and fled. For a while I would chase her around the house, yelling, "Gimme a little whiff!" and she would hide behind the couch from my hateful touch. Eventually I realized that this was wrong of me. I would instead let her in and pretend to have no interest whatsoever in smelling her, and, after not more than a minute or so the cat would approach me and deign to be smelt. I should really be no less impressed by this accord than if I'd successfully communicated with a Papuan tribesman, or decoded a message from the stars.

Whenever I felt embarrassed about factoring a house pet's desires into major life decisions, some grown-up-sounding part of me told myself, *it's just a cat.* It's generally believed that animals lack what we call consciousness, although we can't quite agree on what exactly this is, and how we can pretend to any certainty about what goes on in an animal's head has never been made clear to me. To anyone who has spent time with an animal, the notion that they have no interior lives seems so counterintuitive, such an obdurate denial of the empathetically self-evident, as to be almost psychotic. I suspect that some of those same psychological mechanisms must have allowed people to rationalize owning other people.

Another part of me, perhaps more sentimental but also more truthful, had to acknowledge that the cat was undeniably another being in the world, experiencing her one chance at being alive, as I was. It always amused me to hit or elongate the word "you" in speaking to the cat, as in, "*Yooouu* would probably *like* that!" because it was funny — and funny often means disquieting and true — to remind myself that there really was another ego in the room with me, with her own likes and dislikes and idiosyncrasies and exasperatingly wrongheaded notions about whose water is better. It did not seem to me like an insoluble epistemological mystery to divine what the cat would like when I woke up and saw her face two inches from mine and the Tentative Paw slowly withdrawing from my lip.

I admit that loving a cat is a lot less complicated than loving a human being. Because animals can't ruin our fantasies about them by talking, they're even more helplessly susceptible to our projections than other humans. Though of course there's a good deal of naked projection and self-delusion involved in loving other human beings, too. [20]

I once read in a book about feng shui that keeping a pet can maintain the chi of your house or apartment when you're not there; the very presence of an animal enlivens and charges the space. Although I suspect feng shui is high-end hooey, I learned when my cat was temporarily put up elsewhere that a house without a cat in it feels very different from a house with one. It feels truly empty, dead. Those moments gave me some foreboding of how my life would feel after she was gone.

academic literacies   rhetorical situations   genres   processes   strategies   research MLA / APA   media / design   readings

We don't know what goes on inside an animal's head; we may doubt whether they have anything we'd call consciousness, and we can't know how much they understand or what their emotions feel like. I will never know what, if anything, the cat thought of me. But I can tell you this: A man who is in a room with a cat — whatever else we might say about that man — is not alone.

Engaging with the Text

1. What seems to be Tim Kreider's **PURPOSE** in writing this reflection? Or does he have more than one?

   ▪ 54–56

2. Kreider uses many **SPECIFIC DETAILS** in his reflection. Identify two paragraphs full of details, and discuss what these contribute to his essay. Which detail in the entire essay do you find most revealing (about either Kreider or the cat), most unexpected, or most amusing? Why?

   ▲ 249

3. Although Kreider maintains a loving, positive overall **STANCE** toward his subject, some parts of the essay do display a more detached or skeptical attitude — the **QUESTIONING, SPECULATIVE TONE** that is characteristic of reflections. Identify two such parts. How would the overall impression the essay makes be different without this variation in stance and tone?

   ▪ 64–67

   ▲ 250

4. Kreider includes a brief **NARRATIVE** in his reflection about how he acquired the cat and turned into "Cat Guy." What does this story add to his reflection? Why do you think he put it in the middle of the essay instead of starting out with it?

   ◆ 419–27

5. *For Writing.* Identify something in your life that has been extremely important to you — a pet, a toy, a friend, a car, a place, or something else. Write a **REFLECTION** on the subject expressing your feelings about it. Make sure you include enough **SPECIFIC DETAILS** to help your audience understand why you feel the way you do about your subject.

   ▲ 245–52
   249

69 Texts That Mix Genres

* academic literacies
■ rhetorical situations
▲ genres
○ processes
◆ strategies
● research MLA / APA
□ media / design
▮ readings

DAVID RAMSEY

I Will Forever Remain Faithful

How Lil Wayne Helped Me Survive My First Year Teaching in New Orleans

David Ramsey (b. 1986) was a social studies and writing teacher in the Recovery School District in New Orleans when he wrote this essay, which first appeared in 2008 in the Oxford American: The Southern Magazine for Good Writing. *He is currently a third-grade teacher at Victory Youth Training Academy in the city's Ninth Ward. His writings on both food and music have been published in magazines such as* Slate *and* Men's Journal *and anthologies such as* Best Music Writing *(2009),* Best American Food Writing *(2011), and* Cornbread Nation 5 *(2010). Ramsey also writes fiction, and in 2010 one of his short stories won an award for fiction given by the University of New Orleans.*

1.

Complex magazine: What do you listen to these days?

Lil Wayne: Me! All day, all me.

2. Like a white person, with blue veins

In my first few weeks teaching in New Orleans' Recovery School District, these were the questions I heard the most from my students:

1. "I gotta use it." (This one might sound like a statement, but it's a request—May I use the bathroom?)
2. "You got an ol' lady?" (the penultimate vowel stretched, lasciviously, as far as it'll go).
3. "Where you from?"
4. "You listen to that Weezy?"

I knew that third question was coming. Like many RSD teachers, I was new, and white, and from out of town. It was the fourth question, however, that seemed to interest my students the most. Dwayne Carter, aka Lil Wayne, aka Weezy F. Baby, was in the midst of becoming the year's biggest rapper, and among the black teenagers that made up my student population, fandom had reached a near-Beatlemania pitch. More than ninety percent of my students cited Lil Wayne on the "Favorite Music" question on the survey I gave them; about half of them repeated the answer on "Favorite Things to Do."

For some of my students, the questions *Where are you from?* and *Do you listen to Lil Wayne?* were close to interchangeable. Their shared currency—as much as neighborhoods or food or slang or trauma—was the stoned musings of Weezy F. Baby.

The answer was, sometimes, yes, I did listen to Lil Wayne. Despite 5 his ubiquitous success, my students were shocked.

"Do you have the mix tapes?" asked Michael, a sixteen-year-old ninth grader. "It's all about the mix tapes."

The following day, he had a stack of CDs for me. Version this, volume that, or no label at all.

And that's just about all I listened to for the rest of the year.

3. My picture should be in the dictionary next to the definition of definition

Lil Wayne slurs, hollers, sings, sighs, bellows, whines, croons, wheezes, coughs, stutters, shouts. He reminds me, in different moments, of two dozen other rappers. In a genre that often demands keeping it real via being repetitive, Lil Wayne is a chameleon, rapping in different octaves, paces, and inflections. Sometimes he sounds like a bluesman, sometimes he sounds like a Muppet baby.

Lil Wayne does his share of gangsta posturing, but half the time 10 he starts chuckling before he gets through a line. He's a ham. He is heavy on pretense, and thank God. Like Dylan, theatricality trumps authenticity.

And yet—even as he tries on a new style for every other song, it is always unmistakably him. I think of Elvis's famous boast, "I don't sound like nobody." I imagine Wayne would flip it: "Don't *nobody* sound like me."

Lil Wayne.

4.

Every few weeks, Michael or another student—for this piece, the names of my students have been changed—would have a new burned CD that was supposedly *Tha Carter III*, Lil Wayne's long-anticipated sixth studio album. "This one's official," they would say. I learned to be skeptical even as I enjoyed the new tracks. Nothing "official" would come around until school was out for summer, but Lil Wayne created hundreds of new songs in 2007 and the first half of 2008. *Vibe* magazine took the time to rank his best seventy-seven songs of 2007, and that was not a comprehensive list. These songs would end up on the Internet, which downloaders could snag for free. He also appeared for guest verses on dozens of other rappers' tracks. He thusly managed to rate as the "Hottest MC in the Game" (according to MTV) and the "Best MC" (according to *Rolling Stone*), despite offering nothing new at the record store.

While Wayne claimed to do every song "at the same ability or hype," the quality varied widely. He wrote nothing down (he was simply too stoned, he explained), rapping off the top of his head every time the spirit moved him, which was pretty much all the time. The results were sometimes tremendous and sometimes awkward, but that was half the fun. His oeuvre ended up being a sort of unedited reality show of his wily subconscious.

5. Ain't 'bout to pick today to start running

During the first few days of school, Darius, one of my homeroom students, kept getting in trouble for leaving classes without permission. At the end of the second day, he pulled me aside to tell me why he kept having to use the bathroom: he had been shot in the leg three times and had a colostomy bag.

When I visited him in the hospital a few weeks later—he was there for follow-up surgery—he told me about the dealers who shot him. Darius's speaking voice is a dead ringer for Lil Wayne's old-man rasp. "I told them, Do what you need to do, you heard me? I ain't scared, you heard me?" 15

Then he leaned over and pointed, laughing, to Sponge Bob on the television.

6.

Lil Wayne, rumor has it, briefly went to the pre-Katrina version of our school. Same name and location, but back then it was a neighborhood

academic literacies | rhetorical situations | genres | processes | strategies | research MLA / APA | media / design | readings

high school. The building was wrecked in the storm. Our school, a charter school, is housed in modulars (my students hate this euphemism—they're trailers) in the lot in back. Sometimes I went and peeked in the windows of the old building, and it looked to me like no one had cleaned or gutted it since the storm. It was like a museum set piece. There was still a poster up announcing an open house, coming September 2005.

7.

I taught fifth-grade social studies, eighth-grade writing, ninth-grade social studies. Sometimes I felt inspired, sometimes deflated.

One time, a black student vehemently defended his one Arab classmate during a discussion about the Jena 6: "If you call him a terrorist, that's like what a cop thinks about us." Another day, when I was introducing new material about Africa, a student interrupted me—"I heard them niggas have AIDS!"

8. Pain, since I've lost you—I'm lost too

Our students are afraid of rain. A heavy morning shower can cut atten- 20 dance in half. I once had a student write an essay about her experience in the Superdome. She wrote, without explanation, that she lost her memory when she lost her grandmother in the storm. I was supposed to correct the grammar, so that she would be prepared for state testing in the spring.

9. Keep your mouth closed and let your eyes listen

Lil Wayne is five-foot-six and wiry, sleepy-eyed, covered in tattoos, including teardrops under his eyes. His two camera poses are a cool tilt of the head and a sneer. He means to look sinister, I think, but there is something actually huggable about him. He looks like he could be one of my students—and some of my students like to think they look like him.

The other day, I saw Cornel West on television say that Lil Wayne's physical body bears witness to tragedy. I don't even know what that means, but I do think that Wayne's artistic persona is a testament to *damage.*

10.

One of my favorite Lil Wayne hooks is the chorus on a Playaz Circle song called "Duffle Bag Boy." In the past year, he started singing more, and this was his best turn. He sounds a little like the neighborhood drunk at first as he warbles his way up and down the tune, but his singing voice has an organically exultant quality that seems to carry him to emotional delirium. After a while, he's belting out instructions to a drug courier with the breathy urgency of a Baptist hymn. By the end of the song, the standard-order macho boast, "I ain't never ran from a nigga and I damn sure ain't 'bout to pick today to start running," has been turned by Lil Wayne into a plea, a soul lament.

11.

On New Orleans radio, it seems like nearly every song features Lil Wayne. My kids sang his songs in class, in the hallways, before school, after school. I had a student who would rap a Lil Wayne line if he didn't know the answer to a question.

　　An eighth grader wrote his Persuasive Essay on the topic "Lil Wayne 25 is the best rapper alive." Main ideas for three body paragraphs: *Wayne has the most tracks and most hits, best metaphors and similes, competition is fake.*

12. My flow is art, unique—my flow can part a sea

Once I witnessed a group of students huddled around a speaker listening to Lil Wayne. They had heard these songs before, but were nonetheless gushing and guffawing over nearly every line. One of them, bored and quiet in my classroom, was enthusiastically, if vaguely, parsing each lyric for his classmates: "You hear that? *Cleaner than a virgin in detergent.* Think on that."

academic literacies　rhetorical situations　genres　processes　strategies　research MLA / APA　media / design　readings

Pulling out the go-to insult of high schoolers everywhere, a girl nearby questioned their sexuality. "Y'all be into Lil Wayne so much you sound like girls," she said.

They just kept listening. Then one of the boys was simply overtaken by a lyrical turn. He stood up, threw up his hands, and began hollering. "I don't care!" he shouted. "No homo, no homo, but that boy is cute!"

13.

Lil Wayne on making it: "When you're really rich, then asparagus is yummy."

Lil Wayne on safe sex: "Better wear a latex, cause you don't want that late text, that 'I think I'm late' text." 30

Lil Wayne on possibly less safe sex: "How come there is two women, but ain't no two Waynes?"

14.

Okay, but it's not any one line, it's that *voice*. Just the way he says "car in park" in his cameo on Mario's "Crying Out for Me" remix; it's a soft growl from another planet. It sounds like a threat and a comfort and a come-on all at once.

15. I am just a Martian, ain't nobody else on this planet

Right before you become a teacher, you are told by all manner of folks that it will be (1) the hardest thing you've ever done, and (2) the best thing you've ever done. That seems like a recipe for recruiting wannabe martyrs. In any case, high stakes can blind you to the best moments. One day, I was stressing over what I imagined was my one-man quest to keep Darius in school and out of jail, and missed that a heated dispute between two fifth graders was escalating. Finally, I asked them what was wrong.

"Mr. Ramsey," one of the boys pleaded, "will you *please* tell him that if you go into space for a year and come back to Earth that all your family will be dead because time moves slower in space?"

**16. And to the kids: drugs kill. I'm acknowledging that.
But when I'm on the drugs, I don't have a problem with that.**

On one of his best songs, the super-catchy "I Feel Like Dying," Lil Wayne 35
barely exists. He always sounds high, but on this song he sounds as
though he has already passed out.

A lot of the alarmism about pop music sending the wrong message
to impressionable youth seems mostly overwrought to me, but I'll cop
to feeling taken aback at ten-year-olds singing, "Only once the drugs are
done, do I feel like dying, I feel like dying."

First time I heard a fifth grader singing this in falsetto, I said: "*What
did you say?*"

He said: "Mr. Ramsey, you know you be listening to that song. Why
you tripping?"

My students always ask me why I'm tripping at precisely the
moments when the answer seems incredibly obvious to me.

17.

After Michael cussed out our vice principal, I did a home visit. Michael 40
was one of the biggest drug dealers in his neighborhood, and also one
of my best students.

His mother was roused from bed. She looked half-gone, dazed. Then
she started crying, and hugged me, pulled my head into her body. "No
one's ever cared like this," she said. "Bless you. Thank you."

Michael smiled shyly. "I just want to get in my right grade," he told me.

"We'll find a way to make that happen," I told him.

A few weeks later, I gave him a copy of a *New Yorker* piece on Lil Wayne.

"Actually, that was good," he said, later. "You teach me to write like 45
that?"

18. Born in New Orleans, raised in New Orleans . . .

You live here as a newcomer and locals are fond of saying "this is New
Orleans" or "welcome to New Orleans" by way of explanation. They use it
to explain absurdity, inefficiency, arbitrary disaster, and transcendent fun.

✳ academic literacies   ▪ rhetorical situations   ▲ genres   ○ processes   ◆ strategies   ● research MLA / APA   ▢ media / design   ◧ readings

Enormous holes in the middle of major streets, say, or a drunken man dressed as an insect in line behind you at the convenience store.

Our challenge in the schools is to try to reform a broken system (the "recovery" in Recovery School District doesn't refer to the storm—the district was created before Katrina, when the state took over the city's failing schools) amidst a beautiful culture that is sometimes committed to cutting folks a little slack.

I have heard the following things speciously defended or excused by New Orleans culture: truancy, low test scores, drug and alcohol addiction, extended families showing up within the hour to settle minor school-boy scuffles, inept bureaucracy, lazy teachers, students showing up hungover the day after Mother's Day . . . .

19.

Once, a girl's older sister looked askance at one of my best students after school, and about five minutes later there was a full-on brawl in the parking lot. I lost my grip on the student I was holding back and she jumped on top of another student's mother and started pounding.

On the pavement in front of me was a weave and a little bit of blood. 50 One of my ninth graders was watching the chaos gleefully while I tried to figure out how to make myself useful. He was as happy as I've ever seen him. He shrugged beatifically. "This is *New Orleans!*" he shouted, to me, to himself, to anyone who might be listening.

20.

Sometimes my students tell me they are sick of talking about the storm. Sometimes it's all they want to talk about. Might be the same student. Some students have told me it ruined their lives, some students have told me it saved their lives. Again, sometimes the same student will say both.

21.

From an interview in early 2006:

AllHipHop.com: On the album, did you ever contemplate doing a whole track dedicated to the Hurricane Katrina tragedy?

Lil Wayne: No, because I'm from New Orleans, brother. Our main focus is to move ahead and move on. You guys are not from New Orleans and keep throwing it in our face, like, 'Well, how do you feel about Hurricane Katrina?' I f—king feel f—ked up. I have no f—king city or home to go to. My mother has no home, her people have no home, and their people have no home. Every f—king body has no home. So do I want to dedicate something to Hurricane Katrina? Yeah, tell that b—h to suck my d—k. That is my dedication.

22. I am the beast! Feed me rappers or feed me beats.

Lil Wayne mentions Katrina in his songs from time to time. He has a track that rails against Bush for his response to the storm. But, to his credit, he doesn't wallow in his city's famous tragedy.

The world needs to be told, and reminded, of what happened here. But New Orleans is bigger and more spirited than the storm. So its favorite son can be forgiven for refusing to let it define him. For my students, Lil Wayne is good times and good memories, and enduring hometown pride. All they ask of him is to keep making rhymes, as triumphant and strange as the city itself.

23. Ever since I was little, I lived life numb.

Michael stopped coming to school. His mother told me, "He's a man now. There's nothing more I can do." 55

Darius got kicked out for physically attacking a teacher.

I have lots of happy stories, so I don't mean to dwell on these two, but I guess that's just what teachers do in the summer months, replay the ones that got away.

24.

I read over this, and I got it all wrong. I fetishize disaster. I live in the best city in the world and all I can write about is hurricanes and dropouts.

academic literacies | rhetorical situations | genres | processes | strategies | research MLA / APA | media / design | readings

25.

One time, after they finished a big test I gave them last period, my students started happily singing Lil Wayne's "La La La" on their way outside.

"Come on, Ramsey, sing along, you know it."   60

And so I did. "Born in New Orleans, raised in New Orleans, I will forever remain faithful New Orleans. . . ."

That I *wasn't* from New Orleans didn't much matter, so long as I was game to clap and dance and sing. It was a clear and sunny day, Lil Wayne was the greatest rapper alive, and school was out. It was time to have fun.

Engaging with the Text

1. This essay both narrates a first year teaching and reviews Lil Wayne's music. What is the **PURPOSE** of the essay? What are we meant to take away from it? How are David Ramsey's students and Lil Wayne's lyrics related?

   55–56

2. How does Ramsey **ORGANIZE** his text? Why do you think he chose to organize it in this way? What role do the **HEADINGS** play in the organization? What is the source of those headings?

   268
   604–5

3. Ramsey notes that New Orleans natives often say to newcomers, "this is New Orleans." What does that phrase mean? How is it used in the essay?

4. Throughout his essay, Ramsey inserts **DIALOGUE**. How does the dialogue function in this essay? Whom does he quote, and how is their role central to the essay?

   408–31

5. *For Writing.* Select a favorite artist, and think about how that artist's work relates to something or someone else. Write an essay **ANALYZING** or **REFLECTING** on his or her work. Include images of the work. If you write about a musician and are writing online, add audio.

   94–128
   245–52

ANU PARTANEN

Finland's School Success
What Americans Keep Ignoring

Anu Partanen (b. 1975) is a Finnish writer who splits her time between Finland and the United States and writes for both Finnish- and English-language magazines and newspapers, including the Atlantic, *the* New York Times, *and* Fortune. *She has also worked on the Finnish television show* Pressiklubi (The Press Club), *where she debated news trends and current affairs, and taught magazine writing at a Finnish university. The following essay appeared in the* Atlantic *in 2011.*

EVERYONE AGREES the United States needs to improve its education system dramatically, but how? One of the hottest trends in education reform lately is looking at the stunning success of the West's reigning education superpower, Finland. Trouble is, when it comes to the lessons that Finnish schools have to offer, most of the discussion seems to be missing the point.

The small Nordic country of Finland used to be known—if it was known for anything at all—as the home of Nokia, the mobile phone giant. But lately Finland has been attracting attention on global surveys of quality of life—*Newsweek* ranked it number one last year—and Finland's national education system has been receiving particular praise, because in recent years Finnish students have been turning in some of the highest test scores in the world.

Finland's schools owe their newfound fame primarily to one study: the PISA survey, conducted every three years by the Organization for Economic Co-operation and Development (OECD). The survey compares 15-year-olds in different countries in reading, math, and science. Finland has ranked at or near the top in all three competencies on every survey since 2000, neck and neck with superachievers such as South Korea and Singapore. In the most recent survey in 2009 Finland slipped slightly, with students in Shanghai, China, taking the best scores, but

academic literacies · rhetorical situations · genres · processes · strategies · research MLA / APA · media / design · readings

Finnish schools assign less homework and engage children in more creative play.

the Finns are still near the very top. Throughout the same period, the PISA performance of the United States has been middling, at best.

Compared with the stereotype of the East Asian model—long hours of exhaustive cramming and rote memorization—Finland's success is especially intriguing because Finnish schools assign less homework and engage children in more creative play. All this has led to a continuous stream of foreign delegations making the pilgrimage to Finland to visit schools and talk with the nation's education experts, and constant coverage in the worldwide media marveling at the Finnish miracle.

So there was considerable interest in a recent visit to the U.S. by   5
one of the leading Finnish authorities on education reform, Pasi Sahlberg, director of the Finnish Ministry of Education's Center for International Mobility and author of the new book *Finnish Lessons: What Can the World Learn from Educational Change in Finland?* Earlier this month, Sahlberg stopped by the Dwight School in New York City to speak with educators and students, and his visit received national media attention and generated much discussion.

And yet it wasn't clear that Sahlberg's message was actually getting through. As Sahlberg put it to me later, there are certain things nobody in America really wants to talk about.

During the afternoon that Sahlberg spent at the Dwight School, a photographer from the *New York Times* jockeyed for position with Dan Rather's TV crew as Sahlberg participated in a roundtable chat with students. The subsequent article in the *Times* about the event would focus on Finland as an "intriguing school-reform model."

Yet one of the most significant things Sahlberg said passed practically unnoticed. "Oh," he mentioned at one point, "and there are no private schools in Finland."

This notion may seem difficult for an American to digest, but it's true. Only a small number of independent schools exist in Finland, and even they are all publicly financed. None is allowed to charge tuition fees. There are no private universities, either. This means that practically every person in Finland attends public school, whether for pre-K or a Ph.D.

The irony of Sahlberg's making this comment during a talk at the   10
Dwight School seemed obvious. Like many of America's best schools, Dwight is a private institution that costs high-school students upward of $35,000 a year to attend—not to mention that Dwight, in particular, is run for profit, an increasing trend in the U.S. Yet no one in the room commented on Sahlberg's statement. I found this surprising. Sahlberg himself did not.

Sahlberg knows what Americans like to talk about when it comes to education, because he's become their go-to guy in Finland. The son of two teachers, he grew up in a Finnish school. He taught mathematics and physics in a junior high school in Helsinki, worked his way through a variety of positions in the Finnish Ministry of Education, and spent years as an education expert at the OECD, the World Bank, and other international organizations.

Now, in addition to his other duties, Sahlberg hosts about a hundred visits a year by foreign educators, including many Americans, who want to know the secret of Finland's success. Sahlberg's new book is partly an attempt to help answer the questions he always gets asked.

academic literacies   rhetorical situations   genres   processes   strategies   research MLA / APA   media / design   readings

From his point of view, Americans are consistently obsessed with certain questions: How can you keep track of students' performance if you don't test them constantly? How can you improve teaching if you have no accountability for bad teachers or merit pay for good teachers? How do you foster competition and engage the private sector? How do you provide school choice?

The answers Finland provides seem to run counter to just about everything America's school reformers are trying to do.

For starters, Finland has no standardized tests. The only exception   15
is what's called the National Matriculation Exam, which everyone takes at the end of a voluntary upper-secondary school, roughly the equivalent of American high school.

Instead, the public school system's teachers are trained to assess children in classrooms using independent tests they create themselves. All children receive a report card at the end of each semester, but these reports are based on individualized grading by each teacher. Periodically, the Ministry of Education tracks national progress by testing a few sample groups across a range of different schools.

As for accountability of teachers and administrators, Sahlberg shrugs. "There's no word for accountability in Finnish," he later told an audience at the Teachers College of Columbia University. "Accountability is something that is left when responsibility has been subtracted."

For Sahlberg what matters is that in Finland all teachers and administrators are given prestige, decent pay, and a lot of responsibility. A master's degree is required to enter the profession, and teacher training programs are among the most selective professional schools in the country. If a teacher is bad, it is the principal's responsibility to notice and deal with it.

And while Americans love to talk about competition, Sahlberg points out that nothing makes Finns more uncomfortable. In his book Sahlberg quotes a line from a Finnish writer named Samuli Paronen: "Real winners do not compete." It's hard to think of a more un-American idea, but when it comes to education, Finland's success shows that the Finnish attitude might have merits. There are no lists of best schools or teachers in Finland. The main driver of education policy is not competition between teachers and between schools, but cooperation.

Finally, in Finland, school choice is noticeably not a priority, nor is 20
engaging the private sector at all. Which brings us back to the silence
after Sahlberg's comment at the Dwight School that schools like Dwight
don't exist in Finland.

"Here in America," Sahlberg said at the Teachers College, "parents
can choose to take their kids to private schools. It's the same idea of a
marketplace that applies to, say, shops. Schools are a shop and parents
can buy what ever they want. In Finland parents can also choose. But
the options are all the same."

Herein lay the real shocker. As Sahlberg continued, his core message
emerged, whether or not anyone in his American audience heard it.

Decades ago, when the Finnish school system was badly in need of
reform, the goal of the program that Finland instituted, resulting in so
much success today, was never excellence. It was equity.

Since the 1980s, the main driver of Finnish education policy has been
the idea that every child should have exactly the same opportunity to
learn, regardless of family background, income, or geographic location.
Education has been seen first and foremost not as a way to produce star
performers, but as an instrument to even out social inequality.

In the Finnish view, as Sahlberg describes it, this means that 25
schools should be healthy, safe environments for children. This starts
with the basics. Finland offers all pupils free school meals, easy access
to health care, psychological counseling, and individualized student
guidance.

In fact, since academic excellence wasn't a particular priority on
the Finnish to-do list, when Finland's students scored so high on the
first PISA survey in 2001, many Finns thought the results must be a
mistake. But subsequent PISA tests confirmed that Finland—unlike, say,
very similar countries such as Norway—was producing academic excellence through its particular policy focus on equity.

That this point is almost always ignored or brushed aside in the
U.S. seems especially poignant at the moment, after the financial crisis
and Occupy Wall Street movement have brought the problems of inequality in America into such sharp focus. The chasm between those who can

academic literacies | rhetorical situations | genres | processes | strategies | research MLA / APA | media / design | readings

afford $35,000 in tuition per child per year—or even just the price of a house in a good public school district—and the other "99 percent" is painfully plain to see.

Pasi Sahlberg goes out of his way to emphasize that his book *Finnish Lessons* is not meant as a how-to guide for fixing the education systems of other countries. All countries are different, and as many Americans point out, Finland is a small nation with a much more homogeneous population than the United States.

Yet Sahlberg doesn't think that questions of size or homogeneity should give Americans reason to dismiss the Finnish example. Finland is a relatively homogeneous country—as of 2010, just 4.6 percent of Finnish residents had been born in another country, compared with 12.7 percent in the United States. But the number of foreign-born residents in Finland doubled during the decade leading up to 2010, and the country didn't lose its edge in education. Immigrants tended to concentrate in certain areas, causing some schools to become much more mixed than others, yet there has not been much change in the remarkable lack of variation between Finnish schools in the PISA surveys across the same period.

Samuel Abrams, a visiting scholar at Columbia University's Teachers College, has addressed the effects of size and homogeneity on a nation's education performance by comparing Finland with another Nordic country: Norway. Like Finland, Norway is small and not especially diverse overall, but unlike Finland it has taken an approach to education that is more American than Finnish. The result? Mediocre performance in the PISA survey. Educational policy, Abrams suggests, is probably more important to the success of a country's school system than the nation's size or ethnic makeup.

Indeed, Finland's population of 5.4 million can be compared to many an American state—after all, most American education is managed at the state level. According to the Migration Policy Institute, a research organization in Washington, there were 18 states in the U.S. in 2010 with an identical or significantly smaller percentage of foreign-born residents than Finland.

What's more, despite their many differences, Finland and the U.S. have an educational goal in common. When Finnish policymakers decided to reform the country's education system in the 1970s, they did so because they realized that to be competitive, Finland couldn't rely on manufacturing or its scant natural resources and instead had to invest in a knowledge-based economy.

With America's manufacturing industries now in decline, the goal of educational policy in the U.S.—as articulated by most everyone from President Obama on down—is to preserve American competitiveness by doing the same thing. Finland's experience suggests that to win at that game, a country has to prepare not just some of its population well, but all of its population well, for the new economy. To possess some of the best schools in the world might still not be good enough if there are children being left behind.

Is that an impossible goal? Sahlberg says that while his book isn't meant to be a how-to manual, it is meant to be a "pamphlet of hope."

"When President Kennedy was making his appeal for advancing 　35 American science and technology by putting a man on the moon by the end of the 1960's, many said it couldn't be done," Sahlberg said during his visit to New York. "But he had a dream. Just like Martin Luther King a few years later had a dream. Those dreams came true. Finland's dream was that we want to have a good public education for every child regardless of where they go to school or what kind of families they come from, and many even in Finland said it couldn't be done."

Clearly, many were wrong. It is possible to create equality. And perhaps even more important—as a challenge to the American way of thinking about education reform—Finland's experience shows that it is possible to achieve excellence by focusing not on competition, but on cooperation, and not on choice, but on equity.

The problem facing education in America isn't the ethnic diversity of the population but the economic inequality of society, and this is precisely the problem that Finnish education reform addressed. More equity at home might just be what America needs to be more competitive abroad.

Engaging with the Text

1. According to this essay, what are some of the major differences between how schools are run in the United States and how they are run in Finland? Identify at least three differences, pointing to the sentences that reveal them.

2. What is the answer to the implied question in the **TITLE** of this essay? What do Americans keep ignoring about Finland's school success? Why do you think Americans have not adopted the Finnish system of education? How would a similar system fare in the United States?

344–45

3. Anu Partanen **ENDS** her essay by saying, "the problem facing education in America . . . [is] the economic inequality of society. . . . More equity at home might just be what America needs to be more competitive abroad." Do you agree with her conclusion? Why or why not?

338–42

4. What kind of **EVIDENCE** does Partanen provide to support her argument? How does she use **SOURCES**? How convincing is the evidence and the sources of it?

359–67
445–68

5. *For Writing.* Write an essay responding to Partanen's argument. Do you believe the Finnish system would improve education in the United States, or not? For another perspective, you might read Jonathan Kozol's essay "Fremont High School" on page 716. In your essay, you might mix several genres—to **ARGUE** your own position, **EVALUATE** schools you've attended, and **REFLECT** on your own education.

156–82
197–205
245–52

JEREMY DOWSETT

What My Bike Has Taught Me about White Privilege

Jeremy Dowsett (b. 1979) is a writer and a pastor at a church in Lansing, Michigan. He maintains a blog titled A Little More Sauce, *where he explores topics such as white privilege, racism, and religion. Many of these posts echo points made in his Western Michigan University honors thesis, "Toward an Authentically Anti-Racist Curriculum." The following essay is a 2014 post on* A Little More Sauce *that later appeared in* Quartz, *a digital business news publication.*

THE PHRASE **"WHITE PRIVILEGE"** is one that rubs a lot of white people the wrong way. It can trigger something in them that shuts down conversation or at least makes them very defensive. (Especially those who grew up relatively less privileged than other folks around them.) And I've seen more than once where this happens and the next move in the conversation is for the person who brought up white privilege to say, "The reason you're getting defensive is because you're feeling the discomfort of having your privilege exposed."

I'm sure that's true sometimes. And I'm sure there are a lot of people, white and otherwise, who can attest to a kind of a-ha moment or paradigm shift where they "got" what privilege means and they did realize they had been getting defensive because they were uncomfortable at having their privilege exposed. But I would guess that more often than not, the frustration and the shutting down is about something else. It comes from the fact that nobody wants to be a racist. And the move "you only think that because you're looking at this from the perspective of privilege" or the more terse and confrontational "check your privilege!" kind of sound like an accusation that someone is a racist (if they don't already understand privilege). And the phrase "white privilege" kind of sounds like, "You are a racist and there's nothing you can do about it because you were born that way."

And if this were what "white privilege" meant—which it is not—defensiveness and frustration would be the appropriate response. But privilege talk is not intended to make a moral assessment or a moral claim about the privileged at all. It is about systemic imbalance. It is about injustices that have arisen because of the history of racism that birthed the way things are now. It's not saying, "You're a bad person because you're white." It's saying, "The system is skewed in ways that you maybe haven't realized or had to think about precisely because it's skewed in YOUR favor."

I am white. So I have not experienced racial privilege from the "under" side firsthand. But my children (and a lot of other people I love) are not white. And so I care about privilege and what it means for racial justice in our country. And one experience I have had firsthand, which has helped me to understand privilege and listen to privilege talk without feeling defensive, is riding my bike.

Now, I know, it sounds a little goofy at first. But stick with me. 5 Because I think that this analogy might help some white people understand privilege talk without feeling like they're having their character attacked.

About five years ago I decide to start riding my bike as my primary mode of transportation. As in, on the street, in traffic. Which is enjoyable for a number of reasons (exercise, wind in yer face, the cool feeling of going fast, etc.). But the thing is, I don't live in Portland or Minneapolis. I live in the capital city of the epicenter of the auto industry: Lansing, Michigan. This is not, by any stretch, a bike-friendly town. And often, it is downright dangerous to be a bike commuter here.

Now sometimes it's dangerous for me because people in cars are just blatantly a**holes to me. If I am in the road—where I legally belong—people will yell at me to get on the sidewalk. If I am on the sidewalk—which is sometimes the safest place to be—people will yell at me to get on the road. People in cars think it's funny to roll down their window and yell something right when they get beside me. Or to splash me on purpose. People I have never met are angry at me for just being on a bike in "their" road and they let me know with colorful language and other acts of aggression.

I can imagine that for people of color life in a white-majority context feels a bit like being on a bicycle in midst of traffic. They have the right to be on the road, and laws on the books to make it equitable, but that doesn't change the fact that they are on a bike in a world made for cars. Experiencing this when I'm on my bike in traffic has helped me to understand what privilege talk is really about.

Now most people in cars are not intentionally aggressive toward me. But even if all the jerks had their licenses revoked tomorrow, the road would still be a dangerous place for me. Because the whole transportation infrastructure privileges the automobile. It is born out of a history rooted in the auto industry that took for granted that everyone should use a car as their mode of transportation. It was not built to be convenient or economical or safe for me.

And so people in cars—nice, non-aggressive people—put me in danger all the time because they see the road from the privileged perspective of a car. E.g., I ride on the right side of the right lane. Some people fail to change lanes to pass me (as they would for another car) or even give me a wide berth. Some people fly by just inches from me not realizing how scary/dangerous that is for me (like if I were to swerve to miss some roadkill just as they pass). These folks aren't aggressive or hostile toward me, but they don't realize that a pothole or a buildup of gravel or a broken bottle, which they haven't given me enough room to avoid—because in

academic literacies   rhetorical situations   genres   processes   strategies   research MLA / APA   media / design   readings

a car they don't need to be aware of these things—could send me flying from my bike or cost me a bent rim or a flat tire.

So the semi driver who rushes past throwing gravel in my face in his hot wake isn't necessarily a bad guy. He could be sitting in his cab listening to Christian radio and thinking about nice things he can do for his wife. But the fact that "the system" allows him to do those things instead of being mindful of me is a privilege he has that I don't. (I have to be hyper-aware of him.)

This is what privilege is about. Like drivers, nice, non-aggressive white people can move in the world without thinking about the "pot-holes" or the "gravel" that people of color have to navigate, or how things that they do—not intending to hurt or endanger anyone—might actually be making life more difficult or more dangerous for a person of color.

Nice, non-aggressive drivers that don't do anything at all to endanger me are still privileged to pull out of their driveway each morning and know that there are roads that go all the way to their destination. They don't have to wonder if there are bike lanes and what route they will take to stay safe. In the winter, they can be certain that the snow will be plowed out of their lane into my lane and not the other way around.

And it's not just the fact that the whole transportation infrastructure is built around the car. It's the law, which is poorly enforced when cyclists are hit by cars, the fact that gas is subsidized by the government and bike tires aren't, and just the general mindset of a culture that is in love with cars after a hundred years of propaganda and still thinks that bikes are toys for kids and triathletes.

So when I say the semi driver is privileged, it isn't a way of calling   15 him a bad person or a man-slaughterer or saying he didn't really earn his truck, but just a way of acknowledging all that—infrastructure, laws, gov't, culture—and the fact that if he and I get in a collision, I will probably die and he will just have to clean the blood off of his bumper. In the same way, talking about *racial* privilege isn't a way of telling white people they are bad people or racists or that they didn't really earn what they have.

It's a way of trying to make visible the fact that the system is not neutral, it is not a level playing field, it's not the same experience for everyone. There are biases and imbalances and injustices built into the warp and woof of our culture. (The recent events in Ferguson, Missouri, should be evidence enough of this—more thoughts on that here.*) Not because you personally are a racist, but because the system has a history and was built around this category "race" and that's not going to go away overnight (or even in 100 years). To go back to my analogy: Bike lanes are relatively new, and still just kind of an appendage on a system that is inherently car-centric.

So—white readers—the next time someone drops the p-word, try to remember they aren't calling you a racist or saying you didn't really earn your college degree, they just want you to try to empathize with how scary it is to be on a bike sometimes (metaphorically speaking).

One last thing: Now, I know what it is like to be a white person engaged in racial reconciliation or justice work and to feel like privilege language is being used to silence you or to feel frustrated that you are genuinely trying to be a part of the solution not the problem but every time you open your mouth someone says, "Check your privilege." (I.e., even though privilege language doesn't mean "You are one of the bad guys," some people do use it that way.) So if you'll permit me to get a few more miles out of this bike analogy (ya see what I did there?), I think it can help encourage white folks who have felt that frustration to stay engaged and stay humble.

I have a lot of "conversations" with drivers. Now, rationally, I know that most drivers are not jerks. But I have a long and consistent history of bad experiences with drivers and so, when I've already been honked at or yelled at that day, or when I've read a blog post about a fellow cyclist who's been mowed down by a careless driver, it's hard for me to stay civil.

But when I'm not so civil with a "privileged" driver, it's not because I hate him/her, or think s/he is evil. It's because it's the third time that day I got some gravel in the face. So try to remember that even if you don't feel like a "semi driver," a person of color might be experiencing you the way a person on a bike experiences being passed by a semi. Even if you're listening to Christian radio.

20

———————

*http://alittlemoresauce.com/2014/08/27/the-death-of-mike-brown-and-the-death-of-the-church/

Engaging with the Text

1. Jeremy Dowsett **DEFINES** "privilege talk" as "not intended to make a moral assessment or a moral claim about the privileged at all. It is about systemic imbalance. It is about injustices that have arisen because of the history of racism that birthed the way things are now. It's not saying, 'You're a bad person because you're white.' It's saying, 'The system is skewed in ways that you maybe haven't realized or had to think about precisely because it's skewed in YOUR favor.'" Does this definition help you understand the concept of "white privilege"? Do you think his definition is correct? Why or why not?

   388–98

2. A successful text that mixes genres offers a **CLEAR FOCUS**. What is Dowsett's focus for his essay? How clear and successful is it?

   268

3. Dowsett is clearly writing for an audience that doesn't understand the concept of "white privilege." Identify two specific passages that reveal this intended **AUDIENCE**.

   57–60

4. To help his audience understand the concept of "white privilege," Dowsett compares it to the experience of car drivers who both see and don't see bike riders and as a consequence don't treat them respectfully on the road. How successful do you find this **COMPARISON** for Dowsett's purpose? What other comparison might he have made?

   380–87

5. **For Writing.** Select a concept involving relationships between people, such as patriarchy, political correctness, or helicopter parenting, and **COMPARE** it to a subject with which your targeted audience would be more familiar to help them understand your perspective on the concept. Be sure to offer a **DEFINITION** of your concept and clearly explain your **ANALOGY** for it.

   380–87

   388–98
   386

ALISON BECHDEL

Fun Home

*Alison Bechdel (b. 1960) became a cartoonist and writer after growing
up in Lock Haven, Pennsylvania, where both her parents were high school
English teachers; her father also ran a family-owned funeral home that his
children called the "fun home." This selection is from* Fun Home: A Family Tragicomic *(2006), a best-selling graphic memoir that was made into
an award-winning Broadway musical. In it, Bechdel chronicles her childhood and her coming to recognize both her own homosexuality and her
father's, which she learned of only after his death. Before publishing* Fun
Home, *she had become known for her cartoon strip* Dykes to Watch Out
For, *which followed the lives of a group of lesbian characters over twenty-
five years; the strips were published in gay and lesbian newspapers and
eventually on the web, as well as in twelve book-length collections. In
2012, Bechdel published another graphic memoir,* Are You My Mother?, *
which focuses on her relationship with her mother. Bechdel's work has also
appeared in* Ms., Slate, *the* Village Voice, *the* Advocate, Out, *and many
comic books and anthologies.*

academic
literacies
rhetorical
situations
genres
processes
strategies
research
MLA / APA
media /
design
readings

TWO NIGHTS BEFORE MY FATHER DIED, I DREAMED THAT I WAS OUT AT THE BULLPEN WITH HIM. THERE WAS A GLORIOUS SUNSET VISIBLE THROUGH THE TREES.

DAD! C'MON! LET'S GO UP THE HILL AND SEE IT!

AT FIRST HE IGNORED ME. I RACED OVER THE VELVETY MOSS IN MY BARE FEET.

HURRY UP! IT'S AMAZING!

WHEN HE FINALLY GOT THERE, THE SUN HAD SUNK BEHIND THE HORIZON AND THE BRILLIANT COLORS WERE GONE.

YOU MISSED IT! GOD, IT WAS BEAUTIFUL!

IF THIS WAS A PREMONITORY DREAM, I CAN ONLY SAY THAT ITS CONDOLENCE-CARD ASSOCIATION OF DEATH WITH A SETTING SUN IS MAUDLIN IN THE EXTREME.

YET MY FATHER DID POSSESS A CERTAIN RADIANCE--

--PERHAPS DUE TO HIS HABIT OF EXCESSIVE, EVEN IDOLATROUS, SUNBATHING--

OFF TO CHURCH

--AND SO HIS DEATH HAD AN INEVITABLY DIMMING, CREPUSCULAR EFFECT. MY COUSIN EVEN POSTPONED HIS ANNUAL FIREWORKS DISPLAY THE NIGHT BEFORE THE FUNERAL.

WHY?

WELL, UH...OUT OF RESPECT FOR YOUR DAD.

I HAD BEEN HOPING FOR A MORE BLUNT RESPONSE, LIKE, "BECAUSE YOUR FATHER JUST DIED, YOU IDIOT."

MY NUMBNESS, ALONG WITH ALL THE MEALY-MOUTHED MOURNING, WAS MAKING ME IRRITABLE. WHAT WOULD HAPPEN IF WE SPOKE THE TRUTH?

I DIDN'T FIND OUT.

WHEN I THINK ABOUT HOW MY FATHER'S STORY MIGHT HAVE TURNED OUT DIFFERENTLY, A GEOGRAPHICAL RELOCATION IS USUALLY INVOLVED.

BEECH CREEK — Bruce Bechdel, 44, of Maple Avenue, Beech Creek, well-known funeral director and high school teacher, died of multiple injuries suffered when he was struck by a tractor-trailer along Route 150, about two miles north of Beech Creek at 11:10 a.m. Wednesday.

He was pronounced dead on arrival at Lock Haven Hospital while standing on the berm, police said.

Bechdel was born in Beech Creek on April 8, 1936 and was the son of Dorothy Bechdel, who survives and lives in Beech Creek, and the late Claude H. Bechdel.

He operated the Bruce A. Bechdel Funeral Home in Beech Creek and was also an English teacher at Bald Eagle-Nittany

Institute of Mortuary Science.

He served in the U. S. Army in Germany.

Bechdel was president of the Clinton County Historical Society and was instrumental in the restoration of the Heisey Museum after the 1972 flood and in 1978 he and his wife, the former Helen Fontana, received the annual Clinton County Historical Society preservation ... for the work at their 10-...ctorian house in Beech

IF ONLY HE'D BEEN ABLE TO ESCAPE THE GRAVITATIONAL TUG OF BEECH CREEK, I TELL MYSELF, HIS PARTICULAR SUN MIGHT NOT HAVE SET IN SO PRECIPITATE A MANNER.

gardening and stepped onto the roadway. He was struck by the right front portion of the truck

degree from The Pennsylvania State University. He was also a graduate of the Pittsburgh

...s a member of the ...n Society of America, ...d of directors of the ...k Playhouse, National Council of Teachers of English, Phi Kappa Psi fraternity and was a deacon at the Blanchard

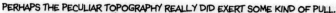

PERHAPS THE PECULIAR TOPOGRAPHY REALLY DID EXERT SOME KIND OF PULL.

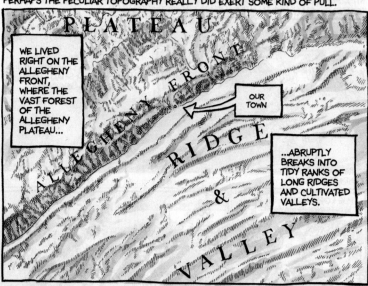

PLATEAU

WE LIVED RIGHT ON THE ALLEGHENY FRONT, WHERE THE VAST FOREST OF THE ALLEGHENY PLATEAU...

ALLEGHENY FRONT

OUR TOWN

...ABRUPTLY BREAKS INTO TIDY RANKS OF LONG RIDGES AND CULTIVATED VALLEYS.

RIDGE & VALLEY

THE APPALACHIAN RIDGES--MANY LONGER THAN HADRIAN'S WALL--HISTORICALLY DISCOURAGED CULTURAL EXCHANGE. MY GRANDMOTHER, FOR EXAMPLE, WAS A BECHDEL EVEN BEFORE SHE MARRIED MY GRANDFATHER. AND IN OUR TOWN OF 800 SOULS, THERE WERE 26 BECHDEL FAMILIES LISTED IN THE PHONE BOOK.

THIS DESPITE THE FACT THAT PEOPLE COULD EASILY DRIVE AROUND THE MOUNTAINS BY THE TIME MY FATHER WAS A CHILD.

DAD

 academic literacies

 rhetorical situations

 genres

 processes

 strategies

 research MLA / APA

 media / design

readings

AND BY THE TIME OF MY OWN CHILDHOOD, THEY COULD DRIVE EVEN MORE EASILY RIGHT ACROSS THEM.

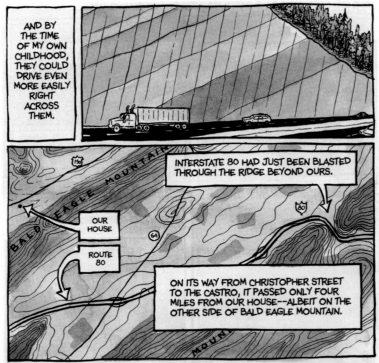

INTERSTATE 80 HAD JUST BEEN BLASTED THROUGH THE RIDGE BEYOND OURS.

BALD EAGLE MOUNTAIN

OUR HOUSE

ROUTE 80

ON ITS WAY FROM CHRISTOPHER STREET TO THE CASTRO, IT PASSED ONLY FOUR MILES FROM OUR HOUSE—ALBEIT ON THE OTHER SIDE OF BALD EAGLE MOUNTAIN.

MOUN...

THIS MASSIVE EARTHEN BERM EFFECTIVELY DEADENED ANY HINT OF NOISE FROM THE GLORIOUS THOROUGHFARE...

...EXCEPT ON STILL, HOT NIGHTS WHEN THE HUMIDITY WAS PARTIC-ULARLY CONDUCTIVE.

OUR SUN ROSE OVER BALD EAGLE MOUNTAIN'S HAZY BLUE FLANK.

(WE SAW LOTS OF SUNRISES IN 1974, THANKS TO THE ENERGY CRISIS AND THE YEAR-ROUND DAYLIGHT SAVINGS TIME IT ENTAILED.)

AND IT SET BEHIND THE STRIP MINE-POCKED PLATEAU...

...TYPICALLY WITH SOME DEGREE OF PYROTECHNIC SPLENDOR, DUE TO PARTICULATES FROM THE PRE-CLEAN AIR ACT PAPER MILL TEN MILES AWAY.

WITH SIMILAR PERVERSITY, THE SPARKLING CREEK THAT COURSED DOWN FROM THE PLATEAU AND THROUGH OUR TOWN WAS CRYSTAL CLEAR PRECISELY BECAUSE IT WAS POLLUTED.

MINE RUNOFF HAD LEFT THE WATER TOO ACIDIC TO SUPPORT LIFE OF ANY KIND.

WADING IN THIS FISHLESS CREEK AND SWOONING AT THE SALMON SKY, I LEARNED FIRSTHAND THAT MOST ELEMENTAL OF ALL IRONIES.

THAT, AS WALLACE STEVENS PUT IT IN MOM'S FAVORITE POEM, "DEATH IS THE MOTHER OF BEAUTY."

I WAS INSPIRED TO POETRY MYSELF BY THESE PICTURESQUE SURROUNDINGS, AT THE AGE OF SEVEN.

SPRING
spring is very nice youknow
not a bit of ice or snow!

I SHOWED IT TO MY FATHER, WHO IMPRO-VISED A SECOND STANZA ON THE SPOT.

LILACS, TULIPS, AND DAFFODILS PEEK THEIR HEADS O'ER THE WINDOWSILLS.

LIMP WITH ADMIRATION, I ADDED HIS LINES TO MY TYPESCRIPT....

...THEN ILLUSTRATED THE PAGE WITH A MUDDY WATERCOLOR SUNSET.

IN THE FOREGROUND STANDS A MAN, MY SAD PROXY, GAZING ON THE UNTIMELY ECLIPSE OF HIS CREATIVE LIGHT.

SPRING
spring is very nice youknow
not a bit of ice or snow!
LiLACS tu lips and daffodils
peak their heads inthewindowsill.

I NEVER WROTE ANOTHER POEM. AND SOON, I ABANDONED COLOR TOO.

WE HAD A HUGE, OVERSIZE COLORING BOOK OF E.H. SHEPARD'S ILLUSTRATIONS FOR *THE WIND IN THE WILLOWS*.

DAD HAD READ ME BITS OF THE STORY FROM THE REAL BOOK. IN ONE SCENE, THE CHARMING SOCIOPATH MR. TOAD PURCHASES A GYPSY CARAVAN.

I WAS FILLING THIS IN ONE DAY WITH MY FAVORITE COLOR, MIDNIGHT BLUE.

WHAT ARE YOU DOING? THAT'S THE CANARY-COLORED CARAVAN!

HERE. I'LL DO THE REST IN YELLOW, AND YOUR BLUE SIDE WILL BE IN SHADOW.

IT WAS A CRAYONIC TOUR DE FORCE.

LOOK. BY ADDING THIN LAYERS OF GOLDENROD AND YELLOW-ORANGE, I GET A RICHER COLOR.

MY MOTHER'S TALENTS WERE NO LESS DAUNTING. ONCE I WENT WITH HER TO A HOUSE WHERE SHE ARGUED WITH A STRANGE MAN, AS IF SHE KNEW HIM INTIMATELY.

A LOT OF WOMEN I KNOW WOULD HAVE BROUGHT THEIR WHOLE FAMILIES TO LIVE OFF YOU. ALL I BROUGHT WAS GRANDMA. GRANDMA IS ALL THE FAMILY I HAVE.

I FEEL VERY FORTUNATE.

THIS WAS ACTING.

I HAVE A RIGHT TO LIVE OFF YOU BECAUSE I MARRIED YOU, AND BECAUSE I USED TO LET YOU GET ON TOP OF ME AND BUMP YOUR UGLIES.

THE AMERICAN DREAM
ALBEE

SHE COULD ALSO PLAY ASTONISHING THINGS ON THE PIANO, EVEN THE MUSIC FROM THE DOWNY COMMERCIAL ON TV.

GRAND VALSE BRILLANTE

SEVERAL YEARS AFTER DAD DIED, MOM WAS USING OUR OLD TAPE RECORDER TO REHEARSE FOR A PLAY. SHE READ FROM THE SCRIPT, LEAVING PAUSES WHERE IT WAS HER CHARACTER'S TURN TO SPEAK.

WHEN SHE CHECKED TO MAKE SURE THE MACHINE WAS RECORDING PROPERLY...   ...SHE REALIZED THAT SHE WAS TAPING OVER MY FATHER'S VOICE.

THIS OWNER CHANGED THE ROOFS, THE PORCHES, THE CHIMNEYS, THE FIREPLACES, THE WALLS, THE WOODWORK, UNTIL IT BECAME A STYLISH TOWN HOUSE SUITABLE FOR A PROSPEROUS LAWYER'S FAMILY.

HE'S NOT TALKING ABOUT OUR HOUSE. HE'S PREPARING A GUIDED TOUR OF A MUSEUM RUN BY THE COUNTY HISTORICAL SOCIETY, OF WHICH HE WAS PRESIDENT.

IT'S JARRING TO HEAR MY FATHER SPEAK FROM BEYOND THE GRAVE.

PROCEEDING TO THE EAST PARLOR, WITH ITS BOLDLY SCROLLED ROCOCO PAPERS AND ITS BORDERED WALL-TO-WALL CARPET, YOU WILL SEE THE SHOWPLACE ROOM OF THE HOUSE.

SYNCHRO START

BUT THE MOST ARRESTING THING ABOUT THE TAPE IS ITS EVIDENCE OF BOTH MY PARENTS AT WORK, INTENT AND SEPARATE.

...RUB HER BACK FOR HER. **KKKKLICK**...AND SMALL, MULLIONED WINDOWS...

THEIR RAPT IMMERSION EVOKES A FAMILIAR RESENTMENT IN ME.

I'M HUNGRY!

I'LL MAKE LUNCH IN FIFTEEN MINUTES.

IT'S CHILDISH, PERHAPS, TO GRUDGE THEM THE SUSTENANCE OF THEIR CREATIVE SOLITUDE.

BUT IT WAS ALL THAT SUSTAINED THEM, AND WAS THUS ALL-CONSUMING.

FROM THEIR EXAMPLE, I LEARNED QUICKLY TO FEED MYSELF.

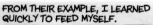

IT WAS A VICIOUS CIRCLE, THOUGH. THE MORE GRATIFICATION WE FOUND IN OUR OWN GENIUSES, THE MORE ISOLATED WE GREW.

OUR HOME WAS LIKE AN ARTISTS' COLONY. WE ATE TOGETHER, BUT OTHERWISE WERE ABSORBED IN OUR SEPARATE PURSUITS.

AND IN THIS ISOLATION, OUR CREATIVITY TOOK ON AN ASPECT OF COMPULSION.

Engaging with the Text

1. The **TITLE** of Alison Bechdel's graphic autobiography, *Fun Home*, refers both to the funeral home in which Bechdel spent a lot of time while growing up and to the fun house in an amusement park. Describe the characteristics that distinguish a fun house from other kinds of buildings. In what ways do the **DETAILS** in this excerpt suggest the idea of an amusement park fun house? Why do you think Bechdel selected this analogy? What does it suggest about the **PURPOSE** of her memoir? 344–45   399–402   55–56

2. What role do the graphic images play in helping Bechdel tell her story? What details do they provide that the words do not, and vice versa?

3. What strategies does Bechdel use in the text and graphics to **GUIDE READERS** through her narrative and help them relate to her struggle to understand her identity? How successful are these strategies in helping readers follow her story? 344–49

4. One of the key features of a text that mixes genres is that it needs a **CLEAR FOCUS**. In what ways does Bechdel's piece accomplish this feature? In your response, consider both the images and the words. 268

5. *For Writing.* Create your own graphic **NARRATIVE** essay that details an early experience of some kind that you had, whether at home, at school, or elsewhere. Think about what insights you want to provide your readers in your account, and focus your piece to convey them. Pay attention to the graphic as well as verbal details you include. You need not draw graphics yourself; if you prefer, you can use images you find elsewhere and integrate them with your own words. 419–27

Acknowledgments

IMAGE ACKNOWLEDGMENTS

Page 40: Courtesy of Jacob MacLeod; p. 73: Courtesy of Emily Vallowe; p. 79: Courtesy of Marjorie Agosín; p. 95: Courtesy of Hannah Berry; p. 96: Courtesy of The Clarks Companies; p. 98: Courtesy of Sorel: p. 99: Courtesy of Danielle Allen. © Laura Rose Photography; p. 105: Seth Wenig/AP; p. 117: urbanbuzz/ Shutterstock.com; p. 118: TOLES © 2007 The Washington Post. Reprinted with permission of UNIVERSAL UCLICK; p. 120: AP Photo/Jeffrey Phelps; p. 121 (top): Courtesy of Ann C. Johns, Ph.D./University of Texas at Austin; p. 121 (bottom): Courtesy of Ann C. Johns, Ph.D./University of Texas at Austin: p. 129: Courtesy of Michaela Cullington; p. 137: © 2010 Larry D. Moore/ Wikimedia Commons; p. 138 (left): Charles Bennett/ AP; p. 138 (right): Mark Duncan/AP; p. 142 (top): Courtesy of Jon Marcus, Photo by Andrew Kubica; p. 142 (bottom): Wesley Hitt/Getty Images; p. 161: Evan Agostini/Invision/AP Photo; p. 163: © Corbis; p. 164: Courtesy of Andrew Leonard; p. 165: YouTube; p. 166: YouTube; p. 167: YouTube; p. 190: Courtesy of Jessica Ann Olson; p. 197: ConsumerReports.org; p. 198: Courtesy of Ali Heinekamp; p. 199: The Kobal Collection; p. 206: The Granger Collection, New York/The Granger Collection; p. 207: Courtesy of Stephanie Huff; p. 216: John Amis/AP; p. 224: Courtesy of Steve Hendrix/The Washington Post; p. 225: Courtesy of Heather Penney; p. 232 (left): Courtesy of Heather Penney; p. 232 (right): Courtesy of The United States Air Force; p. 235: Courtesy of Michael Granof; p. 239: Heather Ainsworth/The New York Times/Redux; p. 244: Wikimedia Commons; p. 265: Steye Raviez/ Hollandse Hoogte/Redux; p. 335: Jim Mone/AP; p. 365: © Reagan Louie; p. 366: RecycleManiacs.org; p. 377: Courtesy of Michiganapples.com; p. 384 (top); © GOOGLE; p. 384 (bottom): © GOOGLE; p. 393: © Swim Ink 2, LLC/CORBIS; p. 404: The Advertising Archives; p. 405: The Advertising Archives; p. 427 (all): Courtesy of The Other Side of Fifty, othersideoffifty.com; p. 448: National Institutes of Health; p. 449: PARS/The New York Times; p. 451 (top): Houston Community College Libraries; http://library.hccs.edu/home; p. 451 (bottom): Houston Community College Libraries, http://library.hccs.edu/home; p. 453: www.wordle.net/ create; p. 454: Permission to publish courtesy of EBSCO; p. 457: The University of Wyoming Library; p. 458: The University of Wyoming Library; p. 516: Jessamyn Neuhaus, "Marge Simpson, Blue-Haired Housewife Defining Domesticity on *The Simpsons*." *Journal of Popular Culture* 43.4 (2010): 761–81. Print; p. 519 (top): Michael Segal, "The Hit Book That Came from Mars." *Nautilus*. Nautilus Think, 8 January 2015. Web. 10 October 2016; p. 519 (bottom): Michael Segal,

"The Hit Book That Came from Mars." *Nautilus*. Nautilus Think, 8 January 2015. Web. 10 October 2016; p. 520: Jessamyn Neuhaus, "Marge Simpson, Blue-Haired Housewife Defining Domesticity on *The Simpsons*." *Journal of Popular Culture* 43.4 (2010): 761–81. Sport Discus with Full Text. Web. 24 Mar. 2016; p. 524 (left): Amana Fontanella-Khan, *Pink Sari Revolution: A Tale of Women and Power in India*. New York: Norton, 2013; p. 524 (right): Amana Fontanella-Khan, *Pink Sari Revolution: A Tale of Women and Power in India*. New York: Norton, 2013; p. 530: John McIlwain, Molly Simpson, and Sara Hammerschmidt. "Housing in America: Integrating Housing, Health, and Resilience in a Changing Environment." *Urban Land Institute*. Urban Land Institute, 2014. Web. 17 Sept. 2016; p. 541: Bettmann/CORBIS; p. 559 (left): Joseph E. Stiglitz, "The Great Divide: Unequal Societies and What We Can Do about Them." New York: Norton, 2015; p. 559 (right): Joseph E. Stiglitz, "The Great Divide: Unequal Societies and What We Can Do about Them." New York: Norton, 2015; p. 567: M. P. Lazette, (2015, February 25). "A Hurricane's Hit to Households." Federal Reserve Bank of Cleveland. Retrieved from www.clevelandfed.org/en/Newsroom%20and%20Events/Publications/Forefront/Katrina.aspx; p. 569: C. F. Guthrie, (2013). "Smart Technology and the Moral Life." *Ethics & Behavior*, 23, 324–37. doi: 10.1080/10508422.2013.787359; p. 570: C. F. Guthrie (2013). "Smart Technology and the Moral Life." *Ethics & Behavior*, 23(4), 324–37. doi:10.1080/10508422.2013.787359; p. 600: Ikea.com; p. 608 (left): The Philadelphia Museum of Art/Art Resource, NY; p. 608 (right): Willem de Kooning (1904–1997)/Private Collection/The Bridgeman Art Library; p. 610a: Reuters/Landov; p. 610b: Reuters/Landov; p. 610b: Reuters/Landov; p. 610d: Reuters/Landov; p. 610e: NASA/Wikimedia Commons; p. 612: ww.loc.gov/rr/record/onlinecollections; p. 613: blog.aai.si.edu; p. 618: www.nps.gov/history; p. 619: Reprinted with permission of Smithsonian Institution; p. 620: Courtesy of Ann M. Lawrence, PhD, University of South Florida; p. 623: Courtesy Richard Bullock; p. 625: Library of Congress/Wikimedia Commons; p. 626: Courtesy of Judy Davis; p. 634 (top): Prezi.com; p. 634 (bottom right): Photo by Bruce Mathews, Courtesy of the Harry S. Truman Library, Independence, Missouri; p. 640: Meghan Hickey; p. 645: Courtesy of Tanya M. Barrientos; p. 649: © Christopher Felver/CORBIS; p. 656 (top): Photo by Jeff Miller/UW–Madison; p. 664: Photo by Jim Harrison/Courtesy of Laurel Thatcher Ulrich; p. 667: John Springer Collection/CORBIS; p. 670: Montgomery County Sheriff's Office/AP; p. 675: Courtesy of Diana George; p. 677: Courtesy Children, Inc.; p. 687: Sasha Frere-Jones Photo by Piera Gelardi/Refinery29 is licensed under a Creative Commons Attribution 3.0 United States License; p. 688: Illustration by Mr. Bingo; p. 693: © The New York Times/Redux; p. 698: Courtesy of Adam Piore; p. 699: Illustration by Ellen Weinstein; p. 704: Illustration by Ellen Weinstein; p. 710: Courtesy of Eleanor J. Bader; p. 716: Steven Senne/AP; p. 717: Photographs by Stephen Buel; p. 718: Photographs by Stephen Buel; p. 725: Courtesy of Alina Tugend; p. 726: Monkey Business Images/Shutterstock.com; p. 731: Courtesy of Alex Weiss; p. 732: © Jagex; p. 735: © Colin McPherson/Corbis; p. 736: The Everett Collection; p. 740 (left): Gustav Schultze, Naumburg, 1882/Wikimedia Commons; p. 740 (right): Newscom; p. 743: Midvale Company Photographs (1883–1953)/Flickr; p. 745: Sebastian Bergmann/Wikimedia Commons; p. 750: Courtesy of Jeremy Adam Smith; p. 765: Courtesy of danah boyd; p. 772 (top): © Editorial Image, LLC / Alamy; p. 772 (bottom): Alamy; p. 774: Alamy; p. 776 (left): Alamy; p. 776 (right): Alamy; p. 779: Cary Conover/The New York Times/Redux; p. 783: Coutesy of Natalie Standiford. Photo by Tobias Everke; p. 787: Courtesy of Chris Suellentrop; p. 803: Röhnert/ullstein bild via Getty Images; p. 813: © Sophie Bassouls/Sygma/Corbis; p. 845: David Corio/Michael

Ochs Archive/Getty Images; p. 846: © GL Archive/ Alamy; p. 847: © Everett Collection Inc./Alamy; p. 849: © YONHAP/epa/Corbis; p. 857: Courtesy of Kevin Harkins; p. 864: Michele McDonald/The Boston Globe via Getty Images; p. 866: Therese + Joel/The New York Times; p. 876: Courtesy of Judith Ortiz Cofer; p. 885 (top): Courtesy of James Hamblin; p. 885 (bottom): Sarah Natsumi; p. 886: Sarah Natsumi; p. 888: Courtesy of The Dumpster Project, dumpsterproject.org; p. 889: Courtesy of The Dumpster Project, dumpsterproject.org; p. 890: Courtesy of The Dumpster Project, dumpsterproject.org; p. 894: Adabel Allen; p. 898: Courtesy of Marcia Brown; p. 899: Courtesy of Winky Lewis Photo; p. 901:Courtesy of Winky Lewis Photo; p. 905: Rex Features via AP Images; p. 906: JAKE NAUGHTON/The New York Times; p. 907: JAKE NAUGHTON/The New York Times; p. 912: © Seth Wenig/AP/Corbis; p. 914: Alamy; p. 915: Alamy; p. 922: Photo by Jonathon Baron; p. 926: Jon Chase/Harvard Staff Photographer; p. 927: U.S. Army photo by Sgt. Chad Menegay, 196th MPAD, 25th Inf. Div., USD-C; p. 931: Joel Travis Sage/Wikimedia Commons; p. 940: Amazur/Wikimedia Commons; p. 947: Courtesy of Geeta Kothari; p. 953: Courtesy of Paula Marantz Cohen. Photo by Diane Pizzuto/Pennoni Honors College, Drexel University; p. 954: pixeldreams.eu/ Shutterstock.com; p. 957: Courtesy of Tim Kreider; p. 958: © 2009 Cartoon by Tim Kreider; p. 965: Courtesy of David Ramsey; p. 967: Chris Pizzello/AP; p. 976: Courtesy of Anu Partanen; p. 977: Sergey Ivanov/ Flickr; p. 984: Courtesy of Jeremy Dowsett; p. 985: Courtesy of Jeremy Dowsett; p. 990 (top): Greg Ruffing/ Redux; p. 990 (bottom): Cover of *Fun Home: A Family Tragicomic* by Alison Bechdel. Jacket art © 2006 by Alison Bechdel. Reprinted by permission of Houghton Mifflin Harcourt Publishing Company. All rights reserved; pp. 991–1002: © 2006 by Alison Bechdel. Reprinted by permission of Houghton Mifflin Harcourt Publishing Company. All rights reserved.

TEXT ACKNOWLEDGMENTS

Marjorie Agosín: "Always Living in Spanish," *The Literary Life*, p. 25. Reprinted by permission of the author.

Danielle Allen: Excerpts from *Our Declaration: A Reading of the Declaration of Independence in Defense of Equality* by Danielle Allen. Copyright © 2014 by Danielle Allen. Used by permission of Liveright Publishing Corporation.

Sam Anderson: "Just One More Game . . ." from the *New York Times Magazine*, April 8, 2012. © 2012 The New York Times. All rights reserved. Used by permission and protected by the Copyright Laws of the United States. The printing, copying, redistribution, or retransmission of the Material without express written permission is prohibited.

E.J. Bader: "Homeless on Campus" from *The Progressive*, July 2004. Copyright © The Progressive. Reprinted by permission.

Rob Baker: "Jimmy Santiago Baca: Poetry as Lifesaver," *Council Chronicle*, Sept. 2008, pp. 23–24. Copyright 2008 by the National Council of Teachers of English. Reprinted with permission.

James Baldwin: "Sonny's Blues" © 1957 by James Baldwin was originally published in The Partisan Review. Copyright renewed. Collected in *Going to Meet the Man*, published by Vintage Books. Used by arrangement with the James Baldwin Estate.

Dennis Baron: "Don't Make English Official — Ban It Instead." Reprinted by permission of the author.

Tanya Barrientos: "Se Habla Español," from the August 2004 issue of *Latina*. Reprinted by permission of the author.

Dave Barry: "Introduction: Guys vs. Men" from *Dave Barry's Complete Guide to Guys: A Fairly Short Book* by Dave Barry, copyright © 1995 by Dave Barry. Used by permission of Random House, an imprint and division of Penguin Random House LLC. All rights reserved.

Glossary / Index

A

abstract, 183–87 A writing GENRE that summarizes a book, an article, or a paper, usually in 100–200 words. Authors in some academic fields must provide, at the top of a report submitted for publication, an abstract of its content. The abstract may then appear in a journal of abstracts, such as *Psychological Abstracts*. An *informative abstract* summarizes a complete report; a briefer *descriptive abstract* provides only a brief overview; a *proposal abstract* (also called a TOPIC PROPOSAL) requests permission to conduct research, write on a topic, or present a report at a scholarly conference. Key Features: SUMMARY of basic information • objective description • brevity

academic writing, 3–9 Writing done in an academic or scholarly context, such as for course assignments. Key Features: evidence that you've carefully considered the subject • clear, appropriately qualified THESIS • response to what others have said • good reasons supported by evidence • acknowledgment of multiple perspectives • carefully documented sources • confident, authoritative STANCE • indication of why your topic matters • careful attention to correctness.

action verb, 256, 258, 415 A VERB that expresses a physical or mental action (*jump, consider*).

active voice, 314 When a VERB is in the active voice, the SUBJECT performs the action: *He sent a gift. See also* passive voice

***ad hominem* argument** A logical FALLACY that attacks someone's character rather than address the issues. (*Ad hominem* is Latin for "to the man.")

Note: This glossary / index defines key terms and concepts and directs you to pages in the book where you can find specific information on these and other topics. Please note the words set in SMALL CAPITAL LETTERS are themselves defined in the glossary / index.

application letters, 253–64 Letters written to apply for a job or other position. Key Features: succinct indication of qualifications • reasonable and pleasing tone • conventional, businesslike form *See also* résumés

arguing, 355–73 A STRATEGY that can be used in any kind of writing to support a claim with REASONS and EVIDENCE.

arguing a position, 156–82 A writing GENRE that uses REASONS and EVIDENCE to support a CLAIM or POSITION and, sometimes, to persuade an AUDIENCE to accept that position. Key Features: clear and arguable position • necessary background • good reasons • convincing support for each reason • appeal to readers' values • trustworthy TONE • careful consideration of other positions

or clearly implied, and requires support by REASONS and EVIDENCE.

"The Clan of the One-Breasted Women" (Williams), 412

classifying and dividing, 374–79 A STRATEGY that either groups (classifies) numerous individual items into categories by their similarities (for example, classifying cereal, bread, butter, chicken, cheese, cream, eggs, and oil as carbohydrates, proteins, and fats) or breaks (divides) one large category into small categories (for example, dividing food into carbohydrates, proteins, and fats). Classification and/or division can serve as the ORGANIZING principle for a whole text.

    characteristics
        clear and distinct categories, 376–78
        rhetorical situation, 378–79
    cubing and, 292
    guidelines
        classifying, 374–75
        dividing, 375–76

cliché, 315–16 An expression used so frequently that it is no longer fresh: *busy as a bee.*

clustering, 291–92 A PROCESS for GENERATING IDEAS AND TEXT, in which a writer visually connects thoughts by jotting them down and drawing lines between related items.

coding, as reading strategy, 19

Cofer, Judith Ortiz, 876–83
Cohen, Paula Marantz, 953–56
Colicchio, Tom, 389

collaboration, 285–88 The PROCESS of working with others.
    face-to-face, 285–86
    group writing projects, 286–87
    online, 286
    writing conferences, 287–88

Columbia Encyclopedia, 455
comfortable, getting, 298
"Coming Home Again" (Lee), 409–10
commas, 315, 409, 483

common ground, 367 Shared values. Writers build common ground with AUDIENCES by acknowledging others' POINTS OF VIEW, seeking areas of compromise, and using language that includes, rather than excludes, those they aim to reach. *See also* inclusive language

comparing and contrasting, 380–87 A STRATEGY that highlights the similarities and differences between items. Using the *block method* of comparison-contrast, a writer discusses all the points about one item and then all the same points about the other item; using the *point-by-point method,* a writer discusses one point for both items before going on to discuss the next point for both items, and so on. Sometimes comparison and/or contrast serves as the ORGANIZING principle for a whole text.
    block method, 382
    figurative language, 385–86

definition, 388–98 A STRATEGY that says what something is. *Formal definitions* identify the category that something belongs to and tell what distinguishes it from other things in that category: a worm as an invertebrate (a category) with a long, rounded body and no appendages (distinguishing features). *Extended definitions* go into more detail: a paragraph or even an essay explaining why a character in a story is tragic. *Stipulative definitions* explain a writer's distinctive use of a term, one not found in a dictionary. Definition can serve as the ORGANIZING principle for a whole text.

description, 399–407 A STRATEGY that tells how something looks, sounds, smells, feels, or tastes. Effective description creates a clear DOMINANT IMPRESSION built from specific details. Description can be *objective, subjective,* or both. Description can serve as the ORGANIZING principle for a whole text.

design, 597–606 The way a text is arranged and presented visually. Elements of design include font, color, illustration, layout, and white space. One component of a RHETORICAL SITUATION, design plays an important part in how well a text reaches its AUDIENCE and achieves its PURPOSE.

dialogue, 408–13 A STRATEGY for includ-ing other people's spoken words to a text.

discovery drafting, 296–97 A PROCESS of DRAFTING something quickly, mostly for the purpose of discovering what one wants to say.

dividing, 375–76. *See also* classifying and dividing

documentation, 496–99 Publication infor-mation about the sources cited in a text. The documentation usually appears in an abbre-viated form in parentheses at the point of CITATION or in an endnote or a footnote. Complete documentation usually appears as a list of WORKS CITED or REFERENCES at the end of the text. Documentation styles vary by discipline. For example, Modern Language Association (MLA) style requires an author's complete first name if it appears in a source, whereas American Psychologi-cal Association (APA) style requires only the initial of an author's first name.

dominant impression The overall effect created through specific details when a writer DESCRIBES something.

evaluation, 197–205   A writing GENRE that makes a judgment about something — a source, poem, film, restaurant, whatever — based on certain CRITERIA. Key Features: description of the subject • clearly defined criteria • knowledgeable discussion of the subject • balanced and fair assessment

evidence, 359–67   In ARGUMENT, the data you present to support your REASONS. Such data may include statistics, calculations, examples, ANECDOTES, QUOTATIONS, case studies, or anything else that will convince your reader that your reasons are compelling. Evidence should be sufficient (enough to show that the reasons have merit) and relevant (appropriate to the argument you're making).

explaining a process, 414–18   A STRATEGY for telling how something is done or how to do something. An explanation of a process can serve as the ORGANIZING principle for a whole text.

types of
   explaining visually, 416–17
   how something is done, 414–15
   how to do something, 415–16

"Gettysburg Address: Two Versions"
(Bass), 332, 338
Ginsberg, Benjamin, 394–95,
396
Gladwell, Malcolm, 415
"Global Warming" (Olson),
190–91
Goodfellow, Peter, 386
Google Books, 458
"Graduation" (Angelou), 419–20
"A Grand, Comprehensive Overview to
Mutual Funds Investing" (Barker),
389
Granof, Michael, 235–37
graphs
for comparing, 383
reading, 24–25
GreatBuildings.com, 402
Grison, Sarah, 23
group writing projects, 286–87
guiding your reader. *See* cueing devices
"Guns and Cars Are Different"
(MacLeod), 40–42
Guterson, David, 334–36, 408–9
"Guys vs. Men" (Barry), 940–46

H

habits of mind, academic, 45–52
Hamblin, James, 884–92
handouts for presentations, 635
Harjo, Susan Shown, 358

hasty generalization, 372   A FALLACY that
reaches a conclusion based on insufficient
or inappropriately qualified EVIDENCE.

Hathi Trust Digital Library, 458

headings
as design element, 604–5
in literary analyses, 215
reading, 13
"Health and Behavioral Consequences
of Binge Drinking in College"
(Wechsler et al.), 341–42
Health Care without Harm, 336
he and she, 316
Heinekamp, Ali, 198–201
Help Wanted: Tales from the First Job Front
(Lewis), 348
Hendrix, Steve, 224–28
Hesser, Amanda, 385
Historical Abstracts, 460
"Homeless on Campus" (Bader),
710–15
Huff, Stephanie, 207–9
Hughes, Langston, 423
Humanities Index, 461
Humanities International Index,
460
Huws, Ursula, 392, 394

I

idea mapping. *See* clustering
"If You Are What You Eat, then What
Am I?" (Kothari), 947–52
illustration. *See* visual
"Immigrant Workers in the U.S. Labor
Force" (Singer), 334
implications, discussing, 339–40
indexes, library, 459–61
informal outlines, 293
informative abstracts, 183–84, 187
InfoTrac, 459

K

keyword A term that a researcher inputs when searching for information electronically.

L

lab report, 399, 402 A writing GENRE that covers the process of conducting an experiment in a controlled setting. Key Features: explicit title • ABSTRACT • PURPOSE • methods • results and discussion • REFERENCES • APPENDIX • appropriate format

layout, 602–3 The way text is arranged on a page or screen — for example, in paragraphs, in lists, on charts, with headings.

letter writing, 295 A PROCESS of GENERATING IDEAS AND TEXT by going through the motions of writing to someone to explain a topic.

N

most often associated with fiction, but it shows up in all kinds of writing. When used in an essay, a REPORT, or another academic GENRE, narration is used to support a point — not merely tell an interesting story for its own sake. It must also present events in some kind of sequence and include only pertinent detail. Narration can serve as the ORGANIZING principle for a whole text. *See also* literacy narrative

O

P

proofreading, 316–17 The final PROCESS of writing, when a writer checks for correct spelling and punctuation as well as for page order, missing text, and consistent use of FONTS. *See also* editing; revising; rewriting

proposal, 235–44 A GENRE that argues for a solution to a problem or suggests some action. Key Features: well-defined problem • recommended solution • answers to anticipated questions • call to action • appropriate TONE. *See also* topic proposal

purpose, 55–56 A writer's goal: to explore ideas, to express oneself, to entertain, to demonstrate learning, to inform, to persuade, and so on. Purpose is one element of the RHETORICAL SITUATION.

Q

questioning A PROCESS of GENERATING IDEAS AND TEXT about a topic — asking, for example, *What? Who? When? Where? How?* and *Why?* or other questions.

S

secondary source, 445–46 An ANALYSIS or INTERPRETATION of a PRIMARY SOURCE. In writing about the Revolutionary War, a researcher would likely consider the Declaration of Independence a primary source and a textbook's description of how the document was written a secondary source.

sexist language, 316 Language that stereotypes or ignores women or men or needlessly calls attention to gender.

working bibliography, 441–43 A record of all sources consulted in research providing all the bibliographic information necessary for DOCUMENTATION including author, title, and publication information.

Submitting Papers for Publication by W. W. Norton & Company

We are interested in receiving writing from college students to consider including in our textbooks as examples of student writing. Please send this form with the work that you would like us to consider to Marilyn Moller, Student Writing, W. W. Norton & Company, 500 Fifth Avenue, New York NY 10110.

Text Submission Form

Student's name _____

School _____

Address _____

Department _____

Course _____

Writing assignment the text responds to _____

_____

_____

_____

_____

Instructor's name _____

(continued next page)

Please write a few sentences about what your primary purposes were for writing this text. Also, if you wish, tell us what you think you learned about writing from the experience writing it.

_____

_____

_____

_____

_____

_____

_____

Contact Information

Please provide the information below so that we can contact you if your work is selected for publication.

Name _____

Permanent address _____

Email _____

Phone _____